Legal Ethics

Theories, Cases, and Professional Regulation

RANDAL N.M. GRAHAM

Faculty of Law
University of Western Ontario

2004
EMOND MONTGOMERY PUBLICATIONS LIMITED
TORONTO, CANADA

Printed in Canada.

Edited, designed, and typeset by WordsWorth Communications, Toronto.

We acknowledge the financial support of the Government of Canada through the Book Publishing Industry Development Program (BPIDP) for our publishing activities.

The events and characters depicted in this book are fictitious. Any similarity to actual persons, living or dead, is purely coincidental.

National Library of Canada Cataloguing in Publication

Graham, Randal N.M.
    Legal Ethics : theories, cases, and professional regulation / Randal N. Graham.

Includes index.
ISBN 978-1-55239-057-3

1. Legal ethics — Canada — Textbooks. I. Title.

KE339.G73 2004   174′.3′0971   C2004-903023-X
KF306.G73 2004

To Garry,
For his professional integrity,
For his kindness and generosity,
And for not objecting when I married his only daughter.

Foreword

I like to think that the seed for this book was planted one day as Professor Graham and I were walking to lunch. He explained to me the approach he was taking in his course on legal ethics and asked if I thought the approach seemed like a good idea. My response was that it was not just a good idea, it was a career-making idea.

The approach in question is that of applying law and economics to the realm of legal ethics. While law and economics has been enormously productive in many other spheres of law, Graham's book is groundbreaking in applying it to the field of legal ethics. It might be objected that ethics, by its very nature, is not suited to the application of the economic approach. This book demonstrates that this objection is quite misguided. As Graham makes clear in his introductory chapters, economics is simply the study of rational choice. Ethical decisions are choices and the lawyers making them are at least as rational as the consumers and business managers to whom economic theory is routinely applied.

The value of an economic approach to legal ethics is made evident in comparison with the traditional approach. The traditional approach to legal ethics has been little more than a series of sermons, where commentators argue for their own ideology. The situation is somewhat as if contracts textbooks focused on the issue of whether breaching a contract is morally wrong. Graham has stripped the ideology out of legal ethics, replaced sermons with substance, and revealed a system in which sensible assumptions about human behaviour allow us to understand and predict the ethical choices being made.

This is not to say that Graham's approach is purely descriptive, with nothing to say about whether a particular rule is good or bad. On the contrary, a systematic understanding of the effect of ethical rules is essential to the designing of rules that are most effective—dare I say "cost-effective"—at deterring undesirable conduct.

In short, I believe that this book will transform the way legal ethics is taught. It certainly should.

Norman Siebrasse
University of New Brunswick Faculty of Law

Preface

There are times when everyone is better off if lawyers breach the rules of ethics. When choosing clients, lawyers should act in cases involving conflicts of interest. From time to time, lawyers should happily divulge their clients' secrets, sacrificing client interests in pursuit of personal gain. In numerous cases lawyers should violate the rules of professional conduct, thwart their clients' legal objectives, and incur the wrath of those who monitor lawyers' ethical choices. The difficulty, of course, is recognizing *when* a lawyer ought to violate prevailing ethical norms.

When should lawyers opt to breach the rules of ethics? Most literature on the topic of legal ethics has approached this question through reliance on amorphous notions such as morality, integrity, professionalism, and honour. Unfortunately, terms such as "morality," "integrity," "professionalism," and "honour" are indeterminate and vague, providing little or no guidance to those who are faced with ethical choices. Given the shifting, nebulous nature of traditional moral terms, moral language lacks the power to govern lawyers' ethical choices, to generate sensible regulations, or to convey verifiable information. As a result, those who wish to study or regulate ethical choices would be wise to avoid reliance on traditional moral terms.

The goal of the present text is to provide a thorough account of legal ethics without reliance on indeterminate moral language. For reasons that will become apparent, my method of pursuing this goal involves the application of microeconomic tools to lawyers' ethical choices. The resulting ethical theory, known as "An Economic Account of Legal Ethics" (or "Ethinomics," for short), focuses on efficiency rather than virtue, on testable hypotheses rather than moral intuitions, and on stable behavioural models rather than metaphysical values. The ultimate goal of the book is to situate legal ethics within an overarching model of human behaviour: the economic model of rational choice. By viewing legal ethics through the lens of economics, this book helps to develop a coherent understanding of each element of the lawyer's ethical universe, forming the basis of a regulatory framework that creates efficient incentives for lawyers faced with ethical problems.

It is important to bear in mind that an economic account of legal ethics does not eliminate the need to consider questions of morality. On the contrary, it provides a way of approaching such questions through the application of testable propositions. Indeed, as we shall see by the conclusion of part I, an economic account of ethical systems *reinforces* many traditional moral claims. Unlike most ethical theories, however, an economic account of ethical systems reaches moral conclusions through the application of reason and reliance on observations concerning the nature of human behaviour. Rather than proceeding from settled notions concerning the nature of good and evil, an economic account of ethical systems allows us to reason *toward* our moral conclusions, providing a rational (rather than purely ideological) means of evaluating lawyers' ethical choices and the regulations governing legal ethics.

While one of the goals of this text is to demonstrate the usefulness of an economic theory of ethical systems, this text does not purport to present a comprehensive treatment of ethical theory and economics. On the contrary, this book is designed to act as an introduction to the important interaction of these two fields. Because of its introductory nature, this book often paints with a broad brush, exploring the general economic principles governing legal ethics while dispensing with unnecessary details. While these details are unnecessary in the present context, they will undoubtedly prove valuable in the future. As a result, one of the goals of this book is to promote the further development of scholarship in this area, and to encourage continuing efforts to gather data concerning the economic effects of ethical choices. As these data are collected, economic predictions concerning lawyers' ethical decisions will continue to grow more powerful, enhancing our ability to understand and regulate the difficult ethical choices lawyers face.

• • •

This book would not have been possible without the support of my friend and colleague, Norman Siebrasse. Professor Siebrasse reviewed numerous drafts of the manuscript, responded to late-night calls concerning revisions to the text, and provided me with copious, useful comments regarding virtually every economic argument in this book. More importantly, after learning of my approach to ethical theory, it was Professor Siebrasse who first encouraged me to publish my ideas. Without Professor Siebrasse's encouragement, I may never have bothered undertaking this project in the first place. As a result, Professor Siebrasse deserves a great deal of the credit for the content (and existence) of this text.

I am grateful for the excellent research assistance provided by Matthew Letson (of the University of New Brunswick) and Erin Kinlin (of the University of Western Ontario). Matthew provided me with a constant stream of interesting cases involving professional misconduct, while Erin reviewed numerous drafts of the text, edited cases, double-checked my calculations, provided critical comments, and sought obscure references in musty law libraries. I would also like to acknowledge the many friends and associates who provided me with suggestions and encouragement throughout the writing process. These included Adam Till, Peter Hogg, Joan Montgomery-Rose, Paul Emond, Margaret Ann Wilkinson, Steven Penney, Karen Davidson, Mitchell McInnes, Peggy Buchan, Heather Ross, Stephen Pitel, Van Lantz, Mary Whiteside-Lantz, Patricia Grant, Veronica D'Souza, and my parents, Peter and Lynn Graham. Last but not least I would like to thank my wife, Stephanie Montgomery-Graham, for tolerating a husband who was constantly distracted by ethical theory and economics during the first six months of our marriage.

Randal N.M. Graham
Toronto
May 2004

Table of Contents

PART II PROFESSIONAL REGULATION

Ethical Theory

CHAPTER ONE

Overview

I. Introduction

A. Avoiding Good and Evil

"Good" and "evil" are troublesome notions. Generations of philosophers, theologians, and even lawyers have proffered definitions of these elusive terms, yet no single set of workable meanings has managed to gain acceptance. Despite the musings of countless well-intentioned theorists, the notions of "good" and "evil" still defy clear definition. As Thomas Hobbes observed:

> divers men, differ not onely in their Judgment, on the senses of what is pleasant, and unpleasant to the tast, smell, hearing, touch, and sight; but also of what is conformable, or disagreeable to Reason, in the actions of common life. Nay, the same man, in divers times, differs from himselfe; and one time praiseth, that is, calleth Good, what another time he dispraiseth, and calleth Evil.[1]

In the absence of a settled definition of "good" or "evil," it seems unwise to rely on either of these notions when constructing a theory of ethics. More importantly, reliance on the ideas of "good" and "evil" may give rise to logical problems. One of the purposes of any ethical theory is to help discern the nature of "good" and "evil." If a goal of ethical theory is to provide a definition of "good" and "evil," it makes little sense to rely on the notions of "good" and "evil" in the development of our ethical theory. Indeed, an ethical theory that begins with settled ideas concerning the meaning of "good" and "evil" (or "moral" and "immoral," "ethical" and "unethical") amounts to little more than an exercise in perfectly circular reasoning. As a result, when trying to make sense of ethical systems, we are well advised to suspend reliance on pre-existing notions of good and evil. This book will accordingly avoid the trap of explaining legal ethics by reference to mystical or inexplicable notions.[2] Instead, this book will attempt to explain all ethical systems (and legal ethics in particular) by reference to more basic, tangible things—namely, scarcity, self-interest, and the human need to survive. In short, this book explains legal ethics by

---

1   Thomas Hobbes, *Leviathan* (New York: Norton & Company, 1997), 87.

2   As David Hume observed in *An Enquiry Concerning the Principles of Morals* (Oxford: Oxford University Press, 1998), 77: "It is full time [that philosophers] should attempt a ... reformation in all moral disquisitions; and reject every system of ethics, however subtle or ingenious, which is not founded on fact and observation."

reference to theories of evolution and economics. Because economics and evolution are so thoroughly intertwined (for reasons that will be seen below),[3] throughout this book the ideas of evolution and economics, together with their impact on the study of legal ethics, are brought together under the rubric of "an economic theory of legal ethics."[4]

The use of economics as a tool for explaining legal ethics presents two immediate problems. First, people are resistant to the idea that ethical systems are based on notions of survival and the maximization of wealth. For mystical reasons, people *want* their theories of ethics to be grounded in metaphysics. According to Robinson and Garratt, for example:

> Human beings seem reluctant to accept that morality is something invented by themselves and so tend to legitimize moral rules by mythologizing their origins.[5]

People want to believe that ethics flow from a supernatural source, from spirituality, or from something within themselves that is far greater than the instinct to survive. From this perspective, any theory that attempts to explain ethics by reference to mundane human needs is considered unpalatable and vulgar. This objection can be overcome quite easily. An economic theory of legal ethics does not exclude the possibility of a god, of spirituality, or of some unseen ethical force that guides us toward the resolution of ethical quandaries. On the contrary, an economic theory simply tells us that whatever forces may be guiding us toward or away from ethical decisions, those decisions can be explained, predicted, and evaluated in economic terms. As John Dewey explains:

> [E]conomics has been treated as on a lower level than either morals or politics. Yet the life which men, women and children actually lead, the opportunities open to them, the values they are capable of enjoying, their education, their share in all the things of art and science, are mainly determined by economic conditions. Hence we can hardly expect a moral system which ignores economic conditions to be other than remote and empty.[6]

Even if ethical decisions are grounded in something more profound than economic reasoning, they usually unfold in the way that economic analysis would predict. Even if God is at the helm, the ethical course that He or She has charted seems to be leading us toward wealth maximization and the assurance of the survival of our species. These concepts fall squarely within the domain of economics. As a result, it makes sense to use the tools of economics to evaluate and predict the ethical choices people make.

---

3   See below, section II, and chapter 2.

4   In the United States, law and economics scholars have only recently started the task of assessing specific rules of legal ethics through the lens of economics. See, for example, George M. Cohen, "When Law and Economics Met Professional Responsibility" (1998), 67 *Fordham Law Review* 273; Richard A. Epstein, "The Legal Regulation of Lawyers' Conflicts of Interest" (1992), 60 *Fordham Law Review* 579; Jonathan R. Macey and Geoffrey P. Miller, "Reflections on Professional Responsibility in a Regulatory State" (1995), 63 *George Washington Law Review* 1105; and David McGowan, "Why Not Try the Carrot? A Modest Proposal To Grant Immunity to Lawyers Who Disclose Financial Misconduct," *Minnesota Legal Studies Research Paper* no. 04-04 (Minneapolis: University of Minnesota Law School, 2004).

5   Dave Robinson and Chris Garratt, *Ethics for Beginners* (Cambridge: Icon Books, 1996), 8.

6   John Dewey, *The Quest for Certainty* (London: George Allen & Unwin, 1929), 269.

The second objection to an economic account of legal ethics is more basic than the first: the study of legal ethics is supposed to be exciting, and economic theory is not. When students embark upon a study of legal ethics, they hope to study impossible conundrums: Should a defence lawyer betray the confidence of her guilty client where doing so would save an infant's life? Should a lawyer help incorporate a company that will wipe out acres of rainforest or destroy a protected species? Should a criminal lawyer defend a racist charged with hate crimes? Should a lawyer stall proceedings against a client in the hope that an elderly, adverse witness will die before the matter can go to trial? These questions seem more interesting than demand curves, mathematical formulas, and other basic tools of economics. Happily, the tools of economics are incapable of siphoning the excitement out of the study of moral choices. On the contrary, they enhance the study of ethics by providing insights into the ways in which real people grapple with difficult ethical questions. Rather than simply asking "what forms of conduct are prohibited under an ethical code?" or "what may a lawyer do when faced with particular moral questions?," an economic inquiry allows us to probe more deeply into legal ethics: What forms of conduct *ought to be* prohibited? When should the lawyer break the law or violate an ethical code on the ground that doing so is in the lawyer's interest? Can a breach of ethical rules create a better legal system? Questions of this nature are *economic* queries. The study of economics is not the study of fiscal policy or accountancy: it is the study of human choices and a compelling method of predicting, analyzing, and measuring those choices and their effect on the real world.[7] Economics provides an elaborate series of tools that can be used in the evaluation of choices. The ethical choices lawyers make are no exception. Like any choice a person faces, an ethical decision involves a series of cost–benefit calculations which ultimately determine the course of action that the decision maker will take. The tools of economics help us understand, evaluate, and predict these kinds of choices.

The remainder of this chapter focuses on a single question: How can economics help us analyze ethical choices? In answering this question, the chapter begins with a general overview of the economic theory of legal ethics, looking at various legal and ethical issues through an economic lens. Following that overview, the chapter moves on to establish the connection between ethical systems and economic drives. The goal of the concluding portions of the chapter is to demonstrate that, despite our human desire to define ethics by reference to metaphysical notions of "good and evil" or "right and wrong," many core ethical concepts owe their origin to the economic ideas of self-interest, scarcity, and wealth maximization. On a fundamental level, we are ethical (or unethical) because we want to survive and prosper. Our ethics flow (at least in part) from economic drives. It therefore seems quite sensible to analyze ethical choices through the use of the tools of economic reasoning.

---

7   As Cooter and Ulen noted in the first edition of *Law and Economics* (New York: Harper Collins, 1988), 11, "[E]conomic concepts such as maximization, equilibrium, and efficiency are fundamental categories for explaining society, especially the behavior of rational people responding to rules of law." In short, "economics" can be defined as the study of rational responses to incentives.

B. A New Perspective

The best way to become accustomed to observing the world through an economic lens is to use concrete examples. The purpose of this section is to demonstrate a basic economic analysis of standard legal relations and to use that analysis to build the groundwork for an economic theory of legal ethics. Consider the following situation.

Example 1.1

Ted is in the business of making widgets. Poonam, whose widget supply is low, wishes to purchase a dozen widgets from Ted for $2,000. Poonam is happy to pay $2,000 for the widgets, because she values them at $2,500. Ted is happy to accept $2,000 for the widgets, because they cost him only $1,500 to produce. As a result, Ted agrees to sell Poonam a dozen widgets in exchange for Poonam's payment of $2,000.

What has Ted *really* agreed to do?

A simple view of this scenario suggests that Ted has agreed to do exactly what he said he would do under the terms of his agreement: Ted has agreed to convey one dozen widgets to Poonam in exchange for Poonam's payment of $2,000. A lawyer or an economist might take a different view. A lawyer, for example, might note that the law of contract requires that Ted *either* deliver the widgets to Poonam *or* pay whatever damages the law requires in the event of a breach of contract. Under a system of expectation damages,[8] those damages would be equal to whatever dollar figure would be sufficient to place Poonam in the economic position she would have occupied had Ted lived up to the terms of his agreement.[9] As a result, a lawyer might not contend that Ted has simply agreed to sell his widgets. On the contrary, from a lawyer's perspective Ted has agreed to *either* (1) deliver the widgets, *or* (2) pay Poonam whatever damages are required to put her into the economic position she would have enjoyed had Ted abided by the explicit terms of the contract. The lawyer views the possibility of breach (and the ensuing legal consequences) as an unstated element of the agreement and an option that Ted has from the moment that the contract is accepted. When he fails to deliver widgets, Ted has not

---

8   The object of expectation damages is to place the victim of a contractual breach into the economic position that he or she would have occupied had the other (breaching) party lived up to the terms of the contract. As Cooter and Ulen point out in *Law and Economics*, 4th ed. (Boston: Pearson Addison Wesley, 2003), 239: "If expectation damages ... achieve their purpose, the potential victim of breach is equally well off whether there is performance, on the one hand, or breach and payment of damages, on the other hand. We say that *perfect expectation damages* leave potential victims *indifferent* between performance and breach."

9   In this example, damages should equal $500 (the economic surplus that Poonam would enjoy as a result of the widget contract). Since Poonam values the widgets at $2,500 and only pays $2,000, she hoped to improve her economic position by $500 through the agreement to purchase widgets. If Ted breaches this agreement, he must replace the $500 gain that Poonam would have received had Ted adhered to the terms of the contract. Since the contract would have given Poonam a $500 benefit, she is neutral as between (1) Ted's adherence to the agreement and (2) receiving a damage payment of $500. Either way, she comes out $500 ahead of where she started.

committed an ethical violation. On the contrary, he has simply opted to take the contractual route of expectation damages rather than the contractual route of widget delivery. By viewing Ted's agreement through the lens of contract law, we change our views concerning the nature of Ted's contractual obligations.

An economic view of example 1.1 takes the lawyer's analysis one step further. What if Ted found someone else (say, Alice) who would be willing to pay $3,000 for one dozen of Ted's widgets? Unfortunately, Ted has only one dozen widgets available for sale: he cannot convey the same 12 widgets to both Poonam and Alice, and he has already agreed to sell the widgets to Poonam. What should Ted do now? Ted can either (1) deliver the widgets to Poonam in accordance with the terms of the agreement, or (2) breach the agreement (paying whatever damages contract law requires) and convey the widgets to Alice in exchange for $3,000.

If Ted adheres to the terms of his agreement, he will deliver the widgets to Poonam and enjoy a profit of $500 (the difference between Poonam's payment of $2,000 and the $1,500 it costs Ted to produce the widgets). If Ted violates his agreement and sells the widgets to Alice, he will enjoy a profit of $1,000—that is, $3,000 from Alice minus (1) the $1,500 cost of producing a dozen widgets and (2) a $500 damage payment to Poonam. By breaching his promise to sell the widgets to Poonam and instead conveying the widgets to Alice, Ted is $500 better off (earning $1,000 by breaching rather than $500 by adhering to the explicit terms of his contract). From an economic perspective, Ted *should* violate the explicit terms of his contract. This is an example of what economists call an "efficient breach" of contract (a concept that will be important throughout part I of this book).[10] Although Ted is breaching the contract (by failing to deliver the widgets to Poonam), in so doing he is making the world (in economic terms) a better place. Poonam is no worse off than she would have been had Ted delivered the widgets (she is equally pleased to receive the widgets, which would have provided her with a $500 economic benefit, or to receive a damage payment equal to $500).[11] Ted is $500 better off by breaching the contract and selling the widgets to Alice. Assuming that Alice values the widgets at more than $3,000 (which she must, since she was wiling to give up $3,000 in exchange for the widgets in question), she is economically better off than she would have been had Ted gone along with the terms of his original agreement. It is efficient for Ted to breach this contract (and sell the widgets to Alice), because the overall gain inherent in the widget sales agreement has increased through Ted's decision to breach the contract. In economic terms, the surplus generated by Ted's relationship with Poonam (that is, the economic gain that would inure to the benefit of all of the relevant parties) is maximized

---

10   In the first edition of *Law and Economics*, supra note 7, Cooter and Ulen provided the following definition of "efficient breach" (at 290-91):

     [A] breach of contract is more efficient than performance of the contract when the costs of performance exceed the benefits to all the parties ... . The costs of performance exceed the benefits when a contingency arises such that the resources necessary for performance are more valuable in an alternative use ... . Incentives for breach are efficient when the transfer of resources to the highest-valued use is accomplished at the lowest transaction costs and in such a way that no one is made worse off by the transfer and at least one person is made better off.

11   See supra note 9.

where Ted breaks his agreement with Poonam, sells the widgets to Alice and (through the payment of expectation damages) puts Poonam into the economic position she would have occupied had Ted adhered to the terms of the original agreement.[12]

Presumably, Poonam and Ted entered their agreement with the principal goal of economic gain. Generally speaking, people enter contracts in order to obtain some form of economic advantage. Since the principal motivation for a contract is economic gain, the best decision for contracting parties to make is whatever decision gives rise to the optimal economic gain. As a result, a rational economist would support Ted's decision to breach the contract with Poonam—the decision to breach the contract maximizes the economic gains that are distributed among all of the relevant players.

The foregoing illustration provides a simplified example of the way in which economics helps us evaluate decisions. Without undertaking an economic analysis, people might support a general rule that breaching a contract is an undesirable act, perhaps even an "unethical" form of behaviour. The economist, by contrast, undertakes a cost–benefit analysis of the decision to breach a contract and analyzes the outcomes that may flow from the choices available to the parties. The economic analysis of the widget sales agreement allows us to see that, in certain situations, breaching a contract might be "the right thing to do" in the sense that it leaves all relevant parties better off than they would have been if they had adhered to the original terms of their agreement. By viewing Ted's contractual obligations through the lens of economics, we come to appreciate (1) the objective of the original agreement—that is, economic gain—and (2) the way in which a breach of the agreement may achieve the goal of economic gain more successfully than adherence to the terms of the agreement.

Our analysis of example 1.1 was an "economic analysis" not because it related to profit or to monetary sums—an economic analysis needn't relate to financial issues. Rather, an "economic analysis" simply refers to any analysis focusing on "the implications of rational choice."[13] Economics is not confined to the study of money, fiscal policy, or the economy. It is the study of rational choices and the impacts that those choices are likely to have on the real world. As a result, we can turn our economic lens toward any system of choices, whether or not the choices in question relate to monetary sums.

---

12   Note that a similar account of expectation damages is frequently used, incorrectly, to prove that expectation damages are necessarily superior to the contractual remedy known as "specific performance" (which, in this instance, would have required Ted to convey his widgets to Poonam). A thorough economic comparison of the remedies of "expectation damages," on the one hand, and "specific performance," on the other, actually reveals that, whichever remedy is chosen, the goods that are the subject of the contract should, in theory, end up in the same individual's hands (the details of this argument are beyond the scope of this book). As a result, this example should not be taken as an economic endorsement of the remedy of expectation damages. On the contrary, it is simply an example of the manner in which a particular rule of law (in this instance, the requirement of expectation damages) can affect the decision-making process of rational individuals.

13   David Friedman, *Law's Order* (Princeton, NJ: Princeton University Press, 2000), 8.

C. Ethical Choices

The form of economic analysis applied in the previous section can be extended into the realm of legal ethics. Consider the "Barristers Oath," an oath that lawyers must take upon their admission to the bar of Ontario:

> You are called to the Degree of Barrister-at-law to protect and defend the rights and interest of such citizens as may employ you. You shall conduct all cases faithfully and to the best of your ability. You shall neglect no one's interest nor seek to destroy any one's property. You shall not be guilty of champerty or maintenance. You shall not refuse causes of complaint reasonably founded, nor shall you promote suits upon frivolous pretences. You shall not pervert the law to favour or prejudice any one, but in all things shall conduct yourself truly and with integrity. In fine, the Queen's interest and the interest of citizens you shall uphold and maintain according to the constitution and law of this Province. All this you do swear to observe and perform to the best of your knowledge and ability. So help you God.[14]

What does this oath mean? From a "plain meaning" perspective, one could argue that the oath entails precisely what it says: the new lawyer swears to "observe and perform" the various promises found within the oath. But what does the oath mean from an economic perspective? Recall example 1.1, above. As we saw in that example, Ted's promise to sell his widgets could be regarded as something *other than* a promise to sell widgets. Instead, it could be regarded as a promise to either (1) sell the widgets, or (2) pay whatever damages might be awarded as a result of his failure to sell his widgets to Poonam. By the same token, the Barristers Oath can be regarded as a promise to either (1) dutifully observe the various promises found within the text of the oath, or (2) submit to whatever penalty might flow from a decision to break those promises. Consider the following example.

Example 1.2

> Norman is a lawyer in the province of Ontario. He has taken the Barristers Oath and has sworn (based on the oath's literal language) to "uphold the Queen's interest ... according to ... the law of [Ontario]." The Law Society of Upper Canada (the body charged with regulating legal ethics in Ontario) has set the penalty for breach of the Barristers Oath at $5,000—this is the only form of punishment the Law Society imposes for violations of the oath.[15]

From an economic perspective, Norman has agreed to *either* uphold the Queen's interest *or* to submit to whatever penalty might flow from his failure to do so. Assume that Norman opposes the monarchy, and took the Barristers Oath because it was the only way that he could become a lawyer. In pursuit of his anti-monarchist agenda, Norman is contemplating a non-violent (yet disruptive) act of civil disobedience (such as a "sit-in" at the Legislative Assembly). Assume that Norman's act of civil disobedience would

---

14   The "Barristers Oath" is found in bylaw 11, s. 6(6) of the *By-Laws of the Law Society of Upper Canada*.

15   This penalty is hypothetical.

(1) violate the language of the oath, giving rise to a fine of $5,000, and (2) violate various provincial laws, giving rise to additional fines totalling $3,000.

Assuming that Norman is a rational person armed with forethought and full knowledge of the costs that flow from a breach of the Barristers Oath, Norman is now equipped with all the tools he needs in order to choose his course of action. He can either (1) abide by the Barristers Oath and adhere to provincial laws, or (2) violate the oath and the relevant laws, incurring fines totalling $8,000. Norman must now engage in a cost–benefit analysis. If Norman would gladly give up $8,000 (or more) in order to rail against the monarchy, he should violate the oath (and related provincial laws) and engage in his contemplated act of disobedience. Norman will be giving up an asset worth $8,000 (namely, the cash required to pay the relevant fines) in exchange for another asset (namely, the right to engage in the contemplated act of disobedience) which Norman values more than $8,000. If Norman sets a personal value of $10,000 on this particular act of civil disobedience (in the sense that he would happily forgo $10,000 of income in order to engage in the relevant act), he will be better off by breaking his oath and paying the relevant fines. In effect, he will have purchased $10,000 worth of civil disobedience for a price of only $8,000. For Norman, that is a bargain.

What is the Law Society's perspective in this scenario? On the facts of this example, the Law Society levies a fine of $5,000 whenever someone breaches the terms of the Barristers Oath. From one perspective, this means that the Law Society has set a *price* of $5,000 for any action that violates the terms of the oath. As Cooter and Ulen note:

> [T]he rules established by law establish implicit prices for different kinds of behavior, and the consequences of those rules can be analyzed as the response to those implicit prices.[16]

From this perspective, there is no question of "good" or "bad" in Norman's decision to breach the oath. Rather, the Law Society has simply set a price for a specific type of behaviour: it costs $5,000 to do anything that conflicts with the promises found within the oath. If Norman chooses to break the oath, he has done nothing sinister or malicious. On the contrary, Norman has simply purchased an asset (the right to engage in certain behaviour) at the price ($5,000) that the Law Society has set. Because the Law Society has set the price at $5,000 per violation, the Law Society should be neutral as between (1) receiving the $5,000 fine, and (2) having Norman refrain from his acts of disobedience. In effect, the Law Society is in the business of selling "ethical indulgences" at prices that it defines.[17] Through its regulation of lawyers' behaviour, the Law Society has established the market price of violations of the Barristers Oath. If the Law Society shows a strong preference for receiving the $5,000 fine, the Law Society has set the market price too high.[18] If the Law Society shows a strong preference for having Norman abide by the terms of the oath rather than paying the fine, the Law Society has set the

---

16   Cooter and Ulen, 1st ed., supra note 7, at 11.

17   Since the Law Society is the only institution in a position to "sell" breaches of the lawyers' ethical code, it could be argued (from an economic perspective) that *the Law Society has a monopoly on unethical behaviour*. This perspective is developed in chapter 4.

18   Note that this is only one possible economic explanation of the Law Society's perspective. Alternative (and, in my view, more sensible) explanations will be developed in chapter 4.

price too low. If this is the case, the Law Society should increase the relevant fine and ensure that only those who are willing to pay a much greater sum (say, $50,000) will be willing to pay the fee to break the oath.

At first blush, an economic view of promise keeping may seem unsettlingly mercenary. For many people, the decision to break a promise seems more troubling than the purchase of an asset. Breaking a vow seems more ethically questionable than purchasing a bicycle or buying groceries. One might think, for example, that Norman's decision to break an oath makes Norman a bad person. He is not merely breaching a contractual obligation and paying the requisite fee—instead, he is breaking an *ethical* obligation and demonstrating a lack of moral fibre. This objection can be overcome through a more thoroughgoing economic analysis.[19] Assuming that the objection is correct and that there are moral implications to Norman's decision to break his promise, the costs of these moral implications can be factored into our ethical calculations. If the "moral element" of oath breaking leads, for example, to feelings of guilt or a reputation for dishonesty, these consequences can be analyzed as economic costs. While it is difficult to place a dollar value on a person's reputation, it is not impossible to do so. Indeed, courts do this rather frequently in cases involving defamation of character. An economist would demand that we take account of these values when deciding whether to take an ethically questionable course of action. When assessing Norman's decision to violate the Barristers Oath, for example, an economist would require Norman to take account of *all* costs (pecuniary and moral) that flow from his decision to break the oath.[20] Any damage to Norman's reputation, any loss of future income due to possible disrepute, or any other losses that flow from Norman's decision to break the oath must be incorporated into the "price" associated with Norman's actions. Norman must determine the value of all these costs and then add these costs to the fines that he will pay. This final sum (made up of fines plus "moral" costs) is the true economic cost of breaking an oath. Where the gains associated with breaking the oath outweigh the total cost, the rational person will break the oath and thereby maximize his or her well-being. While it may be difficult to regard this as a "moral" form of reasoning, it may be easier to see this in more dramatic examples: if

---

19   On a rhetorical level, this objection can also be overcome by reference to precedent. Consider the example of Gandhi (upon whose life Norman's fact situation is loosely based). Gandhi was a lawyer, yet Gandhi engaged in various acts of civil disobedience in order to eliminate the British monarchy's hold on India. This was an economic choice. For Gandhi, the costs associated with civil disobedience (including potential disbarment, imprisonment, and fines) were more than offset by the gains that he associated with an independent India. Gandhi made a rational, economic choice to violate local laws and professional regulations. The asset to be gained (a free India) was worth more to Gandhi than the costs that he incurred. The fact that this choice can be explained by economics has no impact on the "morality" of Gandhi's decisions or behaviour—it simply demonstrates the ability of economics to describe moral decisions.

20   Norman's decision to break the oath will not only impose costs on Norman (in the form of guilt or a bad reputation). On the contrary, this decision will also impose external costs (by diminishing the reputation of lawyers generally, for example, or by impairing the legal system). Presumably, these costs have been factored into the fines that Norman pays ($5,000 to the Law Society and $3,000 to the province). As a result, these "externalities" have already been factored into Norman's decision. If the external costs created by Norman's decision are not fully reflected in the fines, the fines should be increased. This topic is addressed in chapter 4.

Norman's decision to break the oath would save the life of Norman's child, for example, it would be apparent (to many people) that breaking the oath was the right decision. The value of the child's life outweighs the costs that would be associated with a decision to keep a promise (including the relevant financial costs as well as any intangible costs that Norman would incur). Whenever we engage in moral reasoning of this nature—that is, justifying a questionable act by reference to a goal that it achieves—we are engaging in a cost–benefit analysis. This is a basic form of economic reasoning.

The foregoing economic perspective can be summed up rather simply: an individual can do whatever he or she desires as long as that individual is willing to pay the price. In short, "you may continue to do harm to your neighbors so long as you pay a fee for it."[21] Actions are neither intrinsically good nor intrinsically bad; they give rise to various benefits and costs. The study of ethics is simply the study of the manner in which individuals calculate and respond to those costs and benefits. This is essentially an economic inquiry.

The examples of economic analysis set forth in this section are relatively simplistic. Indeed, a more thoroughgoing economic analysis may lead us to question the conclusions that we reached when analyzing ethical and contractual duties. Throughout the remainder of this book, we develop the tools required to undertake a thorough economic analysis that allows us to more carefully balance the costs and benefits of ethical (and unethical) decisions. For now, it is sufficient to note that human actions generate various costs and benefits, and that legal or ethical rules impose costs and provide incentives. The tools of economics allow us to weigh those costs, benefits, and incentives and to determine what a rational person will do when faced with a choice between competing courses of action. This analysis applies to any form of rational choice, including an individual's decision to adhere to (or violate) a code of ethics. As a result, one can use an economic analysis to evaluate the consequences of ethical decisions.

II. The Nature of Ethics
A. Introduction

The illustrations in section I demonstrate the use of economics in the evaluation of ethical choices. While these illustrations may be useful in demonstrating a typical economic analysis, they fail to answer a critical question: while ethics *can* be analyzed from an economic perspective, does it make sense to analyze ethics in this way? Why should we bother applying economic reasoning to ethical issues? The answer to this question may be surprising to those who are unfamiliar with economic reasoning. Although an economic analysis of ethics might initially seem unpalatable, a careful review of ethical systems makes it clear that economics is not only relevant to the study of legal ethics, but also the source from which many important ethical values flow. Simply put, ethics are (at least in part) economic concepts, owing their origins to economic notions. This idea is explored in the following sections of this chapter.

---

21   Per Jansen J (dissenting) in *Boomer v. Atlantic Cement Co., Inc.*, 309 NYS 2d 312, at 321 (Ct. App. NY 1970) (quoted in Cooter and Ulen, 4th ed., supra note 8, at 171).

B. What Are Ethics?

Ethics are a product of human minds.[22] Like poetry, car insurance, fax machines, and income tax, the central ideas that form an ethical system flow from the thoughts of human beings. Like any form of voluntary human behaviour, ethics can be regarded as a form of stimulus response: in response to certain stimuli, human neurons fire in ways that ultimately produce an ethical system. At its core, the subject of ethics is a form of behavioural science—the study of how human beings behave when they decide that certain actions are "right" or "wrong." As a form of human behaviour, the practice of creating and responding to ethical codes should be analyzed like any behavioural system. We must ask *why* people engage in the relevant conduct and *what* people do when pursuing the behaviour in question. What are the stimuli that lead to ethical systems, and what is the nature of the human mind's response?

The first step in analyzing ethics is to consider the root causes of ethical systems. Why is it that humans create (and often adhere to) a series of guidelines that purport to differentiate "right" and "wrong"? A complete answer to this question is beyond the scope of this book. Indeed, there is no single cause of every phenomenon that is embraced by the term "ethics." While our ethical beliefs concerning lying and truth telling might be rooted in reciprocity and self-interest, other ethical beliefs, such as the belief that torturing infants is immoral, might have deep, genetic roots with little or no relation to other ethical values.[23] The fact that these beliefs are often amalgamated under the label "ethics" need not imply a common origin. Indeed, the word "ethics" (like any categorical label) is simply a frequently useful tag that can be used to describe a loosely related group of discrete phenomena.[24] Despite the varying nature of ethical values, however, a significant number of foundational ethical norms share an important feature—they are grounded in economics. The relationship between economics and ethical systems is explored in the following section of this chapter.

C. The Roots of Ethical Systems

One way to observe the economic foundations of ethical values is to imagine a world in which ethics do not exist. What would happen in a world where lies were just as acceptable as truth, where people had no sense of "fairness" or "unfairness," and where no mode of activity could give rise to moral censure? In such a world, many forms of interaction would be costly. Consider the following situation.

---

22   Some readers may find this notion distasteful because it ignores the role of spirituality in ethical reasoning. However, this is not the case. Even if ethical notions are derived from a metaphysical source, the mechanism by which we consider and apply those "spiritual ethics" is, of course, the human mind.

23   This argument should not be taken as a suggestion that the ethic against torturing infants is *not* rooted in reciprocity and self-interest, or that there is no genetic imperative against lying: it simply suggests that individual ethical beliefs may, in fact, be drawn from different sources.

24   The "linguistic" problems inherent in a term such as "ethics," together with the impact of those problems on the economic account of legal ethics, are discussed in chapter 5.

Example 1.3

> Alex and Mina live in a world without ethics. Alex wishes to acquire $10,000 worth of Mina's widgets. Alex values the widgets at $10,000, and hopes to pay as little as possible. Mina incurred a cost of $5,000 making the widgets in question, and she hopes to sell them for the highest possible price.

Because there is no ethical system in this hypothetical universe, Alex's first approach to acquiring Mina's widgets should be theft.[25] It will almost certainly cost Alex less to steal the widgets than it would cost him to purchase the widgets on the market, and (if he is rational) Alex would prefer to maximize his wealth by acquiring the widgets at the lowest possible cost. Alex has no moral compunctions concerning the theft of Mina's property, as moral compunctions do not exist in this hypothetical world. More importantly, no one who detects Alex's theft will hold it against him: theft is not *wrong* in an amoral universe; it is simply another way of doing business.

Knowing that there is nothing preventing Alex from attempting to steal her property, Mina will expend resources in an effort to prevent Alex (and everyone else) from taking her widgets. If she expends sufficient resources on protection (by installing an effective security system in her widget factory, for example), then Alex will be forced either (1) to expend resources in an attempt to circumvent the security system, or (2) to offer to make a mutually profitable exchange.[26] If Alex chooses option 2 (because it is less costly than attempting to circumvent Mina's elaborate security system), a lack of ethics presents additional problems: Mina will almost certainly force Alex to pay her in advance, because she has no reason to believe that Alex will pay her once the widgets are in his clutches.[27] Since no rule of ethics compels Mina to adhere to her side of the agreement, Alex is equally distrustful and will expend substantial resources ensuring that Mina complies with the terms of the agreement. Before Alex willingly parts with his money, he will want to ensure that (1) Mina actually has the widgets that she has agreed to sell, (2) the widgets are of the quality stipulated in the agreement, and (3) Mina will deliver the widgets once Alex's payment has been made. No one else (including the legal system, in the unlikely event that one exists in a non-ethical world) will give Alex these assurances or bear the cost of ensuring that Mina will comply with the contract: no one cares if Mina takes advantage of Alex, because everyone in this hypothetical world is neutral as between ethical and unethical forms of behaviour.[28] The only way to safeguard one's own interests in this universe is to expend resources in pursuit of self-protection.

---

25   For the purposes of this example, we are presuming that I will not simply give you my widgets unless you can offer me something valuable in exchange.

26   A threat of reprisal (by the victim of unethical behaviour) constitutes a cost of self-protection. In order to make good on such a threat, the victim of unethical behaviour will have to expend resources when exacting revenge.

27   For this reason, it is unlikely that credit will be a feature of our non-ethical universe.

28   Indeed, residents of this hypothetical world would have no way of differentiating "ethical" from "unethical" behaviour.

In this example, if Alex does not spend adequate resources monitoring Mina's conduct and preventing her from engaging in unscrupulous behaviour, Mina is certain to take advantage of Alex's trusting nature. She will keep Alex's money and her widgets, and Alex will rue the day that he attempted to make a contract in a non-ethical world. If, by contrast, Alex does expend sufficient resources to ensure Mina's compliance with the agreement, Alex will pay his money, Mina will deliver the widgets, and the exchange will be completed. To bring this contract to fruition, Alex and Mina have each been forced to expend significant resources in order to safeguard their respective interests. Expenditures of this nature, which are known as "transaction costs" in economic circles,[29] are not unique to non-ethical worlds. Indeed, contracting parties in the real world incur costs of this nature every day, performing credit checks, title searches, and other costly actions that are designed to detect and minimize the impact of unscrupulous conduct. In our non-ethical world, however, these costs would be much greater. There is no disincentive to stealing, lying, or cheating in a non-ethical universe. In other words, there are no costs or penalties for behaving unethically. No one will ever feel guilty for having cheated; no one will face social pressure to be honest; and no one has a reason to be fair to arm's-length parties. As a result, individuals in a non-ethical universe have to expend substantial resources in an effort to protect themselves from other people. These other people will then spend their resources attempting to circumvent the protection that others have purchased.[30] The resources that individuals spend on self-protection (and on circumventing each other's protective methods) will be wasted, unavailable for use in productive ventures. This waste is inefficient, because resources could be put to use in more productive ways.

Needless to say, the residents of our hypothetical, non-ethical universe would quickly see their resources dwindling. It seems likely that, in the absence of a pre-existing ethical system, individuals would be compelled to *invent* an ethical system in order to minimize the waste associated with self-protection. The manner in which an ethical system can reduce transaction costs is straightforward. Assume that the first ethic introduced in our community is an ethic against dishonesty and theft. If an individual violates an agreement and cheats a contractual partner out of money, the members of the community will disapprove of the cheating party's actions. The cheater will incur a reputational cost (by being branded a cheater), and it will become increasingly costly for the cheater to transact with other people. Our hypothetical cheater may have to give collateral, make all payments in advance, or pay a premium for goods or services that the cheater purchases.

---

29   Cooter and Ulen, 4th ed., supra note 8, at 91-92, define "transaction costs" as follows:

> Transaction costs are the costs of exchange. An exchange has three steps. First, an exchange partner has to be located ... . Second, a bargain must be struck between the exchange partners. A bargain is reached by successful negotiation, which may include the drafting of an agreement. Third, after a bargain has been reached, it must be enforced. Enforcement involves monitoring performance of the parties and punishing violations of the agreement. We may call the three forms of transaction costs corresponding to these three steps of an exchange: (1) search costs, (2) bargaining costs, and (3) enforcement costs.

30   It is important to note that this hypothetical universe is not a world in which people are basically "bad." It is a universe where there is simply no notion of "good" or "bad," so people tend to behave in whatever manner benefits them the most without regard for any moral considerations.

In other cases, disapproving members of the community may refuse to deal with the cheater altogether.[31] Certain services may become unavailable to the cheater as a result of his or her bad reputation. The cheater may ultimately be forced to be self-sufficient, losing all the advantages that are inherent in cooperative exchange. Provided that our hypothetical cheater is armed with foresight, he or she is now far less likely to engage in unethical conduct. While a cheater might gain $2,000 (for example) by swindling a contractual partner today, he or she stands to lose far more than $2,000 in the future (in the form of social stigma and other losses that flow from moral censure). As Cooter and Ulen note in *Law and Economics*, a society armed with an ethical code

> uses certain non-legal incentives to minimize the occurrence of breach of contract. Of these, one of the most powerful is the value of one's reputation. Because a reputation as a trustworthy contractual partner is sometimes valuable, a reputation as one who breaches contracts is detrimental and may restrain the impulse to engage in breach except in the most serious cases.[32]

Where society imposes a reputational cost on those who cheat contractual partners, the cost of cheating contractual partners may outweigh the gains associated with cheating. If our hypothetical cheater continues down an unethical path, and in so doing consistently incurs costs that outweigh the gains that might be generated through unscrupulous activity, the cheater will quickly squander his or her resources. The presence of an ethical system (which carries with it the possibility of community censure) makes anti-social behaviour far more costly than it otherwise would be. As a result, an individual's ability to profit from anti-social behaviour is significantly diminished where ethical rules exist. To put it bluntly, the presence of an ethical system makes unethical conduct more expensive.

To the extent that the costs of behaving unethically outweigh the gains that an unethically minded person might generate through unscrupulous dealings, rational individuals will abstain from unethical conduct in order to preserve their resources. Through its ability to impose costs on unethical actors, the threat of moral disapproval deters individuals from engaging in unethical behaviour. The diminished likelihood of unethical dealings allows everyone to spend fewer resources on self-protection: when you live in a safe neighbourhood, you can afford to install a less extensive security system. Once an ethical system has been established, resources that would otherwise have been spent on self-protection may now be used in more efficient, productive ways.[33] The presence of an ethical system has effectively diminished the overall cost of interacting with other people. By preserving community resources and promoting collective behaviour, the ethical system makes survival and prosperity far more likely. In other words, one of the principal

---

31   As Friedman, supra note 13, at 145 notes: "Reputation may be the most important method for enforcing agreements in our society, although not the one of most interest to lawyers."

32   Cooter and Ulen, 1st ed., supra note 7, at 289.

33   As we shall see, by adopting an ethical code we are still paying a fee for self-protection. This fee now comes in the form of our decision to refrain from potentially profitable unethical behaviour. We give up one asset (the right to be unethical) rather than another (the costs associated with self-protection), presumably on the basis that the resources expended in self-protection are more valuable than our right to engage in unethical behaviour.

effects of ethical systems is to promote our species' survival and prosperity. The ethical system preserves resources, allows trade and common defence, and permits us to rely on one another to survive. The manner in which ethical systems achieve these goals is through the creation of incentives for cooperative behaviour and disincentives for anti-social conduct. Any system that alters behaviour through the creation of incentives and disincentives is (by definition) an economic system. It accordingly makes sense to use the tools of economics to describe and evaluate the system in question.

The foregoing discussion is not an account of the origin of an actual ethical system: no long-forgotten group of community elders gathered together to produce a schedule of costs that they could impose on all unethical actors.[34] On the contrary, it merely serves to illustrate two points: (1) the ability of an ethical system \to facilitate cooperative behaviour (by reducing costs associated with excessive self-protection and deterring individuals from unethical conduct), and (2) the essentially economic nature of ethical reasoning.

Once the notions of "ethical" and "unethical" (together with the possibility of moral censure) have been established, there are predictable costs associated with the decision to take an unethical course of action. When deciding what actions to take, a rational individual will take into account the outcomes and costs associated with potential decisions. The rational actor will take whichever course he or she believes will bring the greatest gain (meaning the largest possible benefit at the lowest possible cost). When people opt for an ethical course of action, they do so because they believe (generally on a subconscious level) that they will be better off for having adopted an ethical stance. By the same token, an individual who decides to pursue an *unethical* course of action will typically do so because he or she believes that the net gains generated by unethical conduct will be greater than the gains that would have accrued if he or she had adopted an ethical stance. In other words, the decision to be ethical or unethical is rooted in self-interest. Whichever course of action (ethical or unethical) will yield the greatest gain for the relevant actor is the course of action that the actor will choose. The presence of an ethical system does not change the way in which people govern their affairs: they still perform a self-interested cost–benefit computation when deciding how to behave. The presence of an ethical system does not eliminate the spectre of self-interest; it merely changes the costs that must be taken into account when people calculate the costs and benefits of unethical actions.[35] Whether or not an ethical system exists, individuals will inevitably tally the costs and benefits associated with potential courses of action—the presence of an ethical system merely changes the math.

From another perspective, all individuals within an ethical system are engaged in a process of exchange. Each individual (when deciding whether to adhere to a community's ethical code) engages in a cost–benefit analysis, deciding whether to give up one asset—

---

34   Note that modern ethical systems *are* produced in this way: a group of community elders—namely, elected representatives—gathers together (in the legislative assembly) to produce a schedule of costs—namely, legal penalties—they can impose on unethical actors—namely, individuals who violate the law.

35   In 2003, during "Operation Iraqi Freedom," the US government repeatedly claimed that the Iraqi regime would not abuse American captives because it would not be "in the Iraqis' self-interest" to torture captives. This statement is an endorsement of the cost–benefit analysis that is inherent in all ethical decisions, as well as the power of "community censure" to control a self-interested ethical calculation.

that is, the right to engage in and profit from unethical behaviour—in exchange for other assets—for example, a favourable reputation or an increased likelihood that others will act ethically in response. In either case, the decision is driven by the actor's predictions and perceptions concerning the costs and benefits flowing from particular activities. By definition, this is an economic decision. As a result, our decision to adhere to (or depart from) our community's ethical code is essentially an economic choice. This choice is best evaluated through economic analysis.

Throughout this chapter we have seen that ethical systems can be "judged by the structure of incentives they establish and the consequences of people altering their behavior in response to those incentives."[36] On a fundamental level, this is the nature of an economic analysis. An economist observes the rules that govern a system of conduct, considers the incentives and consequences created by those rules, and predicts the outcomes that will be generated as a result of people's responses. Whether those rules relate to money, law, or ethics, they are amenable to an economic analysis. Indeed, wherever humans create a system of penalties and incentives with a view to modifying human behaviour, economics provides a useful means of evaluating that system.

One objection to an economic account of ethical systems (as opposed to systems of law or fiscal policy) relates to the "mystical notions" that were described at the outset of this chapter. People flinch at the idea of ethical systems that relate to profit motives or to economic needs. As John Dewey noted:

> To many persons, the idea that the ends professed by morals are impotent save as they are connected with the working machinery of economic life seems like deflowering the purity of moral values and obligations.[37]

In other words, people prefer to believe that ethics are rooted in philosophical notions beyond the explanatory power of economics. The most obvious of these philosophical notions is altruism: the desire to help others at the expense of one's own needs. Happily, economics is perfectly capable of dealing with altruism and other metaphysical notions. One way in which economics can account for altruism is discussed in the following section of this chapter.

D. Altruism

An economic approach to ethical reasoning strikes many people as a hollow and inaccurate view of ethics. Ethics, it is argued, are not linked to a profit motive: they are rooted in altruistic tendencies inherent in decent human beings. With respect, this objection is premised on an unduly narrow view of economics. Economists are perfectly happy to acknowledge that people are frequently motivated by altruistic aims. Many people (including a few economists I have met) would be happy to give up large portions of their income in order to end child poverty, ease the suffering of the sick, or improve the lives of those who are unable to help themselves. They would sacrifice their property, their

---

36   Friedman, supra note 13, at 11.

37   Dewey, supra note 6, at 269.

security, or their lives in order to achieve a laudable philanthropic goal. Many people might even give to worthy causes without availing themselves of income tax incentives. These people are not anomalies who disprove the economic theory of ethics. An economic theory does not deny the possibility of altruistic motives. Indeed, economics is perfectly able to take account of intangible preferences (such as altruism) when conducting an analysis of ethical decisions. Consider the following example:

Example 1.4

Mary is a philanthropist. She has the opportunity to raise a great deal of money ($100,000) for the purpose of helping Canadian orphans. During the course of her money-raising venture, Mary has the opportunity to embezzle $20,000 from the Canadian Orphan Fund. There is no chance that Mary will ever be caught.

Critics of economic analyses may contend that economics would provide a distorted view of Mary's decision. According to a narrow view of economics, Mary would (in this example) profit $20,000 by embezzling from the charity. If she refrains from taking the money, her profit will be $0. As a result, one could argue that (if ethics are truly rooted in self-interested, economic calculations) a rational person in Mary's position would inevitably choose to embezzle the money. A good economist knows that this is not an accurate picture of Mary's choice. Mary's sense of altruism (in the form of her commitment to the charity) is surely *worth* something to her. She may be happy to forgo a great deal of her own income in order to ensure that the charity prospers. If someone were to approach Mary and offer her a choice between $10 and an end to all child poverty, for example, Mary would surely take the second option. Moreover, Mary may place a high value on her personal sense of right and wrong. She may, for example, be willing to forgo $10,000 of disposable income in order to avoid feelings of guilt associated with stealing from a charity.[38] She may be willing to give up a further $5,000 in order to ensure that all the charity's funds go to appropriate beneficiaries. Finally, Mary may value her sense of self-respect and good character as much as she values $7,000 worth of tradable goods and services. Assuming that Mary would lose self-respect and experience feelings of guilt if she embezzled the charity's funds, she is better off *not* embezzling.[39] The gross benefit Mary derives from embezzling the money is $20,000 (the amount of money embezzled). The cost of embezzling equals the sum of (1) the value that Mary places on her loss of self-respect ($7,000 in our example), (2) the value Mary places on a guilt-free conscience

---

38 Note that individuals act on "intangible preferences" of this nature every day. A simple example is a person who forgoes overtime pay in order to take a weekend off: the person's intangible preference for leisure is, in economic terms, "worth more" than the value of the cash forgone by failing to take the overtime shift. The difficulty involved in calculating figures of this nature will be addressed in chapter 4.

39 The idea that an altruist may be driven by self-interest to pursue altruistic actions is not a new one. As Immanuel Kant noted in *Fundamental Principles of the Metaphysic of Morals* (New York: Liberal Arts Press, 1949), 296, where an individual's actions appear to inure to the benefit of others, "we cannot from this infer ... that it was not really some secret impulse of self-love, under the false appearance of duty, that was the actual determining cause of the will." The topic of self-interest is explored in chapter 2.

($10,000), and (3) the value Mary derives from seeing the charity's funds directed toward needy children ($5,000). The sum of these costs is $22,000, which is $2,000 more than Mary would gain by embezzling the funds. As a result, Mary would be irrational to embezzle the money, because a decision to embezzle results in a net loss of $2,000.[40]

In this overly simplified example, we observe that economics is capable of accounting for ethereal assets (such as self-respect, a guilt-free conscience, and a sense of altruism) that are not readily convertible into cash. While it is theoretically possible to assign a dollar value to such assets (for example, by determining the amount of income that an actor would forgo in order to have the relevant asset), there is no substantive reason to perform this valuation. All that an economic analysis demands is an ordering of preferences: Mary *prefers* an untarnished reputation, a guilt-free conscience, and a successful charity to 20,000 embezzled dollars in her own pocket. We can accordingly say that Mary's altruistic values are (from Mary's perspective) worth more to her than $20,000. As a result, Mary will give up the opportunity to embezzle $20,000 in order to preserve the intangible (but nonetheless valuable) assets represented by her altruistic values. If Mary refrained from embezzling $20,000 yet jumped at the chance to embezzle $100,000, we could safely assert that Mary's altruistic values were (from Mary's perspective) "worth" some dollar amount between $20,000 and $100,000.

E. Valuation of Choices

The use of dollars as a measurement of value when evaluating ethical decisions may seem crass. It might seem vulgar and counterintuitive to put a price on honesty and integrity. The use of dollar values in such cases does not imply that integrity can be purchased or commodified. On the contrary, the use of a dollar figure is simply a matter of convention: a dollar provides a convenient (and relatively constant) measure of value, which is useful when explaining a person's preferences. I may inform you, for example, that I prefer a luxury car to a bowl of ice cream, but this provides you with very little

---

40   The example of Mary's preference for altruism could fall victim to the following critique (put forward by David Friedman, supra note 13, at 239, in another context):

> An economic theory that is free to eliminate anomalies by explaining them away as due to someone's unexplained and peculiar tastes has very little in the way of testability or predictive power. Our objective is explanation, not description. It is possible that people do have those tastes, but if unexplained tastes are the sole reason for the institutions we wish to explain, we have failed to explain them. And our project is much more interesting if we can show that the institutions our tastes favor are in fact efficient, implying that our peculiar tastes are actually an efficient set of norms.

Happily, there is a partial explanation of the efficiency of the human preference for altruistic deeds. This explanation relates to Joseph Butler's notion that "[e]very particular affection, even the love of our neighbour, is as really our own affection, as self-love; and the pleasure arising from its gratification is as much my own pleasure, as the pleasure self-love would have, from knowing I myself should be happy some time hence, would be my own pleasure" (*Fifteen Sermons* (London: G. Bell & Sons, 1949), 168). The economics of Butler's account have been developed elsewhere, but are beyond the scope of the present work. In future chapters, however, we shall see that "unexplained" preferences for altruism or other intangible notions can actually be explained through an economic analysis.

information concerning the relative weight of my preferences. It would be more informative if I asserted that I was perfectly neutral between a luxury car and 10,000 bowls of ice cream: to me, the car is worth exactly 10,000 bowls of ice cream, and (from my perspective) 10,001 bowls of ice cream would be worth exactly one bowl of ice cream more than a car. "Bowls of ice cream," unfortunately, is a cumbersome measure of value. As a result, we convert our valuation to some standard unit of measurement (such as dollars) in order to make our preference ordering more convenient. If we determine (for example) that I value a bowl of ice cream as much as I value $2, and then determine the dollar value that I would subjectively place on each of my other competing preferences (including intangibles such as altruism, revenge, love, and loyalty), we can then proceed to order my various preferences in a rather convenient way, comparing the dollar value I place on loyalty, for example, to the dollar value that I place on other goods, services, or intangible assets.[41] Comparing dollars to dollars is intuitively easier than comparing bowls of ice cream to altruism or embezzled dollars to loyalty. A standard benchmark of value simply facilitates our comparisons and need not imply that loyalty, love, and self-esteem are convertible into cash.

As we have seen, the fact that one cannot purchase loyalty, love, vengeance, self-respect, or other intangibles on the market does not mean that economics is incapable of taking account of these intangible notions when measuring preferences or evaluating choices. The assignment of a dollar value to an asset does not rely on the notion that one could, in fact, purchase the relevant asset for the relevant dollar value. On the contrary, it merely means that our decision maker values the relevant asset just as much as he or she values a particular sum of money (or particular goods or services that the relevant sum of money could supply). In other words, the dollar amounts used throughout this book merely provide a method of assigning relative weight to competing preferences. We could just as easily use a different standard of measurement (such as "happiness units," "utiles," or "karma points") in order to analyze a decision maker's subjective valuation of competing preferences. For the sake of convention, consistency, and simplicity, however, dollar values will generally be used throughout this book.

Now that we have developed the basic tools required for an economic account of ethical systems, it may be useful to consider how the tools of economics could be used to analyze actual ethical breaches. *Adams v. Law Society of Alberta* (2000) and *Law Society of British Columbia v. A Lawyer* (2000), below, accordingly present judicial decisions involving lawyers who were disciplined as a result of their unethical behaviour. When reading the cases that follow, consider three important questions: (1) What costs and benefits did the relevant lawyers consider when deciding to undertake the actions that gave rise to the proceedings against them? (2) Assuming that the decisions remain "good

---

41   It seems unusual to place a dollar value on love and altruism. That being said, it is possible and convenient to do so. Many people can determine (with relative confidence) that they would gladly give up $1 of income in order to have the love of their parents (for example). The fact that an individual can make this assertion makes it clear that comparisons between sums of money and intangible feelings are possible. As Immanuel Kant, supra note 39, at 51, observed, "Whatever has a value can be replaced by something else which is *equivalent* ... . Whatever has reference to the general inclinations and wants of mankind has a *market value*."

law," how will future lawyers decide whether to engage in conduct similar to that of the lawyers being disciplined in these cases? (3) Can the Law Society's perspective be described through the use of economic terms?

Adams v. Law Society of Alberta
(2000), 266 AR 157; 2000 ABCA 240

THE COURT: This is an appeal by Adams from the Decision of the Benchers of the Law Society of Alberta dismissing his appeal from the Decision of the Hearing Committee that he be disbarred from the practice of law. There were dissenting opinions at both the Committee and Bencher levels regarding the disbarment order.

The matter arose regarding four complaints. The first two counts concerned Adams' conviction for sexual exploitation of his 16-year-old client. …

…

Adams was retained by both the complainant, a 16-year-old who was in youth detention, and her boyfriend, who was also in prison. Adams succeeded in getting the complainant released on bail, whereupon she apparently resumed her activity as a prostitute. Adams contacted the complainant on the stroll, discussed her boyfriend's case and asked her what kind of services she provided for her customers. She told him. He had further contact with her at her home and on the stroll and suggested to her that they get together to have sex. The police had observed the complainant working as a prostitute and spoke to her. She related information concerning Adams to the police. She cooperated with the police by giving a statement and consenting to wear a monitoring device when she met with Adams. Adams does not deny that the meeting was for the sole purpose of having sex. Shortly after arriving in the hotel room, the complainant stepped out, and the police entered as Adams was pulling up and zipping up his pants and tucking in his shirt.

In the monitored conversation, Adams had telephoned the Courthouse, advising that he was out of town and would be late for Court. Also in the monitored conversation between the complainant and Adams, she asked him whether he had had sex with a client before, to which he replied that he had not. In response to her question, he admitted having sex with a prostitute in Europe some years earlier.

As indicated earlier, the Hearing Committee was also aware that on September 22, 1994, four months into his Articles, Adams was charged in Edmonton with unlawfully communicating with a person for the purpose of obtaining the sexual service of a prostitute. On December 2, 1994, Adams pled guilty to the charge in Calgary and was granted an absolute discharge. The matters relating to the complainant in this case occurred just two years later in September 1996. …

[As a result of this behaviour, Adams was disbarred by the Hearing Committee.]

Adams' first ground of appeal is that the Hearing Committee overemphasized the harm to the reputation of the legal profession. The question of what effect a lawyer's misconduct will have on the reputation of the legal profession generally is at the very heart of a disciplinary hearing and is clearly best considered by elected members of that profession and the lay benchers appointed to assist in that task and others. It is one of the prime reasons why professional discipline hearings are entrusted to the profession itself.

In this case Adams, twice the age of his young client, and fully aware of her strong desire to have her boyfriend released from jail, persuaded her to have sex with him. At the Committee Hearing, he admitted that his arranging to have sex with his client was "inappropriate." He also admitted that he knew that he was in a trust position with her. He expressed remorse for his conduct and acknowledged to the Hearing Committee that he had dishonoured his profession as a result of his misconduct.

Adams was correct in his assessment that this conduct brought dishonour on the legal profession, as this type of behaviour can lead the public to believe that lawyers are prone to abusing their position of trust. Members of the legal profession must earn the trust of their clients and the public generally, and conduct such as Adams' completely undermines that trust. As such, on reviewing the record, the report of the Hearing Committee and the decision of the Benchers, we are not persuaded that there was an overemphasis of the harm to the reputation of the legal profession.

Adams submits that the Committee failed to give sufficient weight to the good-character evidence. The record shows that the Committee did hear and consider all of the character evidence and referred to those "glowing character references" but decided that those references did not displace or support the facts as found and admitted by Adams as to what had occurred. This ground fails.

···

Adams further contends that the Committee erred in relying upon aggravating factors that were not proven; specifically, it is alleged that the Committee:

(a) speculated as to the complainant's motives and vulnerability;

(b) misapprehended the evidence as to whether Adams offered consideration for sexual favours; and

(c) exaggerated the prevalence of the risk of the sexual misconduct similar to that of Adams.

Adams adopted the dissenting view that the vulnerability of the 16-year-old complainant referred to in the majority Decision was not proved. She did not testify. However, there is no dispute as to her age and the disparity between the ages of Adams and the complainant. Nor is there any dispute as to her anxious desire to have her boyfriend released from jail. While the majority focused on the impropriety of a lawyer pursuing a dual relationship, one personal or sexual and one professional, with a client, they also considered the likely effect on the client's perception or expectation regarding the legal services she would receive. This would be a valid consideration regarding any client's finding herself in that situation and perhaps more so if the client is young. Dr. Pugh characterized the solicitor–client relationship as very special at AB 115:

> … lawyers are perceived by clients to be very special people with very special powers, and this means that the client then is in a very vulnerable position … in his or her

relationship with the lawyer, and it's incumbent upon the lawyer to recognize that nature of this very special trust relationship.

    Mr. Adams set that aside, the almost sanctity of this relationship, and minimized it and discounted it and took advantage of this young woman … .

The understanding that Dr. Pugh had of the importance of the solicitor–client relationship would certainly be within the knowledge of the majority of the Committee. It was in the context of their understanding of that relationship that they spoke of the vulnerability of the young client. We find no error in their discussion of the solicitor–client relationship and the vulnerability of a young client in these circumstances.

Both Adams and the dissenting member of the Committee miss the mark when they focus on the complainant's motive and vulnerability. She did not initiate the proposition of a sexual encounter. It was Adams' desire, despite his acknowledgment that what he proposed was inappropriate, and despite the complainant's reminding question about his having sex with clients.

…

We also agree with the majority of the Benchers' view that the Committee's majority Report was an expression of opinion that there was no evidence that sexual misconduct by lawyers was a serious problem. The discussion was focused less on prevalence than on the comparative seriousness of Adams' misconduct in proposing a sexual relationship with his client as opposed to misappropriating trust funds. The majority contended that perhaps the breach of trust involved in a proposed sexual relationship was even more serious than converting trust funds, for money can be restored but honour cannot. The minority expressly contended that Adams' misconduct was less serious than a case of misappropriation of trust funds, which "in virtually every case … calls for disbarment." This suggestion is troubling, as it implies that the integrity of the person is somehow less important than the integrity of the dollar. We do not diminish the seriousness of the offence of absconding with a client's trust funds. However, we have surely come to a point in our understanding of individual respect where the violation of a person's dignity is at least as important as the value of a bank account. …

Finally, Adams argued that the penalty of disbarment is much more severe than penalties that have been imposed in other similar cases, and that disbarment in this case is manifestly unreasonable. We acknowledge that considering the dispositions in disciplinary matters in other cases and in other jurisdictions can be helpful. But this assessment must be undertaken with due respect to contemporary values in Canadian society. In this regard, we observe that in the past, there has sometimes been a tendency to minimize and excuse misconduct of a sexual nature between the members of some professions and their clients. Further, and in any event, because the relevant facts vary greatly from case to case, care must be taken to consider each complaint in the context of its particular circumstances. As stated earlier, we do not accept the proposition still often invoked in criminal cases, that the most serious disciplinary sanction, disbarment, should be reserved for the most serious misconduct by the most serious offender. In this case, the majority of the Hearing Committee correctly addressed the relevant factors and held that disbarment was the appropriate disposition. Likewise the majority of the Benchers reviewed that disposition and agreed that disbarment was the appropriate order. We do not find that disposition to be manifestly unreasonable. Pursuant to s. 79(1)(c) of the *Legal Profession Act*, the order of the Benchers disbarring Adams is confirmed.

NOTES AND QUESTIONS

1. What motivated Adams to engage in the conduct that gave rise to his disbarment? Is it possible to quantify the "benefits" of this behaviour and to weigh them against the penalty Adams received?

2. Beyond the penalty of disbarment, what "costs" did Adams incur by engaging in the behaviour at issue in this case?

3. Matthew Lawson is a lawyer practising law in Alberta. He is familiar with the decision of the Court of Appeal in *Adams*. Assuming that Matthew (1) had the opportunity to engage in the same type of behaviour that gave rise to the *Adams* case, and (2) was certain that he would be caught and prosecuted, is Matthew likely to refrain from engaging in the relevant behaviour? Under what circumstances would Matthew decide to pursue the behaviour in question despite the court's decision in *Adams*?

4. The court in *Adams* notes that "money can be restored but honour cannot." Does the distinction between "honour" and "money" carry significant implications for an economic account of legal ethics? Why or why not?

5. The penalty in the *Adams* case was disbarment. One purpose of this penalty is to provide a disincentive to other lawyers who are tempted to follow Adams's pattern of behaviour. Is this a sensible penalty, given that the "cost" imposed by disbarment will vary greatly, depending on the projected future earnings a lawyer could enjoy by retaining the right to practise law? Is this any different from a fine, the impact of which will depend greatly on the income of the accused?

Law Society of British Columbia v. A Lawyer
[2000] LSDD no. 19

On September 16, 1997, a citation was issued against [the Respondent] pursuant to the provisions of the *Legal Profession Act* and rule 4-15 of the Law Society Rules by the then Secretary of the Law Society of British Columbia pursuant to a direction from the Chair of the Discipline Committee. The citation directed that this hearing panel enquire into the Respondent's conduct as follows:

1. Your conduct in an interview with Richardson and Kornfeld on November 9, 1995, regarding potential evidence you might give in an action in which Richardson and Kornfeld were counsel, in that you threatened to give evidence damaging to their client's case unless their client, EVL, reached a settlement with you in other litigation outstanding between you and their client.

2. Your conduct in conversations with Richardson on November 14, 1995, and December 3, 1995, regarding potential evidence you might give in an action in which Richardson and Kornfeld were counsel, in that you threatened to give

evidence damaging to their client's case unless their client reached a settlement with you in other litigation outstanding between you and their client. ...

A. Agreed Facts

An agreed statement of facts was filed as Exhibit 3 in the proceeding. It reads as follows:

1. [The Respondent] was called to the Bar of the Province of British Columbia on [date].

2. [EVL and the Respondent] married in 1983. They separated in 1994.

3. [Mr. Pierce] and [EVL] practised law from 1985 to 1995 as a partnership ... in ... British Columbia. The partnership was dissolved in 1995.

4. On June 11, 1990, [EVL] fell into an unmarked hole at a construction site ... At the time of this accident, she was accompanied by [the Respondent] who witnessed the fall.

5. [EVL] entered into litigation with various Defendants in a claim for compensation for personal injuries resulting from the June 11, 1990 accident.

6. [The Respondent] was a potential witness in this litigation because:

    a) he saw the accident occur;

    b) he was [EVL]'s cohabiting spouse and could give evidence as to the effects and extent of her injuries; and

    c) he was [EVL]'s law partner and could give evidence as to her loss of income.

7. The trial of [EVL]'s personal injury action was set for December 1995. Her counsel for this trial were John O. Richardson and Tova Kornfeld.

8. [The Respondent] had acted for [EVL] in settlement negotiations in the personal injury matter prior to the involvement of Ms. Kornfeld and Mr. Richardson as counsel.

9. Litigation in the matrimonial matter between [the Respondent] and [EVL] commenced in April, 1995, and was ongoing for the remainder of 1995. This litigation was acrimonious.

10. Mr. Paul Albi acted for [EVL] in the matrimonial action.

11. [The Respondent] met with Ms. Kornfeld and Mr. Richardson on November 9, 1995, at Ms. Kornfeld's office.

12. On November 14, 1995, [the Respondent] and Mr. Richardson talked by telephone.

B. *Evidence and Findings of Fact*

...

A review of Mr. Richardson's notes of the November 9 meeting, the November 14 telephone conversation and the December 3 telephone conversation make it clear that [the Respondent] sought to link the procurement of a satisfactory resolution of the matrimonial matters with the provision of satisfactory evidence in the personal injury litigation. Neither Ms. Kornfeld, with respect to the November 9 meeting, or Mr. Richardson with respect to all three events, were shaken on their cross-examination and I accepted that their evidence, while not verbatim, is a reasonably accurate record of the conversations which took place. Mr. McAllister says that I should consider [the Respondent's] anger and frustration at the time of the November 9 meeting and characterize his words less harshly. I might be prepared to do so had [the Respondent] not essentially reiterated the issue of "linkage" during his two subsequent conversations with Mr. Richardson. Similarly, although [the Respondent] indicates that on all three occasions, he wished only to make it clear that he was terribly concerned about the effect his evidence might have upon [EVL]'s personal injury litigation, he never indicated that he would simply refuse to testify, perhaps a more logical position and one that he was certainly entitled to take. [The Respondent] says he denied the allegations of blackmail made at the November 9 meeting and yet conducted himself in a manner which resulted in a similar accusation being made by Mr. Richardson during the conversation on November 14. Mr. McAllister also says that [the Respondent] had a vested interest in his wife's lawsuit and would not logically do anything to sabotage her chances of success. While this is so, it is equally true that [the Respondent] stood to accomplish both of his goals: a satisfactory resolution of the matrimonial litigation and a share of the proceeds of the personal injury lawsuit if he succeeded in his threats. ...

I might say that in this case, I am satisfied that the Law Society has proved its allegations of misconduct against [the Respondent] beyond any reasonable doubt on my part.

During the meeting of November 9, [the Respondent] clearly made a linkage between a satisfactory resolution of the matrimonial matter and his provision of evidence in the civil trial. In particular, I note the following extracts from Mr. Richardson's notes:

From the December 3 meeting:

> "I'm not inclined to do a good job for her in Court if she's going to use my testimony to fight me later on in the family case."

> "If a subpoena shows up in my office without a separation agreement, then I'm going to read the documents on my desk which will show she stole $32,000 from me and I will tell the Court which you won't want me to do. If I get a separation agreement with the subpoena, then I'll just chuck all those papers, documents away so the Defence can't find them."

And from the November 14 conversation:

> "I am a big risk to your client ... her biggest risk."

"If I go into that Court room and find out she ripped me off for $32,000, I will tell the jury and she will get nothing. I want a settlement."

"I can't hurt her if I don't "read" the last 10%, i.e. if I don't know for sure."

"I'm 90% sure she ripped me off, it will get her disbarred."

And from the November 9 conversation:

"[The respondent] stated in very clear terms that if [EVL] did not cooperate and come to a settlement on his terms in his matrimonial case that he would expose his allegations of misappropriation of funds, breach of trust. ..."

"He was saying words such as that if we want him on the witness stand she better make a settlement of the matrimonial case this week or next week." ...

Mr. McAllister submits that his client did not form the intent to use "blackmail" or trade his evidence for a settlement with his wife. Mr. McAllister refers me to the case of *R v. Steven David Taylor*, an unreported decision of His Honour Judge Gove of the Provincial Court of British Columbia (Victoria Registry No. 79813-C2). Mr. Taylor, a lawyer, faced charges of uttering threats and conspiracy to utter threats arising out of a telephone conversation intercepted by the Royal Canadian Mounted Police Drug Section. Mr. Taylor satisfied the Court that he did not intend his words to be taken seriously. I accept that words which might otherwise constitute a threat or "blackmail" must be regarded in light of all the circumstances, that they must be considered objectively and within the context of the meeting or conversation in which they occurred. As I have previously stated, had [the Respondent] sought to link his testimony in the personal injury matter with the achievement of a satisfactory result in the matrimonial matter in the first conversation, that of November 9, only, I might have attributed a more innocent connotation to his comments. However, his similar use of linkage in the two subsequent conversations with Mr. Richardson suggest that he intended his words to have their apparent meaning and effect. I am satisfied that on all three occasions, [the Respondent] intended to indicate his willingness to trade favourable evidence in the personal injury matter for a satisfactory result in the matrimonial matter. ...

"Conduct unbecoming a member of the Society" is defined in Rule 1 of the Law Society Rules (1996) as including

"any matter, conduct or thing that is considered, in the judgment of the Benchers or a panel
  a) to be contrary to the best interest of the public or of the legal profession, or
  b) to harm the standing of the legal profession."

This provision, although now found in the Rules rather than the *Legal Profession Act* since December 31, 1998, is identical to the former provision.

"Professional misconduct" is not defined. In the case of *Re Pierce and Law Society of British Columbia* (1993), 103 DLR (4th) 233, Clancy J adopted the following quotation from in *Re a Solicitor*, [1912] 1 KB 302:

"If it is shown," he said, that a solicitor in the pursuit of his profession has done something with regard to it which would reasonably be regarded as disgraceful or dishonourable by his professional brethren of good repute and competency, then it is open to say that he is guilty of "professional misconduct."

Clancy J in *Pierce* goes on to note that a lawyer owes a duty to both the public at large and to the state. To fail in the observance in that duty is professional misconduct, even where that conduct arises in a personal rather than professional capacity. The preface to the Canons of Legal Ethics published in the Professional Conduct Handbook reads, in part, as follows:

A lawyer is a minister of justice, an officer of the Courts, a client's advocate, and a member of an ancient, honourable and learned profession. In these several capacities, it is a lawyer's duty to promote the interests of the state, serve the cause of justice, maintain the authority and dignity of the Courts, be faithful to clients, be candid and courteous in relations with other lawyers and demonstrate personal integrity.

The practice of law requires so much more of a member than the ability to manage his or her business affairs. It requires an awareness and appreciation of the role played by the member in the confluence of contributions which make up our system of justice which, in turn, is at the root of our free and democratic society. [The respondent's] conduct suggests, at least, ignorance of his role in this process and, at worst, a cynical disregard for it.

I find that [the Respondent] professionally misconducted himself with respect to the allegations in Counts 1 and 2 of the schedule to the citation. Although he was represented by counsel in the matrimonial matter, [the Respondent] was clearly acting as his own advocate in his discussions with his colleagues and his threats were directed at [EVL], a former client whom he had represented in the personal injury matter. The several duties to uphold the integrity of the state, the law and our system of justice remain the responsibility of the lawyer at the end of the working day and a failure to perform these duties will result in a finding of professional misconduct even where the misconduct does not occur in the pursuit of the profession, in the strictest sense. I have no doubt that [the Respondent's] conduct in attempting to exact an advantage by threat, is conduct which would be regarded as "disgraceful or dishonourable by his professional brethren of good repute and competency."

I also find that [the Respondent] has been guilty of conduct unbecoming. The Court in *Pierce* determined that the words "the best interest of the public" in Rule 1 referred to the interest of the public in matters of conduct and competence. There is a clear public interest in discouraging conduct of the nature exhibited by [the Respondent] in relation to the circumstances summarized in the citation. Just as clearly, there is the substantial likelihood that public knowledge of such conduct would harm the standing of or public perception of the integrity of the profession as a whole. ...

With respect to Counts 1 and 2 of the schedule to the citation I find that [the Respondent] is guilty of both professional misconduct and conduct unbecoming a lawyer. ...

The primary focus of the *Legal Profession Act* is the protection of the public interest. It follows that the sentencing process must ensure that the public is protected from acts of professional misconduct. Section 38 of the *Legal Profession Act* sets forth a range of penalties, ranging from reprimand to disbarment, from which a panel must choose following a finding of misconduct. An appropriate penalty must ensure that the public is protected and must also take into account the risk of allowing the Respondent to continue in practice.

The decision of the hearing panel in *Ogilvie*, 1999 LSBC 17, while acknowledging that no list of appropriate factors to be taken into account in determining an appropriate penalty could be considered exhaustive or appropriate in all cases, enumerated a series of factors which might be worthy of general consideration. An analysis of each, with reference to the context of the instant case, follows.

A. The Nature and Gravity of the Conduct Proven

The Respondent's proposal to refrain from giving evidence detrimental to EVL's character and credibility in return for a favourable resolution of the matrimonial dispute goes to the very root of his obligations as a "minister of justice" and "officer of the courts."

B. The Age and Experience of the Respondent

The Respondent would have been, perhaps, forty-eight years of age at the time the conduct complained of occurred. By that time, he had been called to the Bar of British Columbia for some eleven years and had significant trial experience before the courts of this Province.

C. The Previous Character of the Respondent, Including Details of Prior Discipline

The Respondent's professional conduct record is summarized in Exhibit 13. At the request of both counsel, I have not considered the matters referred to at Tabs 7, 9 and 11 of the Exhibit. I note that by his seventh year of practice the Respondent had accumulated some twenty complaints concerning his professional conduct and appears to have undergone his first conduct review in August of 1990. That review considered, *inter alia*, concerns about the Respondent's client management skills and the recommendations of the panel included a recommendation "that [the Respondent] seek the assistance of Interlock in order to seek advice which would better enable him to deal with stress and which would allow him to improve his interpersonal skills."

There is no evidence before me as to whether this recommendation was implemented.

Thereafter, the Respondent appears to have undergone several conduct reviews which questioned his judgment in some instances and, more generally, his interpersonal skills. The report of a conduct review which appears at Tab 6 of Exhibit 13 contains the following:

> [The Respondent] was cognizant of his limitations in the area of client skills and indicated to the Sub-Committee that he had made, was and would continue to make efforts

to improve his client skills. He pointed out that there had been fewer complaints regarding his conduct more recently and this was evidence of his attention to this area.

The complaint which gave rise to the conduct review resulted from the alleged failure of the Respondent to refund the sum of $5,000.00 determined to be due to the Respondent's client following a taxation. ...

In February of 1992, the Respondent appeared before a hearing panel facing a citation alleging failure to return a client's file documents following settlement of his accounts. The matter proceeded by way of conditional admission and proposed disciplinary action. The Respondent was reprimanded and ordered to pay costs not to exceed $500.00. In May of 1993, the Respondent faced a further citation for failing to refund funds to his client following settlement of a fee dispute. The panel noted that in relation to the previous disciplinary matter relating to the same sort of conduct, the Respondent had "offered a full apology to the Law Society, stated that he understood his duties and gave assurances that such an incident would not re-occur ..." The panel noted that the misconduct proved appeared to have the same characteristics as that evident in the earlier citation, namely, attempts to obtain a tactical advantage in a threatened dispute or complaint involving the client in circumstances where the Respondent had no right to withhold funds. The panel went on to say:

> It is apparent that the member did not carry out his previously expressed intention. The panel regards withholding of money belonging to another as a matter of utmost seriousness damaging to the reputation of the profession and conduct which should not be tolerated.

The panel imposed a fine of $10,000.00 and costs.

In 1994 the Respondent faced a citation relating to various complaints arising out of the publication of a periodical entitled "Law Notes" by the Respondent. The Respondent was reprimanded and ordered to pay a fine of $3,000.00 and costs.

In October of 1997, the Respondent faced a citation for failing to fulfill financial obligations incurred in the course of practice. He was reprimanded and ordered to pay costs of $5,000.00.

In May of 1998 the Respondent faced a citation for failing to notify the Law Society of an unsatisfied judgment. He was ordered to pay a fine of $3,000.00 plus costs.

In the interval since 1990, the Respondent has spent numerous hours away from his practice attending before conduct review subcommittees or hearing panels as a result of complaints concerning his professional conduct. By my simple calculations, he has paid the sum of $21,500.00 to date exclusive of costs awarded by past panels. When one considers the value of time spent away from his practice in addition to these assessments, the Respondent has paid dearly for his past misconduct. I am left, however, with the lingering sense that the Respondent does not fully understand what some might regard as the basic immutable duties of a practising lawyer which include those enumerated in the preamble to the Canons of Professional Ethics.

D. The Impact Upon the Victim

Counsel have provided me with a copy of the Reasons for Judgment of the Honourable
Madam Justice Allan delivered in the action concerning EVL's claim for compensation as a result of her accident. I am unable to say, from a review of Allan J's Reasons, that the Respondent's failure to testify at the trial prejudiced EVL's claim and
neither am I able to say that evidence he might have offered, by way of corrobora-
tion, might have assisted.

E. The Advantage Gained or To Be Gained by the Respondent

There is no evidence that the Respondent gained any advantage by his misconduct.
He hoped to gain a significant advantage in the matrimonial proceeding by threatening EVL, through her counsel, with harmful evidence should he be called to testify.

F. The Number of Times the Offending Conduct Occurred

The offending conduct occurred on no fewer than three occasions: November 9, 1995,
November 14, 1995, and December 3, 1995. On the occasion of the November 14
conversation, Mr. Richardson clearly indicated that he, Mr. Richardson, regarded the
Respondent's conduct as tantamount to blackmail. The Respondent nevertheless persisted in his misconduct.

*G. Whether the Respondent Has Acknowledged the Misconduct and Taken Steps
   To Disclose or Address the Wrong and the Presence or Absence of Other
   Mitigating Circumstances*

The Respondent has no recollection of the December 3 telephone conversation. With
respect to the November 9 and November 14 conversations, he acknowledges that he
was guilty of an error of judgment. He goes so far as to acknowledge that he left a
potential for misunderstanding as to his true intentions, namely that he was worried
about evidence which had really come to light which might adversely affect EVL's
case should it come to light. He has taken no steps to redress the wrong and has not
addressed the substance of the Law Society's concerns.

   The Respondent was clearly in an agitated state of mind as a result of his domestic
and financial pressures on each of the three subject occasions. One would have understood, in spite of the possibility that he stood to gain from EVL's lost income
claim, had he simply refused to testify on her behalf, given the level of acrimony
between them. In spite of his frustration and agitation, he retained sufficient acumen
to link an advantage in the matrimonial litigation with cooperation in the personal
injury litigation. He was able to maintain his practice and, by all appearances, his
obligations to clients during this same period. I am not satisfied that the Respondent's
emotional state clouded his judgment and robbed him of free thought to the extent
that his actions on the three occasions in question were anything other than voluntary. Mr. McAllister suggests that the failure of experienced counsel, Ms. Kornfeld

and Mr. Richardson, to report the Respondent's misconduct to the Law Society suggests that they did not regard his conduct as being professionally inappropriate. I do not agree. Whatever the reason for their respective failures to complain of the Respondent's conduct, their disinclination to do so cannot in any way be construed as a mitigating circumstance.

H. The Possibility of Remediating or Rehabilitating the Respondent

The Respondent's difficulties with interpersonal issues have been the subject of several prior disciplinary proceedings and conduct reviews. The Respondent does not appear to have followed up on suggestions that he pursue counseling or some other form of assistance in an attempt to improve his skills. He has, as previously indicated, suffered significant financial penalties for his failure to exercise appropriate professional judgment in the past.

I. The Impact on the Respondent of Criminal or Other Sanctions or Penalties

The Respondent has not suffered any criminal or other sanction as a result of his misconduct.

J. The Impact of the Proposed Penalty on the Respondent

The impact of disbarment on the Respondent would be professionally, emotionally and financially devastating. While I have no evidence before me of the Respondent's present financial circumstances, I appreciate that suspension of his right to practise, even for a brief period, will have a significant financial impact on him, particularly as he has only recently succeeded in dealing with his debt load from years ago. I am also aware of all the Respondent's employees and associate whose practice is similar to his own, he also employees six staff members, some of whom might be at least temporarily dislocated by his suspension. I am also mindful of his duties to his clients and the impact of a suspension on his trial schedule.

Without any specific information as to the Respondent's income, I am not in a position to access the impact of a fine upon him. Mr. McAllister refers to the inappropriateness of a "disabling" fine without indicating what the amount of such a fine would be. Given the Respondent's professional conduct record, and the amount he has paid in fines and costs assessments to date, I am not convinced that a fine represents a significant deterrence to him.

K. The Need for Specific and General Deterrence

I am hopeful that an appropriate penalty will deter the Respondent from future acts of this nature. There is also a need to deter others who might misconduct themselves in this fashion by the imposition of an appropriate penalty.

L. The Need To Ensure the Public's Confidence in the Integrity of the Profession

The public must have confidence in the ability of the Law Society to regulate and supervise the conduct of its membership. Only by the maintenance of such confidence in the integrity of the profession can the self-regulatory role of the Law Society be justified and maintained.

M. The Range of Penalties Imposed in Similar Cases

Counsel have been unable to refer me to any authorities of a sufficiently similar nature to assist in determining the issue of penalty. I had considered the case of *Charles Michael Jeffrey*, 1997 LSBC 1 and it has assisted me somewhat. While representing Plaintiffs in difficult litigation, Mr. Jeffrey learned from the trial coordinator that the trial set to begin three days later had been removed from the trial list. He advised the trial coordinator that he would inform opposing counsel of this but did not do so promptly as he wished to leave open the possibility of obtaining a favourable settlement for his clients. Instead, he faxed his clients' latest settlement offer to opposing counsel that same day in the hope that the Defendants would instruct her to settle. Mr. Jeffrey testified that he intended to tell counsel of the adjournment before concluding any settlement and by 3:00 p.m. that day in any event. He telephoned opposing counsel at 2:00 p.m. to see if she had received the settlement offer and did not inform her of the adjournment. Shortly thereafter, opposing counsel learned, from her secretary's call to the Court Registry, that the trial had been adjourned and that Mr. Jeffrey had agreed to pass on this information. When opposing counsel telephoned Mr. Jeffrey to ask why he had not informed her of the adjournment, Mr. Jeffrey implied that he had only recently found out himself. This was untrue, of course, and was intended to mislead opposing counsel. The hearing panel determined that Mr. Jeffrey had misconducted himself in failing to carry out his promise to pass on the information concerning the adjournment to opposing counsel and in attempting to mislead opposing counsel as to when he had learned of the adjournment of the trial on the basis of prior discipline cases, and in spite of Mr. Jeffrey's exemplary record of service to the profession, the hearing panel determined that a one or two month suspension would have been justified had Mr. Jeffrey not already retired from practice. In the event, the panel ordered Mr. Jeffrey to pay an $8,000.00 fine and the sum of $3,000.00 towards the cost of the disciplinary proceedings. Mr. Jeffrey, like the Respondent, had sought to gain an unjustified tactical advantage by the conduct complained of. His misconduct did not suggest, as does the Respondent's, a consistent tactical mechanism. …

Mr. Follett says that disbarment is the only appropriate penalty in these circumstances. I do not agree. The ultimate penalty of disbarment remains reserved for those instances of misconduct at which it can be said that prohibition from practice is the only means by which the public can be protected from further acts of misconduct. I am confident that the Respondent's misconduct may be addressed by a significantly less drastic penalty.

In view of the nature of the Respondent's misconduct as I have characterized it, and taking into account the details of his personal conduct record, I find that a suspension is appropriate and that the appropriate period of suspension is three months commencing March 1, 2000. In arriving at this decision, I have been assisted by the words of Sir Thomas Bingham MR in the case of *Bolton v. Law Society*, [1994] 2 All ER 486, at page 492:

> Because orders made by the tribunal are not primarily punitive, it follows that considerations which would ordinarily weigh in mitigation and punishment have less effect on the exercise of this jurisdiction than on the ordinary run of sentences imposed in criminal cases. It often happens that a solicitor appearing before the tribunal can adduce a wealth of glowing tributes from his professional brethren. He can often show that for him and his family the consequences of striking off or suspension would be little short of tragic. Often he will say, convincingly, that he has learned his lesson and will not offend again. Of applying for restoration after striking off, all these points may be made, and the former solicitor may also be able to point to real efforts made to re-establish himself and redeem his reputation. All these matters are relevant and should be considered. But none of them touches the essential issue, which is the need to maintain among members of the public a well-founded confidence that any solicitor whom they instruct will be a person of unquestionable integrity, probity and trustworthiness. Thus it can never be an objection to an order of suspension in an appropriate case that the solicitor may be unable to reestablish his practice when the period of suspension is past. If that proves, or appears likely to be so the consequences for the individual and his family may be deeply unfortunate and unintended. But it does not make suspension the wrong order if it is otherwise right. The reputation of the profession is more important than the fortunes of any individual member. Membership of a profession brings many benefits, but that is part of the price.

The Law Society will have its costs of this hearing. Failing agreement between counsel as to costs, arrangements may be made to have the matter set down for hearing before me.

NOTES AND QUESTIONS

1. What were the economic costs of the respondent's decision to engage in professional misconduct? What were the benefits that the respondent sought to gain from this course of action? By choosing to adopt his unethical course of action, does the respondent indicate that, from his perspective, the predicted gains associated with the conduct outweighed the predicted losses?

2. Are the penalties imposed by the tribunal likely to have the desired economic effect—that is, will the penalty make lawyers believe that it is not in their economic interest to pursue actions akin to those of the respondent?

3. Did the respondent engage in his unethical actions because he is a self-interested economic actor; because he is a "bad man"; or because of some combination of these factors? How does being a "bad man" relate to economic reasoning?

4. Assuming that the tribunal's decision becomes a stable precedent, and behaviour similar to the respondent's will be punished in a similar way, under what circumstances might future lawyers choose to undertake an unethical course of action similar to that undertaken by the respondent?

5. What was it about the respondent's course of action that made it "unethical"? Is it possible to define the nature of "unethical behaviour"? Is the behaviour "bad" or "unethical" because it imposes costs on others, or for some other, non-economic reason?

6. The tribunal made it clear that one of its goals in punishing the lawyer was to protect "the standing of the legal profession." How does the penalty of disbarment accomplish this objective? Why would the tribunal be interested in accomplishing this objective?

III. The Goals and Functions of an Economic Theory of Ethics

A. Introduction

Previous sections of this chapter have provided an overview of an economic theory of legal ethics. The details of this theory are worked out in later chapters. Before moving on to consider the details and implications of this theory, however, it is important to consider a critical question: what is the *purpose* of an economic theory of legal ethics? This question is briefly addressed below.

B. What an Economic Theory Can Do

The primary goal of any economic theory is to provide an accurate method of describing human choices. In the realm of legal ethics, economics helps describe how people create, abide by, and deviate from ethical codes of conduct, situating these behaviours within an overarching system of human activity. In everything we do, humans respond to various stimuli by considering the outcomes of our actions and selecting the choice that we regard as the "best decision." On a very general level, these "best decisions" are designed to promote the survival of our species. By analyzing ethical systems through the lens of economics and evolution, we can see that ethical choices are not unique: they are governed by the same guiding principles that govern every other choice that human beings make. There is at least some value in a theory that can accurately describe the process of ethical decision making and situate that process within an overarching system of behaviour.

A second goal of the economic theory of legal ethics is to provide a level of structure to our assessment of ethical choices. Rather than generating an ad hoc analysis of individual ethical dilemmas, an economic theory of ethics helps us consider whether there are any unifying threads that permeate our ethical systems. As we shall see, those unifying threads do exist and can be used in our analysis of the choices people make. Rather than relying on unexplained notions of "good" and "evil," an economic model ties decision making to measurable incentives and costs that drive human decisions. By tying ethical decisions to these measurable, objective costs and benefits, an economic theory moves ethical systems out of the mystical realm of the unexplained and into the arena of measurable and testable hypotheses. Through the lens of economics, ethical theories can be subjected to objective, rigorous standards rather than dogmatic (and untestable) conclusions concerning the nature of "right" and "wrong." As Dewey explains:

> With the transfer, these, and all tenets and creeds about good and goods, would be recognized to be hypotheses. Instead of being rigidly fixed, they would be treated as intellectual instruments to be tested and confirmed—and altered—through consequences effected by acting upon them. They would lose all pretence of finality—the ulterior source of dogmatism. It is both astonishing and depressing that so much of the energy of mankind has gone into fighting for (with weapons of the flesh as well as of the spirit) the truth of creeds, religious, moral and political, as distinct from what has gone into effort to try creeds by putting them to the test of acting upon them.[42]

In other words, an economic theory helps demystify the notions of "good" and "evil" and converts them into testable hypotheses. Rather than boldly asserting that "X is ethical" or "God endorses Y," an economic theory allows a fairly objective measurement of the ways in which our ethical choices impact on the world.

Once we come to understand an ethical system as a series of costs and incentives that promote prosperity and survival, we can begin to study the structure of those incentives and the manner in which they promote or discourage particular forms of conduct. As we shall see, economic theory helps us determine whether a particular set of incentives accomplishes the goal of modifying human behaviour in sensible ways. Where a particular body of rules (such as an ethical system) successfully modifies behaviour in a way that promotes prosperity and survival, economic theory can point to the reasons for the success of the relevant system. Where a body of rules fails to provide useful incentives or to generate sensible outcomes, economic theory can help expose and explain this failure while pointing the way toward more efficient systems of incentives. The manner in which an economic theory can help accomplish these objectives is developed throughout the remainder of part I of this book.

C. What an Economic Model Does Not Intend To Do

One of the first objections students raise when confronted by economic theory is that its model of human choices is misguided. Humans, it is argued, do not go about their lives computing the costs and benefits of potential actions. Instead, they simply do what "feels ethical" at the moment. This objection is not a new one. Indeed, Plato voiced this issue in *The Apology*:

> You are sadly mistaken, fellow, if you suppose that a man with even a grain of self-respect should reckon up the risks of living or dying, rather than simply consider, whenever he does something, whether his actions are just or unjust, the deeds of a good man or a bad one.[43]

The answer to this objection has been developed many times in diverse contexts. According to John Stuart Mill, for example, this objection is based on the notion that "there is no

---

42   Dewey, supra note 6, at 263-64.

43   Plato, *Defence of Socrates, Euthyphro, Crito* (Oxford: Oxford University Press, 1997), 41.

time, previous to action, for calculating and weighing the effects of any line of conduct on the general happiness."[44] Mill provides the following rejoinder:

> This is exactly as if anyone were to say that it is impossible to guide our conduct by Christianity, because there is not time, on every occasion on which anything has to be done, to read through the Old and New Testaments. The answer to the objection is, that there has been ample time, namely, the whole past duration of the human species. During all that time, mankind have been learning by experience the tendencies of actions; on which experience all the prudence as well as all the morality of life, is dependent. People talk as if the commencement of this course of experience had hitherto been put off, and as if, at the moment when some man feels tempted to meddle with the property or life of another, he had to begin considering for the first time whether murder and theft are injurious to human happiness. … Nobody argues that the art of navigation is not founded on astronomy because sailors cannot wait to calculate the Nautical Almanack. Being rational creatures, they go to sea with it ready calculated; and all rational creatures go out upon the sea of life with their minds made up on the common questions of right and wrong, as well as on many of the far more difficult questions of wise and foolish. And this, as long as foresight is a human quality, it is to be presumed they will continue to do.[45]

In his economic account of legal systems, David Friedman makes a similar observation:

> Rationality does not mean that a burglar compiles an elaborate spread-sheet of costs and benefits before deciding whether to rob your house. An armed robber does not work out a precise analysis of how shooting his victim will affect the odds of being caught, whether it will reduce the chances by 10 percent or by 20. But if it is clear that it will reduce the risk of being caught without increasing the punishment, he is quite likely to pull the trigger.[46]

Simply put, the truth of economics does not depend on the assumption that individuals go through life with calculators in their hands. On the contrary, economics merely assumes that people tend to make the choices they prefer. Their preferences are based on established notions concerning the costs and benefits of various actions and rough assessments of the consequences that are likely to ensue from choices that are available. All that economics presumes is that people know what they want and have a fairly good idea of how to get it. From these simple assumptions flow an array of powerful tools designed to describe and evaluate all human decisions. Economics is the study of human choices, and a useful way of determining how a system of incentives can be used to direct the choices people make. An ethical system is a prime example of a system of incentives. Economics can accordingly help us study and understand the ethical choices people make.

Law Society of Upper Canada v. Ault, below, presents yet another case in which a lawyer has been accused of behaving unethically. When reviewing the case, consider whether the behaviour of the accused lawyer can be described and evaluated using the

---

44   John Stuart Mill, *Utilitarianism* (Peterborough, ON: Broadview Press, 2000), 32.

45   Ibid., at 32-34.

46   Friedman, supra note 13, at 8.

tools of economics. Did the lawyer consider costs and benefits when embarking on a particular course of action? If not, did the lawyer at least act *as if* he had performed the relevant calculations? Can the tools of economics help us understand the impulses and drives that lead to unethical decisions, and can those same tools be used to design incentives with the effect of preventing unethical choices? Each of these questions will be addressed in greater detail in chapters 3 and 4.

Law Society of Upper Canada v. Ault
[1997] LSDD no. 178

Report of the Discipline Committee

On November 27, 1996 Complaint D297/96 was issued against Frank Arthur Ault alleging that he was guilty of professional misconduct.

The matter was heard in public on May 27, 1997 before this Committee composed of Nancy L. Backhouse, Chair, Marshall A. Crowe and Ronald D. Manes. The Solicitor did not attend the hearing nor was he represented. Christina Budweth appeared on behalf of the Law Society.

...

Facts

4. The Solicitor is 51 years of age. He was called to the Bar in 1975. Prior to his administrative suspension on December 31, 1995 for non-payment of his errors & omissions levy, he practised as a partner in the firm Tavel, Flanigan & Ault in Ottawa. During the period July 31, 1996 to present he has been incarcerated first in the Millhaven Institution and subsequently in the Pittsburgh Institute as a result of the conduct set out below.

5. In late 1989, the Solicitor was a member of the law firm of Gowling and Henderson in Ottawa. He, along with some members of the firm formed an investment company and became involved in a project in Hull, Quebec. The Solicitor was approached by a Mr. Gauthier and offered a half interest in a real estate project. In order to obtain funds to participate, the Solicitor offered his personal line of credit at the Canadian Imperial Bank of Commerce in the amount of $250,000.00. He then borrowed another $100,000.00 from the bank and through efforts which can only be described as loan transactions borrowed a further $162,000.00 for a total of $512,000.00 in debt. Effectively, the Solicitor went from an ordinary lawyer with three children to a real estate investor and speculator at the time coincident with the collapse of the real estate market.

6. Subsequently the Solicitor incorporated Lisgar Square Developments in an attempt to participate in real estate projects which were designed to extract himself from the calamitous debt which he had taken on. As a result, the Solicitor became involved in the series of transactions outlined below which formed the basis of his conviction on criminal charges as outlined in the Complaint.

7. Set out below is a summary of the Solicitor's conduct:

1) INVESTOR: Lynn Sherwood
    PROPERTY: 393 Nelson Street & 338–344 Somerset Street, Ottawa
    NET LOSS: $50 000 + $50 000 = $100 000

   a) In September 1995, Mrs. Sherwood was approached by Sue Rochon, a legal secretary at the firm Tavel, Flanigan & Ault ("Tavel firm"). Ms. Rochon worked for the Solicitor. Mrs. Sherwood held mortgage investments and she was asked by Ms. Rochon whether she would like to invest in second mortgages, paying 11% interest. These mortgages, each in the amount of $50,000, were to be on properties located at 393 Nelson and 338-344 Somerset, in the City of Ottawa. The properties were owned by Lisgar Square and by 1010245 Ontario Inc. (Lisgar Square Management Inc.) respectively. The Solicitor owned both these companies. Mrs. Sherwood was assured by Mrs. Rochon that the investment was secure.

   b) On September 14, 1995 Mrs. Sherwood issued two bank drafts each in the amount of $50,000 payable to the Tavel firm. Mrs. Sherwood did not receive any documentation from the Solicitor or the Tavel firm concerning her investment. On November 16, 1995 Ms. Rochon contacted Mrs. Sherwood to advise her that her funds had not been invested as promised and that they were not secured by mortgages. Mrs. Sherwood was told that The Solicitor had been hospitalized. She was further told that he was being investigated by the Law Society.

   c) Mrs. Sherwood retained a lawyer, Scott McLean, to commence an action against Arthur Ault and the Tavel firm. Mr. McLean was able to determine that Mrs. Sherwood's funds had been deposited to the client trust account of Lisgar Square. Mrs. Sherwood also learned that a third mortgage on 338-344 Somerset Street had been drafted in her name, but not signed. Consequently, Mrs. Sherwood's $100,000 investment was not secured by mortgages as had been promised.

   d) Ms. Rochon was interviewed by the Ottawa Police and she stated that she had been the Solicitor's secretary. She further stated that the two bank drafts totalling $100,000 provided by Mrs. Sherwood had been given to the Solicitor.

2) INVESTOR: William Watkin
    PROPERTY: 34A & 40A MacLaren, Ottawa
    NET LOSS: $25 000

   a) Mr. Watkin stated to the Ottawa Police that in early August 1995 he was advised by his business partner Danny Cantor that John Tavel had offered to arrange a loan of $100,000, which was to be secured by a second mortgage, paying 14%, on a property at 34A and 40A MacLaren Street in Ottawa. Mr. Tavel was acting on behalf of the borrower Lisgar Square (owned by Arthur Ault). The proposal was made to Mr. Watkin and to three other parties. Mr. Watkin met Mr. Tavel and declined the investment because it was felt that a second mortgage did not provide sufficient security. At that time, Mr. Tavel placed a telephone call after which he advised the potential investors that the first mortgagee would waive its first rank mortgage on the property.

b) On September 8, 1995 Mr. Watkin wrote a personal cheque in the amount of $25,000 payable to the Tavel firm. This cheque was deposited in the Tavel firm's trust account. The other investors, each contributing $25,000, included Danny Cantor, Barry Cantor and B & M Cantor Holdings. The Solicitor was the lawyer who reported to the investors. In a reporting letter from the Solicitor dated September 21, 1995, the investors were informed that they held a first mortgage on 34A and 40A MacLaren Street. The Solicitor also provided the investors with a personal guarantee form which he had signed.

c) In November 1995, a cheque drawn on the Solicitor's personal bank account payable to Mr. Watkin, representing interest on the mortgage, was returned as NSF.

d) A property search revealed that Mr. Watkin and the other three investors actually held a fifth mortgage on 34A & 40A MacLaren Street instead of a first mortgage.

3) INVESTOR: Barry Cantor
   PROPERTY: 34A & 40A MacLaren, Ottawa
   NET LOSS: $25 000

a) Mr. Barry Cantor related substantially the same facts to the police as Mr. Watkin. His investment was also $25,000 and a cheque in this amount was issued on September 8, 1995 payable to the Tavel firm.

4) INVESTOR: Danny Cantor
   PROPERTY: 34A & 40A MacLaren / 694 Island Park Drive, Ottawa
   NET LOSS: $25 000 + $32 500 = $57 500

a) Mr. Danny Cantor related substantially the same facts to the police as Mr. Watkin and Mr. Barry Cantor, concerning the MacLaren property. Danny Cantor had invested $25,000 and a cheque in this amount was issued on September 8, 1995 payable to the Tavel firm. Two subsequent interest payments from the Solicitor's personal bank account and from Lisgar Square's account were returned NSF.

b) Mr. Danny Cantor also informed the police that in July 1995 he was contacted by Mr. Tavel who advised him that his partner Arthur Ault was seeking to borrow $65,000 on the security of a first mortgage on the Ault family residence on Island Park Drive in Ottawa. The property was owned by Susan Ault, the Solicitor's wife. The interest rate being offered was 14%. Mr. Cantor stated that because he had known Mr. Tavel for some time, he and B & M Cantor Holdings each advanced $32,500, payable to the Tavel firm.

c) On September 21, 1995 the Solicitor discharged the Cantor mortgage on his Island Park property. Mr. Cantor informed the Police that he had no knowledge of the discharge and that the signature on the discharge was not his signature. The Solicitor has admitted to forging his wife's signature on both the mortgage and discharge documents.

5) INVESTOR: B & M Cantor Holdings
    PROPERTY: 34A & 40 A MacLaren / 694 Island Park Drive, Ottawa
    NET LOSS: $25 000 + $32 500 = $57 500

a) Benes and Morris Cantor were interviewed by the police concerning their
investment in the MacLaren Street property. They related substantially the same
facts as Mr. Watkin, Mr. Barry Cantor and Mr. Danny Cantor. B & M Cantor
Holdings Limited had invested $25,000 and a cheque in this amount was issued
on September 8, 1995 payable to the Tavel firm.

b) Benes and Morris Cantor were also interviewed concerning their investment in the Island Park Drive property. They stated that a cheque payable to the
Tavel firm was issued on July 21, 1995, in the amount of $32,500. As indicated
earlier, the Cantor mortgage was discharged on September 21, 1995.

6) INVESTOR: Benes Cantor
    PROPERTY: 660 Hochelaga, Ottawa
    NET LOSS: $40 000

a) The Ottawa Police interviewed Benes and Morris Cantor concerning their
investment in a property located at 660 Hochelaga Street. The Cantors stated that
they were approached by John Tavel in regards to borrowing $130,000, which
was to be secured by a first mortgage on 660 Hochelaga. This property was nomi-
nally owned by 746722 Ontario Limited. The Solicitor was the owner of this company. On April 3, 1995 B & M Holdings issued a cheque of $80,000 to John Tavel
in Trust. On that same date, Benes Cantor issued a personal cheque of $50,000 to
John Tavel in Trust.

b) A reporting letter sent on the Tavel firm's letterhead, signed by the Solicitor, was sent to Morris and Benes Cantor advising them that their investment was
secured by a first (syndicated) mortgage. Morris Cantor acknowledged receiving
$90,000, thereby reducing the initial investment to $40,000. A property search of
this property revealed that the Morris and Benes Cantor mortgage was not a first
mortgage but rather a third mortgage.

7) INVESTOR: Kisber & Co. Ltd.
    PROPERTY: 660 Hochelaga Drive, Ottawa
                       694 Island Park Drive, Ottawa
    NET LOSS: $200 000

a) The Ottawa Police interviewed Mr. Stephen Kisber, owner of Kisber & Co.
Ltd. Mr. Kisber advised the Police that his investment had been arranged through
the law firm Gibson & Augustine. As a result Kenneth Gibson was also interviewed. He informed the Police that he had represented Kisber & Co. Mr. Gibson
stated that he had been approached by the Solicitor who was seeking to borrow
$200,000. The investment was to be secured by a third mortgage on a property at
660 Hochelaga and a first mortgage on 694 Island Park Drive. As stated earlier,
the Solicitor, through his numbered company, owned the Hochelaga property. The
Island Park Drive property was owned by Susan Ault.

b) A property search of the Hochelaga property revealed that the Kisber mortgage was not a third mortgage but rather a fourth mortgage. Mr. Gibson was informed by the Solicitor's lawyer in November 1995 that the Solicitor forged his wife's signature on the Island Park Drive mortgage. Consequently, Mr. Kisber did not hold a valid mortgage on the Island Park property.

8) INVESTOR: Roy Wilson Real Estate
   PROPERTY: 694 Island Park Drive, Ottawa
   NET LOSS: $50 000

The Ottawa police were not able to interview Mr. Wilson concerning his investment secured by a mortgage on the Island Park Drive property. As stated earlier, the police determined that the Solicitor had forged his wife's signature on the mortgage documents, including the discharge documents, relating to 694 Island Park Drive.

9) INVESTOR: Jacqueline Charbonneau
   PROPERTY: 108 Royal Elm Private, Ottawa
   NET LOSS: $153 000

a) The Ottawa Police interviewed Jacqueline Charbonneau and her lawyer Roger Barrette. Mrs. Charbonneau had purchased a home, located at 108 Royal Elm Private, from Lisgar Square. Mrs. Charbonneau had issued three cheques relating to the purchase. The first cheque, in the amount of $16,750, was made payable to Lisgar Square. The second cheque, in the amount of $158,233.15, was made payable to the Tavel firm. The third cheque, in the amount of $250, was made payable to a sales person.

b) The Caisse Populaire Ste. Anne—Laurier D'Ottawa (Caisse Populaire) held a mortgage in the amount of $153,000 on the property located at 108 Royal Elm Private. The Caisse Populaire did not receive any funds from the Solicitor with respect to the Charbonneau purchase, despite the fact that the Solicitor had received $158,233.15 from the purchaser's lawyer. These funds are no longer in the firm's trust account. The Caisse Populaire has since commenced foreclosure proceedings against the property.

10) INVESTOR: Timothy Walker
    PROPERTY: 106 Royal Elm Private, Ottawa
    NET LOSS: $115 000

a) The circumstances surrounding the Walker matter are similar to the Charbonneau matter, except that in the Walker matter, the Caisse Populaire held a mortgage in the amount of $115,000. This mortgage was never discharged by The Solicitor.

...

Discipline History

10. The Solicitor does not have a past discipline history.

DATED at Toronto this 28th day of February, 1997.

Recommendation as to Penalty

The Committee recommends that Frank Arthur Ault be disbarred.

Reasons for Recommendation

The Solicitor, Frank Arthur Ault is fifty-one years of age and was called to the bar in 1975. Prior to his incarceration for the offenses that give rise to the complaints herein, the Solicitor had achieved a status in the profession that would be envied by most of his colleagues, especially in the Ottawa area in which he was well known for his professionalism. However, between September 1995 and January, 1996, according to the indictment, the Solicitor perpetrated several frauds on persons associated with his practice of law; the frauds consisting of falsifying prioritizations of mortgages such that persons would believe they were being given a certain priority on mortgages, whereas their priority was substantially less.

It appears from the materials that the Solicitor was substantially embarrassed by his financial position to the point that he faced bankruptcy, but rather than endure the bankruptcy, he perpetrated these frauds displaying what was obviously a misguided sense of judgment. Although the Solicitor was considered by his colleagues in the community as an honourable man, hard working and committed professionally, a devoted husband and family man at the core, he suffered from alcoholism and both physical and mental problems which no doubt affected his judgment. But, in reality, it was the crushing debt load that motivated his conduct.

We have before us materials filed on behalf of Mr. Ault which contain several character letters in which prominent members of the professional and local community testify to the Solicitor's worthiness as an individual. Their testimonials to the Solicitor are a tribute to him in the sense that they display a devotion to him, notwithstanding his conduct for which they all express shock.

The Law Society appears to be the last institutional rung in the Solicitor's fall from grace. Notwithstanding his prior exemplary character and the fact that these offenses and the complaints herein are, according to these testimonials, quite out of character, the Solicitor's conduct is egregious. The authorities are quite clear what the obligation of a Committee such as ours is in this situation and that is, notwithstanding the prior good character and the reasons for which the Solicitor misconducted himself, the nature of the conduct here is such that the Solicitor must be disbarred, and that is our recommendation.

Frank Arthur Ault was called to the Bar on March 21, 1975.

ALL OF WHICH IS RESPECTFULLY SUBMITTED.

DATED this 17th day of September, 1997.

Ronald D. Manes, for the Committee

ORDER of Convocation

CONVOCATION of the Law Society of Upper Canada, having read the Report and Decision of the Discipline Committee dated the 17th day of September, 1997, in the presence of Counsel for the Society, the Solicitor not being in attendance and not represented by counsel, wherein the Solicitor was found guilty of conduct unbecoming a barrister and solicitor and having heard counsel aforesaid;

CONVOCATION HEREBY ORDERS that Frank Arthur Ault be disbarred as a barrister, that his name be struck off the Roll of Solicitors, that his membership in the said Society be cancelled, and that he is hereby prohibited from acting or practising as a barrister and solicitor and from holding himself out as a barrister and solicitor.

NOTES AND QUESTIONS

1. Ault was disbarred as a result of the conduct at issue in this case. What "costs" flow from the penalty of disbarment? How do these costs compare with the costs that flow from a fine? Does the penalty of disbarment impose costs on anyone other than the lawyer upon whom this penalty is imposed?

2. The tribunal's decision makes it clear that Ault suffered from alcoholism and other (unspecified) physical and mental problems that affected his judgment. What impact does a disease such as alcoholism have on a theory (such as an economic theory) that is premised on the individual's ability to make rational choices regarding his or her preferred courses of action?

3. Did the penalty imposed in the *Ault* decision accomplish an economic goal? What goals might we hope to achieve through the imposition of penalties?

4. Assuming that *Ault* remains good law, under what circumstances might a future lawyer decide to undertake the course of action that ultimately led to Ault's disbarment?

5. Assume, for the sake of argument, that Ault was incapable of accurately assessing the "present value" of his right to practise law in the future. Does that mean that Ault is incapable of making his decision in an economic manner, or does it simply mean that any decision that Ault makes on economic grounds is likely to be incorrect?

6. Generate a schedule of costs and benefits that Ault might have considered (perhaps subconsciously) when deciding to embark on his unethical course of action. Given that Ault chose to participate in the unethical course of action, can we safely assume that Ault believed that the benefits of the unethical course of action outweighed the cost of the relevant acts? Why or why not?

IV. Conclusion

Chapter 1 has provided an overview of the economic theory of legal ethics. This overview has included repeated references to concepts such as self-interest, utility, efficiency, and profit maximization. In many instances, the references to these ideas have been oversimplified. Chapter 2 is designed to provide a more in-depth look at some of these key economic concepts, paying particular attention to the role these concepts play in evaluating ethical choices. Because these concepts play pivotal roles throughout the remainder of this book, it is important that readers become familiar with them before moving on to subsequent chapters.

CHAPTER TWO

Basic Concepts

I. Introduction

Chapter 1 introduced an economic account of legal ethics. Pursuant to this theory, ethical decisions are portrayed as economic choices. When deciding whether or not to take an ethically dubious action, rational decision makers consider the possible consequences, rank their various preferences, and perform a cost–benefit calculation, ultimately selecting whatever action they believe will generate the optimal outcome. This form of decision making is an economic process, best evaluated through the use of economic tools.

Before using economic theory to describe and evaluate legal ethics, it is important to step back and review the basic tools of economic analysis. The purpose of this chapter is to introduce key economic concepts that can be used in the assessment of ethical choices. The most important of these concepts are scarcity, utility, and maximization. These concepts, together with the analytical framework they establish, are discussed at length in the following sections or this chapter. Readers who are already well versed in basic economic analysis may wish to move on to section IV, where economic tools are applied to ethical choices.

II. Scarcity

A. The Need To Choose

Why must people make choices? Consider the morally charged decision of whether to remain faithful to one's spouse. This decision (like any ethical choice) can be portrayed as a choice between competing options. By remaining faithful, the spouse might maintain a guilt-free conscience, a relatively happy marriage, and an untarnished reputation for fidelity. By philandering, our hypothetical spouse might satisfy sexual desires and a need to experience thrills the spouse associates with illicit behaviour. The choice the spouse makes will depend on the relative value that he or she places on these competing sets of assets. If a happy marriage, a guilt-free conscience, and a reputation for fidelity are worth more to our potential philanderer than the perceived benefits of philandering, he or she will remain faithful at the expense of any enjoyment that philandering might bring. If the perceived benefits of philandering are greater than the value of the spouse's current marriage, reputation, and clear conscience, the spouse will philander at the expense of these resources.[1]

The unstated assumption in this example is that the spouse *is required* to choose between one set of potential consequences (a clear conscience, a good reputation, and a fairly happy marriage) and another set of possible consequences (sexual fulfillment and thrills). The spouse cannot have both.[2] The spouse's selection of one set of consequences will preclude his or her enjoyment of the other. In other words, our hypothetical spouse is constrained in his or her decision. The "constraining factor," forcing the spouse to choose between competing options, is known as "scarcity." Scarcity places limits on an individual's routes to fulfillment, forcing the individual to give up certain options or resources in pursuit of alternative options. The manner in which scarcity forces people to make such choices is explored in the following section of this chapter.

B. The Nature of Scarcity

The notion of scarcity draws our attention to the fact that we live in a world with limited resources. The scarcity of resources makes it impossible for every person to secure the resources needed to fulfill every one of his or her desires. For example, I can either fulfill my desire for entertainment by buying a new TV or fulfill my desire for transportation by paying for car repairs. My choice is constrained by scarcity: I have insufficient funds to purchase both a new TV and car repairs. Because my resources are limited (or scarce), I must select one or the other. In order to have a new TV, I must give up (or at least delay) my car repairs; in order to have my car repaired, I must give up (or at least delay) the acquisition of a TV. At present, I can achieve either the goal of a new TV or the goal of a functioning car, but I cannot achieve both outcomes. I am faced with the problem of scarcity: I have access to insufficient resources to satisfy my desires. Because of scarcity, "decision-makers' opportunities are moderately constrained so that they can achieve some, but not all, of their objectives."[3] As a result, I must choose which objective I will fulfill given the present constraints imposed by scarce resources.

Chapter 1 showed us that any choice between resources is made through a ranking of preferences. Faced with a decision between the purchase of car repairs and the purchase of a new TV, for example, I must decide which of these assets I prefer. Assuming that the two assets have the same market price (say, $2,000), I must determine the relative value I

---

1   The fact that our potential philanderer performs this calculation does not make the philanderer a "bad person" or a moral mercenary. The "goodness" or "badness" of the decision does not lie in its economic form, but in the values that our potential philanderer assigns to the various consequences that his or her decision could bring about. For example, a traditionally "moral" person would place a high value on fidelity, and a low value on "thrills," making it exceedingly likely that our traditionally moral spouse would remain faithful. The spouse is "moral," despite the fact that his or her decision was rooted in a self-interested cost–benefit analysis.

2   More accurately, the spouse *in our example* cannot have both.

3   Cooter and Ulen, *Law and Economics*, 4th ed. (Boston: Pearson Addison Wesley), 219.

assign to each asset.[4] If I would derive $3,000 worth of pleasure from having the new TV and only $2,500 worth of pleasure from a functioning car, I will purchase the new TV and leave my car in disrepair. My need to make this calculation and decide between two options is driven by scarcity: if I had infinite resources I would purchase the TV, the car repairs, and anything else that I considered desirable. In the absence of scarcity there would be no need to make this type of decision. Indeed, Wessels contends that "[s]carcity is the source of all choice."[5] Every choice that an individual must make between resources or competing possibilities arises because of the scarcity of resources.

C. Competition

Scarcity leads to competition. The scarcity of resources does not merely limit my ability to achieve conflicting personal objectives. On the contrary, it also implies that there are insufficient resources for competing individuals to achieve competing goals. Consider a parcel of land. One person wants to use it as a nature preserve; another wants to use the land for mining operations. Our hypothetical parcel of land is uniquely suited to the needs of a nature preserve—it houses the last members of several vulnerable species. The same land is also suited to mining operations—it is rich in mineral deposits that cannot be found in other exploitable land. Unfortunately, the presence of a nature preserve precludes the mining business (in other words, sharing is not an option). In this scenario, land is scarce. Only one of our competing individuals will be able to achieve his or her objective, leaving the other competitor's wishes unfulfilled. As a result, our two competitors need some mechanism for allocating the scarce resource of land.

The law of property is one mechanism for allocating resources. As later sections of this book will demonstrate, a system of ethics frequently serves the same purpose, allocating scarce resources among competing individuals. As we shall see, in the absence of scarcity, there would be no need for a system of ethics at all.

D. Scarcity and Ethics

How does scarcity relate to ethical systems? Consider David Hume's account of the relationship between scarcity and justice:

> Let us suppose that nature has bestowed on the human race such profuse *abundance* of all *external* conveniences, that, without any uncertainty in the event, without any care of industry on our part, every individual finds himself fully provided with whatever his most voracious appetites can want, or luxurious imagination wish or desire. His natural beauty, we shall suppose, surpasses all acquired ornaments: The perpetual clemency of the seasons renders useless all cloaths or covering: The raw herbage affords him the most delicious fare;

---

4   For the purposes of this example, we will assign dollar values to my competing preferences. In reality, this level of specificity is not required. All that is required is an ordering of my competing preferences—that is, a decision regarding which of the two options I prefer.

5   Walter J. Wessels, *Economics*, 3d ed. (Hauppauge, NY: Barron's, 2000), 4.

the clear fountain, the richest beverage. No laborious occupation required: No tillage: No navigation. Music, poetry, and contemplation form his sole business: Conversation, mirth, and friendship his sole amusement. ... It seems evident, that, in such a happy state, every other social virtue would flourish, and receive tenfold encrease; but the cautious, jealous virtue of justice would never once have been dreamed of. For what purpose make a partition of goods, where every one has already more than enough? Why give rise to property, where there cannot possibly be any injury? Why call this object *mine*, when upon the seizing of it by another, I need but stretch out my hand to possess myself of what is equally valuable? Justice, in that case, being totally useless, would be an idle ceremonial, and could never possibly have place in the catalogue of virtues.[6]

Scarcity gives rise to the need for an allocation of resources. Because of scarcity, one individual has access to resources that another person needs. This gives rise to the possibility of conflict.[7] My use of resources may conflict with someone else's, and in pursuing my own interests (and depleting scarce resources) I am causing harm to others by depriving them of assets that they need. We are engaged in what James described as "[t]he wars of the flesh and the spirit in each man, the concupiscences of different individuals pursuing the same unshareable material or social prizes."[8] Where resources are unshareable and scarce, one person is denied what another has. In other words, scarcity leads to deprivation.

In the absence of scarcity there is no possibility of depriving others of the resources they need. To the extent that injury flows from deprivation, scarcity is the ultimate source of harm. As Hume demonstrated, in the absence of scarcity "there cannot possibly be any injury."[9] Without the possibility of injury or harm, there is little need for an ethical system. One can accordingly point to scarcity as a fundamental cause of ethical systems.

The harms that individuals cause through their use of resources can be regarded as costs imposed on other people. Revisit the examples given in chapter 1. In example 1.1, the costs that Ted imposed by breaching his agreement were equal to the loss of economic surplus suffered by his contractual partner (a cost that was offset by the payment of damages). In example 1.4, the harm that Mary would have caused by embezzling funds can be regarded as a cost (in the amount of $20,000) imposed on children who stood to benefit through an alternative use of the funds. The economic theory of ethics holds that one purpose of ethical systems is to minimize such costs and to ensure a fairly "harmless" distribution of scarce resources. By deterring unethical actions (through the imposition of costs on unethical actors), ethical systems minimize the overall costs that result from resource allocation. Ethical systems can accordingly be regarded as a mechanism for coping with scarce resources.

---

6   David Hume, *An Enquiry Concerning the Principles of Morals* (Oxford: Oxford University Press, 1998), 83.

7   See David Friedman, *Law's Order* (Princeton, NJ: Princeton University Press, 2000), 309.

8   William James, *Selected Writings* (London: Orion Publishing Group, 1995), 308.

9   Hume, supra note 6, at 83.

The study of scarcity falls squarely within the domain of economics. The tools of economics are particularly helpful in accounting for the methods by which humans cope with scarcity. Because ethical systems are a mechanism for coping with scarce resources, economics provides a useful means of describing and assessing ethical systems.

Economists use several terms of art when describing the ways in which individuals and communities cope with scarcity. We have already encountered the most important of these terms in chapter 1: "self-interest," "utility," and "maximization." The meaning of these terms, together with the ways in which they assist in the evaluation of ethical choices, is addressed in the following section of this chapter.

III. Self-Interest, Utility, and Maximization

A. Self-Interest

One of the classical assumptions shared by ethicists and economists is that people tend to act in ways that further their own happiness.[10] As Thomas Hobbes noted:

> the voluntary actions, and inclinations of all men, tend, not onely to the procuring, but also to the assuring of a contented, life; and differ onely in the way which ariseth partly from the diversity of passions, in divers men; and partly from the difference of the knowledge, or opinion each one has of the causes, which produce the effect desired.[11]

In other words, all voluntary actions are undertaken for the purpose of increasing the pleasure of the relevant actor. When faced with a climate of scarcity, people will tend to allocate resources in whatever manner they believe will bring them the most happiness. Because individuals tend to allocate resources with a view to their own pleasure, individuals are said to act in their "self interest."

The pursuit of self-interest has often been lauded as the governing principle of all human behaviour. According to Joseph Butler, for example, "no creature whatever can

---

10   The notion of self-interest is traditionally treated differently by ethicists, on the one hand, and economists, on the other. For the ethicist, the notion of self-interest implies that individuals act in ways designed to maximize their pleasure or minimize pain. For the economist, "self-interest" implies that in the process of preference ordering, the only set of preferences that matters to a decision maker is his or her own: the decision maker will ignore the preferences of others when making decisions. Economists have a second assumption, referred to as the assumption of "rationality." Pursuant to this assumption, individuals are assumed to have the capacity to rank potential outcomes from "most preferred" to "least preferred." Where an individual's choices are constrained by scarce resources, individuals make whatever choices they prefer. For the economist, it is irrelevant whether the "preference" is based on traditional notions of "pleasure." The ethicist's use of the term self-interest, by contrast, combines the assumption of rationality with the economic notion of self-interest. Ethical philosophers such as Hobbes, Bentham, and Mill claim that a preference is "preferred" on the ground that it increases the pleasure (or minimizes the pain) of the relevant actor. From the ethicist's perspective, the phrase "I prefer X to Y" is the logical equivalent of "X gives me more pleasure than Y," "X causes me less pain than Y," or "as between X and Y, I find X more pleasurable (or less painful) than Y." Generally speaking, this book will use the term self-interest as it is used by ethicists, combining the economic assumptions of rationality and self-interest.

11   Thomas Hobbes, *Leviathan* (New York: Norton & Company, 1997), 55.

possibly act but merely from self-love."[12] Similarly, Jeremy Bentham argued that the pursuit of personal pleasure (coupled with the avoidance of pain) was the governing force that drove all human decisions. In Bentham's view:

> Nature has placed mankind under the governance of two sovereign masters, *pain* and *pleasure*. It is for them alone to point out what we ought to do, as well as to determine what we shall do. On the one hand the standard of right and wrong, on the other the chain of causes and effects, are fastened to their throne. They govern us in all we do, in all we say, in all we think: every effort we can make to throw off our subjection, will serve but to demonstrate and confirm it.[13]

Arthur Schopenhauer echoed Bentham's thesis, claiming that

> the material basis of [human pursuits] is bodily pleasure or bodily pain. This basis is very restricted: it is simply health, food, protection from wet and cold, the satisfaction of the sexual instinct, or else the absence of these things.[14]

In other words, everything that humans do is driven by the self-interested desire to maximize pleasure and minimize pain. When choosing spouses, spending money, seeking employment, and constructing legal systems, humans inevitably pursue the twin goals of increasing pleasure and decreasing pain. Stated simply, people act in their self-interest. The same is true when people make ethical decisions: when choosing between ethical and unethical courses of action, the decision maker's choices are governed by self-interest. This simple assumption lies at the heart of an economic model of ethical systems.

A self-interest motive does not imply that people like to harm one another, or even that people act without regard for each other's needs. As previous sections of this book have demonstrated, an economic model of ethical reasoning does not deny the existence of altruistic motives.[15] On the contrary, an economic model of ethics draws our attention to the link between altruistic behaviour and self-interest. A person who engages in altruistic behaviour (and in doing so expends or forgoes resources such as time or money) demonstrates an economic preference for altruistic deeds. People engage in altruistic endeavours because they place a *value* on altruism, a value that outweighs whatever assets they forgo in pursuit of their altruistic acts. Consider the following example.

Example 2.1

Steven Suwondo is an employee at a tobacco company. Steven discovers that his employer is illegally adding harmful chemicals to tobacco products in order to increase their addictive properties. Steven decides to report his employer's activities to the press, imperilling his employment on the grounds that "whistle blowing" (in Steven's opinion) is "the right thing to do."

---

12   Joseph Butler, *Fifteen Sermons* (London: G. Bell & Sons, 1949), 168.

13   Jeremy Bentham, *An Introduction to the Principles of Morals and Legislation* (London: The Athlone Press, 1970), 11.

14   Arthur Schopenhauer, *The Pessimist's Handbook* (Lincoln, NE: University of Nebraska Press, 1964), 131.

15   See chapter 1, section II.D.

At first glance, Steven appears to have sacrificed his interests for the benefit of others. From another perspective, however, Steven is simply pursuing his preference for an altruistic action. Assume that Steven knows, with certainty, that he will lose his job if he decides to report his employer's actions. By reporting his employer's illegal activities, Steven is trading one asset (continued access to his current income stream) for another asset that he considers more valuable (the knowledge that people will not be harmed by his employer's activities). Steven reports his employer's activities because, from Steven's perspective, the action is worth taking. To the extent that Steven is giving up some share of personal happiness, he is doing so "for the sake of something which he prizes more."[16] In short, Steven is giving effect to his personal preference. He would rather have the knowledge that he acted for the benefit of the public than continued access to his stream of income. If Steven valued his income more than he valued public health, he would presumably refrain from exposing his employer's behaviour. Because Steven's altruistic action is the choice that he *prefers* (in the sense that he is happier with this decision than he would be with the alternative), Steven can be said to have acted in a way that maximizes his own happiness. In other words, Steven has acted with regard to his self-interest, despite the fact that his actions seem to inure to the benefit of others.

In example 2.1, Steven faced a problem of scarcity. He could either keep his current source of income or secure the public's health by "whistle blowing." He could not do both: the problem of scarcity placed a limit on Steven's routes to personal pleasure, ensuring that Steven could achieve only one of his two objectives. As rational people tend to do, Steven weighed his two alternatives, conducted a cost–benefit calculation and chose the course of action that maximized his pleasure. The fact that Steven (like all people) would tend to choose whatever outcome he preferred demonstrates the notion of self-interest: when faced with competing possibilities, individuals will ultimately choose whatever outcome they prefer. This straightforward (and relatively uncontroversial) point lies at the heart of any economic analysis.

The self-interested nature of Steven's altruistic action does not detract from the "moral quality" of his choice. At first blush, it may appear that Steven's action would be more laudable if he were truly sacrificing his pleasure for the benefit of others. As we have seen, Steven is, in fact, pursuing his own pleasure by giving effect to the outcome he prefers. But one may still regard Steven as "morally admirable," because he *prefers* (or has an interest in) an outcome that results in a personal loss of tangible assets. Steven makes himself happy by helping others rather than by protecting his current source of income. While Steven can be said to have acted in his own self-interest, he has aligned his interests with people who are unable to help themselves. Steven's preference for altruism (an economic preference, the satisfaction of which is in his interest) may also be regarded as an admirable trait. The fact that Steven values altruism more than he values material wealth does not diminish his status as a morally admirable man. Our morality is not determined by the process that we follow when we make ethical decisions, but by the values that we place on competing preferences when making ethical choices.

---

16   John Stuart Mill, *Utilitarianism* (Peterborough, ON: Broadview Press, 2000), 24.

B. Utility

In pursuit of self-interest people have to make decisions. Faced with a climate of scarce resources, people choose between competing possibilities, selecting whatever option they believe will please them most. But how do individuals rank competing possibilities? What are we measuring when we compare competing alternatives? Economists (as well as many ethicists) answer these questions by reference to the notion of "utility," which Jeremy Bentham summarized as follows:

> By utility is meant that property in any object, whereby it tends to produce benefit, advantage, pleasure, good, or happiness (all this in the present case comes to the same thing), or (what comes again to the same thing) to prevent the happening of mischief, pain, evil, or unhappiness.[17]

In other words, the utility of an object is the value it produces. We value a car because it produces a certain amount of utility (perhaps by allowing transportation or enhancing social status). We value a stereo because it produces some other level of utility (perhaps by providing enhanced audio entertainment). As strange as it may seem, we also value our spouses and children for the utility they produce—the "form" of pleasure we recieve from any source is unimportant. To the extent that anything enhances our lives or gives us pleasure, we value that thing for the utility it provides.

The concept of utility embraces far more than mere monetary value: it encompasses anything with the capacity to create happiness or pleasure. The relative value of two items is no more than a relative measurement of the utility they produce: if I assert that I value my wife more than my stereo, for example, I am asserting that my wife provides me with a greater amount of utility than my stereo can provide. When we prefer one object, one principle, or one virtue to another, we prefer it on the ground that it produces more utility than its alternative. As Mill stated:

> [I]f the principle of utility is good for anything, it must be good for weighing these conflicting utilities against one another and marking out the region within which one or the other preponderates.[18]

When we rank competing preferences, we are ranking the utility that is produced by each alternative. When forced to make a choice between alternatives, a rational individual will inevitably select whatever alternative yields the most utility.

When economists assign a dollar value to a particular good or service, they are providing a relative measure of its utility. As we saw in chapter 1, section II.E, the assignment of a dollar value to a particular item does not imply that the relevant item can be purchased in exchange for a sum of money. Instead, the assignment of a dollar value to an asset means that the relevant asset provides the decision maker with *the same amount of utility* as a specified sum of cash. For example, if I say that the love of my dog is worth $10 million, I am asserting that I am just as happy to have the love of my dog as I would be to have $10 million. A $10 million cheque would bring me just as much utility

---

17   Bentham, supra note 13, at 12.

18   Mill, supra note 16, at 32.

as I would get from the love of my dog.[19] It is irrelevant that I cannot buy Rover's affection in the market, or that no one else would conclude that the "fair market value" of Rover's affection is equivalent to $10 million. All that matters to an economist is that, from my perspective, Rover's love provides me with the same amount of utility that I would receive from $10 million. Armed with this knowledge, an economist can begin to make predictions regarding my actions. For example, an economist could assume that I would happily give up Rover's affection in exchange for a sum of money that exceeds $10 million.

The notion of utility can also be applied in the realm of ethics. As we saw in the example concerning the value of Rover's affection, utility does not merely measure the value of tradable goods or services. On the contrary, utility can be used to evaluate anything that people consider valuable, including intangible qualities such as justice, integrity, and other "ethical" virtues. As Hume stated:

> [U]tility … is the sole source of the moral approbation paid to fidelity, justice, veracity, integrity, and those other estimable and useful qualities and principles. It is entirely agreeable to the rules of philosophy, and even of common reason; where any principle has been found to have a great force and energy in one instance, to ascribe to it a like energy in all similar instances.[20]

The principle of utility embodies all that is good in an asset, a virtue, a principle, or an idea. In short, anything that people value can be measured by the principle of utility, regardless of whether the item or idea can be traded. As a result, "ethical virtues" such as honesty, integrity, and fairness can be measured by reference to the relative utility that they yield.

C. Maximization

In section II, above, we noted that a climate of scarcity ensures that there are not enough goods to go around. We value goods for the utility they provide. As a result, the fundamental problem in a climate of scarce resources is that scarcity places limits on utility. People faced with a climate of scarce resources are forced to make choices among the available sources of utility. These choices are made through an ordering of preferences. As Cooter and Ulen note: "[T]he decisionmaker who has ranked outcomes in order of preference and is constrained in his choice will naturally choose the best feasible outcome."[21] The "best feasible outcome" is the one that generates the most utility for the decision maker. In every choice that individuals make, they strive to obtain the optimal level of utility.

---

19   If weighing the relative utility of (1) $10 million plus one apple against (2) the love of my dog, option (1) would be preferable, in that it produces exactly one apple's worth of utility more than the love of my dog. This, of course, assumes that an apple produces a positive amount of utility. If I were allergic to apples or found them repellant, the math would change.

20   Hume, supra note 6, at 98.

21   Cooter and Ulen, *Law and Economics* (New York: Harper Collins, 1988), 234.

The process of striving for the highest possible level of utility is known as "maximization." In pursuit of maximization, individuals select higher utility items over lower utility items, or trade resources that they have for other resources from which they will glean more utility. Cooter and Ulen provide the following summary of the process of maximization:

> Economists usually assume that each economic actor maximizes something: consumers maximize utility (i.e., happiness or satisfaction); firms maximize profits, politicians maximize votes, bureaucracies maximize revenues, charities maximize social welfare, and so forth. Economists often say that models assuming maximizing behavior work because most people are rational, and rationality requires maximization. Different people want different things, such as wealth, power, fame, love, happiness and so on. The alternatives faced by an economic decision-maker give her different amounts of what she wants. One conception of rationality holds that a rational actor can rank alternatives according to the extent that they give her what she wants. In practice, the alternatives available to the actor are constrained. For example, a rational consumer can rank alternative bundles of consumer goods, and the consumer's budget constrains her choice among them. A rational consumer should choose the best alternative that the constraints allow. Another common way of understanding this conception of rational behavior is to recognize that consumers choose alternatives that are well-suited to achieving their ends. …
>
> Choosing the best alternative that the constraints allow can be described mathematically as *maximizing*. To see why, consider that the real numbers can be ranked from small to large, just as the rational consumer ranks alternatives according to the extent that they give her what she wants. Consequently, better alternatives can be associated with larger numbers. Economists call this association a "utility function" … . Choosing the best alternative that the constraints allow corresponds to maximizing the utility function subject to the feasibility constraint. So, the consumer who goes shopping is said to maximize utility subject to her budget constraint.[22]

Our observations concerning scarcity, utility, and maximization lead to one of the key assumptions of economists: when faced with a climate of scarcity, a rational individual will maximize utility. Where nothing impedes exchange, an individual will trade lower utility assets for assets that generate more utility. People want as much utility as they can get, and they will generally attempt to get the largest amount of utility at the lowest possible price.

Most aspects of voluntary human behaviour can be explained in terms of utility maximization. In everything they do, people tend to act as though they are following the principles of economic reasoning: they make their choices and order their affairs in ways that can be explained by reference to utility maximization. This should come as no surprise. The accumulation of resources generally makes survival, reproduction, and successful child rearing much more likely. The resources that we desire are typically (but not exclusively) things that make our existence more comfortable and secure.[23] From an

---

22   Cooter and Ulen, supra note 3, at 15.

23   Many individuals appear to derive utility from destructive "pleasures," such as harmful narcotics or perilous behaviour. This seems to counter the evolutionary argument that the utility of an object is its

evolutionary perspective, the utility of an object can (in many instances) be regarded as the tendency of the object to enhance its user's capacity to survive.[24] As a result, those who are best at maximizing utility are most likely to survive—most likely to pass their genes along to succeeding generations.

Behaviours that increase the likelihood of survival (or, more specifically, increase the likelihood of producing viable offspring) are encouraged through the process of natural selection. As Freeman and Herron note, "Darwin's fourth claim was that the individuals who survive and go on to reproduce, or who reproduce the most, are those with certain, favorable variations."[25] Whatever skills are needed to maximize utility—to accumulate resources that increase our chance of survival—are favourable variations. As a result, those who are more successful in attaining the resources that are required to ensure survival (and the survival of their progeny) will pass on their genetic profiles to succeeding generations. In short, to the extent that the "utility" of an object is a proxy for its tendency to promote our species' survival, natural selection favours utility maximizers. In a contest for survival, the winners will tend to be good economists (or, more accurately, those who act as though they were governed by sound economic reasoning). Our natural predispositions—that is, the instinct to survive and pass our genes along to future generations—ensure that economic principles will govern our behaviour. It is therefore natural that many aspects of human behaviour, including those (such as ethics) that are typically associated with metaphysical notions, are governed by our mundane-seeming desire to accumulate wealth, maximize profit, and ensure our species' survival.

The drive to maximize utility is the foundation of ethical reasoning. As we have seen, ethical systems minimize the costs of collective action and assist us in our quest to maximize utility. Indeed, all ethical decisions can be explained by reference to scarcity and utility maximization. The practical implications of the link between ethics, scarcity, and utility maximization are explored in the following section of this chapter.

IV. Ethical Calculations

A. Introduction

Ethical decisions are made through the application of economic tools. The notions of scarcity and utility maximization permeate our ethical systems, driving individual choices regarding ethical and unethical behaviour. Our assessment of whether or not a particular

---

tendency to promote survival. For economic purposes, it is immaterial whether utility truly promotes survival. The economist simply assumes that, from whatever sources an individual derives his or her utility, the individual's preferences are stable and consistent. This assumption of consistency is fundamental to economics, and allows us to make powerful predictions concerning the choices people make. As we shall see, one need not accept the evolutionary argument in order to accept an economic model that is premised on utility maximization.

24   Indeed, a proponent of evolutionary theory would contend that our species has an over-riding preference for survival, and that more specific preferences (such as preferences for comfort and pleasure) are simply subordinate manifestations of our instinct for survival.

25   Scott Freeman and Jon C. Herron, *Evolutionary Analysis*, 2d ed. (Upper Saddle River, NJ: Prentice Hall, 2001), 55.

act is ethical, or whether we should breach a "rule" of ethics, is made through the use of economic reasoning. Consider the following illustration.

Example 2.2

Garry is a hockey player, playing in a championship final against the top team in the league. During sudden-death overtime, the opposing team's star player takes the puck and charges toward Garry's goaltender. No one but Garry stands between the charging player and Garry's goalie. The only way for Garry to stop the charging player is to trip him, incurring a two-minute penalty.

What should Garry do? Tripping one's opponents violates the rules of hockey. If Garry trips his charging opponent, he will have to endure two minutes in the penalty box and subsequently face retribution on the ice by opposing players. He may also feel guilty. On the other hand, if Garry does *not* trip his opponent, his team is likely to lose the game. Let us assume that (from Garry's perspective) the costs of breaking the "no tripping" rule—that is, the penalty plus the likelihood of retribution, together with any guilt that Garry might feel—are more than offset by the gain that Garry will realize by violating the relevant rule—that is, maintaining his team's chance of winning the game. If Garry is a rational, utility-maximizing individual, he will trip the charging opponent. From Garry's perspective, the utility achieved by stopping a likely goal is greater than the utility achieved by avoiding (1) the penalty box, (2) retribution, and (3) a guilty conscience. As a result, Garry exchanges a less valued (or lower utility) set of assets (freedom from the penalty box, freedom from a guilty conscience, and freedom from retribution on the ice) for a higher utility asset (maintaining his team's chance of winning the championship). While the phrase "utility maximization" is unlikely to enter Garry's puck-addled mind when he makes the decision to trip his opponent, Garry is nevertheless engaged in an economic decision. At a very general level, he will decide (perhaps subconsciously) whether or not "taking a penalty" is worthwhile. This is an ethical decision: it involves the breach of a rule designed to increase player safety and fair play. It is also an economic decision that is guided by utility maximization.

Ethical cost–benefit analyses are not confined to hockey games. Indeed, all of the ethical choices people make are resolved through the unconscious use of economic reasoning. Mill provides a useful example:

[T]o save a life, it may not only be allowable, but a duty, to steal or take by force the necessary food or medicine, or to kidnap and compel to officiate the only qualified medical practitioner. In such cases, as we do not call anything justice which is not a virtue, we usually say, not that justice must give way to some other moral principle, but that what is just in ordinary cases is, by reason of that other principle, not just in the particular case.[26]

In Mill's example, the general ethical rule is that one should neither steal medical supplies nor kidnap doctors. The cost of violating these ethical norms, however, must be

---

26   Mill, supra note 16, at 79.

weighed against the benefit to be obtained through violations. In Mill's example, the benefit to be obtained involves the preservation of life. When deciding whether or not to violate the general rule forbidding the kidnapping of doctors, one must weigh the costs and benefits of the action. This is an ethical decision, and (like all ethical decisions) it is arrived at through the use of "ethical calculus," a series of subconscious calculations weighing the costs and benefits of specific decisions.[27] At its core, this ethical calculus is economic reasoning. The manner in which individuals use this calculus when making ethical choices is addressed in the following section.

B. Simple Utility Calculations

When deciding whether to take a particular course of action, people base their decision on the level of utility that the relevant act will yield. Jeremy Bentham summarized this decision-making process as follows:

> Sum up all the values of all the *pleasures* on the one side, and those of all the *pains* on the other. The balance, if it be on the side of pleasure, will give the *good* tendency of the act upon the whole, with respect to the interests of that *individual* person; if on the side of pain, the *bad* tendency of it upon the whole.[28]

This form of decision making can be symbolized by a simple equation:

$$A - B = X$$

In this equation,[29] A is the sum of the benefits or pleasures to be derived from a proposed course of action (that is, the gross utility gains generated by the act), and B is the sum of all of the costs (or utility losses) generated by the action. X is the figure yielded by subtracting B from A, and represents the net utility that is generated by the proposed activity. Where X is a positive figure (greater than zero), the relevant action yields a net gain in utility. Where X is a negative figure (less than zero), the costs of the act exceed the benefits and result in a net loss. As utility maximizers, rational individuals tend to refrain from acts that lead to a net loss of utility, and tend to take those actions that yield gains. (For the application of this basic equation to "win–win" and "lose–lose" situations, see the box entitled "Double Binds," below.) The application of this equation to ethical choices is illustrated in example 2.3.

---

27 W.D. Ross, in *The Right and the Good* (London: Oxford University Press, 1930), 18, provides a similar, useful example:

> If I have promised to meet a friend at a particular time for some trivial purpose, I should certainly think myself justified in breaking my engagement if by doing so I could prevent a serious accident or bring relief to the victims of one. And the supporters of the view we are examining hold that my thinking so is due to my thinking that I shall bring more good into existence by the one action than by the other.

28 Bentham, supra note 13, at 40.

29 For present purposes, we assume that the gains and losses of utility are certain—that is, the actor knows, with certainty, what benefits will be generated and what costs will be imposed. In subsequent chapters we will introduce the concept of probability, which deals with cases in which the costs or benefits of an action are uncertain.

Example 2.3

Gillian Lefler is a defence lawyer acting for Roy Fleming, who has been charged with rape. Gillian knows, with absolute certainty, that her client is guilty of the offence with which he is charged. The only witness against Gillian's client is Roy's victim, Veronica Hughes.

Veronica is suffering from various mental problems as a result of Roy's assault. She is emotionally unstable and easily confused. Gillian knows that, by pursuing a particularly rigorous cross-examination relating to Veronica's sexual history, she can upset Veronica, cause her to become confused on the stand, and generate inconsistencies in her story. This may undermine Veronica's credibility and increase Roy's chance of acquittal.

Although Gillian receives the same monetary compensation regardless of the outcome of Roy's case, assume that an increased chance of securing a client's acquittal is worth something to Gillian.[30] In this particular situation, Gillian would gladly give up $5,000 of income in order to increase the chance of having her client acquitted. On the other hand, Gillian is an empathetic person: she feels guilty at the prospect of further upsetting and discrediting a victim of a heinous crime. In fact, Gillian would happily forgo $10,000 of income in order to avoid the feelings of guilt she would experience if she tried to rattle Veronica on the stand. Finally, assume that Gillian feels that her duty as a lawyer requires her to seek any lawful advantage that may assist her client regardless of his guilt. Gillian would gladly give up $4,000 rather than fail to fulfill what she perceives to be her professional duties.[31]

Is Gillian likely to engage in the contemplated form of cross-examination? Before answering this question, consider the meaning of the various dollar values we have assigned to Gillian's preferences. By saying that Gillian would "happily forgo" a particular sum of money in exchange for a certain asset, we are saying that the asset in question provides Gillian with the same amount of utility as the specified sum of money. As a result, we can use the relevant dollar value as a proxy for the utility Gillian gains from the relevant asset. We can accordingly enter the relevant dollar values in our ethical calculation. Recall the algebraic expression of ethical choices: $A - B = X$. A represents the "utility gains" that Gillian realizes by pursuing her vigorous cross-examination. In this example, A is the sum of $5,000 (the value Gillian derives from seeing an increase in her client's chance of acquittal) and $4,000 (the value she derives from fulfilling what she perceives to be her duties as a lawyer). B is made up of the costs that Gillian will incur if she engages in the relevant form of cross-examination: $10,000 worth of guilt. Gillian's ethical calculation can accordingly be expressed in the following manner:

---

30   Perhaps Gillian believes that a victory in this case will lead to higher-profile (and higher-valued) cases later on, or enhance her reputation as a "tough defence lawyer."

31   Note that we are making no assumptions regarding the value that Gillian *ought to* place on the relevant outcomes: we are only concerned with Gillian's actual preferences. As we shall see in subsequent chapters, the Law Society has rules in place designed to alter the value of Gillian's preferences in this type of situation.

$$A - B = X$$
$$(\$5,000 + \$4,000) - (\$10,000) = X$$
$$\$9,000 - \$10,000 = X$$
$$-\$1,000 = X$$

In this example, X is a negative figure. In other words, by pursuing the contemplated form of cross-examination, Gillian will experience a net loss of utility.[32] She will feel worse by pursuing the vigorous cross-examination than she would by avoiding it. As a rational person, Gillian is a utility maximizer. She tends to avoid any action that results in a loss of utility. Since the contemplated cross-examination will result in a net loss of utility, Gillian will refrain from discrediting Veronica on the stand. The question of whether this decision makes Gillian a good person, a bad lawyer, or something else is left for future chapters.

Note that Gillian will not actually perform the calculations described above—at least not in the level of detail set forth in the foregoing illustration. As Jeremy Bentham notes:

> It is not to be expected that this process should be strictly pursued previously to every moral judgment, or to every legislative or judicial operation. It may, however, be always kept in view: and as near as the process actually pursued on these occasions approaches to it, so near will such process approach to the character of an exact one.[33]

Rather than performing any detailed calculations, Gillian will simply decide (based on her own subjective preferences) whether her contemplated action increases or decreases her overall state of happiness. Regardless of whether she does the calculations, Gillian's actions will correspond to the predictions generated by our ethical equation. As a result, Gillian will act as though she is governed by economic calculations, despite the fact that she never truly bothers doing the math.

Once we have become accustomed to quantifying ethical values and the consequences that flow from ethical choices, we begin to see the value of an economic theory of ethical systems. The repercussions of ethical (or unethical) decisions can be regarded as prices that are linked to particular choices. The tools of economics allow us to predict the ways in which people respond to prices. As a result, the tools of economics can generate predictions regarding the ethical decisions people make. One way in which economics can help generate such predictions is explored in the following section.

---

32   This example can be turned on its head to achieve the same result. If we asked whether Gillian should *refrain* from the vigorous cross-examination, the benefits of refraining (figure A in our ethical equation) would be $10,000 (the avoidance of guilt), while the costs of refraining (figure B) would be $5,000 (reflecting the diminished chance of acquittal) plus $4,000 (reflecting Gillian's sense of duty). Completing our ethical calculation yields an X with a positive value of $1,000. This means that Gillian will pursue the relevant action. Thus, where the question is "should Gillian pursue the relevant cross-examination," the answer is a resounding "no." Where the question is phrased in the opposite manner, "should Gillian refrain from the vigorous cross-examination," the answer is "yes."

33   Bentham, supra note 13, at 40.

Double Binds

Thus far, we have assumed that individuals make choices as though they apply the equation A − B = X (where A represents the benefits of taking a proposed action, B represents the costs, and X represents the net gain or loss). Our basic account of the decision-making process has resulted in the generalization that individuals take actions that yield a positive value for X, while avoiding actions that yield a negative value for X.

Initially, the foregoing generalization seems to fail to account for "lose–lose" or "win–win" situations. In some cases, all of the decision maker's options seem to generate net losses of utility (a lose–lose situation) or net gains in utility (a win–win situation). The basic decision-making equation (namely, A − B = X) can account for such situations. Consider a typical win–win scenario. A decision maker is offered a choice between a free CD player and a free TV. The decision maker values the CD player at $1,000 and the television at $1,500. How does our equation account for the choice that our decision maker faces? It seems that our equation cannot apply because there is no cost to either choice. Each decision (accepting the television or accepting the CD player) produces a gain. An economist, however, would note that each decision carries an *opportunity cost*. By accepting the television, you forgo your opportunity to accept the CD player. By accepting the CD player, you forgo your opportunity to accept the television. Bearing this in mind, we can now apply our basic calculation to a decision maker's choice as to whether or not he or she should accept the television. Applying our algebraic expression of decisions (A − B = X), A (the benefit of accepting the television) is $1,500. B (the opportunity cost of forgoing the CD player) is $1,000. X works out to $500, a positive figure. Our decision maker should accept the television set. Had we asked the opposite question— namely, "should the decision maker accept the CD player?," A would have been $1,000 (the benefit of accepting the CD player), B would have been $1,500 (the cost of forgoing the television), and X would have been negative $500 (informing our decision maker that he or she should *not* take the CD player). However we phrase our question ("should I choose the CD player?" or "should I choose the TV?"), our equation yields the same answer: you should choose the television, on the ground that you value it more than the CD player.

The mathematics of the lose–lose situation are only slightly more compli- cated. Consider an inescapable choice between (1) paying a $1,000 fine and (2) spending 10 days in jail. Assume that 10 days in jail imposes a cost of $5,000 on our decision maker. Whether our decision maker chooses option 1 or 2, he or she appears to be taking an action that yields a net loss in utility, violating our general rule and taking an action that yields a "negative X" when expressed through the use of our algebraic expression. This is not entirely accurate. Once again, we must factor in the "opportunity costs" of each decision. In a lose–lose situation, however, an opportunity cost acts like a benefit. Returning to our example, if the decision maker chooses option (1) (the $1,000 fine), he or she forgoes the need to incur a cost of $5,000 (the cost of 10 days in prison). In other words, the "benefit" of accepting the $1,000 fine is equal to $5,000 (the value gained by avoiding jail). Thus, the question "should I accept the fine, rather than the prison sentence?" can be expressed through our algebraic expression (A − B = X): A is $5,000 (the value of not going to prison), while B is $1,000 (the cost of paying the requisite fine). This yields an X of $4,000 (a positive X, signifying a "net gain" through acceptance of the option of a fine). In other words, our decision maker should take the fine, because this yields a positive value for X. Choosing the option of jail leads to a negative X equal to −$4,000. Whether we face a lose−lose or a win−win situation, our basic equation (A − B = X) still provides a useful way to describe our approach to making decisions.

C. Maximizing Utility

The use of economics as a tool for analyzing ethical systems allows us to do more than merely add and subtract the costs and benefits of specific ethical choices. Once we have taken the step of accepting ethical systems as a series of price-based incentives, the tools of economics allow us to make complex predictions regarding the manner in which individuals will order their affairs in pursuit of an optimal level of utility. Consider the following example.

Example 2.4

Mark is a philanthropic corporate lawyer practising law in New York City. Mark derives a great deal of utility from his job: he enjoys devoting time to the practice of law. He also derives utility from charitable activities: he enjoys providing pro bono services at a community legal clinic. How much time should Mark devote to each activity?

Economists assume that individuals are capable of ranking the level of happiness (or utility) they derive from various choices. In this example, we must assume that Mark is capable of determining the level of utility he would derive from various combinations of time spent practising law and time spent working at the clinic. For the purposes of comparison, we will assign numerical values[34] to various levels of utility that Mark can achieve through possible combinations of time spent practising law and time spent working at the clinic (the higher the number, the higher the level of utility). For example, assume that devoting 10 hours per week to the clinic and 50 hours per week to practise gives Mark a utility value of 7. Devoting 30 hours per week to the clinic and 60 hours per

---

34   Note that we are now using "non-dollar values" to measure utility. We could just as easily assign dollar values to each level of utility Mark achieves. In this case, each level of utility corresponds to the amount of utility Mark enjoys from a given amount of cash. For example, if we assume that $5,000 provides Mark with a utility value of 5, we could say that any combination of office time and clinic time found on curve 5 = u(x,y) would give Mark $5,000 worth of utility.

week to practise gives Mark a utility value of 9. Spending 30 hours per week at work and zero hours at the clinic gives Mark a low utility level of 2.

It is important to note, at this stage, that the stated utility values are based on Mark's subjective preferences. These preferences are determined by asking Mark what he enjoys (or by observing his activities[35]) rather than by establishing what Mark *ought to* enjoy.[36] Mark has decided that spending 50 hours at work and 10 hours at the clinic makes him less happy (or generates less utility) than spending 60 hours at work and 30 hours at the clinic, while making him happier (or generating more utility) than spending 30 hours at work and no time at the clinic. For economic purposes, we will take these subjective preferences as given, without questioning the propriety or reasonableness of these preferences. The numerical figures given to the competing levels of utility are somewhat arbitrary, designed only to demonstrate the relative level of happiness Mark can generate through competing possibilities.

We can visualize Mark's preferences by graphing the various combinations of clinic time and office time that give rise to various levels of utility. Figure 2.1 shows how various combinations of time compare with one another in terms of the level of utility that they generate for Mark. The x (or horizontal) axis of the graph represents the number of hours spent practising law. The y (or vertical) axis represents the number of hours spent providing pro bono legal services at the clinic. We can plot various combinations of hours spent at work (quantity x) and hours spent at the clinic (quantity y) on our graph. We can then draw lines connecting every combination that gives rise to the same subjective level of utility. For example, all of the combinations of x and y that provide Mark with a utility value of 7 are combined by the curve[37] noted as $7 = u(x,y)$ in figure 2.1.

Each combination of x and y found along curve $7 = u(x,y)$ yields a utility value of 7. In other words, Mark is neutral (or "indifferent") between the various combinations plotted along the relevant curve: they each provide him with the same amount of utility. The curve is accordingly called an "indifference curve": when Mark is ordering his preferences, he is equally happy with all of the combinations found along the same indifference curve. Combinations found on a different indifference curve yield a different level of utility.

The combinations of x and y found along curve $5 = u(x,y)$ yield a utility value of 5. This is lower than a utility value of 7. Because Mark is a utility maximizer, he wishes to achieve the highest level of utility available. As a result, Mark prefers any combination of

---

35   According to Jean-Paul Sartre, *Existentialism Is a Humanism*, quoted in Steven M. Cahn and Peter Markie, eds., *Ethics: History, Theory, and Contemporary Issues*, 2d ed. (Oxford: Oxford University Press, 2002), 448, we must determine preferences by observing behaviour rather than by asking the relevant actor. According to Sartre: "I may say that I like so-and-so well enough to sacrifice a certain amount of money for him, but I may say so only if I've done it. I may say 'I love my mother well enough to remain with her' if I have remained with her. The only way to determine the value of this affection is, precisely, to perform an act which confirms and defines it."

36   Cooter and Ulen, supra note 3, at 22.

37   For those who are unfamiliar with this type of mathematical notation, the notation "$7 = u(x,y)$" simply means that the number 7 represents the utility value of any combination of x and y falling along the relevant curve.

Figure 2.1

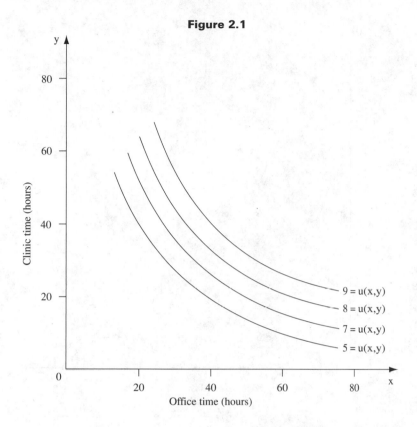

x and y along a high indifference curve (that is, a curve that corresponds to a relatively high level of utility) to any combination found on an indifference curve with a lower utility value.

It seems reasonable to assume that if Mark had infinite time available he would spend an infinite number of hours practising law and an infinite number of hours doing pro bono work at the clinic. Mark derives utility from each activity, and the more time he spends doing both, the greater the utility he will achieve. Unfortunately, Mark is faced with a problem of scarcity. Time is a scarce resource, and Mark does *not* have infinite time to devote to his competing preferences. As a result, Mark must budget his time: scarcity compels him to make a choice between resources. For illustrative purposes, let us assume that Mark has only 80 hours per week to devote to any combination of pro bono work and practice. Figure 2.2 superimposes the line T (indicating the number of hours Mark has available) along the indifference curves shown in figure 2.1. On the left side of this line (the shaded area) are all combinations of x (time spent at the office) and y (time spent at the clinic) that add up to 80 hours or less. In other words, the combinations of x and y found in the shaded areas are the only combinations that Mark can *afford*, given the constraints placed on his time. Combinations found to the right of the shaded area are beyond Mark's reach: he lacks sufficient time to implement any combination of x and y found beyond the shaded area, as they each add up to more than 80 hours.

Figure 2.2

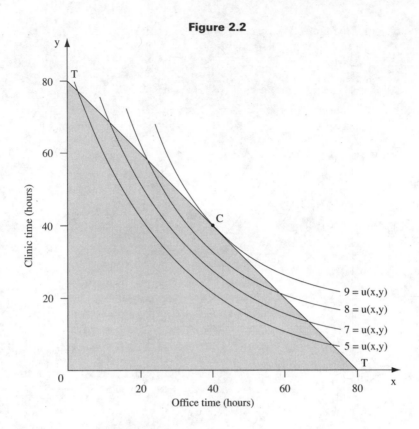

Because Mark is a utility maximizer, he prefers to pick whatever combination of x and y yields the highest attainable level of utility. In other words, Mark will choose a combination of x and y that falls along the highest attainable indifference curve. If we follow line T from left to right, we see that the line intersects several indifference curves. Starting from the left, line T intersects indifference curves with relatively low utility values. As we progress toward the right along line T, we see that it intersects with other indifference curves with higher utility values until it reaches point C, at which point the utility lines it intersects begin to decrease in value. Point C in figure 2.2 is Mark's "constrained maximum": it represents the highest utility value Mark can achieve given the constraints on his resources. In other words, the combination of x and y indicated at point C is the best allocation of time for Mark, given the resources at his disposal.

Because Mark is a utility maximizer, assume that he has decided to choose the combination of x and y suggested by point C. By doing so, Mark has achieved the highest level of utility he can attain through achievable combinations of x and y. Indeed, small movements away from point C can only lower Mark's utility: spending a few extra moments at the office will require Mark to spend less time at the clinic (and vice versa), and movements in either direction take Mark toward lower indifference curves. From Mark's perspective, any reallocation of time that takes him away from point C is inadvisable. Any reallocation of time that takes him toward point C (from any other point in the shaded portion of the graph) is a good idea, because it increases the utility that Mark can achieve.

Indifference curves can be useful in predicting the behaviour of individuals. If we know, for example, that Mark is not allocating his time in accordance with the pattern represented by point C on figure 2.2, we can safely assume that Mark will make adjustments to his schedule that will move him toward the allocation represented by point C. As a utility maximizer, Mark is doing his best to achieve the highest attainable level of utility. He should (and probably will) make small (or "marginal") changes in his behaviour to determine whether they generate an increased level of utility—that is, whether they make him happier. Once Mark's pattern of behaviour arrives at the time allocation that is suggested by point C, Mark will stop making marginal changes in his schedule. He will be as happy as he can be given the available uses of his time, and will eventually settle at the constrained maximum revealed by point C on figure 2.2.

Figure 2.3 demonstrates the effect of marginal changes in Mark's behaviour. Assume that Mark is currently dividing his available time (80 hours per week) in the manner that is represented by point A in figure 2.3. What happens if Mark spends one less minute at the office and one additional minute at the clinic? Mark will lose a certain amount of utility by spending one less minute at the office. However, he will gain an even greater amount of utility by spending that "free minute" at the clinic. In other words, when Mark is at point A in figure 2.3, the utility cost of one minute of office time is less than the utility benefit yielded by one additional minute at the clinic.[38] There is a net increase in utility as a result of a change away from point A and toward point C. In other words, this change makes Mark happier. Mark will accordingly decide to change his schedule and spend more time at the clinic. Mark will continue to reallocate his available time as long as the marginal benefit of his changes is greater than the marginal cost. As soon as the marginal benefit of a change is exactly offset by its marginal cost—that is, the change has no effect on Mark's happiness—Mark will have reached the optimal allocation of time. In economic terms, Mark will have achieved his optimal allocation of resources where "the marginal cost of the last change made equals … the marginal benefit."[39] This occurs at point C in figure 2.3.

Once Mark has arrived at point C, the marginal cost of any change in either direction will be greater than the marginal benefit of any such change. In other words, a change away from point C will result in a net loss of utility: Mark will be less happy after making the relevant change and will accordingly reverse such changes or refrain from making them in the first place. As a result, Mark will tend to settle at point C: as a utility maximizer, Mark will not make changes to his schedule that result in a net loss of utility.

---

38   Note that Mark's decision to spend one additional minute at the clinic can be depicted through the ethical equation developed earlier in this chapter (A − B = X). A would equal the benefit achieved by spending one additional minute at the clinic, B would be the cost of spending one additional minute at the clinic, and X would be the net gain in utility (a positive figure in this example, indicating that Mark should make the change).

39   Cooter and Ulen, supra note 3, at 26.

Figure 2.3

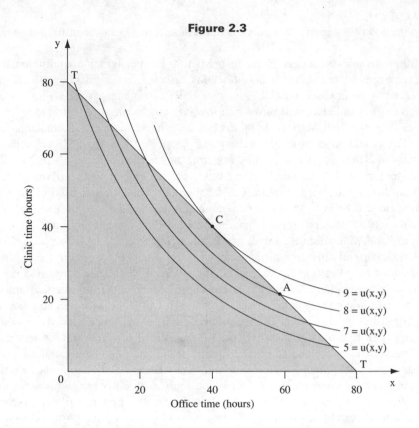

Indifference curves can be used wherever an individual must select between resources for the purpose of maximizing his or her utility. This applies with equal force to the "selection of resources" that is inherent in ethical choices. Revisit example 1.2 from chapter 1, in which Norman was forced to choose between adherence to the terms of the Barristers Oath and various acts of civil disobedience. As we saw in that example, Norman gained utility from breaches of the oath (in the sense that certain breaches of the oath brought him pleasure). He also lost a certain amount of utility from breaches of the oath. Norman (like most rational people) derives at least some utility from money, and every breach of the oath resulted in a loss of $5,000. Norman's ethical decision—that is, his decision whether to breach the terms of the oath—can be represented visually through the use of indifference curves.

Figure 2.4 depicts Norman's ethical choices. The y axis in figure 2.4 represents the fixed-dollar cost (payable as penalties to the Law Society) of any violation of the Barristers Oath. The x axis represents other "bankable income": money that Norman would like to have available for use in obtaining goods or services. The three indifference curves shown in figure 2.4 each connect various combinations of x (money spent on personal consumption) and y (money spent to "purchase" breaches of the Barristers Oath) that yield various utility values for Norman.

Figure 2.4

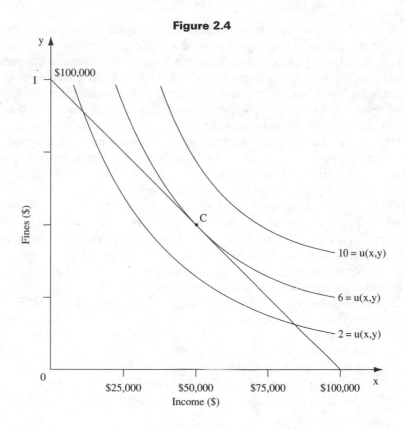

As a utility maximizer, Norman would prefer to purchase (through the payment of fines) an indefinite number of breaches of the Barrister's Oath while still preserving an infinite sum of cash for personal consumption. Norman's ability to acquire these assets, however, is constrained by his disposable income of $100,000 per year (represented by line I in figure 2.4). As a result, Norman can afford only those combinations of fines and expenses that fall below or along line I—that is, combinations that cost $100,000 or less. As we saw in the example regarding Mark's time allocation, Norman will tend to allocate his resource (in this case, income) between fines and other expenses in a way that drives him toward point C (his "constrained maximum"). Any other attainable combination of x and y will generate less utility. As a utility maximizer, Norman will attempt to attain the optimal level of utility he can achieve given constraints placed on his income.

One thing that is revealed by figure 2.4 is that an individual with a greater level of income (who shares Norman's preferences) can afford to breach the Barristers Oath more often—if such a person earned twice as much as Norman, for example, that person could breach the Barrister's Oath twice as often as Norman while still banking twice the money that Norman banks. This is, perhaps, one reason why fixed-dollar fines are not a particularly good way of regulating unethical conduct. It seems counterintuitive to allow the rich to violate ethical norms more frequently than those who have less money. This topic will be explored in greater detail in chapter 4. More importantly, figure 2.4 reveals that we can use the tools of economics to describe, understand, predict, and evaluate a decision maker's actions. As we saw in figure 2.4, Norman's decision of whether or not to violate the Barristers Oath was determined (in part) by the consequences that flowed from violations. Specifically, we saw that the $5,000 fine associated with violations placed limits on the number of times that Norman would break the oath. This rather simple example reveals the interaction of ethics and economics: when a particular form of behaviour carries adverse consequences for a decision maker, those consequences can be regarded as costs that must be considered when a decision maker determines whether or not to engage in the relevant form of conduct. These costs create implicit "prices" for particular activities, and decision makers respond to these prices in the same way that they respond to prices in a market for goods. All things being equal, utility maximizers are less likely to buy something when the price of the relevant article is increased. When we observe the manner in which decision makers respond to particular prices set for ethical violations, we can determine the optimal prices and incentives required to ensure that individuals act in desirable ways. In other words, an economic analysis helps us determine the optimal way to regulate unethical actions. The specific ways in which this can be accomplished are discussed at length in chapters 3 and 4.

Armed with an understanding of scarcity, utility, and the process of maximization, we are now able to deploy these tools in our analysis of the ethical (or unethical) decisions that lawyers make. *Law Society of Upper Canada v. Jaffey* and *Law Society of British Columbia v. Nader*, below, are two cases involving lawyers who were disciplined for unethical behaviour. When reading these two cases, attempt to describe and evaluate the behaviour of each lawyer in terms of scarcity, utility, and utility maximization.

Law Society of Upper Canada v. Jaffey
[1995] LSDD no. 175

Introduction

[The decision of the disciplinary panel in *Jaffey* concerns a solicitor who, among other things, misappropriated nearly $800,000 of his clients' funds. To make matters worse, one of the victims of Jaffey's unethical behaviour was Jaffey's own mother. When reviewing the decision of the disciplinary panel, attempt to describe both Jaffey's behaviour and the decision of the panel in economic terms. Can Jaffey's conduct be expressed through the economic equations we have developed in this chapter? Can his behaviour be explained in terms of utility maximization? Was the disciplinary panel attempting to maximize utility when it held that Jaffey ought to be disbarred? If so, whose utility was the panel attempting to maximize? Did the panel act in its own self-interest? These and other questions will be considered in the notes and questions that follow the decision.]

On December 7, 1994 complaint D315/94 was issued against John Mowat Jaffey alleging that he was guilty of professional misconduct. ...

The facts briefly, in this matter, are that the solicitor John Mowat Jaffey was called to the Bar in 1975. In 1994, he was involved in a series of misappropriations totalling in excess of $785,000. There is evidence that prior to that time he obtained a passport in a false name and on the long weekend of July 1st, 1994, after closing a real estate transaction but not arriving in time at the Registry Office on the Friday, left Canada and flew to Australia.

As well as numerous other victims, he misappropriated over $165,000 from his mother. The solicitor was apprehended by police in Australia and was eventually extradited or brought back to Canada and has been in custody since that time. In February of this year, he pled guilty to charges relating to his misappropriation and received a penitentiary sentence of five years.

The solicitor was previously disciplined by the Society in 1993 and received a reprimand at that time.

It is quite clear in cases of misappropriation that the usual penalty will be disbarment. This is an extremely serious and unsavoury misappropriation, certainly the additional facts of the solicitor's elderly mother being a victim is one that puts this in a particularly distasteful category. The amounts misappropriated have not been re-paid. Clearly, the only appropriate penalty that sufficiently reflects the gravity of this breach of trust is disbarment.

I should add gratuitously that although this is a clear case for disbarment, it never is a happy day when a career ends in this way no matter how unsavoury the actions or the person. This is obviously a tragedy for both the solicitor and his family and his clients. …

Order of Convocation

CONVOCATION of the Law Society of Upper Canada, having read the Report and Decision of the Discipline Committee dated 8th day of June, 1995, in the presence of Counsel for the Society, the Solicitor nor Counsel being in attendance, wherein the Solicitor was found guilty of professional misconduct and having heard counsel aforesaid;

CONVOCATION HEREBY ORDERS that John Mowat Jaffey be disbarred as a Barrister and that his name be struck off the Roll of Solicitors and that his membership in the said Society be cancelled.

NOTES AND QUESTIONS

1. Assume that Jaffey knew, in advance, that he would be disbarred as a result of his behaviour. Further assume that he knew that he would be incarcerated for five years as a result of his unethical actions. Prepare a schedule of the costs and benefits that Jaffey would have weighed had he consciously undertaken the "ethical calculation" developed in this chapter.

2. Can Jaffey's behaviour be explained in terms of utility maximization? Would it be easier to explain Jaffey's behaviour if we were to assume that he believed that there was

only a 20 percent chance that he would be caught and disciplined? The effect of "uncertain punishment" on ethical calculations is explored in chapter 3.

3. How did scarcity give rise to Jaffey's unethical decision? Would Jaffey have acted as he did in a world that was *not* plagued by scarcity?

4. Can the decision of Convocation be explained in terms of utility maximization? How can Convocation hope to maximize its own utility by stripping an individual of the right to practise law?

5. Is it likely that Convocation was *indifferent* as between (1) Jaffey refraining from misappropriating his client's trust money, and (2) Jaffey misappropriating the funds and accepting the penalty of disbarment plus five years in prison? Can we regard disbarment as the "price" that the disciplinary panel has set for behaviour akin to Jaffey's conduct?

6. Note that the members of Convocation claimed that "in cases of misappropriation ... the usual penalty will be disbarment." If the penalty is a "price" for engaging in certain kinds of conduct, with the goal of generating sensible outcomes, shouldn't the penalty depend on the *amount* of money misappropriated? Should a misappropriation of $20 be treated the same as a misappropriation of $800,000? Does an economic analysis require the severity of the penalty to vary with the severity of the ethical breach? This issue is considered in chapter 4.

7. When disbarring Jaffey, Convocation noted that "it never is a happy day when a career ends in this way." Does this mean that the panel members incur a loss of utility when disbarring a fellow lawyer? If so, what benefits offset this utility loss? Attempt to express the Convocation's decision through the algebraic expression of ethical choices $(A - B = X)$.

Law Society of British Columbia v. Nader
[2001] LSDD no. 40

[*Law Society of British Columbia v. Nader* (2001) is another decision involving a lawyer being disciplined for unethical behaviour. In this case, however, the lawyer was not disbarred: he was suspended from practice for a period of 18 months. When reviewing this decision, consider whether or not this "price" fits the behaviour in which Mr. Nader engaged. What is this price designed to do? Additional notes and questions are raised following the decision.]

Mr. Nader represented, on a pro bono basis, a number of people at the APEC Commission of Inquiry. The Commission was appointed in 1998 to inquire into the police response to demonstrations of protesters at the 1997 Asia Pacific Economic Cooperation (APEC) conference at the University of BC campus in Vancouver.

In February, 1999 the Government of Canada agreed to provide funding for a legal team of three lawyers (Mr. Nader and lawyers A and W) to represent certain persons at the hearing. Payment was to be in accordance with a specific pay scale and was to apply for work done and expenses incurred from December 21, 1998 forward.

On April 8, 1999 Mr. Nader rendered a statement of account for payment from the Government of Canada. The account was purportedly for work done and expenses incurred between December 21, 1998 and March 31, 1999. Mr. Nader asked that he be remunerated at the highest level for his category on the basis that he had worked many pro bono hours for those clients for more than a year and a half.

A lawyer who reviewed these accounts for the Government of Canada wrote to Mr. Nader to request an affidavit attesting to the time he had spent on the files and to request access to his time dockets.

After receiving this letter, Mr. Nader raised the matter with lawyer W on the legal team. Mr. Nader said that he had in fact worked part time at a post-secondary institution since 1998, and full time during January and February, 2001 (which was part of the period he claimed to have worked on the APEC files). He admitted that, during that period, he had not actually worked 10 hours a day, six days a week on the APEC inquiry files as indicated on his statement of account.

Soon thereafter, on April 28, Mr. Nader told lawyer A and lawyer W that, by inflating his account, he had sought to be paid for the many hours of work he had done prior to December 21, 1998. The other lawyers advised Mr. Nader that this was no excuse for submitting a false account and that he should resign from the APEC legal team, report his conduct to the Law Society and obtain legal advice.

Mr. Nader sent a letter to his clients in the APEC inquiry indicating that he was resigning as counsel for personal and family reasons. Lawyer A subsequently sent a letter to the clients informing them that Mr. Nader's withdrawal resulted from a demand from the other lawyers on the legal team. At a subsequent meeting with the clients, Mr. Nader disclosed that he had submitted a false statement of account and had been asked to resign.

Mr. Nader wrote to the lawyer representing the Government of Canada to inform him that he would not provide an affidavit verifying his account as he could not swear to its accuracy. He withdrew his account for legal fees and tendered only documentation relating to disbursements. He also advised this lawyer of his resignation from the APEC legal team.

Lawyer A took issue with the accuracy of Mr. Nader's letter. He advised Mr. Nader of this and also demanded that Mr. Nader report himself to the Law Society by May 3, 1999, failing which lawyer A would make the report. Lawyer W endorsed lawyer A's position and urged Mr. Nader to seek legal advice. Both Mr. Nader and lawyer A reported the matter to the Law Society on May 4.

In November, 1999 Mr. Nader admitted to professional misconduct in rendering a statement of account claiming $73,397.50 in legal fees. In the account he falsely stated the hours worked. Although Mr. Nader did not keep time records, he wrongfully billed between $33,000 and $40,000. He was entitled to bill for the balance of the account (at least $33,000 based 385 hours at $85 an hour), but he chose not to resubmit his account for this amount, as an act of contrition.

Decision

By rendering a statement of account that falsely stated the hours worked and the amount he was entitled to bill, Mr. Nader's conduct constituted professional misconduct. ...

We are now concerned with the penalty which follows such misbehaviour.

Given that the primary focus of the *Legal Profession Act* is the protection of the public interest, it follows that the sentencing process must ensure that the public is protected from acts of professional misconduct. Section 38 of the Act sets forth the range of penalties, from reprimand to disbarment, from which a panel must choose following a finding of misconduct. In determining an appropriate penalty, the panel must consider what steps might be necessary to ensure that the public is protected, while taking into account the risk of allowing the respondent to continue in practise.

Criteria to be considered when assessing punishment [are] found in *In the Matter of the Legal Profession Act and Charles Ogilvie*. While not exhaustive, they have been used by many other panels in their consideration of the correct penalty to be meted out. Both counsel have referred to these criteria in their submissions and the panel finds it helpful to do so also. They are as follows:

(a) the nature and gravity of the conduct proven;

(b) the age and experience of the respondent;

(c) the previous character of the respondent, including details of prior discipline;

(d) the impact upon the victim;

(e) the advantage gained or to be gained by the respondent;

(f) the number of times the offending conduct occurred;

(g) whether the respondent has acknowledged the misconduct and taken steps to disclose and redress the wrong and the presence or absence of other mitigating circumstances;

(h) the possibility of remediating or rehabilitating the respondent;

(i) the impact on the respondent of criminal or other sanctions or penalties;

(j) the impact of the proposed penalty on the respondent;

(k) the need for specific and general deterrence;

(l) the need to ensure the public's confidence in the integrity of the profession; and

(m) the range of penalties imposed in similar cases.

(a) The Nature and Gravity of the Conduct Proven

The member was a newly called practitioner. Like all young lawyers who are starting to practise, he did work for free, because he had the time and in the hopes that it would turn into a fee-paying matter. He did this for several months. Eventually, the Government decided that it would fund his clients' legal expenses commencing December 1, 1998. In an attempt to compensate himself for the pro bono work done prior to that date, the member inflated the amount of time he had spent since that date. This is fraud and had the member been successful, it would be a disbarable offence. The only mitigating factor is that, while he did not have a right to be compensated therefore, the member actually did perform the work.

(b) The Age and Experience of the Respondent

The Respondent was, at the time the offence was committed, 35 years old. However, he had only been called to the Bar since May 23, 1997. He stayed on with the firm with which he had articled until it dissolved in late 1997, whereafter he practised in Vancouver as a sole practitioner. He was so practising when the offence was committed.

(c) The Previous Character of the Respondent, Including Details of
    Prior Discipline

There is no evidence of his previous character nor is there any previous discipline problem alleged.

(d) The Impact Upon the Victim

The Government of Canada had agreed to pay the member's proper fees. That would make the public the victim. As a result of his misbehaviour the member was forced to resign from the litigation team at the outset of the hearing and as a result it could be said that his clients, too, were impacted by his misbehaviour. Many of his clients (he represented approximately 30 students) held the judicial system in low esteem. The member's behaviour could not have improved their opinion.

(e) The Advantage Gained, or To Be Gained, by the Respondent

Herein lies the main difficulty of this matter. The member's motives for attempting the theft are complicated. The panel is satisfied that greed was one of these motives. This is confirmed by the amount of money which the member sought to wrongfully receive and by the letter dated April 8, 1999, which accompanied the member's bill, and in which he asked for the highest rate of payment in his category. Were this the only motive, the matter would be simple and the penalty warranted would be the longest period of suspension, if not disbarment. However, the member has been diagnosed as having a medical condition which will in time accelerate his death. He does not at present show any evidence of the disease. His evidence was that, having seen the affect of the disease on his father and being aware that his working life would be shortened, he had to consider ways in which he could make sufficient moneys in a shortened period of time, in order to support himself when he could no longer work. The medical material filed indicates that this is not an unusual consideration which concerns those having this condition. He went on to explain that he had taken on the students on a pro bono basis because he felt that their case was a high-profile matter and would serve to fast-track his career. This he needed because of his medical condition. However, he was finding the stress of the case heavier than he could bear. He was new to the practice of law; the law applicable to obtaining documentation for the hearing was not clear; he had to deal with many clients who did not all have the same instructions and with senior members of the legal team who were dismissive of him. The stress produced by these factors was exacerbated by the fact that he had been advised by his physician not to publicize his medical condition. As a result, he was forced to deal alone with his bouts of depression and anxiety and was unable to explain them to others. The counselling which had been available to him had been withdrawn as a result of governmental cutbacks. He saw one way of relieving his stress as being removed from the APEC matter. However, he felt himself unable to simply resign. He considered, when putting forward his fraudulent bill, that it was a dangerous thing to do but at worse, if he was caught, he would be taken off the case and so relieved from the stress producing situation. He stated that he had in the back of his mind the hope that he would be caught and this would bring his stress to an end. With only two exceptions the bill rendered claimed the maximum amount of hours chargeable in a day (10 hours). The member claimed this amount for 87 days out of a possible 102 days. His bill indicates that on one occasion, he worked 10 hours per day for 21 days straight. The member was aware that Mr. Camp had been appointed specifically to scrutinize the accounts of the legal team. The bill itself invites incredulity. This lends credence to the member's claim that in the back of his mind was the hope that he would be caught. It is inconceivable that such an account would not have been questioned.

Independent evidence supports his contention that he was highly stressed. The medical evidence indicates that people with his problem can suffer from impaired judgment. In addition, to this source of stress, his marriage was deteriorating. He and his wife have since separated.

(f) The Number of Times the Offending Conduct Occurred

The member created only one bill. This took him a day and a half to prepare.

(g) Whether the Respondent Has Acknowledged the Misconduct and Taken Steps To Disclose and Redress the Wrong and the Presence or Absence of Other Mitigating Circumstances

When his account was questioned, the member realized that he could not, as requested, swear an Affidavit to its veracity. Upon discussing the matter with senior counsel who were members of the legal team and being advised to resign and self report to the Law Society, he did so. He did attempt to mislead Mr. Camp about the reason for his inability to swear an Affidavit, and his clients, as to the reason he was retiring as counsel, but when pressed to correct the latter error, did so. He accurately self reported that he had "improperly inflated a statement of account for services." He further acknowledged his misconduct by withdrawing his account. In his appearance before this Panel he admitted his misbehaviour by way of an Agreed Statement of Facts. Although he was entitled to bill the Government for between $33,000.00 and $40,000.00 worth of work actually performed, he did not do so out of a sense of contrition and has undertaken not to do so.

(h) The Possibility of Remediating or Rehabilitating the Respondent

The facts indicate an acknowledgment of his misconduct and a redress of the wrong. The practice of law is inherently stressful. The member will always have his medical condition and be unable to explain his resulting problems to others. However, counselling is now available and he has undertaken to continue with it. Moreover, while the member knew that what he was doing was morally wrong and that he would be in trouble with both his clients and the Law Society were he to be found out, the Panel is of the opinion that had he been able to discuss his problems with senior counsel, he would have realized the seriousness of the act he was about to perform and not have done so.

His actions in immediately resigning from the legal team and self-reporting to the Law Society after discussion with the senior members of the legal team [are] indicative of this.

(i) The Impact on the Respondent of Criminal or Other Sanctions or Penalties

There have been no other sanctions or penalties.

(k) The Need for Specific and General Deterrence

In this case the member knew he had no right to the fees claimed. It was a particularly odious act, given that the payor was not the member's client, but had agreed, without legal obligation, to pay his account. Today the Government of this Province pays out millions of dollars annually in legal fees, to lawyers representing parties adverse in interest. The benefit is that by so doing, people without moneys, in need of representation, can receive it and thereby justice is done. It is necessary that the profession generally realize that they have the same obligations towards the government as they do towards their own client, i.e., to render fair and honest accounts.

(l) The Need To Ensure the Public's Confidence in the Integrity of the Profession

The member presented letters from various of his clients from the Inquiry and from persons concerned to ensure that the complainants in the Inquiry received justice. These letters were all laudatory of the member's behaviour and work ethic. They maintained that they would continue to trust the member. However, one cannot help but wonder whether this would be so had they been the payor of the member's legal fees. One went so far as to state that if the member were unable to practise, people requiring pro bono representation in similar types of matters would be deprived of representation, there being a dearth of counsel having both the willingness and the qualities required to do this type of work. However, it is a fact of life that once counsel start to build up a paying clientele, his or her availability to do pro bono work diminishes accordingly.

The Benchers' primary mandates are the welfare of the public and of lawyers.

Of the two, the responsibility to the public is by far the major one. Here, the member's many clients were made aware of the member's misbehaviour and the reason therefor. Some already lacked a respect for lawyers and the judicial system. The member's actions would only serve to exacerbate this.

(m) The Range of Penalties Imposed in Similar Cases

The Panel has been quoted several cases ranging from outright theft from clients to overbilling the Legal Services Society. The penalties imposed have run from disbarment for the former to suspension for two months for the latter. The latter cases contained elements of incompetence and negligence. These factors do not exist in the matter before us and so the Panel regards the penalty merited as being in the higher range. The member had a degree in philosophy and was aware of the immorality of his act. The Panel is of the opinion that this case falls somewhere in the area of the *Ranspot* case, in which the member was disbarred for 18 months and the *Thomson* case, in which the member was suspended for three years. Of the two, it comes closest to the former, notwithstanding that the amount attempted to be obtained (in excess of $30,000.00) vastly exceeded the amounts in both of the above mentioned cases. Accordingly, the Panel orders that the member be suspended from practice for 18 months as of January 1, 2001. In so ordering, the Panel takes into consideration the following factors:

(a) the inexperience of the member;

(b) the offence was a single occasion;

(c) the member promptly admitted his error;

(d) part of the member's motivation, although misguided, was to remove himself from his major area of stress.

(j) Impact of the Proposed Penalty on the Respondent

This Panel is of the opinion generally that where the motivation of a misbehaviour is financial gain "the punishment should fit the crime" and a fine levied in addition to any other penalty imposed. However, in this case, the forgoing by the member of fees of approximately $33,000.00 to which he was entitled, as an act of contrition, satisfies, in this Panel's opinion, not only that requirement but also the payment of costs which ordinarily follow. As stress is counter-productive to the member's health and was a factor in motivating his misbehaviour, the Panel does not see any value to forcing the member to resume practice with a debt hanging over his head. The member ceased practice in January 2001. The Panel is satisfied that this was brought about in part by his misbehaviour and the discovery thereof and that the period of suspension should take that time into consideration. Also, the Panel is cognizant that given the member's shortened employment future, the period of time he is unable to practise law presents a greater punishment to him that it might to others.

NOTES AND QUESTIONS

1. Although Nader overbilled the government for the services he provided, he *did*, in fact, perform a great deal of work for his clients. Indeed, Convocation noted that Nader was legally (and ethically) entitled to bill the government more than $33,000 for services rendered. After his unethical behaviour was detected, Nader declined to bill the government for the fees to which he was actually entitled, ostensibly out of a sense of contrition. What are the costs and benefits Nader likely considered when he decided *not* to bill the government for services actually rendered? Can the failure to bill the government be seen as an act of utility maximization? How?

2. Construct a list of costs and benefits Nader likely took into account when deciding to overbill the government. Having constructed this list, construct and solve the ethical equation that describes Nader's decision.

3. Can Nader's behaviour be described in terms of utility maximization? Was the disciplinary panel engaged in maximizing behaviour when meting out the relevant penalty?

4. During the course of its decision, the disciplinary panel noted that "[t]he Benchers' primary mandates are the welfare of the public and of lawyers." Is it possible to describe the benchers' actions in terms of self-interest, despite the fact that they are ostensibly acting in the best interest of the public and other lawyers? Note that this topic is discussed in greater detail in chapter 3.

5. The panel seemed particularly concerned with Nader's motives (noting, for example, that Nader was only partly motivated by financial gain). Of what relevance is "motive" when constructing an appropriate penalty for a particular kind of behaviour? If Nader's motive had been entirely stress-related, rather than rooted in greed and financial gain, would this justify the panel setting a different "price" for the behaviour in which Nader was found to have engaged?

6. During the course of its decision, the panel noted that Nader "had a degree in philosophy and was aware of the immorality of his act." Should this be a factor in setting the appropriate penalty? How would Nader's awareness of his action's "immorality" relate to the schedule of costs and benefits he constructed when considering whether to engage in the relevant conduct? Why should the panel consider this factor when designing the "price" for Nader's behaviour?

7. The panel felt that, "given the member's shortened employment future, the period of time he is unable to practise law presents a greater punishment to him than it might to others." Note that this is simply another way of saying that an 18-month penalty deprives Nader of more utility than it would a lawyer without a "shortened employment future." Why would the panel tailor the utility cost of a penalty to the particular preferences and views of a particular lawyer?

8. Are there differences between Nader's unethical conduct and the conduct of John Jaffey (discussed above) that justify the difference in the penalty that each lawyer received? Jaffey misappropriated funds and Nader attempted to receive money that he had never earned. Is Nader morally better than Jaffey because Nader's scheme was exposed? Is Nader in less need of deterrence? Are there economic grounds for the differences in punishment? Are there moral grounds?

9. Note that Nader's victim was the government, rather than a private individual. Does this justify the difference between the penalty Nader received and the penalty that was imposed on Jaffey? Are the decisions of the panels in *Nader* and *Jaffey* consistent? Is there a need for consistency in disciplinary decisions?

V. Conclusion

Chapter 1 introduced the economic theory of legal ethics. Chapter 2 explored basic economic tools and terminology that can be used to assess the ethical decisions that lawyers make. In Chapter 3, we turn our attention to the ethical world of lawyers, using the tools developed in chapters 1 and 2 to describe and evaluate the ways in which lawyers make ethical choices. Throughout chapter 3 and subsequent sections of this book, bear in mind several questions, namely: (1) What use can be made of the predictions generated by an economic analysis? (2) Does an economic analysis provide an accurate portrayal of the decisions lawyers make? (3) Does economic analysis rely on any assumptions that are so unrealistic that the analysis has no value? These questions are addressed in later chapters of this book.

CHAPTER THREE

Lawyers' Ethical Decisions

I. Introduction

Chapters 1 and 2 laid the foundation of an economic account of ethical systems. According to this model, ethical systems can be described in economic terms that explain the motivations and thought processes underlying ethical decisions. Where a decision maker is faced with a choice between ethical and unethical modes of conduct, the decision can be explained and predicted by reference to the economic notions of scarcity and utility maximization. Whether a decision maker chooses to act ethically, unethically, or somewhere in between, that decision can be explained and evaluated through the use of economics.

This chapter focuses economic theory on one particular (and peculiar) ethical system: the system governing lawyers' ethical choices. In pursuit of that objective, the chapter begins with a traditional account of legal ethics, drawing on classical descriptions of the moral (or amoral) universe of lawyers. Subsequent sections of the chapter consider how an economic account of ethical systems can be used to expand upon the traditional accounts of lawyers' ethics, enhancing our ability to understand, evaluate, and predict the ethical choices that lawyers make.

II. Lawyers' Ethics

A. The Moral World of Lawyers

Lawyers inhabit a morally complex universe.[1] Even the most innocuous acts of "lawyering" raise important ethical questions: Can I act for this client in good conscience? Should I help my client pursue an unjust goal? Should I sell my skills to the highest bidder or only to those with righteous aims? Do I have the moral authority to determine whether a client *deserves* my services? Whether a lawyer is in the business of drafting partnership agreements or securing the acquittal of serial killers, questions of this nature inevitably arise in legal practice. Whether meeting with clients, drafting documents, or appearing before the courts, lawyers tread in a realm that is plagued with moral conundrums. Indeed, every act of lawyering carries ethical implications, placing lawyers in positions that test their moral fibre. As Allan Hutchinson notes, "Everything that lawyers do, from the selection of clients

---

1   Some of the text and examples found throughout this chapter are drawn from R. Graham, "Moral Contexts" (2001), 50 *University of New Brunswick Law Journal* 77.

to their involvement in civic affairs, implicates and reflects a lawyer's approach to and understanding of what it means to be an ethical lawyer."[2]

Recent research into the moral world of lawyers has catalogued numerous examples of the daily ethical choices lawyers face.[3] Consider the following typical examples, drawn from recent interviews with lawyers engaged in private practice.

Example 3.1

Lawyer A had recently acquired a junior position at a successful Ontario law firm when the firm's major client asked the lawyer to convey false information to another individual. The client made it clear that, if Lawyer A refused to carry out the client's instructions, the client would end its relationship with the lawyer's firm. Lawyer A knew that failure to satisfy this client would imperil the lawyer's future with the firm.[4]

Example 3.2

Lawyer B represented a client in a litigation matter. Early in the proceedings, it became apparent that opposing counsel (OC) was pressing a frivolous (and unwinnable) case, contrary to the Rules of Professional Conduct. OC was running up fees that served no purpose other than to line OC's own pocket, seriously undermining the interests of OC's own clients. Lawyer B had to determine whether to report OC's actions to a regulatory body.[5]

Example 3.3

Lawyer C was in-house counsel for a manufacturing company that was about to begin selling an unsafe product. While Lawyer C believed that, from an ethical perspective, it was appropriate to dissuade the client from releasing the unsafe product, the lawyer believed that doing so would adversely affect lawyer C's continued employment with the company. Lawyer C accordingly faced a choice between securing continued employment or safeguarding the health and well-being of the client's customers.[6]

As these examples demonstrate, lawyers are frequently faced with puzzling ethical choices. The legal profession is heavily laden with moral quandaries of this nature, constantly testing the lawyer's ability to resolve the ethical issues that surround and penetrate the legal system.

---

2   Allan C. Hutchinson, *Legal Ethics and Professional Responsibility* (Toronto: Irwin Law, 1999), 198.

3   See, for example, Margaret Ann Wilkinson, Christina Walker, and Peter Mercer, "Do Codes of Ethics Actually Shape Legal Practice?" (2000), 45 *McGill Law Journal* 645.

4   Ibid., at 672-73.

5   Ibid., at 659.

6   Ibid., at 669-70.

Surprisingly, lawyers often fail to recognize the moral implications of their profession. Lawyers go about the business of drafting pleadings, merging companies, interviewing witnesses, and arguing cases without reflecting on the ethical implications of their actions. Indeed, many lawyers seem oblivious to moral and ethical issues that are obvious to most outside observers. This lack of moral acuity was highlighted in the infamous case of *R v. Murray* (2000),[7] involving a lawyer (Kenneth Murray) who actively concealed videotape evidence showing his client (Paul Bernardo) taking part in vicious sexual attacks against young women. According to the court in *Murray*, in determining what should be done with the tapes in question Murray "made only a token effort to find out what his obligations were,"[8] and ultimately decided that the issue was "tactical rather than ethical."[9] In other words, Murray believed that his suppression of "hard evidence" of attacks by a serial rapist raised no ethical concerns. It seems unlikely that non-lawyers would have shared Murray's belief.

Murray's perception of lawyers' ethical obligations should come as no surprise. Many lawyers take the view that, despite the seemingly obvious moral challenges facing legal professionals, lawyers operate in a world that is ethically sterile, wholly insulated from moral considerations. This view is common among lawyers, arising in part from the traditional conception of the lawyer's professional role. This traditional conception, together with its role in shaping the ethical attitudes and thought processes of lawyers, is described in the following sections of the chapter.

B. The Traditional Conception of Legal Ethics

The traditional conception of legal ethics portrays the lawyer as a morally neutral agent of the client. According to this model, it is not the lawyer's place to question a client's moral values or to assess the ethical worth of a client's goals. On the contrary, the lawyer turns a blind eye to the moral value of his or her client's projects, using the lawyer's professional skills in whatever legally authorized manner might advance the client's aims. According to Gerald Postema:

> The good lawyer is one who is capable of drawing a tight circle around himself and his client, allowing no other considerations to interfere with his zealous and scrupulously loyal pursuit of the client's objectives. The good lawyer leaves behind his own family, religious, political, and moral concerns, and devotes himself entirely to the client.[10]

---

7   *R v. Murray* (2000), 48 OR (3d) 544 (Sup. Ct. J). The decision in this case is dealt with in greater detail below.

8   Ibid., at 575.

9   Ibid., at 552. Note that at the time Mr. Murray allegedly felt that his actions had no ethical implications, he had not yet viewed the videotapes in question. He had, however, secretly removed the videotapes from the scene of the crime and hidden them from the police at his client's behest. These actions raise important (and, one would think, obvious) ethical concerns that, according to the court in *Murray*, appeared to elude Mr. Murray.

10   Gerald J. Postema, "Moral Responsibility in Professional Ethics" (1980), 55 *New York University Law Review* 63, at 78.

Under this traditional view, the lawyer disregards morality when pursuing a client's interests. Indeed, the legal system forces the lawyer to abandon moral concerns, replacing the lawyer's ethical values with a single-minded devotion to the interests of the lawyer's clientele.

The lawyer's role in furthering client interests is said to justify some rather nasty behaviour. Within the moral bounds of their profession, lawyers act in ways that could be regarded as despicable in any other context. Lawyers mercilessly attack the credibility of witnesses whom they know to be telling the truth. Lawyers assert technical defences (such as limitation periods) in order to help their clients avoid repaying lawful debts. Lawyers engage in "stall tactics," stretching out judicial proceedings in the hope that impoverished parties will abandon valid claims or that elderly parties will die before a matter goes to trial. Lawyers foreclose on orphanages, help polluters, challenge democratic elections, humiliate victims of crime, and defend monsters. Based on any "non-legal" standard of morality, lawyers do a lot of dreadful things. Despite the morally charged nature of these activities, however, many lawyers believe that their actions are insulated from moral censure as a result of the context in which these acts occur. The context of "the legal system," it is argued, immunizes the lawyer from rebuke so long as he or she acts within the lawyer's institutional role.[11] The nature of that institutional role, together with its capacity to insulate the lawyer from moral concerns, is discussed in the following section of this chapter.

C. The Lawyer's Institutional Role

Whenever a lawyer seeks the acquittal of a racist hate-monger, incorporates a company that will wipe out acres of rainforest, or takes any other action that (while arguably legal) seems morally problematic, the lawyer typically seeks refuge in the safety of the lawyer's institutional role. For one reason or another, the lawyer believes that the institution of the legal system bears moral responsibility for the lawyer's ethically questionable behaviour. Perhaps the lawyer believes that the legal system justifies his or her actions by casting responsibility for those acts upon the client. The lawyer is merely acting as the client's agent, making the client aware of legal options, but making few decisions regarding the manner in which the client will proceed. According to this view of the lawyer's role, the lawyer is a morally neutral functionary with no accountability for acts committed in a client's name. It is the client who makes the lawyer draft an agreement to close a factory, destroying a rural community's only industry. It is the client who uses the lawyer to undermine accurate DNA evidence placing the lawyer's guilty client at the scene of a violent crime. The lawyer is not responsible for these actions. On the contrary, the lawyer is merely a morally neutral tool who plays an essentially passive role in carrying out the client's will.

The "neutral-agent" model of the lawyer's professional role, while a common source of comfort among lawyers, seems inherently unpersuasive. After all, even if the lawyer is not directly responsible for the client's morally questionable activities, the lawyer is *helping* the

---

11   See William H. Simon, "Ethical Discretion in Lawyering" (1988), vol. 101, no. 6 *Harvard Law Review* 1083 for an excellent account of the conventional view of "legal amorality."

client commit a morally discreditable act. The decision to help another person undertake an immoral action is hard to justify as a morally neutral choice. Happily, the legal system provides a convenient way around this problem. Rather than simply blaming the client for morally questionable activities, the lawyer can cast the blame directly upon the legal system. This argument, which is referred to as the "neutral-conduit" argument (for reasons that will be seen below), is based on a deeper understanding of the purpose of the lawyer's agency function.

According to the neutral-conduit argument, the lawyer's institutional role is designed to remedy the complexity of the law. Because lawyers are required to respect the limits of the law, any activities that the lawyer undertakes on the client's behalf must be legal. As legal actions, these activities could (in theory) have been carried out directly by the client. Due to the law's complexity, however, the client is unable to proceed without assistance. Though a particular course of action may be legally available to the client, recognizing the availability of that action, or knowing the steps required to undertake a particular act, may require the lawyer's special expertise. The law is confusing and complex. The complexity of the law ensures that no one but a legally trained professional can successfully navigate the legal system. According to Charles Fried:

> [T]he web of perhaps entirely just institutions ... has become so complex that without the assistance of an expert adviser an ordinary layman cannot exercise that autonomy which the system must allow him. Without such an adviser, the law would impose constraints on the lay citizens (unequally at that) which it is not entitled to impose explicitly.[12]

By helping the client cross the barrier of complexity that surrounds the legal system, the lawyer acts as a morally neutral conduit through which an untrained client can gain access to the law. The lawyer is a necessary and neutral component of the legal system, existing only to eradicate the barrier that is presented by the complexity of the law. If the law were not confusing and complex, there would be no need for lawyers at all. As the lawyer is simply an antidote for the complexity of the system, the lawyer has no business evaluating the client's morals. Provided that the client's goals (and the methods used to achieve them) are not prohibited by the law, the lawyer must guide the client through the morass of the legal system, allowing the client to take advantage of whatever benefits the law provides.

The neutral-conduit argument is intuitively appealing. According to this model, the lawyer is merely a remedy for a dysfunctional feature of the legal system. The problem of complexity creates an unintentional barrier that impedes the public's access to the law. The lawyer's only role is to eradicate that barrier. When discharging that function, the lawyer must be careful not to impose additional hurdles that impede the client's access to the law.[13] Most importantly, the lawyer must not impair the client's access to the legal system by inquiring into the client's character or the moral value of the client's objectives.

---

12   Charles Fried, "The Lawyer as Friend: The Moral Foundations of the Lawyer–Client Relation" (1976), 85 *Yale Law Journal* 1060, at 1073.

13   See S.L. Pepper, "Lawyers' Amoral Ethical Role: A Defense, a Problem and Some Possibilities" (1986), *American Bar Foundation Research Journal* 613.

As long as the client's goals are authorized by law (or, at least, not expressly prohibited), the lawyer lacks the moral authority to police the ethical worth of the client's goals. The lawyer must merely apprise the client of the boundaries of the law and assist the client in taking whatever legal steps the client chooses. If lawyers sat in moral judgment over potential clients, they could refuse to act for those who held unpopular ideas. Rather than being ruled by law, society would be governed by the moral whims of lawyers. Rather than eradicating the barrier of complexity, a lawyer who judged the moral value of a client's aims could erect a barrier of morality, forcing the client to adhere to the lawyer's personal code of ethics.

Whether the lawyer is depicted as a morally neutral tool or as a remedy for the complexity of the law, the lawyer is thought to bear no moral responsibility for actions taken in pursuit of a client's interests. Whatever ostensibly unethical actions the lawyer commits, the legal system bears the moral responsibility. All potentially troubling moral issues are eliminated by reference to the institutional role the lawyer serves, leaving the lawyer free to proceed in a neutral manner. As Postema explains:

> [O]nce he has accepted the client's case, the lawyer must represent the client, or pursue the client's objectives, regardless of the lawyer's opinion of the client's character and reputation, and the moral merits of the client's objectives. On this conception, the lawyer need not consider, nor may he be held responsible for, the consequences of his professional activities as long as he stays within the law and acts in pursuit of the client's legitimate aims. Thus, the proper range of the lawyer's concern—the boundaries of the lawyer's "moral universe"—is defined by two parameters: the law and the client's interests and objectives. These factors are the exclusive points of reference for professional deliberation and practical judgment.[14]

The "moral universe" of the lawyer is extremely circumscribed. As long as the lawyer's actions are for the benefit of a client and not explicitly prohibited by the law, the lawyer enjoys a total lack of accountability. Indeed, the lawyer must strive to remain oblivious to all moral considerations. In pursuit of the client's objectives, the lawyer must not be deterred by issues of morality, but must forge ahead despite the harm that pursuit of the client's objectives might inflict upon another. In the words of Lord Brougham:

> An advocate, by the sacred duty which he owes his client, knows in the discharge of that office but one person in the world, the client and none other. To save that client by all expedient means, to protect that client at all hazards and costs, to all others, and among others to himself, is the highest and most unquestioned of his duties; and he must not regard the alarm, the suffering, the torment, the destruction which he may bring upon any other ... he must go on reckless of the consequences.[15]

While working within the context of "the legal system," it is argued, lawyers tread upon a special moral plane. In this region of institutional amorality, standard notions of

---

14   Postema, supra note 10, at 73-74.

15   See W. Forsyth, *The History of Lawyers: Ancient and Modern* (Union, NJ: The Lawbook Exchange, 1996), 380, cited in Allan C. Hutchinson, supra note 2, at 91.

ethics, good behaviour, and propriety have no place. The lawyer disengages his or her moral sensors, pursuing the client's goals with no regard for the suffering that the lawyer's actions might inflict on another. By taking shelter within this ethically sterile role, the lawyer "places the responsibility for all of his acts at the door of the institutional author of the role."[16] The lawyer's own behaviour is systemically amoral, beyond the reach of standard ethical concerns.

The traditional conception of the lawyer's role is attractive for many lawyers.[17] Because all moral and ethical issues are resolved at the institutional level, the lawyer has no need to pay attention to moral issues. The ideal lawyer, it is argued, is one who can remain oblivious to moral or ethical issues that might undermine the lawyer's commitment to a client's objectives. As a result, the lawyer feels no pangs of conscience and endures no moral qualms when acting in pursuit of the interests of a client. As Richard Wasserstrom notes, "the moral world of the lawyer is a simpler, less complicated, and less ambiguous world than the moral world of ordinary life."[18] While ordinary people might be troubled by the ethical implications of their actions, the lawyer is immune to such concerns. Safe in the lawyer's institutional role, the lawyer dons ethical blinders, aware of only two behavioural guidelines—namely, the interests of the client and the limits of the law. However immoral or unethical an action might appear, however terrible the suffering it might cause, the context of the legal system takes the place of the lawyer's conscience. Provided that the lawyer's actions are permitted by the law and serve to further the client's interests, the legal system commands the lawyer to proceed without regard for moral concerns.

The foregoing description of the moral world of lawyers has been reiterated on many occasions.[19] It has also gained some measure of judicial acceptance. When reading the cases that follow, consider the courts' conception of the lawyer's institutional role, as well as the nature of the moral choices that lawyers face when they act in their professional capacity. In each case, consider whether the lawyer is (1) making moral choices or (2) inhabiting an "ethically sterile wasteland" and functioning as a morally neutral tool. Also consider whether the "moral world of lawyers" is, in fact, more straightforward and less ambiguous than the moral world of "ordinary" life.

---

16   Postema, supra note 10, at 74.

17   Note that lawyers are said to be insulated from moral concerns only when acting in their professional capacity. When living life outside the professional sphere, lawyers are (of course) subject to the same moral concerns as everyone else. Because lawyers are thought to abide by one set of morals when occupying a professional role, and a different set of morals when operating outside of that professional role, they are sometimes said to be governed by "role-differentiated morality."

18   R. Wasserstrom, "Lawyers as Professionals: Some Moral Issues," in G.C. Hazard Jr. and D.L. Rhode, eds., *The Legal Profession: Responsibility and Regulation*, 2d ed. (Westbury, NY: Foundation Press, 1988), 162, at 166.

19   See, for example, Wasserstrom, ibid.; S.L. Pepper, supra note 13; and Fried, supra note 12.

Tuckiar v. The King
(1934), 52 CLR 335 (HC Australia)

[The decision of the court in *Tuckiar v. The King* raises several technical issues, including (1) the admissibility of "good character" evidence of a victim, (2) the proper limits of a judge's instructions to the jury, and (3) the racism faced by aboriginal persons in 1930s Australia. For present purposes, however, the most important elements of the decision involve (1) the lawyer's duty of confidentiality, and (2) the role of a lawyer defending a client whom the lawyer knows to be guilty. These issues will be revisited in greater detail in part II, of this book. For now, we shall focus on the nature of the moral choices faced by Tuckiar's lawyer, and consider the extent to which that lawyer was truly insulated from ethical issues.]

THE COURT: This is an appeal by leave from a conviction of murder before the Supreme Court of the Northern Territory, and from the Court's sentence, which was death ... . The prisoner is a completely uncivilised aboriginal native belonging to a tribe frequenting Woodah Island, which lies near Groote Eylandt. On 1st August 1933, a police constable named McColl was killed there by the spear of a native, and the prisoner was brought to Darwin and charged with his murder ... . To prove that it was he who killed McColl, the Crown relied upon two pieces of confessional evidence given by two natives who had been brought with [the prisoner] to Darwin. The first was an aboriginal, called Parriner, whose evidence was interpreted into pidgin English by Paddy [a translator]. The effect of this evidence was that on Bickerton Island, which is a little to the south of Woodah Island, the prisoner told him that the policemen had come up to his camp and taken four lubras [aboriginal women], three of whom were his, that he had been waiting in the jungle for some time for one of his lubras, that he had called and then come out of the jungle, had seen them at the camp, and had run back into the jungle, where he planted himself and sat quiet, that while hiding there, he saw a policeman go past, that he remained still and listened and heard a lubra speak, that he communicated with her by sign language, and told her he was near and would remain, that the policeman came close behind her, whereupon the prisoner signed to her to move aside and then threw his spear, that the policeman clutched the spear with one hand and with the other drawing his pistol fired it three times and then spoke no more ... . The other aboriginal who gave evidence of a confession was a mission boy called Harry. He said, in effect, that the owner of the boat in which they came to Darwin asked him to obtain the prisoner's story. The story the prisoner told him was briefly that on coming back from fishing he had seen the boat in which the police had come to the island, that he had been chased by a black man, who saw him, and had hidden in the jungle, that people had run past him, that after some time he moved into the open, but, seeing nobody, he returned to the jungle, that then hearing the cry of a baby, he looked and saw a white man and a lubra stop, that the white man had sexual relations with the lubra, after which the lubra picked up the baby and both returned to the open space, that the prisoner then communicated by signs with the lubra, who was one of his three lubras, that the white man saw him ... fired at him three times and reloaded, that the prisoner got behind a tree, the white man fired again and the prisoner threw his spear and hit him, that he then ran away and hid in the grass. ...

At the trial at Darwin, the prisoner, who understood no English, was defended by counsel instructed by the Protector of Aborigines. At the conclusion of Parriner's evidence, the Judge asked counsel for the defence whether he had put before the prisoner the story told by the witness and talked it over with him. Counsel replied that he had not done so. The Judge then asked him whether he did not think it proper to discuss the evidence with the accused and see whether it was correct. On counsel stating that he thought it desirable to take that course, the Judge arranged for him to take Paddy the interpreter and discuss the evidence with Tuckiar. The Court adjourned for half an hour to enable this to be done. On the Court resuming, Harry's evidence in chief was taken, but, before proceeding to cross-examine him, the prisoner's counsel said that he had a specially important matter which he desired to discuss with the Judge. He was in a predicament, the worst predicament that he had encountered in all his legal career. The jury retired, and the Judge, the Protector of Aborigines and counsel for the defence went into the Judge's Chambers. On their return, after some discussion of the reasons for the Crown's failure to call as witnesses other constables, trackers and the lubras, the jury were recalled and Harry's evidence was completed. ...

Before the Crown case was quite complete, the jury, who had heard much discussion of the Crown's failure to bring witnesses to Darwin, asked: "If we are satisfied that there is not enough evidence, what is our position?" The Judge reports that he understood them to mean, what was their position if they were satisfied that the Crown had not brought before the Court all the evidence it might have brought. He replied: "You must think very carefully about that aspect of the matter and not allow yourselves to be swayed by the fact that you think the Crown has not done its duty. If you bring in a verdict of 'not guilty' it means that this man is freed and cannot be tried again, no matter what evidence may be discovered in the future, and that may mean a grave miscarriage of justice. Another aspect of the matter that troubles me is that evidence has been given about a man who is dead, and if the jury brings in a verdict of 'not guilty' it may be said that they believe that evidence, and it would be a serious slander on that man. It was the obvious duty of the Crown to bring all the evidence procurable and to have all these matters cleared up entirely, but you must not allow the fact that the Crown has failed in its duty to influence you to bring a verdict of 'not guilty' if there really is evidence of guilt before you on which you can rely. You should go and think about the matter quietly and carefully weigh all the evidence that has been given before you."

Unfortunately a verbatim report of the full summing up was not made and we do not know what direction was given in respect of very important matters, particularly in relation to manslaughter, provocation, and self-defence. But it does appear that, after telling the jury that a decision on any question of fact was entirely for them and they ought not to accept any view he indicated on a question of fact unless in their own independent judgment they agreed with it, the learned Judge proceeded to condemn the story which Harry said the prisoner told him, as an improbable concoction on the part of the prisoner, and, on the other hand, said that the only conclusion from the facts which Parriner said the prisoner narrated to him was that that the homicide amounted to murder. We have also a report upon which we can rely for the two following passages in the summing up to which we attach importance:

> (1) I want you now, if you can, to put all that out of your minds, to look at the matter quietly and dispassionately, and without reference to any observations of that sort—to consider the evidence which has been put before you, and decide whether or not you can act upon that evidence. It may be that owing to the neglect or incompetence or worse of the people who had the preparation of this case for the Crown, a grave miscarriage of justice may occur and a serious slander may be affixed to the name of the dead man. But that is a matter you cannot take into consideration; it is a matter that should be inquired into elsewhere and not here. It is the duty of yourselves to consider only the evidence before you, and to endeavour if you can to avoid any miscarriage of justice. The other matter we cannot, unfortunately, deal with here; the responsibility for that must rest where it may ultimately be fixed.

> (2) You have before you two different stories, one of which sounds highly probable, and fits in with all the known facts, and the other is so utterly ridiculous as to be an obvious fabrication. What counsel for the defence asks you to do is to take up the position that you will not believe either of these stories. Tuckiar has told two different stories to two different boys, and both of these stories have been told to you here in Court. Which one is true? For some reason Tuckiar has not gone into the box and told you which one is true, and that is a fact which you are entitled to take into consideration. You can draw from it any inference you like.

Upon the jury's finding a verdict of guilty, the Judge postponed pronouncing sentence, which, in the case of an aboriginal, is not necessarily death. The prisoner's counsel then made the following statement:

> I have a matter which I desire to mention before the Court rises. I would like to state publicly that I had an interview with the convicted prisoner Tuckiar in the presence of an interpreter. I pointed out to him that he had told these two different stories and that one could not be true. I asked him to tell the interpreter which was the true story. He told him that the first story told to Parriner was the true one. I asked him why he told the other story. He told me that he was too much worried so he told a different story and that story was a lie. I think this fact clears Constable McColl. As an advocate I did not deem it advisable to put the accused in the box.

The learned Judge said: "I am glad you mentioned it, not only in fairness to McColl but also because it proves that the boy Harry was telling the truth in the witness box. I had a serious doubt whether the boy Harry was telling the truth, but it now appears that he was."

When the Court resumed his Honor added: "It did not occur to me at the time, but I think I should have stated publicly that immediately that confession had been made to you, you and Dr. Cook (the Protector of Aborigines) consulted me about the matter and asked my opinion as to the proper course for you, as counsel, to take, and I then told you that if your client had been a white man and had made a confession of guilt to you I thought your proper course would have been to withdraw from the case; but as your client was an aboriginal, and there might be some remnant of doubt as to whether his confession to you was any more reliable than any other confession he had made, the better course would be for you to continue to appear for him, because if you had retired from the case it would have left it open to ignorant, malicious and irresponsible persons to say that this aboriginal had been abandoned and left without any proper defence."

After hearing some evidence upon the subject of punishment, the learned Judge pronounced sentence of death.

We think that this narrative of the proceedings shows that for more than one reason the conviction cannot stand … . In the present case, the jury witnessed the spectacle of the prisoner's counsel, at the suggestion of the Judge, retiring to discuss with the prisoner the evidence of the principal witness against him and see whether it was correct, and of his saying after doing so, that he wished to discuss with the Judge a specially important matter, which put him in the worst predicament that he had encountered in his legal career. Afterwards, the Judge, who had to their knowledge heard counsel's communication, directed them that for some reason the prisoner had not gone into the witness box and told them which of the stories was true and that they were entitled to take that fact into consideration and draw any inference from it they liked. He thus authorized them to make a presumption of guilt from the prisoner's failure to give evidence and the circumstances which had occurred before them were likely to reinforce the presumption with a well-founded surmise of what the Judge had been told by the prisoner's counsel. …

It would be difficult for anyone in the position of the learned Judge to receive the communication made to him by counsel for the prisoner and yet retain the same view of the dangers involved in the weakness of the Crown evidence. This may, perhaps, explain his Honor's evident anxiety that the jury should not under-estimate the force of the evidence the Crown did adduce. Indeed counsel seems to have taken a course calculated to transfer to the Judge the embarrassment which he appears so much to have felt. Why he should have conceived himself to have been in so great a predicament, it is not easy for those experienced in advocacy to understand. He had a plain duty, both to his client and to the Court, to press such rational considerations as the evidence fairly gave rise to in favour of complete acquittal or conviction of manslaughter only. No doubt he was satisfied that through Paddy he obtained the uncoloured product of his client's mind, although misgiving on this point would have been pardonable; but, even if the result was that the correctness of Parriner's version was conceded, it was by no means a hopeless contention of fact that the homicide should be found to amount only to manslaughter. Whether he be in fact guilty or not, a prisoner is, in point of law, entitled to acquittal from any charge which the evidence fails to establish that he committed, and it is not incumbent on his counsel by abandoning his defence to deprive him of the benefit of such rational arguments as fairly arise on the proofs submitted. The subsequent action of the prisoner's counsel in openly disclosing the privileged communication of his client and acknowledging the correctness of the more serious testimony against him is wholly indefensible. It was his paramount duty to respect the privilege attaching to the communication made to him as counsel, a duty the obligation of which was by no means weakened by the character of his client, or the moment at which he chose to make the disclosure. No doubt he was actuated by a desire to remove any imputation on Constable McColl. But he was not entitled to divulge what he had learnt from the prisoner as his counsel. Our system of administering justice necessarily imposes upon those who practice advocacy duties which have no analogies, and the system cannot dispense with their strict observance.

In the present case, what occurred is productive of much difficulty. We have reached the conclusion, as we have already stated, that the verdict found against the prisoner must be set aside. Ordinarily the question would next arise whether a new trial should be had. But upon this question we are confronted with the following statements made by the learned trial Judge in his report—"After the verdict, counsel—for reasons that may have been good—made a public statement of this fact which has been published in the local press and otherwise broadcasted throughout the whole area from which jurymen are drawn. If a new trial were granted and another jury were asked to chose between Parriner's story, Harry's story, and some third story which might possibly be put before them it would be practically impossible for them to put out of their minds the fact of this confession by the accused to his own counsel, which would certainly be known to most, if not all, of them. ... Counsel for the defence ... after verdict made, entirely of his own motion, a public statement which would make a new trial almost certainly a futility."

In face of this opinion, the correctness of which we cannot doubt, we think the prisoner cannot justly be subjected to another trial at Darwin, and no other venue is practicable .... We therefore allow the appeal and quash the conviction and judgment and direct that a verdict and judgment of acquittal be entered.

NOTES AND QUESTIONS

1. Did Tuckiar's lawyer face a moral choice when he agreed to represent a guilty client? Is the client's race (and position of disadvantage) a relevant factor when determining whether or not to take on a guilty client's case?

2. Ignoring, for the moment, the requirements of the rules of professional conduct, was it "ethical" for Tuckiar's lawyer to inform the trial judge that the accused had privately admitted (to his lawyer) that he was guilty of the crime with which he was charged?

3. One of the reasons the lawyer gave for informing the court (and the public) of his client's private confession was to "clear the name" of the deceased police officer, who had been implicated in a sexual liaison with an aboriginal woman in the exculpatory version of Tuckiar's confession. Does this make the lawyer's choice (to publicize his client's confession) a morally correct decision? Was the lawyer engaged in "moral reasoning" when deciding whether or not to inform the court (and the jury) that his client had confessed?

4. Note that Tuckiar's lawyer waited until after the guilty verdict (but before the sentence was handed down) to inform the jury of Tuckiar's guilt. Does this have an impact on the morality of counsel's actions?

5. The court noted that counsel's duty was "to press such rational considerations as the evidence fairly gave rise to in favour of complete acquittal." Explain how this can be

a "moral duty," even where the lawyer knows that the client is guilty of the crime with which he or she is charged. Why did Tuckiar's lawyer express discomfort in the discharge of this duty? Does that make him a particularly moral person, an immoral person, or just a bad lawyer?

6. How would you describe the court's vision of "the role of the lawyer"? Is this a defensible view?

7. Note that the result in this case was that an (apparently) admitted murderer was allowed to go free. Is this a "moral" way of correcting a lawyer's ethical violation? Why or why not? Why would a court choose to grant this remedy in cases involving a breach of the duty of confidentiality?

8. Was Tuckiar's lawyer insulated from the morality of his client's project (that is, seeking acquittal for a crime that he had committed)? Is Tuckiar's lawyer "morally implicated" in his client's conduct by deciding to pursue a vocation (that is, the vocation of a criminal defence lawyer) that requires him to pursue a guilty person's acquittal? Was Tuckiar's lawyer *truly* pursuing "a guilty person's acquittal"?

Rondel v. Worsley
[1969] 1 AC 191

[The decision of the House of Lords in *Rondel v. Worsley* is often held out as the definitive statement of the role of lawyers who appear before the courts. Throughout the decision, the Law Lords make repeated reference to the various duties owed by legal professionals to their clients, the courts, and the public as a whole. When reviewing the court's decision, consider how frequently these duties come into conflict. Also consider whether the "moral world of lawyers" is truly as simple as the traditional model of legal ethics suggests. Finally, consider whether a lawyer's duties to the court, the client, and the public are incompatible with the notion that, when making any kind of decision, individuals (including lawyers) will inevitably be guided by self-interest.]

This was an appeal, by leave of the House of Lords, dated December 1, 1966, from a judgment of the Court of Appeal (Lord Denning MR, Danckwerts and Salmon LJJ), dated October 20, 1966, dismissing the appeal of the appellant, Norbert Fred Rondel, from a judgment of Lawton J, dated December 21, 1965, dismissing the appellant's appeal from the order of Master Lawrence dated May 17, 1965, whereby the master ordered that the statement of claim of the appellant (plaintiff in the action) be struck out and the appellant's action be dismissed on the grounds that the statement of claim disclosed no cause of action. The question raised by this appeal was whether an action lay against a barrister for professional negligence in respect of work done as an advocate. The following further questions were canvassed in argument:

(a) whether, if a barrister had immunity from suit for negligence in connection with work done in or about the court room, such immunity extended to advisory work unconnected with proceedings in court.

(b) whether, if a barrister had any such immunity, the immunity was based upon public policy or the special relationship of barrister and client; and, if so, whether and to what extent such immunity was conferred on solicitors, at least when acting as advocates.

On February 15, 1965, the appellant, Norbert Fred Rondel, issued a writ claiming "damages for professional negligence" against the respondent, Michael Dominic Lawrence Worsley, barrister-at-law, in respect of the respondent's conduct of the appellant's defence on criminal charges at the Central Criminal Court in May, 1959, when the respondent was engaged on a dock brief during the hearing of the charges on which the appellant was found guilty and sentenced to 18 months' imprisonment. ...

LORD REID: My Lords, in 1959 the appellant was charged at the Central Criminal Court with causing grievous bodily harm to one Manning. He was not given legal aid but after the case had proceeded for some time he was informed that he could have a "dock brief." He chose the respondent to be his counsel and, in accordance with his duty as a barrister, the respondent agreed to act for him. During an adjournment he gave to the respondent his account of the affair. The respondent then cross-examined the Crown witnesses and called the appellant and another witness. The appellant was convicted and it is plain that he had no real defence. But he was much aggrieved by evidence that he had used a knife; he wanted to establish that he had inflicted Manning's injuries with his hands alone, or by biting, and apparently the respondent did not ask all the questions or lead all the evidence he had suggested. ...

There is no doubt about the position and duties of a barrister or advocate appearing in court on behalf of a client. It has long been recognised that no counsel is entitled to refuse to act in a sphere in which he practises, and on being tendered a proper fee, for any person however unpopular or even offensive he or his opinions may be, and it is essential that that duty must continue: justice cannot be done and certainly cannot be seen to be done otherwise. If counsel is bound to act for such a person, no reasonable man could think the less of any counsel because of his association with such a client, but, if counsel could pick and choose, his reputation might suffer if he chose to act for such a client, and the client might have great difficulty in obtaining proper legal assistance.

Every counsel has a duty to his client fearlessly to raise every issue, advance every argument, and ask every question, however distasteful, which he thinks will help his client's case. But, as an officer of the court concerned in the administration of justice, he has an overriding duty to the court, to the standards of his profession, and to the public, which may and often does lead to a conflict with his client's wishes or with what the client thinks are his personal interests. Counsel must not mislead the court, he must not lend himself to casting aspersions on the other party or witnesses for which there is no sufficient basis in the information in his possession, he must not withhold authorities or documents which may tell against his clients but which the law or the standards of his profession require him to produce. And by so acting he may well incur the displeasure or worse of his client so that if the case is lost, his client would or might seek legal redress if that were open to him.

Is it in the public interest that barristers and advocates should be protected against such actions? Like so many questions which raise the public interest, a decision one way will cause hardships to individuals while a decision the other way will involve disadvantage to the public interest. On the one hand, if the existing rule of immunity continues there will be cases, rare though they may be, where a client who has suffered loss through the negligence of his counsel will be deprived of a remedy. So the issue appears to me to be whether the abolition of the rule would probably be attended by such disadvantage to the public interest as to make its retention clearly justifiable. I would not expect any counsel to be influenced by the possibility of an action being raised against him to such an extent that he would knowingly depart from his duty to the court or to his profession. But although the line between proper and improper conduct may be easy to state in general terms, it is by no means easy to draw in many borderline cases. At present it can be said with confidence in this country that where there is any doubt the vast majority of counsel put their public duty before the apparent interests of their clients. Otherwise there would not be that implicit trust between the Bench and the Bar which does so much to promote the smooth and speedy conduct of the administration of justice. There may be other countries where conditions are different and there public policy may point in a different direction. But here it would be a grave and dangerous step to make any change which would imperil in any way the confidence which every court rightly puts in all counsel who appear before it.

And there is another factor which I fear might operate in a much greater number of cases. Every counsel in practice knows that daily he is faced with the question whether in his client's interest he should raise a new issue, put another witness in the box, or ask further questions of the witness whom he is examining or cross-examining. That is seldom an easy question but I think that most experienced counsel would agree that the golden rule is—when in doubt stop. Far more cases have been lost by going on too long than by stopping too soon. But the client does not know that. To him brevity may indicate incompetence or negligence and sometimes stopping too soon is an error of judgment. So I think it not at all improbable that the possibility of being sued for negligence would at least subconsciously lead some counsel to undue prolixity which would not only be harmful to the client but against the public interest in prolonging trials. Many experienced lawyers already think that the lengthening of trials is not leading to any closer approximation to ideal justice. ...

There are other arguments which support the continuance of the present rule: they do not appear to me to be conclusive, but they do have weight. I shall only mention one. Suppose that, as in the present case, a convicted man sues his counsel. To succeed he must show not only that his counsel was guilty of professional negligence, but also that that negligence caused him loss. The loss would be the fact that he was wrongly convicted by reason of his counsel's negligence. So after the plaintiff's appeal against conviction had been dismissed by the Court of Criminal Appeal, the whole case would in effect have to be retried in a civil court where the standard of proof is different. That is something one would not contemplate with equanimity unless there is a real need for it.

So the position appears to me to be this: if the present rule were changed there would at least be a grave risk of consequences much against the public interest. And

what is to be the advantage? I do not think that it is enough to say that there might—
or even would—be an occasional case where some client would recover damages
from his counsel. There must be more than that to justify incurring the disadvantages. …

For the reasons which I have given I am of opinion that it is in the public interest
to retain the existing immunity of barristers from action by clients for professional
negligence, at least so far as it relates to their work in conducting litigation and that
would be sufficient to require the dismissal of the present appeal. But to leave the
matter there would, I fear, lead to some misunderstanding or even confusion. The
main reasons on which I have based my opinion relate to the position of counsel
while engaged in litigation, when his public duty and his duty to his client may conflict. But there are many kinds of work undertaken by counsel where no such conflict
would emerge, and there I see little reason why the liability of counsel should be
different from that of members of any other profession who give their professional
advice and services to their clients. The members of every profession are bound to
act honourably and in accordance with the recognised standards of their profession.
But that does not, in my view, give rise to any such conflict of duties as can confront
counsel while engaged in litigation. …

LORD MORRIS OF BORTH-Y-GEST: My lords, this interlocutory appeal, which raises
issues of considerable importance, has been aided in its progress to your Lordships'
House by notable manifestations of patience and indulgence. The issues are of greater
consequence than would seem apparent from a narrative of the somewhat sombre
facts out of which they have, though tardily, emerged. It was as far back as April,
1959, that the appellant went early one morning to a house in West London. A man
named Manning was doorkeeper at the house. At the conclusion of a violent alterca-
tion between the appellant and Manning the latter had the lobe of an ear bitten off and
his hand very severely damaged. The appellant was virtually unhurt. He has said that
he went to the house on behalf of its landlord, a man named Rachman. He has re-
sented any suggestion that he used a knife and has proclaimed that, by the use only of
the strength of his own hands, he tore Manning's hand in half. A consequence of the
encounter was that the appellant was charged. Being committed to the Central Criminal Court he was arraigned before the Recorder of London on Thursday, May 28,
1959. There were two counts in the indictment. The first was that he caused grievous
bodily harm to Manning with intent to do him grievous bodily harm: the second was
that he assaulted Manning occasioning actual bodily harm. The prosecution case was
opened, and then the first witness was called and examined. At that stage the appellant asked for legal aid. The recorder refused that application, but informed the
appellant that he could instruct one of the counsel who were in court to appear for
him. The appellant desired to have the respondent as his counsel and the respondent,
in accordance with the practice and etiquette of the Bar, agreed to act. …

It is in this somewhat uninspiring setting that a question is presented for decision
that for long has been generally regarded as well settled. It must be decided without
regard to the merits or demerits or the tensions of any particular case. As illustrative,
however, of a type of possible action which calls for examination the complaints of
the appellant in this case as they have emerged in the draft of the potential re-amended

statement of claim merit examination. The substance of them was that the respondent failed to put certain questions to witnesses or to call, or to take the necessary steps to call, certain witnesses. There had never been any doubt that it was the appellant who caused the very severe injury to Manning's hand or that it was he who bit off the lobe of Manning's ear. The appellant's case was that he had only acted in self-defence. He now complains that after he had instructed the respondent as to the facts which he said supported his case the respondent (a) failed in examining or re-examining a defence witness to bring out that Manning had associates or friends at the scene of the incident who could have helped him in a fight; (b) failed to cross-examine Manning or a doctor who was a prosecution witness as to the impossibility of the wound having been inflicted by a knife or similar weapon; (c) failed to elicit evidence from the witnesses at the trial or to call or get witnesses to prove that the appellant (as rent collector and caretaker for Rachman) had authority to go to the house in question. The complaint of the appellant was that as a result of these omissions he was wrongly convicted. It may well be open to doubt whether evidence as to some of the matters referred to would have been admissible but I find it unnecessary to consider this point. ...

... [A]n advocate at the English bar, accepting a brief in the usual way, undertakes a duty but does not enter into any contract or promise either express or implied: he takes upon himself an office or duty in the proper discharge of which not merely the client but the court in which the duty is to be performed, and the public at large, have an interest. The court held that the conduct and control of a cause are necessarily left to counsel. They added: "If a party desires to retain the power of directing counsel how the suit shall be conducted, he must agree with some counsel willing so to bind himself. A counsel is not subject to an action for calling or not calling a particular witness, or for putting or omitting to put a particular question, or for honestly taking a view of the case which may turn out to be quite erroneous. If he were so liable, counsel would perform their duties under the peril of an action by every disappointed and angry client."

They also held that "no action will lie against counsel for any act honestly done in the conduct or management of the cause."

It is to be observed that the court accepted that counsel owed a duty: the duty was one which was owed to the client and also to the court and also to the public. The court might have been content to say that as counsel is vested with a discretion as to how he will conduct a case he will have a defence when sued if he asserts that he exercised his discretion honestly. But the court went further and laid it down that for any act honestly done in the conduct and management of a cause no action will lie against counsel. The basis of this would seem to be that as counsel owes a duty to the public and to the court as well as to his client, the public interest and the administration of justice require that he should not be subject to an action in respect of such complaints as "calling or not calling a particular witness, or for putting or omitting to put a particular question, or for honestly taking a view of the case which may turn out to be quite erroneous." The question now arises whether this view is correct and whether today justification for it continues to exist. ...

The advocate has a duty to assist in ensuring that the administration of justice is not distorted or thwarted by dishonest or disreputable practices. To a certain extent every advocate is an amicus curiae. In the Irish case of *Reg. v. O'Connell* it was said by Crampton J that though an advocate for an individual is retained and remunerated for his services "yet he has a prior and perpetual retainer on behalf of truth and justice." His duty to the client is to exercise a reasonable degree of care and skill. In the nature of things that, in turn, involves that he must make decisions which call for the exercise of personal judgment. He must in the honest exercise of his discretion decide what questions to put and what witnesses to call. It would seem to result from this that in most cases it would be an effective answer to an allegation of negligence to say that the course that had been followed in litigation was that which the advocate in the honest exercise of his discretion had deemed it advisable to follow. It is the discretion of the chosen advocate upon which the client must rely. When a case is concluded it can often happen that in retrospect there are cogitations as to whether if this or that additional question had been put or if this or that question had not been put or if some further witness had been called the result might have been different. In many cases it is probable that the result would not have been different. In some cases it might only be those who judicially determined the first case (the judge or members of a jury) who could really supply the answer. If in retrospect it were thought that had a case been differently conducted the result would possibly or probably have been different, it might be that the view would be held that the advocate had honestly exercised his discretion but had been guilty of certain errors of judgment not amounting to negligence. The duty of the advocate is, however, not merely to act honestly: his duty also is to exercise a reasonable degree of care and skill. In the case of such advocates as can and do enter into contractual arrangements the duty arises *ex contractu* but in other cases the duty arises out of and by reason of the relationship between the advocate and the client who has sought his assistance. Though in most cases, by reason of the special and distinctive features of the work of advocates in which personal discretion is so much involved, assertions of negligence could readily be repelled, a cause of action alleging professional negligence could nevertheless always be framed. Is it, then, desirable in the public interest, while rejecting the wide immunity which has hitherto been proclaimed, to retain an immunity relating only to the limited field of the conduct and management of a case in court? Is it, as a matter of public policy, expedient that actions which involve a searching review almost amounting to a re-trial in different actions of previous actions or cases already concluded should not be allowed? Is the administration of justice (which is so much the concern of the community) better promoted if such actions are not countenanced? If it is recognised that there could be some cases where negligence (as opposed to errors of judgment) could be established, is it nevertheless on a balance of desirabilities wise to disallow the bringing of such cases? In my view, the answer to these questions is that it is in the public interest that such actions should not be brought. In this, as in other aspects of the present case, I find myself in general accord with the judgment of Salmon LJ. ...

In his judgment in the Court of Appeal (*Munster v. Lamb*), Brett MR said:

> A counsel's position is one of the utmost difficulty. He is not to speak of that which he knows; he is not called upon to consider, whether the facts with which he is dealing are true or false. What he has to do, is to argue as best he can, without degrading himself, in

order to maintain the proposition which will carry with it either the protection or the remedy which he desires for his client. If amidst the difficulties of his position he were to be called upon during the heat of his argument to consider whether what he says is true or false, whether what he says is relevant or irrelevant, he would have his mind so embarrassed that he could not do the duty which he is called upon to perform. For, more than a judge, infinitely more than a witness, he wants protection on the ground of benefit to the public. …

...

I would dismiss the appeal.

LORD PEARCE: … A further important consideration is the fact that as matters are and have been for centuries a barrister is bound to provide his services to a client who can pay his fee (or whose fees are paid by the public Legal Aid Fund) if the case is one either in the courts or in the advisory sphere in which a barrister normally practises. This has been an essential feature of our law. Many generations of students have been taught to follow Erskine's famous words in which he justified his unpopular defence of Tom Paine: "From the moment that any advocate can be permitted to say that he will or will not stand between the Crown and the subject arraigned in the court where he daily sits to practise, from that moment the liberties of England are at an end."

It is easier, pleasanter and more advantageous professionally for barristers to advise, represent or defend those who are decent and reasonable and likely to succeed in their action or their defence than those who are unpleasant, unreasonable, disreputable, and have an apparently hopeless case. Yet it would be tragic if our legal system came to provide no reputable defenders, representatives or advisers for the latter. And that would be the inevitable result of allowing barristers to pick and choose their clients. It not infrequently happens that the unpleasant, the unreasonable, the disreputable and those who have apparently hopeless cases turn out after a full and fair hearing to be in the right. And it is a judge's (or jury's) solemn duty to find that out by a careful and unbiased investigation. This they simply cannot do if counsel do not (as at present) take on the less attractive task of advising and representing such persons however small their apparent merits. … I agree with Erskine that it would cause irreparable injury to justice if there were any departure from the code which has so long existed, that a barrister cannot pick and choose. To continue to compel him to take cases, yet at the same time to remove his independence and immunity, would seem unfair and unreasonable. Moreover, in a human world such an unfair ruling rarely produces a satisfactory result. It results in evasions and the payment of mere lip-service to the rule—evasions which any fair-minded disciplinary tribunal would in the circumstances find it hard to condemn. And thus evasions would increase. In my view, such a rule would create a harm disproportionate to that which it seeks to remedy.

The independence of counsel is of great and essential value to the integrity, the efficacy, the elucidation of truth, and the despatch of business in the administration of justice. These matters are of paramount importance. The suggested innovation must lessen that independence and do an increasing and inevitable disservice to the administration of justice. I would not, therefore, agree with it … . Moreover, it is important that in respect of these and of other paper work the counsel should not be allowed to pick and choose his clients. If a man, however unreasonable or undesirable, wants to have counsel's advice or paper work he should be entitled to have it. If such a position is to remain unaltered, I do not think that it is either reasonable or desirable to change the present independent immunity of counsel. The loss to the public as a whole would be greater than the gain. It follows that I agree with the majority of the Court of Appeal.

I would dismiss the appeal.

NOTES AND QUESTIONS

1. The House of Lords held that "no counsel is entitled to refuse to act in a sphere in which he practises, and on being tendered a proper fee, for any person however unpopular or even offensive he or his opinions may be, and it is essential that that duty must continue: justice cannot be done and certainly cannot be seen to be done otherwise." Do you believe that all litigators see their role this way? Are there any cases in which a litigator would be "morally right" to refuse to act for a particular client?

2. The following passage from the House of Lords' decision is often used to summarize the lawyer's duty when appearing before the courts:

> Every counsel has a duty to his client fearlessly to raise every issue, advance every argument, and ask every question, however distasteful, which he thinks will help his client's case. But, as an officer of the court concerned in the administration of justice, he has an overriding duty to the court, to the standards of his profession, and to the public, which may and often does lead to a conflict with his client's wishes or with what the client thinks are his personal interests. Counsel must not mislead the court, he must not lend himself to casting aspersions on the other party or witnesses for which there is no sufficient basis in the information in his possession, he must not withhold authorities or documents which may tell against his clients but which the law or the standards of his profession require him to produce.

Is this web of conflicting duties compatible with the notion that lawyers inhabit a "morally sterile wasteland," or that the moral world of the lawyer is uncomplicated? Does the duty to fearlessly raise every issue, advance every argument, etc., truly insulate the lawyer from the morality of his or her client's cause?

3. The court noted that "I would not expect any counsel to be influenced by the possibility of an action being raised against him to such an extent that he would knowingly depart from his duty to the court or to his profession." Is this suggestion compatible with the notion of self-interest? Why or why not? Might a lawyer be morally justified in refusing to act for a client who had a long history of suing his or her lawyers for large amounts of money, causing the lawyers who were sued to waste countless hours in court even where the client's claims were unsuccessful?

4. The House of Lords claimed that "[a]t present it can be said with confidence in this country that where there is any doubt the vast majority of counsel put their public duty before the apparent interests of their clients." Does this reflect your own perception of lawyers' attitudes? Does this reflect what you have been taught in law school?

5. The Law Lords approved of an earlier decision that held that lawyers have "prior and perpetual retainer on behalf of truth and justice." How does this "retainer" relate to the lawyer's duty to seek the acquittal of guilty clients?

6. At the conclusion of his judgment, Lord Pearce noted that if lawyers were to be liable (in negligence) for decisions made in the conduct of a trial, "the loss to the public as a whole would be greater than the gain." Is this an example of the application of economic reasoning to rules governing lawyers' professional conduct? Do you agree with Lord Pearce's application of this decision-making model?

Throughout this chapter we have seen that lawyers are generally discouraged from sitting in judgment on their clients. In other words, lawyers should act resolutely for a client regardless of the lawyer's opinion regarding the merits of the client's claim or the "moral worth" of the client's ultimate goals. The decision of the court in *R v. Delisle* (1999) provides a useful justification for this view of the lawyer's role.

R v. Delisle
(1994), 133 CCC (3d) 541 (Que. CA)

PROULX JA [TRANSLATION]: This appeal essentially raises the issue of the competence of counsel at the trial of the appellant. The appellant was found guilty of assault causing grievous bodily harm and was sentenced to a term of four years' imprisonment. He now seeks to have the judgment quashed on the ground that he suffered irreparable harm because of his counsel's incompetence. ...

A. The Relevant Facts

In the case at bar, it was established, on the basis of the fresh evidence introduced into the record, that the appellant, because of the sudden illness of his lawyer, had to retain the services of another lawyer who had been practising for at most a year. It was also established that the appellant always maintained to his lawyer that he was innocent, that he wanted to testify in his defence and that he even identified Kevin Carl to his lawyer as one of the assailants. I would mention here that the victim had been attacked by a group of individuals and that the main issue the trial judge had to resolve was the identity of the aggressors.

The second lawyer, undoubtedly because of his lack of experience, relied on his impressions rather than undertaking the steps required for effective representation.

Because he did not believe his client's story, he did not even attempt to meet the witness Carl and determined that his client should not testify in his own defence. Following the verdict of guilty but before sentencing, Carl communicated with the lawyer, confiding to him that he was in fact the person responsible for the acts attributed to the appellant. The lawyer then attempted, but in vain, to get the trial judge to reopen the case. In the context of this appeal, Carl gave an affidavit in which he reiterated his participation in the events which led to the conviction of the appellant. He could not be reached, however, to give testimony at the request of the appellant in the context of his motion to call fresh evidence. Furthermore, the transcript of the appellant's and of his lawyer's testimony, which confirms the foregoing, was filed in this Court's record.

B. Counsel's Flagrant Incompetence

It is not astonishing that the Crown here conceded that the appeal must be granted ... . The appellant always maintained that he was innocent. He had indicated to his lawyer the identity of the guilty party and, is it necessary to mention, wanted to testify in his own defence. These instructions of the client were never respected by the lawyer. He thereby imposed on his client his decision not to call him and not to attempt to meet the witness Carl. The lawyer committed a first significant error.

The lawyer's explanation that he did not believe his client's story is also totally unacceptable. The lawyer cannot set himself up as the judge of his client ... . If there is a universal rule of ethics in criminal law which has existed for centuries, it is the rule which provides that counsel must not set himself up as the judge of his own client before the trial begins and then leave it to the trier of fact to decide guilt or innocence. Thomas Erskine, in his address at the trial of Thomas Paine who was charged with seditious libel in 1792, pronounced these words which have inspired both advocates and judges in the centuries which followed: "If the advocate refuses to defend from what he may think of the charge or of the defence, he assumes the character of the judge; nay, he assumes it before the hour of judgment" (*R v. Thomas Paine* (1792), 22 St Tr 357, 412, cited in Pannick, *Advocates* (Oxford University Press, 1992), p. 151).

A little more than a century later, in a decision which has become a classic in the area, *Johnson v. Emerson and Sparrow* (1871), LR 6 Exch. 329 p. 366, Baron Bramwell wrote:

> A man's rights are to be determined by the Court, not by his attorney or counsel. It is for want of remembering this that foolish people object to lawyers that they will advocate a case against their own opinions. A client is entitled to say to his counsel, I want your advocacy, not your judgment; I prefer that of the Court. [Quoted by Mark M. Orkin, Law Society of Upper Canada, in Orkin, *Legal Ethics* (Toronto: Cartwright & Sons, 1957), p. 110.]

One may also consult on this point, Sir David Napley, *The Technique of Persuasion*, 4th ed., 1991, pp. 59-61; Meredith Blake and Andrew Ashworth, "Some Ethical Issues in Prosecuting and Defending Criminal Cases," [1998] *Crim. L Rev.* 16; Stan Ross, *Ethics in Law: Lawyers' Responsibility and Accountability in Australia*, 2nd ed. (Butterworths, 1998), p. 441ff.; and also Daniel Soulez Larivière, *L'avocature* (Éditions du Seuil, 1995) [translation]: "To each their role. To judges to judge, to lawyers to defend. A lawyer who wants to judge his own client is mistaken as to his profession, mixes up respective functions, weakens his own function to the detriment of the entire judicial system."

In the case at bar, counsel for the appellant totally misunderstood the role which was his, by setting himself up as the judge of his client instead of respecting his client's instructions and truly defending his client's interests. Taking into account what we know now as a result of the fresh evidence, this demonstrates even more the danger for counsel of relying upon his impressions.

In conclusion therefore, taking into account the two serious errors committed by counsel for the appellant, each of which is proof of flagrant incompetence and fundamentally violates the appellant's right to make full answer and defence, I am of the view, as the Crown moreover conceded, that irreparable prejudice resulted therefrom justifying the quashing of the judgment and the ordering of a new trial.

For these reasons, I am of the view that the appeal must be granted and a new trial ordered.

NOTES AND QUESTIONS

1. Does the reasoning in *Delisle* justify a general rule that a lawyer should never judge the morality of the client's goals? Does it support the view that lawyers should not refuse to act for clients whom they believe to be immoral?

2. On what grounds should a lawyer form the opinion that his or her client is actually guilty of the crime with which the client is charged? Ignoring the rules of professional conduct (for the moment), what effect should the lawyer's belief in the client's guilt have on the lawyer's conduct of the client's case? Should the lawyer be permitted to raise an affirmative defence—for example, putting forth a false alibi, or suggesting that someone else committed the crime?

III. Problems with the Traditional Model

A. Introduction

Section II introduced a traditional model of legal ethics. Proponents of this model believe that lawyers bear no blame for actions taken in pursuit of a client's goals—indeed, when pursuing client interests, lawyers are well advised to set aside their personal moral qualms. According to this model of legal ethics, lawyers must disregard the ethical implications of their actions and consider only two behavioural guidelines—namely: (1) the limits of the law and (2) the client's interests. Provided that the lawyer respects the boundaries of the law and acts in ways that further the interests of the client, the lawyer can safely ignore the ethical implications of his or her actions. The institution of "the legal system," it is argued, immunizes the lawyer from moral considerations, bearing full responsibility for every morally dubious act the lawyer commits. To the extent that the lawyer's actions appear to be morally problematic, responsibility for those actions is cast upon the legal system, absolving the lawyer of moral accountability. In short, lawyers are said to be systemically amoral, pursuing their tasks without regard for ethical issues.

The traditional account of the lawyer's role is flawed. In reality, the moral world of lawyers is not a morally sterile wasteland in which there are no ethical questions to be answered. On the contrary, the legal profession is fraught with moral issues, constantly challenging the lawyer's capacity to recognize and confront ethical problems. Indeed, the moral world of lawyers is at least as complicated as the moral world of "ordinary life." This critique of the traditional model of lawyer's ethics is developed in the following sections of the chapter.

B. Questioning the "Ethically Sterile Wasteland"

One of the fundamental claims of the traditional account of lawyers' ethics is that the moral world of lawyers is much simpler than the moral world of "ordinary life."[20] As we have seen, proponents of this model claim that lawyers do not need to turn their minds to moral issues: on the contrary, the legal system resolves all of the lawyer's moral problems, eliminating the lawyer's need to consider ethical questions.

The depiction of the lawyer's moral universe as an ethically sterile wasteland is misleading. Assuming that the legal system *does* allow lawyers to disregard the morality of actions taken on behalf of clients (an assumption that will be challenged momentarily), lawyers continue to face a wide array of difficult ethical choices. The most obvious of these choices flow from ethical constraints set out in legislation and professional codes of ethics.[21] These constraints range from the lawyer's fundamental duty of confidentiality to the lawyer's duty to refrain from harming the public image of the legal profession.[22] Even if the lawyer's institutional role *does* justify much of the lawyer's conduct, the rules defining that role require the lawyer to be aware of countless ethical obligations. The lawyer must determine what these obligations entail, and must decide whether or not to abide by these ethical limitations in specific situations. To make matters worse, the lawyer's ethical obligations often conflict with one another. The lawyer owes allegiance to his or her clients, to the courts, to the state, to the public, and to other members of the legal profession.[23] The duties owed to these competing groups are often incompatible. Consider the following examples.

Example 3.4

Pamela Brown is a lawyer representing a defendant on a litigation file. Working late one night, she receives a fax from the plaintiff's counsel that sets out the minimum dollar amount for which the plaintiff is willing to settle. Unfortunately, the fax was not meant for Pamela. Plaintiff's counsel had intended to send it to his articling student, but sent it to Pamela by mistake. Should Pamela pass this information to her client, to whom she owes a duty of loyalty, or should she refrain from taking advantage of

---

20   Wasserstrom, supra note 18.

21   The specific constraints imposed by codes of ethics are discussed in chapters 6, 7, 8, and 9. Several actual codes of ethics are found in the appendixes to this book.

22   See, for example, chapters IV, XIV and XV of the Canadian Bar Association's *Code of Professional Conduct* (reproduced in appendix A).

23   For a thorough discussion of these competing duties, see Beverly G. Smith, *Professional Conduct for Lawyers and Judges*, 2d ed. (Fredericton, NB: Maritime Law Book, 2002), 1:16-26.

procedural errors made by her opponent, to whom she owes a duty of professional courtesy?

Example 3.5

Kelly McEvoy is a criminal defence lawyer representing Justin Potter, who is guilty of the crime with which he is charged. While Kelly examines Justin on the witness stand, Justin proudly asserts that he has no criminal record. Kelly knows this to be false, and was not aware that Justin intended to make this claim in court. The prosecutor fails to detect Justin's lie, and alludes to Justin's lack of a criminal record in subsequent statements before the court. Should Kelly correct this "error" in her capacity as an officer of the court, or should she allow the court to proceed on the basis of Justin's perjured statement?

Example 3.6

Monty Foote has been retained by Mildred Pearson, a vicious criminal who has been charged with the abduction of two young children. Mildred has told Monty, in confidence, that she *did* abduct the children and has hidden them where they are unlikely to be found. The children are still alive, but may die if Monty or his client fails to reveal their current location. If found, the children will be able to identify Mildred as their captor. Should Monty fulfill his duty to the public by safeguarding the lives of children, or should he fulfill his duty to his client by safeguarding information that reveals his client's guilt? Alternatively, should Monty assist his client in using knowledge of the children's whereabouts as a "bargaining chip" in plea negotiations?

In each of these scenarios, the lawyer bears the burden of conflicting obligations. The resolution of conflicts between these competing duties, together with the lawyer's decision to adhere to or depart from the limitations found in laws and codes of ethics, requires the lawyer to make perplexing moral choices. The lawyer's resolution of these conflicts may lead to sanctions including fines, suspension from practice, disbarment, and even criminal prosecution. Far from being "less complicated" than the moral world of ordinary life,[24] the moral world of lawyers is a quagmire of conflicting obligations, requiring the lawyer to navigate a sea of inconsistent duties that delineate the lawyer's moral universe. In the light of the conflicting moral constraints imposed on lawyers, it is difficult to contend that lawyers live in a moral universe that is less ambiguous than the moral world of other individuals.

Perhaps the greatest flaw in the traditional account of legal ethics is its claim that lawyers may disregard the moral value of actions taken on a client's behalf. As we observed in section II.C, above, this claim is rooted in the notion that the lawyer's *raison d'être* is to remedy the complexity of the law. Proponents of this model contend that the

---

24   Wasserstrom, supra note 18.

lawyer's only role is to eradicate the barrier that is created by the complexity of the law, allowing clients to avail themselves of whatever benefits the law provides—benefits that would otherwise be obscured by the confusing nature of the legal system. In other words, the lawyer is a morally neutral conduit through which clients gain access to pre-existing legal rights. When fulfilling this neutral-conduit function, the lawyer has no business policing the moral value of the client's ultimate aims: the lawyer must simply fulfill the neutral-conduit function, allowing the client to proceed in whatever manner the law permits. As a result, the lawyer is relieved of the need to consider moral issues in pursuit of a client's interests. Instead, the lawyer simply takes whatever actions the law allows in pursuit of a client's goals, casting moral responsibility on the client and on the system that is responsible for creating the lawyer's role.

Does the neutral-conduit model truly relieve lawyers of the need to make ethical choices? Certainly not. Indeed, a lawyer's decision to rely upon the neutral-conduit model is *itself* an ethical choice. Consider a simple illustration.

Example 3.7

Emma is a lawyer defending Joe White, a serial rapist. Emma knows that Joe is factually guilty of the crimes with which he is charged. In order to secure Joe's acquittal, Emma launches an attack on the credibility of Riley McKenzie, a witness Emma knows to be telling the truth. By impeaching Riley's credibility, Emma undermines Riley's reputation in the community and secures Joe's acquittal on all charges.

According to the neutral-conduit model, Emma faces no ethical choices in example 3.7. Instead, she merely facilitates her client's ability to take an action that is permitted by the law. If Joe represented himself, he would be permitted to attack Riley's credibility. This option might escape Joe's attention, however, due to the barrier of complexity that obscures Joe's legal rights. By assisting Joe in taking a legal action that would be open to him if he acted for himself, Emma is simply helping her client avail himself of legal options.

The foregoing analysis, which is based upon the neutral-conduit model of legal ethics, is faulty. By undermining Riley's credibility and securing Joe's acquittal in reliance on her neutral-conduit role, *Emma is making an ethical choice*. She is deciding that the right of a factually guilty client to a vigorous defence (or, more generally, the right of *all* defendants to adequate representation) outweighs any harm that innocent witnesses (and the client's future victims) will suffer as a result of Emma's pursuit of the client's goals. The lawyer does not simply rely on the justificatory framework that is provided by the neutral-conduit model—the lawyer *decides* to rely on that framework. In our example, Emma has decided that her commitment to her neutral-conduit function carries more ethical value than her ideological disapproval of the harm that might be done in pursuit of the client's acquittal. This may or may not be a morally sound decision, but it certainly *is* a choice. Rather than relieving lawyers of the burden of moral choices, the neutral-conduit model complicates lawyers' choices by creating another factor to be considered: the importance of the neutral-conduit role. The "moral value" that this role carries, and the question of whether or not that moral value outweighs the harms that might be caused by actions taken in fulfillment of that role, are unavoidable ethical issues that the lawyer must confront. How the lawyer answers such questions is the lawyer's responsibility alone. Blame cannot be placed on the legal system or the client, nor can it be eradicated by a justificatory framework. As a result, the justificatory power of the neutral-conduit model is more illusory than real, leaving the lawyer faced with troubling moral dilemmas that he or she must resolve using his or her own moral sensibilities. In short, lawyers *do* face ethical challenges, regardless of the ethically sterile landscape that is depicted by the traditional view of the lawyer's moral universe.

Whether choosing to pursue a neutral-conduit role or deciphering the conflicting duties imposed by codes of ethics, lawyers are frequently faced with difficult ethical choices. As we saw in chapters 1 and 2, ethical choices can be measured through the use of economics. The same is true of the ethical choices lawyers face. When considering whether to accept a particular client, pursue a particular claim, or even violate a binding code of ethics, lawyers make decisions that can be described, predicted, and evaluated through the use of basic economic tools. The manner in which economics can cast light on lawyers' ethical choices is developed in the remainder of this chapter.

IV. Lawyers' Decisions

There is no magic to the manner in which the economic theory of ethical systems applies to moral decisions made by lawyers. Like any decision, a lawyer's decision to undertake or avoid a particular act can be explained in terms of self-interest and utility maximization. Once the lawyer's decisions have been expressed in basic economic terms, they can be evaluated with economic tools. The purpose of the remainder of this chapter is to apply economic theory to the difficult moral choices faced by lawyers.

For the purposes of this chapter, lawyers' ethical decisions will be divided into two distinct categories—namely: (1) the decision to adhere to (or depart from) the ethical strictures found in oaths and codes of ethics that apply to legal professionals, and (2) the decision to undertake morally dubious (yet legally permissible) acts in pursuit of a client's interests. As we shall see, economic theory is capable of evaluating both types of decision, and effectively reduces each type of choice to a self-interested exercise of utility maximization. The manner in which the economic theory achieves this goal is developed throughout the remainder of the chapter.

V. Oaths and Codes of Ethics

A. Introduction

Upon admission to the Bar, lawyers are called upon to swear a series of oaths that represent the traditional ethical standards of legal professionals. In Ontario, for example, lawyers take the following oaths[25] upon admission to the Bar:

25　The text of these oaths is taken from bylaw 11 of the bylaws of the Law Society of Upper Canada. The Law Society's authority to enact a bylaw prescribing oaths for Ontario lawyers is derived from s. 62(0.1)26 of the *Law Society Act*, RSO 1990, c. L.8. See appendix B to this book.

1. Barristers Oath

You are called to the Degree of Barrister-at-law to protect and defend the rights and interests of such citizens as may employ you. You shall conduct all cases faithfully and to the best of your ability. You shall neglect no one's interest nor seek to destroy any one's property. You shall not be guilty of champerty or maintenance. You shall not refuse causes of complaint reasonably founded, nor shall you promote suits upon frivolous pretences. You shall not pervert the law to favour or prejudice any one, but in all things shall conduct yourself truly and with integrity. In fine, the Queen's interest and the interest of citizens you shall uphold and maintain according to the constitution and law of this Province. All this you do swear to observe and perform to the best of your knowledge and ability. So help you God.

2. Solicitors Oath

You also do sincerely promise and swear that you will truly and honestly conduct yourself in the practice of a solicitor according to the best of your knowledge and ability. So help you God.

3. Oath of Allegiance

You do swear that you will be faithful and bear true allegiance to Her Majesty Queen Elizabeth the Second (or the reigning sovereign for the time being), Her heirs and successors according to law. So help you God.[26]

Similar oaths are required in other jurisdictions. In addition to these oaths, lawyers are required to submit to rules of professional conduct[27] promulgated by the professional body responsible for the regulation of lawyers.[28] As Wilkinson notes: "These codes are the formal statement of the ethical standards of the profession," setting out the moral standards that are expected of practising lawyers in the relevant jurisdiction.[29] Rule 1.03(1)(a) of Ontario's *Rules of Professional Conduct* is typical of the ethical standards established by professional codes of conduct. That rule provides as follows:

[A] lawyer has a duty to carry on the practice of law and discharge all responsibilities to clients, tribunals, the public, and other members of the profession honourably and with integrity.

More specific rules that are found in codes of conduct, such as rules relating to confidentiality, conflicts of interest, professional courtesy, and other professional norms, often

---

26   Section 6(6) of bylaw 11 provides that "[i]mmediately after the court has caused the person to be admitted and his or her name to be enrolled as a solicitor on the rolls of the Society under subsection (5), the presiding judge shall administer in either the English or French language the Barristers Oath, the Solicitors Oath and, if the person so wishes, the Oath of Allegiance." In other words, the Barristers Oath and the Solicitors Oath are mandatory for all lawyers in Ontario, while the Oath of Allegiance to the Queen is voluntary.

27   Ontario's *Rules of Professional Conduct* are available online at http://www.lsuc.on.ca/. Rules proposed by the Canadian Bar Association are set out in appendix A to this book.

28   Legal authority for the creation of a binding code of professional conduct is found in ss. 62.01(4) and (10) of the *Law Society Act*, supra note 25. The authority to mete out penalties for breach of those rules is found in s. 35.

29   Wilkinson, Walker, and Mercer, supra note 3, at 647.

amount to little more than elaborations of the general "integrity rule" encapsulated by general precepts such as rule 1.03(1)(a). By becoming a member of the Bar (and thereby submitting to the authority of the regulatory body governing lawyers in the relevant jurisdiction), lawyers agree to be bound by several ethical precepts of this nature, submitting to whatever penalties flow from violations of the relevant ethical norms.[30]

B. An Economic Perspective

What does it mean when a lawyer swears an oath or agrees to abide by a binding code of ethics? As we saw in chapter 1,[31] an economic view of promise keeping makes it clear that a promise can be regarded as an agreement to either (1) abide by the terms of the promise, or (2) submit to whatever costs might be associated with a failure to keep the promise. When a businessperson agrees to be bound by a contract, for example, he or she agrees to either abide by the contract's terms *or* pay expectation damages. When a suitor pledges fidelity to the object of his or her affections, he or she has agreed to remain faithful *or* to face the repercussions of philandering. When a Benedictine monk agrees to be bound by a vow of silence, he agrees to hold his tongue or face ejection from the Order. The same model applies to a lawyer's submission to oaths and codes of professional conduct. By swearing an oath and agreeing to uphold a code of conduct, the lawyer agrees to either (1) abide by the terms of the oath and the code of conduct, or (2) face whatever costs or penalties might flow from a breach of the relevant ethical norms. As we shall see, the costs and penalties that are associated with breaches of lawyers' oaths and codes of conduct range from rather trivial costs (such as a formal reprimand) to substantial financial penalties and (in the most egregious cases) loss of the right to practise law.

Chapters 1 and 2 demonstrated that every decision a person makes is guided by the notions of self-interest and utility maximization. These notions apply with equal force to lawyers' decisions regarding professional oaths and codes of conduct. Consider the following example.

Example 3.8

Kenneth Lalonde is a lawyer in Ontario. As such, he has agreed to abide by the Barristers Oath, the Solicitor's Oath, the Oath of Allegiance to the Queen, and the Code of Professional Conduct promulgated by the Law Society of Upper Canada.

Kenneth has been approached by Rita Letcher, a particularly litigious Ontario resident. Rita has asked Kenneth to write a letter on her behalf to Mighty Burger Incorporated, alleging that Rita suffered a serious case of food poisoning after ingesting food at Mighty Burger's restaurant. Rita has made it clear to Kenneth that her "serious case of food poisoning" was nothing more than a mild case of indigestion and that the purpose of the

---

30   In Ontario, the Law Society's disciplinary authority is spelled out in rule 6.11 of the *Rules of Professional Conduct*, supra note 27.

31   See chapter 1, section I.B.

letter is simply to scare an undeserved settlement out of the company,
based on the threat of litigation and bad publicity. In the light of recent
incidents involving tainted beef, Rita believes that a solicitor's letter written
on her behalf will secure a settlement of $3,000. She agrees to pay
Kenneth half of that amount. Kenneth believes that if he writes the letter
on Rita's behalf, Mighty Burger will, in fact, pay the sum of $3,000 in order
to avoid court costs and bad publicity.

Assume that Kenneth realizes that by writing the letter on Rita's behalf and pursuing an
undeserved claim for damages, he would be breaching the Barrister's Oath and violating
several rules of professional conduct.[32] Further assume that Kenneth believes that the
Law Society regards breaches of this nature as relatively insignificant (the Law Society
has bigger fish to fry), and that the penalty for this breach would amount to only $1,000.
For the sake of simplicity, assume that Kenneth knows, with absolute certainty, that his
conduct will be detected and prosecuted by Law Society officials, and that the penalty of
exactly $1,000 will be enforced.[33]

Kenneth's decision to accept or reject Rita's offer can be described in economic terms.
As noted above, Kenneth has sworn to abide by a series of oaths and submitted to the
rules of professional conduct. From an economic perspective, this means that Kenneth has
promised to either (1) abide by the terms of the oaths and the code of conduct, or (2) pay
whatever penalties might flow from violations. Kenneth will decide whether to choose
(1) or (2) based on his subjective determination of which choice will do the most to further
his interests. In other words, Kenneth will make his choice based on utility maximization.

Will Kenneth's utility be maximized by accepting Rita's offer or by adhering to the
Barristers Oath and the rules of professional conduct? Surely, Kenneth derives *some*
utility from adherence to professional norms (such as those encapsulated by the Barristers Oath and the rules of professional conduct). It is (to some degree) in Kenneth's
interests to adhere to the rules and oaths because a failure to do so generates several
costs. In this example, the most obvious cost of failing to adhere to the ethical norms of
the legal profession is the $1,000 penalty that is enforced by the Law Society. Additional
costs might include (1) Kenneth's subjective feelings of guilt, and (2) diminished future
income as a result of a tarnished professional reputation. Assume (for present purposes)
that Kenneth places a value of $2,000 on the guilt that he will feel if he accepts Rita's
offer, and a present value of $6,000 on all relevant reputational costs. Further assume that
these are all of the costs that flow from Kenneth's decision. As a result, the "gross utility
cost" (expressed in dollar values) of a decision to take part in Rita's scheme equals the
sum of the $1,000 penalty, the $2,000 cost of guilt, and the $6,000 value Kenneth places
on reputational costs. The total cost of Rita's scheme (to Kenneth) is $9,000.

---

32   See, for example, chapters I, III, and IX of the Canadian Bar Association's *Code of Professional Conduct*
     (reproduced in appendix A).

33   Obviously, the assumptions regarding the penalty and the certainty of enforcement are unrealistic. These
     assumptions will be removed in subsequent sections of this chapter and chapter 4. For now, however, the
     unrealistic nature of these assumptions has no bearing on our analysis of Kenneth's decision-making process.

While it might seem crass to say so, a decision to violate ethical norms is not without its benefits. In example 3.8, Kenneth stands to gain a financial benefit if he accepts Rita's offer. As noted above, Kenneth will gain $1,500 by participating in Rita's unethical scheme.[34] Assume that Kenneth believes that, by helping Rita in this particular scheme, he will make Rita happy and encourage her to involve him in future lucrative endeavours. Kenneth subjectively values this "future business" at $3,000. As a result, the "gross utility benefit" of a decision to violate the applicable ethical norms equals the sum of the immediate financial gain ($1,500) plus the value Kenneth places on future business opportunities that will arise if he participates in this breach ($3,000). The sum of the benefits of this ethical violation is accordingly equal to $4,500.

In chapter 2, we saw that an ethical decision can be reduced to the following algebraic expression: $A - B = X$. In this equation, A is the sum of the benefits to be derived from a course of action (the gross utility gains generated by the act), and B is the sum of all of the costs (or utility losses) the act will generate. X is the figure yielded by subtracting B from A and represents the net utility generated by the proposed action. In example 3.8, figure A equals $4,500 and figure B equals $9,000. Subtracting B from A, we are left with an X that is equal to -$4,500 (a negative figure). As we saw in chapter 2, a "negative X" means that the proposed activity leads to a net utility loss: the costs of the action exceed its benefits. Since Kenneth (like all people) is a utility maximizer, he will attempt to abstain from actions that give rise to utility losses. As a result, our utility-maximizing model (rooted in Kenneth's self-interest) makes it clear that, given the values Kenneth associates with the various costs and benefits flowing from Rita's proposed scheme, Kenneth will refrain from taking the action. The action results in a net loss of utility, so Kenneth will decline Rita's proposal and abide by the terms of his oaths and the rules of professional conduct. This will maximize Kenneth's utility, disappoint Ms. Letcher, and make the Law Society of Upper Canada rather happy.

C. Economic Reasoning and Morality

From one perspective, the decision-making process that was described in the previous section does not appear to be an especially "moral" form of reasoning. One might prefer to believe, for example, that lawyers abide by ethical norms out of a sense of honour or integrity, rather than through the use of subconscious calculations designed to further their self-interest. As we saw in chapters 1 and 2, however, the use of cost–benefit calculations and utility maximization says nothing about the morality of the decision maker in question. Whether a person is diabolical or saintly, he or she will make decisions in a way that coincides with economic theory. The decision maker will subconsciously assign subjective, relative values to the consequences of contemplated actions and select a course of action that gives rise to the most utility. The difference between the moral hero and the villain lies not in the mental process that the decision maker follows, but in the values our decision maker places on competing possibilities. While a highly

---

34   For the sake of simplicity, assume that Kenneth would not have to forgo any financial opportunities in order to participate in Rita's unethical scheme.

moral person might regard another's suffering as an extraordinarily high cost to be weighed when making moral decisions, an amoral person might regard another's suffering as an inconsequential factor. A villain might regard another's suffering as a *benefit* of a potential course of action. The subconscious process of adding and subtracting costs and benefits does not determine a person's "moral nature." Our assessment of the decision maker's morality comes not from the mental process that the decision maker pursues, but from the various values that the decision maker attributes to the consequences that flow from his or her actions. Whether a person is wholly evil, morally pure or (like most of us) a shifting shade of grey, the person's moral decisions will be based on a subconscious cost–benefit calculation. As a result, those decisions can be expressed and evaluated through the use of basic economic tools.

Previous sections of this chapter have suggested that lawyers (like all individuals) make decisions by subconsciously weighing the costs and benefits of the lawyers' competing choices. This decision-making model applies with equal force to the ethical decisions that lawyers make.

The decision of Convocation in *Law Society of Upper Canada v. Clark* provides an excellent example of one lawyer's (somewhat surprising) decision-making process. In this case, the accused lawyer, Bruce Clark, engaged in an unusual pattern of behaviour in pursuit of an undeniably just cause: the protection of the rights of Canada's aboriginal peoples. In pursuit of that objective, Clark (1) accused prominent jurists of complicity in the murder of aboriginal peoples, (2) asserted that many Canadian judges repeatedly committed fraud and treason, (3) attempted to make a citizen's arrest of the entire BC Court of Appeal, and (4) committed a technical assault and the tort of trespass. When reviewing the decisions of the disciplinary committee and Convocation, attempt to construct a schedule of costs and benefits that went into Clark's ethical decisions and describe those decisions through the use of the basic "ethical equation" developed above. Note that, while Clark's conduct was undeniably unusual, his behaviour can nonetheless be explained by reference to the economic notions of self-interest and utility maximization.

Law Society of Upper Canada v. Clark
[1995] LSDD no. 199

CONVOCATION: … Mr. Clark has devoted his career to the advancement of the cause of native rights in Canada. He has studied the subject at the graduate school level, and has obtained a Master of Arts degree in History and a PhD degree in Jurisprudence as a result of his studies in the field of native rights.

For a period of seven years, Mr. Clark lived on a native reserve. He is the author of two academic texts on the subject of the rights of indigenous people in Canada.

All of the particulars in the complaint relate to Mr. Clark's relentless attempts to advance a single legal argument … on his native clients' behalf.

Although space does not permit a complete summary of Mr. Clark's argument, it is based upon the proposition that certain native lands (or "hunting grounds") have never been properly surrendered to the Crown. It follows, he contends, that Canadian courts have no jurisdiction over indigenous people who reside on the unsurrendered lands. Mr. Clark argues that statutes of Canada and the provinces do not apply to indigenous people who live on the unsurrendered lands, and that the affected indigenous people have a right of access to an independent and impartial third party court—as distinguished from non-native Canadian domestic courts—to adjudicate the law.

Mr. Clark goes on to contend that the extraterritorial assumption by the non-native Canadian domestic courts, of jurisdiction over indigenous people living on hunting grounds prima facie constitutes "misprision of treason" and "misprision of fraud" within the meaning of paragraph 6, Part IV of the Royal Proclamation of 1763, which has never been repealed. He adds that the use of the legal term of art "misprision" in the order-in-council relieves his clients of the need to prove intent.

Finally, Mr. Clark argues, by usurping jurisdiction over indigenous people living on unsurrendered hunting grounds, the Canadian government, the legal establishment and the domestic courts are contributing to and are complicit in the genocide of indigenous people. ...

The Findings of the Discipline Hearing Panel

The following allegations of professional misconduct were found established by the discipline hearing panel:

A. While appearing before a justice of the British Columbia Court of Appeal, the solicitor made intemperate statements about the Court which were unsupported by the facts.

B. In the course of his professional practice, the solicitor wrote letters to the following parties which were abusive, offensive and otherwise inconsistent with the proper tone of a professional communication. ...

C. In the course of representing clients in various criminal proceedings, he asserted legal positions for which there was no reasonable basis in evidence, the particulars of which are as follows:

1. He prepared and delivered documentation from a bogus court which purported to influence proceedings relating to outstanding criminal charges against his client, Stephen Snake.

2. He prepared and delivered documentation from a bogus court which purported to convict Judge Fournier ... of various crimes.

3. In submissions made to the court during criminal proceedings brought against Pascal, et al. and Sauls, et al., he accused the British Columbia judiciary and the Crown of conspiracy in crimes of genocide against aboriginal people.

4. While appearing before a panel of the British Columbia Court of Appeal, he attempted to perform a citizen's arrest on the charges of treason and complicity to genocide. ...

In the course of litigation involving the Bear Island Foundation, he made intemperate and unjustified statements about various parties, the particulars of which are as follows:

(i.) In an affidavit which he swore, dated February 2, 1993, he alleged that:

   a. The Attorney General of Ontario was a party to a fraud with respect to concealing relevant evidence from appellate courts, and alleged that the Attorney General of Canada was probably also a party to this fraud;
   b. Chief Gary Potts fraudulently, treasonably and genocidally induced the Supreme Court of Canada to render a decision pursuant to a treaty that is demonstrably void; and
   c. The leaders of the Aboriginal entities who caused a Notice of Change of Solicitors to be delivered by Blake, Cassels and Graydon on February 24, 1993, did so in an attempt to further their fraud, treason and complicity in genocide.

(ii.) In an affidavit which he swore, dated March 15, 1993, he:

   a. implicitly suggested that a decision made by the Honourable Mr. Justice Bolan of Ontario earlier in said litigation might constitute complicity in the crimes of fraud, treason and genocide;
   b. alleged that The Honourable Mr. Justice Bolan wilfully blinded himself to precedents, statutes and facts; and
   c. further alleged that The Honourable Mr. Justice Bolan's refusal to address the precedents, statutes and facts … proved his own criminal liability.

(iii.) In an affidavit which he swore, dated April 20, 1993, he:

   a. alleged that the Attorney General of Canada and the provinces and the judges of the courts of Canada wish to evade the questions as to whether Aboriginal courts have jurisdiction over land;
   b. accused the Attorney General of Ontario of abuse of process and of invoking a criminally illegitimate aspect of non-native court jurisdiction;
   c. alleged that the Attorney General had resorted to chicanery and is guilty of complicity in fraud, treason and genocide and of aiding and abetting the continuation of crimes;
   d. accused The Honourable Mr. Justice Huneault of escaping with his genocidal usurped jurisdiction intact in dealing with a previous motion in the litigation;
   e. alleged that the Attorney General had fraudulently breached an agreement with counsel for the Aboriginal entities;
   f. accused Chief Potts and Rita O'Sullivan (the solicitor's former clients) of participating in a system of patronage and bribery;
   g. accused the Attorney General of Ontario and Canada, as well as unspecified judges, of being guilty of fraud, treason and genocide;
   h. accused The Honourable Mr. Justice Steele of Ontario and the Honourable Chief Justice McEachern of British Columbia of racist attitudes which are fraudulent and treasonable and amount to genocide;
   i. accused the Attorney General of sharp practice and chicanery and of being engaged in a criminal conspiracy on a national scale to pre-empt the law in furtherance of the crimes of fraud, treason and genocide;

   j. accused the Attorney General of cunning chicanery;

   k. accused the Attorney General of sharp practice and chicanery and accused the Canadian domestic courts of racism;

   l. accused the Attorney General of concealing relevant evidence from appeal courts; and

   m. accused The Honourable Mr. Justice Loukidelis of Ontario of judicial complicity in the Attorney General's chicanery.

 (iv.) He made allegations similar to ... above, while making oral arguments before The Honourable Mr. Justice Hineault on March 19, 1993.

  5. When appearing before The Honourable Mr. Justice Roberts of Ontario on June 1, 1993, he:

   B) refused a direct order from The Honourable Mr. Justice Roberts to cease argument on this point and to sit down;

   C) accused The Honourable Mr. Justice Roberts of perpetuating fraud, treason and genocide;

   D) accused The Honourable Mr. Justice Roberts of wilful blindness;

   E) stated that he intended to lay an information against Mr. Justice Roberts forthwith;

   F) alleged that The Honourable Mr. Justice Roberts was afraid to charge the solicitor with contempt; and

   G) stated that he was going to attempt to lay an information against The Honourable Mr. Justice Roberts for complicity in fraud, treason and genocide.

(f) In the course of the said litigation, he caused to be prepared, served and filed affidavits sworn on February 22, 1993; March 15, 1993; and April 20, 1993, in which he was the deponent, notwithstanding the fact that he was also counsel of record for the parties in whose support the affidavits were filed. ...

(h) By engaging in the course of conduct referred to above, he demonstrated his unwillingness to be governed by the Law Society or its Rules and Regulations.

(i) On or about June 6, 1993 in Haileybury, Ontario, the solicitor unlawfully assaulted a member of the Ontario Provincial Police.

(j) On or about June 6, 1993, the solicitor unlawfully trespassed upon certain property in Haileybury, Ontario, in an unjustified and illegal attempt to carry out a citizen's arrest of one James Morrison. ...

The discipline hearing panel found all of the 21 allegations quoted above to have been established. It found a twenty-second allegation, in which it was alleged that Mr. Clark had counselled a subpoenaed Crown witness to refuse to give evidence and to absent herself from the proceedings, not to have been established.

In recommending that Mr. Clark's right to practise law be terminated, the discipline hearing panel explained that it made its recommendation "very reluctantly," and "primarily because of the finding that the solicitor is ungovernable." It added that while some or most of the allegations would not in themselves justify the ultimate penalty of disbarment, the cumulative effect of them, coupled with the finding of ungovernability, left the panel with little choice.

Convocations's Disposition

… Convocation agrees with the discipline hearing panel that Mr. Clark is guilty of professional misconduct, but it does not agree that each of the allegations found established by the panel constitute professional misconduct in the unique circumstances of this case.

Specifically, Convocation does not agree that the allegations relating to what may be described as Mr. Clark's forensic excesses should be considered professional misconduct. Nor does Convocation consider the panel's finding that Mr. Clark is ungovernable by the Law Society to be sustainable.

Finally, in light of its variation of the discipline hearing panel's findings on misconduct—and particularly in light of its rejection of the panel's finding of ungovernability—Convocation has concluded that the termination of Mr. Clark's right to practise is not warranted on the evidence. Convocation accordingly orders that Mr. Clark be reprimanded in Convocation. …

We approach the merits of these complaints by placing great importance on the context in which these arguments are made … . As mentioned above, the discipline hearing panel acknowledged that Mr. Clark's argument (as summarized above) is at the root of the complaint of professional misconduct that the discipline hearing panel and Convocation have been called upon to adjudicate.

Mr. Clark's argument is anything but frivolous. It is the product of intensive study, and reflects a belief that Mr. Clark sincerely holds.

It would be difficult to disagree with Mr. Clark's assertion that the issue that his argument raises is "constitutionally critical." Again, the discipline hearing panel found that Mr. Clark honestly believes that the comments and conduct particularized in the complaint—which are an outgrowth of his argument—were intended to advance the cause of justice and the rule of law.

The "genocide" of which Mr. Clark speaks is real, and has very nearly succeeded in destroying the Native Canadian community that flourished here when European settlers arrived. No one who has seen many of our modern First Nation communities can remain untouched by this reality.

Mr. Clark is not making the kind of arguments that fall to most of us daily in our courts; much of the ordinary work of lawyers relates to the interpretation of a will, the proper understanding of a contract, the ownership of a piece of land, or individual culpability for crime. The issue Mr. Clark raises is one of great significance for an entire people—and for all of us. His commitment to the argument and his conviction respecting its correctness cannot be questioned.

Had this activity been engendered in a context less fraught with significance and emotion, we would take a very different view of Mr. Clark's conduct.

The nature of Mr. Clark's argument is such that the persistent refusal of the Courts—he states, without contradiction, that he has attempted to raise this argument some forty or forty-one times—itself in part engenders his fixed and firm conclusion that his argument is correct. The issue has not been determined by any Court.

It is clear to us that the solicitor has been captured by this argument.

This is an important case because the Solicitor questions the integrity of our system of justice. At the same time, it raises the question of the limits of advocacy.

There can be no question about the right and responsibility of the Law Society of Upper Canada to discipline its members respecting their conduct in court as advocates: *R v. Kopyto* (1987), 39 CCC (3d) 1 (Ont. CA). But advocacy in court is a crucial aspect of freedom of expression guaranteed by the Constitution. In *Edmonton Journal v. Alberta (Attorney General)*, [1989] 2 SCR 1326 at 1336-7, Cory J said:

> It is difficult to imagine a guaranteed right more important to a democratic society than freedom of expression. Indeed a democracy cannot exist without that freedom to express new ideas and to put forward opinions about the functioning of public institutions. The concept of free and uninhibited speech permeates all truly democratic societies and institutions. The vital importance of the concept cannot be over-emphasized. ...

One may well question the effectiveness of Mr. Clark's advocacy. His use of such words as "fraud," "treason," and "genocide" is designed to shock as well as explain, but does not justify the unwillingness of many courts to hear his submissions.

The Law Society should be loath, in professional discipline proceedings, to become the arbiter of lawyers' advocacy techniques. Styles of advocacy vary greatly, and the effectiveness of any particular style is not a matter for Convocation to pronounce on in the context of an allegation of professional misconduct.

It is true that rule 10, and commentary 7 thereto, requires lawyers to treat courts and tribunals with courtesy and respect. There is no necessary conflict between this professional obligation and lawyers' duties to represent their clients "resolutely" (rule 10), "to raise fearlessly every issue, advance every argument, and ask every question, however distasteful, which the lawyer thinks will help the client's case and to endeavour to obtain for the client the benefit of every remedy and defense authorized by law" (rule 10, commentary 2), and "to protect the client as far as possible from being convicted except by a tribunal of competent jurisdiction and upon legal evidence sufficient to support a conviction for the offence with which the client is charged" (rule 10, commentary 10).

The Law Society must always be acutely sensitive to the danger that its disciplinary process may be used to punish vigorous advocacy. The Law Society should act aggressively to protect counsel from attempts to inhibit zealous advocacy on behalf of clients. This duty flows from the Society's responsibility—confirmed in the role statement approved by Convocation—to protect the independence of the bar.

It is important to our decision that the use of what would in most other circumstances rightly be regarded as extravagant, disrespectful and discourteous language, in Mr. Clark's case emanated directly from the legal argument that he was vigorously advancing on behalf of his clients. In attempting to resolve the tension between vigorous advocacy in the face of judicial resistance and the duty to treat the tribunal with courtesy and respect, much will depend on the context.

We are sympathetic, moreover, to Mr. Clark's assertion that the courts have been unwilling to listen to his argument. Though he must accept part of the responsibility for this, it is apparent on the record that he has been prevented by the courts on a number of the occasions in issue from effectively presenting the argument summarized above. Our finding may well have been different if Mr. Clark, having been given a full opportunity to develop his argument, had persisted in attempting to argue a point after the court had ruled against him. Again, the Law Society must promote, rather than inhibit, the right and duty of advocates to protect their clients' interests without unwarranted interference.

The lawyer's duty to resolutely advance every argument the lawyer thinks will help the client's case is of fundamental importance to the proper functioning of our judicial system. Failures to carry out that duty are more prevalent within the system of justice and more harmful to that system than are overzealousness and failures to treat the courts with courtesy and respect. Where the duties do come into conflict, Convocation should be reluctant to find that overzealousness constitutes professional misconduct.

This is not a case involving the distortion or falsification of testimony or the destruction or suppression of documents. (There was, as mentioned above, an allegation that Mr. Clark had advised a subpoenaed witness to absent herself from the proceedings, but that allegation was found by the discipline hearing panel not to have been established on the evidence.) Nor was the court misled in any way by Mr. Clark's argument. No miscarriage of justice was caused. The gravamen of the allegations consists in rudeness, lack of courtesy, and refusal to obey a direct order from a judge.

The Law Society's discipline process is not the only means available for controlling forensic excess. The courts are empowered to physically control the courtroom by ordering removal of any counsel acting improperly and (at least in certain types of proceedings) to order them to pay costs. The ability to call a short adjournment is usually the only measure required. In extreme cases, where all other techniques have been exhausted, a judge may cite a lawyer for contempt. Judges presiding in court are well-positioned to assess the seriousness of excesses in advocacy and to determine whether curative measures are required. Such measures were taken in the incident referred to in paragraph (c)(iv) of the complaint, in respect of which Convocation agrees with the finding of the discipline hearing panel (see below).

The fact that the courts considered it unnecessary to take similar measures in relation to the other particulars in the complaint is a factor that Convocation considered in deciding not to uphold the findings of professional misconduct on those particulars. It does not follow that the Law Society will necessarily exercise its jurisdiction in all cases in which the courts have adopted remedial measures. We also note that the advocacy in question here took place in the context of a serious argument on an issue of public importance. The Law Society's concurrent jurisdiction to discipline lawyers for excesses in advocacy should be reserved for particularly serious and harmful violations.

It is necessary, in the light of the values expressed above, to examine the charges brought against Mr. Clark that deal with the question of improper advocacy.

We do not find his letters abusive or offensive. Nor do we find his statements intemperate nor unsupported by the facts in their context. Indeed, throughout he has begged to be allowed to develop facts to sustain the argument. It is impossible to say there was no reasonable basis in evidence for the legal positions he asserted; he has always been prepared to make a thoughtful and comprehensive argument in each case. There is an entire absence of evidence that the documentation he delivered from a Native tribunal came from a "bogus court"; native tribunals are commonplace throughout Canada and there was simply no evidence about the composition or authority of this one. Though that documentation was intended to influence proceedings in relation to outstanding criminal charges, it was part of a legitimate argument relating to the jurisdiction of the Court before which Mr. Clark was appearing. Indeed, each of the statements alleged to be intemperate and unjustified flow logically and properly from the submissions he was making respecting jurisdiction.

The matter concerning the solicitor's appearance before Mr. Justice Roberts needs to be viewed in context. ...

Beyond doubt, when a direct order to sit down is given by a Judge, counsel must obey it. But in deciding whether the refusal to obey is professional misconduct, the circumstances as a whole must be examined. In this case it is clear that the motion to ask the Honourable Mr. Justice Roberts to disqualify himself for a reasonable apprehension of bias was dismissed before counsel was given any opportunity to articulate the grounds of the challenge; those presumably would be focused upon the role of former Attorney General Kelso Roberts in relation to the issues raised by the jurisdiction argument. In this circumstance, we do not find that the conduct of a solicitor amounted to professional misconduct.

The filing of these affidavits of which the solicitor was a deponent taking into account their content does not, in these circumstances, amount to professional misconduct. The Court was capable of controlling its own record and dealing with that matter directly if it wished.

Three matters remain to be considered.

The first is the attempt to perform a citizen's arrest upon four judges of the British Columbia Court of Appeal (paragraph (c)(iv) of the complaint). ...

It can be seen that this interruption, while serious, unprecedented and indeed hard to comprehend as a rational approach to the issue, caused only a minor disruption of the proceedings.

Second and third, there remains an assault upon a member of the Ontario Provincial Police and a trespass upon the property of James Morrison in an attempt to carry out a citizen's arrest of him. Mr. Clark had become convinced that James Morrison, who was an Indian archivist, had obtained and was concealing a document which would be of crucial significance to the establishment of his argument in a pending case. He resolved to arrest Mr. Morrison and seize the document to safeguard and preserve it for use in Court. Mr. Morrison then called the police who performed their duty and safeguarded him and his property. The evidence indicates that Mr. Clark was told that he could not arrest Mr. Morrison and could not trespass upon his front lawn by an officer of the Ontario Provincial Police. In a polite and non-violent manner he stepped onto the property and when the officer moved to arrest him he moved that officer's hand aside. The assault was technical and the trespass, though momentary, should not have taken place. In the end, no harm was done.

None of these three matters reflect any advocacy whatsoever. There are no issues of freedom of expression at issue unless there is a right to address the court in relation to someone else's cause. We are dealing here with conduct, not with advocacy.

Accordingly, for the reasons given, we find paragraphs (c) (iv), (i), and (j) established.

Ungovernability

As mentioned above, the discipline hearing found established allegation (h) in the complaint, in which it was alleged that by engaging in the course of conduct referred to in previous allegations in the complaint, Mr. Clark demonstrated an unwillingness to be governed by the Law Society or its rules and regulations. The panel advanced as its primary reason for its recommendation that Mr. Clark's right to practise law be terminated (a recommendation that it made "very reluctantly") its finding that Mr. Clark is ungovernable.

Convocation considers the panel's finding of ungovernability to be unsustainable in this case.

Mr. Clark cannot be considered to be ungovernable in the sense in which that term is usually used in discipline proceedings. Though not determinative, it is important that there was no evidence before either the panel or Convocation that he has been disciplined previously since his call to the bar in 1971, almost 25 years ago. The panel recognized that Mr. Clark has been of previous good character.

In the proceedings before the discipline hearing panel and in Convocation, Mr. Clark readily admitted the facts and documents on which the complaint was based. The panel made a point of mentioning in its report that all of the members of the panel were impressed by Mr. Clark's presentation, his thoughtful remarks to the panel, his commitment to his cause, and the obvious sincerity of his beliefs. Convocation was similarly impressed.

The panel based its finding of ungovernability on the fact that Mr. Clark would not undertake to refrain from repeating the conduct that brought him before the Law Society. The panel attached to its report a letter from the Law Society's counsel dated April 21, 1994 and Mr. Clark's reply to that letter dated April 25, 1994. In his reply, Mr. Clark stated that though he had no intention of revisiting his clients' "allegation of law" at the trial level in Canada, he was not prepared to undertake not to repeat the argument that he has been advancing in proceedings that were then pending in the Supreme Court of Canada. Nor was he willing to undertake not to repeat his argument in support of a petition that had been submitted to the Queen, or before "any other appellate or international tribunal that may have or may come to have jurisdiction over genocide."

Particularly in light of our finding that Mr. Clark is not guilty of professional misconduct in respect of many of the particulars referred to in the complaint, we do not think that Mr. Clark's refusal should make him vulnerable to a finding that he is not governable by the Law Society. Indeed, in our view, the Law Society has come quite close to asking Mr. Clark to refrain from making an argument that he believes to be both well founded in law and in the interest of his clients.

The solicitor is not ungovernable. He simply does not agree with the characterization of his conduct by counsel for the Law Society, nor that of the courts that have refused to rule on it, and he will not give up his argument at least until some court has ruled on it.

Conclusion

For these reasons, Convocation concludes that the allegations set forth in paragraphs (a), (b)(i), (b)(ii), (c)(i), (c)(ii), (c)(iii), (e)(i), (e)(ii), (e)(iii), (e)(iv), (e)(v), (f) and (h) do not amount to professional misconduct in the unique circumstances of this case.

Convocation upholds the findings of the discipline hearing panel that Mr. Clark is guilty of professional misconduct in respect of particulars (c)(iv), (i) and (j) of the complaint. ...

Penalty

When informed of Convocation's variation of the discipline hearing panel's findings, the Law Society's counsel, Mr. Brown, very fairly submitted that the appropriate penalty for the professional misconduct found established by Convocation would be a reprimand in Convocation. Convocation adopted Mr. Brown's submission.

The solicitor is currently in Amsterdam. It is our usual practice that reprimands be administered immediately following the decision of Convocation to the solicitor in person. We think it is useful to administer this reprimand in person. Accordingly, Mr. Clark will be asked to attend the January Convocation, at which time he will be reprimanded before Convocation. If he does not appear, he will remain suspended until the reprimand is administered at a subsequent Convocation.

NOTES AND QUESTIONS

1. Did Convocation approve of Clark's conduct? Would it classify Clark's conduct as "ethical" or "unethical"? Did the reason for Clark's ultimate reprimand have anything at all to do with "ethics"?

2. How could Clark's decision be expressed algebraically, following the form of the basic ethical equation developed in chapter 2?

3. Based on the findings of the initial disciplinary panel (which found more than 20 violations of the *Rules of Professional Conduct* and ultimately suggested the penalty of disbarment), it was at least arguable that Clark was behaving in ways that violated the ethical norms governing lawyers. Assuming that Clark was aware of the possibility that he would be disbarred, how can Clark's decision to behave as he did be described as pursuit of Clark's "self-interest"? Was he not pursuing "aboriginal interests" at the expense of his own desires? Why or why not?

4. Is it likely that Clark does *not* personally agree with the position of his clients? If approached by a potential client who wished to fight *against* aboriginal rights, is it likely that Clark (or a lawyer with Clark's apparent beliefs) would feel morally obliged to take the case? Would a lawyer like Clark actually take the case? If not, would the lawyer be likely to accept that he or she had violated an ethical norm, or failed to discharge an important "neutral-conduct" function?

5. Is Clark's "overzealous advocacy" in his clients' best interests? What about future clients? If courts develop an opinion that Clark is eccentric or rude, will future clients be

well advised to retain Clark?[35] What if the major goal of the client is to have his or her plight publicized? Might Clark's erratic behaviour secure publicity for aboriginal groups, and help motivate Parliament to create a political solution?

6. Is Clark principally pursuing (1) his duty to the courts, (2) his duty to the public, (3) his duty to his clients, or (4) his self-interest? Is Clark pursuing some combination of two or more of these duties?

VI. Advancing Client Interests

A. Introduction

Section V developed an economic model describing lawyers' ethical choices. That section focused on the lawyer's decision to abide by (or violate) the various oaths and codes of ethics that apply to lawyers' professional behaviour. The purpose of this section is to extend our economic model of ethical choices to the actions lawyers take on their clients' behalf. Specifically, this section is concerned with two important questions lawyers face—namely: (1) Should I agree to help a client pursue a cause that, while arguably legal, I consider to be immoral or unjust? and (2) Once I have agreed to assist a client, should I advance the client's interests through means which, while legal, violate my personal (rather than professional) moral code? As we shall see, lawyers' answers to these questions can be explained and evaluated using the tools of economics.

The decisions lawyers make in pursuit of a client's interests are typically explained by reference to the neutral-conduit model of lawyers' ethics. That model, which was described in section II.C, above, provides a bleak portrayal of the lawyer's ethical universe. According to this model, the task of the lawyer is to pursue the client's interests while completely disregarding moral concerns. In other words, the neutral-conduit model suggests that lawyers ignore their personal ethical qualms while acting in pursuit of a client's legal rights. Stated bluntly, lawyers make *no* ethical choices when acting in a client's interests, because there are no ethical choices to be made. As long as an action is legal and in the client's interests, the action must be taken regardless of the lawyer's view of the action's ethical implications. As we noted in section III.B, above, this suggestion is ill-founded. In fact, when lawyers consider taking morally dubious actions in pursuit of a client's cause, or consider helping clients pursue causes that the lawyer deems immoral, lawyers do in fact make complex ethical choices. The manner in which economic theory can explain and evaluate these moral choices is developed below.

B. Ethical Decisions Under the Neutral-Conduit Model

How can economics account for ethical choices lawyers make in pursuit of a client's interests? On a very general level, the ethical choices lawyers make when acting on

---

35   Note that Clark eventually made his way to the Supreme Court of Canada. He appeared before that court while I was serving as a law clerk to the late Mr. Justice Sopinka. Before the hearing, I was asked to conduct research into the extent of the court's contempt powers. Court security was noticeably increased on the date of Clark's appearance. Clark's actual appearance before the court led to no unusual incidents.

behalf of clients are the same as every other type of decision: the decision maker subconsciously weighs the potential costs and benefits of a particular course of action, ultimately deciding whether the action generates a net gain in utility. This is true of all types of moral decision, regardless of the context in which the relevant choice is made.

When lawyers act in pursuit of a client's interests, their ethical decisions are somewhat complicated by the justificatory context that is thought to be provided by the neutral-conduit model. The manner in which lawyers' ethical choices, economics, and the neutral-conduit model interact can be explained through the use of an illustration.

Example 3.9

Amanda Moher is a fervent believer in a woman's right to procure abortions. She firmly believes that women have the right to choose to terminate a pregnancy, and that laws impairing that right are immoral and unjust. Amanda is a particularly private person, and (in her professional environment) does not divulge her views regarding abortion.

Amanda is also a recently called lawyer who is working for the Department of Justice. Her first assignment is to prepare arguments defending a recently enacted anti-abortion statute against a constitutional challenge. Amanda does her best to generate arguments in defence of the relevant law. In fact, Amanda's arguments succeed and the anti-abortion law survives the constitutional challenge.

Consider the moral choices Amanda faced in this scenario. In her non-professional life, Amanda is a staunch defender of a woman's right to terminate her pregnancy. If asked to donate money to an anti-abortion group, Amanda will decline. Her decision to refrain from making this donation is easy to visualize in economic terms. The costs of such a donation would include the actual value of the money to be donated, the guilt Amanda would feel if she supported a cause to which she was opposed, and any other costs Amanda would subjectively incur by making it harder for a woman to obtain abortion services. The gains Amanda would generate by making such a donation are negligible: she presumably sees no value in anti-abortion organizations, and is unlikely to feel philanthropic pride as a result of a donation made to a cause with which she disagrees. As a result, the costs of a decision to make a donation would easily outstrip the benefits that Amanda would reap from that decision. As a utility maximizer, Amanda will not choose to make the donation.

Why would Amanda choose to "do her best" to support an anti-abortion law in her professional capacity? If a donation of money to an anti-abortion group would cause Amanda to feel guilty (and accordingly lose utility), surely an expenditure of time, skill, and effort in support of the same cause would generate a similar cost. How is it that Amanda could choose to act in furtherance of an objective that appears to violate her moral code? The answer to this question flows from the neutral-conduit model of lawyer behaviour. While that model is often used to support an inaccurate view of the moral world of lawyers, certain elements of that model are useful in explaining the moral decisions lawyers make. Consider Amanda's decision to assist her client (the government) in its defence of legislation that Amanda considers immoral. What are the moral costs and benefits that Amanda must weigh in deciding whether to help her client in this manner? The following is a plausible list.

Schedule of Costs and Benefits

Costs of Helping the Client Proceed[36]

Guilt: Amanda feels a sense of guilt as a result of her decision to use her skills and legal training in support of a cause she opposes on moral grounds. Since Amanda would be happy to pay $2,000 (but not $2,001) in order to be free of these feelings of guilt, this cost can be assessed at $2,000.

Reputational costs: Amanda may "lose face" among her pro-choice friends. Amanda believes that this cost will be minor, as her friends will accept the fact that Amanda was simply "doing her job." Subjective value: $1,000.

Benefits of Helping the Client Proceed

Career advancement through client satisfaction: If Amanda does an excellent job and impresses her client (the government), she secures her access to future income from this client and improves her chances of career advancement. For the purposes of this example, let us assume that the sum of all "career advancement values" in this case (including a chance of promotion, increased job security, and an enhanced reputation as a skillful lawyer) amounts to $4,000.

Sense of duty: Amanda sees the job of "lawyering" as a noble calling. Indeed, Amanda accepts the neutral-conduit model and believes that a virtuous lawyer is one who provides all clients with access to the benefits of the law, regardless of the lawyer's moral assessment of the client or its projects. Amanda feels a sense of pride when she fulfills this duty, as she fulfills an important role in the legal system (namely, eradicating the barrier of complexity and ensuring that clients are aware of legal opportunities). In this example, Amanda derives the same amount of utility from "pride" as she would derive from earning $2,000.

Net Pecuniary Gain: Amanda is being paid $500 more for this task than she would have been paid for the next most valuable alternative.[37]

Having outlined our schedule of costs and benefits, we may now resort to our algebraic expression of moral decisions: $A - B = X$. Once again, A is the sum of the benefits

---

36   Note that some of the costs and benefits could be determined with mathematical precision. For example, the "career advancement" benefit relates to financial sums that could be quantified with relative precision. Because Amanda is not a real person, and we have no access to her specific financial data, we will simply invent figures for present purposes. The actual value placed on these figures is unimportant for present purposes: the only purpose of this example is to demonstrate the subconscious thought process that governs Amanda's ethical choice.

37   Note that we cannot simply include the gross amount of pay that Amanda receives for her current task. Presumably, if Amanda had not been assigned this task, she would have been assigned an alternative task for which she would be paid. The loss of the money from that alternative task is another form of opportunity cost. Thus, in calculating Amanda's pecuniary benefit, we include only the "net pecuniary benefit" after subtracting the cost of forgone financial opportunities.

to be derived from a course of action (the gross utility gains generated by the act) and B is the sum of all the costs (or utility losses) the act will generate. X is the figure yielded by subtracting B from A and represents the net utility generated by the proposed activity. In Amanda's case, the total benefits are equal to $6,500 (based on the foregoing list of costs and benefits). The costs are equal to $3,000. X (the result of subtracting B from A) accordingly equals $3,500, representing a positive gain in utility. Since Amanda would generate a net gain in utility by defending the anti-abortion law, she will undertake the action despite the fact that she is morally opposed to the content of the relevant legislation.

Example 3.9 demonstrates the link between the neutral-conduit model and the economic account of legal ethics. Clearly, the traditional view of the neutral-conduit model is incorrect: Amanda's role as a neutral conduit did not relieve her of the need to make a moral or ethical choice. The justificatory context that is provided by the neutral-conduit model did, however, have an impact on the decision-making process. Indeed, the neutral-conduit model altered Amanda's moral decision in two ways. First, it diminished the level of guilt Amanda felt as a result of her decision to promote what she perceived to be a morally troubling goal. Because Amanda felt that she was simply "doing her job" (a job that Amanda feels is socially valuable), Amanda feels less guilt when helping the anti-abortion cause in her professional role than she would if she were to assist that cause in a personal capacity. Second, the neutral-conduit model gave Amanda a new value to weigh when making her ethical choice. The benefit described as "sense of duty" in the schedule of costs and benefits is, essentially, Amanda's personal recognition of her neutral-conduit function. Lawyers who endorse the neutral-conduit model believe that lawyers serve an important role in society: they permit their clients to understand and avail themselves of legal opportunities. Lawyers act as remedies for the complexity of the law, ensuring that clients have the opportunity to pursue legal options that they would have failed to recognize without specialized assistance. Like many lawyers, Amanda generates utility by fulfilling this important social role. She feels good about what she is doing. She is serving the cause of "access to justice," and in doing so she generates utility (in the form of pride of accomplishment) that outweighs whatever utility costs (in the form of moral discomfort) Amanda feels as a result of the client's underlying goal. The result is a net gain in utility, which explains why Amanda is happy to take this action despite her moral disapproval of the goal her client pursues.

As we saw in section II.C, above, several legal ethicists have stated that lawyers make no moral choices when pursuing a client's interests. Our economic model reveals the source of this suggestion. Individuals who endorse this view of lawyer amorality simply rank the utility value of the "sense of duty" benefit (that is, the moral benefit of fulfilling the lawyer's neutral-conduit function) at an extremely high figure. Indeed, such individuals are so thoroughly convinced of the high utility value of the neutral-conduit function that they believe that no client is sufficiently distasteful, no legal course of action so morally repugnant, that the utility costs of pursuing a morally dubious action could ever outweigh the utility to be derived from fulfillment of the lawyer's neutral-conduit role. As a result, they believe that lawyers needn't make moral decisions when pursuing client goals. The answer to the question "should I help this client pursue a legal but morally reprehensible act?" is a foregone conclusion. Due to the high value that such ethicists associate with the neutral-conduit function lawyers serve, the answer is always "yes": the utility payoff that is associated with fulfilling the neutral-conduit role, it is argued, will inevitably outweigh the utility cost of pursuing an action that the lawyer feels is morally indefensible.

By concluding that lawyers make no moral decisions in pursuit of client goals, propo-nents of the neutral-conduit model project their own subjective values onto other legal professionals. They assume that the utility benefit of fulfilling the neutral-conduit role must inevitably outweigh the utility cost of pursuing actions that the lawyer considers morally reprehensible. This is presumptuous. More importantly, it fails to correspond to the actual practice of many lawyers, who refuse to act for certain kinds of client based (in part) on the lawyer's moral assessment of the client or the goals the client pursues. Some litigators, for example, refuse to act for criminal defendants who assert the right of free expression as a justification for spreading anti-Semitic propaganda. Some employment lawyers will not represent a union; others will never agree to act for management. Some lawyers will not act for individuals who are accused of spousal abuse. In many cases, the lawyer chooses to withhold his or her services from clients who assert claims that the lawyer feels are unethical or unjust. These lawyers are not anomalies—they simply gain less utility from fulfillment of the neutral-conduit role than they lose by representing a particular type of client or by pursuing a particular type of claim. Lawyers who *do* act for clients whom they consider reprehensible simply place a higher value on fulfillment of the neutral-conduit role. As a result, rather than claiming that lawyers do not face moral decisions when pursuing client interests, the more accurate view is that all lawyers (and indeed, all indi-viduals) *do* subconsciously consider the moral costs and benefits of the actions that they take, even when these actions are taken under the cloak of a justificatory context such as the neutral-conduit model.[38] The neutral-conduit model does not eliminate the need for moral decisions. On the contrary, it simply changes the figures that the lawyer must consider.

Before reviewing judicial and administrative decisions that demonstrate the econom-ics of lawyers' moral decisions in pursuit of client goals, it is important to consider two common questions that may complicate our economic account of legal ethics—namely: (1) Does a lowly associate in a modern "mega firm" have the luxury of making moral decisions? and (2) How can an economic model that is premised on self-interest be applied to legal professionals who, by virtue of their role, are said to act exclusively in pursuit of their clients' interests? These questions are addressed in the following section.

VII. Complicating Factors

A. The Lowly Associate

One objection to an economic model of legal ethics is based on the suggestion that some lawyers lack the freedom to consider ethical issues. As we saw in section II, above, the

---

38   Part of the allure of an economic account of legal ethics is that it does not presume that the decision maker detects an "ethical dimension" to the choice that he or she faces. Whatever decision a person makes, he or she will be guided by utility maximization, whether or not he or she believes that an action has ethical implications. Where the decision maker is aware that a particular activity carries ethical implications, moral costs (such as guilt and reputational costs) will factor into the decision. Where the decision maker does not believe that the decision raises ethical concerns, the decision maker may not factor guilt or reputational costs into his or her subconscious ethical calculations.

neutral-conduit model suggests that lawyers are precluded from making moral decisions as a result of the institutional role that lawyers play. We have already observed how an economic theory of legal ethics has the ability to overcome this objection.[39] A similar objection is that many lawyers lack the authority to make *any* professional choices for themselves. More specifically, junior associates who do the bidding of senior partners at large firms are thought to lack the moral autonomy that is posited by the economic model of legal ethics. A lowly associate, it is argued, lacks the ability to decide whether to take a specific professional action or to act on behalf of clients represented by the firm. Instead, the associate is doomed to carry out the partners' will, regardless of the associate's ethical values.

Consider the hypothetical case of an environmental activist who does exceedingly well in law school, is hired as an associate by a modern "mega firm," and whose first task is to assist in a business deal that will permit the firm's main client to destroy an old-growth forest. The associate may feel that the client's action is morally reprehensible, but may nonetheless help the client on the ground that the associate "has no choice" but to assist in the transaction.

Why does our hypothetical associate feel that he or she has no choice but to assist the firm in pursuing this client's interests? Presumably, it is because of the associate's assessment of the consequences that flow from failure to comply with the firm's instructions. The associate may believe that he or she will be professionally ostracized, kept away from important transactions, or even fired for failing to satisfy the wishes of the partners. These potential consequences, of course, are simply economic costs. The lowly associate still has the choice to refrain from actions that the associate believes to be morally problematic: the cost of making that choice is simply enhanced due to the associate's view of the consequences that flow from that decision. Even lowly associates have the "luxury" of making moral decisions. A moral choice that conflicts with the wishes of the lowly associate's firm is simply more expensive than many other moral decisions. As a result, the lowly associate is similar to other rational actors, taking ethical (or unethical) actions only when the benefits of the action will exceed the action's costs. Like the rest of us, lowly associates are utility-maximizing individuals. Their decisions, though burdened with the powerful incentive to appease a powerful employer, can still be explained by an economic account of ethical choices.

B. Self-Interest Versus Client Interest

When applying an economic model of rational choice to lawyers' decisions, one possible source of confusion flows from the fact that lawyers are often said to act in their clients' "best interests." Earlier sections of this book demonstrated that economics relies on the notion that people are motivated by *self-interest*, and that a rational actor's choices will be governed by the decision maker's desire to maximize his or her own utility. From one perspective, a profession that requires its members to act in furtherance of a client's interests seems incompatible with a self-interest motive. As a result, one might argue that economic models, premised as they are on self-interest and utility maximization, have no application to decisions made by lawyers acting in pursuit of a client's goals.

---

39   See section III.B, above.

Economic models of decision making can and do apply to decisions lawyers make when pursuing client interests. Even when acting in pursuit of a client's interests, lawyers ultimately make decisions based on their own preferences with the goal of maximizing their own utility. When a lawyer acts in pursuit of client interests, the lawyer's ultimate goal is to accomplish several objectives aimed at generating utility for the lawyer— namely: (1) financial gain, (2) professional satisfaction, (3) career advancement or reputational gains that flow from client satisfaction, and (4) fulfillment of a social role the lawyer considers important. Deviation from the interests of the client, by contrast, would soon lead to a loss of the lawyer's employment or, worse still, to the loss of the lawyer's right to practise law. As a result, even when lawyers appear to be acting in the interests of a client, they can be seen to be acting in ways designed to further their own interests and to maximize the utility they can attain.[40]

Even where lawyers act without the expectation of financial rewards (such as cases in which the lawyer provides pro bono legal services), the lawyer's actions can be explained by reference to utility maximization and self-interest. In such cases, the lawyer acts (in part) from an altruistic motive.[41] As we saw in chapter 2, section III.A, the motives of altruists are ultimately grounded in self-interest. As a result, an economic model based on self-interest and utility maximization applies to all decisions lawyers make, even when those decisions are made in pursuit of a client's goals. Although the lawyer is said to act in the *client's* interest, the ultimate factor governing each decision the lawyer makes is the lawyer's perception of his or her *self*-interest. A model premised on utility maximization and self-interest is therefore applicable to the decisions lawyers make.

The decision of the court in *R v. Murray* (2000) is one of Canada's most famous (or infamous) cases involving lawyers' ethics. The case involved Kenneth Murray, one of the lawyers responsible for defending Paul Bernardo (the "Scarborough Rapist," who was also charged with the sexual torture and murder of two teenaged girls). The problem before the court in *Murray* arose from Murray's decision to actively suppress videotape evidence that showed his client engaging in acts of sexual torture, conclusively proving that Bernardo was guilty of several of the crimes with which he was charged. Murray collected the videotapes in a covert fashion and prevented the Crown from discovering their existence. As a result of this behaviour, Murray was charged with attempting to obstruct justice.[42]

When reviewing the court's decision, consider the following questions:

1. Can Murray's decision to represent Bernardo be justified by reference to the neutral-conduit role?

---

40   For an excellent account of the relationship between self-interest and lawyers' professional responsibilities, see George M. Cohen, "When Law and Economics Met Professional Responisbility" (1998), 67 *Fordham Law Review* 273, at 275-79.

41   Aside from pure altruism, lawyers who provide pro bono services may also be motivated by reputational gains and professional marketing.

42   Note that this case involves a criminal charge of attempting to obstruct justice rather than a violation of the *Rules of Professional Conduct*. The decision is still useful in demonstrating the nature of ethical reasoning in the context of the legal profession.

2. Did the neutral-conduit model relieve Murray of the need to make moral decisions in pursuit of his client's goals?

3. Can each of Murray's decisions be explained in economic terms?

4. What types of "costs" (or punishments) ought to be imposed on lawyers who follow Murray's pattern of behaviour?

Additional questions from the court's decision will be raised following the extract.

R v. Murray
(2000), 48 OR (3d) 544 (Sup. Ct. J)

Part One—The Charge

GRAVELY J: The accused, Kenneth Murray, is a member of the Ontario Bar and certified as a specialist in criminal litigation by the Law Society of Upper Canada. He was retained by Paul Bernardo initially in February 1993 in regard to the "Scarborough rapes" and on May 18, 1993, in connection with the murders of Leslie Mahaffy and Kristen French and additional related offences.

On May 6, 1993, on written instructions of Bernardo, Murray attended at the Bernardo home and removed from it videotapes which depicted gross sexual abuse of Kristen French, Leslie Mahaffy, Jane Doe and Tammy Homolka. Without disclosing their existence to the Crown, he retained the tapes for 17 months. Trial motions were to begin on September 12, 1994. On September 2, 1994, Murray, through his counsel, applied to the Law Society of Upper Canada for advice. Accepting that advice Murray appeared before the trial judge, Associate Chief Justice LeSage (now Chief Justice SCO), who directed that the tapes, their integrity protected by suitable undertakings, go to John Rosen, new counsel for Bernardo, at which time Murray was given leave to withdraw as counsel. Rosen, on September 22, 1994, turned the tapes over to the police and they were used by Crown counsel at the trial. A jury found Bernardo guilty on all charges.

Murray now faces this charge of attempt to obstruct justice by concealment of the videotapes.

Part Two—The Facts

The Defence Team

At the material time Murray was a sole practitioner in Newmarket, Ontario. His practice had been restricted to criminal defence work since December 1983. He shared office space with other defence counsel, one of whom was Carolyn MacDonald, who had been at the bar for five years. The office employed secretaries and Kim Doyle, the office manager and law clerk.

When he was retained on the Scarborough rapes and a further charge against Bernardo of assaulting Homolka, Murray asked MacDonald and Doyle to assist him

with the charges on a full time basis. Doyle was responsible for keeping the file orga-
nized, tabulating the vast amount of Crown disclosure documents and preparing legal aid accounts. MacDonald developed the case for trial and was the primary contact person with Bernardo, who was in custody. Murray was lead counsel, but spent
most of his time on his other cases.

57 Bayview Drive

Before his arrest Bernardo lived with his wife, Karla Homolka, in a rented house at
57 Bayview Drive, St. Catharines, Ontario. Between February and April 1993, the
police, for 71 days, conducted an intensive search of the premises, virtually destroying
the interior of the house in the process. On April 30, 1993 the final search warrant
expired and on May 4, Doyle, MacDonald and John Lefurgey (a local lawyer assisting the defence team) attended at 57 Bayview with consent of the landlords to assess
the condition of the house, videotape the interior and decide what possessions of the
Bernardos should be removed. The landlords agreed that the defence team could return
on May 6 to remove the Bernardo belongings. They were also, at that time, to be
allowed 20 minutes alone in the house in order to confer as to which of the Bernardo
possessions might have some relevance to the defence and thus should be taken away.

The Removal of the Videotapes

On May 6, MacDonald and Doyle went to 57 Bayview at 8:30 a.m. and, with the
assistance of the landlords, began to pack up the Bernardo personal effects. Murray
said that on his way to 57 Bayview he got lost and, in attempting to telephone
MacDonald for directions, discovered in his slipcase an unsealed envelope given to
him on May 3, by MacDonald. It contained a letter from Bernardo, which was
wrapped around a sealed envelope. The letter read:

> The following is to be opened only and only if you have entered 57 Bayview. It is
> instructions on what is probably in the house that we need for our defence. Alone they
> may first appear to be irrelevant and thus overlooked but together they can be very
> important. Note: if we can't have access then return the letter intact.
>   What I was worried about is I would be moved and hidden for a few days until our
> possession of the house was up. …

At the top of the page were code words to communicate to Bernardo the results of the
search. The word "successful" was in Bernardo's handwriting. "How about those
Jays," "unsuccessful" and "Leafs" were written by MacDonald and she had drawn an
arrow between the words "unsuccessful" and "Leafs."
     Murray arrived at 57 Bayview at 11:00 a.m. and, as agreed with the landlords, the
defence team was given time alone in the house. Murray then opened the sealed envelope, which contained a map and directions to assist in locating six 8mm videotapes.
     Referring to his note and map, Murray led the way to the bathroom and started to
take apart a pot light while Doyle and MacDonald watched from the doorway. Unsuccessful in finding anything behind the light, he handed the Bernardo instructions to

Doyle, who directed him to another pot light. Murray climbed onto the vanity, dismantled the light and was successful in retrieving six 8mm videotapes. He then reassembled the light and placed the videotapes in his slip case. Doyle and MacDonald hugged each other and Doyle whispered to MacDonald, "what have we got?"

The defence team had lunch together on the balcony of 57 Bayview. Murray told Doyle and MacDonald that they would have to make sure that no one found out about the tapes, and the three of them would have to make a pact that they would be the only ones that ever knew what had been obtained. They shook hands, hugged, and agreed not to say anything to anyone about the tapes. Murray said in his evidence that he knew "they wouldn't tell anybody about the tapes." He felt the discovery of the tapes was a "bonanza" or "gold mine" for the defence.

Murray said MacDonald and Bernardo made up the code words on the instruction letter. "How about those Leafs?" was to be the signal that the search was unsuccessful while "How about those Jays?" meant that the tapes were found. In the afternoon of May 6, Bernardo telephoned Murray at 57 Bayview who said to him, "How about those Jays?"

With the map and directions there was a note from Bernardo that said; "… although we will have to go through them in the future. At this time I instruct you not to view them."

Murray, MacDonald and Doyle packed and removed a large number of items from the house. Murray locked the tapes in a safe or a credenza at his office.

The Homolka Resolution Agreement—Bernardo Charged with Murders

On May 14, 1993 Homolka's defence counsel and Crown counsel entered into a six-page written agreement. Homolka would plead guilty to two counts of manslaughter in relation to the deaths of Kristen French and Leslie Mahaffy, there would be a joint submission that she be sentenced to 12 years' imprisonment and she would provide evidence to assist the Crown.

Sometime between May 14 and 17, 1993 the defence team learned about the charges against Homolka and her release on bail and made the assumption that Homolka had entered into an arrangement with the Crown.

On May 18, 1993 Bernardo was charged with two counts of first-degree murder and additional related offences. Homolka was charged with two counts of manslaughter. Murray's retainer was extended to include the additional charges against Bernardo. Bernardo signed an authorization directing Murray to review the videotapes, make copies and use the tapes as Murray deemed appropriate in Bernardo's outstanding criminal matters.

The Critical Tapes

Of the six videotapes, two ("the critical tapes") form the basis of the charge against Murray.

The critical tapes are indescribably horrible. Leslie Mahaffy was 14 years of age and Kristen French 15 when they were abducted and murdered by Bernardo, assisted by Homolka. The tapes show each of them being forced to participate with Bernardo and Homolka in the grossest sexual perversions. In the course of sexual assaults they are forced to pretend they are enjoying the experience through scripted dialogue, and, in the case of Kristen French, through being instructed to constantly smile at the camera. Obedience is obtained through physical assault and Bernardo threatens each of them with death if they do not perform as directed.

Everyone exposed to the videotapes has been deeply affected by the experience.

Doyle had to review the tapes by way of trial preparation for Rosen. In giving her evidence she broke down at the recollection and said that she saw the tapes nine times, but "a million times in my head."

Rosen, a veteran criminal defence counsel, was obliged to hesitate part way through his evidence as he recollected the images on the tapes. He described viewing the tapes on September 13, 1994 with MacDonald and Clayton Ruby. MacDonald wept beside him as the tapes were shown and Rosen said he himself was extremely upset. Murray described the tapes as "caustic," "corrosive" and "shocking." Even defence counsel, Mr. Cooper, who must in his career have been exposed to almost everything terrible the court system has to offer, was obliged to request a brief adjournment in the course of reading in some of this evidence.

In addition to the dreadful acts perpetrated on Kristen French and Leslie Mahaffy, the critical tapes also show the drugging and sexual assaults of Jane Doe and Tammy Homolka, both 15 years of age.

The critical tapes demonstrate conclusively that Bernardo was guilty of forcible confinement, assault and sexual assault of Kristen French and Leslie Mahaffy and the sexual assault of Jane Doe and Tammy Homolka. They provide strong circumstantial evidence to prove Bernardo guilty of the murders.

The Non-Critical Tapes

Of the "non-critical tapes" two of them portray Homolka in sexual scenes. In one she engages in a sexual display with a prostitute and, in the other, she performs a strip tease and simulates masturbation. Part of the dialogue is:

Bernardo: "What do you enjoy most in life?"
Homolka: "Showing off."
Bernardo: "And?"
Homolka: "Licking little girls."
Bernardo: "And?"
Homolka: "Pleasing my man."

It was anticipated by the defence that these tapes could be used to show that Homolka was not a shrinking, abused wife under the control of Bernardo, but rather a willing participant in gross sexual conduct.

The Crown has no quarrel with Murray's handling of the non-critical tapes.

Murray testified he made no distinction between non-critical and critical tapes, but treated them as making up a package.

. *Copying of the Videotapes*

Sometime in May, after receiving Bernardo's instructions on May 18 authorizing him to review and make copies of the tapes, Murray rented copying equipment. The rental charge of $1,624.95 was never billed to the Ontario Legal Aid Plan. He was afraid, he said, that the disbursement might alert the prosecution to the existence of the tapes and they might be seized under the authority of a search warrant.

In the event, Murray said, he could not make the copying equipment work and he sent it back. He copied the tapes at home using a VHS machine and a camcorder. He said he put a towel over the video screen so no one could see what he was copying and did not watch the tapes except for checking at the end of each tape in fast forward position to ensure that the copying had been accomplished. The originals were placed in a safe in Murray's house and the copies in a safe in his office.

Murray testified that within a week or two after the copies were made in early June of 1993, he was comfortable with his knowledge of the contents of the tapes.

John Rosen's "Advice"

John Rosen is a senior and respected Toronto counsel. Tim Breen was the spousal companion of MacDonald and he was also a legal associate of Rosen. Breen had assisted Murray from time to time on the Bernardo case. On May 18, 1993, while visiting Bernardo and receiving his instructions to review and make copies of the tapes, Murray obtained from him some indication of their contents. That same evening he and MacDonald met with Breen to discuss tactics. The following day, May 19, Breen approached Rosen with a hypothetical question to the effect that if the defence had hard evidence that compromised Homolka's credibility, should it be revealed to the prosecution to ensure that Homolka got charged with murder, or should it be saved for trial? Rosen told Breen there was no obligation to assist in the prosecution, but that defence counsel's first duty is to the client and if the evidence would assist the defence, then it should be held in the file and used to cross-examine the witness at trial: "Hammer her with any hard evidence that compromises her plea, her deal, her credibility." Rosen warned against going to the Crown with the evidence because it would allow the Crown to prepare Homolka for cross-examination at trial.

Neither Breen nor Rosen was told anything about videotapes or the nature of the "hard evidence." Rosen assumed it was something like a diary or a letter or a card written to a friend. Both Murray and Rosen looked upon the issue as tactical rather than ethical. (At this time, Murray had not yet viewed the tapes).

The Defence Plan

Murray testified he had to retain the critical tapes for Bernardo's defence. Bernardo admitted the crimes shown on the tapes but denied killing Leslie Mahaffy and Kristen French. The tapes, Murray said, supported this position. The Crown was going to portray Homolka as an abused, manipulated victim, while the tapes showed the reverse, that she was not afraid and was an enthusiastic participant in the sexual crimes.

He was obliged to keep the existence of the tapes secret so that the Crown could not prepare Homolka for Murray's cross-examination.

It is not entirely clear how Murray planned to utilize the critical tapes. It appears there were two alternatives, to some degree conflicting:

1. Hold back the tapes, tie down Homolka's evidence at the preliminary inquiries and then spring the tapes on her in cross-examination at trial;

2. Tie down Homolka at the preliminary inquiries and then go to the Crown and attempt to negotiate a resolution of the charges against Bernardo on the basis that Murray was holding evidence that would demonstrate that Homolka was incredible. Bernardo would acknowledge guilt on most of the charges and the prosecution could extricate itself from the Homolka deal. If resolution could not be achieved, the tapes would be turned over to the prosecution. While it would be no "surprise" for Homolka at trial, at least she would have been tied down by her evidence at the preliminary inquiries.

Murray stated it was never his intention to "bury" the tapes and, at the very least, they would come out at the trial.

Knowledge by Doyle and MacDonald of Contents of Critical Tapes

Murray chose not to let Doyle or MacDonald have access to the critical tapes. His reason, he said, was that the impact of the tapes upon them would be so great they would not be able to work effectively on the defence file. He wanted to ensure they would "come to trial" with him and he was trying to protect them: "They were both like sisters and I knew what it would do to them. They wouldn't be able to work."

Doyle said she was unable to get a response from Murray as to what was on the tapes, although she frequently asked. She suspected from the beginning that the tapes showed Bernardo involved with the victims. At Murray's request she, on one occasion, looked at a small portion of one of the tapes through the viewfinder of an 8mm camcorder for the purpose of identifying one of the victims.

MacDonald was not a witness at this trial, but I infer from her role as contact person with Bernardo that she must have been told by Bernardo generally what was on the tapes. Murray said he showed her one to two minutes of one of the critical tapes in order to "refocus her." He said the defence strategy was to concentrate on Homolka, but because MacDonald was regularly visiting Bernardo to discuss the case, as he put it, she had "kind of gone soft …":

> Both she and Kim tended to go off into the soft issues. So there was an occasion in the fall of 1993, I said to Carolyn, after one session she came back from the jail, I said "Carolyn, it's time for a reality check." And at that point I provided her with an opportunity to view a portion of one of the critical tapes … . Carolyn watched it for about a minute and a half or two minutes, found it extremely upsetting and from that point on became focused on Karla.

Preferred Indictments and Pre-Trial Cross-Examination of Homolka

Murray said the defence team had planned to use the critical tapes for the cross-examination of Homolka at the preliminary inquiries and at the trial of the domestic assault charge. The Attorney General, however, preferred indictments on the Scarborough rapes and the homicides and related charges and entered a stay of proceedings on the domestic assault charge. In compensation for the loss of the preliminary inquiries the defence was given an opportunity to cross-examine Homolka at the Kingston Penitentiary for Women.

Murray said the arrangements for the cross-examinations were unsatisfactory. There was no judge to make rulings; the exercise was conducted in a small windowless room with the participants sitting around a table; and Homolka appeared to be medicated or tired for the first half-day session. Nonetheless, the cross-examination went on for seven days in May through July of 1994. Questions were put and answered that went beyond the norm for those that might be asked at a preliminary inquiry.

Although Murray was present, the decision was made that MacDonald would conduct the examination based on a cross-examination brief that had been developed continuously from before the end of 1993. There appears to have been little attempt to pin down Homolka using the critical tapes. This would have been difficult for MacDonald to accomplish since she had not seen them. Presumably, also, they were not a part of the cross-examination brief. Murray said he sometimes suggested to MacDonald areas that she might want to cover, based on his knowledge of what was on the tapes.

May 2, 1994—Murray's Resolution Meeting with the Crown—
          "A Room with a View"

At their request Murray met with the representatives of the Crown. The Crown made a resolution proposal which included the concept of somewhat superior prison accommodation for Bernardo. Murray thought the proposal was reasonable and recommended it to Bernardo who turned it down.

Murray did not alert Crown counsel to the existence of any videotapes. Murray said if Bernardo had agreed to the proposed resolution, the tapes, at that point, would have been disclosed.

Murray's Conflict

On May 4, 1994 Bernardo was arraigned before LeSage ACJOC on the homicides and related charges and entered not guilty pleas to all counts.

Towards the end of June 1994 MacDonald told Murray by memo that Bernardo was "spinning off the dial" and Murray should see him and straighten him out, since he was taking a completely untenable position on the homicides. Murray said Bernardo, because of his "super segregation" for 16 months, was losing contact with reality. He believed he was omniscient and knew better than the lawyers.

Murray said that on the visits of July 11 and 12, Bernardo told him he was going to deny having any contact with either Kristen French or Leslie Mahaffy and the tapes were not to be used to contradict this position.

About July 24, 1994 the defence team received disclosure of DNA test results. A stain in the closet of the Bernardo bedroom contained DNA of both Bernardo and Kristen French. Homolka told the police that Kristen French vomited in the closet after having been forced to perform oral sex on Bernardo. Even when faced with the DNA evidence placing him in the house in contact with Kristen French, Bernardo insisted, said Murray, that he would say he had no contact with the girls and the tapes were not to be used. When he was unable to talk Bernardo out of this position, Murray said, he felt obliged to terminate the solicitor–client relationship and he suggested to Bernardo that Rosen take over.

On August 4, 1994 LeSage ACJOC presided over a pre-trial and fixed September 12, 1994 as the date for a change of venue application. Believing that it would be ethically wrong to do so, he said, Murray did not mention his conflict to LeSage ACJOC.

The Approach to John Rosen

At Murray's request, he and Rosen met on August 15, 1994. According to Rosen, Murray asked him to take over the Bernardo defence: "Because I can't handle it. I'm being inundated with motions from the Crown, factums have to be drafted, case books put together, the Crown is preparing motions that I should be bringing and the file is just enormous and I don't have the resources or the wherewithal to do this. You are more experienced than me and I want you to take over the file." After probing further as to the nature of the case and discussing the defence team, Rosen said he asked, "Well, you know, why do you need me?" And Murray's response was, "Look, it's just a difficult case and I just can't handle it." Rosen said Murray mentioned he had a minor conflict that would probably never arise that might require him to be a witness. Rosen said that comment appeared to him to be a casual afterthought and "just a graceful way of saying I need out of this case, I can't do it." In the course of the discussions, Rosen learned the trial had started, that motions were to begin in September and the trial would take about six months, but an adjournment would be obtained to accommodate Rosen's schedule.

Rosen spoke to his family and his partner and, on August 16, left a telephone message at Murray's office that he would not take the brief. When Murray returned the call he appeared to be agitated, according to Rosen, continued to press Rosen and suggested he telephone MacDonald and Breen about the case. When he did that, Rosen said, he received information that made him concerned about the way the case was being conducted and the state of preparation of the file. He said this was a high profile case and if it continued to be badly handled "the profession would receive a black eye." After other discussions, on August 25, Rosen agreed to take over the file provided the client and legal aid agreed and there was a significant adjournment to allow for proper preparation of the defence.

At no time did Murray mention the existence of any videotapes to Rosen.

Murray's version of these meetings is that he had to "sell" Rosen on the file. He had known Rosen for 20 years and planned his approach to appeal to Rosen's ego. As he put it:

All criminal lawyers have an ego. Some are different than others and some have to be fed more than others. I knew that if I went to Mr. Rosen and said, "take it over John, you know, it's an interesting case," he would say, "I'm not interested." But if I said, "John, you've got the experience, you've done a lot of homicides. Tim and Carolyn rely on you a lot. You've the nature to take it over. I've got a conflict, I might become a witness. But you're the one that can do it." With that approach, John saw me asking him for help. He's here, I'm the supplicant.

This approach was successful, said Murray, and Rosen's "ego took over after that."

Rosen and Murray Meet with Bernardo

On August 27, 1994, Rosen and Murray attended the Niagara Detention Centre in Thorold, Ontario so Rosen could be introduced to Bernardo and Murray could tell his client he was getting off the case. Murray spent 15 minutes alone with Bernardo and said he was instructed by him not to tell Rosen about the existence of the tapes. Both counsel then met with Bernardo who was told of the three conditions that had to be met before Rosen took over the file. Bernardo said he was happy with the transfer since he understood Rosen was more experienced and had better skills than Murray. It was agreed that Murray would remain as counsel on the Scarborough rapes.

Bernardo signed Rosen's retainer agreement, which was conditional upon the obtaining of an adjournment of the trial and the issuance of a legal aid certificate. Bernardo also signed an authorization and direction to Murray to "release to my lawyers Rosen Fleming ... all records, reports, files and documents requested by them ... ." A discussion followed, generally about the case, disclosure, experts, Homolka's cross-examination and the change of venue motion. Rosen then gave Bernardo a mini-lecture on the law of homicide and possible defences. There was no discussion about videotapes.

On August 29, 1994, Rosen met with MacDonald and examined the defence file.

The Four Directions

On August 30, 1994 Murray met with Bernardo and had him sign four separate directions:

1. I, PAUL BERNARDO, (a.k.a. Teale), hereby advise Kenneth D. Murray, that I wish to discharge him as counsel of record on the charges of 1st Degree Murder, and related offences, currently before Mr. Justice LeSage, for pre-jury motions, in St. Catharines, Ontario.

2. I, PAUL BERNARDO, (a.k.a. Teale), acknowledge that I wish Kenneth D. Murray to continue to represent me on all matters presently before the Courts of Ontario, with the exception of the St. Catharines charges of First Degree Murder and related charges. FURTHER, it is my express instruction and direction to Kenneth D. Murray that he retain all solicitor and client interview notes, original documents, and other materials I have caused to be in his possession, whether related to the St. Catharines

charges presently before the Courts or not, unless or until I provide him with a specific direction relating to those materials.

3. I, PAUL BERNARDO (a.k.a. Teale), hereby direct Kenneth D. Murray, counsel of record on the offences related to the "Scarborough Rapist" allegations, presently before the Toronto General Division Court, to retain all of my personal writings, client notes and other personal matters, with the contents of the files related to the Scarborough prosecution. I further instruct Mr. Murray not to disclose any of these writings or materials to other counsel retained on my behalf for other offences that are currently before the Court, for which Mr. Murray is not retained, unless I specifically direct the release of such materials, in writing.

4. I, PAUL BERNARDO, (a.k.a. Teale), hereby direct Kenneth D. Murray, presently counsel of record on all my outstanding charges that, with specific reference to the charges of First Degree Murder and related offenses presently in progress in St. Catharines General Division, that I consent to his withdrawing as counsel on these charges. FURTHER, I acknowledge that by consenting to the withdrawal of counsel, I may be unrepresented for the continuation of the trial. Notwithstanding that possibility, because of matters I have discussed with Kenneth D. Murray, it is my instruction and direction that he, under no circumstances, continue to represent me with respect to the St. Catharines charges.

Murray said he took these instructions in order to document what it was that Bernardo was asking him to do. He said he had no intention of following the directions or withholding the tapes from Rosen, or remaining counsel in the Scarborough rapes. The directions were there, he said, for him to act upon or not act upon. The directions would show that it was Bernardo's idea to suppress the tapes.

At this point, Murray's position was precarious:

1. LeSage ACJOC and the Crown were expecting to begin, on September 12, motions in a six-month trial.

2. Murray had not yet disclosed the existence of the tapes to the Crown, although he said that was always his intention.

3. Murray had sold the Bernardo trial to Rosen on the basis that it had academic interest and required Mr. Rosen's superior skills and organizational abilities. Rosen had still not been told about the tapes even though, as Murray put it, "the trial was the tapes."

4. Although Rosen was Bernardo's incoming counsel on the murder charges, Murray had, without notifying Rosen, arranged for Bernardo to sign a series of directions the effect of which was to confirm Murray as counsel on the Scarborough rapes, transfer the tapes and all documents referring to them, from the murder file to Murray's control on the Scarborough rapes, and continue to keep their existence hidden from Rosen.

On the evening of August 30, 1994, Murray, together with MacDonald, met with the Crown prosecutors. Murray advised them he had a conflict and was withdrawing from the case and he was making arrangements for other counsel. He told them the conflict only arose at the beginning of August 1994 and he had spent that month trying to resolve it without success.

Meeting with Lesage ACJOC

Murray had arranged a meeting with LeSage ACJOC for September 1, 1994 for the purpose of informing him that Murray was withdrawing as counsel and Rosen was taking over.

Early on the morning of September 1, 1994, Rosen, Murray and MacDonald got together to discuss what would take place before LeSage ACJOC. Rosen told Murray he should indicate the transfer was not the fault of the client.

At the meeting with LeSage ACJOC, Murray said the private reason was a conflict. The public reason was that the case had taken on an appellate nature and Rosen was better equipped to deal with it by staffing, facilities and ability. Murray said he told this to LeSage ACJOC in order to minimize any prejudice to Bernardo.

Rosen told LeSage ACJOC he needed a lengthy adjournment to get the case properly prepared and to allow him to honour his obligations in other cases.

LeSage ACJOC directed Murray to bring the appropriate application pursuant to the Rules, to be argued in open court on September 12, 1994.

Following the meeting, MacDonald, Murray and Rosen discussed the application Murray was going to bring and what should be included in the supporting affidavit. Rosen told Murray the affidavit would have to be truthful and accurate, that it would be scrutinized first by the prosecution, then by the court, then by the public and then perhaps by the Law Society of Upper Canada, given Rosen's impression that Murray was unprepared and incapable of handling the file. Rosen reminded Murray of his responsibility to protect the client and offered to assist Murray in reviewing the draft materials.

Mr. Cooper Retained and Law Society Advice Sought

On September 1, 1994, Murray contacted Mr. Cooper's office to obtain assistance in getting off the record.

After meeting with his client, Mr. Cooper wrote to the Law Society of Upper Canada for advice. There is no evidence as to the nature of the advice sought.

The Law Society convened a special three-person ad hoc committee, considered the request and, on September 8, 1994, wrote as follows to Mr. Cooper:

Dear Mr. Cooper:

RE: *REGINA vs. BERNARDO*

You have sought the advice of the Professional Conduct Committee ad hoc of the Law Society of Upper Canada on behalf of your client, Kenneth Murray, QC. Based on the information you have provided we wish to advise as follows:

1. Mr. Murray should remove himself as counsel of record for Mr. Bernardo as soon as practicable.

2. Certain material in possession of Mr. Murray should be delivered to His Honour Judge P. LeSage in a sealed packet and to be subject to court determination.

3. We are of the view that Mr. Bernardo should be advised of the steps you intend to take as soon as possible.

Yours truly

Earl Levy QC, Paul Copeland, Colin Campbell QC

Upon receipt of the Law Society letter, Murray attended at the Niagara Detention Centre to update Bernardo on developments. Murray said Bernardo "went ballistic," since the Crown would now inevitably obtain possession of the tapes. He told Bernardo the possession of the tapes could be litigated, but Bernardo, he said, "saw the beginning of the end."

On September 8, 1994, at the request of Bernardo, Rosen visited him in the Niagara Detention Centre. Bernardo showed Rosen a copy of Murray's notice of application for removal as counsel of record. The notice requested that no affidavit need be filed in support of the application. Bernardo told Rosen generally about the contents of the letter from the Law Society and, for the first time, Rosen learned about the existence and contents of the tapes.

Rosen's Application

Rosen said he was concerned that the tapes were being turned over before he, as new defence counsel, had an opportunity to evaluate them and make the appropriate professional and ethical decisions about them. He, accordingly, prepared a notice of application for an order that Murray had been discharged as counsel of record and therefore lacked status to retain the tapes or turn them over to the court. He also wrote Mr. Cooper demanding the evidence and received a reply.

At the hearing of September 12, 1994 before LeSage ACJOC, Mr. Ruby represented Rosen, Mr. Cooper represented Murray and Mr. Stewart appeared for the Crown. After some preliminary skirmishing and a brief adjournment, it was agreed, with the approval of LeSage ACJOC, that the package of videotapes be turned over to Ruby and Rosen on their undertaking they would deal ethically, legally and professionally with it and would preserve its integrity. Murray was allowed to withdraw from the case. Later on in the morning, LeSage ACJOC adjourned the matter to October 7, 1994 to allow Rosen to assess his position.

Murray's Written Summaries

On September 10, 1994, at Mr. Cooper's direction, Murray prepared summaries of the critical and non-critical tapes. At the end of each of the summaries of the non-critical tapes he added comments as follows:

Non-Critical Tape 1

It may have significance to the stalking behaviour the prosecution asserts. The defence may gain some assistance because of the family relations, and the behaviour of the people at the party.

Non-Critical Tape 2

This tape could form potential evidence for a defence, particularly as it relates to Karla's general credibility, her apparent predilection for young girls, and the fact that there appear to be no marks or bruises on her nude body. At her interviews at KPW, she indicated she was beaten repeatedly during the trip to Florida, and on the way back.

Non-Critical Tape 3

All acts are clearly consensual, and the tape does not involve any of the alleged victims.

 It may be potentially of assistance to the defence, particularly as it relates to Karla's credibility.

Non-Critical Tape 4

The tape may have some significance to the defence. It does not depict and [sic] sexual act with Tammy, or any of the other alleged victims.

The summaries of the two critical tapes have no added comments.

Rosen's Reaction to the Tapes

On September 13, 1994 Rosen, Ruby and MacDonald viewed the tapes. Rosen said he was stunned by what he saw, became very concerned about being counsel in the case and wondered what possible defence he would be able to generate in light of the tapes. He realized he might have an obligation to turn the material over to the authorities. It was agreed that Ruby would immediately begin research on this point while Rosen would approach the Crown to see if the case could be settled.

September 16, 1994—Rosen's First Resolution Meeting with the Crown

By September 16, Rosen said, he had concluded he had to turn over the tapes, although his research team was trying to find authority to allow him to keep them. He believed the Crown was aware that the "package" was a collection of tapes. Without disclosing exactly what he had, he planned to see if there was an opportunity for a resolution of the charges.

 At the meeting, Rosen told Crown counsel the defence possessed evidence that, if publicly displayed, would be a tragedy for the families of the victims and would be humiliating to the memory of their children. He suggested if his client were given some interest in resolving the case, it would be unnecessary for the evidence to be used. He offered Bernardo's co-operation in making a clean breast of everything he had done and in submitting to a testing program so that society might find out "… how and why he became who he was … ." Rosen testified he had little else to bargain with because either the Crown would execute a search warrant or the tapes would be given over voluntarily.

 By September 17, according to Rosen, his research team had found in every single case they had looked at, that physical items were not covered by privilege and counsel was held to be obliged to deliver the items to the authorities. On September 18, Rosen wrote to Mr. Stewart at the Crown Law Office. His letter said, in part:

Second, at the present time and subject to an opportunity to properly research and assess the issue, I take the position that the "material" is part of the defence brief and that there is no obligation on the defence to produce it to the prosecution.

Rosen said he wrote the letter, "to attempt to preserve on the record Bernardo's primary position, whether it's tenable or not, which is that it's part of the brief and should stay in the file."

September 20, 1994—Rosen's Second Resolution Meeting

Rosen met again with Crown counsel on September 20. Various avenues of settlement were discussed. Ironically, it appears that Rosen's best chance of settlement lay in the very horror of the tapes. Rosen's evidence was that, at the meeting, Mr. Code, for the Crown, said, "The power of the defence relies on the power of the tapes and the victims may indeed plead to settle."

At the meeting Rosen took the position he had no obligation to turn the tapes over to the Crown and that he had Charter arguments to support that position. In cross-examination he agreed with Mr. Cooper that he might have said, "I don't think I have any ethical obligation to hand it over," but he said his whole position was one of bluff and negotiation and, notwithstanding his own assessment that he was obliged to turn over the tapes, "… other people had different views … ."

The result of the meeting was that Crown counsel wanted first to see the tapes, then they would review their position.

Rosen Relinquishes the Tapes

On September 21, 1994, Rosen and Ruby met with Bernardo for two and one-half hours and received his instructions to turn over the tapes.

On September 22, 1994 the tapes and the copies were delivered to representatives of the Metropolitan Toronto Police and the Niagara Regional Police.

Part Three—Law and Issues

The Indictment

Kenneth Murray is charged:

That from May 6th, 1993 to September 12th, 1994 inclusive in the Regional Municipality of Niagara, Central South Region, and elsewhere in the Province of Ontario, did willfully obstruct or attempt to obstruct the course of justice by concealing certain video tapes for approximately seventeen months which are the products and/or instrumentalities of crime, those video tapes containing scenes depicting the unlawful confinement of Leslie Erin Mahaffy, unlawful confinement of Kristen Dawn French, aggravated sexual assault of Leslie Erin Mahaffy, aggravated sexual assault of Kristen Dawn French, aggravated sexual assault of Tammy Lynn Homolka, aggravated sexual assault of Jane Doe by Paul Bernardo and Karla Homolka, contrary to section 139(2) of the *Criminal Code*.

Crime and Ethics

I have been supplied by counsel with voluminous material on legal ethics.

I want to make clear that my function in this case is limited to deciding if Murray has committed the crime of attempting to obstruct justice, not to judge his ethics. While ethics may integrate with the issue of mens rea, ethical duties do not automatically translate into legal obligations.

...

Justification

... [Murray] cannot ... be said to attempt to obstruct justice if he had legal justification for his conduct.

There is no obligation on a citizen to help the police, but taking positive steps to conceal evidence is unlawful: see *Ingleton v. Dibble*, [1972] 1 All ER 275, [1972] 1 QB 480 (QBDC); *R v. Lajoie* (1989) 47 CCC (3d) 380 (Que. CA); *R v. Lavin* (1992), 76 CCC (3d) 279 (Que. CA); *R v. Akrofi* (1997), 113 CCC (3d) 201 (Ont. CA).

While Mr. Cooper conceded a lay person may not conceal evidence, he argued that defence counsel's obligations to the client dictate a special status that provides reasonable justification in some cases for concealment of evidence, and while the tapes could not be permanently suppressed, these tapes had some exculpatory value and counsel was entitled to temporarily conceal them for defence purposes.

Mr. Cooper did not suggest that confidentiality of the tapes is protected under the umbrella of solicitor–client privilege and no privilege, in my opinion, attaches to this evidence. Solicitor–client privilege protects communications between solicitor and client: see *Solosky v. R*, [1980] 1 SCR 821 at p. 829, 50 CCC (2d) 495 at p. 502. These videotapes are not communications. They are, rather, dramatic evidence of crime and pre-existed the solicitor–client relationship. They are not similar, for example, to a sketch, which might be prepared by a client to help explain a point to his counsel, or even a videotape prepared for that purpose. Murray's discussions with his client about the tapes are covered by the privilege; the physical objects, the tapes, are not. Hiding them from the police on behalf of the client cannot be said to be an aspect of solicitor–client communication. ...

Although Murray had a duty of confidentiality to Bernardo, absent solicitor–client privilege, there was no legal basis permitting concealment of the tapes. In this sense Murray had no higher right than any other citizen. Nor, in my opinion, can it be said that concealing the critical tapes was permissible because they may have had some exculpatory value. They were overwhelmingly inculpatory. Some of the United States authorities, including the *ABA Standards for Criminal Justice: Prosecution Function and Defense Function*, 3rd ed., suggest counsel may retain incriminating physical evidence for a reasonable time for examination and testing. There was no testing contemplated here and, by some time in June 1993, Murray had examined the tapes and knew their contents. He chose to continue to conceal them.

In a line of United States cases beginning with *State ex rel. Sowers v. Olwell*, 64 Wash. 2d 828 (1964), not only is there recognition that solicitor–client privilege does not protect physical evidence, but there is a suggested obligation on counsel to turn over incriminating physical evidence to a prosecutor.

That position appears to have been supported by Canadian commentators, at least with reference to instrumentalities of crime. ...

I am not entirely clear why there exists this almost universal view that incriminating physical evidence must go to the prosecution. In my opinion it does not follow that because concealment of incriminating physical evidence is forbidden there is always a corresponding positive obligation to disclose. In *R v. P. (M.B.)*, [1994] 1 SCR 555, 89 CCC (3d) 289, Lamer CJC said at p. 578 SCR, 304 CCC:

> With respect to disclosure, the defence in Canada is under no legal obligation to co-operate with or assist the Crown by announcing any special defence, such as an alibi, or by producing documentary or physical evidence. ...

Perhaps the general view that there is a turn-over obligation to the prosecution arises from the dilemma counsel faces once improperly in possession of incriminating physical evidence. At that point, almost any step involves potential risk of criminal liability. For example, in Mr. Martin's address ... , he recounts the difficulty created when the murder weapon is dropped on the lawyer's desk.

> What should the lawyer do?
> If he says, "Take the gun and come back after you have disposed of it," he has committed a criminal offence unless, of course, he can persuade a jury at his own trial that his intention was merely to instruct the client that he should leave the pistol at his residence so that it would be available to the police under a search warrant. If he takes possession of the pistol and puts it in his desk or vault a serious problem is created. Obviously, if he buried the pistol in his backyard he would be an accessory after the fact. If he puts it in his desk or vault, may it not be argued that he has just as effectively concealed it?

The ABA Standards, supra, provide generally that defence counsel should return an incriminating physical item to the source after a reasonable period to allow for testing, etc.

Even if that were permissible it was not an option open to Murray. While he had no obligation to assist the police in their investigation or the Crown in its prosecution, Murray could not be a party to concealing this evidence. Having removed the tapes from their hiding place, he could not hide them again. Nor could he implement any instructions from Bernardo that would result in their continued concealment.

Once he had discovered the overwhelming significance of the critical tapes, Murray, in my opinion, was left with but three legally justifiable options:

a) Immediately turn over the tapes to the prosecution, either directly or anonymously;

b) Deposit then with trial judge; or

c) Disclose their existence to the prosecution and prepare to do battle to retain them.

I am satisfied that Murray's concealment of the critical tapes was an act that had a tendency to pervert or obstruct the course of justice.

Mens Rea

The onus is on the Crown to prove beyond a reasonable doubt that it was Murray's intention to obstruct the course of justice.

By putting the tapes beyond the reach of the police and the Crown, Murray clearly intended to impede the prosecution of the case against Bernardo. Defence strategy was based upon concealment of the tapes.

If Murray was aware concealment was unlawful, then the only reasonable inference would be, that by doing so, he intended to obstruct the course of justice.

Murray knew it was unlawful to permanently suppress the tapes. Asked by Mr. Cooper for his reaction to Bernardo's August 30, 1994 direction not to disclose the tapes, Murray said:

> It put me in a position that I was being asked to suppress evidence. I was being asked to do something that was improper, unlawful, unethical and something that I couldn't either under the rules of conduct or professional ethics do. ...

The factual questions of intent then are:

1. Did Murray intend to conceal the tapes permanently or only up to the point of resolution discussions or trial?

2. If the latter, was it his honest belief he was entitled to do so?

Murray's Intention

Murray testified he intended to use the tapes in the defence. With the tapes he could prove Homolka to be a liar and pave the way for Bernardo to give evidence that it was Homolka who committed the murders. The tapes would be used to cross-examine her at trial or in resolution discussions with the Crown.

Mr. Scott argued that Murray's evidence was a tissue of lies, that his intention was to permanently suppress the tapes and he went to Mr. Cooper for advice only when the case was so ill-prepared for trial that Rosen had to be brought in to take over and Murray was faced with giving evidence by affidavit as to his reasons for ceasing to act.

Murray was an enthusiastic witness and his answers at times on cross-examination were more combative than responsive. Perhaps that is natural for an advocate. He was casual with the truth in selling the case to Rosen. I cannot conclude from his demeanour alone that he was untruthful in his evidence. Substantial character evidence was given as to his excellent reputation for integrity and truthfulness.

I am skeptical of Murray's evidence of his intention. I am troubled by the following:

1. Murray's evidence was inconsistent as to his tactical plans to use the tapes. His primary plan seems to have been that, without disclosing them to the Crown, he would surprise Homolka with them on cross-examination at trial. Another plan was that the Crown would get the tapes as soon as serious plea negotiations occurred, or perhaps, he said, negotiations could be concluded without the Crown knowing the contents of the tapes.

2. Murray failed to disclose the existence of the tapes to Rosen.

3. Rosen testified there was nothing in the file when he took over that suggested any use of tapes in the defence.

4. In Murray's summaries of the tapes, he suggested how the non-critical tapes might be used at trial. He had no similar suggestions for the critical tapes.

5. In his resolution discussions with the Crown, Murray made no mention of the tapes.

6. The tapes were not used to tie down Homolka in cross-examination at the Kingston Prison for Women. Nor was there any mention of use of the tapes in the file prepared for that cross-examination. MacDonald conducted the cross-examination without having seen the critical tapes.

7. As of September 1, 1994, 11 days before trial motions were to begin, Doyle and MacDonald (who were said to have spent hundreds of hours preparing the case for trial) had not seen the critical tapes. The absence of consultation with co-counsel MacDonald is bizarre. In a case of this nature, one would normally expect that extensive preparation be conducted with co-counsel and very careful strategies and plans developed as to how the defence is to be approached. There was nothing of that nature apparent here in relation to the critical tapes. ... If the tapes were inevitably going to come out and probably be used at trial, MacDonald eventually had to see them. That would occur in spite of all Murray's efforts to "protect" her.

8. Murray received authorization from legal aid to retain not only MacDonald and Doyle, but also numbers of other individuals to assist in the defence. Tim Lipson and Anne-Marie Hart took over the conduct of the Scarborough Rape charges. Tim Breen was to assist in arguing specific legal points. Dr. Mark Ben-Aron was asked to develop a psychiatric profile of Homolka. He was present at the cross-examination of Homolka at the Kingston Prison for Women. Dr. Fred Jaffe consulted on pathology and Leo Adler and the firm of Helix Biotech provided DNA expertise. Professor Daniel Yarmi advised in the area of psychology. Dr. John Bradford dealt with forensic evidence. Private investigators were instructed to locate background information on Karla Homolka. ... There is no evidence that any of these individuals ever saw the tapes or were briefed on their contents ... . Dr. Ben-Aron was expected to develop a psychiatric profile of Homolka without knowing videotapes existed that showed her apparently revelling in sexual perversions ... . Professor Yarmi no doubt would have been assisted in his analysis of the psychology of the case by viewing Bernardo and Homolka engaged in these crimes. In spite of all this preparation and all the experts and other individuals assisting in preparation for trial without knowledge of the tapes, Murray's evidence was that "the trial was the tapes" and their existence made the case a simple one.

9. Murray on August 30, 1994 had Bernardo sign a series of directions that, if followed, would result in continued concealment of the tapes.

10. It is difficult to conceive how the critical tapes were useful to Bernardo's case. They were damning evidence against him. Murray agreed that once shown the tapes "any jury would have convicted him of sinking the Titanic." While they provided scope for the cross-examination of Homolka, as Rosen said, "the client would have been in a substantially better position if the tapes had never surfaced."

11. When asked by Mr. Cooper why he failed on September 1, 1994 to mention his ethical dilemma to LeSage ACJOC, Murray said:

> Because, as much as I was in a jackpot, the client's interests are paramount to protect. There may be an ethical issue, there may be something that I had to straighten out, but if I had gone to that meeting and said, well My Lord, the reason I want to get off is there's these video tapes that, you know, bury his defence, that the Crown doesn't have and he's told me to hold on to them. Well I couldn't do that … .

This hardly sounds as if Murray, at least at that point, was viewing the tapes as a defence "bonanza."

Mr. Cooper submitted that Murray's explanations should deal with my concerns. While Murray's plans to use the critical tapes at trial were unfocused, it was clear they were to be employed in some way at some stage. Much is explained, he said, by Murray's belief he had to keep the tapes strictly secret in order to retain their tactical value. Rosen could not be told because he was only conditionally on the record for Bernardo. None of the four directions was in fact followed. The tapes were not specifically used in the Homolka cross-examination because of the difficulties mentioned in the evidence and the choice was made to hold back the tapes for their surprise value in cross-examination.

Mr. Cooper argued that Murray should be believed when he says he planned to use the critical tapes for defence purposes. In a careful and detailed review of the evidence, Mr. Cooper examined the position of the defence had the tapes not existed compared to the position with the tapes available.

Without the tapes, he suggested, the evidence against Bernardo was overwhelming. In addition to other pieces of circumstantial evidence, the DNA placed Bernardo in the house and having had sexual connection with one of the victims. The defence would then be faced with Homolka, an eyewitness, who would play her role as innocent, savagely beaten wife, coerced into helping Bernardo commit his crimes. There was little potential for a successful cross-examination of her. It was a "he did it"—"she did it" case, and, with the Scarborough Rapes going in as similar fact evidence, "Bernardo the Stalker" had no chance.

The tapes, suggested Mr. Cooper, gave Bernardo a slim chance. While they show Bernardo in a terrible light, Homolka turns out to be almost as bad. The benefit to the defence was not just that Homolka could be shown as a liar, but also as a person capable of committing murder. She is shown on the tapes administering halothane to her sister and to Jane Doe, and participating in sexual assaults on both of them. The tapes also show her using items of her dead sister's clothing to sexually stimulate Bernardo. For the same purpose she employs a rose which she was then going to put on her sister's grave. Mr. Cooper conceded the tapes were "an atomic bomb" for Bernardo, but, he suggested, "it bombed both ways."

In spite of all the inferences I am tempted to draw against the credibility of Murray based on his actions as I have enumerated them, I am satisfied on the basis of Mr. Cooper's argument that a defence strategy of use of the tapes at trial was reasonably feasible. That lends support to Murray's evidence that he did not intend to permanently suppress them. In this context, I have warned myself about the dangers of hindsight.

Similarly, Murray's alleged plan to use the tapes to negotiate is not unfeasible. Rosen used them for that purpose and they had the *in terrorem* value mentioned by Mr. Code.

Murray was not ready for trial. MacDonald was ill or had resigned from the file and Doyle was on maternity leave. His unpreparedness for trial does not necessarily rule out, however, that a significant reason for giving up the file and finally facing the dilemma with the tapes, was a conflict about instructions from his client.

Murray's evidence that he would at some time disclose the tapes is supported by the fact that MacDonald and Doyle knew they existed. Murray would know that the pact of silence, no matter how solemn, would be unlikely to survive the Bernardo trial if the tapes were ultimately suppressed.

I conclude, therefore, that Murray's explanation as to his use of the critical tapes in the defence of his client is one that might reasonably be true.

Murray's Belief

Assuming he intended to use the tapes for defence purposes, did Murray believe he had a right to conceal them to the extent he did?

Murray testified he believed his conduct was lawful.

Criminal Code s. 139(2) casts a broad net. It does not specifically isolate as criminal the conduct Murray engaged in.

The only official guide given to lawyers in Ontario on this issue is contained in rule 10 of the Law Society of Upper Canada Professional Conduct Handbook. It reads in part:

> 2. ... The lawyer must discharge this duty by fair and honourable means, without illegality and in a manner consistent with the lawyer's duty to treat the tribunal with candor, fairness, courtesy and respect. The lawyer must not, for example: ...
>
>> e) knowingly attempt to deceive a tribunal or influence the course of justice by offering false evidence, misstating facts or law, presenting or relying upon a false or deceptive affidavit, suppressing what ought to be disclosed, or otherwise assisting in any fraud, crime or illegal conduct; ...

The rule provides no guidance as to the nature of evidence that "ought to be disclosed." It is of small help either to counsel or to clients who may believe that both their secrets and their evidence are safe with their lawyers.

While Murray made only a token effort to find out what his obligations were, had he done careful research he might have remained confused. The weight of legal opinion in Ontario is to the effect that lawyers may not conceal material physical evidence of crime, but how this rule applies to particular facts has been the subject of extensive discussion. Lawyers in the United States have been afflicted with the same dilemma. In the materials supplied to me by counsel, there is reference to at least 15 law journal discussions on the issue.

Unlike Murray, Rosen, as soon as he viewed the tapes, realized he was faced with a substantial legal and ethical problem and set up a team of highly experienced counsel to investigate and provide him with an answer. The research team was not unanimous in its opinion, although the majority favoured immediate disclosure. Even after receiving the opinion of his research team, Rosen continued to take the position with the Crown that the tapes need not be produced, albeit, he may have been bluffing.

If I make the assumption Murray intended to use the tapes in the defence, I have no difficulty with the proposition that he may well have believed under the circumstances he had no legal duty to disclose the tapes until resolution discussions or trial.

Part Four—Conclusion

In summary, I find:

1) Murray's concealment of the critical tapes had the tendency to obstruct justice.

2) Murray knew it would be obstructing justice to permanently suppress the tapes.

3) He may not have intended to permanently suppress them.

4) He may have believed he had no obligation to disclose them before trial.

In *R v. W. (D.)*, [1991] 1 SCR 742, 63 CCC (3d) 397, Cory J spelled out what a jury must be told where credibility is a significant issue. A trial judge sitting without a jury must take the same approach. Cory J stated at p. 757 SCR, p. 409 CCC:

The trial judge should instruct the jury that they need not firmly believe or disbelieve any witness or set of witnesses. Specifically, the trial judge is required to instruct the jury that they must acquit the accused in two situations. First, if they believe the accused. Secondly, if they do not believe the accused's evidence but still have a reasonable doubt as to his guilt after considering the accused's evidence in the context of the evidence as a whole … .

In the context of the whole of the evidence, Murray's testimony I find raises a reasonable doubt as to his intention to obstruct justice.

I find him not guilty.

Accused acquitted.

NOTES AND QUESTIONS

1. When Murray viewed the videotapes and learned the extent of Bernardo's culpability, did Murray make a moral decision (that is, a decision that implicated his own ethical values) when deciding whether or not to continue representing a factually guilty client?

2. Assume that Murray had not acted improperly, and had (in accordance with Gravely J's suggestion) simply argued resolutely that the tapes ought to be suppressed. If Murray took this approach after viewing the videotapes, would this action implicate Murray's ethical values? Would it be a moral choice? Construct an ethical equation describing this decision, using your own personal utility preferences.

3. Can the neutral-conduit function justify Murray's decision to covertly search for physical evidence in the accused's home? Is this an ethical (or sensible) action for a lawyer to take? Is this part of a lawyer's job?

4. Assuming that lawyers are taken to be aware of the Court's decision in *R v. Murray*, are subsequent defence counsel precluded from arguing that they did not know that their actions had the tendency to pervert justice or that they had an obligation to disclose similar evidence? If Murray's defences are unavailable to future lawyers, what punishments or incentives might be effective in preventing future incidents akin to Murray's case?

5. Was Murray simply pursuing a neutral-conduit role, or did he (and the rest of his defence team) have a personal stake in winning? When answering this question, consider the following quote from the court's decision:

> The defence team had lunch together on the balcony of 57 Bayview. Murray told Doyle and MacDonald that they would have to make sure that no one found out about the tapes, and the three of them would have to make a pact that they would be the only ones that ever knew what had been obtained. They shook hands, hugged, and agreed not to say anything to anyone about the tapes. Murray said in his evidence that he knew "they wouldn't tell anybody about the tapes." He felt the discovery of the tapes was a "bonanza" or "gold mine" for the defence.

6. If Murray *did* have a personal stake in winning, how does this effect his "utility calculations"?

7. Which of the following actions qualify as "ethical": (1) deciding to act exactly as Murray acted; (2) deciding, upon viewing the critical tapes, to abandon Bernardo's defence and disclose the tapes to the Crown; (3) encouraging Bernardo to agree to disclose the tapes; (4) leaving the practice of law and taking a less "ethically taxing" job? When considering these questions, recall that some proponents of the neutral-conduit model contend that the moral world of lawyers is less complicated than that of ordinary people.

8. After having viewed the tapes, Murray assisted Bernardo in entering a plea of "not guilty" on all counts (including counts related to assaults that were clearly depicted in the tapes). Given that Murray knew that his client had committed the assaults in question, was it ethical for Murray to assist his client in the entering of a "not guilty" plea? Is it *ever* unethical for a lawyer to assist a client in entering a "not guilty" plea? Would it have been ethical for Murray to ask to be removed as counsel once he discovered (1) that his client was guilty, and (2) that his client intended to plead "not guilty"? These issues are addressed in greater detail in part II of this book.

9. What were the reasons Murray ultimately gave for asking to be removed as counsel of record?

10. Rosen attempted to secure a plea bargain by arguing, among other things, that a favourable bargain could eliminate the need to show the tapes in open court, saving the victims' families from the trauma that they would experience if forced to view the tapes. Is this an ethical approach to advocacy? Is it ethical to use the horrific nature of the accused's actions to procure a *lighter* sentence? If Bernardo attempted to make this deal on his own behalf, would that be considered an ethical act?

11. Was Rosen's use of the tapes in plea bargaining justified by the neutral-conduit model? Did the neutral-conduit model relieve Rosen of the need to consider moral issues when deciding to adopt this course of action? How can Rosen's decision be expressed using the ethical equation developed in chapters 1 and 2? Can Rosen's decision be explained by reference to "self-interest"?

12. During plea negotiations, Rosen "bluffed" concerning the nature of his ethical obligations, suggesting that he had no obligation to turn over the tapes. Is "bluffing" just another word for lying? Is this ethical? How does this compare to the dicta of the House of Lords in *Rondel*, above, in which lawyers are said to have an overriding duty to "truth" and "justice"? Does this duty disappear during plea negotiations? Why or why not?

VIII. Getting Caught: Decisions and Uncertainty

A. Introduction

The examples of "ethical decision making" found in earlier sections of this book have been unrealistic in one important way: in each case, decision makers have been assumed to have known, with absolute certainty, whether or not their conduct would be detected and subjected to moral censure. In example 3.8, for instance, Kenneth knew that his behaviour would be detected by the Law Society and that he would be forced to pay a fine of $1,000. Examples in chapters 1 and 2 suffered from similarly unrealistic assumptions: in each example, our decision maker was blessed with the unusual power of knowing, in advance, whether he or she would be detected and punished when engaging in unethical behaviour.

The real world is far less predictable than the world depicted in the preceding examples. Lawyers who violate ethical norms often hope that their conduct will not be detected, but acknowledge a *chance* (rather than an absolute certainty) that they will be caught and punished. When a person considers breaking a community's moral code or violating professional standards, that person rarely knows whether or not he or she will be detected or, if the behaviour *is* detected, how severe the consequences are likely to be. The future consequences of ethical decisions are impossible to predict with perfect accuracy. As a result, it is difficult to predict, with any degree of confidence or precision, the costs and benefits that will flow from our decisions. A realistic model of ethical choices must account for these sources of uncertainty. Economics takes account of uncertainty through the mechanism of "expected-value calculations." These calculations, together with their effect on the economic theory of legal ethics, are discussed in the following sections of this chapter. Readers who are familiar with economics and expected-value calculations should feel free to move on to section IX, below.

B. Expected Values

In order to account for uncertain outcomes in a decision-making model, economists make use of the mathematics of probability. While the notion of probability allows us to generate sophisticated and powerful mathematical models designed to evaluate choices made in conditions of uncertainty, the calculations underlying these models are quite straightforward. Katz and Rosen provide the following useful summary of the relevant mathematics:

> The probability of a given state of the world is a measure of the likelihood that it occurs. If the event cannot happen, its probability is zero; if the event is certain to occur, its probability is one. If it might happen, but not for sure, its probability is somewhere between zero and one. For example, the probability that a heart will be drawn from a fair deck of cards is $13/52 = 1/4$ (or 0.25), the fraction of hearts in the deck. This means that there are 25 chances in 100 that this event will occur, and 75 chances in 100 that it will not. For a given random process, the probabilities of all the states of the world must sum to 1, because it is certain that one or the other of the states of the world will occur. Hence, if there are only two states of the world and the probability of the first occurring is p, then the probability of the second is $(1 - p)$. Because the probability of a heart appearing is $1/4$, the probability of "any other suit" is $1/4$.[43]

Assume that you and 99 of your closest friends have placed your names into a hat. Someone is about to draw a name out of the hat. There is a 100 percent chance that a name will be drawn; that is, the probability that a name will be drawn from the hat is 1, an absolute certainty. There is 1 chance in 100 that the name drawn will be yours—that is, the probability that *your* name will be drawn is $1/100$, or 0.01. Let the probability of your name being drawn from the hat be represented by p: that is, $p = 0.01$. The probability that a name *other than yours* will be drawn from the hat is equal to $(1 - p)$. This equation is derived by taking the 100 percent chance that *some name* will be drawn (a probability of 1), and subtracting from that the 1 percent chance that the name drawn will be yours (a probability of 0.01). In this case, where p equals 0.01, the value of $(1 - p)$ equals $(1 - 0.01)$, which comes out to 0.99. This is another way of saying that there is a 99 percent chance that a name other than yours will be drawn from the hat.

Once we have developed mathematical representations of the likelihood that uncertain events will occur, we can use these mathematics to (1) calculate the value of costs and benefits that may or may not arise, or (2) quantify costs and benefits, the precise values of which cannot be known in advance. Our calculation of such amounts is based on the notion of "expected value," which can be defined as the value of any potential cost or benefit multiplied by the likelihood that the relevant cost or benefit will arise. For example, the expected value of a 50 percent chance of winning a $100 prize is equal to the amount of the potential gain ($100) multiplied by the likelihood that the prize will be won (50 percent, or 0.5). In other words, a 50 percent chance of a $100 gain is worth ($100 × 0.5), or $50.[44] If someone offered you a chance to buy a ticket that yielded a 50

---

43   Michael L. Katz and Harvey S. Rosen, *Microeconomics*, 3d ed. (Boston: McGraw-Hill, 1998), 163.

44   The full calculation is actually ($100 × 0.5) + ($0 × 0.5) = $50. The second set of terms ($0 × 0.5) reflects the 50 percent chance that you will *not* win the $50 prize. In mathematical terms, "expected

percent chance of winning $100, you would be wise to pay less than $50 for the ticket. Based on our expected-value calculation, a 50 percent chance at a $100 prize is worth exactly $50. Paying more than $50 for something worth $50 is a bad idea.

What if our potential prize is not an all-or-nothing proposition? For example, how much should one be willing to pay for a ticket that gave 40 percent odds of winning $100 and a 60 percent chance of winning $30? Once again, we can use expected values to find the answer. In this example, there are two possible outcomes. Let X represent the outcome in which the ticket yields $100. Let Y represent the outcome in which the ticket yields $30. Since the ticket will yield either $100 or $30 (there are no other possibilities), X and Y are the only potential outcomes to consider. The value of the ticket can be determined by adding the expected value of X ($100 multiplied by the 40 percent probability of winning $100) and the value of Y ($30 multiplied by the 60 percent probability of winning $30). The expected-value (EV) calculation looks like this:

$$
\begin{aligned}
\text{EV of ticket} \quad &= \quad (\$100 \times 0.4) + (\$30 \times 0.6) \\
&= \quad (\$40) + (\$18) \\
&= \quad \$58
\end{aligned}
$$

In other words, a ticket yielding a 60 percent chance of winning a $30 prize and a 40 percent chance of yielding a $100 prize has an expected value of $58. A utility-maximizing individual (with nothing better to do with his or her money) would be willing to pay anything up to $58 for such a ticket.[45]

In sum, the expected value of a decision is determined by adding together the values of all potential outcomes of the relevant choice multiplied by the likelihood that the relevant outcome will happen. The manner in which these calculations can be used in an economic theory of legal ethics is described in the following section.

C. Expected Values and Ethical Decisions

The foregoing mathematical tools can be used to supplement our model of the rational decision-making process. Previous sections of this book have demonstrated that decision makers weigh the costs and benefits of the decisions that they make. This assessment of costs and benefits is performed for the purpose of calculating the utility that a potential act will yield. In many cases, the costs and benefits of a decision are uncertain. In these cases, the utility of an action may be difficult to compute: committing a contemplated act may yield a 50 percent chance of a certain benefit, or a 30 percent chance of a certain cost. Where an individual makes decisions under conditions of uncertainty, he or she

---

value" can be defined as the sum of the probabilities of each potential outcome multiplied by the value of each potential outcome. Thus, in a world with three potential outcomes (labeled A, B, and C), the expected value would be calculated as follows: (probability of A × value of A) + (probability of B × value of B) + (probability of C × value of C). It should be noted that, because A, B, and C and the only possible outcomes, the sum of their probabilities must be 1.

45   In reality, we must also assess our ticket-buyer's attitude toward risks. Some people are "risk seekers," who would happily pay more than $58 for our hypothetical ticket, partly for the excitement of "taking a gamble." The economics of "risk preference" are beyond the scope of this book.

cannot predict (with absolute confidence or precision) the utility that a particular act will yield. In such cases, decision makers subconsciously rely on expected values. Consider the following example.

Example 3.10

Tony Sargent is a Canadian lawyer who is thinking of misappropriating $50,000 from his client's trust account. If Tony takes this action, he will gain $50,000. There is a 30 percent chance that Tony will be caught and forced to (1) return the money, and (2) pay a fine of $130,000. If Tony's behaviour is not detected, there will be no fines or penalties. For the purposes of this example, assume that Tony is perfectly amoral—that is, he never feels guilty about his actions, and therefore loses no utility in the form of psychological trauma, nor does he gain utility by virtue of the "thrills" associated with wrongful acts.

The gross utility benefit of taking the money is clear: Tony will gain $50,000 of utility (in the form of the money he takes from his client's account). The costs of Tony's action are uncertain. He *may* have to pay a total cost of $180,000 (in fines plus the return of his client's money). Tony might, however, incur a total cost of $0. If his behaviour is *not* detected, no costs will flow from Tony's unethical action.

How would economic theory describe the decision Tony faces? Recall our basic ethical equation: $A - B = X$. Recall that A equals the sum of the benefits of a potential course of action, and B equals the sum of the action's costs. X, which is generated by subtracting B from A, is the net utility that the relevant action yields. Where X is positive, the benefits outweigh the action's costs and a utility-maximizing individual will take the relevant action. Where X is negative, the action yields a net loss of utility, and a utility-maximizing individual will avoid the relevant act.

In the present example, Tony's action is difficult to describe using our basic model of ethical calculations. This difficulty arises because of the uncertainty that is inherent in figure B: the gross utility costs of Tony's proposed unethical action, which will either be $0 or $180,000 (depending upon whether Tony is caught). If Tony's action is to be described by our ethical equation, we need a mechanism for determining the cost generated through the action Tony proposes. Happily, the notion of "expected values" provides the mechanism we need. Recall the mathematics of probability. A decision to take the money can generate two possibilities for Tony—one in which he is caught and forced to pay a total of $180,000 (state Q), and one in which his behaviour is not detected and he pays no cost at all (state R). According to the facts of our example, there is a 30 percent chance that state Q will come to pass. There is accordingly a 70 percent chance that state R will come to pass (since states Q and R are the only possibilities, and there is a 100 percent chance that either Q or R will happen). In the language of probability, the probability (p) of state Q is 0.3 (or 30 percent), while the probability of state R is $(1 - p)$, or 0.7.

Tony can calculate the "expected cost" of a decision to misappropriate his client's funds by doing a simple calculation. He must add the probabilities of the potential outcomes of his actions multiplied by the costs of these possible outcomes. In this example, the "expected cost" of misappropriating Tony's client's funds equals the sum of

(1) the probability of state Q (0.3) multiplied by the costs associated with that state ($180,000), and (2) the probability of state R (0.7) multiplied by the total costs associated with that state ($0). Tony's expected cost (EC) calculation accordingly looks like this:

$$
\begin{aligned}
EC &= (0.3)(\$180,000) + (0.7)(\$0) \\
&= (\$54,000) + (\$0) \\
&= \$54,000
\end{aligned}
$$

In order to describe Tony's decision in economic terms, we can now insert the expected cost of $54,000 into our ethical equation: A − B = X. A is equal to $50,000 (the gross utility benefit of misappropriating $50,000). B is equal to the *expected* cost of Tony's action—namely, $54,000. X, which is the result of subtracting B from A, is −$4,000. This is a negative figure: the expected costs of Tony's proposed activity exceed the expected benefits. The action will result in a net loss in utility, and (if he is rational) Tony will refrain from the relevant act.[46]

Note that Tony's proposed action gave rise to a *certain* benefit and an *uncertain* cost. If the benefits to be reaped from Tony's action were uncertain, our expected-value model could be used to calculate the "expected benefit" (EB) of the relevant decision. If, for example, Tony's proposed course of action gave rise to a 50 percent chance of generating a $50,000 gross benefit, and a 50 percent chance of generating only a $30,000 gross benefit, we could use our expected-value calculation to determine the expected benefit that these two potential outcomes would provide.[47] Having completed this calculation, the expected benefit figure would have replaced A in our equation. The expected benefit would be compared to the expected cost. If the expected benefit is greater than the expected cost, the decision maker will take the relevant action.

The mathematics of probability lead us to change the meaning of terms found in our algebraic expression of ethical choices. A rational actor will still govern his or her decisions as if he or she followed the equation A − B = X. In conditions of uncertainty, figure A now represents the *expected* benefit of the relevant action (the sum of possible benefits multiplied by the likelihood that each benefit will arise), and figure B now represents the *expected* cost (the sum of possible costs multiplied by the likelihood that each of the costs will be incurred). Having supplemented our basic algebraic expression (A − B = X) with the mathematics of probability, we are now equipped to describe moral decisions in which the decision maker is uncertain of the consequences that might flow from competing courses of action.

---

46   To some readers, the following alternative (yet equivalent) approach will seem more intuitive. There are two possible outcomes of Tony's decision. Either he will be $50,000 better off by taking the money (state Y), or he will be $130,000 *worse* off by taking the money, being caught, and paying the relevant costs (state Z). There is a 70 percent chance of state Y, and a 30 percent chance of state Z. As a result, taking the money yields an expected gain of $35,000 (0.7 × $50,000) and an expected cost of $39,000 (0.3 × $130,000). Subtracting costs from benefits, we are left with −$4,000 (the same figure generated by our ethical equation). However one approaches the relevant mathematics, the outcome is the same—Tony can expect to be $4,000 worse off if he decides to take the money from his client.

47   In this example, the expected benefit (EB) is calculated as follows: EB = (0.5)($50,000) + (0.5)($30,000), which equals $25,000 + $15,000, for a final EB of $40,000.

Cooter and Ulen provide the following useful summary of the economic account of decision making in conditions of uncertainty:

> The basic idea is that rational decision-makers proceed in four steps: first, they determine the probability of each possible state of the world; second, they attach utility to each possible state; next, they multiply the probabilities by the utilities to give the expected utility; and, finally, they choose the action that maximizes the expected utility. To illustrate, suppose Joan and Elizabeth agree to flip a coin for the last piece of pie. Joan will get the remaining piece of pie if, and only if, the coin lands heads. The probability that a tossed coin will land heads is 0.5, so the expected utility from the gamble is 0.5 times the utility value of a piece of pie.[48]

Using this simple technique, we can make useful predictions regarding the manner in which individuals respond to costs and incentives under conditions of uncertainty. As we shall see in chapter 4, expected-value models are particularly useful when designing methods of regulating behaviour.

Before making use of our enhanced model of lawyers' ethical choices, it is important to consider objections to the expected-value model of decisions made in conditions of uncertainty. These objections are discussed in the following section.

D. Criticisms of the Expected-Value Model

There are three important (and closely related) objections to the expected-value model described above. Those objections can be summarized as follows:

1. The model does not reflect the actual practice of decision makers. Rather than valuing costs and benefits, and then multiplying these costs and benefits by the probability that each cost or benefit will arise, decision makers simply do whatever "feels right" in the situations they face.

2. Even if people *were* inclined to proceed in the manner predicted by the expected-value model—that is, multiplying utility values by the probability that those values will arise—they lack the information required to perform these calculations. Unlike Tony in example 3.10, above, real people rarely know that there is, for example, a 30 percent chance of a particular ethical rule being enforced, or that precisely 3 in 10 violations will be punished.

3. Even if people (1) wished to account for probability in their decisions, and (2) had access to reliable information concerning the probability that specific costs or benefits would arise, they lack the capacity to digest and process that information in a useful way that leads to rational choices.

In short, one might argue that people lack the inclination, the information, and the ability to act in the manner portrayed by the expected-value model. As a result, one could contend that the expected-value model presents an inaccurate model of the method by which people make decisions.

---

48   Cooter and Ulen, *Law and Economics*, 4th ed. (Boston: Pearson Addison Wesley, 2003), 431.

E. Responses to Criticisms

The key response to criticisms of the expected-value model is that they are based on a distorted view of what the model purports to do. Like most of economics, the notion of expected value does not purport to describe the *actual* decision-making practice of any particular individual. Instead, it describes trends and general tendencies. Most people (even economists) do not construct elaborate spreadsheets setting out the costs and benefits of their actions. On the contrary, the expected-value model posits that individuals tend to act *as though* they were performing the relevant calculations. While a specific individual may lack the inclination, the information, or the intellectual prowess required to reckon with probabilities, large groups of people tend to act as though they are, in fact, governed by the expected-value model. Consider the following example, drawn from my own experience.

Example 3.11: Student Parking

When I was an assistant professor at the University of New Brunswick, students developed a nasty habit of parking their cars in the faculty lot. Students had learned, through trial and error, that the university's overburdened parking enforcement officers rarely ventured near the faculty of law. As a result, there was a slim chance of parking violations being detected (and, consequently, a slim chance of offenders receiving a ticket). The benefit of parking close to the school (particularly during cold New Brunswick winters) outweighed the cost of a parking violation, particularly when one took into account the minimal chance of receiving a ticket. While the ticket might cost $50, the probability of receiving a ticket was near 0. The convenience of parking near the school was worth something greater than 50×0.0, so students rationally, albeit annoyingly, often parked in the faculty lot [49]

An extension of this example demonstrates the human capacity to respond to sudden shifts in probability. After faculty members complained to the university's central administration, parking officers began making regular trips to the faculty's lot. Students began receiving tickets at increased rates. Students quickly responded to the increased probability of receiving a parking ticket by parking elsewhere. The utility cost of parking farther away (in student lots) was less than the expected cost of a $50 ticket multiplied by the new, increased probability (say, 0.6) that an improperly parked car would receive a ticket. As a result, I and my fellow professors were once again able to find parking. Note that individual students sometimes underestimated the likelihood that they would be ticketed, and (after receiving tickets) ended up regretting their decision to park in the faculty lot. While individual students may have failed to account for the probability of a fine, the preponderance of students responded rationally to the increased probability of fines.

---

49 Note that several students, filled with community spirit and loyalty toward their beleaguered professors (who had to pay for their parking spots), must have assigned a high "guilt value" to parking in the faculty lot, which outweighed the utility to be gained from a prime parking space. These students, to whom I shall be forever grateful, parked in the student lots, even on cold days.

Taken in the aggregate, students made accurate predictions regarding the probability of enforcement and responded as rational utility maximizers. As the likelihood of enforcement rose, the expected cost of illegal parking rose along with it. Students responded by violating the rules less frequently.

There are many instances in which people carefully tailor their behaviour in the manner depicted by the expected-value model. Consider typical driving habits. When a police cruiser is driving beside your car, you are (if you are anything like most drivers) unlikely to exceed the speed limit by more than a trivial margin. When you drive in a heavily patrolled area, you are similarly likely to drive slowly and cautiously. When police are nowhere to be seen, however, and you drive along a stretch of highway where patrol cars could be detected far in advance, you might be inclined to exert extra pressure on the accelerator. This is a response to the probability of enforcement. When the cruiser is beside you, there is a good chance that you will be ticketed if you violate highway laws. When you drive along a long, police-free highway, you are unlikely to be observed by the police (and far more likely to speed). Between these two extremes is the highly patrolled area in which no police cruisers are presently visible. In this case, your decision to speed may depend on numerous factors, such as the current date (more tickets tend to be handed out at the end of a calendar month), current traffic patterns (if everyone else is speeding, you are less likely to be targeted), and the type of car you are driving (sports cars are ticketed more frequently than wood-paneled minivans). In each of these scenarios, you are responding (in rather sophisticated ways) to the probability of enforcement. Although you are unlikely to consciously perform a series of cost–benefit analyses using specific figures regarding probability and cost, you are likely to act as though you had performed those calculations. Taken in the aggregate, people often behave as though they have good information concerning the likelihood that rules will be enforced. As a result, the expected-value model is a useful mechanism for predicting human behaviour.

Even if people have inadequate information concerning the likelihood that rules will be enforced, the expected-value model is still an important tool for predicting human behaviour. As we saw in the examples regarding parking lots and highway traffic, people generally respond to their own *subjective assessment* of the likelihood that costs will be imposed. This accords with the expected-value model. An expected-value model does not depend on the presumption that people have *accurate* information concerning likely costs or benefits. It simply assumes that, once people have formed an opinion regarding the likelihood that costs will be incurred or that benefits will arise, they will use this estimate of probability when deciding whether or not to pursue a particular course of action. Bad information concerning probability may lead to bad decisions, but this is no different from the case in which an individual makes an incorrect assessment of the amount of utility he or she will derive from a course of action. Much in the same way that we observe subjective preferences when determining the utility values that people assign to particular items, we rely on subjective assessments of probability when employing the notion of expected values.[50] As a result, the tendency of any individual to make errone-

---

50   Where a regulatory body wants people to respond to a particular cost or benefit, it becomes the job of the regulatory body to provide information about the likelihood that particular costs (such as fines) will be

ous judgments regarding probability does not impair the usefulness of an expected-value model: the model will simply take into account the decision maker's subjective (and erroneous) view of probability, just as our economic models employ decision makers' private assessments of utility.[51]

F. Expected Values and Cost Assessment

Having overcome the basic objections to the expected-value model, we may now consider the uses to which the model can be put, even in cases where the decision maker lacks useful information regarding probability. One of the most useful aspects of this model can be demonstrated through the following example.

Example 3.12

Marty Kinlin is an amoral lawyer with a business opportunity: he has found an investor (Trina Walsh) who is interested in acquiring 10,000 shares of Investco Ltd. at $6 each. Marty presently owns no shares of Investco, but knows where he can acquire 10,000 shares at a price of $4 each. If Marty buys 10,000 shares at $4 each, and then sells them to Trina at $6 each, he will make a tidy profit of $20,000. Unfortunately, Marty does not have the $40,000 needed to purchase the shares. The only way that Marty can get the money is to misappropriate the sum of $40,000 from his client's trust account. Marty plans to return this $40,000 when the transaction is complete.

Assume that Marty knows that misappropriating $40,000 from a client's trust account (even for a temporary period) is a violation of the code of professional conduct. Further assume that, if detected, Marty's behaviour will result in a fine of $140,000. Finally, assume that Marty has only a vague idea of the likelihood that the Law Society will detect and punish his behaviour.

Given Marty's "vague perception" of the likelihood that he will be caught and punished, how will Marty make his decision? Like all rational actors, Marty will make whichever decision is most likely to maximize his utility.

What is the expected utility of a decision to unlawfully "borrow" $40,000 from a client's trust account? Assume that Marty believes that there is a 90 percent chance that his unethical scheme will be successful—that is, he will successfully borrow the money, buy the shares, and make the profitable sale to Trina. Since this venture will yield a $20,000 profit, the "expected benefit" of this venture is 90% × $20,000. The expected

---

imposed. By skewing an individual's assessment of probability, a regulatory body can alter the individual's behaviour. This topic will be explored in chapter 4.

51   A typical example might be the case where an individual seeks to purchase drugs from a drug dealer, believing that there is a 0 percent chance of getting caught. Even if the drug dealer turns out to be an undercover police officer (such that there was, in fact, a 100 percent chance that our offender would be caught), the offender still responded rationally to a subjective, albeit incorrect, view of probability. The expected-value model is accordingly useful in describing this offender's behaviour.

costs of Marty's venture would be $140,000 (which is the amount of the fine) multiplied
by an unknown probability figure (as we noted, Marty does not know how likely he is to
be punished). Taking account of all the information we have, Marty's "ethical calculation" looks like this:

$$A - B = X$$
$$(0.9)(\$20,000) - (?)(\$140,000) = X$$
$$\$18,000 - (?)(\$140,000) = X$$

Because Marty is unaware of the likelihood of enforcement (represented by the question
mark in the foregoing equations), Marty cannot assess the expected costs of his action
with precision. As a result, Marty cannot determine whether X will be positive (in which
case he will misappropriate the money) or negative (in which case he will not).

How can Marty decide whether or not to take this action? Given his present level of
information, Marty can determine the maximum likelihood of enforcement that will yield
a positive X—that is, the highest value of "?" (the chance of enforcement) that will still
make this action worth taking. Return to our ethical equation:

$$\$18,000 - (?)(\$140,000) = X$$

As we have seen, Marty's action is worth taking if X is greater than zero. As a result, we
can set a value of zero for X and determine the maximum chance of punishment at which
the action is still worth taking:

$$\$18,000 - (?)(\$140,000) = 0$$
$$(?)(\$140,000) = \$18,000$$
$$(?) = \$18,000 / \$140,000$$
$$(?) = 0.129$$

Taking all our information into account, we can see that a probability of punishment
equal to 0.129 (12.9 percent) is the break-even point for Marty's decision. Where there is
a 12.9 percent probability that Marty's behaviour will be punished, the expected benefits
of his decision (90 percent multiplied by $20,000) are exactly equal to the expected costs
(12.9 percent multiplied by $140,000). If the chance of punishment is greater than 12.9
percent, the expected costs of the action (chance of enforcement multiplied by costs) will
be greater than the expected benefits. In those circumstances, X would be negative, and
the action would not be worth taking. We can check our calculation by setting a 13
percent chance of enforcement:

$$A - B = X$$
$$(0.9)(\$20,000) - (0.13)(\$140,000) = X$$
$$\$18,000 - \$18,200 = X$$
$$-\$200 = X$$

Where there is a 13 percent chance of being caught and punished, X is a negative figure
(−$200). In other words, the expected costs of misappropriating the client's money
outweigh the expected benefits of that action by $200 where the Law Society has a 13
percent chance of detecting and punishing the lawyer.

While Marty was uncertain of the likelihood of being caught and punished, the values he *did* know (that is, the benefits of his actions and the costs if he was caught) allowed him to determine the maximum level of enforcement (12.9 percent) at which his action was worth taking. Marty's "vague idea" concerning the likelihood of enforcement may now be useful. While he did not know, with mathematical certainty, the probability of his actions being detected, Marty may be strongly of the view that the chance of being punished is greater than 13 percent. If Marty estimates that the chance of being punished is anything higher than 13 percent, he will decide that his scheme is too risky: if there is more than a 12.9 percent chance of being punished, a decision to misappropriate $40,000 of client funds will yield a net loss in utility. As a rational utility maximizer, Marty would not make that decision.

Example 3.12 demonstrates a critical use of the expected-value model. Using our basic ethical calculation ($A - B = X$) coupled with knowledge of expected values, a rational decision maker can make useful estimates of the level of probability that is required in order to make a particular action worthwhile. Thus, even where a decision maker lacks specific knowledge (or doubts his or her own estimate) of the likelihood that a given cost or benefit will arise, he or she can use the expected-value model to make an educated guess. More important, as we will see in chapter 4, a rational regulator (such as the Law Society or the government) can use this model to make assessments of the level of enforcement required to deter illicit behaviour. Armed with the facts of example 3.12, for example, a rational regulator would know that the relevant regulatory body must set the chance of punishment at higher than 12.9 percent in order to deter individuals from unlawfully borrowing $40,000 out of a client's trust account.[52]

IX. Responding to Punishment

A. Introduction

Throughout this book we have seen that ethical decisions can be described and predicted using the tools of economics. When individuals are faced with a choice to breach or adhere to a particular ethical standard, their decision will be governed by basic economic principles. The decision maker will determine the expected benefits associated with the ethical breach (the benefit generated by breach multiplied by the probability that the benefit will arise), and subtract from that benefit the expected cost of the action (the cost arising from the action multiplied by the probability that the relevant cost will arise). Where the expected benefit exceeds the expected cost, the decision maker will take the relevant action.[53] While decision makers are unlikely to perform these calculations on a conscious level, they inevitably act as though they are governed by the relevant calculations. This is as true of lawyers' ethical choices as it is of typically "economic" choices,

---

52   Note that this assumes that the punishment for misappropriating $40,000 is a fine of $140,000. A more severe punishment, coupled with a lower likelihood of enforcement, could still deter a rational, amoral lawyer. The mathematics supporting this proposition are developed in chapter 4.

53   For a review of the manner in which this model accounts for opportunity costs, refer to the text box, "Double Binds," in chapter 2, section IV.B.

such as a choice of investment vehicles or employment opportunities. In each case, the decision maker will weigh the costs and benefits of a particular decision and make the choice that maximizes utility.

Our observations concerning lawyers' ethical decisions reinforce some basic claims of economics: the rules by which we govern our affairs (together with the punishments for violating those rules) create implicit prices and incentives. People (including lawyers facing ethical decisions) will respond to those prices or incentives in precisely the same way that they respond to market prices and incentives. As the costs associated with an action begin to rise, individuals become decreasingly likely to take the relevant action. Conversely, as the benefits of an action are increased, more and more people are likely to take the relevant action. Using these simple, intuitive guidelines, we can make useful predictions regarding the ways in which people respond to ethical rules. The basic framework for these predictions, together with its application to lawyers' ethical choices, is developed in the closing sections of this chapter.

B. The Rational, Amoral Lawyer

Imagine a world in which the most serious breaches of ethical codes result in the most severe punishments. The more unethical you are, the more this world will punish your behaviour. This seems like an eminently sensible world, and it bears a strong resemblance to the world that we inhabit. A graph of this world's ethical violations and associated punishments looks like figure 3.1.

Note that, given the stated relationship between the seriousness of offences and the severity of punishment—that is, the severity of punishment rises with the seriousness of offences—a typical schedule of punishments (plotted along line P in figure 3.1) will always slope upward as you travel along the x axis. This graphically demonstrates that size of the relevant punishment (shown on the y axis) will rise as the severity of the ethical breach increases.

In order to better understand our graphic schedule of punishments, consider one of the most common violations of legal ethics: the misappropriation of client funds. Assume that the seriousness of an incident of this ethical violation is measured by the amount of money taken. Further assume that the penalty associated with this ethical breach is a fine, the cost of which increases with the seriousness of the breach.[54]

In figure 3.2, both the x and y axes are measured in dollar figures. As you go along the x axis, the seriousness of the breach increases by the amount of money stolen. As you travel up the y axis, the amount of the fine increases. Line E represents one possible punishment schedule: a punishment schedule in which the amount of the fine (shown along the y axis) is exactly equal to the seriousness of the breach (shown along the x axis). Thus, using line E as a schedule of punishments, the fine for taking $3,000 from a client's trust account would be equal to the amount of money taken—namely, $3,000.

---

54   For the purposes of this example, we are assuming that individuals are rational and amoral. The "amoral" assumption eliminates non-pecuniary costs such as guilt. In principle, however, there is no reason that such costs cannot be taken into account. As we noted in chapters 1 and 2, non-pecuniary costs, such as reputational costs and the cost of "moral guilt," can be accommodated by economic theory.

Figure 3.1

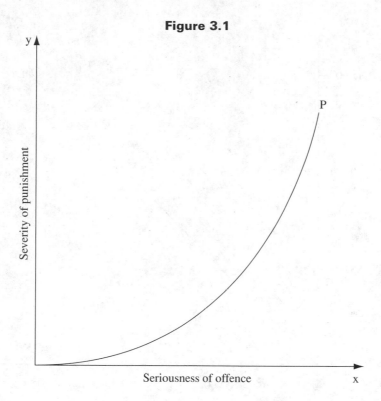

It seems unlikely that a rational, amoral lawyer would be deterred from stealing $3,000 if the only punishment for that offence was to pay the amount of $3,000. Even if the lawyer were to be caught every time that he or she stole a client's money, the lawyer would never be worse off for having taken the client's funds. More importantly, if enforcement falls below the level of 100 percent—that is, if some thefts of client funds went undetected or unpunished—amoral lawyers would always expect to be better off by taking money from their clients. Assuming a 90 percent level of enforcement (which is far higher than the enforcement level in the real world), the gross expected benefit of stealing $1,000 would be $1,000, while the expected cost of stealing $1,000 would be $900 (the $1,000 fine multiplied by the 0.90 probability of its enforcement). Using the expected-value model, lawyers would always expect to be better off by trying to take their client's money.

In order to deter a rational, amoral lawyer from stealing a client's money, the punishment for taking the client's money must be greater in value than the amount of money taken. Our hypothetical, rational regulator is aware of this fact. As a result, the regulator sets a schedule of punishments falling along the line labelled "Nominal Punishment" in figure 3.3.

In figure 3.3, the punishment for misappropriating $X from a client's trust account is some amount greater than $X. For example, the punishment for taking $3,000 of client money (measured along the x axis) is exactly $5,000 (measured along the y axis).

Figure 3.2

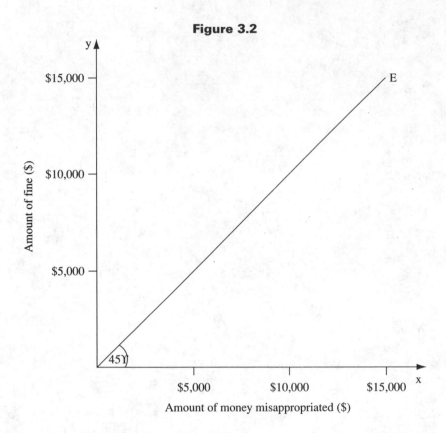

Amount of money misappropriated ($)

As we have seen in this chapter, punishment is uncertain. When calculating the costs of violating an ethical code, one must always reckon with the probability that the relevant conduct will be detected and the punishment will be imposed. In determining whether to commit an ethical violation (including the misappropriation of client funds), our amoral lawyer will calculate the *expected value* of the ethical violation—that is, the benefit of the violation minus the punishment multiplied by the probability of the punishment being imposed.

In figure 3.3, the punishment for misappropriating $3,000 of client funds was $5,000. Now assume that the probability of any offender being caught and punished equals 0.8 (in other words, there is an 80 percent chance that any given offender will be punished). The expected punishment for misappropriating $3,000 of client funds now equals $4,000 (a probability of 0.8 × $5,000). In order to demonstrate the element of uncertainty in punishment, we can add a new line, "expected punishment," to our graph. This line is shown in figure 3.4.

We can now see how a rational, amoral lawyer would respond to a typical schedule of punishments (where the severity of the punishment increases alongside the seriousness of the ethical violation). As we have seen throughout this chapter, a rational lawyer will

Figure 3.3

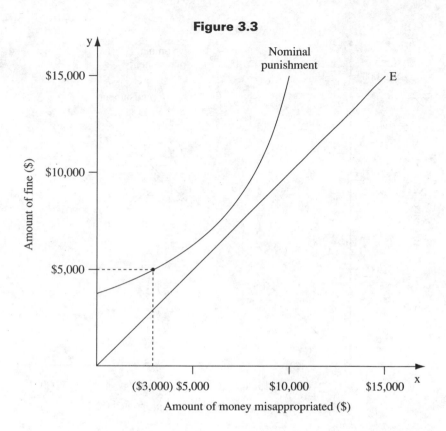

only take an action if its expected benefits exceed its expected costs. In figure 3.4, when nominal punishment is discounted for uncertainty, the expected punishment remains above line E (which represents the "break-even" point, where the cost of a breach is exactly offset by its benefits). As a result, the expected punishment for misappropriating any given amount of money will always exceed the expected benefit. In this model, it never pays to misappropriate money from a client's trust account.[55] Rational lawyers will accordingly refrain from such an action.

What happens if the expected-punishment line slips below line E? This scenario is depicted in figure 3.5. Where any combination of x and y along the expected-punishment line appears below line E (as they do in the shaded area of figure 3.5), the expected punishment of misappropriating money is actually *lower* than the benefit of taking a client's funds. In these circumstances (that is, for any combination of x and y found within the shaded area in figure 3.5) the rational lawyer (who is untroubled by moral

---

55   This assumes, of course, that the lawyer is incapable of taking extraordinary measures designed to
      reduce the chance of detection below the 80 percent figure.

Figure 3.4

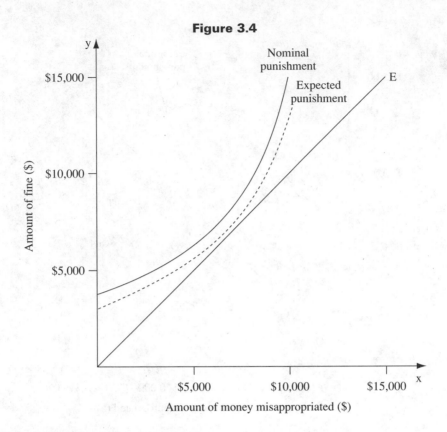

Amount of money misappropriated ($)

issues) will misappropriate client funds: he or she will be better off for having broken the ethical code, because the expected punishment falls below the value of the expected benefit.[56] The Law Society hopes to avoid this situation. The manner in which the Law Society can prevent this situation is discussed in great detail in chapter 4.

C. Summary

The previous sections of this chapter developed an overview of the process governing lawyer's ethical choices. When a lawyer is faced with an ethical dilemma, the lawyer will select his or her course of action based on the consequences that flow from the possible choices. The lawyer will calculate the costs and benefits flowing from possible choices, bearing in mind the probability that the relevant costs or benefits will arise. After performing these calculations (often on a subconscious level), the lawyer will choose whichever action maximizes the lawyer's utility.

---

56   Note that you can use this figure to calculate the most profitable breach—that is, the combination of x and y where the expected punishment line dips below line E by the greatest amount.

Figure 3.5

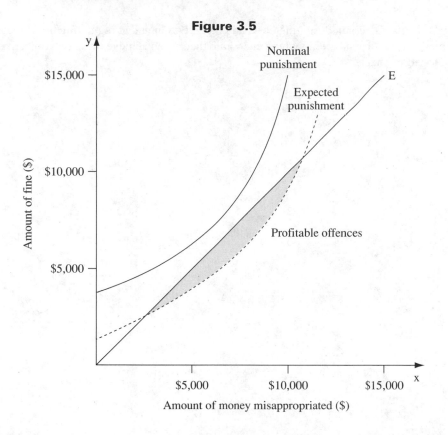

Amount of money misappropriated ($)

NOTES AND QUESTIONS

Revisit the decision in *Adams v. Law Society of Alberta* (2000),[57] discussed in chapter 1, as well as the decision in *Law Society of Upper Canada v. Jaffey* (1995),[58] discussed in chapter 2. This time, establish schedules of costs and benefits for the actions committed by the relevant actors, bearing in mind the likelihood of enforcement. Consider the impact of the likelihood of enforcement on each lawyer's decision to engage in the relevant form of unethical conduct.

X. Conclusion

Chapters 1, 2, and 3 have demonstrated the ability of the economic account of legal ethics to describe the ethical choices made by lawyers. Economic theory, however, is more than merely descriptive. Indeed, the most important aspects of economic theory (in the realm of legal ethics) are (1) its power to predict the actions of rational individuals,

---

57   (2000), 266 AR 157 (CA).

58   [1995] LSDD no. 175.

and (2) its usefulness in designing costs and incentives aimed at regulating the choices of rational actors. The manner in which economic theory can achieve these two objectives is developed in chapter 4.

CHAPTER FOUR

Governing the Profession

I. Introduction

Chapters 1 and 2 developed the basic elements of an economic theory of ethical systems. Chapter 3 applied this theory to lawyers' ethical choices, using economic tools to develop decision-making models that describe, explain, and evaluate the ethical choices that lawyers face. The purpose of this chapter is to look at legal ethics from the perspective of the official body charged with the task of regulating lawyers' professional conduct. In particular, chapter 4 addresses the following questions:

1. Why should an official body bother regulating lawyers' ethics at all? Would it not make more sense to allow unbridled market forces to govern lawyers' ethical conduct?

2. How can economic theory be used to design optimal punishments and incentives aimed at promoting an efficient amount of ethical conduct?

3. What is meant by "optimal punishments and incentives"?

4. What does it mean to have an "efficient amount of ethical conduct"? Would it not be preferable to have a *limitless* amount of ethical conduct—that is, a complete absence of *un*ethical conduct?

While economic theory may not provide complete answers to these questions, it helps to clarify the issues surrounding the regulation of lawyers' ethical conduct and identify the areas in which empirical research is needed in order to ascertain the optimal methods of governing lawyers' behaviour.

Before addressing the economic nature of the regulations governing lawyers' conduct, it is useful to consider the nature and identity of the regulatory body charged with the task of governing lawyers' professional conduct. This topic is addressed in the following section of this chapter.

A. Who Is the Regulator?

Non-lawyers are often surprised to learn that lawyers' professional conduct is not regulated directly by the government. Instead, it is regulated by lawyers themselves. While governments hold the ultimate constitutional power to regulate lawyers and other professionals, in many jurisdictions (including Canada and its provinces) the power to govern the legal profession is delegated to lawyers. In Ontario, for example, the government delegates this power through the *Law Society Act*, which establishes the Law Society of Upper Canada (a body composed of lawyers)[1] as the regulatory body governing lawyers in Ontario.[2] Similar legislative regimes apply in other Canadian provinces. As a result, lawyers in Canada govern themselves and their profession by means of authority granted by the provincial governments. Because (in practice, at least) the power to govern the legal profession is vested in lawyers themselves, the "Bar" (a term that is used to describe those persons having the right to practise law) is said to be "independent" from the government.

Commentators on legal ethics tend to attribute vast importance to "the independence of the Bar" (that is, the freedom of lawyers from day-to-day government oversight). According to Finlayson, for example:

> A vital role of the lawyer is to stand between the citizen and the state, and this role is more important now than ever before ... . Lawyers could not advise citizens as to their responsi-bilities with respect to particular legislation or governmental action if they cannot maintain their independence as individuals. It is almost impossible to do this if the Society that governs them is under the day-to-day control of government. It is imperative that the public have a perception of the legal profession as entirely separate from and independent of government, otherwise it will not have confidence that lawyers can truly represent its members in their dealings with government.[3]

Similarly, Gavin MacKenzie (one of Canada's most prolific commentators on the subject of legal ethics) refers to the independence of the Bar as "one of society's *main means* of ensuring individual rights and freedoms"[4] (emphasis added), noting that the vital impor-tance of an independent Bar makes it evident that "the legal profession cannot be equated with other self-governing professions."[5] In short, many commentators claim that the independence of the Bar is the bulwark of a free and enlightened society, more critical to the survival of our society than other self-regulating professions.

---

1   At the time of writing, the Law Society of Upper Canada is governed by 48 directors known as "benchers," 40 of whom are lawyers elected to the position of bencher by other lawyers in Ontario. The term of office for a bencher is four years. The 8 "non-lawyer" benchers, known as "lay benchers," are appointed by the government of Ontario, and have the same duties as the "ordinary" benchers. The benchers meet once a month at a meeting known as "Convocation," where they make policy decisions relating to the governance of the legal profession.

2   Although the Law Society existed long before the *Law Society Act* (modelled on the Inns of Court of the United Kingdom), its current incarnation, together with all its powers and responsibilities, is constituted by the Act. Governing power is vested in the benchers (see supra note 1). Section 10 of the *Law Society Act*, RSO 1990, c. L.8, gives the benchers authority to "govern the affairs of the Society, including the call of persons to practise at the bar of the courts of Ontario and their admission and enrolment to practise as solicitors in Ontario."

3   George D. Finlayson, "Self-Government and the Legal Profession—Can It Continue?" (1985), 4 *Advo-cates' Society Journal* 1, at 15.

4   Gavin MacKenzie, *Lawyers and Ethics* (Toronto: Carswell, 2001), 27-5.

5   Ibid., at 27-2–27-3.

An independent Bar certainly has advantages.[6] From an economic perspective, however, it is not surprising that most of the sweeping proclamations regarding the fundamental importance of an independent Bar come from those who have the most to lose if the government takes control of the legal profession—lawyers themselves. Lawyers, like many individuals, believe that they are better off if allowed to govern themselves. They prefer to establish their own professional norms, determine who can and cannot be a lawyer, and generally set the rules that govern their own professional lives. Lawyers typically gain utility from self-regulation; they are likely to wince at the thought of government regulation. Like everyone else, lawyers are governed by self-interest and see government intervention as an impediment to the realization of their self-interested goals. Bearing this self-interest in mind, one should be skeptical of a lawyer's claim that a self-governing legal profession is the ultimate guarantor of personal freedoms. An educator is likely to feel that academic freedom is the key to a free society, and that tight-fisted government control of education would unravel the fabric of society to a greater extent than would the government regulation of lawyers. A physician, on the other hand, is likely to think that an independent medical profession—that is, a medical profession free of day-to-day government interference—is the bastion of a free and enlightened society, and that the medical profession "cannot be equated with other self-governing professions."[7] Similar claims could be made by the clergy and other professionals. When assessing claims that a particular profession (if allowed to be free of government intervention) stands between a free society and our descent into barbarism, it is important to bear in mind the notions of self-interest and utility maximization. People act in their self-interest with a view to maximizing *their own* utility. This remains true when people put forth claims concerning the fundamental importance of their own profession (or its freedom from governmental interference), as well as when people pursue their professional calling, argue cases, write exams, select mates, or author books about legal ethics. It is hard to be an economist without becoming a bit of a skeptic.

Despite the alleged importance of an independent Bar, the nature of the body charged with governing lawyers' conduct is not especially important for the purposes of an economic account of legal ethics. Whether lawyers are governed directly by a government or by a subordinate body comprised entirely of lawyers, that body will inevitably govern the profession in the manner predicted by economic reasoning. The actions of the governing body can be explained, predicted, and evaluated by reference to the economic notions of self-interest and utility maximization. The governing body will be motivated by its own self-interest; and it will achieve efficient regulations if the regulations in question have been based on economic analyses of the motives of those people whom the body intends to govern.[8] In short, whether lawyers are regulated directly by the government or by a

---

6   For a full review of these benefits, see MacKenzie, supra note 4, at 27-2–27-6. See also Finlayson, supra note 3 and Arthur Maloney, "The Role of An Independent Bar," *1979 Law Society of Upper Canada Special Lectures* 49.

7   See Mackenzie, supra, note 4, at 27-2–27-3.

8   Some people will immediately balk at the suggestion that the Law Society governs in its own self-interest rather than in the interests of all members of the public. To be sure, there are many instances in which the interests of the Law Society and the interests of the public coincide, such that the Law

subordinate body of lawyers, an economic account of legal ethics is capable of describing and evaluating the regulatory practices of the relevant governing body. More importantly, economic theory can help determine the most effective forms of regulation for the governing body to pursue. Rather than focusing on the motivations of a particular regulatory body, this chapter will assess the regulation of lawyers' ethics through the lens of economics, and consider the most effective methods of regulating lawyers' professional conduct, regardless of the composition of the relevant regulatory body.

B. Why Regulate?

Anyone who has been exposed to economic reasoning has likely encountered the phrase "let the market prevail." The basic idea behind this phrase is that a competitive market for scarce resources leads to an efficient allocation of those resources without the need of regulatory intervention. Consumers' demand for products has an impact on the supply of the goods in question, and the combined effect of supply and demand governs the products' price. The price that is generated by the unregulated interaction of supply and demand will be the *optimal price* for the resource in question—people will ultimately pay whatever price gives rise to an optimal supply of the relevant resources.[9] This "free market"—that is, a market free of government regulation—will give rise to an optimal allocation of whatever resources are found in the relevant market. Any government intervention in the pricing or supply of goods or services is likely to inhibit the market's ability to generate optimal outcomes. In short, an unregulated market leads to efficient allocations of scarce resources, and the government (or other body charged with regulation) has no business interfering in the functioning of the freely competitive market. In the language of economics, "a competitive economy ... generates a Pareto-efficient allocation of resources without any government intervention."[10] In other words, competing individuals acting in their own best interests tend to generate an efficient allocation of resources, without the need of government interference. In the realm of legal ethics, this suggests that an unregulated market for legal services should (in theory) lead to a socially optimal supply of legal services, efficient pricing for legal services, and (most importantly for our purposes) an optimal amount of ethical conduct on the part of legal professionals.[11]

Society's regulations are effective in promoting public welfare. In other instances, however, the interests of lawyers generally (and, therefore, the interests of the Law Society) seem to conflict with the "best interests" of the public. One useful example is rule 3.04 of Ontario's *Rules of Professional Conduct*, which prohibits lawyers from using advertisements that compare the lawyer's fees to the fees of other lawyers. From an economic perspective, one important effect of this rule is to minimize competition and keep lawyers' fees unjustifiably high, to the detriment of the service-seeking public. This is done to benefit lawyers. The self-interested nature of this rule is discussed more thoroughly in section VI.C.

9   See any good text on microeconomics and price theory. An excellent introduction is found in Michael Katz and Harvey Rosen, *Microeconomics*, 3d ed. (Boston: Irwin McGraw-Hill, 1998).

10   Katz and Rozen, ibid., at 399. See also Walter J. Wessels, *Economics* (Hauppage, NY: Barron's Educational Services, 2000), 493: "People, left alone, will select the best goods to consume and produce them in the most efficient manner."

11   The "resource" of ethical conduct can be regarded as one of the products in the market for legal services. When clients retain a lawyer's services, they "purchase" a portion of that lawyer's expertise, work ethic,

Consider the ways in which an unregulated market for legal services might generate an optimal amount of ethical conduct. In an unregulated market, an amoral, self-interested lawyer would engage in unethical practices whenever it was to his or her advantage to do so.[12] When the lawyer decides to engage in unethical conduct, he or she will impose a number of costs on other individuals. For example:

- Unethical lawyers who abscond with client funds impose a direct financial cost upon their clients.
- Unethical lawyers who shirk their duties generate unjustifiable legal fees while making no progress for their clients.
- Unethical lawyers who violate the duty of confidentiality may divulge their clients' secrets, harming their clients by divulging business plans or revealing embarrassing information.
- Unethical lawyers may undermine the public's trust in legal professionals, forcing people who are in search of legal services to spend their time and other resources in search of lawyers who meet a particular ethical standard.

This is by no means an exhaustive list of the costs that flow from unethical lawyers' conduct. Costs of this nature make legal services far less valuable. A lawyer who is likely to abscond with a client's funds is less valuable to that client than a lawyer who can be trusted with client property. Because an unethical lawyer's services are less valuable than the services of an ethical lawyer, individuals who are in need of legal services would be willing to pay less for an unethical lawyer's services.

If clients are willing to pay less for an unethical lawyer's services than they would pay for the services of an ethical lawyer, the average price that clients are willing to pay for legal services varies directly with the public's perception of lawyers' ethical standards. As ethical standards drop, the price of legal services drops as well. To the extent that lawyers would find it more profitable to adopt high ethical standards, our hypothetical, unregulated market for legal services would drive lawyers toward higher ethical standards, improving the ethics of the profession and justifying higher fees for legal services.

In our hypothetical market for legal services, lawyers who develop a reputation for being particularly unethical may find it difficult to attract and maintain clients. In order to attract new clients, lawyers with bad reputations could be forced to reduce the fees they charge for services.[13] In a freely competitive market for legal services, lawyers with

---

time, attention, professional reputation, and commitment to professional ethical standards. The lawyer's own ethical standard (much like the lawyer's work ethic) is thus a "resource" bargained for when individuals hire lawyers. For this reason the notions of "supply" and "demand" can be applied to the economic resource of lawyers' ethics.

12 In other words, our hypothetical lawyer will govern his or her affairs through the $A - B = X$ equation developed in chapters 2 and 3. Where the utility gains (accruing to the lawyer) generated by an unethical action outstrip the utility losses associated with that action, the lawyer will take the action in question.

13 Note that even people who wish to avail themselves of unethical legal services may be unwilling to pay a high price for such services. While the unethical lawyer may be willing to undertake unethical actions for a client, those clients will find it difficult to trust and cooperate with such a lawyer, and may accordingly want to pay less for the lawyer's services.

particulary bad reputations could be priced out of the market. The low fees that they would have to charge in order to compensate for their unethical conduct could render the practice of law unprofitable for such lawyers, driving unethical lawyers out of the legal profession or forcing them to raise their ethical standards.[14] By driving out unethical lawyers or forcing them to raise their ethical standards, the unregulated market for legal services could improve the "average level" of legal ethics in the market.

If our hypothetical, unregulated market for legal services operated in the manner described above, there would be no need for a regulatory body charged with the task of overseeing lawyers' conduct. Lawyers would compete with one another for clients; clients would pay whatever prices they are willing to pay for the level of "ethical dealing" they wish to purchase; and an efficient level of ethical behaviour would be generated through unhindered market forces.[15] Where a lawyer imposed costs on his or her clients by engaging in unethical behaviour, the lawyer would be forced to bear those costs by lowering the prices that he or she charged for legal services. There would be no need for a regulatory body designed to govern lawyers' ethics, as the supply of ethical conduct would rise (or fall) to meet consumer demands. In other words, a perfectly competitive (and unregulated) market for legal services could give rise to the level of ethical conduct demanded by the public. In theory, this is a socially optimal level of lawyers' ethics.

In reality, there is no way of knowing (with absolute certainty) whether a competitive market for legal services would, if left unregulated, generate a socially optimal level of ethical conduct.[16] The actual market for legal services is closely regulated by a powerful body with the authority to promulgate rules designed to control the ethical choices lawyers make.[17] There is, accordingly, no way of observing the level of ethical behaviour that would be generated by a freely competitive market. Instead, the level of ethical conduct we observe is produced by a regulated market that features binding rules of ethics, disciplinary proceedings, and a regulatory body with the power to levy fines, impose suspensions, and exclude potential competitors—that is, lawyers—from the market for legal services (through the Law Society's power of disbarment). The level of ethical conduct we observe in the legal profession is accordingly likely to differ from the level we would observe if the Law Society simply "let the market prevail."

Why does the Law Society bother to regulate lawyers' ethical conduct? If, as we have suggested, a perfectly competitive (and unregulated) market has the capacity to generate a socially optimal allocation of resources (including the "resource" of lawyers' ethics), there is no need for a governing body to step in and impose a regulatory regime. The Law Society could save time, money, and effort by leaving well enough alone, allowing market forces to generate an optimal level of legal ethics.

---

14   Note that the converse of this example may also hold: particularly ethical lawyers may be able to charge more for their services. People seeking a lawyer with a particularly good reputation for ethical behaviour may be willing to pay a premium for those services.

15   A definition of "an efficient level of ethical behaviour" is developed in section VI.E.

16   In sections I.C and D, we will see that it is unlikely that a competitive market for legal services would, in fact, result in an efficient supply of ethical behaviour.

17   The nature and composition of this body is described above in section I.A.

Presumably, the Law Society's decision to regulate lawyers' ethics flows from the assumption than an unregulated market for legal services would lead to something other than a socially optimal level of ethical conduct. For reasons that we will see below, the Law Society is wise to make this assumption. It is unlikely that a freely competitive market for legal services would, in fact, lead to a socially optimal level of legal ethics. As a result, some form of market-correcting mechanism (such as a series of binding rules) is required in order to ensure that the legal profession's ethical standards achieve the level consumers demand.

Why does the Law Society predict that a free market for legal services would produce a suboptimal level of ethical conduct? To understand the answer to this question, it is helpful to be familiar with the notion of "market failure." Where a market failure occurs, a freely competitive market fails to yield a socially optimal allocation of resources. For one reason or another, the relevant market produces too much or too little of a particular resource, calling for regulations (or other corrective measures) designed to optimize the levels at which resources are produced.[18] In the case of the market for lawyers' professional services, which is also the market for legal ethics,[19] the Law Society predicts that a lack of regulation would give rise to market failure, leading to a suboptimal level of legal ethics.

Economists have identified those features of a market that typically give rise to market failure. Two of these features, known as "informational asymmetry" and "negative externalities," can be readily observed in the market for legal services. The presence of these features in a market invariably leads to market failure—that is, a suboptimal allocation of the resources produced in the market. Because these two features are present in the market for legal services, the Law Society wisely predicts that, left to its own devices, the market for legal services will fail to generate a socially optimal level of ethical conduct. These two sources of market failure—namely, informational asymmetry and negative externalities—together with their impact on the market for legal services, are discussed in the following sections of this chapter.

C. Informational Asymmetry

Markets often fail where the parties to an exchange have an imbalance of information. According to Cooter and Ulen:

> When sellers know more about a product than do buyers, or vice versa, information is said to be distributed asymmetrically in the market. ... [S]evere asymmetries can disrupt markets so much that a social optimum cannot be achieved by voluntary exchange. When that

---

18   In some cases, it may be preferable to allow the market failure to continue rather than resort to market-correcting measures. This is the case, for example, where the only plausible regulation is so costly to enforce, or so inefficient in operation, that it leads to a greater waste of resources than the market failure it seeks to correct. In these cases, the regulatory "cure" may be worse than the "disease" of market failure. Only where there is some reason to believe that the relevant regulation will lead to a net improvement in resource allocation should regulation be used to remedy market failure.

19   See note 11, supra.

happens, government intervention in the market can ideally correct for the informational asymmetries and induce more nearly optimal exchange.[20]

The ways in which informational asymmetry can lead to market failure can be seen through the use of the following illustration.[21]

Example 4.1

Brian Lee is the owner of a used car that is in rather poor condition. Fortunately for Brian, the defects in his car are hard to observe. The car's engine cuts out after 45 minutes of continuous operation and will not start again without extensive repairs. Provided that Brian refuses to allow any single test drive to go beyond 45 minutes, potential buyers will not become aware of the car's problems.

If the engine in Brian's car operated properly, Brian's car would be worth $2,000. In its current state, the car is worth only $800 on the market. Brian, who is an expert auto mechanic with a healthy supply of tools and a love of fixing ailing cars, would derive $1,000 of utility from the continued ownership of this car.

Sarah Letson, who is unaware of the deficiencies plaguing Brian's car, believes that she would derive $2,000 worth of utility from the car. Sarah offers Brian $1,800 for the car, and Brian happily accepts.

Assume that Brian and Sarah live in a world where the market for used cars is unregulated. Sellers are not required to provide a warranty regarding their products' fitness, and consumers purchase goods on an "as is" basis.

Consider the flow of utility in the transaction described in example 4.1. Due to his status as an expert auto mechanic, and the utility he gains from fixing cars, Brian derives $1,000 of utility from his relatively useless automobile. Sarah (quite rationally) derives $1,800 of utility from $1,800 of cash. Believing the car to be worth $2,000, Sarah happily exchanges $1,800 for the car, pursuing a $200 net gain in utility. In reality, however, Sarah suffers a utility loss of $1,000 (the $1,800 Sarah paid minus the actual value of $800 that she will derive from the car once she realizes that it is a jalopy). Summing up our utility values, we see that this transaction has led to a utility gain for Brian equal to $800, and a utility loss for Sarah equal to $1,000. The transaction yields a net social utility loss of $200 (Brian's gain less Sarah's loss). In other words, this transaction destroyed $200 of value—rather than generating economic surplus, this transaction has diminished the aggregate economic well-being of the parties to the exchange.

Transactions that yield a net loss of utility are inefficient. As we saw in example 4.1, Sarah's purchase of Brian's car has moved the car from its highest-valued user (Brian, who values the car at $1,000) to a user who values it less (Sarah, who values the car at

---

20   Cooter and Ulen, *Law and Economics*, 4th ed. (Boston: Pearson Addison Wesley, 2003), 47.

21   This example is based loosely on George A. Akerlof, "The Market for Lemons: Quality Uncertainty and the Market Mechanism" (1970), 84 *Quarterly Journal of Economics* 488-500.

only $800), generating an overall loss in social utility. Because this transaction has the effect of diminishing society's overall level of utility, it leads to a less than optimal resource allocation. Transactions of this nature should not occur in a perfect market: as we have seen, a perfectly functioning market ensures an optimal allocation of resources.

Inefficient transactions of the kind described above result from the asymmetrical distribution of information. Brian had full knowledge of the defects plaguing his car, while Sarah had no knowledge of those defects. If Sarah had full knowledge of the quality of Brian's car (and, therefore, full knowledge of the level of utility she would derive from owning the car), she would have refrained from buying the car (at least for the price she offered) and avoided a loss in utility. In a world where buyers have perfect information, Brian's only hope of selling the car would be to (1) find some buyer who (for whatever reason) valued the car in its current condition at more than $1,000 (the subjective utility value Brian places on his car), or (2) repair the car and sell it for some figure that compensates Brian for the price of the car repairs plus the utility Brian derives from owning the car. Transaction 1 or 2 would result in overall gains in social utility, generating economic surplus and an optimal allocation of resources. In short, the presence of perfect information would prevent inefficient transactions and preclude suboptimal resource allocation.

Consider the effect of informational asymmetry in an unregulated market for legal services. When clients purchase a lawyer's professional services, those clients have limited information concerning their lawyer's ethical standards. While some sources of information concerning the lawyer's ethical standards can be found—for example, by consulting the lawyer's peers or investigating the lawyer's professional reputation— consulting these sources may be expensive or time consuming and the information they yield may be inaccurate. Prospective clients may be left with only the lawyer's own self-serving assurances regarding the lawyer's personal ethical standards. As a result, clients lack the ability to assess the level of ethics they will "purchase" when they buy a lawyer's services.

As we saw in chapter 3, individuals who engage in unethical conduct often do so in the hope that their behaviour will not be detected. As a result, unethical lawyers will actively suppress information concerning their ethical standards. Clients who fail to take this into account may find themselves paying more for legal services than those services are worth. While an ethical lawyer can be extremely valuable to a client, a lawyer with low ethical standards may be worthless (or at least less valuable), and may even lead to client losses through the misappropriation of client funds. As a result, clients may follow the pattern demonstrated in example 4.1, inadvertently paying a large sum of money for a resource (namely, the unethical lawyer's services) with no value. Individuals may trade a resource that they value (a large amount of money) for a resource with no value (an unethical lawyer's service). This leads to a suboptimal allocation of scarce resources, providing a clear example of market failure.

Economically savvy consumers living in our hypothetical (and unregulated) market for legal services may not be willing to gamble on their lawyers' ethical standards. On the contrary, rational, clear-minded clients might acknowledge the informational asymmetry that exists in the market for legal services and take it into account when they retain a lawyer. In order to compensate for the fact that they are purchasing goods of an uncertain value (namely, the lawyer's unknowable ethical standards), clients in our hypothetical market may discount the amount of money that they are willing to pay a lawyer. Where they might be willing to pay $400 per hour for a lawyer with an "average" level of ethics, for example, they might be willing to pay far less for a lawyer with lower ethical standards. Since our hypothetical clients cannot know, in advance, the level of ethics exhibited by a particular lawyer, the clients would be willing to pay some figure less than $400 per hour when they purchase legal services.

Where clients discount the price they are willing to pay for legal services as a result of their lack of confidence in lawyers' ethical standards, particularly ethical lawyers may find their services undervalued. Consider a lawyer with a highly developed work ethic. This ethical lawyer works harder than the average lawyer, and his or her professional services may be worth a relatively high dollar figure, say $500 per hour. Due to clients' rational fears concerning their lack of information about lawyers' ethical standards, however, clients may be willing to pay no more than, say, $100 per hour for legal services. In our hypothetical market, $100 per hour may be perfectly adequate to compensate a lawyer who shirks professional obligations, but woefully inadequate for a lawyer with higher standards. Our highly ethical lawyer, if he or she is rational, may decide to leave the market for legal services, choosing instead to find a profession in which a highly developed work ethic is valued and rewarded. Where ethical lawyers find their ethical standards undervalued, they may respond by (1) lowering their ethical standards in the hope of remaining competitive, or (2) leaving the legal profession and seeking alternative employment. Whether our hypothetical lawyer chooses option 1 or 2, the "average level of ethics" of the legal profession drops. Clients who wish to retain a lawyer with a higher ethical standard will find such lawyers unavailable in our hypothetical market. A less than socially optimal level of legal ethics will be available for consumption. Once again, we have an example of market failure.

As we have seen, the informational disparity that exists between lawyers and their clients could result in a market failure—that is, an unregulated market for lawyers' professional services could lead to suboptimal ethical standards. In order to avoid this market failure and promote a higher level of ethical conduct, some market correcting measure is required. The Law Society has introduced market correcting measures in the form of regulations (and related punitive sanctions) governing lawyers' ethical choices. The manner in which the Law Society's regulation of legal ethics helps prevent a market failure is discussed in subsequent sections of this chapter. Before discussing these regulations, we turn our attention to the second source of market failure—"negative externalities."

D. Negative Externalities

A second cause of market failure is the presence of "externalities." Cooter and Ulen describe this source of market failure as follows:

> The second source of market failure is the presence of what economists call *externalities*. Exchange inside a market is voluntary and mutually beneficial. Typically, the parties to the exchange capture all the benefits and bear all the costs … . But sometimes the benefits of an exchange may spill over onto other parties than those explicitly engaged in the exchange. Moreover, the costs of the exchange may also spill over onto other parties. The first instance

is an example of an *external benefit*; the second, an *external cost*. An example of an external benefit is the pollination that a beekeeper provides to his neighbor who runs an apple orchard. An example of an external cost is air or water pollution.[22]

The impact of external costs or benefits (collectively known as externalities) on a typical market can be demonstrated through the use of examples. Consider the following illustration.

Example 4.2

Widgetronics Co. is engaged in the production of electronic widgets. Widgetronics produces what it regards as an optimal number of widgets every year (that is, the amount that maximizes the company's profits). More specifically, Widgetronics produces 200,000 widgets per year with a total production cost of $100,000.[23]

Unfortunately, the production of electronic widgets causes air pollution. This pollution travels to a village downwind of Widgetronics' factory, imposing a cost on the local villagers. Specifically, it costs the village 25 cents to clean the air pollution caused by the production of each widget that is produced by Widgetronics.

Why will the market described in example 4.2 lead to a suboptimal allocation of resources? As a profit-maximizing corporation, Widgetronics will produce whatever number of widgets maximizes the company's profits. This optimal number of widgets depends (to a large extent) on the costs involved in widget manufacturing. A higher production cost will force the company (if it seeks profits) to charge more money for its widgets, decreasing consumer demand for the company's product and (accordingly) the number of widgets manufactured by Widgetronics. As a result, production costs will have an important impact on the company's output.

In example 4.2, Widgetronics has calculated the number of widgets it will produce based on an average cost per widget of 50 cents (it costs Widgetronics $100,000 to produce 200,000 widgets). As we can see from the facts of example 4.2, however, this does not reflect the true *social cost* of widget production—it ignores the costs that widget production imposes on other people. The true cost of producing 200,000 widgets equals $150,000 (the $100,000 cost incurred by Widgetronics plus the $50,000 the village pays to fight pollution), yielding an average cost per widget of 75 cents (rather than the 50 cents on which Widgetronics bases its widget output calculations). Note that the air pollution caused by Widgetronics is as much a cost of widget production as the salary of the widget-production manager.[24] Because part of the cost of producing widgets (the

---

22 Cooter and Ulen, supra note 20, at 44.

23 While this works out to an average cost-per-widget of 50 cents, it is inaccurate to say that it costs 50 cents to produce each widget. In fact, it is very likely that it costs much more to produce the first widget than it costs to produce the last in a batch of 200,000. For this reason, we will simply refer to the "average cost" per widget for the purposes of this example.

24 This point is made more clearly if the removal of air pollution is regarded as a form of waste disposal. Manufacturing firms typically pay for waste disposal as an element of the cost of manufacturing. In

money paid to eliminate air pollution) is borne by the nearby village, Widgetronics ignores this cost in determining the optimal number of widgets that it should manufacture—as a self-interested corporation, Widgetronics will ignore the costs that other people bear.

Because the village downwind involuntarily bears a part of the cost of producing widgets, Widgetronics calculates its optimal widget output based on artificially low production costs. Real production costs equal 75 cents per widget, while Widgetronics' "artificial" production cost equals only an average of 50 cents per widget. Widgetronics acts as if the cost of pollution is zero, when in fact the cost is 25 cents per widget. This allows Widgetronics to charge an artificially low price for widgets (that is, a price that does not fully reflect the cost of widget making), inflating consumer demand for the company's products, and leading to an inefficiently high supply of widgets. If the company truly bore all the costs of manufacturing widgets (including the cost of eliminating the air pollution caused in widget manufacturing), it would have to charge more for its widgets, decreasing (1) consumer demand for widgets, (2) the company's widget output, and (3) the pollution caused by widget manufacturing. Only if Widgetronics takes account of the *actual* cost of widget production will it be driven to manufacture a socially optimal number of widgets.

Example 4.2 shows that the presence of negative externalities may cause producers to produce (and consumers to consume) something other than the socially optimal quantity of resources. Because this amounts to a non-optimal allocation of resources, we can see that the presence of negative externalities is a cause of market failure. This is as true in the market for legal services as it is in the market for widgets. While externalities in our hypothetical widget market cause an inefficient supply of widgets and pollution, however, externalities in the market for legal services can give rise to suboptimal ethical standards.

Consider the impact that negative externalities have on the market for legal services. Revisit the facts of example 3.10 (from chapter 3).

> Tony Sargent is a Canadian lawyer who is thinking of misappropriating $50,000 from his client's trust account. If Tony takes this action, he will gain $50,000. There is a 30 percent chance that Tony will be caught and forced to (1) return the money, and (2) pay a fine of $130,000. If Tony's behaviour is not detected, there will be no fines or penalties. For the purpose of this example, assume that Tony is perfectly amoral—that is, he never feels guilty about his actions and accordingly loses no utility in the form of guilt or psychological trauma, nor does he gain utility simply by virtue of the "thrills" associated with wrongful acts. Further assume that Tony's professional reputation will not be affected by his behaviour.[25]

---

example 4.2, the cost of the company's waste disposal is 25 cents per widget. Rather than paying for its own waste disposal, however, Widgetronics shifts this cost onto the villagers downwind. From this perspective, the villagers are paying one of Widgetronics' important costs of production.

25   While this assumption is unrealistic, it merely serves to simplify the mathematics of the example. In the real world, reputational costs would be another kind of cost that Tony would have to consider when making his self-interested decision.

As we saw in chapter 3, when Tony decides whether or not to misappropriate his client's money, he will act as though he has weighed the gross utility benefit of taking the relevant funds (the $50,000 gain that Tony will enjoy by taking the money) against the potential costs of taking the money (the return of the funds, plus the fines, multiplied by the probability that Tony's behaviour will be detected and punished). Based on the figures in our example, we determined (in chapter 3, section VII.C) that it was not in Tony's interest to take the money, and that Tony would (if he is rational) avoid stealing his client's funds.

If we imagined an unregulated market for legal services, Tony's decision concerning the theft of his client's money would change. Imagine, for a moment, that no penalties would be exacted if Tony chose to misappropriate client funds. There is no law of contract governing Tony's behaviour and no government regulations safeguarding his clients' interests.[26] In these circumstances, Tony (if guided by self-interest and utility maximization) would be sure to take the money. He stands to gain $50,000 by misappropriating the funds, and loses $0 in fines, penalties, and guilt. Tony is $50,000 better off by taking his client's money.

Does this imply that Tony's decision results in an optimal allocation of resources? Certainly not. The only costs that Tony considered when deciding whether or not to take the money were those that he would have had to pay himself. The notion of self-interest makes it clear that Tony ignores the costs his actions will impose on other people. As Cooter and Ulen noted in the first edition of *Law and Economics*:

> [R]ationally self-interested decisionmakers will tend to ignore any external costs they impose on others and to consider only their private costs in making their utility- or profit-maximizing decisions.[27]

In determining whether Tony's decision is *socially* (rather than personally) optimal, however, we must consider the costs that Tony's decision imposes on other people. The following is a non-exhaustive list of possibilities:

1. By misappropriating his client's funds, Tony imposes a direct cost of $50,000 on the client. This cost immediately offsets the $50,000 gain that Tony receives by taking the funds.[28]

2. Tony's client must now spend time and other resources in the search for a new lawyer.

---

26 For many economists, the law of contract is not regarded as a method of regulating transactions; it is a fundamental part of the market mechanism itself. For the purpose of the present analysis, however, it is more useful to consider the law of contract as a regulatory regime. The legal rules of contract law regulate human behaviour by requiring the payment of damages where enforceable promises are breached.

27 Cooter and Ulen, *Law and Economics*, 1st ed. (New York: Harper Collins, 1988), 350.

28 This $50,000 cost is merely a redistributive transfer of wealth (from the client to Tony), and has no direct efficiency implications (that is, the market is no better or worse off with the money in Tony's hands or the hands of the client). In other words, the movement of this money from one person to another does not, by itself, destroy social utility; it merely redistributes that utility. The other costs identified in this list, however, destroy social wealth and therefore undermine efficiency.

3. Tony's actions might erode the confidence of potential clients, eliminating some of the trust they have for legal professionals. Now, when clients seek out legal services, they will spend additional resources screening the lawyers they hire. For example, individuals may spend valuable time interviewing several potential lawyers or contacting former clients to determine the lawyer's professional reputation. The time spent interviewing lawyers gives rise to significant opportunity costs. Potential clients could have spent their resources in more productive ways, but now have to spend them interviewing lawyers.

4. Tony's actions may erode client confidence so much that people may no longer be willing to entrust their funds to lawyers. They may turn to other, less cost-effective means of vindicating their legal rights—for example, by self-representation or personal research.

Each of these costs mirrors the cost of air pollution in example 4.2. Like air pollution, these costs are externalities. They flow from the decisions of an economic actor, yet are borne by someone other than the actor whose behaviour creates the cost. These are direct costs of Tony's choice to take his client's funds, unbargained-for costs that are imposed on other members of Tony's community.[29]

Consider the changes in utility that flow from Tony's decision. Tony gains $50,000 of utility by taking his client's money. His client loses $50,000 of utility through the loss of the money and (unless the client can find another, equally competent lawyer) may also lose whatever utility he or she stood to gain by purchasing Tony's professional services. Potential clients in Tony's community (due to their need to spend resources screening lawyers, or their need to turn to alternative—and more expensive—means of vindicating their legal rights) also lose small amounts of utility as a result of Tony's action. The aggregate of these individual losses may add up to a large amount of lost utility. As a result, the social utility losses flowing from Tony's unethical actions greatly outweigh the utility gain that Tony secures by taking the funds. In other words, Tony's decision to take the money is an inefficient decision, resulting in a net loss of social utility.

Tony's inefficient decision to misappropriate client funds is the result of externalities. Because the costs of Tony's actions were borne by people other than Tony, Tony was driven to make an inefficient decision, resulting in a suboptimal allocation of resources. If Tony had been forced to bear the costs of his decision, he would have chosen not to take his client's funds. As we have seen, the overall social cost of Tony's decision was far greater than the ensuing utility gains. Had Tony been forced to internalize the costs of his decisions (in other words, if Tony were forced to compensate others for the costs that he imposes), he would have made the economically sensible choice—he would have avoided misappropriating the funds. This would have resulted in an optimal allocation of resources, optimizing the social utility flowing from Tony's self-interested choice.

---

29   For reasons that will be discussed below, costs 3 and 4 in the foregoing list should not be considered "compensable," even under a compensatory model of regulation. Instead, they count as "disappearing costs," which are discussed in section IV.B, below.

Tony's decision to misappropriate client funds is emblematic of many unethical choices made by unscrupulous lawyers. These decisions impose a net loss on society but secure a utility gain for the person who makes the unethical choice. The unethical actor imposes externalities on others, securing a personal benefit without paying the relevant costs. This leads to a less than optimal allocation of scarce resources. Once again, this is a form of market failure.

The presence of externalities in the market for legal services, like the existence of informational asymmetries, leads to a suboptimal level of legal ethics. Because the Law Society observes the presence of externalities and recognizes the informational disparities plaguing the market for lawyers' services, it predicts that an unregulated market for legal services would result in market failure. Left to its own devices, the market for legal services would result in an inefficiently high level of unethical conduct. If we are to have an optimal level of legal ethics, we require some mechanism for avoiding market failure.[30] As we shall see, the Law Society's regulatory framework is designed (in part) to avoid market failure, attempting to generate a socially optimal level of ethics.

How can a regulatory framework compensate for market failures and ensure an efficient supply of legal ethics? There are two possibilities. First, the Law Society could force all market actors to internalize the costs of their behaviour, ensuring that market actors (such as lawyers) take only those actions that will lead to optimal resource allocation. In other words, the Law Society could force lawyers to pay the costs imposed by their unethical activities, ensuring that lawyers make unethical choices only where those choices generate net gains in social utility. In essence, this regulatory model parallels the remedial systems governing tort and contract, pursuant to which tortfeasors and contract breachers are forced to pay for the losses that they cause. This regulatory model, referred to as the compensatory model, is discussed in section II, below.

The second plausible method of promoting optimal resource allocation parallels the criminal law. Rather than pursuing a compensatory model, which requires unethical actors to compensate their victims (and accordingly bear the costs of their own choices), the Law Society could construct a quasi-criminal regime designed to deter unethical choices. Instead of forcing lawyers to internalize the costs of their behaviour, a criminal law model (also known as a punishment model) is designed to deter lawyers from engaging in unethical behaviour, setting penalties that are designed to deter and punish unethical lawyers rather than fines aimed at internalizing costs. The punishment model, and its role in shaping the Law Society's method of regulating ethical conduct, is discussed in section VI, below. As we shall see in the concluding portions of this chapter, the compensatory model and the punishment model are not mutually exclusive—indeed, the current (and most sensible) method of regulating lawyers involves a combination of these two regulatory models.

---

30   As noted in note 18, supra, in order to generate efficient outcomes, our market correcting mechanism must itself be efficient. In order to ensure that the cure is not worse than the disease of market failure, regulators must ensure that regulations do not give rise to greater inefficiency than the market failure itself. This may occur where regulations provide unforeseen market-distorting incentives to consumers, where the regulation is unduly expensive to administer or enforce, or where consumers spend significant resources in an attempt to circumvent the regulations.

II. The Compensatory Model

A. Introduction

The previous section addressed the Law Society's reason for regulating lawyers' conduct. As we saw in section I, above, the Law Society's rationale can be explained in terms of market failure. When market failure occurs, resources are allocated in an inefficient manner. In the case of the market for lawyers' professional services, negative externalities and informational imbalances can give rise to market failures, leading to inefficient pricing for legal services and (perhaps more importantly) suboptimal ethical standards among lawyers. As a result, the Law Society does its best to interfere with market forces, constructing a regulatory framework designed to optimize the level of ethical conduct generated in the market for legal services.

Section I demonstrated that a principal cause of market failure is the ability of decision makers to cause negative externalities. Rather than bearing the full cost of their decisions, some decision makers are able to visit the costs of their decisions upon other people. Self-interested decision makers proceed without regard for the costs that they impose on others. Because they are able to ignore a portion of the costs of their decisions, such decision makers frequently make inefficient choices, undertaking actions even when the actions' total cost (including the costs that are imposed on other people) outweighs the total gain. The usual effect of such choices is an inefficient allocation of whatever resources are found in the relevant market, ultimately reducing social utility. This is an example of market failure—something that we hope to avoid.

As we saw in section I, above, the existence of negative externalities is readily observed in the market for lawyers' professional services. When providing legal services, some lawyers are able to act in ways that benefit themselves while imposing unbargained-for costs on others. Externalities in the market for legal services can give rise to an inefficient allocation of scarce resources, including suboptimal levels of ethical conduct. By regulating lawyers' ethics, the Law Society hopes to promote an optimal level of legal ethics, eliminating the inefficiencies caused by the presence of negative externalities.

How might a regulator design a system of rules or regulations with the power to promote an optimal level of ethical conduct? One way to answer this question is to consider other legal regimes designed to overcome market failures caused by negative externalities: two of the most important are the legal systems governing tort and contract.[31] In the realms of tort and contract, legal rules are designed to correct problems caused by decision makers' ability to impose costs on other people. If the remedies employed in the realms of tort and contract have the ability to promote efficient decisions (and eliminate market failures) in those contexts, perhaps a parallel system of rules could be used to promote efficient decisions in the context of lawyers' professional ethics. The general nature of the remedial systems governing tort and contract, together with the ability (or inability) of a similar system to generate optimal levels of ethical conduct, is the topic of the next several sections of this chapter.

---

31   See Katz and Rosen, supra note 9, at 595.

B. Regulating Torts and Contracts

In the realms of tort and contract, tortfeasors or contract breachers injure other people. A reckless driver might injure an innocent victim by smashing into the victim's car; a contract breacher may cause a contractual partner to lose financial opportunities. Injuries of this kind can be regarded as costs created by the behaviour of the person committing the tort or breaching the contract. A person injured by a tortfeasor's reckless driving, for example, incurs the costs of pain and suffering, lost wages, repair expenses, and medical bills—costs that flow directly from the tortfeasor's choice to drive recklessly. In the absence of a regulatory system (such as the regulatory system provided by the law of torts), these costs could be borne by someone other than the party whose actions gave rise to the costs in question. The costs of an automobile collision, for example, might be borne by an innocent victim rather than by the driver whose actions generated the costs. In other words, these costs are externalities—they are borne by someone other than the person whose actions generated the costs.

In the realms of tort and contract, the courts have developed elaborate remedial systems that are designed to eliminate (or redistribute) costs imposed when torts are committed or contracts breached. In many cases, these remedies are designed to achieve two closely related goals. The first (and most important) goal is compensatory—the tortfeasor or contract breacher is forced to compensate whoever is harmed as a result of the tort or breach. The second (closely related) purpose is to ensure that decision makers fully *internalize* costs of their behaviour. Return to the reckless driver example: the tort system requires the driver to compensate injured victims, reimbursing the injured party for pain and suffering, medical bills, repair expenses, and lost wages. When the tortfeasor is made to bear the costs that flow from his or her behaviour, he or she is said to "internalize" the cost of that behaviour; costs that were external—that is, imposed on other people—are now internal—that is, borne by the party who generated the cost. The economic objective of cost internalization (achieved through a compensatory system), together with its potential role in the regulation of lawyers' ethics, is discussed in the following section of this chapter.

C. Internalizing Costs

In contract and in tort, as well as in the market for legal services, the presence of negative externalities can give rise to market failures. In the realms of tort and contract, remedial systems are designed to correct these market failures (and restore efficient resource allocation) by causing decision makers to pay for each of the costs that they impose. In other words, the remedial systems governing tort and contract force decision makers to internalize externalities they create. The concept of internalization can be explained by revisiting the facts of example 4.2.

> Widgetronics Co. produces what it regards as an optimal level of electronic widgets per year—that is, the amount that maximizes the company's profits). More specifically, Widgetronics produces 200,000 widgets per year with a total production cost of $100,000—an average cost of 50 cents per widget.
> Unfortunately, the production of electronic widgets causes air pollution, which travels to a village downwind of Widgetronics' factory, imposing a

cost on the local villagers. Specifically, it costs the village $50,000 to eliminate the pollution caused by Widgetronics' production of 200,000 widgets—an average cost of 25 cents per widget.

As we saw in section I, Widgetronics' production of widgets can be said to create a negative externality: a portion of the true *social cost* of producing widgets (the $50,000 to eliminate air pollution) is borne by someone other than Widgetronics (namely, the innocent people who live in the town downwind). The cost of pollution *is* a cost of widget production, much like the cost of widget-making materials or the wages of Widgetronics' employees. Unlike these obvious costs, however, the cost of air pollution is not paid by Widgetronics: it is paid by the people who live downwind of the widget-making facility. Because this cost of widget production is borne by someone other than Widgetronics, Widgetronics (as a self-interested market actor) ignores this cost of making widgets.

Because Widgetronics is a rational corporation (a corporation that wishes to maximize its own utility), it produces a number of widgets that maximizes the company's profits. When deciding how to maximize its profits, the company must decide (1) the optimal number of widgets to produce, and (2) the price at which it will sell its widgets. When making these decisions, Widgetronics will have to take account of the cost of making widgets. More specifically, Widgetronics will take account of its own *private costs* of widget production—an average cost of 50 cents per widget.[32] As we have seen, this is lower than the true *social cost* of widget production, which would include an additional 25 cents per widget (in respect of air pollution). In effect, Widgetronics is able to save a cost of 25 cents per widget by letting innocent third parties pay this amount. Widgetronics' "cost savings" are passed along to widget consumers. Because Widgetronics enjoys an artificially low cost of production, it can lower the price it charges to its customers. This in turn causes increased consumer demand for the company's widgets, ultimately driving up the number of widgets produced. All told, Widgetronics' ability to cast a portion of widget-production costs on other people generates an inefficiently high supply of widgets, an inefficiently low retail price for widgets, and (most importantly for the purposes of this example) an inefficiently high amount of pollution.

To see how an artificially low production cost can alter the levels of widget production and pollution, imagine that Widgetronics' customers are willing to pay no more than 65 cents for a widget.[33] Based on the facts of example 4.2, when Widgetronics produces 200,000 widgets, the average cost of widget production works out to 50 cents per widget (ignoring the cost of air pollution). This means that, at a production level of 200,000 widgets, Widgetronics' can sell its widgets at a profit of 15 cents per widget.[34] If

---

32   As noted above, this average cost per widget applies at the level of production that Widgetronics has selected. A different average cost would apply if Widgetronics produced a different number of widgets.

33   To make this assumption seem realistic, assume that there is a perfect widget replacement (known as a "gadget") available in the same market, and that the cost of a gadget is 65 cents. If a perfect replacement can be purchased for 65 cents, rational actors would not pay more than 65 cents for a widget.

34   The profit figure is derived by subtracting the private cost of widget manufacturing—namely, 50 cents per widget—from the price that consumers are willing to pay—namely, 65 cents per widget.

Widgetronics had to account for the *social cost* of widget production (that is, the company's cost of producing widgets plus the costs that widget production imposes on other individuals), it would have to pay an average production cost of 75 cents per widget at a production level of 200,000 widgets. Because Widgetronics will be unable to sell its widgets at a profit where the average cost is greater than the amount consumers will pay (65 cents per widget), Widgetronics (if forced to pay for the cost of eliminating air pollution) will have to change its behaviour. Widgetronics might, for example, have to alter the number of widgets it produces, with the goal of producing a number of widgets that gives rise to an average cost of less than 65 cents per widget. If there is no such level of widget production (that is, if the average cost per widget is greater than 65 cents per widget regardless of the number of widgets the company manufactures), Widgetronics would not produce widgets at all. This could be an efficient outcome. If the social cost of producing widgets is always greater than the utility generated from widget production, the efficient level of widget production is zero. While this example of the interaction of manufacturing costs, consumer prices, product supply, and consumer demand is grossly simplified, it does illustrate the ability of negative externalities to give rise to an ineffi- cient allocation of resources. In this example, the efficient level of widget production (and the efficient level of air pollution) may be zero. Due to the presence of negative externalities, however, Widgetronics has produced 200,000 widgets and a large amount of expensive air pollution. This is not the optimal outcome.

How could a regulator correct the inefficiencies generated in example 4.2? One possibility is to charge Widgetronics a fee for any pollution that it produces. If Widgetronics' business creates a cost of $50,000 (in the form of air pollution), a regulator could charge Widgetronics a fee of $50,000 (to be used to eliminate air pollution). Fees of this nature (known in economic circles as "effluent fees" or "Pigouvian taxes")[35] force producers to internalize the costs of their endeavours: a cost that was formerly external (borne by a third party) is now internal (borne by the party whose actions generated the relevant cost). Alternatively, a regulator could require Widgetronics to pay compensatory fees to those who would otherwise bear the cost of air pollution caused by Widgetronics' business. This regulatory method (which parallels the law of torts) would require Widgetronics to pay its "victims" (the people who bear the cost of Widgetronics' pollut- ing activities) whatever amount is required to place them in the position they would have occupied had Widgetronics not polluted the air. Had Widgetronics never polluted the air, the town downwind would never have had to pay a fee of $50,000 to clean it up. Now that Widgetronics *has* polluted the air, and the townspeople *have* been forced to pay $50,000 to eliminate Widgetronics' air pollution, Widgetronics must compensate the town downwind by paying them $50,000.

Assume that a regulator requires Widgetronics to pay the compensatory fee described above—namely, a payment that is equal to the cost of eliminating the pollution caused by Widgetronics' business. How will the imposition of this fee affect the company's con- duct? In calculating the optimal number of widgets to produce, Widgetronics will now

---

35   The phrase "Pigouvian taxes" honours A.C. Pigou, the economist who first described the notion of cost internalization through the imposition of effluent fees.

base its calculations on the true *social cost* of widget production—for example, at a production level of 200,000 widgets, this social cost is equal to 75 cents per widget (the original production cost of 50 cents per widget plus the 25 cent per widget compensatory payment, representing the cost to eliminate air pollution). Widgetronics has, in effect, lost the power to ignore part of the cost of widget production. It must now bear the full cost of producing the company's products. This eliminates the negative externality that gave rise to market failure. Widgetronics will now base the price it charges for its widgets on this new (socially accurate) cost of 75 cents per widget. All things being equal, this should force Widgetronics to charge more for its widgets, which will in turn lead to a drop in consumer demand. The end result is that Widgetronics will now produce a different, *socially optimal* (rather than privately optimal) number of widgets—that is, a number of widgets that allows the corporation to maximize profits while redressing the social costs that are imposed by widget production.[36]

Note that, under a system of compensatory payments, Widgetronics *is not prohibited* from causing air pollution. On the contrary, it is allowed to pollute the air provided that the company pays the cost required to eliminate the pollution. This form of regulation recognizes that we may be *better off* by having Widgetronics pollute the air—if Widgetronics pollutes the air, pays to eliminate the pollution, and still manages to earn profits by producing something consumers want to purchase, the end result of Widgetronics' venture will be an overall gain in social utility. There will be no net losses as a result of air pollution (since Widgetronics has now paid to eliminate the pollution);[37] there will be a net gain (in the form of profit) to Widgetronics; and there will be a net gain for consumers engaging in voluntary exchange—people will only pay $X to buy a widget when they derive more utility from a widget than they do from $X. As a result, our goal in establishing a compensatory regime is not to *prevent* the company from engaging in the relevant form of behaviour. On the contrary, we want the company to continue making widgets so long as widget production generates overall gains in social utility. The goal of our compensatory regime is simply to have the company pay (or internalize) all the costs of its activities. Once the company has internalized these costs, it will produce a number of widgets that maximize social utility.[38] Resources will be distributed in an optimal manner, and market failure will be avoided.

---

36   The "optimal number of widgets" may be zero. If the cost of producing widgets never drops below the maximum price consumers will pay, the business of producing widgets can only be carried on at a loss. If this is the case, the most "profitable" level of widget production is zero.

37   As a technical matter, it should be noted that Widgetronics's damage payment need not (necessarily) be used to eliminate air pollution. Presuming that the town downwind is the recipient of Widgetronics's compensatory fee, the town may decide that it is just as happy with $50,000 and smog-filled skies as it would have been with pollution-free air. However the town downwind chooses to use the compensatory payment, the incentive effects on (1) Widgetronics, and (2) the town itself remain unchanged. Widgetronics will take account of the true social cost of manufacturing when setting its optimal level of production, and the town downwind will lose no utility as a result of air pollution. Any utility lost through air pollution will be perfectly offset by the utility gained through a payment of money damages.

38   At this stage, it should be apparent that too large a compensatory payment will lead to an inefficiently low level of widget production. As a result, a true compensatory regime should do no more than ensure that the person being forced to pay compensation fully internalizes the costs that are imposed by his or her behaviour.

D. Paying the Cost of Ethical Breaches

In section II.B, we noted that damages in tort and contract, while principally designed to compensate victims, can also be explained in terms of cost internalization. Where decision makers injure other people (either physically or financially), we want the decision makers to bear the cost of the injuries they cause. Where a negligent driver collides with a pedestrian, for example, we want the driver to pay for the costs that are imposed on the pedestrian. In theory, the pedestrian should receive an amount of money that replaces whatever utility the pedestrian has lost as a result of the accident. Where an individual breaks a contract, we want the party in breach to compensate the innocent party for the value that the innocent party loses as a result of the breach of contract. In both contract and in tort, one aim of money damages is to have the guilty party bear the costs that his or her decisions have imposed on "innocent victims." In other words, one of the goals of money damages is to ensure that individuals internalize the costs of their decision to breach a contract or commit a tortious act.

How would a compensatory model force unethical individuals to internalize the costs of their unethical decisions? Consider the following example.

Example 4.3

Adam Lantz is a criminal defence lawyer in Toronto. He is currently representing Harry Hufnagel, who has been charged with embezzling over $4 million. Adam does not know whether his client is factually guilty of the offence with which he is charged.

Harry's case involves a great deal of intricate and confusing financial information, calling for the use of forensic accountants and other highly qualified experts. Harry's trial is sure to take a great deal of time. Adam has already spent over 200 hours simply getting ready for it. Adam expects the trial to take at least 4 months, during which he will have to spend countless hours becoming something of an expert in forensic accounting.

On the evening before the trial begins, Adam is offered a job as an "expert legal commentator" for a cable news network. The job requires Adam to start immediately and to withdraw from Harry's case. The demands of the new job preclude Adam from continuing to represent private clients.

If Adam drops Harry's case, Adam will no longer have access to the "income stream" provided by Harry's file. Assume that this costs Adam $90,000. He will, however, generate $150,000 of utility (from salary and fame) if he accepts the new job.

For the purpose of this example, assume that Harry *must* pay Adam for all the hours that Adam has spent preparing for Harry's trial, even if Adam withdraws on the evening of trial (in other words, Harry is not entitled to a refund for the money that he has already paid to Adam). Moreover, no contractual remedy forces Adam to see the trial through to completion.

What will Adam do?

If Adam chooses to withdraw from Harry's case, Harry's defence will be compromised. Harry will have to find a new lawyer, and that lawyer will have to spend whatever time is required to familiarize himself or herself with the intricate facts of Harry's complex case.[39] This will waste Harry's money, the Crown's time, and significant administrative resources. Because of the great expense that is generated when lawyers withdraw in situations of this nature, the *Rules of Professional Conduct* closely regulate a lawyer's ability to withdraw from client files: see chapter XII of the Canadian Bar Association's *Code of Professional Conduct*.[40] Assume that Adam's withdrawal from Harry's case would, in fact, violate chapter XII of the Code. For the purpose of this example, assume that any violation of the Code will be regulated through the imposition of a compensatory fee. Adam will have to internalize whatever costs his actions impose on other people.

In deciding whether to violate the *Code of Professional Conduct* and withdraw from Harry's case, Adam will be guided (at least subconsciously) by the ethical equation developed in chapters 2 and 3—namely, $A - B = X$. In this example, A (which represents the gross utility gains Adam enjoys by violating the *Code of Professional Conduct*) equals $150,000. The value of B is less obvious. Let us assume that Adam feels no guilt as a result of this ethical violation, and that his reputational costs are fairly low (say, $1,000: he was never considered particularly reliable in the first place). In addition, Adam incurs a cost of $90,000 by giving up the fees that he would have received from Harry. Most importantly (for our purposes), Adam will (if he violates the relevant ethical rule) have to pay a compensatory fee equal to the costs that his decision to breach the relevant rule imposes on other people. The amount of this compensatory fee (which is calculated below) will be a component of figure B in Adam's ethical equation. The costs that Adam imposes on others might include the following sums:[41]

- Harry will have to find another lawyer. Assume that the time it takes to find another lawyer creates a "utility cost" to Harry equal to $3,000.
- Harry's lawyer will need time to digest the information concerning Harry's enormously complex case. This will take months of preparation, generating legal fees and utility costs equal to $40,000.[42]
- The Crown lawyers were ready to proceed immediately, but will need to reschedule Harry's case (as well as countless other cases) in order to accommodate the sudden change in counsel. Utility cost: $10,000.

---

39   While this lawyer will have the benefit of Adam's pre-trial notes, it will still take him or her a great deal of time to prepare for Harry's trial.

40   The CBA Code is included in appendix A.

41   In reality, some (but not all) of the "costs" in this list would give rise to claims in contract or in tort. For present purposes, however, we will assume that the only regulatory regime governing Adam's decision is the regime imposed by the Law Society. Whether the costs are compensated through tort law, contract law, direct regulation by the Law Society, or some combination of these regulatory regimes, the impact on Adam's decision is the same: perfect compensation will give rise to perfect cost internalization.

42   Assume that Harry's new lawyer could have earned $40,000 in an alternative endeavour. That lawyer thus gains no net utility as a result of Adam's breach. Instead, Harry simply pays another $40,000 for duplicative preparation.

- Expert witnesses who have prepared for the trial and travelled to the venue will have to be compensated for their wasted time. They will have to be brought to Toronto at some future time (when the newly constituted trial takes place), incurring additional expenses. Utility cost: $10,000.
- Harry's family, firmly convinced of Harry's innocence, incurs utility losses waiting for Harry's day in court. Utility cost: $1,000.

Based on this list of external costs, Adam's compensatory fee equals $64,000: the sum of all costs that Adam's decision to break the rules imposes on other individuals. By paying this fee, Adam bears whatever costs his decision imposes on others: his compensatory payment will compensate those people for their losses.

Having produced a schedule of external costs,[43] we are now equipped with all the information required to predict and describe Adam's ethical choice. Adam's decision can be described through the algebraic expression of ethical choices: $A - B = X$. In this example, we have already seen that A (the gross utility benefits of a decision to break the rule) equals $150,000 (the utility Adam generates through salary and fame). B (the gross utility costs of a decision to break the rule) equals the sum of Adam's reputational costs ($1,000); the income Adam will lose if he abandon's Harry's case ($90,000); and the costs that Adam imposes on other people ($64,000, which Adam will have to internalize through the payment of a $64,000 compensatory fee). The components of B add up to $155,000. Subtracting B from A, we are left with an X of −$5,000: a negative figure. X is negative because the costs of Adam's contemplated act outweigh the gains. Since X is negative, Adam will *not* abandon Harry's case. As a rational, utility-maximizing individual, Adam will refrain from taking actions that lead to losses of utility. Adam will accordingly abide by rule XII of the *Code of Professional Conduct*, continuing to represent Harry and turning down his chance at fame.

Had Adam been allowed to ignore the costs that he imposed on other people, figure B (in Adam's ethical equation) would have been reduced by $64,000. There would have been no compensatory fee for Adam to pay, and all the external costs described above would have remained externalities (that is, they would have been borne by people other than Adam). Since Adam is a self-interested, utility-maximizing individual, his natural inclination is to ignore the costs that his decisions impose on other people. Had Adam been permitted to ignore these costs, he would have abandoned Harry's case on the eve of trial. Adam's decision to abandon's Harry's case would have generated a private gain (to Adam) equal to $59,000 (the $150,000 gain minus the $91,000 cost representing lost fees and diminished reputation). The additional social cost of $64,000 (which Adam imposes on other people) would not have entered into his decision at all, leading Adam to make an inefficient choice (a choice that destroyed $5,000 of social utility).

---

43 Some readers will immediately object to the list of external costs imposed by Adam's behaviour. According to many people, ethical violations do not merely impose costs upon a narrow class of victims. Instead, ethical violations impose a wide array of costs on *all* people, by virtue of the fact that such violations undermine the value of the legal system. For an account of such costs and their role in calculating the utility lost through ethical violations, see section IV.B below.

Through the mechanism of a compensatory fee, Adam has been forced to bear (or internalize) the costs that he imposes on other people, compensating individuals who would otherwise have been harmed (or lost utility) as a result of his decisions. Since the overall effect of this compensatory fee was to make Adam's costs outweigh the gains that he would have generated by breaching an ethical norm, Adam refrained from breaching the ethical norm in question. This had the effect of forcing Adam to make the most efficient decision: the decision that maximized social utility.

Note that the foregoing model of regulation does not guarantee that ethical norms will be respected. If Adam placed an unusually high value on the fame associated with his new job, for example, it might have been worth his while to commit an ethical violation and withdraw from Harry's case. If, for example, Adam would have happily given up $300,000 to have the fame associated with his new job, a breach of the ethical rule would have yielded a net gain in utility. Adam would have happily violated the *Code of Professional Conduct* and paid the relevant fines.[44] This feature of a compensatory model may seem strange. It sounds odd to simply allow people to pay a fee in exchange for the right to engage in unethical conduct. In many instances, however, this is a sensible way to regulate injurious conduct. In fact, this is one way of describing the legal system governing torts. If a tortfeasor is happy to pay the price that flows from a tort (such as trespass, assault, or negligent driving), the tortfeasor simply pays a fee (in the form of compensatory damages) in exchange for the right to engage in tortious conduct. In the realm of tort law, individuals are free to injure other people provided that tortfeasors bear the costs of the injuries they cause. By the same token, the compensatory model of regulation does not prohibit any particular kind of conduct. It simply ensures that individuals bear the cost of their behaviour. The beneficial effects of this form of regulation are discussed in the following section of this chapter. Problems flowing from the compensatory model of regulation are discussed in section V.

III. Advantages of the Compensatory Model

A. Efficient Incentives

In chapters 1 and 2, we noted that one of the principal goals of an economic theory of legal ethics is to determine whether particular rules and regulations generate efficient incentives. When using the phrase "efficient incentives," economists refer to rules or regulations that have the effect of promoting efficient choices (that is, decisions that maximize social utility). Where a rule or regulation leads decision makers to act in ways that generate optimal levels of social utility, the rule or regulation is said to produce efficient incentives.

A compensatory system has the ability to produce efficient incentives. This holds true in the regulation of legal ethics as well as in the more traditional fields of tort and contract. The easiest way to understand the power of a compensatory model to create efficient

---

44   Adam's utility calculation would look like this: $A - B = X$, with A having a value of $300,000 and B having a value of $155,000. Since X is positive, Adam will pursue the act in question.

incentives is through the use of examples. Consider the following illustration, which combines a basic ethical issue (the breaking of a promise) with a typical breach of contract.

Example 4.4

Angela Tasker is the world's most famous actress. She has been hired by an equally famous producer, Steven Bergspiel, to appear in Bergspiel's latest action movie. Tasker and Bergspiel have signed a contract pursuant to which Tasker will be paid the fee of $15 million in exchange for her promise to play the lead role in Bergspiel's film.

Bergspiel is happy to pay Tasker $15 million, since Tasker's participation in the film will increase the movie's profit margin by $30 million (all of which will be paid to Bergspiel). In other words, Bergspiel is giving up an asset valued at $15 million ($15 million worth of cash) in exchange for another asset he values at $30 million (Tasker's promise to appear in the movie). This contract generates a net utility gain of $15 million for Bergspiel.

Tasker prides herself on being an honourable person. She values her reputation as a "promise keeper" as much as she values $10 million. Tasker would feel guilty if she were to break a promise. Indeed, she would be willing to give up $3 million to avoid the feelings of guilt that she would experience if she were to break a promise.

Assume that Tasker is a rational, utility-maximizing individual. Further assume that two days before shooting is to begin for Bergspiel's film, Tasker is offered a part in Lucas George's latest sci-fi thriller, for the outlandish fee of $45 million.

If, as we have stated, Tasker is a rational, utility-maximizing individual, she is going to break her word (the mathematical proof is developed below). For many people (including Tasker), this breach of contract is more than a legal issue. For many people, a breach of contract carries ethical implications. Tasker is breaking a promise that she made in good faith, a promise on which another individual (namely, Bergspiel) has relied. Tasker believes that breaking her promise will impair her reputation as a promise keeper, causing her to lose $10 million worth of utility (representing the value she places on her unblemished record as a promise-keeping actress). On the facts of this example, Tasker would also experience $3 million worth of guilt. Tasker will also lose the $15 million of income that she would have earned by appearing in Bergspiel's film. Tasker's *personal losses* flowing from a breach of Bergspiel's contract would accordingly equal $28 million (the $15 million pay that she forgoes, plus $10 million in reputational costs and $3 million in guilt).

Lawyers will immediately note that Tasker's decision to break her word is not only an ethical issue, it is also a legal issue involving a breach of contract. By violating her contract with the producer, Tasker imposes a cost on her contractual partner—namely, the $15 million gain that Bergspiel would have enjoyed had Tasker adhered to the terms of the original agreement. This $15 million utility loss (suffered by Bergspiel) is a cost imposed by Tasker's breach of contract. Because Tasker is governed by a compensatory regulatory regime (specifically, a system that requires her to pay expectation damages where she breaches a legal agreement), Tasker will be have to compensate Bergspiel for the utility loss he suffers as a result of her decision to breach the contract.

Given the utility gains and losses that flow from a decision to breach this contract, what should Tasker do? Tasker's choice will be "efficient" if it maximizes social utility. Our rule of compensatory damages will be found to produce efficient incentives if it drives Tasker toward efficient decisions. Consider the flow of utility if Tasker breaches the contract. First, consider losses. Tasker will lose $3 million of utility through guilt, $10 million of utility in the form of a tarnished reputation, $15 million of forgone wages, and $15 million that she must pay in compensation to Mr. Bergspiel. Bergspiel suffers no loss of utility as a result of Tasker's breach. Because of the remedy of expectation damages, the utility gain he sought through Tasker's adherence to the contract has been fully replaced through expectation damages. In other words, Bergspiel is neutral as between Tasker's performance of the contract and her payment of $15 million of expectation damages. Whatever utility losses Bergspiel might have suffered through a breach of the agreement have been fully offset through the payment of compensation.[45]

Next, we must consider utility gains that flow from Tasker's decision to breach. Tasker gains the ability to accept a $45 million contract (which will generate $45 million of utility for her). Subtracting losses from gains, we see that Tasker generates an overall gain of $2 million in utility by breaching Bergspiel's contract, even when she is forced to internalize the costs of the relevant breach. As a result, this is an efficient breach of contract, producing an overall gain in social utility. In layperson language, the world is better off because of this breach. Bergspiel is just as happy to have a $15 million damages payment as he would have been to have had Tasker in his movie, and Tasker is happy to have secured an extra $2 million of cash. Lucas George is also better off as a result of Tasker's breach. Presumably, he is willing to pay $45 million to have Tasker in his movie only because he values Tasker's participation in the film more than he values $45 million of cash. In other words, Tasker's acceptance of George's contract generates a gain in utility for George. Finally, it seems likely that the movie-going public will also benefit from this breach. George's willingness to pay Tasker more than Bergspiel was willing to offer likely results from the fact that Tasker's participation in George's movie will lead to more ticket sales than Tasker's participation in Bergspiel's film. In short, the public prefers to see Tasker in George's movie. As a result of Tasker's breach, the movie-going public will see Tasker in the role that they prefer. The net result is that George, Tasker, and the movie-going public are made *better off* as a result of Tasker's breach of the Bergspiel contract, and Bergspiel is no less happy than he would have been had the contract been performed.[46] Because of the remedy of expectation damages, no one suffers utility losses as a result of Tasker's breach, and at least two people (plus the movie-going public) are made substantially happier. Tasker's decision to breach the

---

45   The victim's feelings of neutrality or indifference are further explored in section III.B, which describes the victim's perspective in a compensatory regulatory regime.

46   This type of outcome, where at least one individual is made better off while no individuals are made worse off, is known as a "Pareto-efficient" outcome. It increases social utility without diminishing any single person's utility.

contract maximizes social utility, and Tasker is driven to this decision by a compensatory system of regulation.

What does our economic account of Tasker's breach tell us about compensatory remedies? First, it tells us that a compensatory remedy can produce efficient incentives. We had already seen (in section II.C) that compensatory remedies can prevent decision makers from making inefficient choices that could flow from the presence of negative externalities. Through our account of Tasker's breach, we are now able to see that compensatory damages can also *encourage* decisions that generate overall gains in social utility.

Imagine, for the moment, what would happen if the remedy for breach of contract (or promise breaking) was something greater than expectation damages. Specifically, what would happen if the remedy for breach of contract was the requirement to pay a fine equal to *double* the cost imposed on the victim of breach? In the Tasker example, this punitive remedy would have been equal to $30 million. Taking this new, inflated remedy into account, Tasker would surely have adhered to the Bergspiel contract. From Tasker's perspective, a breach would give rise to a gross utility loss equal to $58 million and a gross utility gain of only $45 million, yielding a net loss (to Tasker) of $13 million. Because decision makers do not pursue utility-losing ventures, a penalty of $30 million would have prevented Tasker from breaching Bergspiel's contract. This might not seem like a terrible thing. After all, breach of contract involves the breaking of an agreement made in good faith between consenting individuals and is something that many people would like to avoid. A heavy penalty (deterring people from breaching agreements) might accordingly seem like a good idea. Unfortunately, our proposed "punitive remedy" (namely, the $30 million fine) also prevents an efficient transaction—one that would have resulted in overall gains in social utility. As we saw in our calculations involving expectation damages, a purely compensatory remedy (with the effect of having decision makers internalize the costs of their decisions), allows (and even encourages) decision makers to breach their contracts where doing so enhances the well-being of all parties. Where a breach of contract generates an overall increase in utility, it seems sensible to promote that breach of contract. If Bergspiel, Tasker, George, and the movie-going public would each prefer (or at least be neutral about) a breach of the original contract, there is no sensible reason to prohibit the breach in question and insist upon performance. If not for Tasker's breach (which was considered a violation of her contract as well as a breach of the ethical norm against breaking one's solemn word), society would have missed out on the opportunity to experience a $2 million gain in social utility.[47] In other words, society is better off as a result of Tasker's breach—at least $2 million of additional wealth has been created. This is referred to as an "efficient breach" of contract, in that more resources are generated by breach of the relevant contract than would have been generated had Tasker adhered to the terms of her agreement. Our suggested punitive remedy (a $30 million fine) would have produced an inefficient choice, one that eliminated our chance at securing a $2 million gain in social utility. The compensatory remedy, by contrast, drove Tasker toward a decision that generated an extra $2 million gain. On the facts of this

---

47   The gain is likely to be larger when one accounts for the utility gains experienced by the movie-going public.

example, only a breach of the Bergspiel contract[48] (governed by a purely compensatory regime) can give rise to optimal resource allocation.[49]

A purely compensatory remedy, with the twin goals of (1) having decision makers compensate those people who they harm through their self-interested decisions, and (2) having decision makers internalize the costs of their behaviour, generally leads to efficient decisions. Where a breach of contract leads to an overall gain in social utility, that breach of contract should not be prohibited. On the contrary, the breach should be encouraged, particularly where the victim of the breach is fully compensated for any foreseeable loss that could have flowed from the breach in question. The victim of the breach is perfectly happy (having received, in the form of damages, the full benefit of the bargain). The breaching party is even happier (having made a decision in his or her self-interest). Most importantly, society gains the benefit of a net gain in utility. It seems silly to impose an inflated remedy where the effect of such a remedy would be to deter breaches of contract that could have made everyone happy. We prefer a compensatory remedy that forces decision makers to internalize the costs of their decisions. *Where decision makers fully internalize the costs that are created by their decisions, they make decisions yielding overall gains in social utility.* In a compensatory regulatory regime, decision makers are forced to bear the full cost of each of their choices. They will therefore make only those choices that generate gains in social utility. In other words, they will make efficient decisions.[50] This is one of the underlying premises of the compensatory model of regulation. Because the compensatory model drives decision makers to make efficient decisions, we can conclude that a compensatory model of regulation has the capacity to produce efficient incentives. This weighs heavily in favour of a compensatory model of regulation, even in the realm of legal ethics.

B. Redressing Wrongs: The Victim's Perspective

Thus far we have been focusing on the ability of a compensatory regime to guide decision makers toward efficient decisions. We have discovered that a compensatory model of regulation has the power to create efficient incentives. When governed by an efficiently

---

48   If Tasker was prohibited from breaching this agreement (by a "penal remedy" requiring a payment of $30 million, for example), it might be possible to achieve an efficient resource allocation through the mechanism of voluntary exchange. George could approach Bergspiel and bargain for the right to have Tasker appear in George's movie rather than Bergspiel's. In the real world, however, this negotiation may give rise to transaction costs that can be avoided if an efficient remedial system simply allows for breach of contract where breach generates an efficient allocation of resources.

49   An additional proof of the "efficiency" of breach in this example deals with the value George places on Tasker's appearance in his movie. George must value Tasker's appearance at more than $45 million. Bergspiel, as we have seen, valued Tasker's appearance at only $15 million. By designing a compensatory remedy with the goal of internalization, we have ensured that a scarce resource (Tasker's ability to appear in a movie) is allocated to its highest-valued user—namely, the one who can use the resource in the most efficient manner. (As we have seen, George can use Tasker's talents in a way that produces more than $45 million in utility.) As a result, society as a whole is better off if Tasker appears in George's movie.

50   David Friedman, *Law's Order* (Princeton, NJ: Princeton University Press, 2000), 24.

run compensatory regime, decision makers are guided toward those choices that yield net gains in social utility. While this goes a long way toward proving the usefulness of a compensatory regime, it might appear to ignore a critical issue: the perspective of individuals who are injured as a result of a decision maker's self-interested activities. As we shall see, when we account for the perspective of a decision maker's victim, the case for a compensatory model of regulation becomes even more compelling. Indeed, one of the key advantages of a perfectly compensatory model of regulation is its ability to satisfy the needs of individuals who are harmed through a decision maker's actions.

How do compensatory regimes address the harms that are suffered by victims of a decision maker's choices? To answer this question, it is useful to consider the nature of harm. From an economic perspective, harm is simply a loss of utility. Where I am harmed by air pollution, for example, I lose whatever utility I associate with unpolluted air. When an accident victim is harmed through the loss of a limb, he or she loses whatever utility he or she gained from (1) the use of the limb, and (2) the absence of the pain that was caused by the relevant injury. All these utility losses are, of course, costs of a decision maker's behaviour. Throughout this chapter we have seen that a compensatory system of regulation requires a decision maker to pay for all of the costs that flow from his or her decisions. As a result, decision makers must bear the utility losses suffered by victims of their choices. The corollary of this proposition is that, once the decision maker has paid for all of the costs that flow from his or her decisions, there will be no costs remaining for anyone else to bear. The victims of the decision maker's choices will not suffer utility losses as a result of the decision maker's behaviour. To the extent that individuals are harmed through a decision maker's choices, the lost utility is replaced by compensation.

The principal goal of any compensatory regime is to replace whatever utility is lost as a result of a decision maker's behaviour. In the realm of tort and contract, this is accomplished through the payment of money damages. If a tortfeasor causes a physical injury, for example, he or she must make up for the victim's lost utility through the payment of a fee (payable to the injured party) that generates an amount of utility that is equivalent to the utility loss of the victim. If a victim loses $800,000 worth of utility in the form of pain and suffering, hospital bills, and lost wages, for example, the tortfeasor must replace this lost utility by paying the victim exactly $800,000.[51] The utility replacement that is achieved through such a compensatory payment is the ultimate goal of compensatory systems. Indeed, the word "compensatory" implies that money damages can *compensate* for whatever utility loss the victim suffers.

Assuming that we are capable of quantifying a victim's utility losses (an assumption that will be challenged in subsequent sections of this chapter), we can calculate the exact amount of money that must be paid in order to make up for the loss a victim suffers. If we are successful in (1) quantifying the victim's losses, and (2) requiring the person who

---

51 Note that, in some instances, the law deviates from a truly compensatory model by placing "caps" on the amount of damage awards relating to certain kinds of losses (such as "pain and suffering" or "lost companionship"). These departures from the compensatory model typically relate to the difficulty involved in quantifying certain categories of harm and the consequent likelihood of overcompensation (which provides inefficient incentives). The problem of loss quantification is discussed at length below in section V.

caused the loss to pay whatever sum of money it takes to eliminate the victim's utility deficit, we have achieved the goal of "perfect compensation." In other words, the payment of money has perfectly compensated the victim for the utility losses he or she has suffered.

The effect of perfect compensation is to render potential victims neutral about the choices a decision maker makes. In the realm of contract law, for example, the victim of a breach of contract should be indifferent as between a decision maker's choice to adhere to the contract or to breach the relevant contract and pay expectation damages. If expectation damages are perfectly compensatory, they will allow the victim of a breach to receive precisely the same amount of utility that he or she would have gained had the contract been performed. If two events give rise to the same amount of utility for a particular individual, that individual is (by definition) equally happy to see either of those two events take place. Since performance of a contract (on the one hand) and breach of contract coupled with perfectly compensatory damages (on the other) each (in theory)[52] gives rise to precisely the same amount of utility for potential victims of breach, a rational person should be neutral as between these two events.

While it is relatively easy to see why a potential victim of a breach of contract would be neutral as between (1) performance of the contract, and (2) a breach of contract coupled with perfect compensation, the notion of "victim neutrality" in the realms of tort and legal ethics is harder for many people to swallow. In the realm of tort (particularly when one considers torts relating to grievous physical injuries), the notion of perfect compensation is especially counterintuitive. Perfect compensation for a physical injury should (in theory) make a potential injury victim neutral as between (1) the absence of an injury, and (2) the occurrence of injury coupled with perfect compensation. According to Cooter and Ulen:

> By the term *perfectly compensatory damages* or *perfect compensation*, we mean a level of damages such that the victim is indifferent between there being no accident and there being an accident with compensatory damages ... perfect compensation is a central concept because it characterizes the level of damages at which the injurer fully internalizes the cost of accidents.[53]

Where an injurer fully internalizes the costs that are imposed as a result of his or her injury-causing actions, there are no costs remaining for an injured party to bear. As a result, the injurer's choice to undertake behaviour that injures another person is (from the injured party's perspective) a costless action. Because the injured party's utility losses are fully offset by utility gains (generated by cash payments), the injured party suffers no loss in utility as a result of the "injuring party's" tortious actions. In effect, perfect compensation makes potential victims indifferent about everyone else's actions, whether or not those actions seem to be injurious.

As noted above, it seems counterintuitive to claim that an individual may be indifferent between (1) the absence of a physical injury, and (2) a physical injury plus a

---

52   Practical difficulties with the assumptions inherent in the notion of perfect compensation are discussed in section V.

53   Cooter and Ulen, supra note 27, at 363.

particular sum of money. Consider a broken arm. What does it mean to be truly neutral as between an unbroken arm (option A) and a broken arm plus a particular sum of money (option B)? Assume that a broken arm results in a utility loss that is valued at $X. In theory, a person who is truly neutral as between options A and B should be willing to agree (in advance) to have a person break his or her arm if the arm breaker was willing to offer more than the sum of $X in exchange for the right to break the victim's arm. If $X plus a broken arm generates precisely the same amount of utility (for our potential victim) as an unbroken arm, a broken arm plus a sum of money *greater* than $X should make the potential victim *happier* (that is, it will generate more utility) than an unbroken arm. This seems fanciful. Few people can readily envision agreeing to have their arm broken for any sum, regardless of the fact that, if their arm were broken in an accident, a court would purport to set the amount of damages required to replace the utility lost through the relevant injury.

The unusual consequences that appear to flow from the notion of perfect compensation do not undermine the usefulness of a regulatory regime based on a compensatory model. Return to the broken arm example. Imagine that a potential victim is offered a choice to either (1) keep his or her unbroken arm, or (2) allow our hypothetical arm breaker to break the victim's arm in exchange for a payment (in advance) of $7 billion. If our potential victim is anything like most people, he or she would at least entertain this offer.[54] It seems likely that a payment of $7 billion (a sum that would eliminate the potential victim's need to work, invest, or worry about money in the future) will more than make up for the pain and suffering (as well as any inconvenience) that flows from a broken arm. This makes it evident that there *is* a sum of money ($7 billion) that provides potential victims with *more* utility than the absence of the contemplated injury. If this is true, there must also be a sum (lower than $7 billion) that leaves the potential victim neutral as between (1) the infliction of an injury plus receipt of the relevant sum, and (2) avoidance of the injury. The fact that this figure may be extraordinarily high (or difficult to prove) does not undermine the validity of the theory underlying a compensatory model. On the contrary, it simply makes the model difficult to apply in certain contexts (such as cases involving broken arms, lost children, or other particularly traumatic forms of injury). The practical difficulties involved in applying compensatory models to such cases (including situations involving breaches of lawyers' ethical standards) are explored in section V.

Assuming, for the moment, that every conceivable form of injury (whether physical or financial) can be expressed in terms of a victim's lost utility, and that the utility lost by a victim can be replaced by a sum of money (a sum of money that may be relatively high in some cases), the existence of a compensatory regime changes the nature of our personal interactions. In the realm of contract law, for example, the presence of a compensatory

---

54   This claim is not based on any scientific study, but on "straw polls" taken by my students at the University of Western Ontario's Faculty of Law and at Osgoode Hall Law School, York University. Students at both faculties agreed that they would enthusiastically accept the offer of $7 billion in exchange for a broken arm. Of course, when accepting this offer, the students knew that they were in no danger of actually having their arms broken (nor were they in any danger of receiving $7 billion).

regime (the remedy of expectation damages) converts a promise to deliver goods (for example) into a promise *either* to deliver the goods *or* to breach the relevant contract and pay expectation damages. When viewed through the lens of a compensatory regime, a contract is nothing more than a mutual guarantee of utility. Each contracting party agrees to supplement the other's utility by a particular sum, either through performance of the specific contractual obligations *or* through the payment of compensatory damages. Because the contract is constructed within the context of a compensatory regime, the possibility of breach (coupled with the payment of expectation damages) is inherent in the contract from the moment of its creation, and the option of breaching the contract (coupled with expectation damages) is simply another route to satisfying the expectations created by the agreement. Provided that our compensatory model does its job, the victim of a breach should be perfectly neutral as between breach of the relevant contract (coupled with expectation damages) and adherence to the terms of the agreement.

The compensatory system governing torts can also alter the way we look at human behaviour. Since tortious conduct is (generally speaking) regulated by a compensatory regime, all people living under that regime are effectively governed by an unspoken agreement: "I will either avoid injurious conduct or I will pay you compensation for the injuries that I cause." The choice to (1) avoid behaviour that causes injuries, or (2) cause an injury and compensate the victim, is (in theory) a perfectly value-neutral choice. If it costs a decision maker something more to avoid causing injury than it costs that decision maker to compensate all victims, the decision maker should be encouraged to injure his or her victims on the ground that injurious actions (coupled with perfect compensation) produce the greatest overall gains in social utility. If a tortfeasor can generate a $3 gain in social utility by causing a $1 injury to a victim, the tortfeasor should cause the $1 injury, compensate the victim (through the payment of $1), and enjoy the overall "profit" of $2. In sum, when living in a perfectly compensatory regime, decision makers should make whatever choices generate the greatest gains in social utility, regardless of the impact on other people. Whatever costs a decision maker imposes on other people, those costs will be internalized by the decision maker, generating efficient decisions and protecting the interests of all potential victims. Because their utility interests are protected, potential victims are perfectly neutral about the decision maker's choices.

The compensatory model, if taken to the extreme (as it has been throughout much of this section), suggests that any injured party can be compensated through the payment of money. Injuries cause a loss in utility to the person who is injured, and money causes a gain in utility to the person who receives it. Thus, money payments can replace the utility lost through any injury. Many readers will find this notion quite distasteful. Some injuries (for example, grievous physical injuries or psychologically troubling injuries such as the loss of a child or spouse) seem to defy compensation through the payment of money damages. It seems crass to argue that a deceased child (for example) can be replaced by money damages. For most people, there is no quantum of money that can replace a lost child. More importantly, even if injuries of this nature *could* be quantified by reference to dollar values, it would be impossible to prove the dollar value that would effectively make up for the victim's lost utility. If injuries of this nature defy perfect compensation, they seem to call into question the very basis of the compensatory model. These criticisms of the compensatory model are well-founded. For many injuries, a payment of money damages is unlikely to give rise to perfect cost internalization or adequate compensation. This problem inherent in the compensatory model will be explored in section V.B, below.

Before exploring the problems that undermine the functioning of compensatory models of regulation, it is useful to consider the manner in which a regulatory regime based on a compensatory model could apply in the regulation of legal ethics. A basic compensatory model of legal ethics, premised on the internalization of costs and the compensation of victims, is explored in the following section of this chapter.

IV. A Compensatory Model of Legal Ethics

A. Introduction

If a regulatory regime based on a compensatory model has the advantages of (1) guiding decision makers toward utility-maximizing choices, and (2) perfectly compensating the victims of injurious behaviour, it seems sensible to suggest that the optimal method of regulating lawyers' conduct is to design a regulatory regime based on the compensatory model. Under this model, lawyers would be forced to internalize whatever utility losses they generated through unethical choices. The effect of cost internalization would be to ensure that lawyers make unethical choices only where the effect of doing so increases society's overall level of utility. As we have seen, the efficient incentives provided by a compensatory regime ensure that decision makers act in ways that maximize social utility. More importantly, a regulatory model aimed at cost internalization would ensure that every lawyer perfectly compensated the people who were injured as a result of any unethical choices that the lawyer made. On a theoretical level, this is an appealing idea. The question whether this model *should* apply in the regulation of legal ethics is considered in subsequent sections of this chapter.

The manner in which the compensatory model could apply in the context of lawyers' ethical choices can be shown through the following example.

Example 4.5

Shelby Dingle is a lawyer in Toronto. Her client, Leila Slade, is planning to sue a local restaurant for $10,000. Leila's claim is based on an alleged instance of food poisoning. According to Leila, the restaurant served her undercooked pork. She contracted trichinosis after eating the pork and suffered severe gastrointestinal discomfort.

Shelby and Leila believe that the claim has a 90 percent chance of succeeding—that is, the expected value of the claim is $9,000 ($10,000 of damages multiplied by a probability of 0.9).

Shelby is an aspiring singer. Two days before she is required to file documents in connection with Leila's claim (to avoid missing a limitation period), a concert promoter offers her a contract to perform as the opening act for famed pop star Brittany Jackson. If she opens for Brittany, Shelby will be paid $60,000. Unfortunately, the concert is in Las Vegas, and Shelby would have to leave immediately. If she decides to perform at the concert,

she will not be able to file Leila's documents in time. If she fails to file
Leila's documents in time, Leila's claim will be statute barred—that is, Leila
will be prohibited from asserting the relevant claim.

For the purposes of this example, assume that Shelby will earn $3,000
if she stays in Ontario and pursues Leila's claim.

What should Shelby do?

Because Shelby is a lawyer in Ontario, she is bound by Ontario's *Rules of Professional Conduct*. Rule 2.01(2) of those rules requires that Shelby live up "to the standard of a competent lawyer." According to rule 2.01(1)(e), a competent lawyer performs his or her duties in a "timely manner." If Shelby fails to file Leila's statement of claim and misses the statute-of-limitations deadline, she will have failed in her duty of competence and violated the rules of professional conduct. For the purposes of this example, assume that only Ontario's Law Society has the power to regulate Shelby's ethical choice. No other regulatory regimes (such as the law of tort or contract) will govern Shelby's behaviour.[55] Further assume that the Law Society has adopted a compensatory regime for regulating lawyers' ethics: where lawyers violate the code of ethics, they must compensate their victims for any damage that the violation causes.

As we have seen throughout the first three chapters of this book, Shelby's decision will be governed by the goal of self-interested utility maximization. In other words, Shelby will act as though her decision is governed by the basic ethical equation developed in chapters 2 and 3—namely, $A - B = X$. Once again, A represents the utility gains that Shelby hopes to secure through a particular course of action. B represents the utility losses (accruing to Shelby) associated with that action. X, which is the result of subtracting B from A, is the net utility gain or loss the relevant act will generate.

In example 4.5, Shelby must decide whether or not she should abandon Leila's claim and accept a contract to perform at the Jackson concert. The utility gain associated with this choice (figure A) is equal to $60,000 (the income Shelby will generate by performing).[56] The utility loss (figure B) associated with this choice is made up of two figures: (1) lost income, and (2) a compensatory damage payment to Leila. The lost income is valued at $3,000 (the income Shelby would have earned had she continued to work for Leila). The compensatory damage payment will equal the amount of any damage that is caused by

---

55   While this assumption is unrealistic, it serves to simplify the analysis. To the extent that tort or contract law *would* provide a remedy for Leila, Law Society regulations (under a perfectly compensatory regime) would give rise to additional remedies only where contract and tort failed to provide a lawyer's victim with adequate compensation. To the extent that contract or tort failed to provide the victim with perfect compensation, the role of Law Society regulations would be to force the lawyer to make up the shortfall. In other words, whether our compensatory regime comprises one regulatory system (such as Law Society regulations) or some combination of multiple regulatory systems (such as tort, contract, *and* Law Society regulations), the overall goal is perfect compensation. Whether perfect compensation is provided by one regime or overlapping systems, the incentive effects on lawyers and their clients will be the same.

56   To the extent that Shelby enjoys performing at the concert, or believes that it will advance her burgeoning singing career, the utility gain may be even higher. For the purpose of simplifying our analysis, however, we will assume that the only gain associated with this choice is the money Shelby is paid for performing.

Shelby's failure to abide by the code of ethics. In this example, Shelby's failure to observe her ethical duties will cause Leila to lose her chance to sue the restaurant. The chance to sue the restaurant was worth $9,000 to Leila (the $10,000 value of the claim multiplied by the 90 percent likelihood that the claim would be successful).[57] Because a decision (by Shelby) to perform at the Jackson concert will deprive Leila of the ability to sue the restaurant, Shelby's decision would impose a $9,000 cost on Shelby. Because she is governed by a compensatory regime, Shelby will (if she breaches the rules of ethics) have to pay Leila the amount that Leila loses as a result of the ethical breach—namely, $9,000. As a result, Shelby's ethical decision can be described mathematically as follows:

$$A - B = X$$
$$\$60,000 - (\$3,000 + \$9,000) = X$$
$$\$60,000 - \$12,000 = X$$
$$X = \$48,000$$

In this example, X is a positive figure ($48,000). Since X is positive, the benefits (to Shelby) of violating the rules of professional conduct exceed the relevant costs, and Shelby will decide to break the rules. She will breach the rules of professional conduct, pay compensatory damages to her client, and embark upon her quest for superstardom. Shelby is better off by breaking the rules of ethics. As a result, Shelby will (and should) violate those rules.

It seems counterintuitive to assert that Shelby "should" breach the ethical duty of competence that lawyers owe to their clients. Consider, however, the nature of this duty, and to whom the duty is owed. This duty of competence is owed to Shelby's client. The ultimate purpose of this duty, like any duty owed by a lawyer to his or her clients, is to preserve the client's utility expectations (as well as the utility expectations of the public). Lawyers owe a duty of competence to their clients because their clients (and other members of the public) *value* competence—that is, they derive utility from it. In our example, we have determined the amount of value Leila places in the competence of her lawyer—namely, $9,000. Because the utility Leila gleans from Shelby's competence has (through Shelby's payment of compensation) been replaced by the utility of money, Leila should be perfectly neutral about Shelby's decision to violate her duty of competence. Leila is just as happy to receive $9,000 from Shelby as she would have been to receive it from the restaurant. Indeed, if (as we have assumed) the figure of $9,000 represents Leila's "investment" in Shelby's adherence to her ethical duty of competence, Shelby could have approached Leila in advance, informed her that she was going to violate her duty of competence by missing the filing deadline, and purchased the right to do so for any sum equal to or greater than $9,000. As a self-interested, wealth-maximizing person, Leila should be happy to make this exchange.

Leila and Shelby are both happy to have Shelby breach the rules of professional conduct where a decision to breach those rules is governed by a compensatory model of

---

57   In reality, the value of this claim to Leila would be $9,000 minus whatever fees Leila would pay to Shelby. We assume, however, that a loser-pays rule applies to Leila's cause of action and the restaurant would pay Shelby's fees.

regulation. How does the rest of the world feel about Shelby's breach? The restaurant Shelby was suing will be happy, since it is no longer faced with a claim for damages.[58] The concert promoter will be happy as well. Presumably, the promoter was willing to pay Shelby $60,000 because he or she valued Shelby's performance more than $60,000: the promoter would have been irrational to exchange $60,000 for a performance that he or she valued less than that amount. Thus, the promoter will gain utility as a result of Shelby's breach. All the relevant players (Shelby, Leila, the restaurant, and the concert promoter) are happier as a result of Shelby's breach. For reasons that will be explained in section IV.B, the rest of society should also be perfectly neutral about Shelby's decision to breach. As strange as it may seem, for reasons that will be seen in section IV.D, even the Law Society should be perfectly neutral about this breach.

Because no one is worse off as a result of Shelby's breach, and at least three parties (namely Shelby, the restaurant, and the concert promoter) are better off as a result, Shelby's breach is an efficient ethical breach that should be encouraged. It is efficient in that it generates net gains in social utility. This gain was secured through the use of a regulatory regime designed around a model of compensation. Had we imposed an inflated penalty (say, a punitive fine of $50,000, or a period of suspension generating a loss of utility that was greater than the amount of the relevant fine), Shelby would have refrained from violating her duty of competence. Leila would have been no worse off than she would have been had Shelby breached her duty and paid compensatory damages. Shelby, however, would have been worse off, losing out on the opportunity to pursue her singing career. More importantly, the concert promoter (and the music-loving public) would have lost a rising star. This eliminates an opportunity for a net gain in utility: an opportunity that could have been realized through the use of compensatory fines.

In theory, a perfectly compensatory regulatory regime ensures that only efficient ethical violations take place. Only where a breach of ethics generates enough utility to compensate all victims will the decision maker pursue a breach of ethics. Inefficient violations (which lead to overall losses in social utility) will be avoided. Because decision makers are forced to bear the costs of their decisions, all of the costs that flow from their decisions (including externalities) will detract from the utility a decision maker enjoys by engaging in an ethical breach. If the costs imposed by the decision maker's ethical violation outweigh the utility gains created by the breach in question, the decision maker (as a self-interested maximizer of utility) will avoid the relevant breach. Our compensatory regime effectively (1) prevents all ethical breaches that cause net losses in

---

58   This is what is referred to as a "positive externality": an external benefit flowing from an economic actor's decision. Astute readers may object to this positive externality. The damage claim against the restaurant was *itself* a component of a compensatory regime (the law of torts), designed to provide the restaurant with efficient incentives. Because the restaurant avoids paying compensation for damages it caused, the restaurant is not provided with efficient incentives to internalize the costs of its activities. This reveals a basic problem of the compensatory model. Even where an economic actor *should* be found liable for a damage-causing action, the actor may be able to escape liability (because its actions were not detected or, as in this example, the damage claimant misses a limitation period). The failure to impose liability on such actors is known as an "enforcement error." Enforcement errors, together with (1) the ability of such errors to undermine compensatory regimes, and (2) the methods used to avoid or combat such errors, are discussed in sections V and VI.

utility, and (2) encourages beneficial (or "efficient") violations of applicable ethical norms—that is, violations that generate net gains in utility. For these reasons alone, it might be sensible to adopt a compensatory model of regulating the ethical choices lawyers make.

B. Costs to Society

In previous sections of this chapter we purported to calculate the utility gains and losses flowing from lawyers' unethical choices. Each of those calculations relied on one un-stated (and unrealistic) assumption: the utility losses flowing from a lawyer's unethical actions are limited to the costs that are borne by (1) the lawyer, (2) the lawyer's clients, and (3) any other party *directly* affected by the lawyer's actions. In example 4.3, for instance, the only losses we considered were those imposed on Adam's client and on the Crown attorneys affected by Adam's choices. In example 4.5, the only costs we included in our analysis were the costs that Shelby's decisions imposed directly on her client. In calculating the losses that flowed from the lawyers' conduct, we ignored any indirect harm—that is, costs imposed on people beyond the lawyer's direct victims—that could be attributed to the conduct of the lawyer whose ethical choices were in question. Until now, we have simply assumed that there *are no* indirect costs that are worth our attention. The only relevant costs are those imposed on the parties who are directly affected by the lawyer's ethical choices.

Scholars in the field of legal ethics (together with practitioners and courts who address the regulation of lawyers' ethical conduct) are unanimous in the view that the negative consequences of a lawyer's unethical actions are not confined to the costs imposed on the lawyer's direct victims. When a lawyer violates the codes of ethics, every member of the public suffers harm—even those who have no contact with the unethical lawyer in question. As Proulx and Layton note, this harm comes in the form of "harm to the administration of justice," which undermines the public's trust in the legal system.[59] The court in *Bolton v. Law Society* (1993)[60] went so far as to claim that the *principal* harm that flows from lawyers' unethical conduct is the erosion of "public confidence in the profession."[61] The court in *Adams v. Law Society of Alberta* (2000)[62] echoed this conten-tion, claiming that lawyers' unethical conduct "brings dishonour on the legal profession [and leads] the public to believe that lawyers are prone to abusing their position of trust."[63] In cases such as these, courts contend that lawyers who violate the codes of professional conduct damage the legal system itself. By diminishing the value of the legal system, it is argued, lawyers harm every person who relies on that system. A lawyer's ethical violation can accordingly be said to generate two kinds of harm—namely: (1) harm to the lawyer's clients and other directly affected parties, and (2) indirect social harm that

---

59   Michel Proulx and David Layton, *Ethics and Canadian Criminal Law* (Toronto: Irwin Law, 2001), 287.

60   [1993] 1 WLR 512 (CA).

61   See MacKenzie, supra note 4, at 26-45.

62   (2000), 266 AR 157 (discussed in chapter 1).

63   See also *Law Society of British Columbia v. A Lawyer*, [2000] LSDD no. 19 (discussed in chapter 1) and *Law Society of British Columbia v. Nader*, [2001] LSDD no. 40 (discussed in chapter 2).

arises as a result of damage done to the legal system. If this account of the harms that flow from ethical breaches is correct, a thorough account of the costs imposed by lawyers' behaviour must contend with social harm as well as with the costs imposed on those directly affected by the lawyer's behaviour.

Commentators who claim that lawyers' unethical actions diminish the value of the legal system are correct. When lawyers engage in unethical conduct, they erode the public's confidence in the administration of justice. This erosion of public confidence generates harm. The nature of this social harm, together with its implications for an economic account of legal ethics, can be revealed through the use of the following illustration.

Example 4.6

Charlie Till is an up-and-coming screenwriter. He has entrusted the only copy of his latest screenplay (a dramatic epic concerning a law professor writing an ethics text) to his lawyer, Heather Sandler. Heather is representing Charlie in his attempt to have the screenplay produced by world-renowned movie producer Eddie Harrington.

Having reviewed Charlie's script, Heather considers it a masterpiece. In fact, she is so taken with the screenplay that she decides (in violation of ethical rules) to claim the screenplay as her own. Without Charlie's knowledge, Heather forwards the screenplay to Harrington, claiming to have written it herself. Harrington loves the screenplay, and buys the option to produce it (from Heather) for $1.2 million.

News of the newly optioned screenplay quickly reaches Charlie, who is furious. Charlie reports his lawyer's actions to the local television station, which broadcasts several reports on Heather's unethical behaviour.

For the moment, assume that Heather's conduct is unregulated. There is no legal regime (criminal, civil, or otherwise) that is capable of regulating her conduct.

Consider the costs that flow from Heather's unethical conduct.[64] By taking advantage of an opportunity that should have been granted to her client, Heather has imposed a cost of $1.2 million on Charlie: funds that should have been paid to Charlie were paid to Heather instead.[65] Heather has also imposed costs upon society as a whole. All members of the public gain utility from a functional legal system. They regard the legal system as a useful public service, one that is funded (in part) through the expenditure of significant

---

64   Because they have no bearing on the present discussion, we will ignore the reputational costs that Heather will incur.

65   Like so many of the costs imposed by unethical behaviour, this is merely an example of redistribution. Money that should have gone to one party has gone to another party. While redistribution has no direct efficiency implications, it can give rise to related losses of social utility. The simplest example is theft. When you steal $20 from my home, you simply redistribute $20 from me to you. This does not erode social utility (because your utility gain fully offsets my utility loss). Fearing future thefts, however, I will now install locking mechanisms on my door. The cost of theft prevention erodes social utility. It imposes costs that would not have existed but for the possibility of theft.

sums of public money. Having been made aware of Heather's unethical actions, members of the public now doubt the efficacy of the legal system, fearing that lawyers will act *against* their clients' interests rather than in pursuit of their clients' legal goals. This is a form of social harm: a loss of public utility that is relevant to our economic account of legal ethics.

To an economist, the public loss of utility flowing from Heather's unethical action does not simply take the form of distrust for the legal system. Instead, it takes the form of an economic distortion that arises when lawyers engage in unethical conduct. The public does not merely feel bad, or lose some unquantifiable level of utility as a result of lawyers' unethical behaviour. Instead, the public (in response to ethical breaches) behaves in ways that give rise to tangible losses. People who *ought to* turn to the legal profession in order to further their interests turn instead to other, less cost-effective methods of pursuing their legal objectives. Fearing that lawyers will violate their confidences or abscond with their resources, people may resort to self-representation or extralegal means to achieve objectives that could be pursued more efficiently by resort to the legal system.[66] Other people may simply abandon any attempt to pursue particular legal objectives, fearing that any attempt to do so will be thwarted by an unethical lawyer's actions. In short, people will deploy their resources in an inefficient manner, giving rise to a suboptimal allocation of resources. As we saw in earlier portions of this chapter, this suboptimal allocation of resources constitutes a market failure: something that the Law Society hopes to avoid.

As an example of the economic distortion described above, consider the impact of Heather's actions on screenwriters in her community. Ordinarily, screenwriters (when attempting to sell their scripts) would entrust their scripts to legal professionals, trusting the lawyers to safeguard the script, pass it along to movie producers and negotiate the terms of the final contract. In many cases, this will be the most cost-effective method of proceeding; indeed, had there been a more cost-effective method of proceeding, rational screenwriters would not have turned to lawyers in the first place. In exchange for legal fees paid by the writer, the lawyer can draw on an array of contacts in the production industry, arranging a sale of the script while minimizing transaction costs. Without a lawyer's intervention, transaction costs would be much higher. The lawyer's contacts, for example, may be accessible to prospective screenwriters only through the expenditure of significant time and money. Once a buyer has been found, the screenwriter (who lacks the lawyer's expertise) may lack the ability to negotiate the most favourable terms of sale. As a result, the optimal way of selling scripts is through a lawyer's intervention. Having witnessed Heather's ethical breach, however, screenwriters in Heather's community fear that lawyers will steal their scripts. As a result, many writers will proceed without a lawyer's assistance, using inefficient (that is, less cost-effective) methods of selling their scripts to movie producers. The resources that are wasted by proceeding without a lawyer are a social cost of Heather's unethical conduct.

---

66   We can safely assume that extralegal means and self-representation are less economically efficient (or cost-effective) than the legal profession itself. If they were not, then the public would already have been using these methods of advancing legal interests rather than resorting to the legal profession, regardless of the public's perception of the profession's ethics.

For present purposes, let us assume that the utility lost through distrust in the adminis-tration of justice—that is, the utility lost through the misallocation of resources that arises when lawyers engage in unethical conduct—can be valued at a particular dollar figure. More specifically, let us assume that Heather's actions (in example 4.6) eroded exactly $50,000 of social utility (which includes, among other things, the excess funds that future screenwriters will spend when plying their trade without the help of legal professionals).[67] When we assess the costs imposed by Heather's actions, this loss of social utility must be added to the costs that Heather has imposed directly on her client (namely, $1.2 million). Taking all these costs into account, we see that Heather imposes a total cost of $1,250,000 through her breach of ethical rules. This figure encompasses all of the harm that flowed from Heather's breach of ethical norms.

Let us now assume that the Law Society regulates lawyers' behaviour through a compensatory model of regulation. Where lawyers commit a breach of ethical rules, they must make a compensatory payment to redress the harm they have caused. How might this compensatory model apply in example 4.6?

Initially, it seems attractive to suggest that a perfectly compensatory model should require Heather to pay $1.2 million to Charlie as well as $50,000 to the public (or to the public's representative, such as the government or the Law Society). One might argue that only by paying both forms of compensation can Heather compensate for all the harm she has caused. While this seems intuitively attractive, it is technically incorrect. A damage payment to Charlie (in the amount of $1.2 million) is all that is needed to correct the utility losses flowing from Heather's unethical actions.

Consider the impact of a perfectly compensatory payment to Charlie Till. In this example, Heather will pay Charlie $1.2 million, returning him to the level of utility he would have experienced were it not for Heather's ethical violation. The effect of this compensatory payment, as we have seen throughout this chapter, is to make Charlie perfectly neutral as between (1) Heather's adherence to ethical norms, and (2) Heather's breach of ethical norms coupled with perfect compensation. In other words, Charlie is perfectly happy to have Heather violate the rules of ethics and pay perfect compensation. He is just as happy with $1.2 million from Heather as he would have been with $1.2 million from Harrington.[68]

How will the rest of the public feel if Heather is forced to compensate Charlie for the losses caused by Heather's unethical conduct? Will the public require a $50,000 payment to restore its lost utility? While intuition suggests that the answer to this question should be yes, that intuition is incorrect. Instead, the public's $50,000 utility loss is avoided through Heather's $1.2 million payment to Charlie. This effect can be observed if we consider the nature of the social utility that was lost as a result of Heather's breach.

---

67   As we shall soon see, the value of this figure is unimportant. This social cost can be eliminated without being directly addressed by regulatory intervention.

68   Again, if Charlie is *not* indifferent between these two options, than we have failed in our goal of perfect compensation. A perfectly compensatory payment makes the victim indifferent between breach, on the one hand, and compliance plus damages on the other. If the victim prefers compliance, the damage payment is not high enough. If the victim prefers breach, the damage payment is too high.

As we noted above, the public's lost utility was not merely a reflection of hurt feelings. On the contrary, it reflected a loss of confidence in the administration of justice. Having observed a lawyer commit an unethical action to the detriment of her client, the public feared that lawyers would continue to act unethically, absconding with client assets or otherwise undermining their clients' interests. As a result, members of the public became reluctant to employ a lawyer's services. This reluctance to rely on the legal system was the source of social harm. People who should have turned to lawyers turned to other (less efficient) methods of furthering their objectives. In effect, the public took expensive precautions to avoid even greater utility losses at the hands of unethical lawyers. These precautionary measures wasted the public's scarce resources, ultimately generating a loss in social utility.

The public's reluctance to rely on legal professionals flows from the fear that unethical lawyers will impose utility losses on their clients. Where a compensatory system forces lawyers to perfectly compensate their victims, this reluctance disappears. To the extent that lawyers *do* behave unethically and impose costs on their clients, those lawyers will be forced to compensate their clients through the payment of money damages. Presuming that the Law Society's compensatory regime of regulating lawyers' ethics functions perfectly, it is impossible for clients to be harmed where lawyers engage in ethical breaches. In effect, the client's utility expectations are insured. Either the lawyer will preserve the client's utility through adherence to the code of professional conduct or the lawyer will restore the client's utility through a payment of money damages. Either way, it is impossible for the client to lose utility through a lawyer's ethical choices. There is no need to (1) waste resources guarding against a lawyer's unethical behaviour, or (2) turn to alternative (less efficient) methods of furthering legal objectives. The public will no longer be reluctant to rely on lawyers' services whenever a lawyer's services might be useful. Since the public no longer needs to turn to (inefficient) alternatives to a lawyer's professional services, the social utility loss that is occasioned by ethical breaches is avoided. In short, the social cost of ethical breaches disappears where lawyers are made to compensate the *direct* victims of their unethical conduct. For this reason, we can safely ignore the *indirect* costs of unethical conduct when designing our compensatory regime. Social costs will disappear provided that the direct victims of lawyers' unethical behaviour receive perfect compensation.

To clarify the notion of "disappearing" social costs, revisit the situation of screenwriters in the community described in example 4.6. Having observed Heather's act of stealing a script, these writers were inclined to proceed without a lawyer's assistance. This gave rise to a misallocation of resources: an erosion of social utility that amounts to social harm. If these writers now observe that Heather must pay Charlie the sum of $1.2 million (the sum that Charlie would have earned had Heather adhered to the code of ethics), these writers will no longer feel the need to avoid the use of legal services. If a lawyer steals a script, he or she must pay the writer whatever sum the writer would have earned by selling the script in question. In short, these writers have nothing to lose by hiring a lawyer. The writers will once again use a lawyer's services whenever it is efficient to use those services. The social costs of Heather's unethical decision (the costs that arose where people refrained from using the legal system) have completely disappeared. This leads us to one of the most interesting and compelling aspects of the compensatory model of regulation. *Where a compensatory model requires a decision maker to compensate all (and only) the direct victims of the decision maker's actions, any indirect costs of the decision maker's actions disappear.*[69]

To many readers, the notion of disappearing social costs seems fanciful. Indeed, it seems quite likely that even the most efficient compensatory regime would be unable to eliminate public skepticism concerning lawyers' ethics. Despite the presence of a compensatory regime, many potential clients are likely to avoid reliance on a lawyer's professional services out of fear that the lawyer will undermine (rather than further) the client's interests. In short, the social costs of ethical breaches remain in place, despite the presence of a compensatory regime. In truth, this objection is well-founded. It does not, however, flow from a flaw in the theory of compensatory regimes. On the contrary, it flows from our practical inability to implement a perfectly compensatory system of regulation. While our theoretical model ensures that lawyers compensate victims of unethical behaviour, causing related social costs to disappear, the reality is that lawyers can often avoid making compensatory payments. Lawyers may be judgment-proof, they may avoid detection or prosecution, or they may find alternative means of avoiding the need to compensate people who are harmed by the lawyer's ethical violations. Where lawyers avoid the need to compensate the victims of unethical conduct, they fail to restore the utility of their victims, and (more importantly for our purposes) the social costs of unethical actions remain in place. Potential clients remain fearful that their lawyers will undermine their legal interests and people avoid the legal system out of concerns regarding lawyers' ethical conduct.

While the ability of lawyers to avoid paying perfect compensation represents a significant flaw in the compensatory model, it does not force us to abandon the use of a compensatory model of regulation. Instead, it simply suggests that we should supplement the compensatory model where it fails to generate socially optimal outcomes. The most sensible method of overcoming the flaws in the compensatory model is discussed below in section VI.

In section III.A, we saw that a compensatory model of regulating legal ethics has the power to compel lawyers to make efficient ethical choices. In section III.B, we saw that the compensatory model has the capacity to render potential victims neutral concerning lawyers' ethical breaches. In the present section, we have seen that even the social costs that flow from a lawyer's breach of ethics can be redressed (at least in theory) through the compensatory model. Having considered the perspectives of (1) lawyers, (2) victims, and (3) the general public, we have only one perspective left to consider: that of the body charged with regulating lawyers' ethical choices. That perspective is described below in section IV.C.

---

69   This hypothesis can be tested by applying it to the crime of embezzlement. Assume that all embezzlers are immediately detected and required to compensate the victims of their crimes. What form would this compensation take? If we were successful in forcing all embezzlers to compensate their victims, would it be sensible for people to spend resources *preventing* embezzlement? Consider how this parallels the regulation of lawyers' ethical choices.

EXERCISE

Using the tools developed in previous sections of this chapter, prepare an analysis of the ethical decision described below.

Example 4.7

Janette Hiotte is a criminal lawyer in Ontario. Her client, Scott Wayteve, has been charged with aggravated assault. Janette believes that Scott is factually innocent of this crime, and has prepared a strong case that she believes will lead to Scott's acquittal. Janette does not want to call Scott as a witness, for fear that his surly demeanor will not sit well with the jury.

During the course of Scott's trial (before a judge and jury), the judge pointedly asks Janette (in front of the jury) whether Scott has a criminal record. Scott does, in fact, have an extensive criminal record, although none of the prior offences involved violence. It was improper for the judge to ask this question. Neither the judge nor the jury is entitled to an answer. Information concerning Scott's prior offences is inadmissible on the issue of Scott's guilt or innocence of the crime for which he is currently being tried.

If Janette answers yes, she is undermining her client's chance of acquittal, prejudicing the jury, and violating her duty of confidentiality. If she answers no, she is committing a serious ethical breach by lying to the tribunal.[70] Janette believes that the only option she can exercise without committing a serious breach of ethics is to inform the judge that the court is not entitled to ask this question. Unfortunately, she believes that a failure to answer the question in front of the jury would unduly prejudice her innocent client, causing the jury to believe that Scott had something that he wanted to hide. Even moving for an immediate mistrial could undermine Scott's interests, requiring him to be tried yet again for an offence that Janette believes he did not commit. As a result, Janette opts to lie to the court, saying that Scott does not have a criminal record. The Crown does not rebut this claim.

Assume that Janette's lie is a violation of the *Rules of Professional Conduct*. Further assume that Janette's lie will be uncovered at the conclusion of Scott's trial and that her breach of ethical norms will be punished through the imposition of a compensatory fine.

Consider Janette's subconscious ethical calculation.

1. What utility gains would Janette experience by breaching the rule against lying to a tribunal?

2. What utility losses does Janette cause through her violation?

---

70   See rule 4.01(2)(e) of Ontario's *Rules of Professional Conduct*: "When acting as an advocate, a lawyer shall not ... knowingly attempt to deceive a tribunal or influence the course of justice by ... misstating facts."

3. Who experiences these losses?

4. Generate reasonable figures for each of these benefits and costs and consider whether a compensatory regime might provide efficient incentives in this case.

5. Consider whether a penal system of ethical rules (with inflated fines that go beyond the level of perfect compensation or prison terms that generate large losses of utility) can generate the same set of outcomes.

After working through this problem, it should be evident that (in theory, at least) a carefully tailored regulatory system based on perfect compensation has the capacity to optimize the level of ethics present in the market for legal services. Such a system would ensure that only efficient ethical breaches would take place and that victims would be perfectly compensated whenever a lawyer violated ethical norms.[71]

Before considering the flaws inherent in the compensatory model of regulating lawyers' ethics, one last issue remains to be considered: the perspective of the body that is responsible for regulating lawyers. How would the Law Society feel about a compensatory system designed to regulate a lawyer's ethical conduct? That issue is considered in the following section of this chapter.

C. The Regulator's Perspective

In section III.B, we noted that a perfectly compensatory system of regulation has the effect of rendering individuals neutral about a decision maker's choices. In the realm of contract law, for example, the availability of expectation damages renders rational people neutral about a contractual partner's choice to either (1) abide by the provisions of a contract, or (2) breach the contract and pay expectation damages. Because we assume that our compensatory system generates perfect compensation, we accept that any utility that is lost through breach of contract is immediately replaced through the payment of expectation damages. Contractual partners are guaranteed to receive the level of utility that they sought when agreeing to enter the contract, regardless of their fellow contractor's choice to breach or adhere to the relevant agreement.

If legal ethics are governed by a perfectly compensatory system, the public should be neutral as between (1) a lawyer's adherence to ethical norms and (2) the lawyer's decision to breach the relevant norm and pay compensatory damages. By the same token, a regulatory body that purports to represent the public interest (such as the regulatory body governing lawyer's ethical choices) should be neutral as between the lawyer's

---

71   There is a strong argument that an action that *appears to be* unethical may appear ethical if it is carried out for sufficiently noble goals. The meaning of ethical in such cases is open to question. An action that is (in most instances) unethical may become "ethical" if undertaken for good reasons. Happily, the meaning of ethical and unethical is unimportant for the purposes of an economic theory. At present, we are simply evaluating the efficiency of actions and determining whether we can regulate harmful (or cost-imposing) actions through a system of compensation. The question whether a particular act qualifies as good or evil does not arise. Value judgments such as these are difficult to make with any confidence or precision. Our ability (or inability) to fully articulate the nature of goodness and evil, or to generate determinate definitions of ethical and unethical, is discussed at length in chapter 5.

adherence to ethical standards and the lawyer's decision to breach those ethical standards and pay perfectly compensatory damages. Common sense dictates that, if the *victims* of a lawyer's unethical actions are rendered neutral about the lawyer's unethical choices, the regulator should be indifferent about the lawyer's choices as well—there is no reason for a regulator to be upset if everyone else in society is happy. If the regulator showed a marked preference for having its rules obeyed even when a breach of the relevant rules was more efficient (and, therefore, in society's best interests), that regulator would be acting *against* society's interests, demanding thoughtless obedience for no reason apart from the regulator's own desire for power. The Law Society should (in theory) have no vested interest in forcing people to behave inefficiently.

The impact of a compensatory model on the regulator's perspective can be demonstrated through a simple illustration. Consider the following example.

Example 4.8

Alarmed at increased rates of tardiness among lawyers, the Law Society of Wupovia (a fictitious nation) has promulgated a new rule of professional conduct: the rule of timely appearance. Pursuant to this rule, all lawyers who are late for court appearances must pay $1 million to the Wupovian Law Society. A portion of that $1 million payment will be used to compensate all people who lose utility as a result of the lawyer's tardiness. The remainder of the $1 million fine will be used to fund the Law Society's important social programs.

Presumably, the $1 million penalty will ensure that there are few very tardy lawyers in Wupovia. If, however, someone had the remarkable ability to earn more than $1 million by being late for a court appearance, that person would breach the rule, pay the $1 million fine and make a profit.

How would the Law Society feel if, given the facts of example 4.8, a Wupovian lawyer breached the rule of timely appearance (by being two minutes late for court) and willingly paid a fine of $1 million? Presumably, the $1 million penalty is far more than is required to redress the utility losses flowing from a two-minute delay. For the purposes of this example, let us assume that the lawyer's delay gives rise to costs equalling $10,000. After receiving the lawyer's payment of $1 million, the Law Society could pay the amount of $10,000 to compensate those who were prejudiced by the two-minute delay.[72] The Law Society could then keep the remaining $990,000 to fill its coffers.

It seems reasonable to assert that the Law Society of Wupovia would be immensely pleased with our tardy lawyer's ethical breach. As a rational, self-interested regulatory body, the Law Society gains utility from cash. It can accomplish a great deal of important philanthropic work with $990,000. Because the Law Society has set the penalty for

---

72 For the purpose of this example, assume that the figure of $10,000 includes the cost of administering and enforcing the penalty. If the amount of a compensatory fine does not account for the costs of enforcement, it does not truly compensate for all the costs that are generated by the act that gives rise to the fine. In short, the costs of enforcement are costs of the behaviour that is subject to the compensatory model.

breach of the timely appearance rule at more than the amount required to compensate those people who lose utility through our hypothetical lawyer's two-minute delay, it profits from the violation of the timely appearance rule. All things being equal, it seems likely that the Law Society *prefers* to see our hypothetical lawyer break the rule and pay the fee of $1 million. This breach adds close to $1 million to the Law Society's coffers while causing an insignificant (and easily remedied) amount of harm.

If there is a punitive dollar figure (namely, $1 million) that makes the Law Society *prefer* the breach of a rule of professional conduct to compliance with that rule, there must be some lower dollar figure that renders the Law Society neutral as between (1) compliance with the relevant rule, and (2) a breach of the rule coupled with payment of the relevant dollar figure. This lower dollar figure is the figure at which all utility losses that are caused through breach of the rule are compensated through the payment of the fine. Where the compensatory fine for an ethical violation is just enough to compensate all those who lose utility as a result of the violation, the Law Society should be neutral (or "indifferent") as between adherence to the ethical rule and a breach of the rule coupled with compensation. If the Law Society shows a marked preference for breach of the rule plus payment of the fine, it has set the fine too high; it now profits from each ethical violation. (In other words, the Law Society enjoys net gains in utility when individuals breach a rule of professional conduct.) If the Law Society shows a marked preference for adherence to the rule (rather than breach of the relevant rule coupled with payment of a fine), it has set the fine too low.[73] In pursuit of the goal of perfect compensation, the Law Society should attempt to set the fine such that it is indifferent between breach of the rule (plus payment of the fine) and adherence to the relevant obligation.

To some people, it may seem perfectly sensible to let the Law Society profit where lawyers violate the *Rules of Professional Conduct*. As we have seen, however, only a penalty (or, more accurately, a compensatory fee) set at the level of perfect cost internalization has the effect of generating efficient incentives. If a breach of the rules of professional conduct can generate more utility than it costs to all concerned, then that breach of ethical norms should be encouraged. In example 4.8, the presence of an inflated fine (namely, $1 million) precludes efficient breaches of the timely appearance rule, unless those breaches are so lucrative that they generate more than $1 million of profit. If lawyer X could generate $800,000 of social utility—perhaps by performing some valuable public service—by being one minute late for court, the threat of a $1 million sanction would preclude this efficient breach of ethical norms. Indeed, *any* utility gains less than $1 million would be prevented by the threat of the $1 million fine. Violations that could have generated hundreds of thousands of dollars of utility are prevented, prohibiting sensible breaches that could improve the overall welfare of society. As a result, the compensatory model of regulation posits that regulators should set the price of breach at no more (and no less) than the amount required to compensate the victims of ethical breaches.

---

73   A Law Society that always prefers adherence to its rules gains utility from unswerving obedience to its own commands, regardless of the interests of other members of society. A Law Society of this nature would be inefficient and tyrannical.

Once the Law Society has set fines at a level that is just enough to compensate the victims of ethical breaches, it has achieved the goal of perfect internalization. All persons regulated by the relevant regime will fully internalize the costs of their decisions, breaching ethical rules only when those breaches lead to gains in social utility. As we have seen in this discussion, this level of fine also leaves the Law Society neutral as between adherence to an ethical rule and a breach of the rule coupled with compensation. In the final analysis, a perfectly compensatory system of regulation has four significant effects: (1) it creates efficient incentives for decision makers, (2) it perfectly compensates the victims of a decision maker's choices, (3) it causes indirect social costs (discussed in section IV.B) to disappear, and (4) it renders a rational regulator indifferent as between adherence to ethical norms and breach of the norm plus compensation. In theory, at least, this seems like a perfect system.

At this stage, many readers will be skeptical about the ability of a compensatory system to govern lawyers' ethical choices. This skepticism is well-founded. As we shall see in the following section of this chapter, practical problems inherent in the compensatory model make it unlikely that a compensatory model—without significant modification—would provide an adequate method of governing lawyers' ethical choices. The chief difficulties flowing from the compensatory model are discussed in the following section of this chapter.

V. Problems with the Compensatory Model

A. Introduction

A compensatory model of regulation can be marvelous: it promotes efficient behaviour, fully compensates those who have been harmed by a decision maker's choices, and renders rational regulators indifferent about a decision maker's actions. All told, compensatory models are sophisticated and elegant, promoting efficient choices, and optimizing the allocation of scarce resources. Unfortunately, a purely compensatory model (without significant modification) provides an inadequate method of regulating the ethical choices lawyers make.

To many people, a compensatory model of regulation seems (on an intuitive level) inappropriate as a method of governing lawyers' ethical conduct. Rather than imposing a total ban on unethical conduct, a compensatory model *encourages* lawyers to breach the rules of legal ethics whenever a breach results in a gain of social utility. This strikes many people as problematic. Sometimes, it is argued, we want to eliminate some feature from a market—for example, pollution, war, or unethical behaviour—even when an efficient market would produce a positive quantity of that feature. Proponents of this argument may consider an optimal amount of unethical conduct to be zero, despite the fact that an unregulated market (even a very efficient one) might produce a positive quantity. In the case of legal ethics, for example, it seems sensible to contend that the Law Society prefers to see no unethical conduct at all. To many people, this seems far more plausible than the contention that the Law Society should be neutral as between (1) ethical conduct, and (2) unethical conduct coupled with the payment of perfect compensation. To many people, this intuitive reason is enough to reject a compensatory model of regulating lawyers' ethics.

   As we have seen throughout this chapter, there are compelling economic arguments that justify the conclusion that a rational regulator *should* be neutral as between (1) ethical conduct, and (2) unethical conduct coupled with perfect compensation. The intuitive argument against the application of a compensatory model of legal ethics is an insufficient justification to reject the use of compensatory models in the regulation of lawyers' ethical choices. There are, however, three practical reasons for concluding that a compensatory model of regulation, despite its theoretical advantages, is incapable (at least without significant modification) of governing lawyers' ethical choices. These three reasons can be summarized as follows:

1. Some of the harms caused by a lawyer's unethical conduct seem to defy the notion of perfect compensation.

2. Even if all of the harms caused by a lawyer's unethical conduct were amenable to the goal of perfect compensation, it would be to impossible to calculate the level of compensation required to replace the utility lost as a result of the harm in question.

3. Many unethical actions are undertaken in the hope that the relevant act will not be detected—that is, unethical lawyers hope (and often expect) that they will not be caught. Where the chance of being caught (or the chance of being forced to compensate all victims) is less than 100 percent, the expected cost of compensation may be less than the gain to be generated from engaging in unethical behaviour, even where the unethical action leads to an overall loss of social utility. In other words, a compensatory model may encourage unethical actions, even where those actions impose a drain on society.

Each of these problems is addressed in the following sections of this chapter.

B. Non-Compensable Harm

In each of the examples we have encountered in this chapter, the utility losses experienced by the victims of a decision maker's choices have been expressed in dollar values. In many cases this is relatively uncontroversial. When I commit a tort and destroy your $25,000 car, for example, the dollar value of the harm that I have caused is easy to calculate—it equals $25,000 (the value of the asset I have destroyed). In cases of this nature, it is easy to achieve the goal of perfect compensation. I simply pay my victim whatever sum of cash compensates for the loss of utility that was caused by my behaviour. Cases of this kind are easily governed by a compensatory model of regulation. If I am forced to compensate you (through a payment of $25,000) in the event that I destroy your $25,000 car, I will make the choice to destroy your car if (and only if) I value the right to do so more than I value $25,000. In other words, the requirement of perfect compensation provides me with efficient incentives, ensuring that I will make efficient choices. It also renders you (the victim) perfectly neutral about my behaviour. You are just as happy to have a damage payment of $25,000 (and a ruined automobile) as you are to have your car in its undamaged state. My efficient incentives and your indifference have been achieved through the mechanism of perfect compensation. In cases of this nature—that is, where the damage done is readily converted into an ascertainable dollar figure—the goal of perfect compensation is attainable.

While it is relatively easy to replace a lost car with a specific sum of cash, some kinds of harm do not seem amenable to the goal of compensation. Consider the murder of a child. How much compensation would it take to leave a child's parents "indifferent" as between (1) having their child remain alive, and (2) having a murdered child plus compensatory damages? According to many theorists,[74] questions of this nature are impossible to answer. If this question *could* be answered by reference to a dollar figure, then we should (theoretically) be able to approach the child's parents in advance and purchase the right to kill their child for any amount that is greater than the compensatory sum. This notion is so repellant to many people that they believe no dollar figure is capable of replacing a living child.[75] In all cases, it is argued, the parent would rather have the child than any quantity of money.[76] If there is no sum of money that is capable of replacing a lost child, then the goal of compensation is unattainable.

Many of the forms of conduct regulated by the criminal law impose harms that appear to be ill-suited to the goal of compensation. Cooter and Ulen provide the following illustration:

> Consider a thought experiment regarding a crime. How much money would you require in order to agree to allow someone to assault you with a hammer? This question does not make much sense. The concept of indifference is difficult to apply to crimes like assault. Consequently, the relevant law cannot take as its goal the perfect compensation of victims and the internalization of costs by injurers.[77]

Like the loss of a child, the loss of a spouse, or perhaps the loss of a limb, a whack in the head with a hammer is hard to quantify in monetary terms. It thus seems (to many people) difficult to contend that the goal of perfect compensation is attainable in such cases. There is no sum of money that makes me indifferent as between (1) a lack of injury, and (2) a grievous, hammer-related wound plus compensation. If perfect compensation is unattainable, there is no dollar figure that can make a victim indifferent as between (1) falling victim to the conduct and receiving a damage payment, and (2) remaining free from the type of harm the conduct causes. Similarly, there is no dollar figure that will provide efficient incentives to decision makers wondering whether to

---

74   See, for example, Cooter and Ulen, supra note 20, at 452.

75   Some economists would contend that all utility-depleting behaviour can, in principle, be compensated through the payment of money damages. Harm diminishes utility and cash replaces utility. For such economists, compensation for a lost child may be an astronomical sum, but achieving the goal of perfect compensation would not be "impossible" in principle.

76   Note that the notion of "non-compensability" (even as it relates to children) may be a matter of perspective. In some poor countries, children are sometimes sold into slavery so that the rest of the family can purchase food and other goods. Parents who make this choice are deciding that a quantity of money is capable of compensating them for their child. In North America, one effect of our general standard of living is to make this type of transaction inconceivable.

77   Cooter and Ulen, supra note 20, at 452.

engage in the relevant form of conduct. Where a decision maker would always prefer to be free from the relevant harm than to have the harm plus compensatory damages, the harm is said to be "non-compensable." Where the harm caused by a particular act appears to be non-compensable, it is difficult to regulate that act by reference to a regime that is premised on perfect compensation.[78]

Many of the harms generated through a lawyer's ethical breaches are thought to defy the notion of perfect compensation. Consider, for example, the case of *Szarfer v. Chodos* (1986).[79] In that case, Szarfer's lawyer (Mr. Chodos) breached the rules of confidentiality, using confidential information (related to Mr. Szarfer's impotence) to begin an affair with Mr. Szarfer's wife. The harm imposed in cases such as *Szarfer v. Chodos* may be difficult to quantify in economic terms. In other cases, a lawyer's breach of ethical rules may deprive a client of an unquantifiable opportunity or result in an unjustifiable prison sentence. In cases such as these, it could be argued that, due to the nature of the harm caused by the lawyer's ethical breach, the goal of perfect compensation is hard (or perhaps impossible) to achieve. If that is the case, it is difficult to contend that a compensatory model is capable of regulating the behaviour that gave rise to such non-compensable losses.

While I am sympathetic to the notion that the loss of a spouse or child cannot be fully replaced by a payment of money damages, I am less convinced that the utility lost through a lawyer's unethical conduct could not, at least in principle, be perfectly offset through damage payments. Courts routinely award compensatory damages for cases involving ephemeral losses such as damage to reputation, pain and suffering, or lost opportunities. Even in the case of *Szarfer v. Chodos*, the court ordered a damages payment that was designed to compensate Szarfer for the lawyer's breach of confidentiality (and the ensuing affair between the lawyer and Mr. Szarfer's spouse).[80] If damages have the capacity to compensate for ephemeral losses such as these, surely they have the power to provide compensation for most losses imposed by lawyers' violations of ethical norms. This can be confirmed by a simple thought experiment. Attempt to imagine all of the ethical violations that a lawyer might commit. Now assume that, if you fall victim to an ethical violation, the lawyer will be required to provide you with $20 million. It seems likely that most clients would be willing to accept a large number of ethical breaches if the result was a damage payment of $20 million. There must accordingly be some figure (lower than $20 million) that makes lawyers' clients neutral as between (1) adherence to the lawyer's code of professional conduct, and (2) a breach of the code coupled with perfect compensation. It is at least arguable that the harms that are generated through a lawyer's ethical breaches are, in principle, compensable through the payment of money damages. While compensation *in principle* might be feasible, however, compensation *in*

---

78   While there are economic techniques for deriving a value for ostensibly non-compensible harms—for example, the technique known as Hand rule damages—these techniques are widely regarded as inaccurate. Largely because of their inaccuracy, the details of such economic techniques are beyond the scope of this chapter.

79   (1986), 54 OR (2d) 663 (HCJ); aff'd. (1988), 66 OR (2d) 350 (CA) (discussed in detail in chapter 6).

80   The sum was $43,663. See chapter 6.

practice may be unattainable. For many violations of lawyers' ethical standards, it is difficult to calculate or quantify (with any degree of confidence or precision) the harms that lawyers' ethical violations cause. The problem of quantification, and its impact on the compensatory model, is dealt with in the following section of this chapter.

C. Quantifying Harms

The previous section of this chapter highlighted one supposed limitation of the compensatory model of regulation. Stated simply, it is widely believed that some forms of harm defy the notion of compensation. While that claim is, at least in the realm of legal ethics, not especially compelling, it does point toward a weakness in the compensatory model, a weakness that is relevant to the regulation of lawyers' ethical conduct. Even if all forms of harm *are* theoretically compensable, it may be impossible to establish the *level* of compensation required to replace the utility lost through certain forms of harm. In other words, even where compensation is possible in principle, it is (as a practical matter) impossible to prove the dollar figure that can compensate for certain types of losses. Cooter and Ulen provide the following useful example:

> Even if perfect compensation *is* possible in principle, it may be impossible in fact. Let us suppose, for example, that a level of compensation exists that makes Jonny indifferent about whether Frankie lops off Jonny's arm. It would be impossible to prove this level in court. The obstacle to proof is that arms are not bought and sold in a market; there is no objective way to know how much the loss is worth to Jonny. If the court asks Jonny what amount he feels would compensate for the loss, he may not know the answer, or he may answer by exaggerating. When there is no market to induce people to reveal their subjective valuations, economists say that there is a "problem of preference revelation." When perfect compensation is possible in principle, it may be impossible in fact because of the problem of preference revelation.[81]

In this example, we are assuming that there *is* a level of compensation that renders Jonny neutral about the loss of a limb. Even assuming that such a level of compensation exists, however, we are left with a problem of preference revelation. There is no reliable source of evidence that can guide us in the quantification of the utility loss that Jonny suffers through the loss of his arm. We cannot simply ask Jonny how much he valued his arm, as his claim is likely to be unreliable (he is likely to exaggerate the value of the arm so that he will receive a higher amount of compensation). Nor can we look to an objective source of price information such as a market for the purchase and sale of limbs. As a result, the utility value inherent in Jonny's preferences cannot be revealed to the court. We have a problem of preference revelation.[82] If the goal of compensation is to

---

81   Cooter and Ulen, supra note 20, at 452.

82   While Cooter and Ulen's example is useful in explaining the difficulties of loss quantification, it does not reflect the common practice of courts. In the real world, courts calculate the value of lost limbs all the time (in tort cases involving injuries of this nature). Indeed, it was once common practice for lawyers to consult "meat charts" (that is, price lists regarding the value of damage to certain parts of a person's body) when deciding how much compensation to seek for injured clients.

force decision makers to pay whatever level of compensation is needed to offset the losses their decisions impose, we *must* accurately assess the victim's preferences. We must discover the dollar value that generates perfect compensation for the loss that has been suffered by the victim. In order to do this, we must quantify the utility value of the victim's loss. As we have seen in Cooter and Ulen's example, however, proving the value of this loss may be impossible with respect to certain harms. If you cannot quantify the value of the victim's loss, you cannot achieve the goals of (1) perfect compensation, and (2) perfect cost internalization. In cases such as this, a compensatory system is an ineffective method of regulation.

Many of the harms generated by lawyers' ethical violations give rise to the problem of preference revelation. How much damage is caused when a lawyer violates a client's confidentiality? How much utility is lost when a lawyer violates the rules regarding undisclosed conflicts of interest? While losses of this nature might be easily calculated in many cases, they frequently give rise to problems of preference revelation. Consider, once again, the decision in *Szarfer v. Chodos*, in which the court was asked to calculate the level of compensation that could compensate Mr. Szarfer for (among other things) the affair between his wife and Mr. Chodos. How would Szarfer prove the level of utility that he lost through his affair? His self-serving assertions are likely to be inaccurate (Szarfer has an incentive to lie about the utility he has lost in the hope of receiving an inflated damage award). More importantly, there is no market mechanism capable of revealing the amount of utility lost when a lawyer has an affair with the client's spouse. At best, a court faced with problems akin to the issue in *Szarfer v. Chodos* will simply guess at the level of compensation that is appropriate. To the extent that this guess is incorrect, the compensatory sum will fail to (1) generate efficient incentives, and (2) offset the utility losses experienced by the victim. As this example reveals, in the context of lawyers' ethical decisions, the problem of preference revelation may prevent the compensatory model from succeeding in its task of generating efficient incentives. If we are to benefit from the advantages of a compensatory model, we must augment the compensatory model in a way that "compensates" for the difficulties created by the problem of preference revelation.

If the standard compensatory model is an inadequate method of regulating lawyers' ethical conduct, how can regulators supplement the compensatory model in a way that can prevent the market failure (that is, the suboptimal level of legal ethics) that is likely to be generated by the market for lawyers' services? Before answering this question, we must consider the final (and most important) reason that the compensatory model has difficulty regulating the ethical (or unethical) choices that legal professionals make. That flaw, and its implications for the regulation of lawyers' ethical conduct, is described in the following section of this chapter.

D. Getting Caught

One of the most attractive features of the compensatory model is its ability to provide efficient incentives. As we saw above in section III, the compensatory model of regulation forces people to internalize the costs of their decisions, theoretically ensuring that individuals will make only those choices that give rise to net increases in social utility. Unfortunately, the nature of legal ethics is such that purely compensatory models have difficulty producing efficient incentives. Because of the nature of unethical behaviour, a purely compensatory model would often fail to produce efficient incentives, ultimately giving rise to suboptimal levels of ethical conduct. As we saw above in section I.B above, this is a form of market failure—the very thing the Law Society hopes to avoid.

Why does a compensatory model of regulation sometimes fail to provide lawyers with efficient incentives when it comes to making ethical choices? Consider the following example.

Example 4.9

Shonagh Girgis is a lawyer in New York. She is thinking about submitting inflated dockets to her client, HugeCo Industries, Inc.—that is, Shonagh is thinking of billing HugeCo Industries for more hours of billable work than she actually performed on the client's behalf. Specifically, Shonagh is considering an addition of 20 hours to her docket. At her rate of $400 per hour, Shonagh's false docket will provide her with exactly $8,000 of extra income. Because her firm's bill to HugeCo is fairly large (over $200,000), Shonagh believes that her false dockets will go unnoticed. In fact, she is 100 percent certain that HugeCo will not detect her behaviour and that she will, in fact, be able to collect her extra $8,000.

It will take Shonagh 30 minutes to construct a believable docket that contains the extra 20 billable hours. In other words, Shonagh will have to expend time and effort pursuing her ill-gotten gain. Assume that 30 minutes of Shonagh's time is worth $200 to Shonagh (in other words, had she used her time in an alternative pursuit, she could have generated $200 of income).

Shonagh believes that her only chance of detection is through the monitoring activities of state Bar officials. Once she has collected her fee from HugeCo, Shonagh believes that there is a 20 percent chance that Bar officials will discover her padded dockets and force her to reimburse HugeCo's $8,000. This reimbursement is the only sanction Shonagh will face as a result of her behaviour: New York lawyers (in this fictitious example) are regulated by a purely compensatory regime.

Assume that Shonagh has no conscience (in other words, she will not feel guilty if she engages in unethical behaviour). Finally assume that if Shonagh is caught, she will incur reputational costs in the amount of $5,000.

What will Shonagh do?

Ignoring, for the moment, Shonagh's view that her behaviour is unlikely to be detected, the decision Shonagh faces can be depicted as follows:

$$A - B - X$$
$$\$8,000 - (\$5,000 + \$8,000 + \$200) = -\$5,200$$
$$X = -\$5,200$$

In this example, figure A (the benefit of submitting padded dockets) equals $8,000, the direct monetary gain that Shonagh receives by padding dockets. Figure B (the costs that

Shonagh will incur if she submits her padded dockets) has three components—namely: (1) the $5,000 reputational cost that Shonagh will incur if she decides to pad her dockets, (2) the $8,000 of compensation that Shonagh must pay to HugeCo, and (3) the $200 of income Shonagh forgoes by preparing the falsified docket. If A and B have been calculated correctly, Shonagh will not submit the padded dockets: subtracting B from A, we are left with a negative X (−$5,200). The costs of this unethical choice exceed its benefits. As a rational decision maker, Shonagh will not pursue an action that gives rise to a loss of utility.

Based on the facts that we have considered thus far, it seems that a compensatory model of regulation would do a wonderful job of regulating Shonagh's conduct. First, it would ensure that Shonagh's client was reimbursed for any costs that it incurred as a result of Shonagh's actions. Second, it would ensure that Shonagh internalized all of the costs of her decisions. This gives rise to efficient incentives, driving Shonagh to pad her dockets only if the act in question could give rise to an overall gain in social utility. Since the act in question does not give rise to a gain in social utility (in this example it destroyed $5,200 of social utility), the compensatory model would ensure that Shonagh refrained from padding her dockets. Unfortunately, we have ignored an important fact. Shonagh, like many unethical actors, believes that her unethical actions are unlikely to be detected.

In chapter 3 we noted that many unethical actors undertake unethical actions with the hope that their behaviour will not be noticed. They take steps designed to ensure that no one knows of their unethical behaviour. If unethical acts are undetected (or if other enforcement errors prevent the payment of compensation),[83] decision makers can avoid paying some of the costs that flow from their decisions. Revisit the facts of example 4.9. Shonagh believes that there is only a 20 percent chance that the act of padding dockets will be discovered. This has an important effect on her decision. In order to paint an accurate picture of the decision Shonagh faces, we must take account of her views regarding the probability that her unethical act will be discovered. As we saw in chapter 3, section VIII, this can be done by using expected value calculations. Specifically, we must multiply the costs and benefits in Shonagh's ethical equation by the probability that each of those costs and benefits will arise.

If we account for probability, figure A in Shonagh's ethical equation will not change. The gross utility gain of submitting an inflated docket is $8,000 (an $8,000 benefit multiplied by a probability of 1.0). However, figure B changes when we account for probability. There is (according to Shonagh) an 80 percent chance that her unethical behaviour will not be detected by the body charged with regulating lawyers. If Shonagh's behaviour is not detected, she will never be forced to compensate her victim, and her professional reputation will remain untarnished. As a result, there is an 80 percent chance that Shonagh's only cost will be the $200 she forgoes by creating false dockets—there is an 80 percent chance that Shonagh's only cost will be $200. If Shonagh *is* caught, she will have to pay

---

83   Other enforcement errors include (1) a failure to bring a suit against Shonagh, or (2) an erroneous finding of no liability (due to the plaintiff's failure to discharge the burden of proof). Where either of these enforcement errors take place, the likelihood of enforcement falls below 100 percent.

compensation to HugeCo and incur related reputational costs. There is a 20 percent chance that this will happen. For the purposes of illustrating Shonagh's ethical choice, we must multiply Shonagh's reputational costs and the costs of compensation by the likelihood that those costs will arise (0.2).

Bearing in mind Shonagh's assessment of the probability that her behaviour will be detected, Shonagh's ethical equation should be rewritten as follows:

$$A - B = X$$
$$\$8,000 - [(0.2)(\$5,000) + (0.2)(\$8,000) + \$200] = X$$
$$\$8,000 - [(\$1,000) + (\$1,600) + \$200] = X$$
$$\$8,000 - \$2,800 = X$$
$$\$5,200 = X$$

In this more accurate depiction of Shonagh's choice (a version that takes account of the probability that Shonagh's behaviour will be detected), figure A still equals $8,000 (the extra fee that Shonagh collects), but figure B now equals the sum of (1) the $200 of income Shonagh forgoes when she prepares her falsified docket plus (2) the sum of her reputational costs and compensation *multiplied* by the likelihood that Shonagh will have to pay those costs (a probability equal to 0.2). Taking these figures into account, we see that a decision to pad dockets yields a net expected benefit equal to $5,200 (a positive X). In other words, Shonagh *will* pad her dockets, given the low probability that her act will be detected.

It is important to note that Shonagh's decision to pad her dockets was inefficient. Even if she escapes detection, Shonagh's decision gives rise to an overall loss of social utility (but a gain in Shonagh's personal utility). Shonagh's gain from the action (if she is not detected) equals $7,800 (the ill-gotten money that she collects less the income she forgoes preparing the dockets). HugeCo's loss from the action equals $8,000. Taking all relevant people into account, Shonagh's act leads to an overall loss of $200.[84] In other words, Shonagh's act destroys $200 dollars of value even if Shonagh evades detection. This means that Shonagh's act of "docket padding" is inefficient.

Once we bear in mind the realistic assumption that many unethical acts go undetected, we are forced to admit that a compensatory model of regulation, despite its many advantages, has difficulty regulating lawyers' ethical decisions. Specifically, a purely compensatory model of regulation cannot work for ethical breaches with a low probability of detection. As we have seen in example 4.9, a purely compensatory model can make inefficient unethical choices profitable (for the unethical lawyer in question) where the likelihood of enforcement falls below 100 percent. Our purely compensatory model (coupled with a low probability of enforcement) led Shonagh to pursue a choice that resulted in a $200 loss of social utility. If the compensatory model had functioned correctly, Shonagh would not have padded her dockets. Unfortunately, the model did not

---

84   The loss is actually somewhat greater. Because people like Shonagh pad their dockets, regulatory officials (such as the Law Society) must expend resources attempting to detect and prevent such behaviour. Absent unethical conduct, these costs of enforcement would not arise. As a result, the costs expended on enforcement can be regarded as a cost of unethical behaviour.

function correctly: since the likelihood of enforcement fell below 100 percent, a purely compensatory model led Shonagh to make an inefficient choice.[85]

Even where an unethical action leads to a net loss in social utility, a compensatory model (coupled with a less than 100 percent chance that compensation will be required) leads lawyers to take unethical actions in pursuit of personal gain. In other words, where the likelihood of enforcement falls below 100 percent, a compensatory model fails to generate an optimal allocation of resources. In the realm of legal ethics, a purely compensatory model can fail to prevent market failure. This undermines the usefulness of the compensatory model of regulation.

As a general rule, a compensatory model is ineffective in creating efficient incentives where enforcement errors diminish the chance that adequate compensation will be collected. In other words, where there is a less than 100 percent chance that compensatory orders will be enforced, a purely compensatory model provides inadequate means of ensuring that victims of the relevant conduct will receive their compensation. If there is a low probability that decision makers will have to compensate victims, there is a significant chance that decision makers will not be required to internalize the cost of their decisions. As we saw in section I.D, above, where they can avoid the need to internalize the costs of their decisions, decision makers make inefficient choices.

The impact of enforcement errors—that is, a failure to force decision makers to bear the cost of choices that they make—on a compensatory model is easiest to see through a simple thought experiment. If the only punishment for stealing $100 is the requirement that you return $100 if you are caught, you are better off if you attempt to take the money, provided only that there is a less than 100 percent probability that you will be caught. If you are caught, you are no worse off than you were before you stole the $100 (presuming that the theft was easy, and did not require you to expend resources). If you are *not* caught, you are $100 better off. The *expected benefit* of a decision to take money is always positive in a compensatory system where the likelihood of enforcement falls below 100 percent.[86]

Because it is practically impossible to ensure that every unethical act will be detected, or that those that are detected will be successfully prosecuted, we must accept the fact that a compensatory model will have difficulty creating efficient incentives in the realm of legal ethics. Where unethical acts go undetected, a compensatory model can fail to force decision makers to make efficient ethical choices. The result is a suboptimal level

---

85   Note that failure to detect is not the only enforcement error that can undermine liability. Even if unethical behaviour is detected, it may not be subjected to sanctions. Many cost-imposing parties are found "not liable" on the ground that the victim fails to discharge the burden of proving that the cost-imposing action took place (or that the cost-imposing party was the one who imposed the cost). If these factors diminish the likelihood that compensatory damages will be paid, the probability of enforcement is diminished to a level below 100 percent.

86   Assuming that there is a 50 percent probability of enforcement in this example, the expected cost of taking $100 is (0.5)($100), or $50. The benefit to the thief equals $100. Thus, the net expected benefit of taking $100 is $50 where there is a 50 percent chance of being caught (and the only repercussion is compensation). Since there is a net benefit, it is profitable for thieves to steal money where (1) they are regulated by a purely compensatory model, and (2) there is less than a 100 percent chance of enforcement.

of ethical behaviour—something that the Law Society hopes to avoid. As a result, we must search for a method of supplementing compensatory models in cases where unethical acts are difficult to detect or where compensation is difficult to enforce. The supplementary method that is most likely to be successful (and the method that is currently used in many jurisdictions) is discussed in section VI, below.

E. Conclusion

In the opening sections of this chapter we noted that an unregulated market for legal services is likely to produce a suboptimal quantity of ethical conduct. In other words, there would be a market failure—the market for legal services would produce less of a product (legal ethics) than consumers would like to consume. This is another way of saying that, absent some form of regulatory intervention, lawyers (as a group) are likely to be less ethical than we would want them to be. In section I, we suggested that there were two possible ways of correcting the market failure that would exist in a free market for legal services: (1) a compensatory model of regulation, paralleling the legal regimes governing tort and contract law; or (2) a punishment model of regulation paralleling the criminal law.

The last several sections of this chapter demonstrated the workings (and failings) of a compensatory model of regulation. Theoretically, this model is attractive: lawyers would be made to compensate all of their victims, decision makers would make efficient decisions, and regulators would be neutral as between unethical choices (coupled with the payment of compensation) and compliance with prevailing ethical norms. More importantly, a compensatory model would eliminate the need to define amorphous words such as "ethical" and "unethical." Rather than asking whether a particular form of conduct counted as ethical, we could ask whether a lawyer's acts imposed unbargained-for costs on other people. Wherever a lawyer imposed costs on other people, the lawyer would compensate those people, thereby internalizing the cost of the lawyer's conduct. The unanswerable question of whether or not a particular act counts as ethical or unethical never arises.

The compensatory model of regulation is, in fact, the primary method of regulating lawyers' ethics. In most cases, the compensatory model of regulation is imposed on lawyers without the Law Society's intervention—the law of tort or contract has the effect of forcing lawyers to compensate the victims of the lawyer's unethical behaviour. As a result, the Law Society is compelled to intervene only in cases where the compensatory model that is provided by the law of tort and contract fails to provide lawyers with efficient incentives.

Despite the many (theoretical) advantages of a compensatory model, we have concluded (in sections V.A through D) that, for important practical reasons, a compensatory model would, in many cases, have difficulty regulating lawyers' ethical choices. As a result, we must augment our compensatory model in ways designed to overcome the problems inherent in a purely compensatory system. As we shall see, the most efficient augmentation of the compensatory model involves a regulatory regime that parallels the criminal law. This regulatory regime, and its role in supplementing the compensatory model of regulation, is discussed throughout the remainder of this chapter.

VI. The Punishment Model

A. Introduction

The last several sections of this chapter have considered the usefulness of a compensatory model of regulation. In the context of legal ethics, the goal of the compensatory model is to ensure that lawyers compensate the victims of their unethical activities. This has the effect of achieving an optimal level of ethics by ensuring that lawyers internalize the costs of their decisions.

Generally speaking, the laws of tort and contract constitute compensatory regimes that have the effect of regulating lawyers' ethical decisions. When lawyers violate the terms of their retainers, or engage in actions that have the effect of imposing costs upon the lawyers' clients, the "regulatory regimes" created by private law (namely, the law of tort and contract) often require lawyers to compensate their victims, thereby (1) forcing lawyers to internalize the costs of their behaviour, and (2) driving lawyers toward an efficient level of ethical behaviour. If the regulatory regimes created by private law were sufficient to drive lawyers toward efficient ethical choices, the Law Society would have no need to intervene—the compensatory model that is created by private law would have the effect of eliminating the market failures that could otherwise be created by externalities and informational assymetry. Unfortunately, practical issues relating to lawyers' ethical choices often prevent the compensatory model from achieving its lofty goals when it comes to regulating lawyers' ethics. Lawyers' unethical actions may give rise to harms that are not amenable to the goal of compensation, and enforcement errors (such as a failure to detect unethical conduct) may allow lawyers to evade the need to compensate their victims.

We now turn our attention to a supplementary model of regulating legal ethics: a model that can be used to help us overcome the failings of a compensatory model where that model fails to give rise to optimal outcomes. For the purposes of this book, we will refer to this model as the "punishment model" of regulation. Much like the goal of the compensatory model, the ultimate aim of the punishment model is to generate an efficient allocation of scarce resources. The punishment model pursues this goal through somewhat different means than its compensatory cousin. Rather than forcing lawyers to compensate the victims of their choices, the punishment model aims to prevent unethical choices in the first place. The ways in which this goal is pursued by the punishment model, coupled with this model's role in shaping lawyers' ethical decisions, are discussed throughout the remainder of the chapter.

B. The Goals of the Punishment Model

The principal goal of the punishment model is deterrence. While a compensatory model seeks to *regulate* cost-imposing behaviour by having decision makers internalize the costs of their decisions, the punishment model seeks to *stop* certain forms of cost-imposing behaviour. Where the compensatory model makes decision makers prefer to take a cost-imposing action only when the relevant action generates an overall gain in social utility, the punishment model is designed to ensure that decision makers generally prefer not to engage in the relevant form of cost-imposing behaviour. When decision makers consistently prefer to refrain from engaging in a regulated form of behaviour, decisions makers are said to be "deterred" from engaging in the relevant conduct.

How does a punishment model pursue the goal of deterrence? Broadly speaking, the punishment model is designed to make illicit acts so costly that it is generally not in a decision maker's interest to pursue the act in question. In the language of economics, the goal of the punishment model is to ensure that the expected cost (to the actor) of an illicit form of conduct usually exceeds the expected benefit (to the actor) of the type of behaviour in question. The following illustration demonstrates one of the ways in which this goal can be accomplished.

Example 4.10

Jerome Cutter is a lawyer in Alberta. He has acted as plaintiff's counsel in several cases against PuffCo, a multinational tobacco corporation.

Jerome is considering writing a letter to PuffCo on behalf of a client named Jim McCallum. The proposed letter would assert that McCallum has used PuffCo's products for ten years and is now suffering from throat cancer. In the letter, Jerome would assert that McCallum is willing to avoid legal action in exchange for a one-time settlement payment equal to $10,000. Based on his past experience with PuffCo, Jerome believes that PuffCo will attempt to avoid the bad publicity flowing from a trial by offering Jim a settlement of at least $5,000.

Unfortunately, Jim McCallum does not exist. Indeed, the contents of Jerome's proposed letter are the product of Jerome's vivid imagination, representing nothing more than a scheme to gain an unwarranted settlement from PuffCo. Jim believes that he will gain an undeserved $5,000 settlement from PuffCo if he undertakes his scheme. He also believes that there is only a 50 percent chance that his unethical behaviour will be detected.

Writing the letter and receiving the settlement payment will take some time and effort. The time and effort that Jerome will spend on this project represents a cost to Jerome equal to $100.

If Jerome were regulated by a purely compensatory regime (and unencumbered by feelings of guilt or fear of reputational repercussions), he would be sure to write the letter to PuffCo (thereby violating several important ethical rules).[87] We can predict this result using the ethical equation developed in chapters 2 and 3: $A - B = X$. As we have seen, figure A in this equation represents the expected benefits of a proposed course of action, B represents the expected costs, and X represents the net utility generated by the proposed course of conduct. Taking account of the figures noted above (and assuming that Jerome is governed by a compensatory model), Jerome's subconscious ethical calculation looks like this:

---

87   See, for example, Ontario's *Rules of Professional Conduct*, rule 6.01 and rule 4.01(2) (available online at http://www.lsuc.on.ca/).

$$A - B = X$$
$$\$5,000 - [\$100 + (0.5)(\$5,000)] = X$$
$$\$5,000 - \$2,600 = X$$
$$X = \$2,400$$

In this example, the expected benefit of a decision to assert the fraudulent claim equals $5,000 (the amount of PuffCo's payment). The expected costs equal the sum of (1) $100 (representing the time and effort it takes Jerome to assert the claim), and (2) a $5,000 compensatory payment multiplied by the probability (0.5) that Jerome's unethical act will be discovered. Taking these figures into account, our ethical equation yields an X equal to $2,400 (a positive figure). Since X is positive, a decision to write the letter generates a gain in utility for Jerome. Jerome will accordingly write the letter.

Note that, on the facts of this example, the compensatory model would lead Jerome to make a socially inefficient decision (a decision that leads to an overall loss in social utility). In other words, the social costs of Jim's actions would outweigh the relevant gains. If the compensatory model functioned correctly, it should have prevented Jerome from engaging in actions leading to overall losses of social utility. Because of the possibility that Jerome will evade detection, however, the compensatory model fails to achieve the desired result. The chance of non-enforcement (the 50 percent chance that Jerome will evade the need to compensate his victim)[88] lowers the expected costs of Jerome's proposed unethical choice to the point that Jerome will make a socially inefficient choice despite the presence of our regulatory model.

How would a punishment model overcome the problems inherent in a compensatory regime? Consider, once again, the goals of the punishment model. The purpose of the punishment model is to deter potential offenders from engaging in particular forms of cost-imposing behaviour. In other words, the goal of the punishment model is to ensure that the expected cost (to the actor) of an illicit course of action exceeds the benefit that the actor expects to gain. In example 4.10, this could be achieved by *supplementing* (but not replacing) the requirement of compensation with an additional punitive sanction greater than $4,800.[89] Consider, for example, what would happen if the additional punitive sanction for pursuing a fraudulent claim of damages were set at double the amount of the fraudulent claim. Under this regime (which combines compensation with punitive sanctions), Jerome's decision could be described as follows:

---

88   The diminished chance of enforcement could be caused by several factors. In this example, it is caused by the difficulty involved in observing Jerome's behaviour. In other cases, it could be caused by (1) high costs of pursuing compensatory remedies, (2) failure of an accuser to discharge a burden of proof, or (3) an erroneous finding of no liability. Where any of these enforcement errors occur, the likelihood of enforcement drops below 100 percent.

89   This is because there is a 50 percent chance that Jerome's behaviour will be detected. If Jerome faces a 50 percent chance of a $4,800 fine (in addition to the requirement of compensation), this adds an expected cost of $2,400 (0.5 × $4,800) to Jerome's subconscious ethical calculation. This cost of $2,400 offsets Jerome's expected gain. As a result, a fine of any amount greater than $4,800 (coupled with a 50 percent chance of enforcement) makes it unprofitable to Jerome to write the letter.

$$A - B = X$$
$$\$5,000 - [\$100 + (0.5)(\$5,000 + \$10,000)] = X$$
$$\$5,000 - [\$100 + \$7,500] = X$$
$$\$5,000 - \$7,600 = X$$
$$X = -\$2,600$$

Now that Jerome faces a sanction beyond the level required to compensate his victim, it is no longer in his interest to write the fraudulent settlement letter. While the gross utility benefits flowing from the unethical choice remain unchanged, the gross utility costs (represented by figure B in our equation) have changed dramatically. Now, in addition to the requirement that he return the victim's money, Jerome will (if he is caught) have to pay an additional fine equal to twice the value of the fraudulent settlement. Despite the fact that Jerome is only 50 percent likely to be detected, the expected cost of his unethical action now exceeds the benefit that he hopes to generate through his activities. As a result, it is no longer in Jerome's interest to pursue a fraudulent settlement. Recognizing that a choice to write the letter leads to a net loss in his personal utility, Jerome will refrain from writing the fraudulent letter. The punishment model, when coupled with our standard compensatory regime, will succeed in deterring Jerome from violating his ethical duties.

Example 4.10 demonstrates the basic function of the punishment model. Stated broadly, the punishment model seeks to impose punitive sanctions on offenders, thereby ensuring that the costs associated with illicit behaviour generally exceed the gains decision makers can generate by engaging in the relevant form of conduct. In the realm of legal ethics, a regime designed around the punishment model would be designed to make ethical violations "more expensive" for offenders, so that the costs (to offenders) of ethical breaches outweith any gains that the offender hoped to secure by breaching an ethical obligation. When the punishment model functions perfectly, the benefits to be gleaned from unethical conduct rarely justify acceptance of the relevant punitive cost. In other words, rational individuals will generally be deterred from engaging in unethical behaviour.

Many readers will have noted that the punishment model is, in essence, the regulatory model we apply in the context of the criminal law. Such readers may also note that, if the punishment model aims to deter *all* criminal conduct (an issue that will be dealt with momentarily), it is not entirely successful. If the punishment model successfully set penalties such that people were always deterred from taking part in criminal conduct, we would not observe crime in the real world. Unfortunately, we do. It accordingly appears that either (1) the goal of *absolute* deterrence is not, in fact, the goal of the punishment model, or (2) something prevents the punishment model from achieving the goal of absolute deterrence. As we shall see in section VI.E, the first of these two possible explanations is correct. An efficient punishment model is not designed to deter *all* illicit behaviour. The arguments supporting this counterintuitive claim are developed in later sections of this chapter.

Before developing a more detailed account of the punishment model and its use in the regulation of legal ethics, it is important to answer a fundamental question: what sorts of unethical conduct should be deterred? What should count as "unethical conduct" for the purposes of a punishment-focused regime? This topic is addressed in the following section.

C. What Acts Should Be Punished?

One of the fundamental goals of any system of regulation is to maximize social utility by minimizing costs. In other words, legal rules are designed to eliminate or reduce the damage caused by various cost-imposing actions. Where a particular action typically generates net losses of social utility, that activity should be regulated such that we can minimize or eliminate those losses. Where an action imposes *no* net costs on society, that action should not be regulated at all. In other words, the acts that should be regulated pursuant to *any* model of regulation (including the punishment model) should, at a minimum, be limited to those that give rise to net losses in social utility.

Should *all* actions that give rise to net losses in social utility be regulated through a punishment model? Certainly not. As we saw in sections II to V, many cost-imposing actions can be regulated efficiently by a compensatory regime. Torts and breaches of contract impose a wide array of costs upon their victims, but we regulate these actions through a compensatory regime rather than through a model based on punitive sanctions. It would be inefficient to govern tort and contract through the use of the punishment model. If we deterred all breaches of contract, for example (by subjecting contract-breachers to punitive sanctions), efficient breaches of contract would be prevented. Breaches of contract that would make everyone happy (including the so-called victim of the breach) would be precluded through the use of punitive sanctions.[90] Similarly, if we prohibited tortious conduct and subjected all tortfeasors to punitive sanctions, we would prevent efficient torts.[91] If we simply *prohibited* every cost-imposing action, and sub-jected all cost-imposing people to punitive sanctions, we would effectively prohibit many actions that would have otherwise had the effect of generating overall gains in social utility. If the goal of regulation is to maximize social utility, overuse of the punishment model would prevent the realization of this goal.

In most situations, the compensatory model of regulation is the ideal method of regulating cost-imposing behaviour. Where a decision maker's choices generate negative externalities, the decision maker should be required to internalize those externalities through the payment of compensation. Where this takes place, decision makers will make choices that are socially efficient—that is, choices with the effect of maximizing social utility. In short, the compensatory model provides decision makers with efficient incentives, driving them toward socially optimal choices. In most cases, the compensatory model provides the perfect system of regulating behaviour, preventing those actions that erode social utility and encouraging those behaviours that give rise to utility gains.

If the compensatory model is the optimal design for a regulatory regime, we should abandon, supplement, or alter that model only where it fails to achieve its objectives. We should depart from the compensatory model only in cases where that model fails to (1) generate perfect compensation, (2) eliminate negative externalities, or (3) create efficient incentives for decision makers. Where the compensatory model fails to achieve

---

90   For examples of efficient breach, coupled with discussions of why such breaches should be permitted, see example 1.1 (in chapter 1) and example 4.4 (in chapter 4), above.

91   For an example of an efficient tort, and a discussion of why such torts should be permitted, see section II.C.

these three goals, we may need an alternative (or supplementary) model (such as a punishment-based model) to promote efficient behaviour.

As we saw in section V, economists have identified those situations in which the compensatory model typically fails—namely: (1) when the regulated action causes harms for which compensation is impossible in principal or in practice, or (2) when decision makers have the ability to avoid detection or liability, diminishing the expected costs created by the compensatory model. Because we have already identified those forms of behaviour that cannot be regulated through the use of compensatory regimes, we have gone a long way toward defining the kinds of behaviour that should be governed through the use of a punishment model. Stated simply, we should prohibit and punish only those activities that (1) impose costs on other people, and (2) cannot be regulated effectively by a compensatory regime. More specifically, we should punish decision makers whose decisions impose costs on other people and meet either or both of the following two conditions:

1. The decision maker's action gives rise to harm for which compensation is impossible in principal or in practice.

2. The decision maker's action is one that is likely to give rise to enforcement errors—that is, the actor has the ability to evade detection or otherwise avoid the need to compensate victims.[92]

Where a decision maker's actions meet the foregoing criteria, the compensatory model often fails to give rise to efficient decisions. If we govern such activities through a compensatory model, or fail to govern such activities altogether, uninternalized externalities may give rise to market failures. In order to prevent the market failures that may flow from such activities, we attempt to deter decision makers from pursuing such activities in the first place. Only where deterrence is needed (because the goal of compensation is elusive) should an act be governed by a punishment model of regulation.

As we saw in section V, many of the unethical actions lawyers take meet the criteria for acts that should be punished. In many cases, a lawyer's unethical actions impose harms for which compensation may be impractical or impossible. For example, where lawyers (1) violate confidentiality, (2) act in cases involving undisclosed conflicts of interest, or (3) assist their clients in pursuing illegal goals, they give rise to a host of harms that are not amenable to the goal of compensation. More importantly, several of the acts prohibited by the rules of professional conduct are difficult to detect and prosecute, giving rise to a low probability that the lawyer will be made to compensate those who suffer as a result of his or her unethical choices. Indeed, part II of this book focuses on a lawyer's specific ethical obligations, and demonstrates that breaches of those duties often qualify as actions calling for punishment and deterrence. Many of the acts that violate the

---

92   In the context of criminal law, a third reason for employing the punishment model relates to the inability of decision makers to afford compensatory payments. Where a defendant is judgment proof—that is, he or she cannot be ordered to pay compensation as a result of a lack of funds—punitive sanctions (such as imprisonment) may be the only alternative. Due to the presence of a mandatory insurance regime in the context of legal practice, the problem of judgment-proof defendants is not considered in this chapter.

lawyer's core ethical duties—namely, violations of duties relating to confidentiality, conflicts of interest, and advocacy—satisfy the conditions required for acts that should be deterred and punished. In cases such as these, our compensatory regime must be augmented by supracompensatory sanctions (such as punitive fines) if we are to generate optimal outcomes. As we shall see, the Law Society does, in fact, supplement the basic compensatory model with punitive sanctions when it regulates violations of lawyers' ethical duties.[93] It therefore appears that the regulators have done an excellent job in selecting the forms of lawyer behaviour that ought to be regulated and punished through the use of punitive sanctions.

Among all of the lawyer's specific ethical duties, there is one (imposed by Ontario's *Rules of Professional Conduct*) that does not seem to fit the category of behaviour that should be punished and deterred. The relevant rule is found in paragraph (c) of Ontario's rule 3.04(1), which provides as follows:

> Subject to subrule (3), a lawyer or a law firm may advertise their services or fees in any medium including the use of brochures and similar documents provided that the advertising:
>
>   (a) is not false or misleading; ... [and]
>
>   (c) does not compare services or charges with other lawyers or law firms.

Paragraph (a) is sensible: false or misleading advertising would certainly impose costs on other people. People would make decisions based on inaccurate information, frequently taking actions that they might have avoided if they had access to better information. As a result, a breach of paragraph (a) would give rise to utility losses for the victims of the relevant lawyer's behaviour. Paragraph (c), however, which prohibits price comparison, is difficult to defend. Since "false or misleading" advertising is already prohibited by rule 3.04(1)(a), paragraph (c) deals only with information that (1) is true, (2) is not misleading, and (3) compares the price for the lawyer's services with the prices that are charged by other lawyers.

It is difficult to see how advertising in contravention of rule 3.04(1)(c) qualifies as a behaviour that gives rise to net losses of social utility—in other words, it is difficult to see how such advertising qualifies as a form of cost-imposing behaviour. From a common-sense perspective, it seems that the public would be better off with *more* information about the relative costs of lawyers' professional services. Provided that the information is not misleading (which it cannot be, given the presence of rule 3.04(1)(a)), such information helps individuals make informed decisions when they seek a lawyer's professional assistance. Simply put, advertisements comparing prices would result in utility *gains* for many consumers. Rule 3.04(1)(c) therefore fails to satisfy the first condition of the punishment model: the model should be used only to regulate those behaviours that impose utility losses on society. Rule 3.04(1)(c), by contrast, prohibits conduct that gives rise to overall gains in social utility.

---

93   In reality, the Law Society is almost exclusively concerned with the supplementary role of punitive sanctions. In most cases, the Law Society relies on the law of torts to provide lawyers' victims with compensation, and goes on to punish lawyers only where the remedy of compensatory damages fails to provide the lawyer with efficient incentives. This is an efficient manner of proceeding. Only where other legal methods fail to generate compensation should the Law Society concern itself with compensatory goals.

From an economic perspective, the true purpose of rule 3.04(1)(c) is easy to understand. As we noted at the outset of this chapter, the Law Society is composed of lawyers, and like any individual or regulatory body, the Law Society acts in its own best interests. If lawyers began openly comparing their prices with the prices of other lawyers, individuals searching for lawyers would be able to seek out lawyers who provide comparable service for lower prices. All things being equal, people would like to pay as little as possible for any good or service. If people have ready access to the information required to engage in comparative pricing, they will naturally choose the lawyer who charges the lowest fee for comparable service. This would lead to price competition among lawyers, forcing lawyers to lower their fees in order to undercut their competitors. As any competent competition lawyer will tell you, competition of this nature is good for the public. The only utility losses flowing from advertising that violates rule 3.04(1)(c) are the utility losses suffered by lawyers who must charge less for their services. In other words, rule 3.04(1)(c) is anomalous. It is designed to protect lawyers' interests to the detriment of the public. The rule lowers social utility by diminishing the level of accurate, non-misleading information available to consumers who are in search of legal services. An economic analysis makes it clear that, since the behaviour targeted by rule 3.04(1)(c) does not lead to net losses of social utility, that behaviour should not be prohibited at all.[94]

Despite the existence of anomalies such as Ontario's rule 3.04(1)(c), the regulations established in professional codes of conduct are typically well-crafted. Generally speaking, the behaviours subjected to punitive sanctions by the rules of professional conduct do, in fact, satisfy the criteria of behaviours that should be punished: (1) they generate externalities; (2) those externalities involve costs that are not amenable to the goal of compensation; and (3) the people who engage in such behaviours are often able to avoid detection, regulation, and the payment of compensation. The specific behaviours targeted by the Law Society's rules and regulations are discussed at length in part II of this book.

Having defined the kinds of behaviour we want to deter, the next logical question is this: *how* do we deter unethical actions? The general model of deterrence, based on choices made by rational individuals, is discussed in the following section of this chapter.

D. The Rational Lawyer Revisited

The previous section described the nature of the activities that a punishment-focused system of regulation should deter. Before considering the specific methods of deterring those activities, it is important to consider the nature of the individuals whose behaviour we are modifying through the punishment model. If we can understand the conditions under which a rational person will commit an unethical action, we can determine how to change those conditions such that a rational person will no longer undertake the unethical act. By understanding the rational person's reasons for committing unethical acts, we can

---

94   I would like to thank Norman Siebrasse of the University of New Brunswick for drawing this anomaly to my attention. I would also like to thank Heather Ross of the Law Society of Upper Canada for her helpful comments on this particular rule of professional conduct. Ms Ross pointed out that many benchers of the Law Society vigorously oppose rule 3.04(1)(c).

determine the optimal method to deter a rational person from engaging in the relevant form of conduct.

The economic model of rational decision making was described in chapter 3. Specifically, section IX.B of chapter 3 demonstrated the conditions in which a rational, amoral person will decide to make an unethical choice. Review that section now, focusing on the following questions:

1. In what circumstances will an amoral lawyer undertake an unethical action?

2. How does the lawyer's morality affect the decision-making model described in section IX.B of chapter 3?

3. How can the Law Society develop a combination of punitive and compensatory sanctions that will have the effect of deterring rational actors from engaging in unethical courses of action?

The answers to questions 1 and 2 are discussed at length in chapter 3, section IX.B. The answer to question 3 is discussed below in section VI.F. Before answering that question, it is important to redefine the economic goals of the punishment model and reconsider the nature of the harms that flow from lawyers' unethical choices. These issues are addressed in the following section.

E. An Optimal Amount of Unethical Conduct

Section VI.B claimed that the ultimate goal of the punishment model is deterrence. That is not entirely true. While deterrence can be regarded as the *primary* goal of the punishment model, it is important to remember the fundamental reason for pursuing this goal in the first place. Our reason for deterring unethical conduct through the use of a punishment model, like our reason for requiring cost internalization under compensatory regimes, is to maximize social utility. As we saw in section I.B, above, the fundamental goal of regulation is to eliminate the causes of market failure. Where (and only where) the market fails to generate an efficient allocation of scarce resources—that is, an allocation of resources with the effect of maximizing social utility—regulators should step in to correct the failure of the market. The principal goal of regulation is to maximize utility. As a result, we should pursue the goal of deterrence only where pursuit of this goal will have the effect of maximizing social utility. In situations where deterrence has the effect of *reducing* social utility, we should not pursue the objective of deterrence.

Throughout the previous sections of this chapter, we have assumed that deterrence preserves social utility. How, then, can deterrence have the effect of *diminishing* social utility? The answer is revealed through the following illustration.

Example 4.11

Imagine that we live in an odd society in which there is only one unethical act per year. We do not know who will commit that act (we have a different unethical actor every year), but we know that he or she will be a lawyer. Once a year, a mystery lawyer violates one of the rules of professional conduct, imposing an average cost of $100,000 per year through a single breach of the rules.

The Law Society is interested in putting an end to these annual ethical breaches. As a result, it considers hiring prosecutors, investigators, and a disciplinary committee in order to detect, prosecute, and punish unethical lawyers. The Law Society's hope is that the presence of a disciplinary regime will put an end to (or deter) each of the annual ethical breaches.

Prosecutors, investigators, and disciplinary committees do not do their work for free (and even if they did, the time they spent doing their disciplinary work would impose significant costs by taking them away from other endeavours). In order to ensure that our disciplinary regime is effective in deterring the annual ethical breaches, we must spend $250,000 of public funds. Assume that there is no way to deter the ethical breaches without spending at least $250,000.

On the facts of this example, should the Law Society deter the annual ethical breaches, or should it allow the ethical breaches to continue?

In example 4.11, society is (on the whole) better off if we refrain from deterring the annual ethical breaches. If we let unethical lawyers go unpunished, society will lose an average of $100,000 per year through unethical lawyers' actions. By contrast, if we deter all ethical breaches by creating an effective disciplinary regime, society will save the $100,000 cost imposed by ethical violations. These savings come, however, at a cost of $250,000. On the facts of our example, society is (on the whole) $150,000 better off by leaving ethical breaches undeterred. In this example, the optimal number of ethical breaches is 1 breach per year, rather than 0, given the money that it costs to deter unethical conduct.

It should be obvious that example 4.11 is unrealistic. In the real world, there are *many* ethical breaches every year, and the annual social cost of ethical breaches is far greater than $100,000. More importantly, we are unable to predict (with any confidence or precision) the annual costs that will be imposed by ethical breaches. Despite its air of unreality, however, example 4.11 reveals an important fact about deterrence. Deterrence is costly. This is as true in the real world as it is in the odd society that was depicted in example 4.11. Deterrence can sometimes be so costly that it is *more expensive*—that is, imposes more social costs—than the behaviour that we initially hoped to deter. "Buying" deterrence in these circumstances is irrational. It makes no sense to spend $20 of your money just to deter a thief from stealing a single dime. By failing to deter (and letting the thief run off with your dime), you would be $19.90 better off.[95]

Deterrence is so expensive in the real world that we allow *many* unethical actions to go undeterred each year on the grounds that it would cost too much to deter those ethical

---

95 To further develop this example, assume that you have an asset worth $5. It is vulnerable to theft. The only way to lessen the likelihood of theft is to hire a guard at a cost of $20 per hour, or to buy a $10 lock. Both costs of precaution are unjustifiable. In this example, the unjustifiable costs of precaution parallel the unjustifiable costs of deterrence in the punishment model.

breaches.[96] As a result, we deter only those ethical breaches that we are willing to deter. We purchase the level of deterrence for which the public is willing to pay. As we try to *increase* our level of deterrence, the project of deterrence becomes increasingly costly. As we shall see, the more unethical acts we hope to deter in the real world, the more it costs to deter each additional ethical violation.

Why is deterrence so expensive? As we saw in example 4.11, deterrence is achieved by raising the costs borne by people who participate in acts we hope to deter. More specifically, deterrence is achieved by raising the *expected costs* that decision makers face if they engage in the actions that we hope to deter. There are only two ways of manipulating expected costs. We can either (1) change the likelihood that unethical actions will be detected and punished, or (2) alter the nominal value of the punishment we impose—for example, by raising the dollar value of a fine.[97]

Increasing the likelihood of punishment can be costly. To detect and punish additional offenders, we must pay more investigators, fund more prosecutions, or hire more prosecuting attorneys—three expensive methods of achieving higher levels of deterrence. Increasing the nominal value of a punishment can also be costly: if we raise the nominal value of a fine, for example, some offenders will no longer have the ability to pay the fine in question. Where offenders cannot bear the cost of our fine, we must resort to more expensive forms of punishment (such as suspension or disbarment). Suspension and disbarment impose significant social costs. The lawyer's staff will lose their employment, the lawyer's clients lose their lawyer, the lawyer's family loses a source of economic support, hearings in which the lawyer was involved will be delayed, and (during the period of suspension or disbarment) there will be fewer lawyers available to serve clients (in other words, it will be harder to find a lawyer). By increasing the nominal value of a fine to the point where offenders cannot pay, we have imposed costs on society through the use of socially (rather than privately) costly sanctions.[98] As a result, increasing the nominal value of a punishment, much like increasing the likelihood of punishment, increases the costs society bears in order to purchase more deterrence. In short, buying more deterrence is always costly.[99]

---

96   This should come as no surprise. If we spent all public money on murder prevention, for example, we might be able to deter all murders. We do not spend our money in this manner, and we leave several murders undeterred. This is not because we like to have the occasional murder, but because deterrence is costly and there are other things that we would like to do with public money.

97   This notion is explored in greater detail in section VI.F.

98   This is even more obvious where the alternative to a fine is imprisonment. A fine costs the offender money, while incarceration costs society money (in the form of money spent to feed and house the prisoner during the period of imprisonment).

99   An additional cost of increasing the severity of punishment involves the possibility of wrongful convictions. No matter how efficient our punishment model is, the risk of wrongful conviction exists. The possibility of being wrongfully convicted is a cost of practising law. This cost rises as the nominal value of punishment increases. Where nominal punishment is too high, the risk of wrongful conviction multiplied by the cost of punishment may rise so high that it makes the practice of law unattractive. If a prospective lawyer knows that there is a significant possibility of wrongful disbarment (for example) despite not having done anything wrong, he or she will likely choose another profession. The only way

Having considered the *costs* of deterrence we can redefine the goal of the punishment model. If the ultimate goal of regulation is to maximize social utility, the goal of the punishment model cannot be to deter *all* offences regardless of the cost of deterrence. On the contrary, the goal of the punishment model must be *efficient deterrence*—that is, deterrence that has the effect of maximizing social utility. As David Friedman notes:

> The correct rule ... is to prevent an offense if and only if the net cost from the offense occurring is greater than the cost of preventing it. The reason we do not increase the punishment for murder may be, and probably is, that although we would like to prevent more murders than we do prevent (indeed, we might like to prevent all murders), the cost of doing so is more than we are willing to pay.[100]

Where deterring a breach of ethics generates higher social costs than the breach itself, we are better off by letting the offender breach the relevant ethical norm. Doing otherwise would diminish social utility, much like spending $20 to save a dime. In short, too much deterrence is an inefficient use of scarce resources.[101]

The tools of economics allow us to graphically demonstrate the interaction of the costs of deterrence and the costs of unethical actions. In figure 4.1, the horizontal axis measures the level of deterrence that society achieves, expressed as a percentage of total deterrence (from a low of 0 percent at the left-hand side of the figure, where no unethical actions are deterred, to a high of 100 percent, representing total deterrence, at the right). The vertical axis measures social utility using dollars as a convenient unit of measurement. Line D depicts the marginal cost of various levels of deterrence. As we move along line D from left to right, we deter a larger percentage of unethical activities through the expenditure of additional public funds.[102]

Line B depicts the marginal benefit gained by generating various levels of deterrence. It is important to note that line B does not measure the *total* social benefit achieved at

---

to avoid wrongful punishments is to increase the costs of enforcement: to have more investigators working to ensure that only guilty parties are, in fact, convicted.

100 Friedman, supra note 50, at 226.

101 The notion of "too much deterrence" can be explained by a thought experiment. Imagine a world in which we could deter all crime, but at a cost of all public money. While we would have a world free of crime, we would have no money left for education, hospitals, or other worthy projects. As a result, we would be better off leaving some crime undeterred and pursuing other goals that were more important than total deterrence. In the realm of legal ethics, the Law Society could spend all of its resources on prosecuting unethical lawyers. This would, however, leave no more resources for public education, lawyer referral services, or other valuable functions that the Law Society supplies.

102 Note that line D slopes up and to the right. This is because the first dollars spent on deterrence have a greater impact on deterrence than dollars we spend later. Placing one police officer on a street (at a cost of $50,000, for example) may diminish crime in the neighbourhood by 30 percent. Each additional officer may diminish the level of crime by successively lower amounts (the second officer may lower the crime rate by an additional 20 percent, for example, still at a cost of $50,000). As Cooter and Ulen, supra note 20, at 471-72, note, "[O]fficials undertake easy deterrence before resorting to harder deterrence. Consequently, achieving additional reductions in crime becomes increasingly costly. For example, reducing crime by an additional 1 percent is easier when crime has already been reduced by 5 percent than when crime has already been reduced by 95 percent."

Figure 4.1

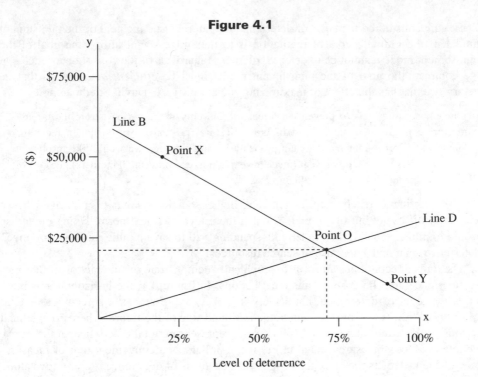

various levels of deterrence. Instead, it measures the marginal benefit generated by making incremental changes in the level of deterrence we achieve. For example, point X on line B demonstrates that, by moving from a level *just below* 20 percent deterrence to the level of *exactly* 20 percent deterrence, society generates a benefit equal to $50,000. Point Y, by contrast, demonstrates that society gains an additional $10,000 of utility by moving from a level of deterrence just below 90 percent to a level of exactly 90 percent. Since the benefit of a small reduction in unethical conduct tends to diminish as we deter more and more unethical actions, Line B slopes downward. This represents the intuitive notion that changing the level of deterrence from 0 to 10 percent, for example, generates more social benefit than changing the level of deterrence from 80 to 90 percent.

We will achieve the socially optimal level of deterrence (and, therefore, the socially optimal amount of unethical activity) when the cost of eliminating (or deterring) one additional unethical action is exactly offset by the benefit that is achieved by eliminating that particular action. This point is found at point O in figure 4.1. If we eliminate any *more* unethical conduct (such that we move to the right of point O), the cost of eliminating those unethical actions will be greater than the benefit we receive by eliminating the relevant breaches. Each unethical act that we deter beyond point O costs us more (through expenditures on deterrence) to deter than it would cost to simply allow the act to occur.

This would result in a net loss of social utility. We may be spending $20 to save a dime. As a result, we should deter no additional ethical infractions once we have reached the level depicted at point O in figure 4.1.

Note that point O appears at a level of deterrence that is below 100%. In other words, we are leaving some ethical breaches undeterred. This is the same as saying that the optimal amount of unethical conduct in society is a quantity greater than zero. We maximize social utility by leaving some unethical actions undeterred. This demonstrates the conclusion that, as long as deterrence is costly, we will not (and should not) deter all unethical actions. Instead, we will allow some unethical conduct to continue (by failing to spend sufficient resources to detect and punish the relevant ethical breaches). This allows us to use our resources in a more efficient manner, perhaps through expenditures on other valuable programs that the Law Society offers.

The conclusion that the optimal level of unethical conduct is greater than zero leaves some people perplexed. Would it not be preferable to have a world that was free of unethical conduct? Of course it would, but this is the wrong question. The question is not "would it be better to have no unethical conduct at all?" but "would it be better to *eliminate* all unethical conduct?" The regulation of legal ethics is premised on the existence of unethical behaviour. If there were no unethical behaviour in the real world there would be no need for punishment in the first place. The presence of unethical conduct gives rise to market failure, and market failure calls for efficient regulatory intervention. We would be happier if there were no market failure—that is, no unethical conduct. Unfortunately, unregulated markets fail to yield a world that is free of ethical breaches. Given that unethical conduct does exist, we are compelled to spend our money to deter it. If we take the costs of enforcement seriously, we are driven to conclude that we cannot efficiently put an end to all unethical conduct. Instead, we should spend our scarce resources to purchase deterrence only where our expenditures generate gains in social utility. To do otherwise diminishes public utility at a faster rate than the ethical breaches that we hope to deter. As long as deterrence continues to be expensive, the optimal level of unethical behaviour is going to be higher than zero.

Once we have managed to (1) identify those behaviours that our system of regulation should deter, (2) observed the impact of penal sanctions on a rational person's choices, and (3) considered the costs of deterrence and their relationship to the goals of the punishment model, we are armed with all the information we need in order to make specific claims about the appropriate penalties for the acts we hope to deter. The general theory of optimal punishments, together with the mathematics underlying that theory, is discussed in the following section of this chapter.

F. Setting Penalties

What is the best way to penalize an act we hope to deter? How can we ensure that the penalties we select help us achieve the goal of deterrence? Is it possible to ensure that our punishments are sufficiently high to deter unethical actions, yet not so high that they also generate inefficient deterrence—that is, deterrence that is more costly than the acts that it deters? In order to answer each of these questions, we must develop a theory of optimal punishment.

The theory of optimal punishment has long been debated by scholars, philosophers, religious leaders, and parents of naughty children. Throughout most of history, the prevailing view regarding punishment has been accurately summed up by a simple axiom: "Let the punishment fit the crime." John Stuart Mill expressed this view as follows:

> [T]he test of justice in penal infliction is that the punishment should be proportioned to the offense, meaning that it should be exactly measured by the moral guilt of the culprit.[103]

In other words, the size of the proper penalty must depend on the magnitude of the culprit's moral guilt. The difficulty with Mill's formulation, of course, is that moral guilt is difficult to measure. As we have seen throughout this book, morality is an indeterminate notion, incapable of guiding us (with any degree of confidence or precision) toward the accurate measurement of the gravity of offences, let alone the nature or magnitude of punishments that are proportionate to those offences. A rational model of regulation calls for a more precise method of evaluating the gravity of offences and determining the appropriate size of the punishments that attach to those offences. Happily, economic theory provides some useful assistance. The tools of economics allow us to carefully measure the relative gravity of offences and design and implement sanctions that are capable of deterring those offences. In other words, economic theory can help us design optimal punishments.

In the previous section of this chapter (and in section IX.B of chapter 3), we saw that rational individuals commit unethical actions where (and only where) the expected benefits of the unethical act outweigh the act's expected costs. Where the expected cost of violating a particular ethical norm exceeds the expected benefit of violating that norm, a rational actor will refrain from violating the norm in question. In such cases, the application of our ethical equation (developed in chapters 2 and 3) yields a negative X: a net loss of utility for the decision maker in question. Since rational decision makers will not pursue an activity that causes them to suffer a net loss of utility, a rational actor will not undertake an unethical action where the expected cost of the relevant act exceeds the expected benefits. As a result, if we want to deter an individual from engaging in a particular activity, we must raise the expected cost of that activity to the point where it exceeds whatever benefits might be experienced by a person who engages in the relevant form of behaviour.

The foregoing discussion leads to a simple guideline for the setting of appropriate penal sanctions:

> *The penalty attached to any act we wish to deter should ensure that the expected cost of engaging in the activity exceeds the expected benefit of engaging in the activity.*

Where a penalty meets this condition—that is, where the penalty ensures that the expected costs (to the offender) of the prohibited act outweigh the expected benefits (to the offender) of engaging in the action—our penalty will deter decision makers from undertaking the relevant act.

Viewed from an economic perspective, penalties are prices. When we establish penal sanctions for a particular activity, we are establishing a price for that activity. As we have seen, our goal in establishing this price is to alter the expected cost of engaging in a

---

103   John Stuart Mill, *Utilitarianism* (Peterborough, ON: Broadview Press, 2000), 372.

particular activity. When we impose a fine for littering, for example, we increase the price (or expected cost) of littering. By contrast, where we decrease the fine associated with speeding, we lower the price (or expected cost) of speeding. Whenever we calibrate the penalties associated with a particular course of action, we are modifying the expected costs of the relevant activity. Our goal in setting penalties, as we noted above, is to modify the expected costs associated with particular forms of conduct such that people will be efficiently deterred from engaging in the relevant forms of behaviour.

As we saw in section VIII.B of chapter 3, the notion of expected cost relates to two variables—namely: (1) the nominal value of any cost associated with a particular activity, and (2) the likelihood that the cost will be imposed. The expected cost of a punishment can be called the "expected punishment." As Cooter and Ulen note, "When the probability of punishment is multiplied by its severity, the result is the expected punishment."[104] The expected punishment flowing from a $50 fine that is imposed 25 percent of the time, for example, is $12.50 (a $50 nominal fine multiplied by a 0.25 probability of enforcement). In order to modify the expected punishment flowing from this fine, we can alter either of our two variables: we can increase (or decrease) the current nominal value of the fine ($50), or we can increase (or decrease) the current probability of enforcement (0.25). If we want to increase the expected punishment associated with any particular act, we can either make the punishment associated with that activity more *certain*—that is, we can increase the likelihood that the punishment will be imposed—or more *severe*—that is, we can increase the nominal value of the punishment in question, perhaps by raising the value of a fixed-dollar fine. The mathematics involved in setting expected punishments can be revealed through the use of an example. Consider the following illustration.

Example 4.12

Brewster is a lawyer in Ontario. He is considering violating the Law Society's false-advertising rule. The expected benefit (to Brewster) of violating the rule equals $49,999.99. Brewster will be deterred if (and only if) the expected cost of violating the rule is at least $50,000.

Assume, for the purpose of this example, that Brewster is rational and completely amoral (in other words, Brewster will suffer no guilt or other moral costs). Further assume that Brewster already has a bad reputation and will suffer no reputational costs as a result of a decision to breach the rule. In other words, the only expected costs that Brewster will suffer if he violates the rule flow from whatever penalty the Law Society imposes.

As noted in this example, an expected punishment (EP) equal to $50,000 will be sufficient to deter Brewster from violating the Law Society's rule against false advertising. This level of expected punishment could be achieved by imposing a $50,000 fine every single time that a lawyer violated the rule against false advertising. A $50,000 nominal fine (NF) levied 100 percent of the time (a probability, or p, equal to 1.0) yields an expected punishment of $50,000. The expected punishment is calculated as follows:

---

104   Cooter and Ulen, supra note 20, at 474.

$$EP = NF \times p$$
$$EP = \$50,000 \times 1.0$$
$$EP = \$50,000$$

The same EP can be generated by setting different values for both NF and p. For example, we can achieve an expected punishment of $50,000 by increasing the fine to $100,000 and enforcing it only 50 percent of the time:

$$EP = NF \times p$$
$$EP = \$100,000 \times 0.5$$
$$EP = \$50,000$$

Because the expected cost is still equal to $50,000, the imposition of a $100,000 fine 50 percent of the time will be enough to deter Brewster from violating the rules regarding false advertising. However we modify the severity of our fine or the certainty of enforcement, the same level of deterrence will be achieved provided that the product of certainty and severity—that is, the product of p and NF—is equal to $50,000. An expected punishment of $50,000, however that figure is generated, is just enough to deter Brewster from breaching the advertising rules.

Table 4.1 demonstrates several combinations of fines and punishments that generate the minimum expected punishment (namely, $50,000) that is required to deter Brewster from violating the Law Society's rules regarding false advertising. Although the fines levied range from $50,000 to $250,000, and the probabilities of enforcement range from a high of 1.0 (a 100 percent chance of enforcement) to a low of 0.2 (a 20 percent chance of enforcement), each expected punishment in table 4.1 equals $50,000. Each combination of nominal fines and probabilities of enforcement proposed in table 4.1 yields exactly the same level of deterrence. Any combination would be effective in deterring Brewster on the facts of example 4.12. More generally, every combination in table 4.1 would be effective in deterring *any offence* that generated an expected benefit (to the offender) lower than $50,000.

If the combinations of severity and certainty (or nominal fines and probability) set out in table 4.1 each provide the same level of deterrence, which combination is most efficient? This is another way of asking which of the five combinations listed in table 4.1 is the optimal punishment for an offence that is deterred through the imposition of an expected punishment of $50,000. If, as we demonstrated in section VI.E, the economic goal of the punishment model is efficient deterrence, the optimal punishment is likely to be the last option in table 4.1—namely, a fine of $250,000 applied with a probability of 0.2.

Why is the most efficient punishment the sanction that combines the highest fine with the lowest probability of enforcement? The answer relates to the ultimate goal of the punishment model—namely, the maximization of social utility. If, as we have suggested, each of the combinations listed in table 4.1 generates the same level of deterrence, we should select whichever combination costs society the least amount of money. If we could deter 50 percent of all unethical activities by paying either $1 million or $5 million, we should take the cheaper option and use the remaining $4 million for other purposes. This leads to a second observation concerning optimal punishments:

Where two or more punishments yield the same expected cost (and therefore generate the same level of deterrence), the optimal punishment is the least expensive.

Table 4.1   Expected Punishments

Nominal fine (NF)	Probability of enforcement (p)	Expected punishment (NF × p)
$ 50,000	1.0	$50,000
$ 62,500	0.8	$50,000
$100,000	0.5	$50,000
$200,000	0.25	$50,000
$250,000	0.2	$50,000

When choosing between two equally effective forms of punishment, we should choose the least expensive of our options.

In table 4.1, the least expensive combination is likely to be the $250,000 fine administered with a probability of 0.2. This is because we need only enforce this fine 20 percent of the time in order to achieve the desired level of deterrence. As we saw in section VI.E, above, enforcement is expensive. A higher probability of enforcement requires a larger expenditure of resources. We must have more prosecutions, hire a larger number of prosecutors, expend more scarce judicial resources, and spend more money on the detection of unethical activities (through the hiring of additional Law Society watchdogs, for example). Increasing the probability of detecting and punishing lawyers' unethical conduct can dramatically raise the costs of enforcement. As a result, a low probability of enforcement is dramatically less expensive than a high chance of enforcement. Increasing the size of the fine (rather than its probability of enforcement) is usually less expensive than raising the chance of enforcement. A high fine is (in most cases) no more expensive to collect than a low fine.[105] As Cooter and Ulen point out, "fines are so cheap to administer that they yield a profit to the state, at least so long as the fine is not too large relative to the offender's income."[106] Given that certainty of punishment (through increased enforcement efforts) is expensive, and severity of punishment (through increases in the size of a fine) is relatively inexpensive, "large fines with low probability are typically more efficient than low fines with high probability."[107]

Our preference for more severe punishments (with a low probability of enforcement) changes dramatically when we move away from low-cost punishments (such as fines) to high-cost punishments (such as suspension from practice or disbarment). As we saw in the previous section, suspension and disbarment impose a variety of costs on society. In

---

105 Note that the situation changes if the fine becomes so high that the offender cannot pay. In these situations, we must turn to more expensive punishments such as suspensions or disbarment. As we see below, in such cases it may be more efficient to raise the probability of enforcement and lower the fine.

106 Cooter and Ulen, supra note 20, at 474.

107 Ibid.

many cases, periods of suspension or disbarment may be more expensive than added enforcement efforts. It may cost $20,000 per month to hire more prosecutors and thereby raise the likelihood of enforcement (for example), but suspension may cost far more per month in wasted judicial resources, social assistance (for the lawyer's jobless staff members), and lost productivity.[108] If this is the case, efficient deterrence may require a higher probability of enforcement coupled with shorter periods of suspension. In these circumstances, the penalty of 1 month of suspension coupled with a probability of 1.0 may be a more efficient penalty than 10 months of suspension applied with a probability of 0.1, despite the fact that both yield the same expected punishment—namely, an expected suspension of 1 month.

The foregoing account of inexpensive punishments (such as fines) and expensive punishments (such as suspension) leads to the conclusion that, all things being equal, it is more efficient to punish unethical lawyers through the use of fines before resorting to the costly punishment of suspension or disbarment.[109] The "optimal punishment" for an unethical action should, in most cases, include the maximum fine that the unethical lawyer can bear. Only when the capacity of the lawyer to pay fines has been exhausted should we move on to incapacitate the lawyer through the expensive enforcement mechanism of suspension or disbarment. To do otherwise would simply be too costly.[110]

The foregoing account of optimal punishment asserted that, "all things being equal," fines are preferred over suspension or disbarment. Unfortunately, all things are rarely equal. In many instances, the Law Society may prefer disbarment to a fine—for example, in the case where the offender is declared ungovernable[111] and future ethical breaches are inevitable. In such cases, the Law Society may prefer to suspend or disbar the offender for a number of reasons. The Law Society has an interest in excluding unethical persons from the practice of law (through the power of disbarment), because this bolsters the public's perception that unethical people are not allowed to be lawyers. Moreover, the Law Society may predict that a particular offender is so likely to reoffend that the penalty

---

108 For a more thorough account of the costs of disbarment, see section VI.E.

109 This simply paraphrases Cooter and Ulen, supra note 20, at 475, who state that "efficiency requires exhausting the ability to punish criminals cheaply with fines before resorting to the costly punishment of imprisonment."

110 One element of punishment that we have ignored is stigma. In reality, stigma is one of the most important (and efficient) elements of a punitive system. Stigma is rather inexpensive, and imposes real costs on offenders. Stigma is useful in that, unlike fines (which have less of an impact on wealthy offenders), stigma has a disproportionately heavy impact on the wealthy. A high-earning lawyer is likely to suffer more from the stigma of a disciplinary proceeding than a lawyer who is struggling—that is, the impact on the wealth of the wealthy lawyer will be greater. More importantly, provided that the Law Society's disciplinary proceedings are made public, the imposition of penalties generates public information concerning the lawyer's ethical standards. This information can be used to overcome the problems caused by informational asymmetry, discussed in section I.C. The impact of stigma (in the form of reputational costs) has already been observed in several examples in chapter 3. For a more thorough account of the economic effect of stigma, see Friedman, supra note 50, at 231-32.

111 See the decision in *Law Society of Upper Canada v. Clark*, [1995] LSDD no. 199, for an example of a lawyer who was alleged to be ungovernable. The *Clark* decision is set out in chapter 3.

of disbarment is actually *less* expensive than the imposition of a series of fines through costly prosecutions. If disbarment seems inevitable (due to the likelihood of recidivism) it may be least expensive to disbar the unethical lawyer sooner rather than later. Most often, however, the penalty of suspension or disbarment is reserved for those cases in which the appropriate expected punishment is so vast that it calls for a greater fine than the offender can afford. If the lawyer is unable to pay the cost of the requisite fine (together with perfect compensation), the imposition of the fine cannot function as a deterrent. In such cases, the Law Society's only method of achieving efficient deterrence is to penalize the lawyer through the removal of the right to practise law.

G. Calculating Optimal Punishments

Thus far, we have considered the relative merits of fines, suspension, and disbarment and considered the combinations of severity and probability that generate deterrence in the least expensive manner. What remains is to consider the method of calculating the appropriate expected punishment for any particular violation of the rules of professional conduct. The mathematics required for calculating optimal punishments have already been developed (in the context of criminal law) by David Friedman.[112] The following discussion is simply an application of Friedman's excellent work in the context of the regulation of lawyers' ethics.

Assume that there is a particular type of ethical infraction that imposes a cost of $100,000 every time that it is committed. Assume that the expected punishment for this ethical violation is currently set at $50,000 (through one of the combinations listed in table 4.1, above). Finally, assume that we can deter *one more infraction* if we raise the expected punishment to $50,002.

If we raise the expected punishment to $50,002, we will prevent a loss of $100,000 (the social damage that would have been caused by the extra offence we have deterred). Let us assume, however, that increasing the expected punishment to $50,002 requires us to spend an extra $10,000 on enforcement.[113] Should we increase the expected punishment to $50,002, or leave it where it is (at $50,000)?

It is tempting to leap to the conclusion that we should automatically increase the expected punishment to $50,002. After all, this increase deters one more offence that would have cost society $100,000, and this added deterrence cost us only $10,000 in increased enforcement costs. In order to provide a thorough answer to this question, however, we must consider all the costs and benefits that flow from the act we are deterring. In particular, we must account for the preferences of the offender who we hope to deter.

What does our hypothetical offender hope to gain from the proposed unethical activity? In our example, the answer must be something between $50,000 and $50,002. Recall that by raising expected punishment to $50,002, we are deterring one more offender who

---

112 Friedman, supra note 50, at 227-29.

113 We may have to hire more investigators or prosecutors, thereby raising the costs of enforcement.

would not have been deterred had the expected punishment been set at $50,000. We can therefore assert that this offender generates somewhere between $50,000 and $50,002 of utility by engaging in the unethical act. For the sake of simplicity, assume that the offender's gain is equal to $50,001.[114]

If the offender's action causes $100,000 worth of damage, and generates $50,001 in gains to the offender, the net social damage caused by the offender's action is $49,999. By deterring this offence, we have saved $49,999 of net social utility. As we noted above, the cost we incurred to generate this savings equalled $10,000. The increase in expected punishment yields a net social benefit of $39,999. Since this represents a net gain in social utility, we should increase the expected punishment to $50,002.

If we hope to achieve the socially optimal level of deterrence, we should continue to increase the expected punishment for this ethical infraction as long as doing so generates net gains in social utility—that is, as long as the cost of increasing the punishment is less than the amount of net social damage we prevent through added deterrence. As David Friedman notes, this "process stops when the last offence deterred costs just as much to deter as the net damage it does."[115]

Once this process stops—that is, once we have deterred the last ethical infraction worth deterring—we will have designed the optimal punishment for this particular infraction. If we were to increase our expected punishment, the value of the deterrence that we gain would be offset by the cost incurred to generate that deterrence—for example, we may spend $20,001 to prevent $20,000 of net damage. Once we have reached this level of deterrence, additional levels of deterrence cost more than they are worth. As a result, we should increase expected punishment no further.

To enhance the precision of our economic account of optimal punishments, we can convert our general description into a series of simple equations.[116] First, we can express the net damage caused by any ethical infraction:

Equation 4.1

net damage = damage done – gain to offender

Next, we can determine the utility gain experienced by the marginal offender—that is, the offender who is "just barely deterred" by a marginal increase in expected punishment. Because the offender was not deterred by a lower expected punishment, and is just barely deterred by a marginal increase in that punishment—for example, the offender was not deterred by a $50,000 expected punishment, but *was* deterred by a $50,002 expected punishment—we can safely assume that the gain to this newly deterred offender would

114   It may seem counterintuitive to weigh the offender's preferences against those of "innocent victims" and the rest of society. Our reason for doing so is developed below.

115   Friedman, supra note 50, at 228.

116   The following equations simply paraphrase David Friedman's account of optimal criminal sanctions, applying Friedman's conclusions in the realm of legal ethics. See supra note 50, at 228, for Friedman's account of optimal punishment. For more detailed mathematics, visit http://www.daviddfriedman.com.

have been roughly equal to the newly enhanced expected punishment. Thus, for the marginal offender:

Equation 4.2

gain to offender = expected punishment

Because the gain to this offender is roughly equal to the expected punishment, we can return to equation 4.1 (net damage = damage done – gain to offender) and substitute "expected punishment" for "gain to offender":

Equation 4.3

net damage = damage done – expected punishment

This formula, which defines the net damage of the marginal offence, will be useful in designing optimal punishments.

Earlier we noted that the goal of optimal punishment is achieved where the last offence deterred costs just as much to deter as the net damage that it causes. This optimal punishment can be represented as follows:

Equation 4.4

cost of deterring one more offence = net damage

In equation 4.3, we saw that the net damage of the marginal offence is equal to the damage to the victim minus the expected punishment. As a result, we can safely replace "net damage" in equation 4.4 as follows:

Equation 4.5

cost of deterring one more offence = damage done – expected punishment

By simply rearranging equation 4.5, we come to the following conclusion:

Optimal Punishment

expected punishment = damage done – cost of deterring one more offence

As a result, the optimal punishment for any ethical infraction is achieved where the punishment equals the damage done by the relevant infraction minus the cost of deterring one more infraction. Where this level of punishment is achieved, we have achieved the optimal level of deterrence: the highest level of deterrence for which we are willing to pay.

What does the theory of optimal punishment tell us about the regulator's method of establishing penal sanctions? According to David Friedman:

> The solution to the problem of setting the level of punishment combines elements of two
> different intuitions: punishment equal to damage done ("an eye for an eye," "make the

punishment fit the crime") and enough punishment to deter. If catching and punishing criminals is easy and inexpensive, the optimum is about equal to damage done; enforcement and punishment costs are unimportant, so we simply design our system to deter all inefficient and only inefficient crimes.[117]

Under the conditions proposed by Friedman, the punishment model would deter only inefficient offences. Where the gain to the offender exceeds the damage that is created by the offence—for example, in cases where some valuable social goal is pursued through a breach of ethical rules—the offence is economically efficient and will not be deterred by the optimal punishment. As a result, our optimal punishment can (and should) have the effect of deterring a lawyer from misappropriating a client's trust account, for example, without deterring Gandhi from violating the rules of professional conduct in pursuit of his home country's independence. The former offence is inefficient—that is, the damage it causes outweighs gains to the offender—while the latter is efficient—the gains outweigh the damage. Under these conditions, the theory of optimal punishments helps ensure that only inefficient offences are deterred.[118]

Our account of optimal punishments was based (in part) on the "net damage" caused by ethical breaches. In other words, when assessing the level of damage caused by ethical breaches (and designing the relevant sanction), we subtracted the utility gains enjoyed by the offender. This effectively counts the offender's gain as a social benefit, reducing the overall social cost of unethical behaviour. To some readers, this seems counterintuitive. Why should our definition of net damage subtract the utility gains of unethical lawyers from the utility losses suffered by their victims? In short, why should optimal punishments account for gains enjoyed by "villains"? Cooter and Ulen raise this issue:

> According to the standard view among economists, as mentioned, the criminal's benefit partly offsets the victim's cost. Moralists, however, might say that the criminal's illicit gain should not count as a social benefit. Ordinarily people reach different conclusions on different examples. To illustrate, most people agree that the benefit enjoyed by a person who steals food from an unoccupied cabin to save his life when lost in the wilderness should count as a social gain, and most people agree that the pleasure felt by a rapist (if there is such a pleasure) should not count as a social gain commensurate with the victim's pain.[119]

---

117 Friedman, supra note 50, at 229.

118 In more realistic conditions, where enforcement is expensive, the theory of optimal punishment still deters only inefficient offences. It does not, however, deter *all* inefficient offences. Where an offence is inefficient and enforcement is expensive, the optimal punishment will fail to deter those inefficient offences for which deterrence would be too costly. Thus, while an offence may be inefficient in that the gains to the offender are lower than the damage that is caused, deterring that offence may be even *more* inefficient, costing more to deter than would be lost by allowing the offence to continue. In this sense, failure to deter this class of inefficient offences is, from a social-welfare perspective, efficient. See section VI.E for a more thorough explanation.

119 Cooter and Ulen, supra note 20, at 471.

Similarly, Friedman notes that

> costs and benefits ought to have a moral as well as an economic dimension. I have a right to
> my life and property, so my loss as a victim of murder or theft counts. You do not have a
> right to my life and property, so the loss to you when we prevent you from killing or
> robbing me does not count.[120]

To be useful, however, an economic account of ethical systems *must* account for the
gains or losses that are experienced by offenders. The embezzler's gain from embezzlement *must* be counted against the victim's loss. To understand why, return to the introductory portions of chapter 1. There we saw that reliance on vague notions such as
"good" and "evil" when defining ethical systems gives rise to circular reasoning. If the
purpose of ethical theory is to help us define the notions of good and evil, it makes little
sense to start with settled notions of what counts as good and evil behaviour. By the same
token, if our economic theory does not account for the gains and losses experienced by
so-called unethical actors, our economic theory becomes empty. As Friedman notes:

> If instead of treating all benefits to everyone equally we first sort people into the deserving
> and the undeserving, the just and the unjust, the criminals and the victims, we are simply
> assuming our conclusions. Benefits to bad people don't count, so rules against bad people
> are automatically efficient. We cannot deduce moral conclusions from economics if we start
> the economics by assuming the moral conclusions.[121]

In short, our ethical theory is meant to tell us what counts as ethical or unethical. In
making this determination, we must count the costs and benefits that everyone in our
universe experiences; we must define an act as "unethical" based (in part) on the costs
and benefits that flow from the relevant act. If we ignore the costs and benefits experienced by any class of people in our universe, we are assuming our conclusions and
engaged in nothing more than ideology. One of the features of the economic theory of
ethical systems is that it allows us to view behaviour through a more objective lens,
avoiding reliance on unstated assumptions regarding what counts as ethical or unethical.
As a result, we must count all gains and losses that flow from particular actions, regardless of our beliefs regarding the moral value of the relevant actor.

Once we have decided what behaviour is to be declared unethical and determined the
method of designing the optimal penalty for specific unethical acts, we have designed the
perfect punishment-based system of regulation. The goal of perfect punishment is, of
course, unattainable given our present state of knowledge. We cannot always measure the
net damage caused by a particular infraction, nor can we accurately determine the precise
cost that is incurred in deterring one additional ethical infraction. What we can do,
however, is estimate net damage and the costs of added deterrence with far more accuracy than we can measure the extent of a particular lawyer's moral guilt. As a result, the
theory of optimal punishment is a more precise guide in the setting of penal sanctions

---

120 Friedman, supra note 50, at 229.

121 Ibid., at 230.

than vague references to the "moral culpability" of an offender. To the extent that we can generate useful estimates concerning the net damage caused by a lawyer's unethical conduct, and estimate the costs required to raise our system's level of deterrence, we can use the theory of optimal punishments as an additional tool in the design of functional regulatory regimes. In the future, as we collect empirical data concerning (1) the true costs of deterrence and (2) the damage caused by lawyers' unethical behaviour, the theory of optimal punishment will become even more important.[122]

We have now considered all of the elements of the both the "compensatory model" and the "punishment model" of regulating lawyers. We have seen the effects of compensatory payments, generating efficient incentives and perfectly compensating victims. We have observed those cases in which a purely compensatory model fails to generate optimal outcomes in the regulation of lawyers' ethical choices. We have decided what counts as "punishable" behaviour, and considered the costs of deterrence. We have determined when deterrence is inefficient. We have also laid the groundwork for the design of optimal sanctions. Armed with the tools we have developed in our discussion of the compensatory and punishment models of regulating lawyers, we are now ready to evaluate the Law Society's actual methods of regulating lawyers' ethical behaviour. As we have seen throughout this chapter, the Law Society (in conjunction with the courts) does, in fact, employ a combination of compensation and punitive sanctions when governing lawyers' ethics. Generally speaking, we rely on tort and contract to ensure that victims of unethical lawyer behaviour receive appropriate compensation, and the Law Society supplements the compensatory model by generating supracompensatory punitive sanctions such as fines, suspension, or disbarment. The combination of compensation and punitive sanctions is designed with the objectives of (1) generating efficient incentives and deterrence, and (2) providing victims with appropriate compensation. The remainder of this chapter provides us with our first opportunity to use the tools of economics to evaluate the sanctions that are actually used to govern lawyers' ethics. Part II of this book, which includes chapters 6 through 9, allows us to repeat this analysis in a more detailed manner, considering each of the core ethical obligations that are created in professional codes of conduct.

VII. Case Study: Wijesinha

The decision of the Law Society's Disciplinary Committee (together with the decision of Convocation) in *Law Society of Upper Canada v. Wijesinha* (1998) provides a useful case study regarding the Law Society's theory of punitive sanctions. The case involves a solicitor who was convicted of attempting to obstruct justice and subsequently charged with professional misconduct. The Supreme Court of Canada, in *R v. Wijesinha* (1995) (reproduced below) upheld Wijesinha's conviction for attempting to obstruct justice as

---

122   The first Canadian studies collecting empirical data regarding lawyers' ethics have already begun. See, for example, Margaret Ann Wilkinson, Christina Walker, and Peter Mercer, "Do Codes of Ethics Actually Shape Legal Practice?" (2000), 45 *McGill Law Journal* 645. As this work continues, economic theory's predictions regarding individual choices and the regulator's decisions will become even more powerful.

well as Wijesinha's sentence of 15 months in prison. The decision of Convocation (reproduced in full below, together with the recommendations of the Disciplinary Committee) deals with the charge of professional misconduct. For present purposes, we are primarily concerned with the decision of Convocation and the recommendations of the Disciplinary Committee. However, because of the sparse factual account those decisions provide, we begin by reproducing the factual account provided by the Supreme Court of Canada. When reading these decisions, consider the economic impact of the penalties imposed on Wijesinha. Specific notes and questions follow Convocation's decision.

R v. Wijesinha
[1995] 3 SCR 422

Factual Background

The appellant was for a number of years a Crown Attorney in the city of Toronto. He left that position and set up his own practice specializing in the defence of persons charged with drinking and driving offences. On December 17, 1991, he was convicted of four counts of attempting to obstruct justice and sentenced to 15 months' imprisonment.

The evidence at the trial revealed that on March 23, 1989, the appellant approached Constable Stade, who was a breathalyzer operator, with a proposal. He suggested to Stade that he would pay him $250 for each successful referral of persons who had failed the breathalyzer test. The appellant gave Stade some business cards to give to people he referred to the appellant, and told him to mark the business cards in a particular manner. In that way, the appellant would know that it was Stade who had referred the prospective client. In the course of his conversation with Stade, the appellant stated that Constable Thompson was already referring people to him for the same amount. He suggested that Stade might wish to confirm this with Thompson. Stade told the appellant that he would think about his proposal.

Stade disclosed the appellant's proposition to a colleague and reported it to his superiors, who decided that an investigation should be conducted. Stade was instructed to feign agreement with the appellant's proposal. Pursuant to those instructions, Stade met the appellant at the courthouse on March 30 and told him that he would participate in the fee-for-referral scheme. At the police station, Stade signed a form consenting to the interception of his conversations and, while wearing a bodypack, met with Constable Thompson on April 4. In the course of the conversation, Thompson confirmed that he was referring persons to the appellant and was receiving $250 for each person who became a client.

When the police investigators obtained this information, they called the Law Society Discipline Committee for advice. The investigators also sought the views of Crown counsel who expressed the opinion that, as long as the appellant was not seeking to have a witness give false evidence, the appellant's fee-for-referral scheme did not amount to a criminal offence.

At the invitation of the appellant, Stade went to his home on April 7. He was wearing a bodypack. In the course of their conversation, the appellant confirmed his arrangement with Thompson and instructed Stade as to the manner in which he was to mark his business cards. He told him that the referred persons were to be called "fish." During the same conversation, the appellant told Stade that he was aware of the danger that Stade might be wearing a bodypack and that he would never ask a police officer to change his evidence.

After the meeting at the appellant's house, discussions took place between the police investigators, the Law Society and Crown Counsel. As a result of these discussions, Stade was told to go along with the appellant's scheme. In June of 1989, Stade referred four persons to the appellant and gave each of them a business card marked in the manner suggested by the appellant. Three of these persons retained the appellant to defend them.

On June 19, Stade phoned the appellant at his office to inquire whether there were any "fishes" yet, to which the appellant replied that there were. The two men agreed to meet at the appellant's home the next evening. Once again Stade wore a bodypack and recorded their conversation. The appellant confirmed that he had been retained by three of the persons and paid Stade $750 in cash, and encouraged him to send more clients. He suggested that Stade could make up to $10,000 per year and wondered if Stade knew of anyone else who might refer prospective clients to him. Although the police did not pursue their investigation of the appellant, they continued to communicate with and supply information to the Law Society. In the fall of 1989, the police provided the Law Society with the evidence which they gathered from their investigation. The Law Society then commenced its own investigation. It advised the appellant of the nature of his alleged misconduct and gave him details of the evidence. The Law Society followed its usual procedure and invited the appellant to respond to the allegations.

In preparing his response, the appellant spoke to Constable Thompson as well as to the three clients who had been referred to him by Stade. He asked each of them to sign a statutory declaration which he had prepared. All four complied with his request.

The statutory declaration signed by the three clients contained a paragraph stating that:

> At no time did any police officer direct or suggest that I retain [the appellant]. At no time did any police officer give me any business cards of [the appellant].

The declaration signed by Thompson stated that the appellant had never paid or offered to pay him any money for referring potential clients to him. At trial, the three clients and Thompson testified that these portions of the statutory declarations were false.

On January 11, 1990, the Law Society received the four statutory declarations, together with a letter from the appellant responding to the allegations brought against him. The Law Society did not inform the police of the statutory declarations it had received, but continued with its investigation. On March 15, 1990, the appellant was charged with professional misconduct pursuant to the provisions of the *Law Society Act*, RSO 1980, c. 233. In the fall of that same year, the police received information that the appellant had requested another former client to sign a false affidavit concerning his referral by an officer. As a result of this information, they resumed their investigation of the appellant. The police learned that the Law Society believed that the statutory declarations which the appellant had submitted to it were false. The police obtained copies of the declarations together with the letter from the appellant to the Law Society. The appellant was subsequently charged with four counts of attempting to obstruct justice.

At the trial, the appellant challenged the admissibility of the wiretap evidence, the statutory declarations and the *viva voce* evidence which pertained to them. They were all ruled admissible by the trial judge. The appellant was convicted at trial on the four counts of attempting to obstruct justice. The conviction was unanimously upheld in the Court of Appeal. At the conclusion of the hearing before this Court, the appeal was dismissed with reasons to follow.

[The Supreme Court of Canada upheld the appellant's conviction as well as his sentence to 15 months in prison.]

Law Society of Upper Canada v. Wijesinha
[1998] LSDD no. 89

The Facts

The evidence in support of the Complaint was received in the form of an Agreed Statement of Facts supported by a Document Book, both of which were filed as Exhibits. In view of the seriousness of the matter, the evidence will be reviewed in some detail.

The Solicitor was called to the Bar in 1966. Prior to that time, he practiced law for 14 years in Ceylon. He practiced as an assistant Crown Attorney in Metropolitan Toronto between 1966 and January, 1988 when he established a private practice as a sole practitioner. He then restricted his practice to criminal defence work and specialized in the defence of impaired driving and related charges.

On December 17, 1991, the Solicitor was found guilty after 8 days of trial before Mr. Justice Trainor of the Ontario Court (General Division) sitting with a jury of four counts of wilfully attempting to obstruct, pervert or defeat the course of justice by knowingly submitting to the Law Society of Upper Canada with intent that they should be acted upon by the Law Society as if they were genuine:

i. a Solemn Declaration given under oath by Kenneth Langille on November 24, 1989;

ii. a Solemn Declaration given under oath by Merrill Lee Roache on November 24, 1989;

iii. a Solemn Declaration given under oath by Norman James McMath on November 24, 1989;

iv. a Solemn Declaration given under oath by Anthony Thompson on December 11, 1989;

knowing the Declarations to be false, contrary to section 139(2) of the *Criminal Code of Canada*.

Copies of the Declarations in question are attached as Appendices 1 to 4 respectively.

On January 8, 1992 a conviction was entered on Count 1. Mr. Justice Trainor granted a conditional stay in respect of Counts 2, 3 and 4 on the basis that all matters arose out of the same transaction. Also on January 8, 1992 the Solicitor was sentenced to 15 months' incarceration. The Solicitor appealed his conviction to the Court of Appeal for Ontario and sought leave to appeal his sentence. On February 18, 1994 the Court of Appeal ordered that the appeal against conviction be dismissed. The Court further ordered that the application for leave to appeal against the sentence be granted and that the appeal also be dismissed. The Solicitor subsequently appealed to the Supreme Court of Canada which appeal was heard on May 31, 1995 before a panel of a full Court. The Supreme Court similarly dismissed the appeal.

Based on the Solicitor's admission and the facts as agreed, the Committee found the solicitor guilty of professional misconduct.

Recommendation as to Penalty

The Committee is divided in its recommendation as to penalty. The recommendation of the majority of the Committee as explained in this Report and Decision is that the Solicitor be disbarred.

Reasons for Recommendation

Regarding penalty, the following facts are also germane. The Solicitor is presently 67 years of age. He ceased to practice on May 1, 1991. He has no prior discipline history. He has now served his sentence imposed by Mr. Justice Trainor. While he did not appear on the occasion of the hearing, a letter was filed on his behalf, a copy of which is attached as Appendix 5. Finally, the Solicitor noted that while he respects the findings of the various Courts, he respectfully disagrees with them.

On the occasion of this hearing, counsel for the Law Society and the Solicitor made a joint submission that the Solicitor should be granted permission to resign. Having regard to the nature of the misconduct in question, the Committee made it clear that there was concern about such a disposition. This resulted in further submissions which included reference to the applicable authorities.

The parameters governing the issue of penalty are found in Section 34 of the *Law Society Act*. Specifically, in the case of a member found guilty of professional misconduct, a range of dispositions are available to Convocation up to and including disbarment.

Regarding the principles to be applied, these have been variously stated in the authorities. Obviously, any disposition must reflect the obligation that the profession be governed in the public interest. With this in mind, general deterrence is an important consideration to reinforce the expectation that misconduct will be treated seriously, and to deter others from similar actions. Specific deterrence must also be considered to protect against the possibility of repetition as far as the member is concerned. At the same time, the interests of the member must also be considered and rehabilitation, where possible, encouraged.

It is instructive to focus on these foregoing principles having regard to the facts in question. First, with regard to the principle of general deterrence, it must be borne in mind that the specific misconduct here goes to the heart of the Society's regulatory regime. Furthermore, the conduct was initiated by a member whose daily practice was premised on the integrity of the very process he sought to subvert, namely, the sanctity of the oath and the accuracy of sworn evidence. The Solicitor in this case has violated his duty to the Court and his duty to the profession as well as his duty to himself. It would be difficult to conceive of facts where the principle of general deterrence is of less application. In short, there should be very little latitude where the issue of false testimony is concerned.

Regarding specific deterrence, this is not a significant factor to be considered. It is common ground that future misconduct on the part of the Solicitor is not a concern.

With regard to the rehabilitation of the member, this consideration is also less significant. The member has not practiced since May, 1991 and does not intend to practice in the future. Indeed, as he acknowledges in his letter attached as Appendix 5, it would be virtually impossible for him to appear in any Court in the Province at any time in the future.

The real issue, therefore, is whether there are mitigating factors found in the evidence such that the maximum penalty should not be imposed.

Having regard to the authorities, one of the factors which has served as mitigation in other cases has been the Solicitor's motivation for the activity in question. For instance, if the misconduct were the result of dire personal circumstances such as illness, serious economic straits or the collapse of a member's personal life, the penalty might be moderated. Here, we had no evidence of such circumstances.

Also central to a number of the authorities is the issue of remorse. Again, in the evidence before us there was no suggestion of contriteness. To the contrary, the member emphasized that he disagreed with the findings made in the Courts.

At its highest, to the extent that there is a mitigating factor, we are asked to find this in the member's personal circumstances. That is, we are asked to depart from the maximum penalty on the basis of compassion. While one can be sympathetic to the member's situation, it does not necessarily, without more, constitute a sufficient mitigating factor to reduce a penalty otherwise applicable.

That there was a joint submission calling for the Committee to grant permission to resign is a significant factor to be considered. However, the recommendation as to penalty must reflect the independent view of the Committee based on both the submissions and the record. It is of significance in our view that the Solicitor chose not to appear. There were no witnesses called nor testimonials filed beyond the Solicitor's own letter. Having regard to the circumstances and the other evidence, compassion alone does not serve to diminish the penalty which in our view is applicable. On the basis of the record before us, the appropriate penalty is disbarment. ...

Dissent

. . .

I write to recommend to Convocation that permission to resign be the penalty imposed upon the Member. I am disposed to this even though I have read the well-reasoned recommendation of the majority in this matter. Further, I am disposed to pay great deference to the joint submission of the two experienced counsel appearing on this matter.

I adhere to the view that joint submissions should be endorsed unless outside the range. Although the Committee was provided with cases involving false/improperly sworn affidavits/statutory declarations (e.g. Linton, decision of Convocation September 26, 1996 and Janjua, decision of Convocation of March 25, 1993) where suspensions were imposed, I believe that there is no serious dispute that the range of penalty here is permission to resign versus disbarment.

Further, there can be no dispute that the misconduct here is very serious and strikes at the very heart of the administration of justice. While under investigation by the Law Society the Member caused the Law Society to receive false affidavits intended to divert suspicion from himself. With obvious forethought and planning the Member set upon a path to personally benefit himself. His offences are of the gravest sort, more aggravated by his 22 years as a respected Crown Attorney who daily worked to uphold the law and respect for the judicial system.

However, there is no evidence put before the Committee to detail the cause and effect of these false affidavits. Simply put to us was the conviction. Without more I am constrained to make further findings of aggravation or mitigation regarding the facts.

However, I also look to the personal facts of the individual member and still am of the view that permission to resign is the appropriate penalty. Those personal facts are set out in the letter the Member submitted dated July 31, 1997 and which is attached as Appendix 5 to the majority reasons herein. That letter describes a man so distraught over the way he let down himself, his family, his friends, neighbours, and Sri Lankan community both in Canada and his native country, that suicide was an option. When dissuaded from that course of conduct, he has chosen to merely await the "inevitable" instead.

Clearly, this is a man who has looked deeply in the mirror. The Member need not be physically present before me to be able to see the broken man he now is. He makes no excuses and I respect that as too often the assignment of blame is the preoccupation of these hearings. The Member's letter may be taken as bluntly spoken but I see it in a different light.

I note that the Member voluntarily quit practising in 1991 and has sought to formally resign since then but has been prohibited from doing so while discipline matters remain outstanding. The Committee was told that the appeal from the General Division conviction was in regards to technical matters only. The sentence of 15 months was not "light." There was no dispute (albeit there was disagreement with the General Division finding) in the finding of professional misconduct before us. There is no prior discipline history but rather an exemplary career. I find the old adage applies: "The bigger they are, the harder they fall." No one knows that better than the Member.

I have carefully reviewed the cases submitted to us in support of the joint recommendation and realize that not one is close to being "on all fours" with the case at hand. But the cases preferring permission to resign are instructive for the making of that recommendation alone. Each case was equally worthy of disbarment ... .

In the decisions of *McLaughlin* and *Woolcott*, both before Convocation on January 26, 1984, the misconduct included misappropriations and other matters of the nature of failing to file, etc. and permission to resign was recommended. In *McLaughlin*, as in the present case there were no excuses made and no medical evidence presented.

In the *Boughner* matter (in camera Committee Report of March 9, 1994) the remorse of the Member was as obvious as I so find here.

In *Loney* (Convocation decision of June 27, 1996) the list of misconduct was long. Mr. Loney was found to be ungovernable. He offered no explanation, no plan, no hope for change, no options. He filed no character evidence and no psychiatric report as here. Yet the Committee admitted, Loney "engenders in us compassion and a desire to help" and recommended permission to resign failing which there should be disbarment.

In *Ducas* (Convocation decision of November 28, 1996) the list of misconduct was huge and included numerous offending incidents involving improper affidavits. With a prior discipline record and a finding of ungovernability, the joint recommendation of permission to resign was followed. In *Gardner* (Convocation decision of January 23, 1997) the single bencher sitting found "the two purposes for which penalties are imposed in a discipline matter are (1) the protection of the public and (2) the protection of the reputation of the profession." These could be met by accepting the joint recommendation for permission to resign.

The desired end result will be achieved by either penalty. In fact it is already being achieved by the Member having voluntarily ceased to practise since 1991. Even though the Member did not attend before us, his letter spoke volumes without straining the ear. The Member retained counsel to appear before us, and much co-operation must have fostered the Agreed Statement of Facts before us and the joint submission. In all the circumstances I am compelled to pay deference to that submission.

I therefore recommend that the Member be granted permission to resign failing which, he shall be disbarred.

· · ·

Order of Convocation

CONVOCATION of the Law Society of Upper Canada, having read the Report and Decision of the Discipline Committee dated the 23rd day of February, 1998, in the presence of Counsel for the Society, the Solicitor not being in attendance but represented by J. David Hobson, QC, wherein the Solicitor was found guilty of professional misconduct and having heard counsel aforesaid;

CONVOCATION HEREBY ORDERS that Walter Kingsley Wijesinha be granted permission to resign his membership in the said Society, and thereby be prohibited from acting or practising as a barrister and solicitor, and from holding himself out as a barrister and solicitor.

NOTES AND QUESTIONS

1. What was Wijesinha's reason for offering police officers $250 for referrals? Can this be explained in terms of utility maximization? Presuming that Wijesinha knew that the Law Society would regard this action as an unethical action, can you describe Wijesinha's subconscious ethical calculation?

2. Why might the Law Society have considered Wijesinha's referral-for-cash scheme an unethical form of conduct?

3. Can Wijesinha's decision to rely on false affidavits be explained in terms of utility maximization? Attempt to generate an equation explaining Wijesinha's decision (based on the $A - B = X$ equation developed in chapters 2 and 3). What are the costs that flowed from Wijesinha's decision? What are the benefits? What is the probability that these costs and benefits will arise?

4. Could Wijesinha's conduct be regulated (efficiently) through the use of a compensatory model? Why or why not?

5. Note that the penalty of disbarment (or permission to resign) is, from a certain perspective, the equivalent of a fine: one can determine the present value of the income stream a lawyer could expect to generate over any particular period. By removing the lawyer's right to practise law during that period, you remove the lawyer's right to a stream of income. The present value of this income stream can be expressed in dollar values, and compared to the nominal value of a fine. Bearing this in mind, how would you calculate the cost of the penalty that was imposed on Wijesinha?

6. From an economic perspective, how is the cost of disbarment different from the cost of resignation? Which of these two penalties would have a greater deterrent effect? Which of these two penalties costs society more to impose?

7. Based on what we know concerning the theory of optimal punishments, was the penalty imposed on Wijesinha an optimal penalty?

8. Would the Law Society's penalty have changed had Wijesinha not already been sentenced to 15 months in prison? In other words, does the fact that Wijesinha has already been penalized have any impact on the penalty that the Law Society imposes? Should it? How would this relate to the goals of efficient deterrence?

9. If the goal of a penalty is deterrence, why were the solicitor's age and disciplinary history relevant to a determination of the appropriate penalty? Why was the likelihood of future offences a factor?

10. Why are an offender's personal circumstances relevant to a determination of the appropriate penalty? For example, the court notes that illness or dire personal consequences may serve as a mitigating factor in the determination of the appropriate penalty. Why? Why is motive a relevant factor?

11. Why is remorse a relevant factor in setting penalties? Is there an economic reason for considering remorse? When answering this question, consider the relationship between remorse and the likelihood of future infractions. How can remorse be expressed in terms of utility, and how does this utility value relate to the penalty that is ultimately imposed?

12. Did the penalty imposed by Convocation make sense? Would you have recommended a different penalty had Wijesinha not already been imprisoned for 15 months?

VIII. Conclusion

This chapter considers the perspective of the regulatory body charged with the task of governing lawyers' ethical choices. As we have seen, this perspective can be described and evaluated using the tools of economics. This should come as no surpise: as we saw in chapter 3, the ethical choices lawyers make can be predicted and described using the tools of economics. If lawyers' choices can be described and evaluated through the tools of economics, the *modification* of those choices (which is the goal of regulation) should also be explained by reference to economic principles. Indeed, this chapter has demonstrated that the tools of economics generate particularly useful insights concerning the regulation of lawyers' ethical conduct. Using the tools of economics, we can consider the goals of possible regulatory systems, evaluate the specific methods that are employed by those systems, and consider which methods have the effect of driving lawyers toward an optimal amount of ethical conduct. Even if economic theory fails to provide a complete account of the regulations governing lawyers' ethical conduct, it goes a long way toward explaining the economic motives underlying violations of ethical norms and describing the issues that must be considered when designing effective methods of preventing or curtailing lawyers' ethical violations. As a result, the tools of economics serve as useful additions to the "toolkits" of those responsible for governing lawyers' ethics.

Chapters 1 through 4 have laid the groundwork for an economic theory of legal ethics. To many people, this theory seems intuitive. Lawyers (like all other individuals) inevitably act in ways that give effect to their personal preferences, and the regulator will attempt to modify those personal preferences through the imposition of sanctions. The goal of setting those sanctions is to alter lawyers' economic preferences—to make lawyers *prefer* to behave in ways that promote an efficient legal system. While many people wholeheartedly embrace an economic account of legal ethics, however, others find the theory hard to swallow. Many people simply refuse to accept the ability of an economic theory to explain the workings of an ethical system. While many opponents of the economic theory of legal ethics will base their objections on ephemeral (and largely inexplicable) notions such as spirituality or morality,[123] others will raise more concrete questions concerning the power of economics to predict and evaluate the ethical choices lawyers make. Chapter 5 describes and assesses the most frequently raised objections to the economic account of legal ethics. As we shall see, economic theory has the power to respond to each objection. Indeed, by the end of chapter 5, we shall see that economic theory is far more powerful and useful than the alternative methods used for explaining the complex ethical choices lawyers make.

---

123 Note that this is not intended to deny the value of spirituality or morality in general. On the contrary, I simply question the value of concepts such as spirituality and morality in the design of functioning regulatory systems. As we have seen, these notions fail to generate testable outcomes and tend to vary according to the ideology of whoever is making a claim based on spirituality or morality. More importantly, it may be considered improper (in a society that values freedom of conscience and religion) to impose a spirituality-based or morality-based system of regulation on all lawyers. As a result, economic theory may be the preferable method of describing the regulation of legal ethics. Additional reasons for abandoning reliance on the notions of morality and spirituality are considered in chapter 5.

CHAPTER FIVE

Objections

I. Introduction

A. Ethinomics

Chapters 1 through 4 have situated the topic of legal ethics within an overarching model of human behaviour: the behavioural model described by economics. By viewing legal ethics through the lens of economics, we have seen that legal professionals make decisions in accordance with the process of utility maximization. When faced with any decision (including moral or ethical choices), lawyers act as though they are governed by subconscious assessments of the costs and benefits flowing from the available choices. When choosing between two options (such as a choice to breach or to adhere to a code of ethics) the lawyer will weigh the costs and benefits flowing from each competing option, ultimately selecting whichever option does the most to further his or her personal interests. Through a basic understanding of self-interest and utility maximization, we have (in chapter 1 through 4) generated a coherent theory of lawyers' ethical choices—one that has allowed us to explain (1) the motives of lawyers who commit unethical actions, (2) the perspective of people who are harmed by ethical breaches, and (3) the economic principles that regulators can (and often do) use when trying to regulate lawyers' ethical choices. In sum, the tools of economics have allowed us to develop a sophisticated, coherent understanding of each element of the lawyer's ethical universe.

The economic account of legal ethics is an extension of a very old idea. The school of thought known as utilitarianism, championed in the 18th and 19th centuries by Jeremy Bentham and John Stuart Mill,[1] was rooted in the notion that ethical choices are governed by economic principles. Bentham and Mill persuasively argued that all decisions (including moral and ethical choices) are governed by the decision maker's assessment of the costs and benefits flowing from competing possibilities. Writing in 1789, Bentham developed the elements of "felicific calculus," the basic mathematics that explain, predict, and evaluate ethical choices.[2] As a result, the theories presented in this text are not entirely new ideas. Instead, this text builds on the best ideas developed by Bentham and

---

1 See Jeremy Bentham, *An Introduction to the Principles of Morals and Legislation* (London: The Athlone Press, 1970) and John Stuart Mill, *Utilitarianism* (Peterborough, ON: Broadview Press, 2000).

2 Dave Robinson and Chris Garratt, *Ethics for Beginners* (Cambridge: Icon Books, 1996), 71.

Mill, applying modern economics to utilitarian thought and deploying the ensuing behavioural model into the field of legal ethics. The resulting theory of ethical decisions—known as "ethinomics" among my students—provides a rational and persuasive method of analyzing lawyers' ethical choices. Through the application of ethinomic principles, we can describe, evaluate, and predict the ethical choices lawyers make, ultimately designing rational regulatory models aimed at minimizing the harms caused by unethical behaviour.

B. Remaining Objections

In laying the foundations of ethinomics, chapters 1 through 4 dealt with several objections to the application of economic principles to ethical decisions. In chapter 1, for example, we confronted the notion that economic analysis is incapable of accounting for altruistic actions,[3] as well as the objection to the practice of assigning dollar figures to the values that are at stake in ethical choices.[4] In chapters 3 and 4 we considered whether or not the expected value model—that is, the model which posits that people account for probability in the decision-making process—is an accurate reflection of the ways in which real people make decisions.[5] While we have already answered each of these objections to ethinomics, there are still objections remaining. The two most important of these objections can be referred to as (1) the "rationality objection," which relates to key assumptions underlying any utilitarian model of ethical choice, and (2) the "indeterminacy objection," which suggests that it is impossible to generate *any* coherent theory of ethical choice, let alone a theory rooted in economics. This chapter confronts these two objections.

II. Rationality

A. The Objection

The notion of "rationality" is fundamental to economics. Indeed, one accurate definition of economics is "the science of rational choice." In explaining and predicting the choices that individuals make, economists rely on the assumption that people tend to behave *rationally*. In the context of an economic analysis, "rationality" implies that people tend to make decisions by weighing the various costs and benefits flowing from alternative choices,[6] ultimately selecting whatever option the decision maker prefers. As Cooter and Ulen note, "rationality holds that a rational actor can rank alternatives according to the

---

3   See chapter 1, section II.D.

4   See ibid., section II.E.

5   See chapter 3, section VIII.E and chapter 4, section V.D.

6   As we have seen throughout chapters 1 through 4, this analysis may be undertaken consciously (as it is
     when people choose between investment opportunities) or unconsciously (as it often is when people
     choose a spouse or a leisure activity).

extent that they give her what she wants."[7] People assess the "net pleasure" (or utility) that competing options yield, and—in the language of economists—select whatever option maximizes their utility. For the economist, this model of decision-making behaviour is the essence of rationality.

The economic model of behaviour rests upon the assumption that decision makers are (1) aware of their own preferences, and (2) able to rank their various preferences in order. Confronted with the need to choose between competing options, a rational person weighs the costs and benefits associated with each option, using the tally of costs and benefits to determine which of the options the decision maker prefers. If a person lacks this ability (that is, if the person defies the economic assumption of rationality), economics can tell us little about this decision maker's choices.

The assumption of rationality is often easy to accept. When people purchase cars, select insurance, hire lawyers, or choose between competing employment opportunities, they engage in a conscious ordering of preferences. They assess the costs and benefits flowing from each available option and choose whichever alternative they prefer (that is, they select the option that provides them with the highest amount of utility). For decisions involving financial opportunities and the acquisition or use of tangible assets, this model of rationality accords with our experience. However, when applied to other kinds of personal choices—for example, choices involving moral or ethical issues—the notion of rationality is more difficult to accept. Real people, it is argued, make non-financial decisions without resorting to comparisons of competing costs and benefits. Instead, they simply do "what feels right" in the relevant circumstances, relying on intuition, psychological factors, religious training, or indefinable notions such as "goodness" and "morality." Because people do not appear to approach certain categories of choice (including moral and ethical choices) in a predictable, rational manner, the theory of economics, with its reliance on the assumption of rationality, seems incapable of describing or predicting personal choices of this nature.

The rationality objection has intuitive appeal. In the real world, people often behave in ways that seem to defy the notion of rationality. Every day we observe people who, despite the availability of reliable information concerning the costs and benefits of particular choices, persist in making decisions that seem irrational. My wife, for example, insists that I am irrational every time I buy a video game instead of making additional contributions to a retirement savings plan. The world is filled with similar illustrations:

- Despite persuasive (and well-publicized) evidence concerning the long-term health effects of obesity, North Americans continue to follow a diet that is unduly high in calories and fat, while refraining from engaging in adequate exercise. Indeed, the obesity rate in North America has dramatically *increased* in recent years, even as information concerning the high cost of obesity has become more widely available.
- Many individuals choose to smoke cigarettes despite repeated, credible warnings concerning cigarettes' negative impact on smokers' hearts and lungs.

---

7   Cooter and Ulen, *Law and Economics*, 4th ed. (Boston: Pearson Addison Wesley, 2003), 15.

- Many individuals choose to drop out of secondary school, despite the availability of well-publicized (and reliable) information concerning the long-term income benefits of a higher education.
- Even when they are presented with statistics concerning the low probability of winning the lottery, people persist in buying tickets. They do so even when it is pointed out that the expected cost of purchasing lottery tickets is always higher than the expected benefit of winning.
- Many upper-year law students choose to spend their time engaged in drunken revelry, watching television, or otherwise neglecting their legal studies, even after having discovered (in first-year law) that doing so can lead to regret, poor grades, and diminished job opportunities.

If the people described in the foregoing examples were truly engaged in a rational weighing of costs and benefits, it is argued, they would not make the bad decisions described above. Rational people would stay in school, refrain from smoking, watch their weight, save their money, and study diligently for each of their exams. They might even invest in retirement savings instead of buying video games. Whenever decision makers act in ways they are likely to regret, they appear (at first blush) to have failed to weigh the costs and benefits of their actions. In short, they appear to defy the economic assumption of rationality. If people make *irrational* decisions, it is argued, economics can do little to help us analyze the decisions people make.

The foregoing arguments concerning rationality—especially those that question my penchant for buying video games—are based on a misconception of the economic notion of rationality. In the context of an economic analysis, rationality does not require decision makers to place competing preferences in any particular order—people are free to prefer a high-fat diet to good health or a single night of drunken shenanigans to an A on a torts exam. The *wisdom* of a decision maker's preferences is, in most instances, beyond the concern of economic analysis. As Cooter and Ulen note:

> It is important to note that the preferences … are *subjective*. Different people have different tastes, and these will be reflected in the fact that they may have very different preference orderings … . Economists leave to other disciplines, such as psychology and sociology, the study of the source of these preferences. We take … tastes or preferences as given, or, as economists say, as *exogenous*, which means that they are determined outside the economic system.[8]

The fact that people make decisions that seem irrational does not compel us to conclude that those decisions are irrational in the context of an economic analysis. For the economist, the notion of rationality relates to the *process* by which people make decisions, not the *quality* of the decisions people make. The economic assumption of rationality merely assumes that people weigh the costs and benefits of particular possibilities. The *value* of those costs and benefits is subjective; it is determined outside the boundaries of the economic system. A person who prefers a regular diet of bacon and

---

8   Ibid., at 22.

scotch to a healthy and functional cardiovascular system, for example, will give effect to the relevant preference by consuming bacon and scotch. The person believes, from his or her perspective, that the benefits of a diet of bacon and scotch (for example, flavour and the pleasant effects of inebriation) outweigh the costs (for example, a shortened lifespan, diminished mental capacity, and obesity).[9] The fact that this decision may be unwise does not relate to its rationality. From an economic perspective, the decision is said to be rational because it was based on an ordering of *the decision maker's* preferences. The fact that a wiser person might assign different values to the competing costs and benefits of the bacon-and-scotch diet does not make that person particularly rational, or reveal our bacon-and-scotch consumer to be irrational. Provided that an individual's choices are based on *his or her subjective assessment* of competing costs and benefits, designed with a view to maximizing utility, that decision maker is rational from an economic perspective.[10] In sum, even people who make apparently silly choices count as rational individuals. They simply assign their own peculiar values to the costs and benefits of their actions.

While the technical meaning of rationality in the context of an economic analysis helps to alleviate some concerns of those who raise the rationality objection, it still leaves our original question unanswered. Does the assumption of rationality (even when confined to its technical meaning) hold when people are faced with *ethical* decisions? While people might accept the model of rational choice in the context of ordinary decisions, they might nonetheless object to the assumption of rationality in the realm of ethical choices. Even if people can be said to make almost all of their choices—including very unwise decisions—by resorting to an assessment of competing costs and benefits, one might argue, this model of rational choice does *not* apply where ethical choices are concerned. Instead, ethical choices are governed by ephemeral factors that are incapable of expression by resort to typical economic tools. They are not governed by rationality, but by metaphysical factors that are beyond the reach of economists' calculations.

It is impossible to disprove the assertion that ethical choices are driven by indefinable forces or metaphysics. As a result, those who believe in a metaphysical explanation of ethical choices are unlikely to accept that people behave in a rational manner when deciding whether or not to behave ethically. This particular branch of the rationality objection cannot be overcome given our present state of knowledge concerning metaphysical forces. Of course, it is similarly impossible to prove that ethical choices *are* governed by metaphysical forces. Proponents of rationality and proponents of metaphysics cannot be made (by force of reason) to accept each other's position. Indeed, it would be pointless to bother trying. Proponents of each position are likely to feel that their opponents simply fail to understand the true nature of human decisions. Such arguments

---

9   To be more accurate, this decision maker takes account of expected values. He or she does not simply weigh ill health against the pleasures of scotch and bacon, but considers the cost of ill health *multiplied* by the likelihood of its occurrence.

10   Note that the decision does not become *irrational* if the decision maker later changes his or her mind. Preferences are not assumed to be constant over time. I may prefer to eat lobster tonight and steak tomorrow. In order to count as a rational person, I need only have the capacity to order my preferences *right now*. The order in which I rank my preferences is permitted to change tomorrow.

tend to break down to battles of will rather than reason. As a result, any attempt to change the views of metaphysicians is beyond my present powers.

It is, of course, entirely possible that the metaphysicians are right. Ethical choices may be governed by forces that are beyond the dismal science of economics. The assumption of rationality, with its unswerving faith that choices are grounded in rational computations of costs and benefits, may be wholly inapplicable in the realm of ethical choice. If the metaphysicians are right, however, and the theory of rational choice cannot account for ethical choices, there is little point in trying to regulate lawyers' ethics at all. As we shall see in the following section of this chapter, it seems unlikely that *any* regulatory regime can be effective where its subjects fail to act in a rational manner—if people are irrational, they cannot be regulated through the use of the regulatory tools that are available given our present state of knowledge. As a result, the bodies currently charged with the task of regulating lawyers' ethics each assume that lawyers behave rationally, even when lawyers consider ethical choices. All disciplinary panels, all courts, and all regulatory bodies charged with the task of regulating lawyers' conduct—even those who do not purport to rely on economic theory—rely heavily on the assumption that, when making ethical choices, lawyers engage in a rational weighing of costs and benefits. The inescapable nature of the assumption of rationality, together with its role in shaping current methods of regulating ethics, is discussed in the following section of this chapter.

B. Current Regulatory Practice

Utilitarian ethicists are not alone in assuming that rationality governs ethical choices. On the contrary, all of the bodies currently regulating lawyers' ethical choices—while rarely employing economic terms to describe their practices—rely heavily on the assumption that ethical choices are based on rational calculations of costs and benefits.

The unspoken reliance of courts and regulatory officials on the economic notion of rationality is revealed when the relevant bodies discuss *deterrence*. When designing or meting out penalties for a breach of ethical standards, courts and regulatory officials consistently state that their main goal is to deter future ethical infractions.[11] Consider the following passage from *Law Society of British Columbia v. A Lawyer* (2000),[12] which involved a lawyer who violated the rules of professional conduct:

> I am hopeful that an appropriate penalty will deter the Respondent from future acts of this nature. There is also a need to deter others who might misconduct themselves in this fashion by the imposition of an appropriate penalty.

The disciplinary panel in *Law Society of Upper Canada v. Wijesinha* (1998)[13] held that, when imposing a penalty in response to a lawyer's violation of ethical standards,

---

11   See Gavin MacKenzie, *Lawyers and Ethics* (Toronto: Carswell, 2001), 26:43-44, where he notes that, when disciplining lawyers accused of ethical infractions, "the discipline hearing panel focuses on ... the need for deterrence."

12   [2000] LSDD no. 19 (reproduced in chapter 1), at para. 64.

13   [1998] LSDD no. 89, at para. 14.

general deterrence is an important consideration to reinforce the expectation that misconduct will be treated seriously, and to deter others from similar actions.

Similar statements can be found in countless cases, including *Schwartz v. Kujawa*
(2001),[14] *Law Society of British Columbia v. Dent* (2002),[15] and *Law Society of British
Columbia v. Nader* (2001),[16] in which the tribunal held that "the need for specific and
general deterrence" is one of the primary goals of punishing lawyers who engage in
unethical practices. In each of these decisions, courts and regulatory bodies make it clear
that, where violations of lawyers' ethical standards are concerned, the primary goal of
imposing penalties is to deter future unethical behaviour.[17]

What does all of this talk of deterrence have to do with the assumption of rationality?
Consider the meaning of deterrence. At its most basic level, the word "deter" refers to
the act of making people prefer to refrain from taking a particular course of action. As the
disciplinary tribunal noted in *Nova Scotia Barrister's Society v. Steele* (1995),[18] deterrence is "the effect a penalty may have on others who would be inclined to the same
misconduct as the offender but would fear suffering the same penalty." As we have seen
in the foregoing cases, deterrence is accomplished through the imposition of penalties. A
penalty, of course, is just another word for costs. As a result, the goal of deterrence—
namely, the goal of making people prefer to refrain from undertaking particular actions—is
achieved by raising the costs associated with those actions. When we impose penalties
for unethical behaviour, we are attempting to drive people toward ethical decisions by
making unethical choices more expensive. If we believe that deterrence works, we must
believe that raising the costs that are associated with a particular course of action makes
it increasingly unlikely that people will participate in the relevant form of behaviour.

In each of the judicial and administrative decisions referred to in this chapter (and in
every case in which a court imposes a penalty with the goal of achieving deterrence), the
courts assume that *deterrence works*. They assume that if they increase the costs that are
associated with a particular form of behaviour, they will decrease the likelihood that
people will engage in that behaviour. This reveals the courts' reliance on the assumption
of rationality. If deterrence works in the regulation of lawyers' ethical conduct—if
increasing the costs associated with unethical conduct lowers the likelihood that lawyers
will engage in unethical conduct—then lawyers *must* be weighing costs and benefits
when considering ethical choices. In other words, the assumption of rationality must be
accurate in the context of ethical choices. If lawyers do not consider the costs and
benefits of their actions when considering whether or not to behave unethically, then
increasing the costs associated with unethical behaviour (through the imposition of
penalties) should have no impact on such lawyers' ethical choices. Because courts and

---

14   270 F3d 578 (8th Cir. 2001).

15   [2002] LSBC 01 (Disciplinary Panel).

16   [2001] LSDD no. 40 (reproduced in chapter 2), at para. 27.

17   See also *Law Society of British Columbia v. Johnson*, [2001] LSDD no. 6 and *Law Society of Upper
      Canada v. Dyment*, [1995] LSDD 180.

18   [1995] LSDD no. 261, at para. 11.

regulators repeatedly act on the belief that deterrence works—that increased penalties do, in fact, reduce the likelihood that lawyers will engage in unethical actions—those courts and regulators must believe that lawyers' choices (even moral and ethical choices) are governed by subconscious computations of the costs and benefits flowing from competing possibilities. In other words, they assume that lawyers are rational when considering ethical choices.

It should come as no surprise that courts and regulators assume that people are rational when making ethical choices. If people were not rational, there would be little need for courts and regulators at all. Given our present state of knowledge, behaviour can be regulated only through the granting of benefits or the imposition of costs. We can grant benefits (such as rewards) in response to behaviour that we want to encourage; we can impose costs (such as fines, suspension from practice, or imprisonment) in response to behaviour that we wish to curtail. If people do not account for costs and benefits when considering how to behave, we cannot (through regulatory action) affect their choices at all. If people are irrational when considering ethical choices—if they do not make ethical choices by comparing costs and benefits—we are incapable (by regulatory action) of affecting the ethical choices people make. In the context of the regulation of lawyers' ethical choices, all of the money spent designing enforceable regulatory regimes, all of the money spent enforcing such regimes, and all of the money spent compensating judges, tribunals, and legislative drafters is spent without a purpose. Since we do not appear to regard expenditures on the regulation of lawyers' ethics as a waste of resources, we must admit that we accept that lawyers are rational when considering ethical choices. Indeed, we are so convinced that lawyers account for costs and benefits when considering ethical choices that we spend significant sums creating regulatory bodies for the purpose of modifying the costs and benefits flowing from unethical conduct.

Our review of the present practices of regulatory and judicial bodies reveals that all of these bodies—even those that do not purport to rely on economic principles—repeatedly act on the assumption that lawyers are rational when considering ethical choices. In other words, the assumption of rationality lies at the heart of current regulatory practices. As a result, the economic theory of legal ethics, with its assumption of rationality in the context of lawyers' ethical choices, simply relies on assumptions already made by courts and regulatory officials. If the assumption of rationality does not hold in the realm of lawyers' ethical choices, we have not merely discovered a problem with the economic theory of legal ethics. We have undermined the fundamental beliefs of every regulatory body charged with the task of governing lawyers' ethical choices. It is not merely the economic theory of legal ethics that stands or falls with the assumption of rationality. If the assumption of rationality is unwarranted, then all of our laws based on deterrence fall as well.

The goal of this section has been to respond to the objection that the assumption of rationality is unjustified. As we have seen, this objection can be answered in two ways: first, by pointing out the narrow, technical meaning of "rationality" in the context of an economic analysis, and second, by pointing out that the assumption of rationality lies at the heart of every regulatory regime; it is not merely a quirk of economics. We are compelled (by virtue of the limitations of our regulatory powers) to assume that lawyers are rational—whether or not we choose to accept an economic account of legal ethics. As a result, while we need not discount the skeptical views of metaphysicians, we must nonetheless accept the basic assumption of rationality if we hope to regulate human behaviour at all.

As we noted at the outset of this chapter, the assumption of rationality is only one of two principal objections to the economic account of legal ethics. The second objection, known as the "indeterminacy objection," is discussed throughout the remainder of this chapter.

III. The Indeterminacy Objection

A. Introduction to Indeterminacy

The second major objection to ethinomics—known as the indeterminacy objection—has nothing to do with the economic branch of ethinomics, but relates instead to our theory's status as a theory of ethical choice. According to those who raise the indeterminacy objection, it is *impossible* to generate a coherent theory of ethics. Because terms such as "ethical" and "unethical" are *indeterminate*—that is, they carry no settled meaning—any attempt to design a system explaining the nature of ethical choices is an exercise in futility. If the objective of explaining ethical choices is an unattainable goal, ethinomics is a theory without a point.

The basis of the indeterminacy objection is easy to understand.[19] The indeterminists hold that the language in which ethics and morality is discussed (including words such as "ethical" and "unethical," or "moral" and "immoral") carries no determinate meaning. Instead, such words are shifting, nebulous variables that defy clear definition. Starting from this premise, the indeterminists conclude that statements such as "cannibalism is unethical" or "voluntarism is ethical" are incapable of conveying verifiable information. The statement "cannibalism is unethical," for example, can never be shown (by empirical evidence) to be either true or false. It may seem true to *some readers*, who believe (before encountering this sentence) that cannibalism is inadvisable and that it conforms to the reader's preconceived idea of what it means to be unethical. To other readers, perhaps those who come from societies in which cannibalism is practised, the statement may *seem* false. It is impossible, by force of reason or empirical investigation, to verify the statement "cannibalism is unethical" without making a value judgment that is internal to the reader. There is no physical measurement of "unethical" or "ethical" to which the subject of the sentence can be compared, no objective arbiter of what it means to be ethical in all contexts. If the sentence carries any meaning at all, it is (at most) the author's expression of his or her dislike of the practice of consuming human flesh, or perhaps a command to the reader to stop eating humans—the statement "cannabalism is unethical" may be equivalent to the phrase "don't eat people!"—it is neither true nor false, but simply an edict or command. That may tell us something about the author, but nothing at all about the nature of ethics or its relationship to particular kinds of action. According to indeterminists, all uses of ethical language fall prey to this critique: they are

---

19   For a more thoroughgoing account of indeterminacy in the context of *all language*—that is, an account that is not restricted to the impact of indeterminacy on the language of ethical theory—see Randal N. Graham, *Statutory Interpretation: Theory and Practice* (Toronto: Emond Montgomery, 2001), chapter 2.

incapable of settling the meaning of ethical terms in a way that makes it possible to verify or disprove moral statements. In short, because words such as "ethical" and "unethical" are completely indeterminate, "it is impossible to find a criterion for determining the validity of ethical judgments."[20]

The indeterminacy that is inherent in ethical statements can be revealed through a simple example. Consider a debate between two people who disagree about abortion. One debater may utter the statement "abortion is ethical." The other may disagree, stating that "abortion is unethical." How can you verify one claim or disprove the other? Any attempt to do so falls back on further indeterminate claims: "it is good for women to have power over their bodies," or "it is immoral to stop the beating of a living, foetal heart." Statements of this nature cannot be verified by appeals to empirical data. Indeed, they rely on no data at all; no verifiable truths that can be used to prove the content of the relevant moral statements. We might agree, for example, that abortion allows women to have control over their bodies, but we are unable to prove whether that degree of control is "good." Similarly, we may agree that abortion stops a beating foetal heart, but we cannot prove that stopping a foetal heart counts as "immoral." Claims concerning the morality of any form of conduct rely on the author's own beliefs rather than any external fact. Because they rely on the author's subjectively held values and are couched in amorphous language such as "ethical" and "moral," statements such as "X is ethical" or "Y is moral" have no verifiable meanings. Any theory that relies on similar statements— any theory that purports to generate moral or ethical truths—is accordingly doomed to failure.

Over the last 300 years, a large proportion of ethical scholarship has focused on the notion of indeterminacy. Writing in 1789, for example, Bentham noted that ethical statements (such as "murder is unethical") carried no discernable meaning. In Bentham's view, a person making such a statement should consider the nature of the words contained within it:

> [L]et him examine and satisfy himself whether the principle he thinks he has found is really any separate intelligible principle; or whether it be not a mere principle in words, a kind of phrase, which at bottom expresses neither more nor less than the mere averment of his own unfounded sentiments.[21]

Similarly, Jean-Paul Sartre notes that ethical language is so nebulous that it lacks the power to govern human behaviour. According to Sartre:

> No general ethics can show you what is to be done; there are no omens in the world. The Catholics will reply, "But there are." Granted—but, in any case, I myself choose the meaning they have.[22]

---

20   Alfred Jules Ayer, "Language, Truth, and Logic," in Steven M. Cahn and Peter Markie, eds., *Ethics: History, Theory and Contemporary Issues*, 2d ed. (New York: Oxford University Press, 1998), 490.

21   Jeremy Bentham, "An Introduction to the Principles of Morals and Legislation," in Cahn and Markie, supra note 14, at 328.

22   Jean-Paul Sartre, "Existentialism Is a Humanism," in Cahn and Markie, supra note 20, at 448.

In other words, there are no knowable ethical precepts that are sufficiently verifiable that they are able to provide guidance to people faced with ethical choices. Words such as "ethical" and "unethical" are inescapably indeterminate, vulnerable to perpetual redefinition by those who use the terms. Their meaning is inherently subjective, indefinable, and incapable of conveying information with precision.

In recent years, the strongest proponents of the indeterminacy objection have been adherents to the emotivist school of thought. These are ethical scholars (led by A.J. Ayer) who believe that ethical statements (such as, "X is ethical") are nothing more than simple expressions of emotion. James Rachels summarizes emotivist scholarship as follows:

> What made emotivism more sophisticated than earlier versions of subjectivism was its analysis of moral language. The key idea exploited by the emotivists was that *not every utterance is meant to be true or false*. An imperative—"Don't do that!"—is neither true nor false. It does not convey information; rather, it gives an instruction about what is to be done. Similarly, a cheer—"Hurrah"—is not a statement of fact, not even the fact that we like something. It is merely a verbal manifestation of an attitude. According to the emotivists, ethical "statements" are like this. They are not used to state facts; they are, really, disguised imperatives or avowals. Thus, when someone says "Lying is wrong," it is as if he or she had said "Don't lie!" or "Lying—yech."[23]

In other words, statements such as "sleeping with a client is unethical" mean nothing more than "don't sleep with your clients!" or "sleeping with clients—boo!" Such utterances are not subject to empirical verification. They simply convey instructions to the audience or express the author's privately held beliefs. In short, there is no *truth* inherent in moral claims—they are simply avowments or commands.

Not surprisingly, many moralists object to the emotivists' strident claims concerning the non-verifiable nature of ethical truths. Ayer responds to this objection as follows:

> Some moralists claim to settle the matter by saying that they "know" that their own moral judgments are correct. But such an assertion is of purely psychological interest, and has not the slightest tendency to prove the validity of any moral judgment. For dissentient moralists may equally well "know" that their ethical views are correct. And, as far as subjective certainty goes, there will be nothing to choose between them.[24]

Since there is no way to conclusively settle debates between competing ethical claims, Ayer concludes that there is little point in analyzing any ethical statement. According to Ayer:

> Fundamental ethical concepts are unanalyzable, inasmuch as there is no criterion by which one can test the validity of the judgments in which they occur … . For in saying that a certain type of action is right or wrong, I am not making any factual statement, not even a statement about my own state of mind. I am merely expressing certain moral sentiments. And the man who is ostensibly contradicting me is merely expressing his moral sentiments.

---

23   James Rachels, "Modern Ethical Theory," in Cahn and Markie, supra note 20, at 453.

24   Ayer, supra note 20, at 489.

So that there is plainly no sense in asking which of us is in the right. For neither of us is asserting a genuine proposition.[25]

Ayer concludes that

[t]he exhortations to moral virtue are not propositions at all, but ejaculations or commands which are designed to provoke the reader to action of a certain sort. Accordingly, they do not belong to any branch of philosophy or science.[26]

In short, *there are no moral truths* to be discovered. There is no moral Rosetta Stone to help us firmly define words such as "ethical" and "unethical" and no way of verifying or evaluating competing moral claims. On the contrary, moral claims are merely emotive ejaculations, designed to provoke specific actions rather than to generate meaningful information.

If the claims of indeterminists are correct—if there are no empirical facts underlying moral statements such as "sleeping with clients is unethical"—then any theory purporting to be a theory of ethics rests on shaky ground. To the extent that ethical theories invoke ostensibly indeterminate concepts such as "moral" and "ethical," those theories amount to nothing more than a series of unverifiable claims and exhortations. Ethinomics, as we have seen throughout this book, purports to be a theory of ethics. As a result, emotivists' claims, rooted in the indeterminacy objection, may have the power to undermine the basic tenets of ethinomics. The impact of the indeterminacy objection on the theory of ethinomics is discussed in the following section of this chapter.

B. Response

The indeterminacy objection does not reveal a flaw in ethinomics. On the contrary, it reveals one of ethinomics' greatest features. A core advantage of an *economic* account of legal ethics is that it does not insist on a settled, determinate meaning of moral language. The economic account of legal ethics does not require words such as "moral" and "immoral" or "ethical" and "unethical" in order to describe and regulate lawyers' professional conduct. Instead, ethinomics relies on verifiable quantities (such as economic costs and benefits) in its effort to account for lawyers' behaviour.

The power of ethinomics to design workable regulatory regimes without reliance on indeterminate concepts can be seen through a review of the examples used in chapters 1 through 4. Consider a random sampling of the various forms of conduct we have discussed throughout this book.

- *Breach of contract.* In chapter 1, we saw that harms flowing from breach of contract can be avoided by forcing contract breachers to compensate their victims through the payment of perfect expectation damages.
- *Violations of lawyers' oaths.* In chapters 1 and 3, we saw that violations of the Barristers Oath or Solicitors Oath could be regulated efficiently by forcing the oath breaker to bear whatever costs might flow from a breach of the relevant oath.

---

25   Ibid., at 489-90.
26   Ibid., at 488.

- *Breaches of confidentiality, impermissible withdrawal, theft of trust funds, and other breaches of professional codes.* In chapters 3 and 4, we saw that much of the harm flowing from violations of professional codes of conduct can be avoided through a compensatory model of regulation. Where the compensatory model of regulation fails to eliminate such harm, it can be supplemented by a punishment model of regulation that enhances social welfare and minimizes the relevant harm.

For every form of behaviour we have encountered, ethinomics is able to generate an appropriate method of dealing with the behaviour in a way that minimizes harm and encourages gains in social utility.[27] We achieve these key objectives without discussing the issue whether the relevant conduct counted as moral or ethical, or whether questions of morality even arise. The economic solution to breach of contract, for example, is the same whether one considers contractual breaches to be moral, immoral, or amoral. Regardless of the moral quality of a breach of contract, harm is minimized (and social welfare encouraged) where the contract breacher pays the victim expectation damages. Similarly, the economic solution to breaches of confidentiality does not require an assessment of the morality of a breach of confidence. To the extent that a lawyer imposes harm through a violation of confidentiality, that lawyer should be forced to redress the harm through compensation. Again, the question of whether the breach of confidence is an immoral form of conduct is immaterial. Regardless of the moral quality of the relevant conduct, the economic solution remains the same. The economic solution to any form of cost-imposing behaviour deftly avoids the question of whether or not the behaviour is immoral. Instead, questions of ethics and morality are left to moral philosophers. Ethinomics simply gets on with the job of minimizing harm and promoting overall gains in social utility.

By focusing on the quantifiable (and empirically verifiable) notion of economic harm, ethinomics works to minimize the quantifiable harms that are generated by individual choices. Where an act imposes costs, ethinomics can determine how to cope with the relevant action and minimize whatever harm the action causes. These goals are achieved without regard for the moral quality of the relevant form of behaviour. Without reliance on the indeterminate language of ethical theory, ethinomics helps us minimize the harms that flow from *any* form of conduct. That should make even the strictest of the moral philosophers grin. Indeed, if the advocates of the indeterminacy objection are correct, ethinomics may represent the *only* workable form of ethical theory. By (1) focusing on quantifiable economic harms, and (2) eschewing reliance on indeterminate concepts such as moral and immoral, an economic account of ethical systems provides a practical and achievable solution to the problem of social harm and encourages us to maximize the welfare of the community. What more can one demand of a theory of lawyers' professional conduct?

---

27 Recall that, in some instances, the optimal method of regulation is to refrain from acting. If any active form of regulation would cause more harm than the behaviour we hope to curtail, the cost-imposing behaviour should be allowed to continue. Ethinomics reminds us that we should be unwilling to use a cure that is more costly than the disease.

IV. Conclusion

Throughout this chapter, we have confronted the two principal objections to the economic theory of legal ethics—the rationality objection (which relates to the economic branch of our theory) and the indeterminacy objection (which relates to the "ethical" branch of ethinomics). As we have seen, neither objection truly reveals a flaw in the economic theory of legal ethics. On the contrary, each demonstrates its value. Our response to the rationality objection, for example, demonstrated that *all* attempts to regulate moral or ethical conduct are compelled to rely on the assumption that humans are governed by rational choice—that all human decisions, even decisions relating to moral and ethical issues, are rooted in subconscious computations of competing costs and benefits. All models of regulation, even those that do not purport to rely on economic concepts, are premised on the belief that people are governed by rationality. Economics merely makes this notion explicit and gets on with the job of minimizing the costs of human behaviour.

Our response to the indeterminacy objection was even more instructive. Through an analysis of the notion of indeterminacy, we discovered one of the fundamental benefits of the economic theory of legal ethics. While other ethical theories rely on indeterminate notions such as moral and immoral, an economic theory avoids such notions and moves on to minimize costs. By focusing on quantifiable economic costs, ethinomics provides a mechanism to increase social welfare without reliance on the indeterminate terms of ethical theory. In short, by avoiding reliance on good and evil or ethical and unethical, ethinomics provides a theory of human behaviour that can help us avoid the harms that may be generated by individual choices, leading us toward the goal of maximizing social welfare.

Without starting from a position of indeterminacy—such as reliance on vague notions of good and evil—the economic account of legal ethics has confirmed some of our moral intuitions. In chapters 3 and 4, we saw that punishment should be carefully tailored to fit offences, victims should be fully compensated for the harms they suffer, harm to society should be minimized, and gains in social welfare should be encouraged. Each of these seemingly moral conclusions flows from an economic perspective—a perspective grounded in verifiable facts and simple assumptions. By starting with a series of observations and reliable assumptions concerning the way that humans behave, we have created a thorough account of legal ethics—an account that is firmly grounded in observable fact and logic. The fact that we have managed to confirm our basic moral intuitions along the way says something about the value of those intuitions, but even more about the value of economics. While our moral intuitions appear (in many cases) to be correct, economics provides a way of *reasoning toward* those intuitions, rather than simply moralizing from them. We do not begin by assuming that we have reliable knowledge of good and evil or the ability to define the essential nature of morals or ethics. Instead, we simply assume that people are rational and act to further their own interests. Equipped with no more than these two meagre assumptions and a willingness to follow them to their logical conclusions, we have managed to cobble together a coherent and cohesive theory of human behaviour—a fairly healthy return on our investment. Starting with only a few simple assumptions and a deep commitment to logic, ethinomics can (1) provide us with the ability to account for each of the moral and ethical choices lawyers make, and (2) help us design a rational regulatory system with the effect of minimizing the harms that flow from ethical breaches. It is difficult to see how one could object to such a theory.

Professional Regulation

Introduction to Part II

Part I of this book presented an economic account of legal ethics. Pursuant to this theory, ethical decisions are portrayed as economic choices. When deciding whether or not to take an ethically dubious course of action, rational decision makers consider the possible consequences, rank their various preferences, and perform a subconscious cost–benefit calculation, ultimately selecting whatever action they believe will maximize utility. As we have seen, this form of decision making is an economic process, best evaluated through the use of economic tools. In demonstrating the economic theory of legal ethics, part I also described the traditional theories that have been used to describe and explain lawyers' ethical choices. In particular, chapter 3 reviewed the neutral-agent and neutral-conduit models of legal ethics, pointing out why those traditional models are inadequate accounts of the complex ethical world that lawyers inhabit.

Part II applies the theories of part I to specific ethical obligations of lawyers. In particular, part II focuses on (1) the ethical duties relating to integrity and confidentiality (chapter 6); (2) situations in which lawyers are permitted (or required) to disclose or use a client's information (chapter 7); (3) ethical duties relating to conflicts of interest (chapter 8); and (4) lawyers' ethical obligations relating to advocacy (discussed in chapter 9).

CHAPTER SIX

Integrity and Confidentiality

I. Introduction to Specific Ethical Duties

In many jurisdictions, lawyers' ethical duties are spelled out in codes of conduct. In Canada, for example, lawyers are typically governed by binding codes of conduct promulgated by the law society of the province in which the lawyer practises. In most cases, these codes are modelled on the Canadian Bar Association's Code of Professional Conduct ("the CBA Code"), a non-binding code that purports to establish (or at least describe) the ethical obligations that are owed by legal professionals. Similar non-binding codes (on which binding codes are based) are found in other jurisdictions. In the United States, for example, the American Bar Association ("the ABA") has promulgated model rules of professional conduct on which many American states have based their own binding codes.[1]

The CBA Code begins by setting out the most general of the lawyer's ethical duties. This duty, commonly known as the duty of Integrity, is the fundamental ethical obligation from which many other ethical duties flow. Chapter I of the CBA Code provides (in part) as follows:

> The lawyer must discharge with integrity all duties owed to clients, the court, other members of the profession and the public.

According to the CBA's official commentaries regarding the lawyer's duty of integrity, "[i]ntegrity is the fundamental quality of any person who seeks to practise as a member of the legal profession." The commentary further provides that "[i]f personal integrity is lacking, the lawyer's usefulness to the client and reputation within the profession will be destroyed regardless of how competent the lawyer may be."[2] Finally, the commentary notes that "[t]he principle of integrity is a key element of each rule of the Code."[3] In other words, the duty of integrity is the cornerstone of the lawyer's ethical duties, providing the foundation upon which other ethical obligations are built.

---

1   Binding codes refer to codes of conduct that create binding ethical obligations, the breach of which can give rise to professional sanctions.

2   Canadian Bar Association Code of Professional Conduct, chapter I, commentary.

3   Ibid.

The foundational nature of the duty of integrity is made particularly clear in Ontario's *Rules of Professional Conduct*. Indeed, Ontario's rules do not purport to establish a separate duty of integrity, but choose instead to elevate integrity to the level of an over-arching principle designed to guide the interpretation and application of each of the lawyer's ethical duties. According to rule 1.03(1) of Ontario's *Rules of Professional Conduct*:

> 1.03(1) These rules [namely, *all* the *Rules of Professional Conduct*] shall be interpreted in a way that recognizes that:
>
> (a) a lawyer has a duty to carry on the practice of law and discharge all responsibilities to clients, tribunals, the public, and other members of the profession honourably and with integrity;
>
> (b) a lawyer has special responsibilities by virtue of the privileges afforded the legal profession and the important role it plays in a free and democratic society and in the administration of justice, including a special responsibility to recognize the diversity of the Ontario community, to protect the dignity of individuals, and to respect human rights laws in force in Ontario
>
> (c) a lawyer has a duty to uphold the standards and reputation of the legal profession and to assist in the advancement of its goals, organizations, and institutions;
>
> (d) the rules are intended to express to the profession and to the public the high ethical ideals of the legal profession;
>
> (e) the rules are intended to specify the bases on which lawyers may be disciplined; and
>
> (f) rules of professional conduct cannot address every situation, and a lawyer should observe the rules in the spirit as well as in the letter.

As a result of these provisions, a lawyer's behaviour is held up to a general standard of integrity that requires lawyers to discharge each of their more specific ethical duties in a manner that is consistent with this overarching principle. Where a lawyer is alleged to have breached the rules of professional conduct, the content of those rules (as well as the offending lawyer's conduct) will be measured by reference to the general notion of integrity.

It is important to note that the duty of integrity may apply to far more than a lawyer's *professional* conduct. According to the CBA Code, chapter 1, commentary 3, for example, "questionable conduct on the part of the lawyer in either *private life or professional practice* will reflect adversely upon the lawyer, the integrity of the legal profession and the administration of justice as a whole" (emphasis added). It thus appears that a lawyer found to lack integrity in his or her personal life could be subjected to disciplinary action. Indeed, there are several cases in which lawyers *have* been disciplined as a result of a lack of integrity demonstrated by "deviant conduct" in the lawyer's personal life.[4]

The term "integrity" is not self-defining. Much like "good," "evil," "moral," "immoral," "ethical," and "unethical," "integrity" is an indeterminate word, seemingly incapable of providing clear guidance in the application of rules of professional conduct. Indeed, it is

---

4   See, for example, *Cwinn v. Law Society (Upper Canada)* (1980), 28 OR (2d) 61 (Div. Ct.). This case (and others like it) is discussed in more detail by Gavin MacKenzie in *Lawyers and Ethics: Professional Responsibility and Discipline*, 3d ed. (Toronto: Carswell, 2001), 26.8.

hard to see what the overarching principle of integrity adds to the more specific rules of professional conduct. At best, it may be nothing more than a harmless marketing statement, promoting the view that lawyers possess a desirable virtue. At its worst, the notion of integrity could be used to entrench a particular group's political ideology. It is not difficult to imagine a time when belonging to a particular political organization, exhibiting particular sexual preferences or practices, or adhering to the tenets of a particular religion might have been held to reflect poorly upon an individual's integrity, thus supporting an allegation of "conduct unbecoming a lawyer" and leading to the imposition of professional sanctions. Whenever an arbiter is empowered to evaluate another person's behaviour through the use of broad and indeterminate terms, that arbiter has the power to suffuse the relevant term with his or her own ideology, impregnating the term with unstated cultural norms and personal biases.[5] It is difficult to order one's affairs in response to terms that either (1) provide decision makers with no specific guidance, or (2) allow an arbiter to shape and mould those terms in response to unstated personal preferences or political ideologies.

As we have seen throughout this book, one of the virtues of an economic account of legal ethics is its ability to minimize our reliance on indeterminate terms. Rather than assessing a lawyer's behaviour with a view to determining whether that behaviour is "good," "ethical," "moral," or characterized by "integrity," an economic theory of legal ethics focuses on the notion of efficiency. Instead of asking whether the lawyer's behaviour measures up to the amorphous standard of integrity, an economic theory considers the nature and extent of costs imposed by the lawyer's behaviour, compares those costs to the benefits achieved by the relevant conduct, and determines whether the benefits of the act exceed its costs. By assessing a lawyer's conduct through the lens of economics, we are able to give meaning to otherwise indeterminate notions—perhaps an action counts as ethical where it maximizes social (rather than only personal) utility; perhaps a lawyer has integrity where he or she internalizes the costs of actions and pursues efficient forms of professional conduct. Through the use of economics, we can provide clearer guidance regarding the meaning and application of the rules of professional conduct, avoiding reliance on indeterminate terms such as "integrity" and "morality." The manner in which economic theory can help define specific ethical obligations is considered throughout part II of this book.

Happily, the amorphous nature of the word "integrity" has, in recent years, managed to work very little mischief in the application of lawyers' professional norms. Indeed, integrity seems to have become little more than a rhetorical device, invoked to damn or praise a lawyer's conduct when the relevant lawyer faces a claim that he or she has

---

5   Professor Constance Backhouse provided an excellent example of the potential for "ideological appropriation" in her analysis of the word "professionalism." According to Backhouse, professionalism has been used (historically) by the legal profession to exclude certain disadvantaged groups from the practice of law. Because professionalism has an indeterminate meaning, self-interested groups can appropriate that term to promote their own political ideology. Professor Backhouse's comments were presented in a speech and paper entitled "Gender and Race in the Practice of Law" at the First Colloquium on Professionalism hosted by the Chief Justice of Ontario's Advisory Committee on Professionalism (University of Western Ontario, October 20, 2003).

violated one of the more specific rules of professional conduct. Because the rule of integrity tends to be relegated to this purely supplementary role, it is best not to view it as a separate obligation of the lawyer. Instead, the principle of integrity (whatever it might entail) is best seen as a component of each of the more specific rules of professional conduct. As a result, the rule of integrity will not be given separate treatment in this text. Instead, it will be considered only in connection with more specific ethical obligations. The first of these specific obligations, the lawyer's duty of confidentiality, is the topic of the remainder of this chapter.

II. The Duty of Confidentiality

A. Introduction

Like the generic duty of integrity, the lawyer's duty of confidentiality is widely regarded as one of the defining features of the legal profession. The duty of confidentiality is considered one of the hallmarks of the lawyer's professional calling, providing for the foundation of trust and loyalty upon which the solicitor–client relationship is based.

The lawyer's duty of confidentiality is set out in chapter IV of the CBA Code. That chapter provides (in part):

> The lawyer has a duty to hold in strict confidence all information concerning the business and affairs of the client acquired in the course of the professional relationship, and should not divulge such information unless disclosure is expressly or impliedly authorized by the client, required by law or otherwise permitted or required by this Code.

This language is mirrored in several provincial codes of professional conduct.[6] For example, section 2.03(1) of Ontario's *Rules of Professional Conduct* provides as follows:

> A lawyer at all times shall hold in strict confidence all information concerning the business and affairs of the client acquired in the course of the professional relationship and shall not divulge any such information unless expressly or impliedly authorized by the client or required by law to do so.

In the United States, the American Bar Association's Model Rules of Professional Conduct set out the duty of confidentiality in rule 1.6:

> (a) A lawyer shall not reveal information relating to representation of a client unless the client consents after consultation, except for disclosures that are impliedly authorized in order to carry out the representation, and except as stated in paragraph (b).
>
> (b) A lawyer may reveal such information to the extent the lawyer reasonably believes necessary:
>
> > (1) to prevent the client from committing a criminal act that the lawyer believes is likely to result in imminent death or substantial bodily harm; or

---

6   See, for example, chapter 5 (rule 1) of the BC's *Professional Conduct Handbook*; section 3.06 of Quebec's *Code of Ethics of Advocates*; and chapter 4 of Manitoba's *Handbook of Professional Conduct*.

(2) to establish a claim or defense on behalf of the lawyer in a controversy between the lawyer and the client, to establish a defense to a criminal charge or civil claim against the lawyer based upon conduct in which the client was involved, or to respond to allegations in any proceeding concerning the lawyer's representation of the client.

These statements simply codify one of the legal profession's longstanding traditions: clients are entitled to expect that their lawyers will maintain the confidence of the client's private information. Where the lawyer violates the client's confidence, the lawyer departs from fundamental professional obligations, giving rise to the possibility of fines, civil liability, and removal of the lawyer's right to practise.[7]

B. Rationale

Why do we compel lawyers to abide by a duty of confidentiality? This duty has typically been explained by reference to the integrity (meaning "proper functioning," rather than "morality") of the adversary process. The duty of confidentiality is thought to assist in the courts' ability to generate reliable verdicts. The duty of confidentiality achieves this objective by ensuring that lawyers advise their clients and prepare their clients' cases based on a full appreciation of the facts relating to the client's needs. As Beverley Smith notes:

> The rationale underlying this duty which is expected of the lawyer by the client is a powerful but simple one. In order that the lawyer may do the best for the client within the bounds of the law applicable to the situation, the lawyer must know everything which is pertinent to the matter at hand. This may entail the revelation of facts which could be damaging to the client should they reach other ears. Unless granted some privilege to do otherwise the lawyer's lips are to be kept sealed as to *all* that passes between the lawyer and the client. This position of trust has usually the effect of encouraging the client to be candid in dealings with the client's legal advisor.[8]

Similarly, Proulx and Layton explain the rationale for the rule of confidentiality as follows:

> [T]he client who is assured of complete secrecy is more likely to reveal to his or her counsel all information pertaining to the case. The lawyer who is in possession of all relevant information is better able to advise the client and hence provide competent service. The client's legal rights are furthered, as is the truth-finding function of the adversarial system.[9]

If the lawyer is in possession of all the client's information, he or she is able to fully advise the client of all the relevant legal options. In adversarial proceedings (including cases involving criminal liability), the lawyer needs full information in order to uphold

---

7 The various remedies available for breach of the duty of confidentiality are reviewed in the cases dealt with in this chapter.

8 Beverley G. Smith, *Professional Conduct for Lawyers and Judges* (Fredericton, NB: Maritime Law Book, 2002).

9 Michel Proulx and David Layton, *Ethics and Canadian Criminal Law* (Toronto: Irwin Law, 2001), 170-71.

the client's legal rights. The central role that confidentiality plays in legal systems can be demonstrated through a simple example.

Example 6.1

Anna Topol stands accused of killing her spouse, Mitchell Smith. Mitchell was an abusive husband and father, frequently beating Anna and her two small children. Anna felt trapped in her relationship, unable to extricate herself and her children from their terrible family situation. On the night of November 5, when Mitchell returned drunk from a night on the town and began acting in a menacing, threatening manner, Anna shot him in the back. He died immediately.

Assume, for the purposes of this example, that the facts of Anna's case support a successful plea of self-defence based on battered spouse's syndrome. Further assume that Anna is unaware of the fact that her actions are legally justified by virtue of the doctrine of self-defence.

If Anna believes that any information she provides her lawyer may be used against her, she might be unwilling to provide her lawyer with accurate information concerning the crime with which she is charged. Indeed, Anna might be inclined to deny involvement in the killing of her husband—from Anna's perspective, this may appear to be the only way to avoid the imposition of criminal sanctions. If Anna simply denies involvement in the crime, forensic evidence may prove that she did kill her husband. This could result in a conviction, despite the fact that Anna's behaviour could have supported a valid defence. If Anna knows that information provided to her lawyer will be held in strict confidence, however, she can safely apprise the lawyer of the relevant information without fear that the lawyer will use that information against her interests. Armed with a thorough appreciation of the facts of Anna's case, the lawyer is fully equipped to argue the case in the manner that is most likely to lead to a just result. On the facts of this example, it is only through Anna's reliance on her lawyer's duty of confidentiality that the court is equipped to render the proper verdict (that is, the verdict that is "just," or the verdict that conforms with the applicable legal principles). As we can see through this example, courts may be more likely to learn the "truth," and therefore render reliable verdicts, where lawyers preserve the confidentiality of their clients' information.

What are the economic interests that are protected by the lawyer's duty of confidentiality? In individual cases, the most obvious interest protected is the privacy of the client. Lawyers come into possession of information that many clients consider awkward or embarrassing, and the client would lose utility if such information were disclosed. In more compelling cases, clients may lose opportunities or incur legal liabilities as a result of the lawyer's disclosure of the client's information. As we have seen in the above example, however, the interests of the client are not the only interests protected by the lawyer's duty of confidentiality. The duty of confidentiality (in the words of Proulx and Layton) furthers the "truth-finding function" of the courts.[10] Where lawyers violate

---

10   Ibid.

confidentiality, they undermine the public's willingness to provide lawyers with adequate information, ultimately jeopardizing the courts' ability to render reliable verdicts. Where the functioning of the judiciary is impaired, all members of the public lose a portion of the utility they have invested in the integrity and reliability of the legal system. As a result, a lawyer's departure from the obligation of confidentiality imposes a cost on every person who relies on the legal system.

Chapter 4 made it clear that certain forms of economic interests are difficult to protect through the use of a compensatory model of regulation. Specifically, chapter 4 demonstrated that a compensatory model is often inadequate in cases where (1) compensation is impossible in principle or in practice, or (2) there is a possibility that the actor responsible for imposing a cost will evade liability. In cases of this nature, the compensatory model must be replaced or supplemented with a model that relies on punitive sanctions. As we have seen, violations of confidentiality may give rise to harms that are not amenable to the goal of compensation. While the harm to the lawyer's client may be compensable through civil liability, the harm to the legal system is (in principle and in practice) hard to quantify for the purposes of a compensatory regime. More importantly, lawyers who violate confidentiality are (in many cases) able to avoid detection and liability: as we shall see throughout the cases in this chapter, there are many ways in which lawyers can evade detection and punishment for violations of confidentiality.[11] Where enforcement errors of this nature can occur—that is, where unethical lawyers avoid the need to compensate their victims—a compensatory model fails to provide efficient incentives. As a result, a compensatory model is inadequate (by itself) as a method of governing lawyers' use of clients' information. Instead, a supplementary punishment model is required, supplementing the requirement of compensation with punitive sanctions designed to deter lawyers from violating their ethical obligations.

When lawyers violate confidentiality, the laws of tort and contract will require the lawyer to compensate the victim of the breach of the lawyer's obligation. In order to make up for the failings of an exclusively compensatory regime, the law societies of various jursidictions supplement the law of tort and contract through the creation of a punitive regulatory regime. Where lawyers breach the duty of confidentiality, the aim of the Law Society is not simply to have those lawyers compensate their victims. The Law Society's goal is also to punish the lawyer to an extent that ensures that breaches of confidentiality are no longer in the lawyers' interests. The Law Society attempts to price breaches of confidentiality out of the market, making such breaches so expensive that lawyers would generally prefer to preserve the secrecy of their clients' information. In other words, in dealing with violations of confidentiality, the goal of the Law Society is deterrence.

When reviewing the cases that follow, consider the subconscious, ethical calculations pursued by the lawyers who are alleged to have violated their duty of confidentiality. In

---

11   The decision of the court in *Szarfer v. Chodos* (1986), 54 OR (2d) 663 (HCJ), discussed below in section IV, provides a perfect example. In that case, the lawyer's conduct was discovered only because the lawyer's client happened to stumble across the lawyer as the lawyer was making use of the client's confidential information. Had the client not encountered the lawyer at the relevant time, it is likely that the lawyer would have evaded detection.

some cases, these alleged violations are excused by the judiciary. Is economic theory able to explain these judicially approved breaches of confidentiality? Is it sensible to explain the duty of confidentiality by reference to economic notions, or should this duty be explained by reference to integrity and morality? How do the courts and the Law Society construct appropriate remedies when lawyers are found to have violated confidentiality? These and other questions are explored in the sections that follow.

III. Overview

The decision of the Supreme Court of Canada in *Smith v. Jones* (1999) (reproduced below) deals with the nature and extent of solicitor–client privilege. It is important to recognize that solicitor–client *privilege* is not the same as the lawyer's ethical duty of confidentiality. The lawyer's duty of confidentiality is much broader than solicitor–client privilege. As Proulx and Layton note:

> [C]rucial distinctions exist between a lawyer's ethical duty of confidentiality and legal–professional privilege. First, the privilege applies only in proceedings where the lawyer may be a witness or otherwise compelled to produce evidence relating to the client. The ethical rule of confidentiality is not so restricted, operating even where there is no question of any attempt to compel disclosure by legal process. Second, legal–professional privilege encompasses only matters communicated in confidence by the client, or by a third party for the dominant purpose of litigation. Once again, the rule of confidentiality is broader, covering all information acquired by counsel whatever its source. Third, the privilege applies to the communication itself, does not bar the adduction of evidence pertaining to the facts communicated if gleaned from another source, and is often lost where other parties are present during the communication. In contrast, the rule of confidentiality usually persists despite the fact that third parties know the information in question or the communication was made in the presence of others.[12]

As a result, the lawyer's duty of confidentiality is much broader in scope than solicitor–client (or legal–professional) privilege, encompassing all of the duties and information caught by solicitor–client privilege as well as a great deal more.

While the decision in *Smith v. Jones* deals with solicitor–client privilege, it is nonetheless particularly relevant to a discussion of lawyer–client confidentiality. The *Smith v. Jones* decision deals with the judicial creation of a public-safety exception to solicitor client privilege, allowing disclosure of information in cases when death or bodily harm may flow from a failure to divulge the information. If that exception exists, it has obvious implications for the lawyer's duty of confidentiality: if the lawyer is permitted (or required) to divulge the client's information in support of public safety, that information is no longer protected by the lawyer's duty of confidentiality.

The decision in *Smith v. Jones* is important for several reasons. First, it provides an excellent discussion of the rationale of both solicitor–client privilege and the lawyer's

---

12   Proulx and Layton, supra note 9, at 173. See also MacKenzie, supra note 4, at 3-3.

duty of confidentiality. Second, it discusses the circumstances in which the lawyer's duty of confidentiality must yield to competing policy concerns. Most importantly (for present purposes), the decision in *Smith v. Jones* shows the depth of the court's commitment to the lawyer's duty of confidentiality. Indeed, the court is reluctant to permit the disclosure of confidential information even where disclosure is needed to save a person from death or bodily harm. The reason for the court's reluctance to erode the duty of confidentiality flows from the view, noted above, that confidentiality is vital to the proper functioning of the legal system.

When reading the court's decision in *Smith v. Jones*, consider the following questions:

1. Is the court engaged in an economic analysis when it balances the duty of confidentiality against competing policy concerns?

2. Can the court's decision be explained by reference to the ethical equation developed in chapters 2 and 3? If so, what are the benefits to be gained by requiring (or permitting) disclosure? What are the costs?

3. If a lawyer disclosed a client's information in order to save another's life, would that lawyer be considered "unethical" under a standard conception of morality (whatever that might mean)? Can economic theory explain this moral judgment?

4. Is there any point in requiring confidentiality in cases in which disclosure could save a person's life? Could a penal sanction succeed in deterring an ethical lawyer from divulging client confidences if lives depended on the release of the information?

Smith v. Jones
[1999] 1 SCR 455

CORY J (L'Heureux-Dubé, Gonthier, McLachlin, Iacobucci, and Bastarache JJ concurring): The solicitor–client privilege permits a client to talk freely to his or her lawyer secure in the knowledge that the words and documents which fall within the scope of the privilege will not be disclosed. It has long been recognized that this principle is of fundamental importance to the administration of justice and, to the extent it is feasible, it should be maintained. Yet when public safety is involved and death or serious bodily harm is imminent, the privilege should be set aside. This appeal must determine what circumstances and factors should be considered and weighed in determining whether solicitor–client privilege should be set aside in the interest of protecting the safety of the public.

I. Factual Background

Solicitor–client privilege is claimed for a doctor's report. Pending the resolution of that claim the names of the parties involved have been replaced by pseudonyms. The appellant, "James Jones," was charged with aggravated sexual assault of a prostitute.

His counsel referred him to a psychiatrist, the respondent, "John Smith," for a forensic psychiatric assessment. It was hoped that it would be of assistance in the preparation of the defence or with submissions on sentencing in the event of a guilty plea. His counsel advised Mr. Jones that the consultation was privileged in the same way as a consultation with him would be. Dr. Smith interviewed Mr. Jones for 90 minutes on July 30, 1997. His findings are contained in an affidavit he submitted to the judge of first instance. They set out the basis for his belief that Mr. Jones poses a continuing danger to the public.

Dr. Smith reported that Mr. Jones described in considerable detail his plan for the crime to which he subsequently pled guilty. It involved deliberately choosing as a victim a small prostitute who could be readily overwhelmed. He planned to have sex with her and then to kidnap her. He took duct tape and rope with him, as well as a small blue ball that he tried to force into the woman's mouth. Because he planned to kill her after the sexual assault he made no attempt to hide his identity.

Mr. Jones planned to strangle the victim and to dispose of her body in the bush area near Hope, British Columbia. He was going to shoot the woman in the face before burying her to impede identification. He had arranged time off from his work and had carefully prepared his basement apartment to facilitate his planned sexual assault and murder. He had told people he would be going away on vacation so that no one would visit him and he had fixed dead bolts on all the doors so that a key alone would not open them.

Mr. Jones told Dr. Smith that his first victim would be a "trial run" to see if he could "live with" what he had done. If he could, he planned to seek out similar victims. He stated that, by the time he had kidnapped his first victim, he expected that he would be "in so deep" that he would have no choice but to carry out his plans.

On July 31, Dr. Smith telephoned Mr. Jones's counsel and informed him that in his opinion Mr. Jones was a dangerous individual who would, more likely than not, commit future offences unless he received sufficient treatment.

On September 24, 1997, Mr. Jones pled guilty to aggravated assault and the matter was put over for sentencing. Sometime after November 19, Dr. Smith phoned Mr. Jones's counsel to inquire about the proceedings. On learning that the judge would not be advised of his concerns, Dr. Smith indicated that he intended to seek legal advice and shortly thereafter commenced this action.

The *in camera* hearing took place in December 1997. Dr. Smith filed an affidavit describing his interview with Mr. Jones and his opinion based upon the interview. Mr. Jones filed an affidavit in response. On December 12, 1997, Henderson J ruled that the public safety exception to the law of solicitor–client privilege and doctor–patient confidentiality released Dr. Smith from his duties of confidentiality. He went on to rule that Dr. Smith was under a duty to disclose to the police and the Crown both the statements made by Mr. Jones and his opinion based upon them. Henderson J ordered a stay of his order to allow for an appeal and Mr. Jones promptly appealed the decision.

The Court of Appeal allowed the appeal but only to the extent that the mandatory order was changed to one permitting Dr. Smith to disclose the information to the Crown and police. The order was stayed to permit Mr. Jones to consider a further appeal. It also directed that pseudonyms be used, that proceedings be heard in camera and that the file remain sealed pending further order. This order is discussed in greater detail below. The sentencing of Mr. Jones on the aggravated assault charge was adjourned pending the outcome of this appeal.

II. Analysis

A.   The Nature of the Solicitor–Client Privilege

Both parties made their submissions on the basis that the psychiatrist's report was protected by solicitor–client privilege, and it should be considered on that basis. It is the highest privilege recognized by the courts. By necessary implication, if a public safety exception applies to solicitor–client privilege, it applies to all classifications of privileges and duties of confidentiality. It follows that, in these reasons, it is not necessary to consider any distinctions that may exist between a solicitor–client privilege and a litigation privilege.

The solicitor–client privilege has long been regarded as fundamentally important to our judicial system. Well over a century ago in *Anderson v. Bank of British Columbia* (1876), 2 Ch. D 644 (CA), at p. 649, the importance of the rule was recognized:

> The object and meaning of the rule is this; that as, by reason of the complexity and difficulty of our law, litigation can only be properly conducted by professional men, it is absolutely necessary that a man, in order to prosecute his rights or to defend himself from an improper claim, should have recourse to the assistance of professional lawyers … to use a vulgar phrase, that he should be able to make a clean breast of it to the gentleman whom he consults with a view to the prosecution of his claim, or the substantiating of his defence … that he should be able to place unrestricted and unbounded confidence in the professional agent, and that the communications he so makes to him should be kept secret, unless with his consent (for it is his privilege, and not the privilege of the confidential agent), that he should be enabled properly to conduct his litigation.

Clients seeking advice must be able to speak freely to their lawyers secure in the knowledge that what they say will not be divulged without their consent. It cannot be forgotten that the privilege is that of the client, not the lawyer. The privilege is essential if sound legal advice is to be given in every field. It has a deep significance in almost every situation where legal advice is sought whether it be with regard to corporate and commercial transactions, to family relationships, to civil litigation or to criminal charges. Family secrets, company secrets, personal foibles and indiscretions all must on occasion be revealed to the lawyer by the client. Without this privilege clients could never be candid and furnish all the relevant information that must be provided to lawyers if they are to properly advise their clients. It is an element that is both integral and extremely important to the functioning of the legal system. It is because of the fundamental importance of the privilege that the onus properly rests upon those seeking to set aside the privilege to justify taking such a significant step.

As Lamer CJ stated in *R v. Gruenke*, [1991] 3 SCR 263, at p. 289, 67 CCC (3d) 289:

> The *prima facie* protection for solicitor–client communications is based on the fact that the relationship and the communications between solicitor and client are essential to the effective operation of the legal system. Such communications are inextricably linked with the very system which desires the disclosure of the communication.

The solicitor–client privilege was originally simply a rule of evidence, protecting communications only to the extent that a solicitor could not be forced to testify. Yet now it has evolved into a substantive rule. As Dickson J (as he then was) wrote in *Solosky v. The Queen*, [1980] 1 SCR 821, at p. 836, 105 DLR (3d) 745, 50 CCC (2d) 495, "Recent case law has taken the traditional doctrine of privilege and placed it on a new plane. Privilege is no longer regarded merely as a rule of evidence which acts as a shield to prevent privileged materials from being tendered in evidence in a court room."

Lamer J (as he then was) expanded on this statement in *Descôteaux v. Mierzwinski*, [1982] 1 SCR 860, at p. 875, 141 DLR (3d) 590, 70 CCC (2d) 385, when he discussed the content of this substantive rule:

> It is quite apparent that the Court in [*Solosky*] applied a standard that has nothing to do with the rule of evidence, the privilege, since there was never any question of testimony before a tribunal or court. The Court in fact, in my view, applied a substantive rule, without actually formulating it, and, consequently, recognized implicitly that the right to confidentiality, which had long ago given rise to a rule of evidence, had also since given rise to a substantive rule.
>
> It would, I think, be useful for us to formulate this substantive rule, as the judges formerly did with the rule of evidence; it could, in my view, be stated as follows:
>
> 1. The confidentiality of the communications between solicitor and client may be raised in any circumstances where such communications are likely to be disclosed without the client's consent.
> 2. Unless the law provides otherwise, when and to the extent that the legitimate exercise of a right would interfere with another person's right to have his communications with his lawyer kept confidential, the resulting conflict should be resolved in favour of protecting the confidentiality.
> 3. When the law gives someone the authority to do something which, in the circumstances of the case, might interfere with that confidentiality, the decision to do so and the choice of means of exercising that authority should be determined with a view to not interfering with it except to the extent absolutely necessary in order to achieve the ends sought by the enabling legislation.
> 4. Acts providing otherwise in situations under paragraph 2 and enabling legislation referred to in paragraph 3 must be interpreted restrictively.

As the British Columbia Court of Appeal observed, solicitor–client privilege is the privilege "which the law has been most zealous to protect and most reluctant to water down by exceptions." Quite simply it is a principle of fundamental importance to the administration of justice.

B. Limitations on Solicitor–Client Privilege

Just as no right is absolute so too the privilege, even that between solicitor and client, is subject to clearly defined exceptions. The decision to exclude evidence that would be both relevant and of substantial probative value because it is protected by the solicitor–client privilege represents a policy decision. It is based upon the importance to our legal system in general of the solicitor–client privilege. In certain circumstances, however, other societal values must prevail.

(1) Innocence of the Accused

One exception to solicitor–client privilege was set out in *R v. Dunbar and Logan* (1982), 68 CCC (2d) 13, 138 DLR (3d) 221 (Ont. CA). Martin JA, speaking for the court, ruled that solicitor–client privilege must yield to the right of accused persons to fully defend themselves. At p. 44 he wrote:

> No rule of policy requires the continued existence of the privilege in criminal cases when the person claiming the privilege no longer has any interest to protect, and when maintaining the privilege might screen from the jury information which would assist an accused.

The House of Lords recently considered this issue in *R v. Derby Magistrates' Court*, [1995] 4 All ER 526. It held that solicitor–client privilege was absolute and permanent. It could not be set aside even when to do so would allow an accused to present a full answer and defence to a criminal charge. With great respect, I prefer the reasoning of Martin JA. Despite the strength and importance of the privilege, it remains subject to certain well-defined and limited exceptions. These exceptions are not foreclosed and may be expanded in the future, for example, to protect national security. However the question of further exceptions need not be considered in these reasons. It is significant and worthy of observation that *Dunbar and Logan*, *supra*, was cited with approval by this Court in *R v. Seaboyer*, [1991] 2 SCR 577, at p. 607, 83 DLR (4th) 193, 66 CCC (3d) 321 (*per* McLachlin J), and in *A. (L.L.) v. B. (A.)*, [1995] 4 SCR 536, 130 DLR (4th) 422, 103 CCC (3d) 92, *sub nom. R v. Beharriell* (*per* L'Heureux-Dubé J). At para. 69 of *A. (L.L.) v. B. (A.)*:

> When the enforcement of a privilege means that the accused will be limited as to his or her right to make full answer and defence to criminal accusations, this Court has strongly tended to favour disclosure. ... Even the solicitor–client privilege, which has been elevated to a "fundamental civil and legal right" ... will be overridden to allow the accused to make full answer and defence to criminal charges[.] [Citations omitted.]

(2) Criminal Communications

A second exception to solicitor–client privilege was set out in *Descôteaux v. Mierzwinski*, *supra*. Lamer J for the Court, held that communications that are criminal in themselves (in this case, a fraudulent legal aid application) or that are intended to obtain legal advice to facilitate criminal activities are not privileged. At p. 893 this appears:

There are certain exceptions to the principle of the confidentiality of solicitor–client communications, however. Thus communications that are in themselves criminal or that are made with a view to obtaining legal advice to facilitate the commission of a crime will not be privileged, *inter alia*.

(3) The Public Safety Exception

In *Solosky*, *supra*, an inmate in a federal penitentiary asked this Court to make a declaration that all properly identified correspondence between solicitors and clients would be forwarded to their destinations without being opened. The inmates' privilege was in conflict with the *Penitentiary Act*, RSC 1970, c. P-6, and with Regulation 2.18 of the Penitentiary Services Regulations, which allowed the institution's director to censor any correspondence to the extent the censor considered necessary.

In his decision, Dickson J ruled that the inmate's privilege must yield when the safety of members of the institution is at risk. In his reasons at p. 840, he implicitly limited the solicitor–client privilege. He wrote:

> The result, as I see it, is that the Court is placed in the position of having to balance the public interest in maintaining the safety and security of a penal institution, its staff and its inmates, with the interest represented by insulating the solicitor–client relationship. Even giving full recognition to the right of an inmate to correspond freely with his legal adviser, and the need for minimum derogation therefrom, the scale must ultimately come down in favour of the public interest.

In certain circumstances, therefore, when the safety of the public is at risk the solicitor–client privilege may be set aside.

Courts in other jurisdictions have considered the issue of public safety exceptions to privilege, particularly in doctor–patient relationships. Obviously these cases do not deal with solicitor–client privilege. However they do support the position that other privileges are subject to the public interest. Moreover, they assist in determining the approach that should be taken to the consideration of the issue of privilege. Further these cases are useful in exploring certain issues that arise in this case, for example, how the victim class can be identified and how specific the potential victim or class of victims must be.

I would emphasize that these cases are not being examined with a view to establishing a tort duty on doctors to disclose confidential information when a public safety concern arises. That issue is not before the Court and must not be decided without a factual background and the benefit of argument.

(A) AMERICAN DECISIONS

In *Tarasoff v. Regents of University of California*, 551 P.2d 334 (Cal. 1976), the Supreme Court of California considered whether psychologists and psychiatrists have a duty to warn a potential victim when they were or should have been aware that a patient presented a serious danger to an identifiable person.

In that case a patient under the care of the respondents, a psychologist and two psychiatrists employed by the University of California, confessed to his psychologist his intention to kill a young girl, who was readily identifiable from his description. The psychologist contacted the police who questioned and briefly detained the patient but released him because he appeared rational. Two months later, the patient killed the girl. Her parents brought an action against the therapists for failure to warn them of the danger to their daughter.

Tobriner J of the California Supreme Court at p. 340 wrote:

> When a therapist determines, or pursuant to the standards of his profession should determine, that his patient presents a serious danger of violence to another, he incurs an obligation to use reasonable care to protect the intended victim against such danger. The discharge of this duty may require the therapist to take one or more of various steps, depending upon the nature of the case. Thus it may call for him to warn the intended victim or others likely to apprise the victim of the danger, to notify the police, or to take whatever other steps are reasonably necessary under the circumstances.

He went on to observe that the public interest in maintaining access to mental health treatment had to be balanced against the public interest in safety. At p. 346:

> We recognize the public interest in supporting effective treatment of mental illness and in protecting the rights of patients to privacy … and the consequent public importance of safeguarding the confidential character of psychotherapeutic communication. Against this interest, however, we must weigh the public interest in safety from violent assault.

At p. 347, he concluded:

> We conclude that the public policy favoring protection of the confidential character of patient-psychotherapist communications must yield to the extent to which disclosure is essential to avert danger to others. The protective privilege ends where the public peril begins.

In *Thompson v. County of Alameda*, 614 P.2d 728 (Cal. 1980), county officials were aware of the violent propensities of a juvenile delinquent in their care. These violent propensities were directed toward young children. The county released the juvenile delinquent from custody into the care of his mother. Within 24 hours, he had sexually assaulted and murdered the five-year-old who lived next door. The parents of the victim sued the county for, *inter alia*, failing to warn them. The Supreme Court dismissed their suit.

In reaching its decision, the majority of the court held that *Tarasoff, supra*, was distinguishable because the victim in *Tarasoff* "was the known and specifically foreseeable and identifiable victim of the patient's threats" (p. 734). Richardson J explained and distinguished the decision in *Tarasoff* in this way at p. 734:

> [W]e made it clear that the therapist has no general duty to warn of each threat. Only if he "does in fact determine, or under applicable professional standards reasonably should have determined, that a patient poses a serious danger of violence to others (does he bear) a duty to exercise reasonable care to protect the foreseeable victim of that danger." …
>
> Unlike *Johnson* [*v. State of California*, 447 P.2d 352 (Cal. 1968)] and *Tarasoff*, plaintiffs here have alleged neither that a direct or continuing relationship between them and

County existed through which County placed plaintiffs' decedent in danger, nor that
their decedent was a foreseeable or readily identifiable target of the juvenile offender's
threats.

The court thus explicitly limited the duty to warn to cases in which the danger to a
particular victim was foreseeable. At p. 735, Richardson J wrote:

Bearing in mind the ever present danger of parole violations, we nonetheless conclude
that public entities and employees have no affirmative duty to warn of the release of an
inmate with a violent history who made nonspecific threats of harm directed at nonspecific victims.

In California, the duty to warn was thus restricted to cases in which specific threats of
harm were directed against specific victims.

This position was reiterated in *Brady v. Hopper*, 570 F. Supp. 1333 (D. Colo. 1983).
James Brady and two others were suing Dr. John Hopper, John Hinckley's psychiatrist, in tort for the injuries they suffered during Hinckley's attempt to assassinate
President Reagan. The court dismissed their claim, finding that Hinckley had made
no threats upon which a duty to warn could be based. Moore J wrote at p. 1339,
"Nowhere in the complaint are there allegations that Hinckley made any threats regarding President Reagan, or indeed that he ever threatened anyone." It was determined that the duty to warn did not arise until such time as both the threat and the
possible victim could be identified. Something more than a merely speculative risk
of harm to unidentifiable persons was necessary (at p. 1338):

[O]nce the patient verbalizes his intentions and directs his threats to identifiable victims,
then the possibility of harm to third persons becomes foreseeable, and the therapist has
a duty to protect those third persons from the threatened harm.

The reasons in *Brady v. Hopper* made it clear that the duty to warn should not be
interpreted in such a wide and encompassing manner that therapists would become
responsible for all their patients' violent actions. Such a test would be unreasonable
and upset the balance between public safety and the importance to society of cultivat-
ing confidential relationships. Moore J wrote at p. 1339: "In my opinion, the 'specific threats to specific victims' rule states a workable, reasonable, and fair boundary
upon the sphere of a therapist's liability to third persons for the acts of their patients."

There is much to commend these well-reasoned American decisions. Yet they lead
me to believe that two observations should be made. First, it will not always be necessary to identify a specific individual as the victim. Rather it may be sufficient to
engage the duty to warn if a class of victims, such as little girls under five living in a
specific area, is clearly identified. Second, although Moore J speaks of the patient
"verbaliz[ing] his intentions," I believe it is more appropriate to speak of a person
making known his or her intentions. While speech is perhaps the most common means
of making intentions known, it is certainly not the only manner of indicating a clear
intention. It could be accomplished soundlessly yet with brutal clarity by thrusting a
knife through a photograph of the intended victim.

(B) UNITED KINGDOM DECISIONS

The leading case in the United Kingdom on balancing the duty of confidentiality and the duty to disclose is *W. v. Egdell*, [1990] 1 All ER 835 (CA). Although the facts differ somewhat from this case, enough similarities exist to make the reasoning set out in the two concurring judgments helpful to the considerations that must be given to the case at bar. In that case W. pled guilty to manslaughter after committing a series of killings. As a result of a finding of diminished responsibility he was confined to a mental institution. Ten years later, he applied pursuant to the appropriate regulations for a conditional discharge, or a transfer to a regional secure unit. To this end, through his solicitors, W. consulted Dr. Egdell, a psychiatrist, who was to report on his mental state. His report did not support W.'s application for transfer. Rather he expressed grave concerns regarding W.'s lack of remorse and his continuing interest in homemade bombs and fireworks. As a result, W. withdrew his application.

Shortly thereafter, Dr. Egdell telephoned the tribunal that was to review W.'s application to ask whether it had received a copy of his report. He learned that it had not and that the application had been withdrawn. He telephoned W.'s solicitors for permission to forward his report to the assistant medical director of the hospital in which W. was incarcerated and was refused. Nonetheless, Dr. Egdell forwarded his report to the hospital, which then forwarded it to the Home Office. Both of these copies were sent without W.'s permission or knowledge.

By chance, several days later W.'s file was due for a three-year review under the *Mental Health Act*. It was then that his solicitors learned that Dr. Egdell's report had been forwarded to the hospital. W. began proceedings, seeking an injunction to prevent the mental health review tribunal from disclosing or considering Dr. Egdell's report, for the delivery of all copies of the report to him, and for damages for breach of the duty of confidence.

In their concurring judgments, Sir Stephen Brown P and Bingham LJ affirmed the trial judge's ruling dismissing W.'s suit. Bingham LJ said at p. 848, "[T]he law treats such duties [of confidentiality] not as absolute but as liable to be overridden where there is held to be a stronger public interest in disclosure." Both justices agreed with the trial judge that the threshold for disclosure was met. The harm that could result if W.'s mental illnesses were not adequately recognized and treated was serious, and the displacing of doctor–patient confidentiality was justified in light of the existing circumstances. The fact that W. had already committed murder was obviously significant. Sir Stephen Brown P wrote at p. 846:

> The balance of public interest clearly lay in the restricted disclosure of vital information to the director of the hospital and to the Secretary of State who had the onerous duty of safeguarding public safety.
>
> In this case the number and nature of the killings by W must inevitably give rise to the gravest concern for the safety of the public.

In the United Kingdom the duty on a doctor not to disclose is never absolute. Further, the duty to disclose must be evaluated in the context of the existing circumstances and the specific facts presented.

C. The Public Safety Exception and Solicitor–Client Privilege

The foregoing review makes it clear that even the fundamentally important right to confidentiality is not absolute in doctor–patient relationships, and it cannot be absolute in solicitor–client relationships: *Solosky, supra*. When the interest in the protection of the innocent accused and the safety of members of the public is engaged, the privilege will have to be balanced against these other compelling public needs. In rare circumstances, these public interests may be so compelling that the privilege must be displaced. Yet the right to privacy in a solicitor–client relationship is so fundamentally important that only a compelling public interest may justify setting aside solicitor–client privilege.

Danger to public safety can, in appropriate circumstances, provide the requisite justification. It is significant that public safety exceptions to the solicitor–client privilege are recognized by all professional legal bodies within Canada. See, for example, Chapter 5, s. 12, of the British Columbia Professional Conduct Handbook:

> **Disclosure to prevent a crime**
>
> 12. A lawyer may disclose information received as a result of a solicitor–client relationship if the lawyer has reasonable grounds to believe that the disclosure is necessary to prevent a crime involving death or serious bodily harm to any person.

See as well the even broader Rule 4.11 of the Law Society of Upper Canada's Professional Conduct Handbook.

Quite simply society recognizes that the safety of the public is of such importance that in appropriate circumstances it will warrant setting aside solicitor–client privilege. What factors should be taken into consideration in determining whether that privilege should be displaced?

(1) Determining When Public Safety Outweighs Solicitor–Client Privilege

There are three factors to be considered: First, is there a clear risk to an identifiable person or group of persons? Second, is there a risk of serious bodily harm or death? Third, is the danger imminent? Clearly if the risk is imminent, the danger is serious.

These factors will often overlap and vary in their importance and significance. The weight to be attached to each will vary with the circumstances presented by each case, but they all must be considered. As well, each factor is composed of various aspects, and, like the factors themselves, these aspects may overlap and the weight to be given to them will vary depending on the circumstances of each case. Yet as a general rule, if the privilege is to be set aside the court must find that there is an imminent risk of serious bodily harm or death to an identifiable person or group.

(A) CLARITY

What should be considered in determining if there is a clear risk to an identifiable group or person? It will be appropriate and relevant to consider the answers a particular case may provide to the following questions: Is there evidence of long-range planning? Has a method for effecting the specific attack been suggested? Is there a prior history of violence or threats of violence? Are the prior assaults or threats of violence similar to that which was planned? If there is a history of violence, has the violence increased in severity? Is the violence directed to an identifiable person or group of persons? This is not an all-encompassing list. It is important to note, however, that as a general rule a group or person must be ascertainable. The requisite specificity of that identification will vary depending on the other factors discussed here.

The specific questions to be considered under this heading will vary with the particular circumstances of each case. Great significance might, in some situations, be given to the particularly clear identification of a particular individual or group of intended victims. Even if the group of intended victims is large, considerable significance can be given to the threat if the identification of the group is clear and forceful. For example, a threat, put forward with chilling detail, to kill or seriously injure children five years of age and under would have to be given very careful consideration. In certain circumstances it might be that a threat of death directed toward single women living in apartment buildings could in combination with other factors be sufficient in the particular circumstances to justify setting aside the privilege. At the same time, a general threat of death or violence directed to everyone in a city or community, or anyone with whom the person may come into contact, may be too vague to warrant setting aside the privilege. However, if the threatened harm to the members of the public was particularly compelling, extremely serious and imminent, it might well be appropriate to lift the privilege. See in this regard *Egdell, supra*. All the surrounding circumstances will have to be taken into consideration in every case.

In sum, the threatened group may be large but if it is clearly identifiable then it is a factor—indeed an essential factor—that must be considered together with others in determining whether the solicitor–client privilege should be set aside. A test that requires that the class of victim be ascertainable allows the trial judge sufficient flexibility to determine whether the public safety exception has been made out.

(B) SERIOUSNESS

The "seriousness" factor requires that the threat be such that the intended victim is in danger of being killed or of suffering serious bodily harm. Many persons involved in criminal justice proceedings will have committed prior crimes or may be planning to commit crimes in the future. The disclosure of planned future crimes without an element of violence would be an insufficient reason to set aside solicitor–client privilege because of fears for public safety. For the public safety interest to be of sufficient importance to displace solicitor–client privilege, the threat must be to occasion serious bodily harm or death.

It should be observed that serious psychological harm may constitute serious bodily harm, as this Court held in *R v. McCraw*, [1991] 3 SCR 72, at p. 81, 66 CCC (3d) 517:

> So long as the psychological harm substantially interferes with the health or well-being of the complainant, it properly comes within the scope of the phrase "serious bodily harm." There can be no doubt that psychological harm may often be more pervasive and permanent in its effect than any physical harm.

(C) IMMINENCE

The risk of serious bodily harm or death must be imminent if solicitor–client communications are to be disclosed. That is, the risk itself must be serious: a serious risk of serious bodily harm. The nature of the threat must be such that it creates a sense of urgency. This sense of urgency may be applicable to some time in the future. Depending on the seriousness and clarity of the threat, it will not always be necessary to impose a particular time limit on the risk. It is sufficient if there is a clear and imminent threat of serious bodily harm to an identifiable group, and if this threat is made in such a manner that a sense of urgency is created. A statement made in a fleeting fit of anger will usually be insufficient to disturb the solicitor–client privilege. On the other hand, imminence as a factor may be satisfied if a person makes a clear threat to kill someone that he vows to carry out three years hence when he is released from prison. If that threat is made with such chilling intensity and graphic detail that a reasonable bystander would be convinced that the killing would be carried out the threat could be considered to be imminent. Imminence, like the other two criteria, must be defined in the context of each situation.

In summary, solicitor–client privilege should only be set aside in situations where the facts raise real concerns that an identifiable individual or group is in imminent danger of death or serious bodily harm. The facts must be carefully considered to determine whether the three factors of seriousness, clarity, and imminence indicate that the privilege cannot be maintained. Different weights will be given to each factor in any particular case. If after considering all appropriate factors it is determined that the threat to public safety outweighs the need to preserve solicitor–client privilege, then the privilege must be set aside. When it is, the disclosure should be limited so that it includes only the information necessary to protect public safety. See in this respect *Descôteaux, supra*, at p. 891.

(2) Extent of Disclosure

The disclosure of the privileged communication should generally be limited as much as possible. The judge setting aside the solicitor–client privilege should strive to strictly limit disclosure to those aspects of the report or document which indicate that there is an imminent risk of serious bodily harm or death to an identifiable person or group. In undertaking this task consideration should be given to those portions of the report which refer to the risk of serious harm to an identifiable group; that the risk is serious in that it involves a danger of death or serious bodily harm; and that the serious risk is imminent in the sense given to that word in para. 84 above. The requirement that the disclosure be limited must be emphasized. For example, if, a report contained references to criminal behaviour that did not have an imminent risk of serious bodily harm but disclosed, for example, the commission of crimes of fraud, counterfeiting or the sale of stolen goods, those references would necessarily be deleted.

D. Application of the Public Safety Exception to Solicitor–Client Privilege to the Case at Bar

(1) Clarity

Would a reasonable observer, given all the facts for which solicitor–client privilege is sought, consider the potential danger posed by Mr. Jones to be clear, serious, and imminent? The answer must, I think, be in the affirmative. According to Dr. Smith's affidavit, the plan described by Mr. Jones demonstrated a number of the factors that should be considered in determining the clarity of the potential danger. They are the clear identification of the victim group, the specificity of method, the evidence of planning, and the prior attempted or actual acts that mirror the potential act of threatened future harm.

It is apparent that Mr. Jones had planned in considerable detail attacks on prostitutes on Vancouver's Downtown Eastside. He had gathered materials together that he planned to use to achieve his ultimate goal of forcing a prostitute to become his "sex slave" before killing her. He had arranged for vacation time from his job and had modified his basement apartment to ensure that no one else could enter. Mr. Jones had proceeded so far as to take rope and duct tape with him and had planned to shoot the intended victim in the face to obliterate her identity. Perhaps most important, he had called the initial assault to which he pled guilty a "trial run." These factors should be considered together with Dr. Smith's diagnosis of Mr. Jones, namely that he suffered a paraphiliac disorder with multiple paraphilias (in particular, sexual sadism), personality disorder with mixed features, and some antisocial features and drug abuse difficulty. The original planning and the prior attack on a prostitute emphasize the potential risk of serious bodily harm or death to prostitutes in the Downtown Eastside of Vancouver.

Although Mr. Jones attempted to explain his failure to seek treatment for fear of a longer sentence and the danger he would be exposed to in prison, this does not affect the gravity of the threatened attack on prostitutes. The combination of the factors referred to in the paragraph above meets the standard of clarity necessary to set aside solicitor–client privilege. The potential victim or group of victims is identifiable. Mr. Jones had already acted once in committing the crime for which he is waiting to be sentenced. It is clear that he intended to act again. The risk of serious bodily harm or death was readily apparent and the group of victims was readily identifiable. The harm potentially caused was of the utmost gravity.

(2) Seriousness

The seriousness of the potential harm, a sexually sadistic murder, is clearly sufficient. The fact that Mr. Jones has after careful and detailed planning already committed an assault upon a prostitute supports the finding that the potential harm caused would be extremely serious.

(3) Imminence

The most difficult issue to resolve is whether the risk of serious bodily harm can be termed "imminent." Mr. Jones was arrested on September 17, 1996, for the assault he had committed three days earlier. He consulted Dr. Smith on July 30, 1997. Dr. Smith contacted Mr. Jones's counsel the following day to inform him that, in Dr. Smith's opinion, Mr. Jones was a dangerous individual. About three months later, some 14 months after Mr. Jones's arrest, Dr. Smith telephoned Mr. Jones's counsel again and learned that his (Dr. Smith's) concerns would not be addressed in the sentencing hearing. He then began these legal proceedings. Mr. Jones has been in custody since December 15, 1997, pursuant to the order of Henderson J. Mr. Jones was thus at liberty from September 14, 1996, to December 15, 1997, a period of almost 15 months. During that time he did not carry out his plan to attack and kill another prostitute. Moreover, Mr. Jones has not carried out a series of attacks over a period of time, which would lead to the conclusion that another attack was imminent. He has been charged and convicted of only one incident.

No evidence was adduced as to whether Dr. Smith considered that a future attack was imminent. It is noteworthy that, first, he waited over three months to contact Mr. Jones's counsel. Second, there is no evidence that he believed it was probable Mr. Jones would commit a serious attack in the near future. Yet it must be remembered that Dr. Smith did take it upon himself to call Mr. Jones's counsel regarding the sentencing hearing. Even more significantly, Dr. Smith undertook these proceedings so that his report and opinion might be considered in the sentencing of Mr. Jones.

There are two important factors that indicate that the threat of serious bodily harm was indeed imminent. First, Mr. Jones admitted that he had breached his bail conditions by continuing to visit the Downtown Eastside where he knew prostitutes could be found. Second, common sense would indicate that after Mr. Jones was arrested, and while he was awaiting sentence, he would have been acutely aware of the consequences of his actions. This is of particular significance in light of his fear of being attacked while he was in jail.

Let us assume that the evidence as to imminence of the danger may not be as clear as might be desired. Nonetheless, there is some evidence of imminence. Furthermore, the other factors pertaining to clarity, the identifiable group of victims, and the chilling evidence of careful planning, when taken together, indicate that the solicitor–client privilege must be set aside for the protection of members of the public.

The judge of first instance very properly limited disclosure of Dr. Smith's affidavit to those portions of it which indicated that there was an imminent risk of death or serious bodily harm to an identifiable group comprising prostitutes located in the Downtown Eastside of Vancouver. In light of these conclusions, the solicitor–client privilege attaching to Dr. Smith's report, to the extent provided by the order of Henderson J, must be set aside.

E. Appropriate Procedures To Adopt

Dr. Smith chose to bring a legal action for a declaration that he was entitled to disclose the information he had in his possession in the interests of public safety. However, this is not the only manner in which experts may proceed. Although it is true that this procedure may protect the expert from legal consequences, there may not always be time for such an action. In whatever action is taken by the expert, care should be exercised that only that information which is necessary to alleviate the threat to public safety is revealed.

It is not appropriate in these reasons to consider the precise steps an expert might take to prevent the harm to the public. It is sufficient to observe that it might be appropriate to notify the potential victim or the police or a Crown prosecutor, depending on the specific circumstances. ...

III. Disposition

The file will be unsealed and the ban on the publication of the contents of the file is removed, except for those parts of the affidavit of the doctor which do not fall within the public safety exception. Subject to this direction the order of the British Columbia Court of Appeal is affirmed and this appeal is dismissed without costs.

NOTES AND QUESTIONS

1. How does the court determine whether a particular public policy (such as public safety or national security) is capable of overriding a lawyer's duty of confidentiality? Attempt to explain this decision in terms of utility maximization. To the extent that the disclosure of a client's information constitutes a breach of the client's expectations, can disclosure of information in the name of public safety be explained in terms of "efficient breach" (discussed in chapter 1)? Should a client (such as Mr. Jones) whose confidence is breached in reliance on the public-safety exception be entitled to compensatory damages from the person who divulges the client's confidence? Would this ensure that only efficient breaches took place?

2. Note that Mr. Jones's counsel, who had read the client's psychological report and was aware of the danger that his or her client posed to the public, did not attempt to disclose the relevant information. Can economics help explain this decision? Was that lawyer making a moral choice, or pursuing an amoral role required by the neutral-conduit model (discussed in chapter 3)?

3. Is it permissible for a lawyer to disclose confidential information in cases where failure to do so might result in a wrongful conviction? If so, why is a lawyer not allowed to disclose confidential information where doing so could prevent a *wrongful acquittal*?

4. At one point in its judgment, the court opines that "only a compelling public interest may justify setting aside solicitor–client privilege." Is this correct? Are there circumstances in which a compelling *private* interest (such as the lawyer's own pecuniary interest) may justify a violation of confidentiality? What if the client refuses to pay the lawyer, and the lawyer must disclose the existence and general nature of the retainer in order to sue the client for non-payment of fees? Can this be explained in terms of public interest? Can it be explained in terms of the maximization of social utility? Additional situations in which the duty of confidentiality yields to public and private interests are discussed in chapter 7.

5. The court claims that "[t]he disclosure of planned future crimes without an element of violence would be an insufficient reason to set aside solicitor–client privilege because of fears for public safety." What about an act of ecoterrorism, designed to destroy an

important natural resource? Is it rational to limit disclosure to cases involving particular kinds of public harm, or should the court simply allow the disclosure of confidential information whenever disclosure maximizes social utility? In what circumstances might the courts allow a lawyer to violate confidentiality in cases where the client plans to commit a non-violent (yet especially harmful) crime?

6. In order to rely on the "public safety" exception discussed in *Smith v. Jones*, the person or group threatened with death or serious bodily harm must be readily "identifiable." Why? What if a client informed a lawyer of the client's plan to carry out "sniper" attacks on randomly selected victims? Could a court justify a loss of confidentiality in such cases?

7. Do you agree with the court that members of a particular profession—namely, prostitutes—in the downtown core of a very large city—namely, Vancouver—constitute an "identifiable group" for the purposes of the public safety exception? Would "all lawyers in Toronto" constitute an identifiable group? Should they?

8. Note that the exception developed in *Smith* is now embodied in rule 2.03(3) of Ontario's *Rules of Professional Conduct*. That rule provides as follows:

> Where a lawyer believes upon reasonable grounds that there is an imminent risk to an identifiable person or group of death or serious bodily harm, including serious psychological harm that substantially interferes with health or well-being, the lawyer may disclose, pursuant to judicial order where practicable, confidential information where it is necessary to do so in order to prevent the death or harm, but shall not disclose more information than is required.

9. For an excellent review of the economic basis of the rule of confidentiality, see George M. Cohen, "When Law and Economics Met Professional Responsibility" (1998), 67 *Fordham Law Review* 273. In that article, Cohen contends that "confidentiality rules are an essential part of agency relationships (and agency law) generally because in the absence of such rules, the informational advantage the agent has would enable the agent to use information about the principle to the principle's disadvantage. Applied to the lawyer-client context, the fundamental purpose of confidentiality rules is to help minimize lawyer-client agency costs." Do you agree with Cohen's formulation of the economic basis of the lawyer's duty of confidentiality? How does it relate to the rationale discussed in section II.B, above?

IV. Use of Information

As we have seen throughout this book, a decision maker will tend to violate ethical norms when a violation maximizes the decision maker's utility. A lawyer will decide to violate confidentiality, for example, where the benefits (to the lawyer) of the relevant violation exceed the costs of violating the ethical norm (including the expected cost of whatever punishment will be imposed by the Law Society, and any compensating payments required under tort and contract law). As we saw in chapter 4, if the Law Society seeks to deter lawyers from engaging in unethical behaviour, it must establish punitive sanctions, making ethical violations so "expensive" that the benefits of engaging in the relevant form of conduct rarely exceed the costs (to the lawyer) of the ethical violation.

By pricing violations of client confidence "out of the market," the Law Society hopes to minimize the social costs that flow from the lawyer's access to the client's information.

If our goal in regulating the duty of confidentiality is to minimize the social costs that flow from violations of this ethical obligation, it is important that we define the ethical duty in a way that takes account of *all* the costs and benefits that may flow from the lawyer's access to the client's confidential information. As a result, we cannot limit our definition of "breach of confidence" to those cases in which the lawyer *discloses* the client's information. A lawyer's access to a client's information makes it possible for the lawyer to harm the client without disclosing the information—for example, the lawyer may take advantage of a secret business opportunity that the client planned to pursue. By the same token, it is possible for a lawyer to benefit from a client's secret information without disclosing the relevant information. Thus, even where confidentiality (strictly speaking) is maintained, the lawyer might harm the client through the lawyer's personal use of the client's private information. If our goal is to minimize the harms that flow from a lawyer's access to the client's private information, we must not only regulate the lawyer's disclosure of that information, but any "use" the lawyer makes of the information to the detriment of the client or the benefit of the lawyer.

A lawyer's use (as opposed to disclosure) of client information is discussed in the CBA Code, rule IV, commentary 5. That commentary provides (in part) as follows:

> The fiduciary relationship between the lawyer and the client forbids the lawyer to use any confidential information covered by the ethical rule for the benefit of the lawyer or a third person, or to the disadvantage of the client.

As a result, the CBA Code clearly prohibits "use" as well as "disclosure" of confidential information. Consult Ontario's *Rules of Professional Conduct* (available online at http://www.lsuc.on.ca). Do these rules apply to use as well, or only to disclosure?

The decision of the court in *Szarfer v. Chodos* (1986) (reproduced below) demonstrates the court's response to cases in which a lawyer benefits (and a client is harmed) through the lawyer's access to the client's information, despite the fact that the lawyer keeps the information confidential. When reading the court's decision, it is important to note that this is not a disciplinary proceeding, but a private suit for tort damages. In other words, the lawyer's former client is seeking a payment of damages in response to the lawyer's use of the client's private information. As we saw in chapter 3, the role of tort damages is to force tortfeasors to internalize the costs of their behaviour, compelling them to make efficient decisions and ensuring that their victims are compensated. It should also be noted, however, that the lawyer involved in *Szarfer* (Mr. Chodos), after having been ordered to compensate his client through the payment of money damages, was also subjected to disciplinary proceedings and suspended from practicing law for six months.[13] To the extent that Chodos had already compensated his client through the payment of money damages, what was the point of imposing this additional sanction? For an answer to this question, consult section V of chapter 4.

---

13   See *Law Society of Upper Canada v. Chodos*, [1996] LSDD no. 42.

Szarfer v. Chodos
(1986), 54 OR (2d) 663 (HCJ); aff'd. (1988), 66 OR (2d) 350 (CA)

CALLAGHAN ACJHC:

Nature of Claim

The plaintiff claims general, special and punitive damages from the defendant as a result of an alleged breach of fiduciary duty arising from their relationship as solicitor and client. The plaintiff claims the defendant utilized confidential information for his own advantage and placed his personal interest in conflict with his duties as a fiduciary. In addition, the plaintiff pleads that the defendant's conduct was a breach of the contract between the parties resulting in damages. In the alternative, the plaintiff claims the defendant having full knowledge of the vulnerable mental and physical condition of the plaintiff, acted in wanton disregard of such knowledge and inflicted mental suffering on the plaintiff thereby committing an intentional tort or, alternatively, the defendant acted negligently in inflicting the aforesaid injury thereby causing the damage claimed. The plaintiff is a social services employee who was born in Poland in 1946. He came to Canada with his family in 1957 and married his wife Cecile in 1968. One child of the marriage was born in 1971 and a further child was adopted in December, 1983.

The plaintiff left school at the age of 16 after completing grade 8 in Grace Street Public School in Toronto and thereupon commenced work as an upholsterer. He studied hairdressing and completed a course therein in 1965 and thereafter worked as a hairdresser until October, 1978. In June, 1978, as a result of a fall he suffered a severe fracture of his left wrist and arm. He was off work for approximately eight weeks when he returned to his employment as a hairdresser. As a result of the fracture he had great difficulty in performing his duties as a hairdresser and was dismissed in October, 1978, by his employer. He was unable to obtain full-time employment; however, he did work part-time as a hairdresser and in January, 1979, he consulted the defendant with a view to commencing an action against his former employer for wrongful dismissal.

The defendant is a solicitor who carries on the practice of law in the City of North York in the Municipality of Metropolitan Toronto. He was called to the Bar of this province in 1974 and entered his present partnership in June of 1977. The defendant had acted for the plaintiff in relation to his claim for compensation from the Workers Compensation Board as a result of the accident of June, 1978. He had also acted for the plaintiff in a small claims court claim in 1978. The defendant specialized in litigation.

The Wrongful Dismissal Action

The plaintiff's fracture of the left arm was severe and he encountered difficulty in the healing process. His arm required further surgery in September, 1979, in the area of the wrist. Thereafter he was unable to work as a hairdresser on a permanent basis. From the date of the injury in June, 1978, for a period of approximately five months, he was unable to collect either his unemployment insurance payments or his compensation from the Workers' Compensation Board. He was placed on a rehabilitation programme that required daily attendance at a rehabilitation clinic. In the course of that treatment he suffered an anxiety attack resulting in hyperventilation which required his confinement in an infirmary for approximately one hour. Eventually, the Workers' Compensation Board agreed to retrain the plaintiff and he entered the social service workers programme at Seneca College in September, 1980. In the interim his wife, who was a legal secretary, assumed the burden of providing for the family. This situation placed a strain on the marriage relationship which did not abate when the plaintiff returned to college for retraining. In addition to the marital strain, the plaintiff was depressed as a result of his circumstances and sought professional assistance from a psychiatrist, Mr. H. Fenigstein, from whom he took group psychotherapy from June, 1980, until some time in the spring of 1981.

The wrongful dismissal action proceeded through the normal steps until February, 1981, when the defendant at a continuing education programme of the Law Society of Upper Canada became aware of the possibility of a claim for damages arising as a result of mental distress in relation to a wrongful dismissal. On February 25, 1981, the defendant arranged to discuss with the plaintiff and his wife the possibility of advancing such a claim in the then pending lawsuit. The plaintiff gave the defendant instructions to proceed with such a claim and in support thereof the defendant interviewed the plaintiff and his wife on several occasions with reference thereto. On March 12, 1981, the plaintiff's wife forwarded a typed statement to the defendant (ex. 3, Tab 8) in which she outlined the strains that had been placed upon the marriage relationship as a result of the plaintiff's failure to obtain work and indicated that they had discussed separation because their interests were no longer the same. …

The plaintiff's wife had on several occasions worked as a legal secretary on a temporary basis in the defendant's law office. On May 12, 1981, the defendant completed dictating his written submissions. His secretary was unavailable and he asked the plaintiff's wife if she would type the submissions for filing in court the next day. Mrs. Szarfer agreed and attended at the defendant's office at approximately 6:00 p.m. She was going out that night at 8:15 p.m. and completed typing the submissions at approximately 8:00 p.m. The submissions were filed the next day. On May 21, 1981, judgment was delivered in the aforesaid action and the plaintiff's claim was dismissed with costs. Although an appeal was launched on the plaintiff's behalf by other solicitors, the appeal was abandoned some time thereafter.

The Affair

The defendant had known Mrs. Szarfer since 1978 when they met on a social occasion. As indicated, she had worked for the defendant on several occasions for one to two weeks at a time as a temporary legal secretary. On May 12, 1981, after completing typing of the submissions, Mrs. Szarfer left the defendant's law office and went out for dinner with some friends. At approximately 11:00 p.m. she returned to the defendant's office and she and the defendant engaged in sexual relations. This liaison continued for a period of approximately six weeks with clandestine meetings either in the defendant's office or in adjacent hotels. The evidence establishes approximately two to three meetings a week.

On June 26, 1981, the plaintiff who was assisting his brother as a delivery man in the latter's business was cutting through the parking-lot of the Tower Motel at the corner of Keele and Wilson Ave. in the City of North York. As he passed through that lot he spotted his wife's car parked therein. Believing she was having lunch in the hotel he went in to join her. He was unable to locate her in either the dining-room or the bar and sat down for a moment in the foyer. At that point he observed his wife and the defendant get out of the elevator. The plaintiff was shocked. He was unable to move. He was not seen by his wife or the defendant and shortly after they left he left the lobby. That afternoon, he telephoned his wife and advised her that he was aware of the affair. He then moved out of the marital home and moved in with his brother.

On June 27, 1981, the plaintiff suffered an anxiety attack while driving his car and was taken by ambulance to the emergency department of the North York General Hospital after being found by the Provincial Police in his motor vehicle on Highway 401 honking the horn thereof. He was suffering numbness in both arms, was hyperventilating and was emotionally upset.

The plaintiff remained in the hospital until July 6, 1981, when he was released. The final diagnosis upon release was that of "neurotic depression with hysterical features." While in the hospital he had been visited by his wife on several occasions and had on one occasion enjoyed a week-end pass with her. Upon his discharge from the hospital the plaintiff returned to live with his wife in the matrimonial home. On several occasions he treated his wife violently. On one occasion his violence attained life-threatening proportions. His brother-in-law intervened to prevent an attack on his wife with a knife. In August, 1981, he instructed counsel to approach the defendant with a view to settling this matter. The defendant in a display of cold indifference to the plaintiff and his concerns advised that he would defend any proceeding initiated. This action was accordingly commenced.

On September 19, 1981, the plaintiff was readmitted to the North York General Hospital suffering a depressive reaction. He remained therein until September 24th, when he was again discharged and was referred to the Mental Health Clinic for joint sessions with his wife and he was advised to seek ongoing psychiatric therapy. Shortly after his release on this occasion, he continued with his retraining programme at Seneca College but encountered considerable difficulty in the field work which required him to work in psychiatric wards of hospitals and homes for the aged. The plaintiff had been successful in the first year of his studies but encountered considerable difficulties in the second year. He was, however, able to complete his retraining programme and in June, 1982, commenced employment with the Municipality of Metropolitan Toronto Community Services Department. He is presently employed in that department. He is still living with his wife and in 1983 together they adopted a child which adoption has assisted in strengthening the marriage bond. The plaintiff still is under psychiatric treatment although his condition has improved over the past two years.

Psychiatric Evidence

The plaintiff is presently under the care of Dr. Hung-Tat Lo, a psychiatrist … . He has treated the plaintiff weekly with psychotherapy. On the first admission to hospital, Dr. Lo diagnosed the plaintiff's condition as that of neurotic depression with hysterical features. He found no psychotic symptoms but he did find cognitive impairment particularly with regard to short-term memory. This impairment prevented the plaintiff from recalling details of the incident leading to his hospitalization. This lack of memory, which is evident in the plaintiff's testimony, is a result of hysterical amnesia. It is Dr. Lo's diagnosis that the plaintiff is presently suffering from adjustment disorder causing him to develop symptoms of anxiety depression coupled with surges of anger, rage and irritability along with periods of confusion and forgetfulness which in turn have led to great marital strain and occupational insecurity. The evidence establishes that prior to June 26, 1981, the plaintiff was suffering from a depression as a result of his marital and financial difficulties. He apparently, however, was able to cope with those difficulties at that time and had embarked upon a course of retraining with a view to rehabilitating himself as a social service worker. Dr. Lo testified that the discovery of the affair was a severe traumatic blow to the plaintiff and was the cause of his present psychiatric problem which is that of a post-traumatic neurosis. It was Dr. Lo's view that the plaintiff was a man who looked up to and respected professionals and had a deep and abiding trust in both his wife and the defendant, his solicitor. This personality characteristic increased the severity of the blow attendant upon the discovery of the affair. His memory impairment on his admission to the hospital in June of 1981 is a symptom of the severity of the shock to the plaintiff. In Dr. Lo's view, the plaintiff's "post-traumatic neurosis" will abate with the successful resolution of these proceedings in some six to twelve months. ...

I conclude that the discovery by the plaintiff of the affair between his wife and the defendant resulted in a genuine traumatic emotional disorder. He sustained a form of traumatic neurosis arising out of an acute situational distress which led to hospitalization. Absent the insult caused by the discovery of the affair, he would not have required hospitalization and the subsequent out-patient psychiatric care that he is presently undergoing. He presently suffers from post-traumatic neurosis with an anxiety depression consequent upon the discovery of the affair and will require treatment by way of psychotherapy for a further six- to twelve-month period. While his condition has improved over the past two years, residual emotions such as anger, rage, irritability, periods of confusion and forgetfulness together with nightmares are continuing and relate to the traumatic effect of discovering the affair.

Credibility

The plaintiff alleges that the defendant utilized confidential information for his own advantage in that in exploring the basis for the claim for damages for mental distress in the wrongful dismissal action he became fully aware of the strains in the marriage relationship between the plaintiff and his wife and used this knowledge to effect the affair. The plaintiff testified that he advised the defendant of the difficulty they were encountering in their sexual relations. The defendant claims that he never inquired into those relations once he ascertained that the marriage was under a considerable strain as a result of the financial difficulties the parties were encountering and the plaintiff's inability to return to work. What the defendant actually knew is relevant for the purposes of determining whether or not he utilized confidential information for his own advantage and placed his personal interests as a result in conflict with those of his client. The defendant in addition to meeting with the plaintiff and his wife on February 25, 1981, also discussed the state of the marriage with the plaintiff's sister, Mrs. Rosenberg. He requested and received from the plaintiff's wife a type-written memorandum forwarded to him on March 12, 1981 (ex. 3, Tab 8). That memorandum sets forth at length the marital difficulties the parties were encountering. From that memorandum, the contents of which the defendant read, and the evidence of their meetings, I am satisfied that he knew there was a great strain in the marriage relationship between Mr. and Mrs. Szarfer and that they were arguing all the time. He was aware that Mrs. Szarfer was complaining that the plaintiff had become lazy and his nerves were bothering him, that his health was impaired. He knew she was very upset and angry about the fact that the plaintiff had gone back to school and that she, for that period of time, was the sole means of family support. He was also aware of the fact they had very little to talk about and that Mrs. Szarfer felt the plaintiff was not the same man she married and did not enjoy being in the same room with him. The defendant also knew that Mr. Szarfer had gone heavily into debt by way of borrowing in order to support the family during this period of crisis. He was also aware that Mr. and Mrs. Szarfer had discussed separation.

The plaintiff testified that he advised the defendant that he and his wife were having sexual problems and that he was impotent. The defendant claimed he did not inquire into such matters. It was submitted to the court on behalf of the defendant that the plaintiff's evidence should not be accepted in this regard as that the inconsistencies between his evidence and the statements attributed to him in the medical records (ex. 1, Tabs 1 and 2) indicate that he is not to be believed. In so far as those records are concerned, I am satisfied that at the time they were taken the plaintiff was in a confused state suffering from a severe depression. In his evidence the plaintiff corrected many of the statements found in the medical records and I accept his evidence in that regard. I am also of the view that I should accept the plaintiff's evidence in relation to whether or not the defendant in discussing the claim for mental distress explored fully the matrimonial relationship between the parties including their sexual relations. I have arrived at that conclusion, firstly, because in the circumstances it was natural to inquire into that aspect of the marital relationship having regard to the nature of the claim being advanced. The defendant conceded in cross-examination that in retrospect his position did not make sense. While the defendant testified that he was only concerned with the strain placed on the marital relations as a result of their financial problems I find that he in fact inquired into the marital sexual problems separate and apart from the financial problem. This is confirmed by his trial notes wherein under item 12 thereof he purported to explore, in examining the plaintiff, the mental problem under two aspects, namely, marital and financial.

Secondly, while I accept the defendant's evidence that prior to discoveries on this matter he had not reviewed in detail his file, I regretfully must conclude that his answers on that discovery leave a great deal to be desired. Some of them (Qq. 89 to 95) were just incorrect. He so conceded on cross-examination. Notwithstanding the fact that he knew they were incorrect he made no effort to notify either his counsel or counsel on the other side as to the correct state of affairs. Again when asked on discovery as to his knowledge about the state of the plaintiff's marriage he indicated that he was not aware of any particular problems (Qq. 134 to 139). Such an answer was also incorrect. He was well aware of the matters set forth above, and as indicated, was fully aware of the difficulties the plaintiff and his wife were encountering in their sexual relations. These transparent inconsistencies have led me to conclude that he was endeavouring to cover up the true state of his knowledge in relation to this tragic affair.

In addition to his knowledge of the state of the marriage, the defendant was fully aware of the background and stress under which the plaintiff was living. As indicated, he knew that the plaintiff was in a precarious financial situation and had borrowed large sums of money to maintain his home. He was aware that after the operation in 1979 the plaintiff could no longer earn his livelihood as a hairdresser. He knew that the plaintiff had never been unemployed in 15 years. He was aware of the anxiety attack that the plaintiff suffered in 1979 as a result of his difficulties with the Workers' Compensation Board. He knew that the plaintiff was living in pain from the injury to his wrist and was constantly on medication as a result. He knew the plaintiff was unable to secure a steady income or permanent employment. He was aware that the plaintiff was suffering from aggravation and stress as a result of his inability to obtain such employment.

He also knew that from June 24, 1980, until March, 1981, the plaintiff was attending group psychotherapy sessions under the treatment of Dr. H. Fenigstein, a psychiatrist (ex. 3, Tab 7). I am satisfied that Dr. Fenigstein's letter of March 4, 1981, was in the defendant's file in relation to the plaintiff's case and he was aware of its contents.

In relation to Mrs. Szarfer, the defendant of course was aware of the difficulties she was encountering in the marriage. He knew that she had a heart condition and that the marriage was subjecting her to constant fights and quarrels. In addition she had the strain of providing a source of income while the plaintiff returned to Seneca College for retraining. He also knew that as a result of the difficulties the family had encountered, Mrs. Szarfer felt that she and her husband had lost a very important part of their relationship and possibly their love for each other. In these circumstances the defendant made arrangements for payment of his bill of costs in the wrongful dismissal action with Mrs. Szarfer. He forwarded that bill to her on June 1, 1981, while the affair was continuing. The account was in the amount of $3,382.30. Mrs. Szarfer paid approximately $2,000 on the account, part of which came from an income tax refund due the plaintiff. The defendant claims that the balance of the account has been written off. Mrs. Szarfer agreed initially to pay the defendant's account either prior to trial or shortly thereafter. Unfortunately, because of the financial strain she was unable to make such payment and the defendant agreed to accept payments over a period of time. Accordingly, Mrs. Szarfer's position has to be assessed in the light of not only what the defendant knew about her but also the fact that she was the one who was undertaking to pay the account in relation to the wrongful dismissal action. Mrs. Szarfer was vulnerable and the defendant knew it as a result of knowledge gained in relation to the claim for damages for mental distress in the wrongful dismissal action.

Aside from the evidence with reference to the account, the foregoing information in relation to the plaintiff, his wife and their marital relationship was all within the knowledge of the defendant on May 12, 1981. It was obtained in confidence and it bore the stamp of confidentiality. A person who has obtained such information is not allowed to use it for activities detrimental to the person who made the confidential communication. This prohibition on use remains even when all features of such information may have been published or can be ascertained by actual inspection by any member of the public in documents such as court documents: *Seager v. Copydex Ltd.*, [1967] 2 All ER 415, per Lord Denning MR at p. 417.

I am satisfied that the evidence establishes that the marriage in issue was a normal relationship until the unfortunate accident of June, 1978, when the plaintiff broke his wrist. Thereafter his inability to continue in his chosen profession along with the difficulties he was encountering with the Workers' Compensation Board and obtaining other employment caused him great anxiety and placed him in a condition of aggravation under stress. I am satisfied that there was no infidelity on his part and that he was unaware of any infidelity on the part of his wife until June 26, 1981. I accept the evidence of Dr. Lo and Dr. Berry that the discovery of the affair caused him to sustain, as above-mentioned, a traumatic neurosis. While he was susceptible to such a mental disorder he had not up until that point suffered such a disorder. He was coping with his daily problems and looking forward to his retraining and his new profession as a social service worker. His present condition was caused, in my view, by the discovery of the affair. While Mrs. Szarfer was not called to testify in these proceedings, and no doubt her evidence would have been helpful, I accept the explanation of counsel (exs. 5 and 6) that her present condition is such that it would have been extremely harmful to her to require her to testify in these proceedings. In these circumstances, therefore, it is necessary to determine whether or not there has been an unauthorized use of confidential information by the defendant.

Law

The fiduciary relationship between a lawyer and his client forbids a lawyer from using any confidential information obtained by him for the benefit of himself or a third person or to the disadvantage of his client. The crucial question for decision is whether or not the defendant used confidential information for his own purposes or to the disadvantage of the plaintiff. It is conceded that the defendant was in a fiduciary relationship with the plaintiff and owed him all the duties of a fiduciary. The highest and clearest duty of a fiduciary is to act to advance the beneficiary's interest and avoid acting to his detriment. A fiduciary cannot permit his own interest to come into conflict with the interest of the beneficiary of the relationship. The equitable principle is stated in Waters, *Law of Trusts in Canada*, 2nd ed. (1984), at p. 710:

> It is a fundamental principle of every developed legal system that one who undertakes a task on behalf of another must act exclusively for the benefit of the other, putting his own interests completely aside. In the common law system this duty may be enforceable by way of an action by the principal upon the contract of agency, but the modes in which the rule can be breached are myriad, many of them in situations other than contract and therefore beyond the control of the law of contract. It was in part to meet such situations that Equity fashioned the rule that no man may allow his duty to conflict with

his interest. Stated in this way, Equity has been able since the sixteenth century to provide a remedy for a whole range of cases where the person with a task to perform has used the opportunity to benefit himself.

… Once the fiduciary relationship is established, as it is in this case, the onus is on the trustee to prove that he acted reasonably and made no personal use whatsoever of the confidential information: see Waters, *supra*, p. 736; *Krendel v. Frontwell Investments Ltd. et al.*, [1967] 2 OR 579 at p. 584, 64 DLR (2d) 471 at p. 476.

In engaging in sexual intercourse with the plaintiff's wife, the defendant was acting in his own interest and to his personal benefit. I cannot help but conclude that his actions were also to the detriment of his client's interest. Upon discovery of the affair, the client's trust in the solicitor was destroyed. Such conduct which vitiates trust, the essential element of a solicitor–client relationship, and results in physical injury to the client, is a breach of the conflict-of-interest rule referred to above.[14] The defendant has not discharged the onus of proving that he acted reasonably in the circumstances. That in itself is sufficient to hold him liable for damages.

Furthermore, however, I am satisfied that he used confidential information for his own purposes in order to obtain the delights and benefits of the affair. The defendant had known Mrs. Szarfer since 1977 but had no sexual relationship with her until May of 1981. He did not acquire details of the Szarfers' marital and sexual problems until March or April of 1981. At that time he obtained the intimate knowledge of the emotional and mental problems of both the plaintiff and his wife. He obtained such information as part of the process of the wrongful dismissal action. The plaintiff's mental state and the plaintiff's sexual problem were issues in that action. As a solicitor he undertook to prosecute the claim for wrongful dismissal including a claim for damages for mental distress and the state of the marriage and all the information related above was an indivisible part of the task undertaken by him as a solicitor. Again, he was aware of Mrs. Szarfer's vulnerability as a result of the information he obtained about the marriage. I have not accepted the defendant's denial that he did not have any information respecting the marriage except financial nor can I overlook his denial of not knowing of the possibility of the marriage break-up even though his trial notes disclosed that he intended to examine on that very issue at trial of the wrongful dismissal action. These matters together with the time factors involved have led me to conclude that the defendant in fact did use the confidential information that he obtained from the plaintiff and his wife for his own purposes and I so find. In so doing, the defendant was in breach of his professional duty to his client, the plaintiff, and that breach was the cause of the plaintiff's post-traumatic neurosis. The breach constituted professional negligence and demonstrated an unreasonable lack of skill and fidelity in his professional and fiduciary duties as a lawyer. …

In this case the injury to the plaintiff was not caused by the adultery. The injury was caused by the defendant's use of confidential information for his own purposes. While the adultery forms part of the core facts of this claim, and is admitted, the

---

14   The conflict-of-interest rule is discussed in chapter 8.

action itself is founded on the allegation that the plaintiff's mental and emotional status was adversely affected by the defendant's misuse of confidential information and that, in my view, constitutes a viable cause of action for damages. ...

Exemplary Damages

The defendant stood in a fiduciary relationship to the plaintiff. He failed to discharge his duty to the plaintiff in that he used the confidential information obtained as to the marital relationship between the plaintiff and his wife for the benefit of himself. His conduct was dishonourable. Integrity is the fundamental quality of a lawyer. Trustworthiness is the essential element in the true lawyer-client relationship. While the affair was in one sense a private activity, it destroyed the essential trust between the plaintiff and the defendant which is the hallmark of the solicitor–client relationship. However, I am not satisfied in these circumstances that this is an appropriate case for exemplary damages. The defendant's conduct while deserving of condemnation cannot be characterized as sufficiently high-handed and arrogant in relation to the plaintiff's rights to warrant imposition of such damages.

In result, therefore, there will be judgment for the plaintiff in the sum of $43,663 with interest thereon.

NOTES AND QUESTIONS

1. As noted in the introduction to the case, Szarfer was suing his lawyer for compensation. The utility loss giving rise to the claim for compensation flowed from a psychological disorder (caused by Chodos) leading Szarfer to "develop symptoms of anxiety depression coupled with surges of anger, rage and irritability along with periods of confusion and forgetfulness." As compensation for this loss, the court ordered Chodos to pay Szarfer $43,663. Does this mean that the court believed that Szarfer would be indifferent as between (1) freedom from his psychological problems, and (2) the existence of those psychological problems plus a payment of $43,663? Does it make sense to speak of *compensatory* damages in this context? Is it likely that Mr. Szarfer could be rendered indifferent about Chodos' affair with Mrs. Szarfer?

2. Note the following passage from the court's decision:

> A person who has obtained such information is not allowed to use it for activities detrimental to the person who made the confidential communication. This prohibition on use remains even when all features of such information may have been published or can be ascertained by actual inspection by any member of the public in documents such as court documents

Why should the duty to refrain from acting on confidential information apply when the lawyer could have learned that information from other sources? Is this "fair"? How does this relate to the rationale underlying the duty of confidentiality?

3. During the course of its judgment the court noted that "[a] fiduciary cannot permit his own interest to come into conflict with the interest of the beneficiary of the relationship." Is this inconsistent with the assumption that all actors, regardless of their ethical

obligations, will ultimately act in their self-interest? For an answer to this question, review section VII.B, chapter 3.

4. Describe Chodos' ethical violation by reference to the basic ethical calculation described in chapters 2 and 3 (namely, A – B = X). When defining figure A, bear in mind the court's description of the benefits Chodos gleaned from using Szarfer's confidential information:

> In engaging in sexual intercourse with the plaintiff's wife, the defendant was acting in his own interest and to his personal benefit.

Similarly, the court notes that Chodos obtained "delights and benefits" from the affair. Note that these non-monetary sources of utility can be considered in the ethical calculation. For a review of the way in which non-pecuniary benefits can be expressed in terms of monetary value, review section II.E in chapter 1.

5. Note that the court refrained from imposing punitive damages in this case and, instead, simply ordered compensation. Given the fact that Mr. Chodos had hoped to avoid detection and punishment, is it sensible to rely on a compensatory model of regulation? In answering this question, (1) review the discussion of "the punishment model" in chapter 4, and (2) bear in mind the fact that Chodos ultimately *was* suspended for six months as a result of his behaviour.

V. The Interests Protected

The decision of the court in *Geffen v. Goodman Estate* (1991) (reproduced below) deals with the extent of the lawyer's duty of confidentiality after the lawyer's client has died.[15] As we shall see, the duty of confidentiality continues even after the client's death (see, for example, the commentary to Ontario's rule 2.03(1), which provides that the duty of confidentiality "survives the professional relationship and continues indefinitely after the lawyer has ceased to act for the client, whether or not differences have arisen between them").[16] In *Geffen v. Goodman Estate*, the court considered the circumstances in which a lawyer could disclose information concerning a client who had died, despite the continued existence of the ethical duty of confidentiality.

Given that the lawyer's obligation of confidentiality continues after the client's death, what is the nature of the utility interest protected by the lawyer's duty of confidentiality? For the purposes of this discussion, we may assume that the dead have no concept of utility. As a result, we can ignore the preferences of the dead. If the dead have no

---

15   Like the decision in *Smith v. Jones*, above, the decision in *Geffen v. Goodman Estate* actually deals with solicitor–client privilege, rather than the lawyer's duty of confidentiality. Given that the duty of confidentiality embraces (and goes beyond) the doctrine of privilege, however, any holding that privilege extends after the client's death applies with even greater force to the duty of confidentiality. Similarly, any order that the lawyer may (or must) disclose privileged information after the lawyer's client has died carries obvious implications for the lawyer's duty of confidentiality.

16   Similarly, the commentary to rule 1.6 of the ABA's model rules provides that "[t]he duty of confidentiality continues after the client–lawyer relationship has terminated." See also the CBA Code, rule 4, commentary 4.

observable preferences (and are therefore immune from utility losses), what is the point of protecting confidentiality even after the client has died? Does the protection of confidentiality have utility implications for people other than the lawyer's deceased client? When considering these questions, refer to the discussion of the rationale of the obligation of confidentiality (found in section II.B, above).

Geffen v. Goodman Estate
[1991] 2 SCR 353

WILSON J: The respondent, Stacy Randall Goodman, as executor of his mother's estate and on his own behalf, commenced an action claiming that he and his siblings were entitled to certain property left to his mother, Tzina Goodman, by his grandmother, Annie Sanofsky. The appellants, Sam, William and Ted Geffen are the brothers and nephew of Stacy's mother. They are the trustees of a certain trust agreement in which Stacy's mother is named as the settlor and under which the trust property is to be distributed amongst all of Annie Sanofsky's grandchildren. This appeal concerns the validity of the trust agreement.

1. The Facts

Annie Sanofsky had four children, Sam, Ted, Jack and Tzina. Sam and Ted Geffen are both successful businessmen currently living in the United States. Their brother Jack is an insurance underwriter who lives in Edmonton. Their sister Tzina, (Mrs. Goodman) now deceased, had a less than trouble-free life. She first came under the care of a psychiatrist while a teenager. Psychiatric intervention became a common feature of her existence. She was hospitalized many times over the years and was eventually diagnosed as suffering from bipolar affective disorder, formerly known as manic depressive disorder, and immature personality. Tzina's illness caused strain in her family relationships. Her disorder tended to drive people away from her. Although she married and had children she did not have much contact with her children after her separation from her husband. Her contact with them was purely casual.

In 1968, with the help of her son Jack, Annie Sanofsky executed a will providing for a life estate to her daughter Tzina and directing that on Tzina's death her estate should be distributed to all of her (Annie's) grandchildren. At the time of their mother's death the four children were surprised to learn that a new will had been executed in 1975 which superseded the 1968 will. Under the new will Annie Sanofsky left the property which had been her home outright to her daughter Tzina, provided bequests of $1000 each to her sons, and directed that the residue of her estate be held in trust for Tzina during her lifetime and pass on Tzina's death to her (Tzina's) children.

The three Geffen brothers, not surprisingly, were unhappy with the way in which their mother had disposed of her estate. They thought it unfair that their children had been cut out of the will. Their sister agreed. They were especially concerned, however, with their mother's decision to bequeath her home in Calgary outright to their sister. Tzina had a history of mental illness and they feared that her disability would interfere with her capacity to act responsibly in relation to the property she had inherited. They were particularly concerned that Tzina might divest herself of the assets she needed for her own support. If this happened they might be called upon to contribute to her support. They, along with their sister, decided to seek legal advice as to whether or not the second will was valid.

They retained the services of Mr. Pearce, a Calgary lawyer, and explained the situation to him. Jack Geffen acted as spokesman for the family. The options open to Tzina were canvassed. It was suggested that the house be transferred by Tzina to her brothers' children. A disagreement ensued between Tzina and her brother Jack. She did not like the idea of transferring title to the house immediately, leaving herself with only a life interest in it. Mr. Pearce suggested that she take some time to think things over. The meeting disbanded, the brothers paid for the consultation and all concerned returned to their respective homes.

Mrs. Goodman thereafter had only casual contact with her brothers but continued to seek the advice of counsel and communicated with Mr. Pearce on several occasions. As a result of these consultations it was suggested to Mrs. Goodman that the Calgary residence be put into a trust for her for life with her brothers as trustees but that she would retain the right to dispose of the property by will. This suggestion was vehemently rejected by Jack but accepted by Ted and Sam Geffen. Jack indicated that he would have nothing further to do with the trust and it was agreed that Ted's son William would replace him as a trustee.

Mr. Pearce then went ahead and prepared the trust deed. The trust property was conveyed to the trustees on terms that Mrs. Goodman retained a life interest in the Calgary residence and that on her request the trustees would consider a sale of the property so long as the sale was in Mrs. Goodman's best interests. The trust deed further provided that upon Mrs. Goodman's death the trust property would be divided equally among her surviving children, nephews and nieces, i.e., all Annie Sanofsky's grandchildren.

After the deed was executed Mrs. Goodman was apparently not too sure of the effect of what she had done. She attempted twice to put the property on the market. Her attempts were thwarted by Mr. Pearce. Mrs. Goodman died in May of 1984, leaving a last will and testament in which she left her entire estate to her children. ...

At trial the plaintiffs submitted that the trust agreement was entered into by Mrs. Goodman as a result of the undue influence of the defendants and Jack Geffen. Hutchinson J first dealt with the admissibility of Mr. Pearce's [the lawyer's] evidence and in particular the argument that it should not have been received since it was privileged. Having concluded that Mr. Pearce's testimony was properly admitted the trial judge turned to its import. He said at pp. 220-21:

> I accept Mr. Pearce's testimony that during his initial dealings with Mrs. Goodman during the period of his initial interview up to at least 7th February 1980 Mrs. Goodman fully understood the nature and effect of the arrangements evidenced by the trust agreement. I am satisfied that Mrs. Goodman was the initiator of the instructions to Mr. Pearce, following periods of independent thought by her, to draw the trust agreement in

accordance with his suggestion that this would be an alternate method of holding the Calgary residential property so as to ensure that she had a place to live during her lifetime and that she intended to include all of the ultimate beneficiaries of the trust named therein, including her own children.

Based on the testimony of the solicitor as well as the other witnesses, Hutchinson J found on the evidence that the Geffen brothers did not in fact influence their sister into signing the trust agreement. ...

Solicitor–Client Privilege

The trial judge's admission of the evidence of Mr. Pearce, the solicitor who drafted the trust agreement, is challenged by the respondents. Mr. Pearce's evidence is crucial in this case for two reasons. First, it may help to ascertain what the precise circumstances surrounding the deceased's entry into the trust agreement were. And secondly, this evidence is vital to the determination of whether Mrs. Goodman received independent advice concerning the proposed transaction.

At trial Hutchinson J admitted Mr. Pearce's evidence and justified doing so on two distinct grounds. First, he held that the circumstances of this case were analogous to the wills context where a recognized class of exceptions to the rule regarding the inadmissibility of communications between solicitor and client has been well established. At pages 223-24 of his reasons he said:

> I can find no logical reason why the exception to the solicitor–client privilege that exists in cases where the succession of property turns on the validity of a will would not apply to the present case. In the present case, the trust agreement entered into by Mrs. Goodman is being challenged by the plaintiff, who claims that undue influence was placed upon Mrs. Goodman to execute the agreement. There really is no distinction between an allegation of undue influence when it arises in the case of the execution of a will as opposed to the execution of a trust document when in each case the testator or the settlor has since died. In both cases, it is the duty of the court to ascertain the true intention and the capacity of the deceased. In my view, it is in both the interest of the client and the interest of justice that the relevant evidence of the solicitor, Mr. Pearce, be admitted in evidence.

In the alternative, he found that even if no analogy could be drawn to contests over succession rights, the privilege that existed between Mrs. Goodman and Mr. Pearce had been waived. At page 224 he said:

> In the present case, the plaintiffs are legal representatives of the deceased Mrs. Goodman. By raising no objection to the testimony of Mr. Pearce and by electing to extensively cross-examine him, the plaintiffs have impliedly waived any solicitor–client privilege that might have existed between Mr. Pearce and Mrs. Goodman. It is obvious that the defendants who were charged with the responsibility of carrying out the terms of the trust for the benefit of the ultimate beneficiaries named therein have also waived the solicitor–client privilege on behalf of such beneficiaries by the fact of their having called Mr. Pearce as a witness.

In the Court of Appeal Hetherington JA expressed her concurrence with Hutchinson J's first ground but made no mention of his alternative finding. The majority did not address the evidentiary issue.

In this Court the respondents attacked this aspect of the trial decision. They maintain that the trial judge erred in drawing an analogy between the wills exception and this case and that the general rule as to solicitor–client privilege should have been applied. To them Mr. Pearce as solicitor should not have been permitted to testify and the court itself should have put a stop to his evidence. ...

It has long been recognized that communications between solicitor and client are protected by a privilege against disclosure. The classic statement of the rationale behind this rule was made over one hundred and fifty years ago by Brougham LC in *Greenough v. Gaskell* (1833), 1 My. & K 98, 39 ER 618, at p. 103 and at pp. 620-21, respectively:

> The foundation of this rule is not difficult to discover. It is not (as has sometimes been said) on account of any particular importance which the law attributes to the business of legal professors, or any particular disposition to afford them protection, though certainly it may not be very easy to discover why a like privilege has been refused to others, and especially to medical advisers.
>
> But it is out of regard to the interests of justice, which cannot be upholden, and to the administration of justice, which cannot go on, without the aid of men skilled in jurisprudence, in the practice of the Courts, and in those matters affecting rights and obligations which form the subject of all judicial proceedings. If the privilege did not exist at all, every one would be thrown upon his own legal resources; deprived of all professional assistance, a man would not venture to consult any skilful person, or would only dare to tell his counsellor half his case.

More recently, this Court has described the privilege as a "fundamental civil and legal right": see *Solosky v. The Queen*, [1980] 1 SCR 821, at p. 839. Thus, while at one time it was thought that the privilege belonged to the solicitor and not to his client, there is now no doubt that the privilege belongs to the client alone. One consequence of this is that confidential communications between solicitor and client can only be divulged in certain circumscribed situations. The client may, of course, herself choose to disclose the contents of her communications with her legal representative and thereby waive the privilege. Or, the client may authorize the solicitor to reveal those communications for her. Even then, however, the courts have been cautious in allowing such disclosures, so much so that they have assumed for themselves the role of ensuring that without the client's express consent a solicitor may not testify. Thus, in *Bell v. Smith*, [1968] SCR 664, this Court held that there had been a violation of solicitor–client privilege when a former solicitor of the plaintiffs in a motor vehicle accident claim was subpoenaed by the defendants and testified as to the settlement discussions that had taken place. Spence J said at p. 671:

> It is rather astounding that Mr. Schreiber should be subpoenaed to give evidence on behalf of the defendants as against his former clients and that he should produce his complete file including many memoranda and other material all of which were privileged

as against the plaintiffs and whether the plaintiffs' counsel objected or not that he should be permitted to so testify and so produce without the consent of the plaintiffs being requested and obtained.

Lord Chancellor Eldon said, in *Beer v. Ward* (1821), Jacob 77, 37 ER 779, at p. 80:

> ... it would be the duty of any Court to stop him if he was about to disclose confidential matters ... the Court knows the privilege of the client, and it must be taken for granted that the attorney will act rightly, and claim that privilege; or that if he does not, the Court will make him claim it.

So important is the privilege that the courts have also stipulated that the confidentiality of communications between solicitor and client survives the death of the client and enures to his or her next of kin, heirs, or successors in title: see *Bullivant v. Attorney-General for Victoria*, [1901] A.C. 196; *Stewart v. Walker* (1903), 6 OLR 495; and *Langworthy v. McVicar* (1913), 25 OWR 297.

An exception has, however, developed to permit a solicitor to give evidence in wills cases and a variety of explanations for this exception to the general rule concerning solicitor–client privilege have been advanced by commentators and courts alike. In *Wigmore on Evidence* (vol. 8, (SS) 2314), for example, the author suggests that, in so far as issues relating to the execution or contents of a will are concerned, the rationale underlying the exception relates to the testator's desire for secrecy. At page 610 of vol. 8, Professor Wigmore states:

> But for wills a special consideration comes into play. Here it can hardly be doubted that the execution and especially the contents are impliedly desired by the client to be kept secret during his lifetime, and are accordingly a part of his confidential communication. It must be assumed that during that period the attorney ought not to be called upon to disclose even the fact of a will's execution, much less its tenor. But, on the other hand, this confidence is intended to be temporary only. That there may be such a qualification to the privilege is plain.

In those cases dealing with the validity of a will as opposed to its execution or contents Professor Wigmore acknowledges that the secrecy rationale does not fully explain why a testator's communications with his solicitor should be admitted. In such circumstances he suggests at pp. 612-13 that a solicitor may testify as to the state of mind of the testator since, if the testator were insane or unduly influenced, his utterances were "obviously not confidentially made with reference to the secrecy of the fact of insanity or undue influence, for the testator of course did not believe those facts to exist and therefore could not possibly be said to have communicated them." Professor Wigmore then goes on to cite numerous American cases in which a solicitor has been permitted to testify where the validity of a will has been challenged on the ground that the testator was unduly influenced.

Professor Phipson, on the other hand, appears to be of the view that a different rationale supports the exception to the solicitor–client privilege in the wills context. In his opinion, any time claimants have a joint interest with the client in the subject matter of the communication, whether dealing with wills or some other matter, no privilege attaches. Hence, he states that as between joint claimants under a testator as to communications between the latter and his solicitor, the privilege does not apply: see *Phipson on Evidence* (13th ed. 1982), at p. 300. In *The Law of Evidence in Civil Cases* (1974), the authors argue that Canadian courts have approached the admissibility of this sort of evidence in a unique way, although the same result has been arrived at. For instance, in *Stewart v. Walker*, *supra*, it was alleged that the testator had died intestate. The deceased's solicitor, however, had in his possession a copy of a will providing that he, the solicitor, was to be left the greater part of the deceased's estate and was appointed as sole executor. It was contended that the solicitor should not be permitted to give evidence as to the existence or validity of the will. The Ontario Court of Appeal, however, felt that the solicitor should have been permitted to testify, saying at pp. 497-98:

> The nature of the case precludes the question of privilege from arising. The reason on which the rule is founded is the safeguarding of the interests of the client, or those claiming under him when they are in conflict with the claims of third persons not claiming, or assuming to claim, under him. And that is not this case, where the question is as to what testamentary dispositions, if any, were made by the client. As said by Sir George Turner, Vice-Chancellor, in *Russell v. Jackson* (1851), 9 Ha. 387, at p. 392: "The disclosure in such cases can affect no right or interest of the client. The apprehension of it can present no impediment to the full statement of his case to his solicitor … and the disclosure when made can expose the Court to no greater difficulty than presents itself in all cases where the Courts have to ascertain the views and intentions of parties, or the objects and purposes for which dispositions have been made." It has been the constant practice to apply the rule here stated in cases of contested wills where the evidence of the solicitors by whom the wills were prepared, as to the instructions they received, is always received. And the application of a different rule in this action would deprive the plaintiff of a considerable part of the proof of his case.

Similarly, In *Re Ott*, [1972] 2 OR 5 (Surr. Ct.), where the issue was whether the testator by tearing it up intended to revoke a later will and revive an earlier one, Anderson Surr. Ct. J held that the discussion that took place between the deceased and his solicitor at the time of the destruction of the will was admissible. At page 11 he said:

> … [S]ince it is of essence to the case to find out the intention of the testator when he destroyed the will whether or not he was revoking his will unconditionally or whether he was only tearing it up on condition that an earlier will was thus revived, the whole issue turns on this question and it would seem to me that to invoke the privilege of the client, after the client is deceased would make it impossible for the Court to determine the intention of the testator in tearing up the will. In the interests of justice, it is more important to find out the true intention of the testator.

In the present case the respondents argue that no analogy can be drawn between these wills cases and the situation here. I disagree. It is implicit in their argument that the common law has as yet only recognized an "exception" to the general rule of the privileged nature of communications between solicitor and client when dealing with the execution, tenor or validity of wills and wills alone. Their argument is reminiscent of earlier days when the "pigeon hole" approach to rules of evidence prevailed. Such, in my opinion, is no longer the case. The trend towards a more principled approach to admissibility questions has been embraced both here and abroad (see, for example, in Canada, *Ares v. Venner*, [1970] SCR 608 (hearsay), and *R v. Khan*, [1990] 2 SCR 531 (hearsay), and in the United Kingdom, *Director of Public Prosecutions v. Boardman*, [1975] AC 421 (HL) (similar fact)), a trend which I believe should be encouraged.

In my view, the considerations which support the admissibility of communications between solicitor and client in the wills context apply with equal force to the present case. The general policy which supports privileging such communications is not violated. The interests of the now deceased client are furthered in the sense that the purpose of allowing the evidence to be admitted is precisely to ascertain what her true intentions were. And the principle of extending the privilege to the heirs or successors in title of the deceased is promoted by focusing the inquiry on who those heirs or successors properly are. In summary, it is, in the words of Anderson Surr. Ct. J in *Re Ott*, *supra*, "[i]n the interests of justice" to admit such evidence. …

5. Disposition

I would allow the appeal, set aside the decision of the Court of Appeal, and restore the decision of the trial judge. The appellants are entitled to full reimbursement from the trust property for their actual and reasonable costs (including legal fees) incurred in defending the respondent's lawsuit.

NOTES AND QUESTIONS

1. If, as the court contends, the benefit of confidentiality "belongs to the client alone," what is the point of enforcing the duty of confidentiality once the relevant client has died? Are there some aspects of this duty which enure to the benefit of the courts? To other people?

2. What is the point of holding that the benefits of a solicitor's duty of confidentiality pass on to the successors of the client? In what circumstances might a client's successors have a utility interest in the maintenance of the lawyer's duty of confidentiality?

3. Would the functioning of the legal system be impaired if clients knew, in advance, that their private information could be disclosed after they died? Why or why not?

VI. Promoting Justice

Like the decision of the court in *Geffen v. Goodman Estate*, above, the decision of the court in *R v. Jack* (1992) (reproduced below) deals with the ability of a lawyer to divulge confidential information received from a former client. Unlike *Geffen v. Goodman* estate, however, the goal of disclosure in *R v. Jack* was not simply to determine the intentions of a now-deceased client. Rather, the goal of disclosure in *R v. Jack* was to determine whether the former client had been murdered. When reading the court's decision, consider whether the court is attempting to further the interests of the lawyer's former client or whether it is pursuing the broader social goal of "promoting justice." Is the court in *Jack* engaged in its own economic analysis?

If the goal the court in *R v. Jack* pursues can be defined as "the promotion of justice," consider whether *R v. Jack* could sow the seeds of a much broader exception to confidentiality involving any case in which social utility could be maximized by disclosure.[17] The topic of exceptions to the duty of confidentiality will be considered in greater detail in chapter 7. For present purposes, the goal of our analysis of the court's decision in *Jack* is to consider the court's view of the rationale underlying the duty of confidentiality.

R v. Jack
(1992), 70 CCC (3d) 67 (Man. CA)

SCOTT CJM: After one of the longest jury trials in Manitoba history, Brian Jack was convicted of second degree murder in the death of his wife Christine. He now appeals his conviction. What makes this case unique is that her body has never been found despite a massive search for her which commenced shortly after an admitted domestic quarrel with the accused on December 17, 1988. Much of the 39-day trial was taken up with evidentiary problems which arose because there could be no proof of cause of death. ...

Background

In December, 1988, Christine Jack, the accused and their two young children resided at 170 Alburg Dr. in the City of Winnipeg. Christine Jack was employed by the child guidance clinic as a speech therapist. She also had a part-time business called Kinder Spirit which manufactured and sold children's clothing.

Evidence was led by the Crown, much of it over the objection of counsel for the accused, about the nature of the relationship between the accused and his missing wife. This evidence disclosed that a marriage that had been for many years an idyllic one had begun to disintegrate in the fall of 1988 due, in part at least, to the failure of the accused's business and the inevitable pressures that it placed on the marriage. No less than 13 witnesses testified about the state of the marriage and, in particular, the deteriorating relationship between the spouses.

In November, 1988, Christine Jack and a close friend, Cheryl McMillan, spent a few days in Grand Forks, North Dakota. On her return, Christine Jack told the accused she no longer had feelings for him and wished to end the marriage. The accused and Christine Jack attended on a psychiatrist who specialized in family counselling. The accused told friends and acquaintances that it was his constant desire to keep the marriage together.

---

17   Like several of the cases in this chapter, the decision in *R v. Jack* deals with privilege, rather than confidentiality. However, since the question in *R v. Jack* is whether confidential information can be disclosed despite the existence of privilege, the decision has obvious implications for the duty of confidentiality. If a lawyer is permitted to disclose information despite the existence of solicitor–client privilege, the lawyer is necessarily permitted to breach the duty of confidentiality as well.

Evidence tendered by the Crown disclosed that in and around December, 1988, Christine Jack met and spoke with a number of her friends, including the witnesses Donna Henry, Cheryl McMillan, Connie Matthes, Alfred Kircher and Earl Weber. She also spoke to her parents, Mr. and Mrs. Reiter, and to an old family friend, Lidijia Jankovec. She made comments to all of them regarding her feelings and future intentions. Statements to these persons were admitted by the trial judge as original evidence of the state of mind of Christine Jack. Evidence was also admitted of an appointment and a meeting that Christine Jack had with a lawyer a few days before her disappearance.

From all of this evidence the picture that emerges is one of a loving, caring mother who would not willingly abandon her children, family and friends whatever the personal provocation. Equally clear is that she had made up her mind the marriage was finished and had determined, once the holiday season was over, to effect a separation. ...

The Trial

The preliminary hearing in this matter commenced on May 10, 1989, and proceeded intermittently over a number of months, concluding in September, 1989. The trial was set for May 7, 1990, but was adjourned on a motion by the Crown on May 2, 1990, to enable DNA blood typing to be completed. In fact, the DNA testing was not completed by the time the trial commenced on September 10, 1990, and no such evidence was tendered.

At the opening of the trial, the Crown addressed the jury as follows: "This is a very rare and very unique case insofar as the Crown cannot lead evidence before you with respect to the finding of the deceased." The Crown called 44 witnesses. Family and friends of Christine Jack testified that they had not seen or heard from her since December 17, 1988, despite much publicity surrounding her disappearance and the massive police search.

During the course of the trial there was a further belated disclosure by the Crown that there had been reports of other alleged sightings of Christine Jack and the Blazer. The defence made a motion for a mistrial. The motion was denied by the trial judge, but on defence counsel's application the court called two witnesses, Donna Pike and Shirley Garbutt. Both witnesses were employed as waitresses at the Charter House hotel restaurant, and both testified that they saw a person whom they believed to be Christine Jack in the Charter House restaurant on December 23, 1988. They also testified having notified the Winnipeg police department almost immediately thereafter. Ms. Pike testified that the police did not attend on her until September, 1989, after a police officer had first disclosed evidence of alleged sightings while testifying at the preliminary inquiry. The police never interviewed Ms. Garbutt.

On further application by the Crown, the court called George Gershman as a witness. Mr. Gershman was the manager of the Charter House hotel. He testified that he saw a woman on the premises, but it was not the person whose picture he had seen in the newspapers.

At the conclusion of the evidence for the Crown and the three witnesses called by the court, the defence made a motion for a directed verdict so as to withdraw the charge of murder from the jury. The motion was denied. The defence did not call any evidence.

The Crown addressed the jury on November 13, 1990. The defence addressed the jury on November 14, 1990. The charge to the jury commenced at 10:00 a.m. on November 15, 1990, and concluded at 9:30 p.m. A recharge of the jury concluded at 11:02 p.m. the same day. The next day the jury returned a verdict of guilty of second degree murder.

The Legal Issues

. . .

4. Admissibility of the evidence of the lawyer whom Christine Jack consulted a short time before her disappearance.

Although tendered by the Crown as "state of mind" evidence, it is argued that in fact the contents of privileged communications were disclosed during the lawyer's evidence—this being so in the absence of a waiver of the privilege by the client. It is asserted that the privilege can be raised in the interests of justice by any interested party, including the individual accused of the homicide of the person for whose benefit the privilege exists. ...

Solicitor–Client Privilege

On Wednesday, December 14, 1988, some three days before her disappearance, Christine Jack consulted a lawyer specializing in family law. Over the objections of counsel for the accused who asserted solicitor–client privilege, the lawyer was allowed to testify as to the general nature of the meeting, but not to the specific dialogue. In the course of doing so, she indicated that Christine Jack was under stress "as most people who are going through separation, but she had clearly made up her mind where she was going and what she was going to do." She also testified that she explained the legal options and remedies available to Christine Jack.

In ruling that the evidence was admissible, the trial judge accepted the Crown's submission that the evidence was being tendered not as an exception to the hearsay rule so as to make relevant proof of the truth of the contents of an otherwise privileged communication, but simply (again) to prove the state of mind and future intentions of Christine Jack. He relied on the decision of *R v. Dunbar and Logan* (1982), 68 CCC (2d) 13, 138 DLR (3d) 221, 28 CR (3d) 324 (Ont. CA), as authority for the proposition that when the client no longer has any interest to protect, there is no rule requiring the continued preservation of solicitor–client privilege.

In support of his ruling, he referred to the American concept of a "good faith determination" which is used in cases where an express waiver cannot be obtained. He concluded that, in any event, it was in the best interests of Christine Jack to waive the privilege. (It should be noted that the American approach allows the contents of confidential communications to be revealed.)

Legal privilege attaches to certain kinds of confidential information passing from clients to lawyers during the course of proceedings. In *Ott v. Fleishman*, [1983] 5 WWR 721, 46 BCLR 321, 22 BLR 57 (SC), McEachern CJBC (as he then was) defined confidential information as follows (at p. 723):

> I do not propose to attempt a comprehensive definition, but for practical purposes any information received by a lawyer in his professional capacity concerning his client's affairs is *prima facie* confidential unless it is already notorious or was received for the purpose of being used publicly or otherwise disclosed in the conduct of the client's affairs.

In the unique circumstances of this case, I am of the opinion that the evidence given by Christine Jack's lawyer did not constitute a communication of confidential information received by the lawyer from the client. In its context, it was simply a recitation of the lawyer's advice and opinion as to the general tenor of the meeting, and her conclusion as to the client's state of mind and future plans. ...

Furthermore, in my opinion, solicitor–client privilege does not attach in the circumstances of the case. In argument, strong reliance was placed by the accused on the case of *Bell v. Smith* (1968), 68 DLR (2d) 751, [1968] SCR 664, 46 BCLR 321, where Spence J, writing for the court, said (at p. 751):

> Because the solicitor owes to his former client a duty to claim the privilege when applicable, it is improper for him not to claim it without showing that it has been properly waived. Especially is this so when, as here, the circumstances are such as to make it most unlikely that a waiver would be given. Also, because it is improper to induce a breach of duty, I have serious doubts about the propriety of putting to a solicitor questions that involve the disclosure of confidential information without first bringing in evidence of a proper waiver. In any case, because the client's privilege is a duty owed to the Court, no objection ought to be necessary and the evidence in violation of the privilege should not be received.

Relying on the emphasized passage above, the accused concedes that the privilege exists in favour of the client (Christine Jack), but asserts that it can be invoked by anyone whose interests might be adversely impacted by the disclosure. Further support is found by the accused in *R v. Solosky* (1979), 50 CCC (2d) 495, 105 DLR (3d) 745, [1980] 1 SCR 821, where Dickson J (as he then was) referred to the privilege existing "out of regard to the interests of justice."

In my opinion, the accused's position is not tenable. In this case the person in whose favour the privilege exists is alleged to have been killed by the very person who claims to benefit from the privilege. It is clearly in the best interests of Christine Jack, and in the "interests of justice," that the privilege be waived as it was in this case by her lawyer.

The basic rule is that the claim to privilege can only be made by the person whose privilege it is: see *Wigmore on Evidence* (McNaughton rev. 1961), vol. 8, p. 111, 2196:

> It follows that the claim of privilege can be made solely by the person whose privilege it is. The privilege (as the common phrasing runs) is purely personal to himself. Whether he chooses to permit disclosure without objection, or whether he prefers to exercise the exemption which the law concedes to him, is a matter resting entirely between himself and the state (or the court as its representative). The party against whom the testimony is brought has no right to claim or to urge the exemption on his own behalf.

In *McCormick on Evidence*, 2nd ed. (1972), it is noted at p. 192 that, "the privilege is not designed to protect the fact-finding process but is intended to protect some 'outside' interest," namely, a party to legal proceedings. The privilege does not arise as a result of some undefined duty to the court. *Bell v. Smith*, *supra*, simply stands for the proposition that a court will not knowingly allow a solicitor to act in breach of a duty to a client when the information will clearly be used against the interests of the client. The underlying basis of the rule as to solicitor–client privilege is public policy favouring candour between lawyers and their clients. It is a privilege which the client alone has the power to invoke except in extraordinary circumstances such as here when the client is not available. It cannot be invoked by a party whose interest in the proceedings is manifestly contrary to that of the client.

The Supreme Court of Canada in admitting communications between a deceased person and her solicitor in *Geffen v. Goodman Estate* (1991), 81 DLR (4th) 211 at p. 235, [1991] 5 WWR 389, 80 Alta. LR (2d) 293, said per Wilson J:

> In my view, the considerations which support the admissibility of communications between solicitor and client in the wills context apply with equal force to the present case. The general policy which supports privileging such communications is not violated. The interests of the now deceased client are furthered in the sense that the purpose of allowing the evidence to be admitted is precisely to ascertain what her true intentions were. And the principle of extending the privilege to the heirs or successors in title of the deceased is promoted by focusing the inquiry on who those heirs or successors properly are. In summary, it is, in the words of Anderson Surr. Ct. J in *Re Ott*, *supra*, "[i]n the interests of justice" to admit such evidence.

With respect to other heads of privilege, the courts have recently shown a tendency to allow evidence to be introduced in "the interests of justice" where the benefit to the administration of justice clearly outweighs in importance any public interest that might be protected by upholding the claim for privilege: see, for example, *Bergwitz v. Fast* (1980), 108 DLR (3d) 732, 18 BCLR 368, 1 ACWS (2d) 180 (BCCA); *Hamulka v. Golfman* (1985), 20 DLR (4th) 540, [1985] 5 WWR 597, 35 Man. R (2d) 189 (CA), and *Merrill Lynch v. Granove*, [1985] 5 WWR 589, 35 Man. R (2d) 194, 33 ACWS (2d) 18 (CA). This is exactly what was done, albeit in the interests of the accused, in *Dunbar and Logan*, *supra*, relied on by the trial judge.

I have no difficulty in concluding in the circumstances of this case that if the evidence of the lawyer strayed into communications of a confidential nature, it was in the interests of both the client, Christine Jack, and the administration of justice that the communications in question be admitted in evidence. ...

Conclusion

In all of the circumstances of this complex and difficult case, I have come to the conclusion that the appeal must be allowed because of the error in the trial judge's charge with respect to the Charter House witnesses. A new trial is ordered on the charge of second degree murder. ...

NOTES AND QUESTIONS

1. According to the court,

> the evidence given by Christine Jack's lawyer did not constitute a communication of
> confidential information received by the lawyer from the client. In its context, it was simply
> a recitation of the lawyer's advice and opinion as to the general tenor of the meeting, and
> her conclusion as to the client's state of mind and future plans.

Does this mean that lawyers can now divulge their clients' states of mind and future
plans, together with a recitation of any advice that the lawyer has given the client? Would
this make sense, given the rationale underlying the ethical duty to keep client information
confidential? Should the decision in *R v. Jack* receive a more limited application?

2. What would be more likely to impair the utility interests of the public in this case:
disclosure of confidential information or refusal to allow the disclosure of confidential
information? By allowing disclosure in this case, is the court doing so on the ground that
there is no "harm" to be compensated or no "harmful conduct" to be deterred? To the
extent that the court creates an exception to confidentiality in this case, how would you
describe that exception? In what circumstances will that exception apply?

3. Whose utility interests is the court maximizing by permitting disclosure of the
relevant information?

4. The court notes that privilege "cannot be invoked by a party whose interest in the
proceedings is manifestly contrary to that of the client." If Christine Jack is merely
missing (rather than dead), how are her husband's interests "manifestly contrary" to those
of his missing wife? In making this statement, is the court presuming that Brian Jack
killed his wife? Is this assumption (which lies at the heart of the court's decision to
permit the disclosure of the information) contrary to the presumption of innocence?

VII. Duty To Assert

Because of the nature of the interests it protects, many people assume that the duty of
confidentiality is a passive duty only: it requires the lawyer to *refrain* from disclosing or
using the client's information, but places no active burden on the lawyer. This assumption is unwarranted. In many cases, the obligation of confidentiality imposes a positive
duty to "assert confidentiality when information is sought by a third party."[18] This may
include the duty to object to search warrants concerning the contents of a lawyer's files,
or the duty to raise a claim of privilege when the lawyer's testimony (relating to confidential information) is sought in legal proceedings. The lawyer's *positive* duty to assert
confidentiality is discussed in *Bell v. Smith* (1968) (cited immediately below).

---

18   Proulx and Layton, supra note 9, at 191.

Bell v. Smith
[1968] SCR 664

SPENCE J: ... The circumstances involved are rather intricate and of the most unusual nature and it is, therefore, necessary to relate them in some detail. On August
27, 1962, the plaintiff James Bell was operating a motor vehicle owned by the plaintiff Kenneth Bell, his father, and with passengers the plaintiffs Helen Bell, his mother,
and David Grey Bell (properly called David Guy Bell) and Marjorie Bell. The vehicle came into contact with one owned by the defendant John William Charles Smith
due, to what was alleged by the plaintiffs, to be the negligence of the said defendant
Smith. One Commiski, an employee of the Pilot Insurance Company, recommended
that the plaintiffs consult either Mr. Henry Schreiber, QC or Mr. John Agro, QC to
act on their behalf. The plaintiffs chose to consult Mr. Henry Schreiber. Due, it was
said, to the continued serious physical conditions of the various plaintiffs, a statement of claim was not issued until November 12, 1965. A statement of defence was
issued on December 21, 1965, and issue was joined on December 22, 1965.

On January 6, 1966, the various plaintiffs were examined for discovery, and on
January 11, 1966, the solicitors for the defendants gave notice of motion of an application for leave to make a payment into Court in full satisfaction of the claims of the
plaintiffs. These examinations for discovery and this notice of application for leave
to pay into Court seem to have very much increased the tempo of the discussions for
settlement of the action between the solicitors for the plaintiffs and for the defendants. The solicitor for the plaintiffs conferred with his client Mrs. Helen Bell by
telephone almost immediately after the examinations for discovery and then the various plaintiffs attended his office on January 10th and on January 12th. During these
latter occasions there were telephone conversations between the solicitors for the
plaintiffs and for the defendants, and the amounts of the settlements were discussed
in great detail. The record contains many long memoranda setting out how various
amounts were arrived at.

The plaintiff Helen Bell has testified that, after a very long conference on January
12, 1966, she and her co-plaintiffs agreed to the settlement which was proposed and
which her then solicitor, Mr. Schreiber, said was the utmost he could obtain from the
solicitor for the defendants. Mr. Schreiber seems to have been greatly concerned at
the possible penalty in costs which the plaintiffs would have incurred had the application for leave to pay into Court been granted and then the payment made there-
under ... exceeded what the plaintiffs would have recovered at trial.

So soon as the plaintiffs had, with great reluctance, expressed their agreement to
settle in the amounts outlined by Mr. Schreiber in this conference, he telephoned at
once to Mr. Agro, the solicitor for the defendants, to inform him of such agreement,
and on the same day wrote a letter in which he set out the matter. ...

... The plaintiff Helen Bell testified that having attempted on that very day, January 12, 1966, to telephone to Mr. Schreiber to say that the plaintiffs had recanted
from their agreement to settle on the basis outlined, she succeeded, on January 13,
1966, in giving that message to Mr. Schreiber's secretary who undertook to pass it on
to her employer. She continued that then they were telephoned by the said secretary

on January 14th and asked to come down to Mr. Schreiber's office immediately. Helen Bell continued in her testimony to outline a conference in Mr. Schreiber's office on January 20th and her letter of the same date to Mr. Schreiber in which she demanded an increase in her claim in the amount of $75,000. ...

On February 7, 1966, a notice of motion was served on the various plaintiffs. This was for an application to be presented on February 10, 1966, at 10:00 a.m. for judgment in accordance with the settlement purported to have been made on January 12, 1966. So soon as the plaintiff Helen Bell received service of notice of that application, she wrote to Mr. Schreiber. The last two sentences of that letter read:

> The notice of motion contains an affidavit of John L. Agro setting out certain facts we believe to be incorrect.
>
> The matter is of serious interest and unless we receive a reply of your intentions by telephone (No. 772-3224) arrangements will be made to have counsel defend the motion and have you removed as solicitor on the record.

On February 8, 1966, that is, the next day, Mr. Schreiber served a notice of motion on the solicitor for the defendants to be heard at the same time as the motion for judgment. The relief asked in Mr. Schreiber's motion was for an order to set aside the settlement in the action and to restore the said action to the list of actions to be tried at this sitting of the Court. Also on February 8th Helen Bell and the other plaintiffs signed a notice of change of solicitors from Mr. Schreiber to Messrs. Ballachey, Moore and Hart. I should add that by a document entitled "Notice of Dispute" and dated February 4, 1966, the various plaintiffs had given notice to both Mr. Schreiber and Mr. Agro that "out of court settlement offered in full satisfaction of each of their claims is not acceptable and is refused and further take notice that it is their desire to proceed to trial by judge and jury for proper and just assessment for specific and general damages." On February 10, 1966, the motion for judgment in accordance with the settlement came on for hearing before Richardson J in Hamilton. Mr. Agro appeared for the applicants and Mr. Ballachey for the respondents.

It would appear that the first witness called by the applicants on the application was Henry L. Schreiber, the solicitor who had acted, until February 8, 1966, for the plaintiffs. It is Mr. Ballachey's recollection that he objected to Mr. Schreiber's giving evidence. Mr. Ballachey so testified on examination upon an affidavit which he had filed and to which reference will be made hereafter. The record in the appeal case shows no such objection but that record purports to be only "[e]xtract from proceedings *viva voce* evidence submitted on the motion." Mr. Agro executed an affidavit on June 2, 1967, and he states in para. 5 thereof:

> H.L. Schreiber, Esq., the former counsel for the Plaintiffs, appeared under subpoena and gave evidence on behalf of the Defendants. Mr. Ballachey raised no objection to giving of evidence by Mr. Schreiber.

[In other words, the plaintiffs' former lawyer was called to give evidence regarding the plaintiffs' acceptance of the defendant's original settlement offer. In giving his evidence, the plaintiff's former lawyer produced the plaintiffs' entire file, containing all the confidential information he had learned during the course of his professional engagement.]

"Counsel should not give a proof of evidence of what occurred at a hearing in which he was professionally engaged." This quotation is from 3 Hals., 3rd ed., p. 68, referring to the Annual Statement of the General Council of the Bar, 1937, p. 7. Under the circumstances of this case, counsel for both parties no doubt felt that they could not properly discharge their duty to their clients without submitting to the Court of Appeal evidence by affidavit followed on one side by cross-examination. I am not suggesting that this was improper under the circumstances. However, this shows how important it is to have all Court proceedings conducted in such way that there can be no justification for such a course of action. That this resulted in the Court being invited to choose between conflicting statements made under oath by distinguished members of the bar clearly demonstrates the wisdom of the aforementioned rule and the desirability of taking every precaution to ensure that the paramount interests of the clients will not require it to be broken.

This regrettable occurrence was occasioned by insufficient concern for a fundamental rule, namely, the duty of a solicitor to refrain from disclosing confidential information unless his client waives the privilege.

It is rather astounding that Mr. Schreiber should be subpoenaed to give evidence on behalf of the defendants as against his former clients and that he should produce his complete file including many memoranda and other material all of which were privileged as against the plaintiffs and whether the plaintiffs' counsel objected or not that he should be permitted to so testify and so produce without the consent of the plaintiffs being requested and obtained. Lord Chancellor Eldon said, in *Beer v. Ward* (1821), Jacob 77 at p. 80, 37 ER 779:

> … [I]t would be the duty of any Court to stop him if he was about to disclose confidential matters … the Court knows the privilege of the client, and it must be taken for granted that the attorney will act rightly, and claim that privilege; or that if he does not, the Court will make him claim it.

Because the solicitor owes to his former client a duty to claim the privilege when applicable, it is improper for him not to claim it without showing that it has been properly waived. Especially is this so when, as here, the circumstances are such as to make it most unlikely that a waiver would be given. Also, because it is improper to induce a breach of duty, I have serious doubts about the propriety of putting to a solicitor questions that involve the disclosure of confidential information without first bringing in evidence of a proper waiver. In any case, because the client's privilege is a duty owed to the Court, no objection ought to be necessary and the evidence in violation of the privilege should not be received. …

In view of this state of most regrettable confusion, I am of the opinion that the plaintiffs should have a right to have their action tried in open Court and that the appeal must be allowed. …

Appeal allowed; new trial ordered.

NOTES AND QUESTIONS

1. At one point in the judgment, the Supreme Court of Canada says that it has "serious doubts about the propriety of putting to a solicitor questions that involve the disclosure of confidential information without first bringing in evidence of a proper waiver." Does this create an additional duty relating to confidentiality—namely, a duty not to question other lawyers about a client's confidential information?

2. The court claims that "the client's privilege is a duty owed to the Court." Does this conform to what you know about the rationales underlying the duty of confidentiality? Is the court endorsing the view that the court *itself* loses utility where the lawyer breaches the duty to keep client information confidential? In what sense can the duty of confidentiality be regarded as a duty owed both to the lawyer's client and to the courts?

3. What is the appropriate remedy for the breach of confidentiality that occurred in this case? Should the offending lawyer be disbarred? Should he be forced to compensate his former clients for the cost of their new trial? What remedy would promote efficient incentives? What remedy would promote the goal of deterrence?

4. What gains did the offending lawyer pursue by disclosing his former client's information? Can his behaviour be described by reference to our basic ethical equation?

VIII. Legislative Erosion

Because the lawyer's duty of confidentiality can prevent the disclosure of information that could be vital to a court's determination of a disputed factual issue, it is often seen as an impediment to the truth-finding function of the courts. As Gavin MacKenzie notes, "the lawyer's duty of confidentiality is often an obstacle to the search for truth."[19] This is particularly evident in the criminal justice system, where lawyers often hold conclusive proof that their clients are, in fact, responsible for the crimes with which they are charged. As a result, laypersons often question the wisdom of the lawyer's ethical duty of confidentiality. Why should lawyers be permitted to withhold evidence of a crime? Issues of this nature have frequently led commentators to claim that "[t]he duty of confidentiality is sometimes invoked by lawyers to justify behaviour that is considered by most non-lawyers to be monstrous."[20]

Because of the public's disdain for the duty of confidentiality in cases where a lawyer may hold evidence that a client committed a crime, legislatures have (from time to time) enacted laws eroding the protection provided by the duty of confidentiality in criminal cases. The court in *R v. Fink* (2002) (reproduced below) was faced with a legislative provision the effect of which was to impair a client's right to confidentiality. Section 488.1 of the *Criminal Code* (reproduced in the court's decision) permitted law enforcement officials to seize files from a lawyer's office for the purposes of gathering evidence

---

19   MacKenzie, supra note 4, at 3-2.

20   Ibid., at 3-1.

against the lawyer's clientele.[21] While the section gave the opportunity for the lawyer to assert solicitor–client privilege, that opportunity could be lost in a wide array of circumstances. The court's decision in *R v. Fink* concerns the extent to which the relevant legislation violates s. 8 of the Charter, in part because of s. 488.1's erosion of the client's right to confidentiality.[22]

When reviewing the court's decision, consider the following questions: What were the interests that the legislature balanced when enacting s. 488.1 of the Code? Can the legislature's decision be represented by reference to utility maximization? If so, what are the benefits of s. 488.1? What are its costs? Does the court in *Fink* agree with the legislature's cost–benefit analysis? To the extent that the court departs from the legislature's cost–benefit analysis, does it simply disagree with the legislature's method of maximizing social utility, or is the court pursuing a different goal? Is the court considering a different set of costs and benefits, or is the court simply assigning different utility values to the same costs and benefits that the legislature considered?

R v. Fink

(2002) 216 DLR (4th) 257 (SCC)[23]

ARBOUR J (McLachlin CJC, Iacobucci, Major, Bastarache, and Binnie JJ concurring): These appeals bring into question the constitutionality of s. 488.1 of the *Criminal Code*, RSC 1985, c. C-46, which sets out a procedure for determining a claim of solicitor–client privilege in relation to documents seized from a law office under a warrant. The issue is brought before this Court by way of three separate appeals from the provinces of Alberta (*Lavallee, Rackel & Heintz v. Canada (Attorney General)*), Newfoundland and Labrador (*White, Ottenheimer & Baker v. Canada (Attorney General)*) and Ontario (*R v. Fink*), ...

For the reasons that follow, I am of the view that s. 488.1 is unconstitutional and must accordingly be struck down pursuant to s. 52 of the *Constitution Act, 1982*.

I. Facts: The Three Appeals

The facts of these cases are not controversial, nor are they determinative. Accordingly, all three matters can be briefly summarized as follows.

In Lavallee, the RCMP obtained a search warrant in the regular form and wording pursuant to s. 487 of the *Criminal Code* on January 16, 1996. The search was to be executed on the following day at the law firm of Lavallee, Rackel & Heintz, in the

---

21   Authority to conduct the relevant search was technically created by s. 487 of the Code. Section 488.1, however, purported to set out the circumstances in which a claim of privilege could be advanced.

22   Once again, this decision relates to privilege, rather than confidentiality. However, to the extent that s. 488.1 permitted a loss of solicitor–client privilege, it also (necessarily) gave rise to a loss of confidentiality.

23   The full style of cause of the several appeals heard together in this case is *Lavallee, Rackel & Heintz v. Canada (Attorney General)*; *White, Ottenheimer & Baker v. Canada (Attorney General)*; *R v. Fink*.

City of Edmonton, targeting correspondence, estate files, trust records and other documents in relation to Mr. Andy Brent Polo, an individual suspected of money laundering and of being in possession of proceeds of crime. When the RCMP arrived at the law firm to execute the warrant, a solicitor who was familiar with the documents in question claimed solicitor–client privilege. The searching officers accordingly followed the procedure set out in s. 488.1 of the *Criminal Code*: the documents were sealed in envelopes, summarily identified and taken into police custody. The next day, January 18, 1996, counsel retained by the law firm moved in the Court of Queen's Bench to fix a date and place for a judicial determination of privilege in reference to the seized documents in accordance with s. 488.1(3). In April 1996, the law firm gave notice of a constitutional question, alleging the unconstitutionality of s. 488.1 of the *Criminal Code*. The law firm and Mr. Polo also moved to quash the warrant but the application was denied in part by Dea J: (1997), 199 AR 21 (QB). In 1998, Veit J struck down s. 488.1 as unconstitutional: (1998), 126 CCC (3d) 129, 160 DLR (4th) 508 (Alta. QB). The appeal from that order was dismissed unanimously by the Court of Appeal for Alberta: (2000), 143 CCC (3d) 187, 184 DLR (4th) 25.

In *White*, a search warrant was obtained to search the law offices of Raymond P. Whelan, including all storage facilities occupied by him at the law firm of White, Ottenheimer & Baker, in the City of St. John's, Newfoundland. The warrant authorized officers of Revenue Canada to search the premises for documents relating to Daley Brothers Ltd. and Mr. Terry Daley who were suspected of the offences described in ss. 239(1)(a) and (d) of the *Income Tax Act*, RSC 1985, c. 1 (5th Supp.). When the search was executed on June 30, 1998, a partner in the appellant law firm claimed solicitor–client privilege with respect to the targeted documents and, as a result, pursuant to s. 488.1 of the *Criminal Code* and s. 232 of the *Income Tax Act*, the documents were sealed and taken into police custody. On July 9, 1998, the law firm moved to set a date and time for the determination of privilege under both s. 488.1(3) of the *Criminal Code* and s. 232(4) of the *Income Tax Act*. On January 29, 1999, the appellants applied for a declaration that s. 488.1 of the *Criminal Code* and s. 232 of the *Income Tax Act* are contrary to s. 8 of the *Canadian Charter of Rights and Freedoms*. Halley J of the Supreme Court of Newfoundland, Trial Division, dismissed the application. The Court of Appeal allowed the appeal in part, resorting to the remedial techniques of severance and reading-in to salvage the impugned section of the *Criminal Code*: (2000), 146 CCC (3d) 28, 187 DLR (4th) 581.

In *Fink*, a search warrant was executed at the law firm of Turkstra, Mazza Associates on February 8, 1999, in the City of Toronto, targeting documents relating to the appellant Jeffrey Fink who was suspected of various counts of fraud over $ 5,000. As [a] result of the claim of solicitor–client privilege made on behalf of the appellant by counsel, the search was carried out according to the procedure set out in s. 488.1 of the *Criminal Code* and the documents were taken into police custody. On November 11, 1999, the appellant applied to the Ontario Superior Court of Justice for an order declaring s. 488.1 to be inconsistent with s. 8 of the Charter. Dambrot J dismissed the application: (2000), 143 CCC (3d) 566. Goudge JA, for a unanimous court, allowed the appeal and declared s. 488.1 to be unconstitutional and of no force and effect: (2000), 51 OR (3d) 577, 149 CCC (3d) 321, 193 DLR (4th) 51.

II. The Impugned Provisions

Definitions

488.1(1) In this section,

"custodian" means a person in whose custody a package is placed pursuant to subsection (2)

"document," for the purposes of this section, has the same meaning as in section 321;

"judge" means a judge of a superior court of criminal jurisdiction of the province where the seizure was made;

"lawyer" means, in the Province of Quebec, an advocate, lawyer or notary and, in any other province, a barrister or solicitor;

"officer" means a peace officer or public officer.

Examination or seizure of certain documents where privilege claimed

(2) Where an officer acting under the authority of this or any other Act of Parliament is about to examine, copy or seize a document in the possession of a lawyer who claims that a named client of his has a solicitor–client privilege in respect of that document, the officer shall, without examining or making copies of the document,

    (a) seize the document and place it in a package and suitably seal and identify the package; and

    (b) place the package in the custody of the sheriff of the district or county in which the seizure was made or, if there is agreement in writing that a specified person act as custodian, in the custody of that person.

Application to judge

(3) Where a document has been seized and placed in custody under subsection (2), the Attorney General or the client or the lawyer on behalf of the client, may

    (a) within fourteen days from the day the document was so placed in custody, apply, on two days notice of motion to all other persons entitled to make application, to a judge for an order

        (i) appointing a place and a day, not later than twenty-one days after the date of the order, for the determination of the question whether the document should be disclosed, and

        (ii) requiring the custodian to produce the document to the judge at that time and place;

    (b) serve a copy of the order on all other persons entitled to make application and on the custodian within six days of the date on which it was made; and

    (c) if he has proceeded as authorized by paragraph (b), apply, at the appointed time and place, for an order determining the question.

Disposition of application

(4) On an application under paragraph (3)(c), the judge

    (a) may, if the judge considers it necessary to determine the question whether the document should be disclosed, inspect the document;

    (b) where the judge is of the opinion that it would materially assist him in deciding whether or not the document is privileged, may allow the Attorney General to inspect the document;

(c) shall allow the Attorney General and the person who objects to the disclosure of the document to make representations; and

(d) shall determine the question summarily and,

(i) if the judge is of the opinion that the document should not be disclosed, ensure that it is repackaged and resealed and order the custodian to deliver the document to the lawyer who claimed the solicitor–client privilege or to the client, or

(ii) if the judge is of the opinion that the document should be disclosed, order the custodian to deliver the document to the officer who seized the document or some other person designated by the Attorney General, subject to such restrictions or conditions as the judge deems appropriate, and shall, at the same time, deliver concise reasons for the determination in which the nature of the document is described without divulging the details thereof.

Privilege continues

(5) Where the judge determines pursuant to paragraph (4)(d) that a solicitor–client privilege exists in respect of a document, whether or not the judge has, pursuant to paragraph (4)(b), allowed the Attorney General to inspect the document, the document remains privileged and inadmissible as evidence unless the client consents to its admission in evidence or the privilege is otherwise lost.

Order to custodian to deliver

(6) Where a document has been seized and placed in custody under subsection (2) and a judge, on the application of the Attorney General, is satisfied that no application has been made under paragraph (3)(a) or that following such an application no further application has been made under paragraph (3)(c), the judge shall order the custodian to deliver the document to the officer who seized the document or to some other person designated by the Attorney General.

Application to another judge

(7) Where the judge to whom an application has been made under paragraph (3)(c) cannot act or continue to act under this section for any reason, subsequent applications under that paragraph may be made to another judge.

Prohibition

(8) No officer shall examine, make copies of or seize any document without affording a reasonable opportunity for a claim of solicitor–client privilege to be made under subsection (2).

Authority to make copies

(9) At any time while a document is in the custody of a custodian under this section, a judge may, on an *ex parte* application of a person claiming a solicitor–client privilege under this section, authorize that person to examine the document or make a copy of it in the presence of the custodian or the judge, but any such authorization shall contain provisions to ensure that the document is repackaged and that the package is resealed without alteration or damage.

Hearing in private

(10) An application under paragraph (3)(c) shall be heard in private.

Exception

(11) This section does not apply in circumstances where a claim of solicitor–client privilege may be made under the *Income Tax Act*.

. . .

IV. Analysis

A. Law Office Searches

Before the 1970s, law office searches were seldom employed in the course of criminal investigations. But since that time, there has been an observable trend in Canada and the United States towards more aggressive investigatory methods which include the issuing of warrants to search law offices for evidence of crime. See generally L.H. Bloom Jr., "The Law Office Search: An Emerging Problem and Some Suggested Solutions" (1980), 69 Geo. LJ 1, wherein the author partially attributes "the sudden and recent emergence of the law office search" (p. 7), in the United States to the Watergate scandal, which he claims lowered the public esteem of lawyers in general. See also J.E. Davis, "Law Office Searches: The Assault on Confidentiality and the Adversary System" (1996), 33 *Am. Crim. L Rev.* 1251.

In Canada, the enactment of s. 488.1 of the *Criminal Code* (originally s. 444.1) in 1985 was in fact the legislative response to a line of cases culminating in this Court's decision *Descoteaux v. Mierzwinski*, [1982] 1 SCR 860, 70 CCC (2d) 385, 141 DLR (3d) 590, that set out guidelines for the issuing of search warrants for law offices. From the outset, Canadian courts expressed serious concerns about the dangers of law office searches in light of solicitor–client privilege, and urged Parliament to create protective measures akin to those found in the *Income Tax Act*. Section 488.1 was designed to address these concerns and, in the words of the Minister of Justice, "establish a sealing procedure with respect to seized documents that will ensure protection of solicitor–client privilege" (House of Commons, Standing Committee on Justice and Legal Affairs, Minutes of the Proceedings and Evidence, January 22, 1985, Issue No. 5, at 5:9). As it will be explained further in these reasons, s. 488.1 of the *Criminal Code* falls short of providing the protection it promised and, indeed, unconstitutionally jeopardizes solicitor–client privilege. ...

It seems clear from this background that s. 488.1 of the Code was enacted in an effort to address the specificity of the searches of lawyers' business premises and, in particular, to ensure that privileged communications made to a lawyer were properly exempted from the reach of that investigative technique. At the same time, to the extent that s. 488.1 only applies "[w]here an officer acting under the authority of [the *Criminal Code*] or any other Act of Parliament is about to examine, copy, or seize a document in the possession of a lawyer," it is clear that the provision was never intended to supersede the common law principles pertaining to the issuance of a warrant in the law office context, as discussed by Lamer J in *Descoteaux, supra*. That is,

s. 488.1 does not attempt to deal with the process for authorizing the search of law offices but merely with the manner in which they are carried out. The question before us is whether this attempt reached the constitutional mark. Not all communications between a solicitor and a client are covered by privilege (*Solosky, supra*, at p. 829). In the context of civil litigation, for example, affidavits of documents are produced, identifying documents that would otherwise be discoverable, but that are claimed as privileged and thus exempt from disclosure.

In the context of a criminal investigation, the privilege acquires an additional dimension. The individual privilege holder is facing the state as a "singular antagonist" and for that reason requires an arsenal of constitutionally guaranteed rights (*Irwin Toy Ltd. v. Quebec (Attorney General)*, [1989] 1 SCR 927 at p. 994, 58 DLR (4th) 577). It is particularly when a person is the target of a criminal investigation that the need for the full protection of the privilege is activated. It is then not an abstract proposition but a live issue of ensuring that the privilege delivers on the promise of confidentiality that it holds.

It is critical to emphasize here that all information protected by the solicitor–client privilege is out of reach for the state. It cannot be forcibly discovered or disclosed and it is inadmissible in court. It is the privilege of the client and the lawyer acts as a gatekeeper, ethically bound to protect the privileged information that belongs to his or her client. Therefore, any privileged information acquired by the state without the consent of the privilege holder is information that the state is not entitled to as a rule of fundamental justice.

It is in that context that we must ask whether Parliament has taken all required steps to ensure that there is no deliberate or accidental access to information that is, as a matter of constitutional law, out of reach in a criminal investigation.

E. The Constitutional Failings of Section 488.1 Identified in the Proceedings Below

As stated above, the appellate courts of Alberta, British Columbia, Newfoundland, Nova Scotia and Ontario all held that the procedure set out in s. 488.1 unconstitutionally offended to the rights enshrined in s. 8 of the Charter. In coming to that conclusion, these courts identified several problems within the provisions of s. 488.1 which, either directly or indirectly, compromise the integrity of solicitor–client privilege.

(1) Absence or Inaction of Solicitor

The courts below all found that privilege may be lost through the absence or the inaction of the solicitor. Pursuant to s. 488.1(2), the sealing procedure is only engaged if "a lawyer ... claims that a named client of his has a solicitor–client privilege" in respect of the documents. If the solicitor is not present at the time and place of the search, the officers conducting the search must give the lawyer a reasonable opportunity to make the claim of privilege, as directed by s. 488.1(8). If no claim is made, they may seize the documents and freely examine their contents, thus causing the privilege to be lost. Similarly, the privilege may also be lost if the solicitor is present but fails to claim the privilege for whatever reason (incompetence, sickness or out of sheer nervousness arising out of having his or her office searched). See *Lavallee*, *supra*, at paras. 28 and 37; *White*, *supra*, at para. 21; *Fink*, *supra*, at para. 34, and *Festing* [*v. Canada (Attorney General)* (2001), 206 DLR (4th) 98 (BCCA)], at para. 17.

(2) The Naming of Clients

Courts have also identified another offensive aspect of s. 488.1(2) in the requirement that the lawyer name the client whose privilege is being threatened in order to engage the sealing procedure with respect to that client's documents. The name of the client may very well be protected by solicitor–client privilege, although this is not always the case. See *Thorson v. Jones* (1973), 38 DLR (3d) 312 (BCSC); R.D. Manes, M.P. Silver, *Solicitor–Client Privilege in Canadian Law* (1993), at p. 141. Where the name of the client is indeed privileged information, s. 488.1(2) compels the lawyer to choose between two different privileged items: the name of the client or the confidential documents targeted by the search. In these situations, s. 488.1(2) requires that one privilege be sacrificed so that the other may be salvaged. See *Lavallee*, *supra*, at para. 50; *White*, *supra*, at para. 21; *Fink*, *supra*, at para. 39; *Festing*, *supra*, at para. 17, and [*Canada (Attorney General) v. Several Clients and Several Solicitors* (2000), 189 NSR (2d) 313 (SC)], at para. 38.

(3) No Notice Given to Client

The courts below also criticized the fact that s. 488.1 fails to ensure that all interested clients are notified when their documents are about to be turned over to the investigators. Indeed, the procedure does not provide for the mandatory notification of privilege holders. This absence of notice is particularly striking when, as described above, the solicitor is absent or fails to act, thus irremediably depriving the client of the opportunity to assert his or her solicitor–client privilege. The absence of notice is the first step in a series of consequences which can be fatal to maintaining the confidentiality of privileged documents. See *Lavallee*, *supra*, at paras. 28-39; *White*, *supra*, at para. 21; *Fink*, *supra*, at para. 42; *Festing*, *supra*, at para. 17, and *Several Clients*, *supra*, at para. 38.

(4) Strict Time Limits

If the privilege is not asserted at the time of the search, for whatever reason, the seized documents may be examined by the investigating officers and prosecutors. Even if solicitor–client privilege is asserted at the time of the search, it may still be lost if the client or solicitor fails to move for "a place and day ... for the determination of the question whether the document should be disclosed" within fourteen days of the search and seizure, as provided by s. 488.1(3)(a)(i) of the *Criminal Code*. In *Lavallee*, Cote JA further observed at para. 41: "The looming '14-day time' limit under s. 488.1(3) is really only 10 to 11 days, because the subsection says that 2 days' notice must be given. In view of the *Interpretation Act*, RSC 1985, c. I-21, s. 27(2), that will eat up at least 3 days. Since the lawyer needs authority to move in court, and since only the client owns the privilege and can move, the 10 or 14 days might well be missed." This time limit was held to be unreasonably strict and unworkable by the courts below. This procedural rigidity is exacerbated by the fact that no time extension can be granted without the consent of the Crown. See also *White*, *supra*, at para. 21; *Fink*, *supra*, at para. 34; *Festing*, *supra*, at para. 17, and Several Clients, *supra*, at para. 38.

(5) Absence of Discretion

Even in cases where the privilege has been asserted at the first opportunity, if the strict procedures outlined above are not followed, the Code provides that the court has no remedial discretion to relieve the privilege holder from his or her default and maintain the confidentiality of the information claimed to be privileged. This means that if an application is not made within 14 days of the search for a judicial determination of the validity of the claim of privilege, and if the consent of the Attorney General cannot be obtained for an extension of time, the judge has no discretion under the Code and must order that the documents seized and held under seal be turned over to the prosecution. Pursuant to s. 488.1(6), "the judge *shall* order" (emphasis added) that the documents be delivered to the prosecuting authorities. See *Lavallee*, *supra*, at para. 28; *White*, *supra*, at para. 1; *Fink*, *supra*, at para. 35. The courts in *Festing*, *supra*, and *Several Clients*, *supra*, also found this aspect to be particularly offensive.

(6) Access of the Attorney-General Prior to Judicial Determination

Finally, some appellate courts took issue with the fact that, pursuant to s. 488.1(4)(b), the Attorney General may be allowed to inspect the documents where the judge is of the opinion that it would materially assist the court in determining the question of privilege. Several courts held that this subsection effectively nullifies solicitor–client privilege before it is even determined that such privilege exists. The courts were of the view that the Crown does not need to inspect the documents in order to make meaningful submissions with regards to the seized documents and that the issue of privilege could be determined without allowing the Attorney General to access the seized documents. In the first instance of *Festing*, Romilly J opined at para. 82: "I fail to see how disclosure to the prosecuting authority for the purposes of determining privilege is a practical necessity. I appreciate that eventually someone will have to see the documents in order to decide privilege. But surely that someone does not have to be the prosecuting authority" ((2000), 31 CR (5th) 203). See also *Fink*, *supra*, at para. 34; *Festing*, *supra*, at para. 19; *Several Clients*, *supra*, at para. 41.

The legislative deficiencies described above were held to impair solicitor–client privilege beyond any tolerable constitutional limit by the appellate courts of British Columbia (*Festing*, *supra*), Nova Scotia (*Several Clients*, *supra*) and Ontario ... who accordingly all struck down s. 488.1 of the *Criminal Code*. While it endorsed the grounds identified in *Lavallee* in finding that s. 488.1 was unconstitutional, the Court of Appeal for Newfoundland (*White*, *supra*) ultimately decided that the section could be saved in accordance with the guidelines given by this Court in *Schachter v. Canada*, [1992] 2 SCR 679, 93 DLR (4th) 1, and by resorting to legislative severance and reading-in. More will be said on the issue of remedy further in these reasons.

F. Section 488.1 Violates Section 8 of the Charter

The proper approach to the constitutional issues here is under s. 8 of the Charter, and there is no need to undertake an independent s. 7 analysis. This was properly explained in *Fink* by Goudge JA, at para. 15:

> While a seizure undertaken by the state in the course of a criminal investigation can be said to implicate s. 7 and while solicitor–client privilege is encompassed within the principles of fundamental justice, I think s. 8 provides a sufficient framework for analysis. If the procedure mandated by s. 488.1 results in a reasonable search and seizure of the documents in the possession of a lawyer, it surely accords with the principles of fundamental justice and vice versa.

If the procedure set out in s. 488.1 results in an unreasonable search and seizure contrary to s. 8 of the Charter, it follows that s. 488.1 cannot be said to comply with the principles of fundamental justice embodied in s. 7. See also *Re Motor Vehicle Act*, [1985] 2 SCR 486, 23 CCC (3d) 289, 24 DLR (4th) 536. In *R v. Edwards*, [1996] 1 SCR 128, 104 CCC (3d) 136, 132 DLR (4th) 31, at para. 33, Cory J stated that "[t]here are two distinct questions which must be answered in any s. 8 challenge. The first is whether the accused had a reasonable expectation of privacy. The second is whether the search was an unreasonable intrusion on that right to privacy." A client has a reasonable expectation of privacy in all documents in the possession of his or her lawyer, which constitute information that the lawyer is ethically required to keep confidential, and an expectation of privacy of the highest order when such documents are protected by the solicitor–client privilege. This is not at issue in this case. I will therefore proceed immediately to the second step of the s. 8 analysis, namely the reasonableness of the statutory intrusion on the privacy interests of solicitor's clients.

At this stage, the issue is whether the procedure set out by s. 488.1 results in a reasonable search and seizure of documents, including potentially privileged documents, in the possession of a lawyer. Indeed, s. 8 only protects against unreasonable searches and seizures: *Hunter v. Southam Inc.*, [1984] 2 SCR 145, 14 CCC (3d) 97, 11 DLR (4th) 641. In commenting on the fact that a reasonable search and seizure is permitted under s. 8 of the Charter, Dickson J (as he then was) stated, at pp. 159-60:

> This limitation on the right guaranteed by s. 8, whether it is expressed negatively as freedom from "unreasonable" search and seizure, or positively as an entitlement to a "reasonable" expectation of privacy, indicates that an assessment must be made as to whether in a particular situation the public's interest in being left alone by government must give way to the government's interest in intruding on the individual's privacy in order to advance its goals, notably those of law enforcement.

Since *Hunter*, this Court has striven to strike an appropriate balance between privacy interests on the one hand and the exigencies of law enforcement on the other.

See *R v. Araujo*, [2000] 2 SCR 992, 2000 SCC 65, 149 CCC (3d) 449, 193 DLR (4th) 440; *R v. Golden*, 2001 SCC 83 [reported 159 CCC (3d) 449, 207 DLR (4th) 18]. Sometimes, however, the traditional balancing of interests involved in a s. 8 analysis is inappropriate. As it was stated in *R v. Mills*, [1999] 3 SCR 668, 139 CCC (3d) 321, 180 DLR (4th) 1, at para. 86, "the appropriateness of the balance is assessed according to the nature of the interests at stake in a particular context, and the place of these interests within our legal and political traditions." Where the interest at stake is solicitor–client privilege—a principle of fundamental justice and civil right of supreme importance in Canadian law—the usual balancing exercise referred to above is not particularly helpful. This is so because the privilege favours not only the privacy interests of a potential accused, but also the interests of a fair, just and efficient law enforcement process. In other words, the privilege, properly understood, is a positive feature of law enforcement, not an impediment to it.

Indeed, solicitor–client privilege must remain as close to absolute as possible if it is to retain relevance. Accordingly, this Court is compelled in my view to adopt stringent norms to ensure its protection. Such protection is ensured by labeling as unreasonable any legislative provision that interferes with solicitor–client privilege more than is absolutely necessary. In short, in the specific context of law office searches for documents that are potentially protected by solicitor–client privilege, the procedure set out in s. 488.1 will pass Charter scrutiny if it results in a "minimal impairment" of solicitor–client privilege.

Minimal impairment has long been the standard by which this Court has measured the reasonableness of state encroachments on solicitor–client privilege. Recently, in [*R v. Brown*, 2002 SCC 32], in defining the scope of the "innocence at stake" exception to solicitor–client privilege, this Court insisted that the judge order the "production of only those communications that are necessary to allow an accused, whose innocence is otherwise at stake, to raise a reasonable doubt as to his guilt" (para. 77). In *Jones, supra*, this Court held at para. 77 that even where public safety is at stake, there must be a clear and imminent risk of serious bodily harm or death to an identifiable person or group before solicitor–client privilege can be compromised. Moreover, where it is determined that these criteria are met, the majority in *Jones* held that "[t]he disclosure of the privileged communication should generally be limited as much as possible" (para. 86). Major J, dissenting on another point, agreed at para. 28 that "solicitor–client privilege is a fundamental common law right of Canadians … . Anytime such a fundamental right is eroded the principle of minimal impairment must be observed." As I noted earlier in these reasons at para. 20, the minimal impairment standard was also applied in *Descoteaux, supra*, where Lamer J instructed justices of the peace to be "particularly demanding" when issuing warrants to search law offices, so to "limit the breach of this fundamental right [solicitor–client privilege] to what is strictly inevitable" (p. 891).

Does s. 488.1 more than minimally impair solicitor–client privilege? It is my conclusion that it does.

While I think it unnecessary to revisit the numerous statements of this Court on the nature and primacy of solicitor–client privilege in Canadian law, it bears repeating that the privilege belongs to the client and can only be asserted or waived by the client or through his or her informed consent (*Solosky, supra*; *Descoteaux, supra*; *Geffen, supra*; *Jones, supra*; *McClure* [[2001] 1 SCR 445]; *Benson, supra*. In my view, the failings of s. 488.1 identified in numerous judicial decisions and described above all share one principal, fatal feature, namely, the potential breach of solicitor–client privilege without the client's knowledge, let alone consent. The fact that competent counsel will attempt to ascertain the whereabouts of their clients and will likely assert blanket privilege at the outset does not obviate the state's duty to ensure sufficient protection of the rights of the privilege holder. Privilege does not come into being by an assertion of a privilege claim; it exists independently. By the operation of s. 488.1, however, this constitutionally protected right can be violated by the mere failure of counsel to act, without instruction from or indeed communication with the client. Thus, s. 488.1 allows the solicitor–client confidentiality to be destroyed without the client's express and informed authorization, and even without the client's having an opportunity to be heard.

In that respect I note that s. 488.1(8), which requires the investigative officers to give reasonable opportunity for a claim of solicitor–client privilege to be made before examining, making copies or seizing any documents, is limited to a claim "to be made under subsection (2)." The claim under subs. (2) is of course the claim that the lawyer is required to make, at the time of the search, in order to trigger the further procedural protections provided for in s. 488.1. Therefore, under this statutory scheme, reasonable opportunity has to be provided to the privilege keeper, but not to the privilege holder, to ensure that the privileged information remains so. This positive obligation on counsel shifts the burden of guaranteeing the respect for Charter rights from the state to the lawyer. I stress here that I am making no adverse assumption about the competence, professionalism and integrity of lawyers. However, in the context of searches of law offices, it cannot simply be assumed that the lawyer is the alter ego of the client. The solicitor–client relationship may have been terminated long before the search. This of course does not displace the duty of loyalty owed by the solicitor to the client. But law office searches may place lawyers in a conflict of interest with their clients, or may place them in conflict regarding their ongoing duties to several present and former clients. I cannot see how s. 488.1(8), limited as it is, can raise this entire procedural scheme to a standard of constitutional reasonableness when it fails to address directly the entitlement that the privilege holder, the client, should have to ensure the adequate protection of his or her rights. Indeed, because of the complete lack of notification provisions within the s. 488.1 scheme, the client may not even be aware that his or her privilege is threatened.

In cases where it would not be feasible to notify the potential privilege holders that they need to assert their privilege in order to bar an intrusion by the state into these protected materials, at the very least independent legal intervention, for instance in the form of notification and involvement of the Law Society, would go a long way to afford the protection that is so lacking under the present regime. Indeed, this is done routinely as a matter of practice in Quebec, and occasionally elsewhere. For a detailed description of the practice in Quebec, see *Maranda v. Quebec (Judge of the Court of Quebec)* (2001), 161 CCC (3d) 64 (Que. CA), at paras. 34 to 38, application for leave to appeal granted May 16, 2002 (No. 28964) [163 CCC (3d) vi].

I stress here again that the enactment of s. 488.1 represents an attempt to respect the solicitor–client privilege. However, in order to respect the constitutional imperatives, the enactment must strive to ensure that the chances of the state's accessing, through a search warrant, privileged information to which the state has no right of access, are reduced to their reasonable minimum. In my view, since the right of the state to access this information is, in law, conditional on the consent of the privilege holder, all efforts to notify that person, or an appropriate surrogate such as the Law Society, must be put in place in order for the section to conform to s. 8 of the Charter.

Another fatal flaw in the current statutory scheme is, in my view, the absence of judicial discretion in the determination of the validity of an asserted claim of privilege. I am not unduly concerned with the apparently strict time limits imposed by the Code for this issue to be dealt with, as I believe that a proper interpretation of these provisions would permit a court to relieve a party from its default to comply with the statutory time line, for instance on consent, in the interest of justice. However, I cannot see how one can read a residual judicial discretion in s. 488.1(6) which confers an entitlement on the Crown to access the seized documents if an application has not been made, or has not been proceeded with, with the dispatch required by s-ss. (2) and (3). The language is clear, "the judge shall" order the documents released to the prosecution. Short of replacing the word "shall" with the word "may" by way of constitutional remedy, a point to which I will return below, I cannot see how, as a matter of sound statutory interpretation, one can interpret this provision as containing an element of judicial discretion. Again, measured against the constitutional standard of reasonableness in s. 8 of the Charter, this mandatory disclosure of potentially privileged information, in a case where the court has been alerted to the possibility of privilege by the fact that the documents were sealed at the point of search, cannot be said to minimally impair the privilege. It amounts to an unjustifiable vindication of form over substance, and it creates a real possibility that the state may obtain privileged information that a court could very well have recognized as such. In my view, reasonableness dictates that courts must retain a discretion to decide whether materials seized in a lawyer's office should remain inaccessible to the state as privileged information if and when, in the circumstances, it is in the interest of justice to do so.

I also find an unjustifiable impairment of the privilege in the provision in s. 488.1(4)(b), which permits the Attorney General to inspect the seized documents where the applications judge is of the opinion that it would materially assist him or her in deciding whether the document is privileged. This particular aspect of s. 488.1 was disapproved of by the Law Reform Commission of Canada who felt that "granting the Crown access to confidential communications passing between a solicitor and his client would diminish the public's faith in the administration of justice and create a potential for abuse" (p. 60). See Law Reform Commission of Canada, Report 24, Search and Seizure (1984), Recommendation Seven, at p. 58. I agree. As Goudge JA stated at para. 40 of his reasons in *Fink*, *supra*: "The effect of this provision is the complete loss of the protection afforded by the very privilege that may subsequently be determined to apply." It should be noted however that while the substantive aspect of the privilege is irremediably lost by operation of s. 488.1(4)(b), its evidentiary component remains untouched and continues to protect the privileged documents from being entered into evidence. See *Borden & Elliot* [*v. The Queen* (1975), 30 CCC (2d) 337 (Ont. CA)], at p. 343. However, in my opinion and as Southey J recognized in that case, "it would be small comfort indeed" for the privilege holder that the law prevents the introduction of his or her confidential documents into evidence when their contents have already been disclosed to the prosecuting authority. Ultimately, any benefit that might accrue to the administration of justice from the Crown's being in a better position to assist the court in determining the existence of the privilege is, in my view, greatly outweighed by the risk of disclosing privileged information to the state in the conduct of a criminal investigation. I also cannot understand the logic of the argument that the Crown should be trusted not to use information obtained under that provision if it subsequently proved to have been the proper subject of a privilege. If, as would be the case under this provision, the conduct of the Crown examining the documents would have been entirely lawful, it is difficult to understand why the Crown should then refrain from making use of such knowledge lawfully acquired. In the end, this provision is unduly intrusive upon the privilege and of limited usefulness in determining its existence.

In short, in my opinion, s. 488.1 fails to ensure that clients are given a reasonable opportunity to exercise their constitutional prerogative to assert or waive their privilege. Far from upholding solicitor–client confidentiality, s. 488.1 permits the privilege to fall through the interstices of its inadequate procedure. The possible automatic loss of protection against unreasonable search and seizure through the normal operation of the law cannot be reasonable. Nor can the provision be infused with reasonableness in a constitutional sense on the basis of an assumption that the prosecution will behave honourably and, for instance, initiate a review under s. 488.1(3), if neither the client nor the lawyer has done so, or refrain from exercising the right to inspect the sealed documents, even though authorized to do so by the reviewing judge, as contemplated by s. 488.1(4)(b). As Cory J observed in *R v. Bain*, [1992] 1 SCR 91 at pp. 103-4, 69 CCC (3d) 481, 87 DLR (4th) 449: "Unfortunately it would seem that whenever the Crown is granted statutory power that can be used abusively then, on occasion, it will indeed be used abusively. The protection of basic rights should not be dependent upon a reliance on the continuous exemplary conduct of the Crown, something that is impossible to monitor or control." Even more so, I would add that the constitutionality of a statutory provision cannot rest on an expectation that the Crown will refrain from doing what it is permitted to do.

For these reasons, I find that s. 488.1 more than minimally impairs solicitor–client privilege and thus amounts to an unreasonable search and seizure contrary to s. 8 of the Charter. The appellants did not make any submissions on the issue of whether s. 488.1 could be saved under s. 1 of the Charter in the event it was found to be unconstitutional, as I have found it to be. Although this Court has left open the possibility that violations of ss. 7 and 8 could be saved under s. 1 in exceptional circumstances, this is clearly not such a case. See *Re BC Motor Vehicle Act* [[1985] 2 SCR 486]; *Hunter, supra*; *Suresh v. Canada (Minister of Citizenship and Immigration)*, 2002 SCC 1, at para. 78 [reported 208 DLR (4th) 1]. See also D. Stuart, *Charter Justice in Canadian Criminal Law* (3rd ed. 2001), at pp. 24-25 and 245. In particular, if, as here, the violation of s. 8 is found to consist of an unjustifiable impairment of the privacy interest protected by that section, everything else aside, it is difficult to conceive that the infringement could survive the minimal impairment part of the *Oakes* test. See *R v. Heywood*, [1994] 3 SCR 761 at pp. 802-3, 94 CCC (3d) 481, 120 DLR (4th) 348. I therefore conclude that s. 488.1 could not be saved by s. 1: while effective police investigations are indisputably a pressing and substantive concern, s. 488.1 cannot be said to establish proportional means to achieve that objective inasmuch as it more than minimally impairs solicitor–client privilege. ...

[The court went on to strike the section down].

NOTES AND QUESTIONS

1. According to the court in *R v. Fink*, "[t]he name of the client may very well be protected by solicitor–client privilege, although this is not always the case." This is another instance in which the lawyer's duty of confidentiality is broader than solicitor–client privilege. Generally speaking, lawyers are ethically bound not to identify their clients or to disclose the fact that a particular individual may have consulted them. The CBA Code makes this clear in chapter IV, commentary 3, which provides that "[a]s a general rule, the lawyer should not disclose having been consulted or retained by a person unless the nature of the matter requires such disclosure."[24]

2. Can the court's decision be described in terms of the maximization of social utility? Can the legislature's decision to enact s. 488.1 be described in the same terms? To the extent that both the legislature and the court were attempting to maximize social utility, where did they part company?

3. Design a schedule of costs and benefits considered by the legislature when it enacted s. 488.1. Were these same costs and benefits weighed by the court in *R v. Fink*? Did the legislature err in selecting appropriate costs and benefits, or did it simply weigh the competing costs and benefits incorrectly?

4. The court notes that "privilege favours not only the privacy interests of a potential accused, but also the interests of a fair, just and efficient law enforcement process. In other words, the privilege, properly understood, is a positive feature of law enforcement, not an impediment to it." What does this say about the utility interests protected by solicitor–client privilege (and, by extension, the lawyer's duty of confidentiality)?

IX. Guiding Principles

The decision of the Ontario Court (General Division) in *Stewart v. Canadian Broadcasting Corporation* (1997) (reproduced below) provides a useful summary of the law surrounding the lawyer's duty of confidentiality, as well as a summary of the policies underlying that ethical duty. These summaries are presented in the context of a rather famous lawyer's alleged use of confidential information in a television program. The issue of lawyers' appearances in the media is becoming increasingly important: lawyers are frequently

---

24   This is also provided for in the commentaries to Ontario's rule 2.03(1).

asked to appear on television to comment on the administration of justice. In many cases, they are asked to comment on cases in which they appeared as counsel. In these cases, they run the risk of violating the lawyer's duty of confidentiality.

Note that, pursuant to rule 6.06(1) of Ontario's *Rules of Professional Conduct*, lawyers are permitted to make public statements. Indeed, the commentaries to that rule suggest that lawyers are encouraged to comment publicly on "the effectiveness of existing statutory or legal remedies, on the effect of particular legislation or decided cases, or to offer an opinion about cases that have been instituted or are about to be instituted." The basis of this suggestion is that lawyers are regarded as experts in the administration of justice, and the public values their input regarding the current state (and shortcomings) of the law. Surely, this is an important role for lawyers: lawyers are uniquely able to identify defects in the legal system and call for whatever changes are required to improve the functionality of that system. As a result, lawyers serve an educative function. One could accordingly argue that society has an interest in the ability of lawyers to freely discuss the judicial system and its flaws. Where such discussions involve cases in which the lawyer appeared as counsel, a careful balancing of interests is required, weighing the lawyer's function as a critic and educator against his or her duty as a guardian of the client's confidential information. Like all balancing of interests, the weighing of society's interest in confidentiality, on the one hand, against society's interest in lawyers' freedom to criticize the legal system, on the other, is a cost–benefit analysis that can be described through the tools of economics. When reviewing the court's decision in *Stewart*, attempt to describe it in the economic terms developed throughout part I of this book.

Note that the numbering of the *Rules of Professional Conduct* has changed since the date of this decision. In particular, the court's repeated references to "rule 4" should now be read as references to Ontario's rule 2.03, which deals with confidential information.

Stewart v. Canadian Broadcasting Corporation
(1997), 150 DLR 4th 24 (Ont. Ct. Gen. Div.)

MACDONALD J:

Introduction

On November 27, 1978 the plaintiff Robert Stewart ran over Judy Jordan with his automobile and dragged her to her death. He was convicted of criminal negligence causing death. Following conviction, he discharged his counsel and retained the defendant Edward L. Greenspan, QC to represent him during sentencing and to appeal the conviction. The appeal was dismissed in January 1981 and Mr. Stewart began serving his sentence of three years' imprisonment. He was released on parole after 11 months and began rebuilding his life.

On November 17, 1991, when Mr. Stewart believed that he had put the past behind and re-established himself, the defendant Canadian Broadcasting Corporation broadcast a one-hour episode of the program known as "The Scales of Justice" on its national television network. This episode known as *Regina v. Stewart* was a re-enactment of the plaintiff's crime and trial created by the defendants Scales of Justice Enterprises Inc. and CBC. Mr. Greenspan appeared on air as the host and narrator. Mr. Greenspan had also been, with Mr. George Jonas, one of the incorporators of Scales of Justice Enterprises Inc. (hereinafter Scales) and one of the guiding minds in the development of the concept which became the television program known as "The Scales of Justice" (hereinafter the program). There is a substantial dispute respecting the extent of Mr. Greenspan's involvement in making the *Regina v. Stewart* episode.

The plaintiff instituted this action as a result of the broadcast, which was seen by close to one million viewers. I dismissed the action against CBC in oral reasons delivered earlier.

The Issues as Pleaded

The plaintiff pleads that Mr. Greenspan breached implied terms of his contract that he would keep in confidence any information provided to him by virtue of his representation of Mr. Stewart, and that he would act in Mr. Stewart's best interests in relation to any transaction touching upon the subject of the sentencing or appeal. Mr. Stewart also pleads that Mr. Greenspan owed a fiduciary duty of loyalty which obliged him to act in Mr. Stewart's best interests during the course of any transaction relating in any way to the sentencing or appeal. The plaintiff pleads that these implied contractual terms and solicitor's duties "were intended to and did survive the termination of the contractual relationship" between Mr. Greenspan and Mr. Stewart. In paragraph 25 of the statement of claim, Mr. Stewart pleads that Mr. Greenspan breached these contractual terms and the fiduciary duty of loyalty in a number of ways, as follows:

a) he permitted or, alternatively, did not oppose the portrayal of a case in which he represented an accused as the subject of a "The Scales of Justice" episode;

b) he permitted the defendant production company, over which he had control, to participate in the production notwithstanding his role as the plaintiff's counsel;

c) he failed to warn the plaintiff that the defendants contemplated making the production;

d) he provided resource material and other information for use in the preparation of the production;

e) he appeared in the production;

f) through his speech in the production, he identified himself as the plaintiff's solicitor;

g) through his speech in the production, he endorsed the findings of fact made at the trial of the plaintiff;

h) he put his own financial interests before the interests of the plaintiff;

i) he put his own self-promotion or self-aggrandizement before the interests of the plaintiff;

j) through publicizing the plaintiff's conviction ... he increased the adverse effect of that conviction on the plaintiff despite the fact that he had been specifically retained to minimize such an effect; and

k) he made his speech in the production without appreciation or control over the context in which it was to be used.

. . .

Mr. Greenspan's statement of defence contains the following assertions:

— The script for and the enactment of the plaintiff's crime and trial were taken solely from the public record and not from any confidential information from Mr. Greenspan.

— Mr. Greenspan's participation in the programme was for the primary purpose of educating the public as to the judicial process.

— In his capacity as the plaintiff's former solicitor, Mr. Greenspan acted fairly, reasonably and properly and fulfilled his obligations to the plaintiff.

— Neither the rules of professional conduct of the Law Society of Upper Canada, nor any other professional ethical rules made it improper for Mr. Greenspan to appear in and take part in the broadcast.

The Trial of Regina v. Stewart

It is necessary to consider some of the evidence presented at the criminal trial, the findings of the trial judge, the way in which Mr. Stewart's defence was conducted, prior to Mr. Greenspan's retainer and Mr. Greenspan's sentencing submissions, but not for the purpose of re-trying any of the issues which arose in that trial. His Honour Judge Graburn, the trial judge, has determined conclusively what Mr. Stewart did to Judy Jordan. His findings of fact were not challenged on appeal and cannot be challenged in this trial. It is necessary to consider these matters now because they explain the nature of Mr. Greenspan's retainer, they are the context in which any fiduciary duties began, and they establish the extent to which the broadcast was based on information disclosed in open court and which therefore became public knowledge. The transcript of the criminal trial was part of the joint documents exhibit put in evidence on consent. ...

Judy Jordan was in her late twenties, married and a dancing instructor. She lived with her husband in an apartment building at 6010 Bathurst Street, on the northwest corner of Rockford Road in Toronto. Shortly before midnight on November 27, 1978 she was returning from a dancing class and was walking near the front of her apartment building, in its circular driveway, when she was struck by Mr. Stewart's vehicle.

Mr. Stewart was 30 and a family man with an unblemished background. He lived a short distance north of the accident scene. He had spent the day working. At about 6:00 p.m., he consumed one or two beers and then went to dinner at a restaurant with some co-workers, where he drank a moderate amount. At about 11:00 p.m. he left the restaurant and took an indirect route home because of weather conditions and to avoid police spot-checks. He was feeling ill. He entered Bathurst Street south of the accident scene and drove north. He was unable to contain a bowel movement. He decided to make use of trees which he saw adjacent to 6010 Bathurst Street.

Mr. Stewart entered the circular driveway in a counter-clockwise direction and drove slowly around a traffic island. His vehicle struck Mrs. Jordan and knocked her down. As the Stewart vehicle continued in motion it passed over her and she became entangled in its undercarriage. Mr. Stewart did not stop at the apartment building. He drove out of the circular driveway, stopped briefly, headed west on Rockford Road and turned his lights off.

Mrs. Jordan's piercing and very loud screams commenced in the circular driveway. Witnesses testified to hearing her screams while they were as high in apartment buildings as the 11th floor, some with their windows closed. Their recollections varied widely as to the length of time the screaming lasted. Graburn J made careful findings about where the screaming stopped, on conflicting evidence. Mrs. Jordan's body came loose from the Stewart vehicle on Torresdale Avenue, about one quarter mile from 6010 Bathurst Street.

Mrs. Jordan died from a fractured skull and a lacerated brain inflicted at the point where her screaming stopped. Blood of her rare type, skull fragments and brain tissue were found on the undercarriage of Mr. Stewart's vehicle. Scalp hairs similar to Mrs. Jordan's and associated tissue were found wrapped around the drive shaft.

Mr. Stewart was arrested on December 18, 1978 when police examination of vehicles like his disclosed that pieces of fan shroud, found along the route Mrs. Jordan had been dragged, matched damage to the fan shroud of his vehicle. ...

Until his conviction, Mr. Stewart was represented by counsel who had been a formidable leader of the criminal defence bar for many years. With the benefit of hindsight, it is likely that his health was failing at the time of the Stewart trial. Sadly, he suffered from a degenerative brain disorder and died not long after the trial. While the transcript discloses that counsel represented Mr. Stewart effectively in a number of areas, including the presentation of evidence directed to Mr. Stewart's lack of knowledge that Mrs. Jordan was under his car, it also discloses lapses of judgment which are relevant herein.

The transcript of the criminal trial shows that Mr. Stewart's first counsel took the position that Mrs. Jordan was lying in the circular driveway as a result of the actions of a third party when Mr. Stewart ran over her. He suggested in cross-examination that Mrs. Jordan had been pushed into the roadway. He questioned the relationship between Mr. and Mrs. Jordan, apparently attempting to implicate Mr. Jordan in her death. He also suggested that Mrs. Jordan had been killed by drug dealers with whom she was allegedly involved. An alleged friend of hers had been found murdered, supposedly as a result of involvement in drugs. These allegations were rejected out of hand by Graburn J in his reasons for judgment. As well, when counsel led Mr. Stewart's evidence-in-chief, some of his language was abrasive and appeared to be dismissive of Mr. Stewart's testimony. Mr. Stewart testified before me that his relationship with his first counsel was very poor by the time of conviction, and I have no doubt this was so.

Consequently, upon conviction, Mr. Greenspan was retained. I will address at a later point the facts and issues surrounding his retention. I address now Mr. Greenspan's representation of Mr. Stewart in respect of sentencing. I accept Mr. Greenspan's evidence that he immediately contacted the Crown Attorney, Mr. Stephen Leggett, QC who led him to believe that the Crown was considering asking for a very substantial prison term. I accept as well that Mr. Leggett led Mr. Greenspan to believe that he had a poor impression of Mr. Stewart. In an effort to soften the Crown's position, Mr. Greenspan sought to convince Mr. Leggett that Mr. Stewart's former counsel, not Mr. Stewart, was responsible for the unsavoury aspects of his defence. ...

From all of the above, I find as follows. Mr. Greenspan knew when acting for Mr. Stewart respecting sentence that the media coverage of Mr. Stewart's crime and trial had been very negative and had gone so far as to portray him as an inhumanely cruel and wicked person, which is the relevant definition of "monster" from the *Oxford English Dictionary*. Mr. Greenspan recognized that the public abhorred Mr. Stewart because of the nature of his crime, the perception that he had attacked his victim and her family which arose from counsel's trial tactics, and the extensive and very critical media coverage. Mr. Greenspan recognized that he should address in his sentencing submissions both public abhorrence of Mr. Stewart and the public interest implicit in the objectives of sentencing. He recommended to Mr. Stewart that he authorize a public apology to the Jordan family as part of the sentencing submissions to the court, and Mr. Stewart agreed. Graburn J accepted the apology as genuine because he took it into account in sentencing, as described. I also accept that it was genuine. Based on the evidence before me, Mr. Stewart was in fact not complicit in his first counsel's trial tactics. I accept that his desire to disassociate himself from counsel's assertions was not merely tactical, but was also based on a genuine absence of complicity. He felt that counsel was handling the trial very badly. There were substantial difficulties communicating with counsel because of his nature at that time. In his first meeting with Mr. Greenspan, Mr. Stewart was particularly critical of counsel's statements about Mrs. Jordan and her husband.

In his submissions, Mr. Greenspan did not accept the media and public perceptions of Mr. Stewart as intractable and unappeasable. He sought to modify those views. The public apology was significant in that regard. Mr. Greenspan's words of apology were addressed to Graburn J in court, but their import went beyond the court to specific members of the public, namely the Jordan family. They were not parties to the prosecution. They were the members of the public most affected by the trial tactics of former counsel. The presence of the media and the extensive coverage of this proceeding mean that the apology to those members of the public was made in full public view. It was stated to be a public apology. ...

In my opinion, the public apology made in open court and directed to members of the public taken together with Mr. Greenspan's reply to the Crown's submissions establish clearly that Mr. Greenspan went beyond submissions directed solely to sentence, and undertook the task of attempting to change through the sentencing hearing how Mr. Stewart was viewed by the public. ...

I find that the transcript of the criminal trial establishes that Mr. Greenspan made use of the court as a public forum from which to influence public perceptions of Mr. Stewart. He sought to have the court's words of judgment influence the court of public opinion, in whose hands Mr. Stewart would be indefinitely. ...

Mr. Greenspan knew that Mr. Stewart's imprisonment would be no longer than a fixed and certain time period and that at some point, he would be released. He also knew that Mr. Stewart, like all imprisoned convicts, would face the task on release of resuming his life. In Mr. Stewart's case, Mr. Greenspan knew that he would face the task of resuming his life in a society in which the amalgam of negative feelings about his crime and negative feelings about his counsel's attacks on his victim and her family could last indefinitely. Mr. Greenspan knew this because he held the view that public abhorrence of Mr. Stewart due to media reports about the conduct of the trial had a life of its own. He made that assertion to Graburn J. I find that, in this extraordinary case, Mr. Greenspan went to extraordinary lengths as counsel to protect his client from the public. He not only addressed the public's legitimate interests and perceptions which would influence the sentence imposed by the court, he also addressed the risk that individual members of the public would sanction Mr. Stewart after his release from prison into its midst. …

Preparing the Regina v. Stewart Episode

. . .

a) Alleged Wrongful Disclosure of Confidential Information

The concept of confidentiality is a chameleon, taking different legal hues from the circumstances in which it is found. It may arise in respect of information because of the nature of the information itself, because of the nature of the relationship between the persons giving and receiving the information, or both. In some cases, confidentiality gives rise to an obligation resting on the recipient to maintain the secrecy in which the information was shrouded before it was communicated to the recipient. Secrecy may also be required of a recipient despite relatively widespread knowledge of the information. Confidentiality may also give rise to an obligation resting on the recipient not to disclose or to make use of communicated information even though that information is so widely known that it is public knowledge.

The confidentiality obligations I now address have the complexion of information communicated to a lawyer by his client, or coming to the lawyer's attention through acting for the client, and regarded as secret. The colouration suffusing these obligations is that of private and hidden matters, known in this case only to a few people who were, with the exception of Mr. Stewart himself, linked by professional involvement in his defence and bound by lawyer and client obligations to him. I will address other aspects of confidentiality at a later point.

It will be recalled that the radio broadcast is not the subject of this litigation. The plaintiff relies on it because it depicted an interview between Mr. Greenspan and Mr. Stewart in the Don Jail which allegedly disclosed information between lawyer and client which Mr. Greenspan was required to hold in confidence. Even though the interview scene did not find its way into the television broadcast, Mr. Swadron argues that the radio script containing confidential information was the basis of the television script, and says that supports the argument that Mr. Greenspan breached fiduciary or contractual duties by his participation in the television broadcast.

Mr. Tait and Mr. Jonas wrote the radio script. Mr. Tait, Mr. Jonas and Mr. Greenspan all testified that Mr. Greenspan provided no information of any nature respecting the *Stewart* case for the purpose of creating either the radio script or the television script. Mr. Greenspan was the source of, or responsible for some script content, as discussed subsequently. Both Mr. Tait and Mr. Jonas testified that the interview between Mr. Stewart and Mr. Greenspan in the radio broadcast was fictionalized. I find that it was fictionalized. I find that Mr. Greenspan did not disclose confidential (meaning secret) information about his meeting with Mr. Stewart in jail which found its way into the radio program. I reject this allegation as completely unfounded.

It is also alleged that Mr. Greenspan disclosed to Scales or its employees that the relationship between Mr. Stewart and his first counsel was failing during the course of trial, which information Mr. Greenspan then repeated in his narration of the television broadcast. The termination of counsel's retainer at the end of trial is a matter of public record. A distinction is therefore drawn between the failing relationship during the course of trial, said to be confidential information not publicly known, and the termination of the retainer.

I also reject this allegation as completely unfounded. I have already found as a fact on the basis of Mr. Greenspan's evidence that one of his first steps on Mr. Stewart's behalf was to speak to Mr. Leggett to disassociate Mr. Stewart from the actions of his former counsel. In my opinion, it is likely that Mr. Leggett already knew that relations between Mr. Stewart and his counsel had been failing during trial, for the following reasons. Mr. Leggett had been present in court when counsel led Mr. Stewart's evidence in chief, using language which was abrasive and which I have found was dismissive of Mr. Stewart's testimony. The words of Mr. Stewart's counsel found in the transcript were undoubtedly sufficient to let Mr. Leggett know that the professional relationship was strained. Mr. Stewart then terminated counsel's retainer. Mr. Leggett knew of this because the sentencing was adjourned to give Mr. Greenspan time to prepare. Viewed together with what had happened between Mr. Stewart and his counsel in court, termination of the retainer was probably sufficient to confirm to Mr. Leggett that the relationship had been failing during the trial. Mr. Greenspan then disclosed that Mr. Stewart was not behind the unsavoury defence tactics. In my opinion, that probably provided new information to Mr. Leggett about Mr. Stewart, but not about the state of his relationship with his first counsel. In my opinion, Mr. Greenspan's disclosure that Mr. Stewart was not behind his counsel's tactics probably confirmed what Mr. Leggett already knew about the relationship between Mr. Stewart and his first counsel at trial. In any event, Mr. Greenspan made this disclosure with Mr. Stewart's authority, pursuant to the very broad discretion given to Mr. Greenspan in the retainer document.

In addition, Mr. Jonas testified that he spoke with Mr. Leggett to gather information about the Stewart case. I find that Mr. Leggett was fully co-operative and forthcoming with Mr. Jonas, given that he played his own part in the radio broadcast. Mr. Jonas testified that it was Mr. Leggett, not Mr. Greenspan who told him about the failing relationship between Mr. Stewart and his first counsel during trial. I accept this evidence as factual and find that Mr. Greenspan did not disclose this information to Scales.

Allegations that counsel wrongfully disclosed confidential (meaning secret) information about a client are serious allegations. It should be clearly recognized that there
is no truth, not even a hint of it, in these serious allegations against Mr. Greenspan.

. . .

The Role of Counsel

... Mr. Greenspan's evidence was that rule 4 of the *Rules of Professional Conduct*
(which I will consider shortly) bars counsel from disclosing confidential information, and that is the extent of the fiduciary responsibility respecting the affairs and
business of a former client. Mr. Greenspan's position is that the rule is exhaustive
respecting fiduciary responsibilities. Once the information is in the public domain,
Mr. Greenspan testified that it is the lawyer's choice whether to discuss that information publicly, subject to any contractual constraint. Mr. Greenspan also testified that,
respecting matters in the public domain, in a conflict between the truth and the client,
"you go with the client" by perhaps not "telling it all," and that is an obligation which
is broader than the rules.

Mr. Greenspan testified that he spoke with the late Mr. J.J. Robinette, QC in the
early to mid-1980s on several occasions respecting publishing information about his
cases. According to Mr. Greenspan, they discussed the *Rules of Professional Conduct*
and "how these things are done." Mr. Robinette was then co-operating in a book
about his professional life and had provided to Scales transcripts of the *R v. Dick* trial
in which he had been defence counsel. He had played himself in the radio presentation about that trial. Mr. Greenspan testified that he formed the view that Mr. Robinette
did not obtain the consent of his former clients to whatever was mentioned in the
book or said on radio about Ms. Dick and her case. Apart from Mr. Greenspan's
testimony, there is no evidence which proves that Mr. Robinette did or did not obtain
any consents from former clients. Mr. Robinette was alive at the time of trial. It was
accepted by all counsel that he was not available to testify.

Mr. Greenspan also testified that Mr. Frank Scott, QC provided material, played
himself, and narrated the television production of *Roncarelli v. Duplessis* without the
consent of his former client, Roncarelli. Again, there is no evidence which proves
more than Mr. Greenspan's belief that Mr. Scott did not obtain the consent of his
former client.

Mr. Greenspan also testified that the late Mr. Arthur Maloney, QC also co-operated
with Scales.

It was from observing leading lawyers like these that Mr. Greenspan formed the
view that nothing prevented him from involving himself in the production and
broadcast of *Regina v. Stewart*, despite his former client's objections to the type of
show he was helping to present. In my opinion, evidence about the conduct of leading
lawyers respecting former clients and their cases is relevant to the determination of
when fiduciary duties arise, the nature and the extent of any such duties, and whether
they are breached in the circumstances under consideration. The evidence before me
is that Mr. Robinette, Mr. Scott, Mr. Maloney and other leading counsel, some now
Judges, have spoken or written or provided information about former clients and their

cases in a variety of circumstances. Counsel have spoken about former clients or their cases in legal circles for educational purposes, for example at Law School seminars. Some counsel have co-operated with the Osgoode Society, which is dedicated to the preservation of legal history, by recording their professional memoirs or co-operating in the publication of books about their professional lives.

It is therefore argued that the conduct of leading counsel demonstrates the absence of fiduciary constraints upon public use or discussion of information in the public domain which is about former clients or their cases. In my opinion, this evidence is too general and non-specific to support any such assertion. In some cases there is some sparse evidence and in other cases, there is no evidence about the information which was used or discussed publicly by these counsel, the nature of their professional relationships with their former clients (except for the most general information about the issues in the litigation), the relationship between the information used or discussed publicly by counsel and the issues respecting which they were retained, the existence or absence of consent or objection by a client, the existence or absence of fiduciary duties, or breach of fiduciary duties in the particular circumstances. There is no evidence about whether former clients were aware of the use or publication of any information by their counsel. It is therefore possible that existing fiduciary obligations were not asserted by the clients. With the exception of the approximate date of Mr. Robinette's involvement in the broadcast about Ms. Dick and the date of the book of his professional life, I have little information about when counsel's public use or discussion of client information took place. Counsel other than Mr. Robinette may well have used or discussed client information when fiduciary principles were less developed and thus were less containing than they are now.

In Mr. Robinette's case, the Dick broadcast was in approximately 1982 and the book about him was in 1984. It was also around that period that Mr. Greenspan spoke with Mr. Robinette as mentioned, and received telephone calls from him after various of the Scales radio broadcasts. The radio broadcasts ended in about 1985. The only evidence about the substance of Mr. Robinette's advice or position or views is Mr. Greenspan's view that Mr. Robinette clearly conveyed to him that he had no discomfort with talking about clients. In my opinion, this is Mr. Greenspan's interpretation of Mr. Robinette's statements. It was admitted on the agreement that Mr. Robinette was not available to testify. What weight should this evidence be given? Even if this is regarded as Mr. Robinette's own views, because Mr. Robinette was unavailable to testify, the circumstances to which Mr. Robinette felt such views should properly apply is not addressed. In any event, Mr. Robinette's opinions and views about fiduciary issues between 1980 and 1985 probably did not take into account the significant developments in this area and the ongoing evolution of fiduciary principles as of the broadcast in 1991.

Consequently, I find that the above evidence about the conduct of leading counsel respecting public discussion of former clients and their cases is too superficial and too subject to substantial questions to establish the professional or fiduciary standards they probably followed in the circumstances of this case, as I have found them to be. Consequently, I find this evidence to be of very little assistance in the resolution of fiduciary issues herein.

As a result of Mr. Greenspan's reliance in 1991 upon dated information about the fiduciary issues which could arise from his involvement in the *Regina v. Stewart* broadcast, I conclude that in 1991 he was not clear in his own mind about fiduciary principles. Mr. Greenspan was far from alone in this.

(ii) The Rules of Professional Conduct

There was frequent reference at trial to various rules of professional conduct and accompanying commentaries of the Law Society of Upper Canada. They play a larger part in Mr. Greenspan's defence than they do in the plaintiff's case. He pleaded that no requirement in the rules or in any other professional ethical rules made it improper for him to participate in the broadcast in issue. To the extent that the plaintiff alleged a breach of the rules, Mr. Greenspan pleaded his right to freedom of expression as guaranteed by s. 2(b) of the *Canadian Charter of Rights and Freedoms*, and that, if the rules infringe that right, it is not demonstrably justifiable in a free and democratic society. At trial, Mr. Greenspan's position was different. He sought shelter under the rules, arguing that they support his position that he was not bound by fiduciary duties which were breached by his actions. His counsel did not raise any aspect of the Charter. In his written outline of argument on Mr. Greenspan's behalf, Mr. Jack put his position as follows:

> The Court is not, of course, obliged in any given case to limit itself to the regulatory rules, nor should it cede its jurisdiction to decide the cases before it. Rather, the Court is asked to consider that, where the regulatory rules have addressed the issues, as here, and where those rules are clearly in accordance with the overall standards of the profession as they relate to the factual circumstances at hand ... and where the regulatory rules and standards are reasonable, as they are here, it is not necessary to go further. The Court should hold in such a situation, that the substance of the fiduciary duty is embodied in the applicable regulatory rules and professional standards, and that no further standards are necessary to be applied in order to do justice in the case at hand.

In my opinion, the rules and commentaries have two limiting features which are significant here:

1. The *Law Society Act*, RSO 1990, c. L.8, gives the Law Society through Convocation the power to regulate lawyers' conduct. The Act does not give Convocation the power to regulate clients or their rights. In any event, in the rules and commentaries relevant to the issues herein, Convocation has not attempted to regulate clients or their rights.

2. The rules and commentaries are not an all-inclusive code governing lawyers' conduct in every circumstance which may arise in professional life. They address only specific issues, and do so in a variety of ways ranging from mandatory to advisory. ...

Fiduciary principles require consideration of all relevant circumstances. This brings into consideration in this case the relevant rules and commentaries of the Law Society.

However, it is necessary to note that it is fiduciary principles which the court must apply herein, not just the relevant rules and commentaries.

Mr. Gavin MacKenzie testified on Mr. Greenspan's behalf. I found him to be careful in his attention to the issues, responsive to questioning in a non-adversarial way, and intent upon assisting the court in the discharge of its responsibilities. Mr. MacKenzie's qualifications to express opinions respecting Mr. Greenspan's conduct and compliance with the Rules of Professional Conduct, or with other ethical requirements were not challenged. He is a Bencher of the Law Society of Upper Canada and a member of its professional conduct committee and discipline committee (policy section). He was formerly a member of the Law Society's special committee on reform of the Rules of Professional Conduct. From 1990 to 1993, he was Senior Counsel—Discipline for the Law Society. He has acted frequently as counsel in professional conduct and discipline matters and has taught in the professional responsibility section of the Bar Admission Course. He is the author of *Lawyers and Ethics: Professional Responsibility and Discipline* (Toronto: Carswell 1993), a leading text in the area. In order to give his opinion, it was frequently necessary for Mr. MacKenzie to address matters of law. This was permitted so that he could develop his opinion respecting factual issues as he saw fit, and so that his evidence would disclose the assumptions or influences which shaped his conclusions. Clearly, Mr. MacKenzie is highly qualified respecting matters of professional conduct, ethics and discipline. It should be noted however that, while his views respecting the law were informative and insightful, domestic law is not the province of the expert witness. It is for the court to determine and apply.

The facts which Mr. MacKenzie was asked to assume for purposes of his opinions are important. They are set out fully in his testimony and in his written report, which is also evidence on consent. The significant assumptions are as follows:

a) The script for the broadcast in issue was prepared not on the basis of information or documents that were obtained from Mr. Greenspan, certainly not confidential information, but rather on the basis of the trial transcript and other publicly available information.

b) The trial, the appeal and Mr. Greenspan's retainer were all at an end by the time of Mr. Greenspan's involvement in the broadcast in issue.

c) It was not within Mr. Greenspan's power to cancel the program. He could have decided that he did not wish to participate, but the broadcast would have been aired in any event.

d) Mr. Greenspan's involvement gave the highest chance for a sympathetic portrayal of the events. Mr. Stewart's case was put in a better light than might have been without Mr. Greenspan's contribution.

e) Various eminent lawyers have participated in Scales of Justice programs, thereby demonstrating widespread support for the idea of the program among lawyers generally and among leading members of the Bar.

f) Mr. Greenspan was paid a fee for his services as host and narrator. His firm
was also paid a fee for reviewing scripts.

g) Mr. Greenspan did not seek Mr. Stewart's consent.

I turn now to the rules and commentaries which may apply.

Rule 4: Confidentiality of Information[25]

The rule is as follows:

> The lawyer has a duty to hold in strict confidence all information concerning the busi-
> ness and affairs of the client acquired in the course of the professional relationship, and
> should not divulge any such information unless expressly or impliedly authorized by
> the client or required by law to do so.

Some of the commentaries are not relevant. The relevant commentaries are:

Guiding Principles
1. The lawyer cannot render effective professional service to the client unless there
   is full and unreserved communication between them. At the same time the client
   must feel completely secure and entitled to proceed on the basis that without any
   express request or stipulation on the client's part matters disclosed to or discussed
   with the lawyer will be held secret and confidential.
2. This ethical rule must be distinguished from the evidentiary rule of lawyer and
   client privilege with respect to oral or documentary communication passing between
   the client and the lawyer. The ethical rule is wider and applies without regard to the
   nature or source of the information or the fact that others may share the knowledge.
3. As a general rule, the lawyer should not disclose having been consulted or retained by a particular person about a particular matter unless the nature of the
   matter requires such disclosure.
4. The lawyer owes the duty of secrecy to every client without exception, and whether
   it be a continuing or casual client. The duty survives the professional relationship
   and continues indefinitely after the lawyer has ceased to act for the client, whether
   or not differences may have arisen between them.
5. The fiduciary relationship between lawyer and client forbids the lawyer from using any confidential information covered by the ethical rule for the benefit of the
   lawyer or a third person, or to the disadvantage of the client. Should the lawyer
   engage in literary works such as an autobiography, memoirs and the like, the lawyer should avoid disclosure of confidential information. ...
8. The Rule may not apply to facts which are public knowledge, but nevertheless the
   lawyer should guard against participating in or commenting upon speculation concerning the client's affairs or business.

---

25   Note that the numbering of Ontario's rules has changed since the date of this decision. Confidentiality is
     now dealt with in rule 2.03.

The commentaries which I have quoted are all "guiding principles" and therefore amplify or clarify the rule or its application.

The allegations of breach of confidence by disclosure of secret information are without substance. There remains the issue of whether public information gathered by Mr. Jonas from public sources which found its way into the script and the public information added to the script by Mr. Greenspan, all of which was then repeated on air by Mr. Greenspan, amounts to a wrongful disclosure of confidential information, contrary to this rule. There is also the issue of whether the information omitted from the broadcast by Mr. Greenspan, namely Mr. Stewart's lack of complicity in his first counsel's trial tactics and his apology for them, was information Mr. Greenspan was required not to disclose by this rule. In my opinion, the exaggeration of the distance that Mr. Stewart dragged Mrs. Jordan screaming in agony is not "information concerning the business and affairs of the client acquired in the course of the professional relationship" because of its inaccuracy. However, the question remains of whether broadcasting accurate information, less critical of Mr. Stewart, was open to Mr. Greenspan, given the obligations contained in this rule.

The rule itself expresses the confidentiality obligation in mandatory terms. It establishes a duty of strict confidence. It is also expressed very broadly, covering "all information concerning the business and affairs of the client acquired in the course of the professional relationship ... ." Commentary 2, a guiding principle, extends the confidentiality obligation beyond lawyer and client privilege. The confidentiality obligation does not depend on the information being received from the client. It applies without regard to the "nature or source" of the information. It does not depend on the information being unknown to others. Widely known information may still be confidential information within this rule. At the same time, commentary 8 recognizes that the rule may not apply to facts which are public knowledge.

Commentary 4 refers to "the duty of secrecy." The rule itself refers to "a duty of strict confidence." In my opinion, commentary 4's reference to "the duty of secrecy" refers to what the rule itself says.

Secrecy does not, in the context of this rule, refer only to hidden and private information because the rule, guided by the principle in commentary 2, constrains the lawyer respecting widely known information. Given this, I see "secrecy" and "strict confidence" as synonymous. Properly interpreted, commentary 4, a guiding principle, provides that the duty of strict confidentiality "survives the professional relationship and continues indefinitely after the lawyer has ceased to act for the client."

Commentary 5 figures prominently in Mr. Greenspan's defence. It has two parts. The first part advises that "the fiduciary relationship between lawyer and client forbids the lawyer from using any confidential information covered by the ethical rule for the benefit of the lawyer or a third person, or to the disadvantage of the client." Convocation has not imposed an obligation. It reminds lawyers of the obligation imposed by fiduciary principles. In the second part of this commentary, Convocation does not forbid a lawyer from engaging in literary works etc. but states that in them, the lawyer "should avoid disclosure of confidential information." The only suggestion in the commentary that a lawyer publishing such information may not be subject to a duty of strict confidence pursuant to the rule is found in the non-mandatory statement that the lawyer "should avoid" disclosure of confidential information. This commentary does not say that in literary works of the described type, the lawyer is freed from any duty of strict confidence which otherwise applies. In my opinion, the proper interpretation of this commentary is that the rule itself, containing a duty of strict confidence, means that a lawyer should avoid disclosure of confidential information in literary works. This part of commentary 5 is an advisory admonition respecting literary works and it does not dilute the rule. It explains what a lawyer should do in particular circumstances because of the rule. To hold otherwise would constrain disclosure of confidential information except in cases of literary disclosure, and that interpretation is inconsistent with a "strict duty."

My conclusions respecting the application of rule 4 and its commentaries herein are as follows. Mr. Greenspan did not disclose secret information, as I have held. All information which was broadcast except for the exaggerated distance Mrs. Jordan was dragged screaming had been known to the public for years, through coverage of Mr. Stewart's crime, its investigation and prosecution. All of that information was public knowledge within the meaning of commentary 8 and did not fall within rule 4's constraining language. The exaggeration was misinformation which is not within the rules. The rule neither prohibits what was broadcast nor prevents the broadcast of the omitted information which was also public knowledge, as a result of Mr. Stewart's consent to its disclosure in 1979. Given the legislative intent found in the *Law Society Act*, rule 4 may influence, but cannot and does not have the effect of exempting a lawyer from any fiduciary obligations to a client or former client which apply to a literary or other publication, including a television broadcast.

A duty of loyalty is not articulated in a separate rule. It arises in rule 4 through commentary 5's mention of fiduciary relationships between lawyers and clients, which of course include loyalty obligations. It also arises in commentary 4 which provides that confidentiality duties continue indefinitely after the lawyer has ceased to act. A duty of loyalty arises as well in rule 5 which addresses conflicts of interest, to which I now turn.

[A discussion of conflicts of interests has been removed.]

Fiduciary Issues

(a) General

Mr. Stewart's crime, trial and sentence were the subject of public controversy and widely known in 1978 and 1979. This extensive information, made known through the justice system and published by the media, was public knowledge. This information remained public knowledge in 1991 even if, with the passage of time, it had faded to the fringes of public awareness.

In 1991, Mr. Stewart did not have the legal right to preserve any decreased public awareness of this public knowledge. The law did not shield him from what he had done, or from the public's right to know how its justice system had dealt with him and his conduct, or from the media's right to remind the public about this public information. Recognizing these ongoing realities is not the same as saying that the law requires Mr. Stewart to pay indefinitely for his wrongdoing. There is no such obligation in law. His sentence was the full measure of what the law required him to pay, and Mr. Stewart served it years ago.

Mr. Stewart's claim is narrower and more specific than an attack on media re-publication of public information. Mr. Stewart takes the position that, regardless of the public nature of information about his crime, trial and sentencing, and regardless of the media's right to re-broadcast it, Mr. Greenspan owed him a fiduciary duty of loyalty which arose from their concluded counsel and client relationship, which duty did not allow Mr. Greenspan to participate as he did in this broadcast.

Confidentiality was pleaded to be an implied contractual term. That has not been established. The tort of breach of confidence was not pleaded. Confidentiality is also raised as an aspect of the alleged breach of the fiduciary duty of loyalty. The evidence establishes no disclosure of secrets between counsel and client, and further establishes that all information in the broadcast in question was public knowledge with the exception of the exaggeration of the distance Mr. Stewart dragged Mrs. Jordan screaming in agony. That exaggeration did not disclose a version of the facts proven to have been confidential, as distinct from subject to the alleged fiduciary duty of loyalty. In my opinion, confidentiality considerations are irrelevant to the determination of fiduciary issues in this case. In *Canadian Aero Service Ltd. v. O'Malley* (1973), 40 DLR (3d) 371 (SCC), misuse of confidential information was alleged to be a breach of fiduciary duty. Laskin J (as he then was) stated for the court at p. 388 that he did not see that the question of confidentiality was relevant to the enforcement of a fiduciary duty, and that the fact that breach of confidence may itself afford a ground of relief does not make it a necessary ingredient of a successful claim for breach of fiduciary duties. In *LAC Minerals Ltd. v. International Corona Resources Ltd.* [(1989), 61 DLR (4th) 14 (SCC)], Sopinka J for the majority held at pp. 63 and 64 DLR that the presence of conduct that incurs the censure of a court of equity in the context of a fiduciary duty cannot itself create that duty. Consequently, the fact that confidential information is obtained and misused cannot itself create a fiduciary obligation. One of the possible incidents of a fiduciary relationship is the exchange of confidential information and restrictions on its use. However, where "the essence of the complaint" is misuse of confidential information, Sopinka J held that the appropriate cause of action is breach of confidence and not breach of fiduciary duty.

… If a fiduciary duty of loyalty barred Mr. Greenspan from participating in the broadcast of what was, with the exception mentioned, public information, it is not, in my opinion, consistent with the principles of fiduciary obligations to describe this duty as a duty of confidentiality.

In other circumstances, confidentiality and fiduciary issues intersect. In *Breach of Confidence* (Oxford: Clarendon Press, 1984) Francis Gurry states at p. 158 that "[t]he obligation of confidence can itself be regarded as a fiduciary obligation which defines for its own purposes its own class of fiduciaries." See also Goff and Jones, *The Law of Restitution*, 4th ed. (London: Sweet & Maxwell, 1993) at pp. 662 ff. and pp. 679ff. for a discussion of fiduciary's obligations respecting confidential information. …

(c) The Duty that Arises from This Relationship

It is trite but necessary, I think, to begin by noting that Mr. Greenspan was not bound
to be Mr. Stewart's advocate forever. This is consistent with rule 5, commentary 13
of the *Rules of Professional Conduct* which does not prohibit a lawyer from acting
against a former client. It advises when a lawyer may not act, and when it is "not
improper" for a lawyer to act. This standard of the profession demonstrates that a
lawyer is not bound indefinitely to serve the former client's interests which were the
subject of the earlier retainer. In my opinion, that obligation ends when the retainer
ends. However, the end of the lawyer and client relationship as such does not end the
fiduciary relationship. Duties arising from that fiduciary relationship may well re-
strain the lawyer from speaking about the former client's issues or business which
were the subject of the concluded retainer, or from taking steps which affect them.

In my opinion, the fundamental principles which Dubin JA restated in *Re R. and
Speid* [(1983), 3 DLR (4th) 246] included the nature of a lawyer's ongoing fiduciary
duties to a former client. This was done through quoting part of Gale J's reasons in
Tombill Gold Mines [[1955] 1 DLR 101]. Gale J did not just speak of an existing
principal and agent relationship such as an existing lawyer and client relationship, he
spoke of an existing fiduciary relationship. That fiduciary relationship survives the
termination of the lawyer and client relationship and the end of the duties which are
solely part of it.

... In determining the nature of the duty which arises from the fiduciary relationship in issue, there is an area of limited agreement in the reasons in *Hodgkinson v.
Simms* [(1994), 117 DLR (4th) 161] which I believe to be relevant. In the reasons of
La Forest J the following is quoted from the paper presented by Professor P.D. Finn,
at the Professional Responsibility Seminar, University of Auckland on May 29 1987,
entitled "Conflicts of Interest and Professionals" at p. 15 (see La Forest J's reasons at
p. 185 DLR):

> In some spheres conduct regulation would appear to be becoming an end in itself and
> this because there can be a public interest in reassuring the community—not merely
> beneficiaries—that even the appearance of improper behaviour will not be tolerated.
> The emphasis here seems, in part at least, to be the maintenance of the public's accep-
> tance of, and the credibility of, important institutions in society which render "fidu-
> ciary" services.

· · ·

Mr. Jack submitted that substantially all of the information about Mr. Stewart, his
crime and trial was public information before Mr. Greenspan was retained. He therefore argued that Mr. Greenspan was not bound by a fiduciary duty of loyalty to refrain
from involvement in republishing public information, which he learned through the
media. In my view, the nature of a counsel and client relationship in general, and this
one in particular show again the limitations of casting the duty herein in terms of
confidentiality, which this submission does. In the case of criminal defence counsel,
information is frequently in the public domain by the time counsel is retained. Frequently, a crime has been committed, a victim has gone to police and the processes of

justice have been brought to bear, with appropriate and necessary publication of information and media scrutiny. In a sensational case like Mr. Stewart's, particularly one involving flight to avoid prosecution, much information is public knowledge before the accused is identified and charged and, often, before counsel is retained. It is noteworthy that such public information probably would not prevent the existence of a fiduciary duty based on confidentiality. Rule 4 of the *Rules of Professional Conduct* indicates that a duty of confidentiality on the part of counsel may apply to information which is widely known. When the fiduciary duty is one of loyalty, unrelated to confidentiality, and in respect of the public disclosure and use of information by counsel, pre-retainer publication is of very little significance. I am of the view that Mr. Greenspan's fiduciary duty of loyalty to Mr. Stewart was not materially altered, diluted or destroyed by the pre-retainer publicity or by the fact that Mr. Greenspan first learned about Mr. Stewart and his case from publicly disseminated information. When Mr. Greenspan became counsel and that information became the subject of his professional services, it also became the subject of a fiduciary relationship. It therefore became the subject of a fiduciary duty moulded by the public issues and factors, among others. Those public issues and factors included public knowledge of the case, public perceptions and mis-perceptions of Mr. Stewart, and Mr. Greenspan's professional services in respect of public perceptions such as abhorrence and mis-perceptions such as those arising from first counsel's tactics. The fiduciary duty in issue therefore arises in part from what Mr. Greenspan said and did in public as counsel, it applies to what he said and did in public as broadcaster and, in my opinion, it is not defeated by what others said and did publicly before that fiduciary duty of loyalty arose.

(d) Breach of Fiduciary Duty

For the above reasons, Mr. Greenspan breached his fiduciary duty of loyalty to Mr. Stewart in the following ways:

— He favoured his financial interests over the plaintiff's interests as alleged in sub-paragraph 25(h) of the statement of claim.

— He put his own self-promotion before the plaintiff's interests as alleged in sub-paragraph 25(i) of the statement of claim.

— By the way he publicized his former client and his former client's case in 1991, he undercut the benefits and protections he had provided as counsel, and therefore, increased the adverse public effect on the plaintiff of his crime, trial and sentencing, which falls within sub-paragraph 25(j) of the statement of claim.

It is alleged in sub-paragraph 25(f) that Mr. Greenspan breached his fiduciary duty through his speech in the production in which he identified himself as the plaintiff's solicitor. In my opinion the evidence confirming this is relevant to the above breaches, but this is not a breach in itself.

. . .

Damages

. . .

I assess the compensation which Mr. Stewart is entitled to recover from Mr. Greenspan in the amount of $2,500.00. The amount of profit which Mr. Greenspan is obliged to disgorge to Mr. Stewart is $3,250.00. ...

Disposition

For the above reasons, I grant judgment in favour of the plaintiff against Mr. Greenspan only in the amount of $5,750.00.

The action is otherwise dismissed.

NOTES AND QUESTIONS

1. Greenspan is alleged to have "put his own self-promotion or self-aggrandizement before the interests of the plaintiff." Is this inevitable, given the economic assumptions regarding self-interest and utility maximization discussed in chapter 2? It should be obvious, by now, that the answer to this question is no. Why?

2. The court considers it important to "establish the extent to which the broadcast was based on information disclosed in open court and which therefore became public knowledge." Why? In answering this question, consider the commentary to rule 2.03(1) of Ontario's *Rules of Professional Conduct*, which provides (in part) that the duty of confidentiality "applies without regard to the nature or source of the information or the fact that others may share the knowledge." Further note that the court in *Stewart* makes it clear that "[c]onfidentiality may also give rise to an obligation resting on the recipient not to disclose or to make use of communicated information even though that information is so widely known that it is public knowledge."

3. Consider the actions of Stewart's original trial lawyer. According to the court in *Stewart*, this lawyer "questioned the relationship between Mr. and Mrs. Jordan, apparently attempting to implicate Mr. Jordan in her death. He also suggested that Mrs. Jordan had been killed by drug dealers with whom she was allegedly involved." Leaving aside the issue of confidentiality for the moment, is this line of argument ethical? By implicating Jordan's husband in Jordan's death, was this lawyer committing an unethical action, or could his actions be described by the words of the commentary to Ontario's rule 4.01, which requires the lawyer "to raise fearlessly every issue, advance every argument, and ask every question, however distasteful, which the lawyer thinks will help the client's case and to endeavour to obtain for the client the benefit of every remedy and defence authorized by law. The lawyer must discharge this duty by fair and honourable means, without illegality and in a manner that is consistent with the lawyer's duty to treat the tribunal with candour, fairness, courtesy, and respect and in a way that promotes the parties' right to a fair hearing where justice can be done"?

4. Does the decision in *Stewart* imply that lawyers have a duty to act as stewards of their former clients' public images? Why or why not?

5. Based on the holdings in *Geffen* and *Jack* (discussed in sections V and VI, respectively), would Greenspan have been permitted to appear in the "Scales of Justice" program (featuring Mr. Stewart's case) after Mr. Stewart died?

6. What weight does the court in *Stewart* give to Greenspan's evidence concerning the practices of eminent members of the Ontario Bar? Why might this information be relevant?

7. At one point during the proceedings, "Mr. Greenspan pleaded his right to freedom of expression as guaranteed by s. 2(b) of the *Canadian Charter of Rights and Freedoms*, and that, if the [*Rules of Professional Conduct*] infringe that right, it is not demonstrably justifiable in a free and democratic society." To what extent must the duty of confidentiality yield to the lawyer's right to freedom of expression? In your opinion, which right— namely, the client's right to confidentiality or the lawyer's right to free expression— should be given primacy?

8. What was the court's goal in awarding damages of $5,750—compensation for harm inflicted on Mr. Stewart; deterrence for Mr. Greenspan; or deterrence for lawyers' generally? From an economic perspective, what ought to have been the goal of the court's decision?

9. Note that rule 2.03(6) of Ontario's *Rules of Professional Conduct* provides that "[i]f a lawyer engages in literary works, such as a memoir or an autobiography, the lawyer shall not disclose confidential information without the client's or former client's consent." In addition, the commentary to Ontario's rule 6.06(1), which deals with public appearances, provides that "[p]ublic communications about a client's affairs should not be used for the purpose of publicizing the lawyer and should be free from any suggestion that a lawyer's real purpose is self-promotion or self-aggrandizement."

X. Conclusion

The cases discussed in this chapter have set out the basic elements of the lawyer's duty of confidentiality, one of the core ethical norms of the legal profession. Like any ethical duty, however, the duty of confidentiality is not absolute. As we have seen throughout this chapter, there are circumstances in which the lawyer's duty to preserve the confidentiality of a client's information must give way to competing policy concerns. Specific situations in which the lawyer may be permitted (or required) to divulge or use a client's confidential information are discussed in greater detail in chapter 7.

CHAPTER SEVEN

Exceptions to Confidentiality

I. Introduction

Chapter 6 introduced two of the defining features of the lawyer's ethical universe: the duty of confidentiality and solicitor–client privilege. These defining features, however, are far from absolute—in several of the cases discussed in chapter 6, the courts carved out exceptions to both privilege and confidentiality, permitting (or even requiring), the use or disclosure of information where some competing public policy outweighed the interests protected by non-disclosure.

The purpose of this chapter is to take a closer look at exceptions to solicitor–client privilege and, more generally, exceptions to the lawyer's duty of confidentiality. The chapter considers several possible exceptions to the lawyer's duty of confidentiality—namely:

1. exceptions relating to the lawyer's self-interest;

2. exceptions allowing disclosure in support of an accused's right to make full answer and defence;

3. exceptions allowing disclosure in support of public safety;

4. cases in which disclosure is required by law;

5. cases in which disclosure is authorized by the client;

6. exceptions allowing disclosure where the relevant information is a matter of public knowledge; and

7. a more general exception where the values protected by non-disclosure are outweighed by whatever values will be advanced by disclosure—that is, a general exception for cases in which social utility is maximized through disclosure.

When reading the sections that follow, consider the following questions: Is there a need to establish a series of "pigeonhole" exceptions to confidentiality, or should the courts move toward a more generalized exception permitting disclosure wherever disclosure maximizes social utility? Do the current, specific exceptions to confidentiality support or undermine the purposes of the ethical duty of confidentiality? Are the current exceptions sensible? Even if there were no exceptions, would the Law Society be likely to discipline lawyers who disclosed their clients' confidences in the situations that are currently covered by the specific exceptions? These and other questions will be explored in the sections that follow.

II. Lawyer Self-Interest

Many people are surprised to learn that one of the most well-established exceptions to the ethical rule of confidentiality relates specifically to the lawyer's self-interest. In many cases where the lawyer's self-interest is at stake, the lawyer is permitted to disclose or use a client's otherwise confidential information. To those who are familiar with economic theory, a "self-interest" exception should come as no surprise: as we saw in chapter 2, individuals inevitably act in their self-interest. This is as true of regulators as it is of other people or organizations. Since the bodies charged with the task of promulgating lawyers' professional codes of conduct are composed of legal professionals (see chapter 4), it should come as no surprise that various rules of professional conduct (and exceptions to those rules) are designed, at least in part, to further the interests of members of the legal profession. As a result, it is not especially shocking to learn that one of the key exceptions to the lawyer's duty of confidentiality arises in cases in which disclosure of a client's information is required in order to further the self-interest of a lawyer.

In what situations might a lawyer's personal interests justify the disclosure of a client's confidential information? The most obvious instance involves the collection of fees. As we saw in chapter 6, the fact that a client has hired a particular lawyer is generally considered confidential information—in many cases, the lawyer is not permitted to divulge the fact that he or she has been retained by a particular individual. Imagine a world in which there are no exceptions to this rule. What would happen if the client simply refused to pay the lawyer for services rendered, or alleged that the lawyer's fees were unreasonable? Because the lawyer could not disclose the fact that he or she had been retained by the client, or divulge the nature of the work undertaken for the client, there would be no means of enforcing payment. The lawyer could not sue the client for non-payment of fees, because this would involve disclosure of the existence of the retainer. In short, the lawyer would have no means of proving that he or she had acted on behalf of the relevant client. The existence of the contract between the lawyer and the client would be considered confidential, leaving the lawyer unable to prove that he or she had performed services that gave rise to the lawyer's right to collect a fee. If the lawyer is to prove entitlement to fees, the lawyer must be allowed to divulge the existence of the retainer. As a result, some exception to the rule of confidentiality is required in order to ensure that lawyers can enforce retainer agreements.

Cases involving fee-recovery are not the only situations in which a lawyer has a personal stake in disclosing confidential information. Consider a case in which a former client alleges that the lawyer has engaged in professional misconduct. Assume, for example, that a client has alleged that the lawyer has misappropriated money from the client's trust account. In order to defend against this allegation, the lawyer may find it necessary to lead evidence of (1) the nature of the relationship with the client, (2) the receipt of funds from the client, (3) transactions involving the use of the client's funds, and (4) the client's instructions with respect to the use of those funds. Absent some exception to the rule of lawyer-client confidentiality, all these pieces of information would be considered confidential. The lawyer would not be entitled to divulge or use the relevant information, and the lawyer would be unable to defend against the allegation that he or she had misappropriated the funds. Once again, some exception to confidentiality is required in order to allow the lawyer to safeguard his or her interests: an exception is required to permit the lawyer to defend against charges of impropriety.

As a result of the concerns expressed above, lawyers are permitted to disclose a client's otherwise confidential information for the purpose of collecting fees or defending against a charge of impropriety. These exceptions to the general rule of confidentiality are explicitly spelled out in many codes of professional conduct. Commentary 10 to chapter IV of the CBA Code, for example, provides as follows:

> Disclosure [of a client's confidential information] may also be justified in order to establish or collect a fee, or to defend the lawyer or the lawyer's associates or employees against any allegation of malpractice or misconduct, but only to the extent necessary for such purposes.

Similarly, Ontario's rule 2.03 provides (in part) as follows:

> (4) Where it is alleged that a lawyer or the lawyer's associates or employees are:
>   (a) guilty of a criminal offence involving a client's affairs,
>   (b) civilly liable with respect to a matter involving a client's affairs, or
>   (c) guilty of malpractice or misconduct,
> a lawyer may disclose confidential information in order to defend against the allegations, but the lawyer shall not disclose more information than is required.
>
> (5) A lawyer may disclose confidential information in order to establish or collect the lawyer's fees, but the lawyer shall not disclose more information than is required.

In the situations described by the foregoing provisions, lawyers clearly have the right to divulge or use a client's otherwise confidential information in order to safeguard their personal interests. In these cases, the lawyer will not be subjected to professional sanctions. The economic implications of this exception to confidentiality will be explored in the notes and questions below.

The decision of the Ontario Court of Appeal in *R v. Dunbar* (1982), below, deals with the lawyer's self-interest exception to confidentiality and solicitor–client privilege. Specifically, *Dunbar* involves a lawyer's ability to divulge privileged information in the face of a former client's allegation that the lawyer has broken the law. When reviewing the decision, pay particular attention to the effect of the court's holding that the client's former lawyer will be entitled to divulge the confidential information.

It should be noted that the last several pages of the court's decision in *Dunbar* are devoted to another potential exception to the lawyer's duty of confidentiality, referred to as the "innocence-at-stake" exception. This exception suggests that a lawyer may be entitled to divulge a client's confidential information in cases in which the information is needed in order to help an accused make "full answer and defence." This exception, which raises its own peculiar policy concerns, is dealt with in detail in section III.

R v. Dunbar
(1982), 68 CCC (2d) 13 (Ont. CA)

MARTIN JA: The appellants, Kenneth Logan and John Dunbar, were tried along with Kevin Bray on an indictment containing three counts charging them with first degree murder. …

The appellants, the co-accused Bray and the deceased Talbot were members of a Windsor motor cycle club known as the Lobos. The deceased Talbot was a drug dealer, the deceased Ladouceur was his son and the deceased Kathryn Furdal was living with Talbot. The three deceased were killed on Sunday evening, January 25, 1976, at Talbot's home. Their bodies were found the following day in the living-room area of the house.

Talbot had a bullet wound in the head and one in the abdomen, his skull had been fractured and he had numerous stab wounds. Kathryn Furdal had multiple stab wounds and her skull had been shattered by a blow administered with a good deal of force. Ladouceur had been shot in the head twice and had a scalp wound caused by a blow of considerable force.

Parts of a shot-gun were found about the room, but the barrel of the shot-gun was never found. The bullets found in the deceased and the cartridges found in the living-room were all fired from the same .25 calibre gun which, according to the firearms examiner, could resemble a .22 calibre weapon. The knife wounds were probably made by a knife of the stiletto type.

The case for the Crown against the appellants, as it went to the jury, was based primarily on the testimony of two young women, Kerena Girard and Roberta Bearhope, and on the testimony of the co-accused Bray. …

The co-accused Bray testified in his own defence, as did the appellants. Bray testified that he had known Talbot for some time and that he and Talbot had purchased the house where Talbot was killed. Bray and Talbot were partners in the business of trafficking in drugs. He said that on the evening of January 25th, he was picked up around 7:30 p.m. by one O'Connor, a probationary member of the Lobos Club, and went to the club. They left the club shortly afterwards and spent several hours driving around, visiting various people and trying to obtain some marijuana. As they were driving on Walker Rd. shortly before midnight, he recognized Logan's car. They followed Logan and when they eventually caught up with him, Bray went over to Logan's car where he saw both the appellants. Dunbar told him to get into Logan's car, which he did, after telling his companion that he was going with the appellants.

Bray testified that Dunbar had a double-barrelled shot-gun with the butt ripped off. He said the shot-gun had blood and long hair on it. When Bray asked what had happened, the appellants told him that they had just killed Talbot. Bray testified that Dunbar and Logan threw the shot-gun in the river and that Dunbar also pulled out what looked like a .25 calibre hand-gun which he also threw in the river along with his jacket. Bray became frightened and tried to run away, but they caught up with him and told him to get back into the car. They then drove to Kerena Girard's apartment and en route, according to Bray, Logan said "[t]oo bad the broad and the kid had to go too but that is the way it is." When they arrived at the apartment, Kerena Girard was there, and also a young man. After the young man left, Logan asked for a pair of scissors which Girard obtained for him. Logan then began cutting up his gloves in the wash-room. Girard had also testified that Logan cut up his blood-stained gloves and flushed the pieces down the toilet. ...

The Solicitor–Client Privilege Issue

. . .

It is necessary to set out in some detail the factual background against which the issues on this branch of the appeal arise.

The trial of the appellants and their co-accused, Bray, commenced on October 16, 1978. After the appellants had completed their evidence, Mr. Tuck, Bray's counsel, announced on the morning of November 8, 1978, that his client had decided to testify. At the request of Bray's counsel the trial judge adjourned the trial until the afternoon.

Mr. Ducharme, Dunbar's counsel, advised the trial judge that he had been taken completely by surprise by Bray's decision to give evidence incriminatory of his client. He indicated to the trial judge that he would be making an application to reopen his client's case and to call further evidence concerning Bray. Mr. Tuck, Bray's counsel, stated that it was only on the previous night that he had heard from Bray what he believed to be the full and true story. His instructions up to that morning were that Bray would not be testifying. Mr. Tait, Logan's counsel, indicated to the judge that his client now wished him (Tait) to testify.

The trial judge ruled that he would first allow Bray to testify. Then in the light of that testimony he would hear representations from counsel for the appellants with respect to reopening their cases. Mr. Tait requested an adjournment for the balance of the day to permit defence counsel to locate witnesses. He indicated for the first time that it might be necessary for Logan to retain other counsel. He later informed the judge that he had been retained by all three accused the night of the arrest and that his instructions had always been received from all three accused at the same time.

Bray then testified as to the events of the night of January 25, 1976, previously summarized. He also said that two days after the killings, at Dunbar's suggestion, he went to see the police because he was a co-owner of the house in which the murders took place. He testified that the statement he gave to the police at that time was largely false. Bray testified that after being charged, he was "offered five years for accessory after the fact." He did not say by whom the offer was made. He also said that at another point, Mr. Thompson, his former counsel, told him that the Crown would be willing to "let [him] go" if he testified against his co-accused. He said that at about the time of the preliminary hearing, Mr. Thompson told him that the Crown would be willing to accept a plea of guilty to a charge of conspiracy to commit bodily harm for which Bray would receive a sentence of six to eight months. He initially accepted this offer but immediately changed his mind because he thought that there was still a chance that Logan and Dunbar might escape conviction. Moreover, the appellants assured him that if things went badly at the trial, they would tell the truth in order to clear Bray. ...

Mr. Ducharme, Dunbar's counsel ... disclosed that he had conducted joint interviews and felt that he, too, could not participate further in the trial. During the discussion it was disclosed that around August 14, 1978, Bray had provided Mr. Tait with two handwritten statements: one, six pages in length and the other, one page in length. When it appeared that the trial judge might not be prepared to grant an adjournment to permit Logan and Dunbar to retain other counsel, Mr. Ducharme requested that he be given an opportunity to speak to Mr. Cooper. Upon resuming, Mr. Ducharme informed the trial judge that, based upon his discussion with Mr. Cooper, he felt that he could continue to act for Dunbar, but Mr. Tait said he felt that he could not continue to act for Logan. The trial judge refused to grant an adjournment, and instructed Mr. Ducharme not to ask questions about matters of a privileged nature in his cross-examination of Bray. Mr. Ducharme asked that a *voir dire* be held with respect to the way in which certain written statements of Bray came into Ducharme's possession. The trial judge refused this request because in his opinion a relationship of confidentiality existed between Bray and Ducharme.

Mr. Ducharme then disclosed that there was a third written statement of Bray which had been found by Dunbar in Bray's cell and taken apparently without Bray's consent. The trial judge held that this document was also privileged.

Bray refused to waive the solicitor–client privilege.

With the consent of all counsel we received on the appeal the affidavit of Patrick Ducharme to which are marked, as exs. "A" and "B," two handwritten documents. Mr. Ducharme deposes to the fact that the documents marked as exhibits to his affidavit were given to him at the trial by Mr. Tait and that they are the documents that he sought permission to use at the trial. Both documents are dated August 14, 1978. The first consists of three pages and is unsigned. The second is signed by Kevin D. Bray and consists of nine pages. Both documents refer to a third document (presumably the document taken by Dunbar from Bray's cell) which consists of two pages of handwritten notes. The substance of the documents dated August 14, 1978, is that Bray's former lawyer, Mr. Thompson, discussed with him the two proposals outlined in Bray's examination-in-chief, previously mentioned, whereby Bray in exchange for his testimony against his co-accused would either be released or permitted to plead guilty to conspiracy to cause bodily harm for which he would receive lenient treatment. It is implicit in the statements that his former lawyer was suggesting that he lie in order to incriminate Dunbar and Logan. He asserts in his statements that Dunbar and Logan have never admitted to him that they were in any way involved in the murders. The third document which we also received consists of handwritten notes in different handwriting to the statements dated August 14, 1978, and are supposedly the notes of Mr. Thompson indicating the points that Bray would be required to cover in his testimony. It should be said at once that there is no evidence of wrongdoing on Mr. Thompson's part other than the allegations made by Bray in his testimony and in the statements. The handwritten notes are capable of an innocent construction depending upon what Bray told Mr. Thompson.

The learned trial judge ruled that all three documents were privileged. He said:

> Mr. Ducharme says quite simply that he at no time acted for Mr. Bray and Mr. Bray being a witness, privilege does not attach. Mr. Tuck has indicated that his client will not waive the matter of privilege and says the documents are privileged. ...

It has been revealed to this Court that apparently the three accused were interviewed on several occasions by each of the three counsel appearing before me. In other words, Mr. Ducharme has talked on occasion to Mr. Bray in the cells as well as his own client, Mr. Dunbar. I am not passing on the propriety of what went on, I am simply saying this, that to me Mr. Bray talked to Mr. Dunbar [sic] as one "seeking legal advice and with the intention of confidentiality." He, therefore, fulfills the requisite of privilege. I feel, therefore, I do not need a *voir dire* to determine whether the evidence is admissible and I quite clearly find that Mr. Ducharme had the position I outlined with Mr. Bray and that privilege attaches to their discussions.

Mr. Ducharme mentions that a paper was found in the cell by someone and he also wishes to cross-examine on this. I hold this to be the same as the other document. No questions, therefore, will be asked either about any documents attached to Mr. Bray unless Mr. Bray waives that privilege.

Mr. Tuck has indicated that he does not waive the privilege but I think I should hear the same from Mr. Bray and if he does not waive the privilege, I shall direct that Mr. Ducharme ask no questions of Mr. Bray on any of these points either written or verbal.

Patently, the trial judge in referring to Mr. Bray talking to "Mr. Dunbar" as one seeking legal advice meant to say "Mr. Ducharme."

Following his ruling the trial judge asked Bray's counsel to explain to his client the "matter of waiving privilege." Bray stated and his counsel confirmed that he did not wish to "waive [his] privilege."

Mr. Rosenberg for the appellants contended that the trial judge erred in holding that the documents were privileged because:

1. The solicitor–client privilege never attached to the documents, since Bray intended that they be communicated to the co-accused and their counsel, and hence the communications were not intended to be confidential.

2. That even if the two documents dated August 14, 1978, were privileged when made as a communication to Mr. Tait at a time when he was acting for both Bray and Logan, the privilege became inapplicable as between Bray and Logan when a subsequent controversy arose between the joint clients.

3. The privilege, if it initially attached to the documents, was destroyed when Bray at the trial made an imputation of fraud against his former solicitor, Thompson, and also against Mr. Tait, and they were entitled to testify as to how the documents came into existence in order to rebut the allegation of misconduct.

4. That if the third document, found in Bray's cell, was initially privileged, the privilege was lost when Bray allowed it to fall into Dunbar's hands.

Mr. Rosenberg further contended that in any event, the trial judge erred in ruling that the documents were privileged without holding a *voir dire* to determine the circumstances in which the documents came into existence and under which they came into the possession of counsel for the accused Logan and Dunbar.

[The court went on to hold that solicitor–client privilege had attached to the documents at the moment of their creation. It then considered whether the privilege attaching to those documents was waived by virtue of subsequent developments.]

Whether Bray Waived the Privilege by His Testimony Imputing Misconduct to His Former Counsel

Counsel for the appellants contended that Bray's evidence at the trial imputing misconduct to his former solicitor Thompson and to Mr. Tait constituted a waiver of the privilege.

Bray, in his examination-in-chief, did not make any imputations of misconduct against either Mr. Tait or Mr. Thompson, but he clearly did so in cross-examination.

Dean Wigmore states that when the client alleges a breach of duty by the attorney the privilege is waived as to all communications relevant to that issue: 8 *Wigmore on Evidence* (McNaughton Rev.), p. 638. In *McCormick on Evidence*, 2nd ed., the author states at p. 191:

> As to what is a controversy between lawyer and client the decisions do not limit their holdings to litigation between them, but have said that whenever the client, even in litigation between third persons, makes an imputation against the good faith of his attorney in respect to his professional services, the curtain of privilege drops so far as necessary to enable the lawyer to defend his conduct. Perhaps the whole doctrine that in controversies between attorney and client the privilege is relaxed, may best be based upon the ground of practical necessity that if effective legal service is to be encouraged the privilege must not stand in the way of the lawyer's just enforcement of his rights to be paid a fee and to protect his reputation. The only question about such a principle is whether in all cases the privilege ought not to be the same qualification, that it should yield when the evidence sought is necessary to the attainment of justice.

In cross-examination, counsel for Dunbar asked Bray whether he had ever said to anyone that he could not give evidence against Dunbar and Logan because it would be a lie to which Bray replied: "Mr. Tait directed Ken. He said, well, if you were in his position I'd tell you to do this and I just wrote it down."

> Q. Did you want to write it down?
> A. Well, at the time I had no choice. Ah Logan and Dunbar were there and were coming on heavy to me.

Bray later testified as follows:

> Q. Yes, what did you say in Mr. Tait's presence?
> A. I can't really remember what exactly, what I said, I didn't say very much
> Q. I suggest to you that you said that you could never lie about these gentlemen and that you could not say under oath that they were involved in this crime because you know that would be swearing under oath or telling a lie under oath; is that true?
> A. That is what Mr. Tait directed Ken and Ken told me and I wrote it down.

Bray was also cross-examined about the alleged "deal" which he had been offered whereby he would be allowed to plead guilty to a lesser offence and receive a sentence of six to eight months. He gave the following testimony:

> Q. Okay. And each of those deals, you get nothing, six or eight months, the deal was you had to be sure and implicate these two gentlemen; isn't that right?
> A. Yeah.
> Q. The evidence had to dovetail, had to match?
> A. Um-hmm.
> Q. Except for that part of the evidence that affected you; right?
> A. I told Thompson that I would not lie.
> Q. All right.
> A. I'm not lying.
> Q. Did he want you to lie?
> A. Yeah, I think he did.
> Q. Your lawyer wanted you to lie about this; is that what you are saying?
> A. On another occasion, yeah.
> Q. Do you think Mr. Thompson will back you on that?
> A. I don't know if he would.
> HIS LORDSHIP: Just rephrase your question, Counsel, and don't argue with the witness, please.
> MR. DUCHARME: : Mr. Thompson, your former lawyer, wanted you to lie; is that right?
> A. In so many words, yeah.
> Q. And I suggest to you the lie that he wanted you to give was that these two individuals were involved in this crime and you refused to do that?
> A. No, he wanted me to say I drove the car.
> Q. He wanted you to say what?
> A. That I drove the car.
> Q. That you drove the car?
> A. That's right.
> Q. That is all he wanted you to say?
> A. Plus a few other things, too.

Bray later testified that Mr. Thompson had given him certain notes relating to matters with respect to which Bray's testimony would have to "dovetail" with the Crown's case. These notes as previously indicated appear to be document No. 3 which were also ruled to be privileged. The trial judge ordered counsel to desist from this line of questioning.

Mr. Doherty contended that since Bray had not made imputations against Mr. Tait and Mr. Thompson in his examination-in-chief, the eliciting by cross-examination of the imputations against his former counsel did not dissolve the privilege. With respect, I do not think the principle that an allegation of fraud by the client against the solicitor relaxes the privilege so far as is necessary to enable the lawyer to defend his reputation is confined to imputations against his lawyer made during examination-in-chief.

It appears to be clear that where the client on direct examination testifies to a privileged communication in part, this is a waiver as to the remainder of the privileged consultation or consultations on the same subject. Dean McCormick suggests that unless the client was surprised or misled the same rule should apply where part of the communication is revealed on cross-examination and that the decisions to the contrary are hardly supportable. See *McCormick on Evidence*, 2nd ed., pp. 194-5: 8 *Wigmore on Evidence* (McNaughton Rev.), p. 637, fn 3, where the learned editor comments that the ruling in *Foley v. Poschke* (1940), 32 NE 2d 858, that a statutory provision for waiver upon the "voluntary testimony" of the client did not include testimony given on cross-examination since it is not "voluntary" seems incorrect since the client on cross-examination could have invoked the privilege.

I see no valid reason why Bray's imputations against his former lawyers on cross-examination should not constitute a waiver of the privilege so far as it is necessary to enable them to defend themselves against the imputations, on the same basis that a partial disclosure of a communication on cross-examination constitutes a waiver of the privilege as to the balance of the communication.

Whether the Solicitor–Client Privilege Must Yield Where the Privileged Communication Might Assist an Accused To Prove His Innocence

In *R v. Barton*, [1973] 1 WLR 115, Caulfield J enunciated a broad exception to the solicitor-and-client privilege. He held that the privilege must yield where to uphold the privilege would permit the withholding of evidence from the jury which might enable an accused to establish his innocence or to resist an allegation by the Crown. In that case, the accused was charged with fraudulent conversion and the falsification of accounts alleged to have been committed while employed as a legal executive with a firm of solicitors. The accused served a subpoena on a partner of the firm to give evidence at the trial and to produce certain documents. The solicitor claimed that the documents were protected by the solicitor–client privilege.

In ruling that the documents were admissible, Caulfield J said at p. 118:

> I think the correct principle is this, and I think that it must be restricted to these particular facts in a criminal trial, and the principle I am going to enunciate is not supported by any authority that has been cited to me, and I am just working on what I conceive to be the rules of natural justice. If there are documents in the possession or control of a solicitor which, on production, help to further the defence of an accused man, then in my judgment no privilege attaches. I cannot conceive that our law would permit a solicitor or other person to screen from a jury information which, if disclosed to the jury, would perhaps enable a man either to establish his innocence or to resist an allegation made by the Crown. I think that is the principle that should be followed.

Sir Rupert Cross, in commenting on the principle enunciated by Caulfield J states that the merits of the doctrine are obvious but its precise implications and limitations, if any, have not been worked out: see *Cross on Evidence*, 5th ed., p. 291. This principle would also appear to be accepted by the learned editors of *Phipson on Evidence*: see *Phipson on Evidence*, 12th ed., p. 242.

In *R v.* Barton, *supra*, the solicitor from whom the privileged information was sought to be obtained was not a co-accused. One limitation of the wide principle enunciated by Caulfield J that suggests itself is that an accused ought not to be required to disclose privileged information, the disclosure of which might assist a co-accused to the detriment of the accused who is required to disclose the privileged communication. Assuming for the present purpose that the privilege protecting communications by Bray to his solicitors was not destroyed by his subsequent imputations against them, the removal of the privilege, while it might assist his co-accused, might be damaging to Bray. The interests of Bray as well as his co-accused must be balanced in deciding whether the privilege must yield in the interests of the co-accused.

Different considerations will apply on a new trial of Logan and Dunbar. Generally speaking, if a communication or a document has attracted privilege it remains privileged, unless waived or otherwise dissolved. The privilege continues after the end of the litigation and even after the death of the client: see 8 *Wigmore on Evidence* (McNaughton Rev.), pp. 630-1; *Phipson on Evidence*, 12th ed., p. 248. The doctrine "once privileged always privileged" has, however, been enunciated in civil cases. The privilege enures for the benefit of successors in title of the person able to claim it.

No rule of policy requires the continued existence of the privilege in criminal cases when the person claiming the privilege no longer has any interest to protect, and when maintaining the privilege might screen from the jury information which would assist an accused.

Sir Rupert Cross, in discussing the duration of the privilege, say in *Cross on Evidence*, 5th ed., p. 286:

> A time may come when the party denying the continued existence of the privilege can prove that the party relying on it no longer has any interest to protect, as where the solicitor for the unsuccessful plaintiff in a civil action takes a statement from a witness who is subsequently prosecuted for perjury, and the prosecution wish to ask the solicitor what the witness said to him.

Bray having been acquitted, a balancing of interests at a new trial of the appellants favours the admission of the communications of Bray to his former solicitors, notwithstanding that privilege initially attached to the communications (and even if, contrary to the view I have expressed, the privilege was not lost by Bray's imputation of fraud against his former solicitors), where the admission of the communications assists the appellants in resisting the allegations made against them. The principle enunciated in *R v.* Barton, *supra*, is, in my view, properly invoked in those circumstances.

Mr. Doherty, as I understood his argument, contended that the documents and handwritten notes were of such little weight in support of the appellants' defence, that the destruction of the privilege was not warranted in order to place before the jury the specifics of those documents. The jury was made fully aware, Mr. Doherty submitted, that Bray admitted that he had previously told other people, including his lawyers, that to the best of his knowledge his co-accused were not involved in the killings, but that he was now saying that his previous statements were false, and that his testimony implicating the appellants was true.

Accepting Mr. Doherty's submission that the documents were not of such value in assisting the defence in resisting the allegations made against them to justify their admission on the principle of *R v.* Barton, *supra*, at a time when Bray was a co-accused, different considerations will, in my opinion, apply at a new trial of the appellants. I agree that the documents, and particularly the handwritten notes, are not of great value in support of the appellants' defence. I am unable, however, to say that a jury would not attach any weight to them.

To sum up: in my view privilege attached to the three documents. The privilege with respect to document No. 3 was lost when Dunbar removed it from Bray's cell. The privilege with respect to the documents dated August 14th was removed in so far as it was necessary to enable Mr. Thompson and Mr. Tait to refute the imputations of fraud made against them. Accordingly, Mr. Thompson and Mr. Tait were entitled to give evidence to refute the allegations of fraud.

Refusal To Permit Dunbar To Reopen His Case

After Bray had completed his evidence, counsel for Dunbar applied to reopen his case to call as witnesses, Tait and Thompson, Bray's former solicitors. The trial judge refused the application.

If the trial judge had been correct in his view that the communications between Bray and his former solicitors remained privileged, then, of course, he would not have erred in refusing the application to permit the case of Dunbar to be reopened in order to call Tait and Thompson, since their evidence would have been inadmissible. As previously indicated, however, I am of the view that the privilege had been removed by Bray's imputation against Tait and Thompson in cross-examination to the extent that the removal was necessary to permit Tait and Thompson to refute those allegations. It seems clear that counsel for the appellants did not foresee that Bray would give testimony incriminatory of their clients. Indeed, Mr. Tuck, counsel for Bray, stated that his instructions up to the morning of the day that Bray testified were that Bray would not be testifying, and that he had only heard the previous night what he believed to be the full and true story.

If, as I have held, the testimony of Thompson and Tait was admissible to refute the imputation of fraud against them, then the application to reopen the case should properly have been granted: see Archbold, *Pleading, Evidence & Practice in Criminal Cases*, 40th ed. (1979), pp. 414-5. …

[Appeal allowed; new trial ordered.]

NOTES AND QUESTIONS

1. Consider the nature of the allegations made against Mr. Bray's former lawyers. Were Bray's lawyers ever "officially" accused of misconduct? Was it likely that Bray's allegations of misconduct would be used to support charges against the lawyers? If not, what purpose was served by allowing the lawyers to disclose their client's private information?

2. What is the likely effect of disclosure in this case? Will it have the effect of protecting the lawyers' personal interests, or will it simply have the effect of undermining Bray's credibility?

3. Should the self-interest exception apply only in cases in which the lawyer actually faces a personal cost (such as a fine, a penalty, a reputational cost, or the inability to collect the lawyer's fee)? Conversely, should confidentiality and privilege automatically disappear when the client besmirches the lawyer's character or ethics? If so, what is the rationale of the self-interest exception?

4. Were Bray's allegations of impropriety likely to have any effect on Thompson's professional reputation? If not, what is the purpose in allowing the disclosure of confidential information in this case?

5. What are the economic implications of the lawyer's self-interest exception? Could it be argued that this exception is designed as a mechanism for maximizing social utility? How can we explain the self-interest exception in terms of utility maximization? When answering this question, consider the effect of this exception on (a) the availability of legal services, (b) the willingness of lawyers to act on behalf of criminal defendants of questionable character, and (c) the ability of a criminal defendant to adopt a strategy that may give rise to an acquittal.

6. According to George M. Cohen, "When Law and Economics Met Professional Responsibility" (1998), 67 *Fordham Law Review* 273, at 294, "the self-defense exception fits within agency theory. Absent the self-defense exception, self-interested lawyers would be more reluctant to represent clients who ... might attempt to use an absolute confidentiality obligation to unfairly hold up the lawyer's fees or otherwise blackmail the lawyer."

III. Innocence at Stake

One of the fundamental values of our nation's legal system is the notion that innocent persons should not be convicted of offences. Indeed, it is often suggested that we would prefer to see 10 guilty individuals go free rather than seeing 1 innocent person go to jail. In many cases, a lawyer may be in possession of confidential information that could have the effect of securing the acquittal of an innocent accused. This carries implications for the lawyer's duty of confidentiality. Consider the following illustration.

Example 7.1

Scott Trbovich is on trial for murder. Although there were no witnesses to the crime with which he is charged, Scott has no alibi and circumstantial evidence makes it appear that he is guilty.

In reality, Larry Sizzler committed the crime with which Scott has been charged. Unfortunately, there is no evidence linking Larry to this crime. Police never suspected Larry's involvement. Larry's former lawyer, Amy Hamilton, is aware of Larry's guilt, because Larry confessed to Amy soon after he murdered the victim.

Before the conclusion of Scott's trial, Larry Sizzler died of a heart attack. Larry's confession to Amy is confidential, and this confidentiality survives

> Larry's death. Amy, who has been monitoring the progress of Scott's trial, believes that Scott will be convicted, despite the fact that he is innocent.
>   Should Amy be permitted to disclose Larry's confession?

As we saw in section II, above, the Ontario Court of Appeal (as a result of its holding in *Dunbar*) would answer this question in the affirmative. This flows from the court's proposal of a general innocence-at-stake exception to the lawyer's duty of confidentiality. Pursuant to this exception, lawyers are entitled to divulge a client's confidences where (1) the client no longer has an interest in keeping the relevant information confidential, and (2) the disclosure of the information would allow an accused to make full answer and defence to a criminal charge. In the case of *Smith v. Jones* (reproduced in chapter 6), the Supreme Court of Canada endorsed this exception to the lawyer's duty of confidentiality. As a result, the innocence-at-stake exception to confidentiality appears to have become a feature of Canadian law.

Given the widespread acceptance of the notion that innocent people ought to be protected against the possibility of unjust convictions, readers may be surprised to learn that not all countries share Canada's apparent enthusiasm for an innocence-at-stake exception to the duty of confidentiality. Indeed, England's House of Lords explicitly rejected this exception in *R v. Derby Magistrates' Court* (1995), reproduced below, a case that was considered and rejected by the Supreme Court of Canada in *Smith v. Jones*. The decision of the House of Lords in *Derby Magistrates' Court* provides a thorough analysis of the policies implicated by the innocence-at-stake exception. After reviewing that decision, compare it to the holding of the Supreme Court of Canada in *Smith v. Jones*, above, and consider which decision is more compelling.

R v. Derby Magistrates' Court
[1995] 4 All ER 526

LORD TAYLOR OF GOSFORTH CJ: ... On 3 April 1978 a 16-year-old girl was murdered. Although she was stabbed many times, a number of the wounds were shallow and the cause of death was strangulation. On 9 April the appellant was arrested. He at first denied involvement but subsequently admitted being solely responsible for the murder. On 10 April he made a statement to that effect (the first account). In it he alleged that the girl had sexually assaulted and provoked him whereupon he had stabbed her. Proceedings were commenced against him charging him with murder. Preparations for trial were well advanced when, on 6 October 1978, a psychiatrist visited the appellant. Following that visit, on 8 October, the appellant changed his story. He made a statement alleging that his stepfather had killed the girl. Although he, the appellant, was present and took some part he did so under duress (the second account).

In November 1978, after a trial at the Crown Court at Nottingham in which the appellant relied upon the second account, he was acquitted.

On 14 December 1978, when interviewed by a senior police officer, the appellant repeated his first account that he alone had killed the girl. However when his solicitor arrived he retracted that confession.

On 16 April 1980 the appellant made a statement to the police reaffirming the second account.

On 1 April 1987 the mother of the deceased girl issued a writ against the appellant and his stepfather alleging assault and battery against both. In July 1991 the civil action came on before Rougier J. It lasted some five days and the appellant gave evidence implicating his stepfather, who did not give evidence. On 30 September 1991 Rougier J gave judgment. He held that on the evidence before him he was sure that the sole cause of the girl's death was strangulation by the stepfather but that so far as the stab wounds were concerned the appellant and his stepfather were joint tortfeasors.

On 7 July 1992 the stepfather was arrested and charged with murder. On 8 October 1992 the stipendiary magistrate refused a motion to stay the proceedings on the basis that they were an abuse of process. An application for judicial review of that decision was refused by the Divisional Court in February 1994.

On 20 June 1994 committal proceedings against the stepfather began. The appellant was called on behalf of the Crown to give evidence. In the course of cross-examination he was asked about instructions he had given to the solicitors acting for him in 1978 between his giving the first account and the second account. The appellant declined to waive his privilege. Accordingly, an application was made on 21 June for the stipendiary magistrate to grant a witness summons directed to the solicitor seeking the production of privileged documentation, in particular—

> All attendance notes and proofs of evidence which disclose the factual instruction of [the appellant] in defence of the charge of murder in 1978, coming into existence prior to 8th October 1978 and to exclude advice given to him by solicitors and or counsel.

The Derby stipendiary magistrate granted a witness summons pursuant to s 97 of the *Magistrates' Courts Act* 1980 in the terms sought ... the Divisional Court certified the following question:

> Whether a witness summons may properly be issued under s 97 of the *Magistrates' Courts Act* 1980 to compel production by a prosecution witness in committal proceedings of proofs of evidence and attendance notes giving factual instructions to his solicitor which (a) may contain or record previous inconsistent statements by the witness; and/or (b) which are the subject of legal professional privilege which has not been waived. ...

On 5 April 1995 your Lordships' House gave leave to appeal. ...

I now turn to the second main issue in the case, which would arise only if the conditions for issue of a witness summons under s 97 of the 1980 Act were satisfied, but which raised a discrete ground of appeal. Mr Francis submitted that the documents covered by the witness summons are protected by legal professional privilege, and are therefore immune from production. In the course of the committal proceedings the appellant was asked whether he was willing to waive privilege. After consulting his solicitor he replied that he was claiming privilege both in respect of his criminal trial in 1978, and in respect of the civil trial in 1991.

The stipendiary magistrate considered that it was his duty to weigh the public interest which protects confidential communications between a solicitor and his client against the public interest in securing that all relevant and admissible evidence is made available to the defence. In his view the balance came down firmly in favour of production. The appellant could no longer be regarded as having any recognisable interest in asserting privilege. The overriding consideration was the need to secure a fair trial for the stepfather. In holding that he was obliged to weigh competing public interests against each other, the stipendiary magistrate was following the decision of the Court of Appeal, Criminal Division in *R v. Ataou* [1988] 2 All ER 321, [1988] QB 798. If *R v. Ataou* was correctly decided, then the stipendiary magistrate was plainly entitled to take the view he did. Indeed, McCowan LJ in the Divisional Court described the balancing exercise which he had carried out as flawless. I would not disagree. For there could be no question of the appellant being tried again for murder, and it is most improbable that he would be prosecuted for perjury.

The important question remains, however, whether *R v. Ataou* was correctly decided, and in particular whether, when there is a claim for privilege in respect of confidential communications between solicitor and client, there is a balancing exercise to be performed at all. Mr Francis submits that there is not. He points out that in the long history of legal professional privilege there is no hint of any such exercise having been performed prior to the decision of Caulfield J in *R v. Barton* [1972] 2 All ER 1192, [1973] 1 WLR 115. So it will be necessary to look briefly at the history of the privilege, and then to consider the underlying principles on which it is based. But before doing so, it is convenient to start with the two decisions which, according to Mr Francis, have introduced a new and erroneous element into the law.

In *R v. Barton* the defendant was charged with fraudulent conversion, theft and falsification of accounts alleged to have been committed in the course of his employment as a legal executive with a firm of solicitors. A partner in the firm of solicitors was served with a subpoena to produce certain documents which had come into existence while he was acting as the solicitor to the executors of certain estates. The partner took the point that the documents were protected by legal professional privilege. Caulfield J held that the documents must be produced. After referring to a passage from *Cross on Evidence* (3rd edn, 1967) p 240, he continued ([1972] 2 All ER 1192 at 1194, [1973] 1 WLR 115 at 118):

> I think the correct principle is this, and I think that it must be restricted to these particular facts in a criminal trial, and the principle I am going to enunciate is not supported by any authority that has been cited to me; I am just working on what I conceive to be the rules of natural justice. If there are documents in the possession or control of a solicitor which, on production, help to further the defence of an accused man, then in my judgment no privilege attaches. I cannot conceive that our law would permit a solicitor or other person to screen from a jury information which, if disclosed to the jury, would perhaps enable a man either to establish his innocence or to resist an allegation made by the Crown. I think that is the principle that should be followed.

It should be borne in mind that Caulfield J's decision was one of first impression. It was given as an interlocutory ruling in the course of a criminal trial on circuit. It may be doubted whether he had any books available other than *Cross on Evidence*, *Archbold* and perhaps *Phipson on Evidence*; and the only case cited, *Wheeler v. Le*

Marchant (1881) 17 Ch D 675, is concerned with a different question altogether, namely the protection of communications between a solicitor and a third party.

R v. Barton was cited in the New Zealand decision of *R v. Craig* [1975] 1 NZLR 597, and a Canadian case, *R v. Dunbar and Logan* (1982) 138 DLR (3d) 221. These were the only authorities referred to in the decision of the Court of Appeal in *R v. Ataou* [1988] 2 All ER 321, [1988] QB 798.

The facts of *R v. Ataou* were that the appellant was charged with conspiracy to supply a controlled drug. His co-accused pleaded guilty, and elected to give evidence for the prosecution. Counsel for the appellant wished to cross-examine him about a previous statement which was said to be favourable to the appellant. The co-accused claimed privilege. The trial judge upheld the claim for privilege and the appellant was convicted. His appeal against conviction was allowed. The Court of Appeal stated the following principle ([1988] 2 All ER 321 at 326, [1988] QB 798 at 807):

> When a communication was originally privileged and in criminal proceedings privi-
> lege is claimed against the defendant by the client concerned or his solicitor, it should
> be for the defendant to show on the balance of probabilities that the claim cannot be
> sustained. That might be done by demonstrating that there is no ground on which the
> client could any longer reasonably be regarded as having a recognisable interest in
> asserting the privilege. The judge must then decide whether the legitimate interest of
> the defendant in seeking to breach the privilege outweighs that of the client in seeking
> to maintain it.

Applying that principle, the court held that there were only two factors which tended to show that the co-accused "continued to have a recognisable interest in asserting the privilege," namely the adverse influence it might have on the judge when he came to sentence the co-accused, and the risk of a prosecution for perjury. If the trial judge had carried out a balancing exercise, as the Court of Appeal said that he should have done, he would very likely have held that these two factors were outweighed by the appellant's interest in using the document to discredit the co-accused.

Thus under the principle stated in *R v. Ataou*, if it be correct, the judge is required to approach an application for production of documents protected by legal privilege in two stages. First he must ask whether the client continues to have any recognisable interest in asserting the privilege and, secondly, whether, if so, his interest outweighs the public interest that relevant and admissible documents should be made available to the defence in criminal proceedings.

So stated, the principle seems to conflict with the long established rule that a document protected by privilege continues to be protected so long as the privilege is not waived by the client: once privileged, always privileged. It also goes against the view that the privilege is the same whether the documents are sought for the purpose of civil or criminal proceedings, and whether by the prosecution or the defence, and that the refusal of the client to waive his privilege, for whatever reason, or for no reason, cannot be questioned or investigated by the court. I therefore turn briefly to the history of the privilege to see to what extent these traditional views are borne out by the authorities.

The first case to which we were referred, and the earliest case cited in 9 Holdsworth's History of English Law pp 197-202, is *Berd v. Lovelace* (1577) Cary

62, 21 ER 33. Since the report is very short, it can be quoted in full:

> Thomas Hawtry, gentleman, was served with a subpoena to testify his knowledge touch-
> ing the cause in variance; and made oath that he hath been, and yet is a solicitor in this
> suit, and hath received several fees of the defendant; which being informed to the Mas-
> ter of the Rolls ... ordered that the said Thomas Hawtry shall not be compelled to be
> deposed, touching the same, and that he shall be in no danger of any contempt, touch-
> ing the not executing of the said process. ...

Holdsworth points out that the decision in *Berd v. Lovelace* followed very shortly
after the *Perjury Act* 1562 (5 Eliz 1 c 9) by which it was established for the first time
that all competent persons could be compelled to testify.

Two years later, in *Dennis v. Codrington* (1579) Cary 100, 21 ER 53, the same
rule was applied to counsel:

> The plaintant seeks to have Master Oldsworth examined touching a matter in variance,
> wherein he hath been of counsel; it is ordered he shall not be compelled by subpoena,
> or otherwise, to be examined upon any matter concerning the same, wherein he the said
> Mr. Oldsworth, was of counsel. ...

At first it was thought that the reason for the privilege was that a lawyer ought not, in
honour, to be required to disclose what he had been told in confidence. But this explanation was rejected in the *Duchess of Kingston's Case* (1776) 20 State Tr 355, [1775-
1802] All ER Rep 623. In that case Sir Cecil Hawkins, the Duchess's doctor, objected
that he should not, in honour, be compelled to give evidence against her at her trial
for bigamy. His objection was overruled. But this did not affect the development of
legal professional privilege. By the end of the eighteenth century it was already well
on the way to being established on its present basis.

In *Wilson v. Rastall* (1792) 4 Term Rep 753, [1775-1802] All ER Rep 597 it was
decided that the privilege was confined to the three cases of counsel, solicitor and
attorney. There was reference in that case to an earlier case of bribery tried at Salisbury
before Lord Hardwicke, in which a Mr Reynolds wished to give evidence as to what
he had learnt while acting as the defendant's attorney. He was rebuked by Buller J for
being willing to reveal the secrets of his former client:

> ... I strongly animadverted on his conduct, and would not suffer him to be examined:
> he had acquired his information during the time that he acted as attorney; and I thought
> that the privilege of not being examined to such points was the privilege of the party,
> and not of the attorney: and that the privilege never ceased at any period of time. In
> such a case it is not sufficient to say that the cause is at an end; the mouth of such a
> person is shut for ever. (See 4 Term Rep 753 at 759, [1775-1802] All ER Rep 597 at 599.)

The case is thus clear early authority for the rule that the privilege is that of the client,
which he alone can waive, and that the court will not permit, let alone order, the
attorney to reveal the confidential communications which have passed between him
and his former client. His mouth is shut forever.

Although the rule was thus established by the end of the eighteenth century, the
reason for the rule was not fully developed until two cases heard and decided by Lord

Brougham LC, one after the other, at the beginning of 1833. In *Greenough v. Gaskell* (1833) 1 My & K 98, [1824-34] All ER Rep 767 the question was whether the privilege was confined to cases where legal proceedings were already in contemplation. Lord Brougham LC held it was not. As to the reason for the rule, he said (1 My & K 98 at 103, [1824-34] All ER Rep 767 at 770):

> The foundation of this rule is not difficult to discover. It is not (as has sometimes been said) on account of any particular importance which the law attributes to the business of legal professors, or any particular disposition to afford them protection, though certainly it may not be very easy to discover why a like privilege has been refused to others, and especially to medical advisers. But it is out of regard to the interests of justice, which cannot be upholden, and to the administration of justice, which cannot go on, without the aid of men skilled in jurisprudence, in the practice of the Courts, and in those matters affecting rights and obligations which form the subject of all judicial proceedings. If the privilege did not exist at all, every one would be thrown upon his own legal resources; deprived of all professional assistance, a man would not venture to consult any skilful person, or would only dare to tell his counsellor half his case.

In *Bolton v. Liverpool Corp* (1833) 1 My & K 88, 39 ER 614 the defendant in civil proceedings sought inspection of the plaintiff's case to counsel to advise (though not apparently the advice itself) and filed a bill of discovery in equity for that purpose. Not surprisingly the defendant failed. Lord Brougham LC said (1 My & K 88 at 94, 39 ER 614 at 617):

> It seems plain, that the course of justice must stop if such a right exists. No man will dare to consult a professional adviser with a view to his defence or to the enforcement of his rights. The very case which he lays before his counsel, to advise upon the evidence, may, and often does, contain the whole of his evidence, and may be, and frequently is, the brief with which that or some other counsel conducts his cause. The principle contended for, that inspection of cases, though not of the opinions, may always be obtained as of right, would produce this effect, and neither more nor less, that a party would go into Court to try the cause, and there would be the original of his brief in his own counsel's bag, and a copy of it in the bag of his adversary's counsel.

Numerous cases throughout the nineteenth century repeated the same themes. Thus in *Holmes v. Baddeley* (1844) 1 Ph 476 at 480-481, 41 ER 713 at 715 Lord Lyndhurst LC said:

> The principle upon which this rule is established is that communications between a party and his professional advisers, with a view to legal proceedings, should be unfettered; that they should not be restrained by any apprehension of such communications being afterwards divulged and made use of to his prejudice. To give full effect to this principle it is obvious that they ought to be privileged, not merely in the cause then contemplated or depending, but that the privilege ought to extend to any subsequent litigation with the same or any other party or parties … . The necessary confidence will be destroyed if it be known that the communication can be revealed at any time.

In *Anderson v. Bank of British Columbia* (1876) 2 Ch D 644 at 649 Jessel MR said:

The object and meaning of the rule is this: that as, by reason of the complexity and difficulty of our law, litigation can only be properly conducted by professional men, it is absolutely necessary that a man, in order to prosecute his rights or to defend himself from an improper claim, should have recourse to the assistance of professional lawyers, and it being so absolutely necessary, it is equally necessary, to use a vulgar phrase, that he should be able to make a clean breast of it to the gentleman whom he consults with a view to the prosecution of his claim, or the substantiating his defence against the claim of others; that he should be able to place unrestricted and unbounded confidence in the professional agent, and that the communications he so makes to him should be kept secret, unless with his consent ... that he should be enabled properly to conclude his litigation.

In *Southwark and Vauxhall Water Co v. Quick* (1878) 3 QBD 315 at 317-318 Cockburn CJ said:

The relation between the client and his professional legal adviser is a confidential relation of such a nature that to my mind the maintenance of the privilege with regard to it is essential to the interests of justice and the well-being of society. Though it might occasionally happen that the removal of the privilege would assist in the elucidation of matters in dispute, I do not think that this occasional benefit justifies us in incurring the attendant risk.

In *Pearce v. Foster* (1885) 15 QBD 114 at 119-120 Brett MR said:

The privilege with regard to confidential communications between solicitor and client for professional purposes ought to be preserved, and not frittered away. The reason of the privilege is that there may be that free and confidential communication between solicitor and client which lies at the foundation of the use and service of the solicitor to the client; but, if at any time or under any circumstances such communications are subject to discovery, it is obvious that this freedom of communication will be impaired. The liability of such communications to discovery in a subsequent action would have this effect as well as their liability to discovery in the original action.

In *Calcraft v. Guest* [1898] 1 QB 759 at 761, [1895-9] All ER Rep 346 at 348 Lindley MR said:

I take it that, as a general rule, one may say once privileged always privileged. I do not mean to say that privilege cannot be waived. ...

I may end with two more recent affirmations of the general principle. In *Hobbs v. Hobbs and Cousens* [1959] 3 All ER 827 at 829, [1960] P 112 at 116-117 Stevenson J said:

... privilege has a sound basis in common sense. It exists for the purpose of ensuring that there shall be complete and unqualified confidence in the mind of a client when he goes to his solicitor or when he goes to his counsel that that which he there divulges will never be disclosed to anybody else. It is only if the client feels safe in making a clean breast of his troubles to his advisers that litigation and the business of the law can be carried on satisfactorily ... . There is ... an abundance of authority in support of the proposition that once legal professional privilege attaches to a document ... that privilege attaches for all time and in all circumstances.

In *Balabel v. Air-India* [1988] 2 All ER 246, [1988] Ch 317 the basic principle justifying legal professional privilege was again said to be that a client should be able to obtain legal advice in confidence.

The principle which runs through all these cases, and the many other cases which were cited, is that a man must be able to consult his lawyer in confidence, since otherwise he might hold back half the truth. The client must be sure that what he tells his lawyer in confidence will never be revealed without his consent. Legal professional privilege is thus much more than an ordinary rule of evidence, limited in its application to the facts of a particular case. It is a fundamental condition on which the administration of justice as a whole rests.

How then did Mr Goldberg seek to restrict or disapply the operation of legal professional privilege in this case?

In his written case the only argument put forward was that the appellant did not consult his lawyers with a view to obtaining advice in the course of their ordinary professional employment, but with a view to forwarding his criminal purpose of deceiving the jury. The case was thus said to fall within the exception recognised by Stephen J in *R v. Cox and Railton* (1884) 14 QBD 153, [1881-5] All ER Rep 68. The argument was not that the privilege had to be balanced against some other public interest, but rather that the communications were never privileged at all. I need not take further time on this point, since it was formally abandoned by Mr Goldberg towards the end of his oral argument.

Apart from *R v. Cox and Railton*, Mr Goldberg submitted that in other related areas of the law, privilege is less sacrosanct than it was. He points to the restrictions recently imposed on the right to silence, and the statutory exceptions to the privilege against self incrimination in the fields of revenue and bankruptcy. But these examples only serve to illustrate the flaw in Mr Goldberg's thesis. Nobody doubts that legal professional privilege could be modified, or even abrogated, by statute, subject always to the objection that legal professional privilege is a fundamental human right protected by the European Convention for the Protection of Human Rights and Fundamental Freedoms (Rome, 4 November 1950; TS 71 (1953) Cmd 8969), as to which we did not hear any argument. Mr Goldberg's difficulty is this: whatever inroads may have been made by Parliament in other areas, legal professional privilege is a field which Parliament has so far left untouched.

Mr Richards, as *amicus curiae*, acknowledged the importance of maintaining legal professional privilege as the general rule. But he submitted that the rule should not be absolute. There might be occasions, if only by way of rare exception, in which the rule should yield to some other consideration of even greater importance. He referred by analogy to the balancing exercise which is called for where documents are withheld on the ground of public interest immunity and cited the speeches of Lord Simon of Glaisdale in *D v. National Society for the Prevention of Cruelty to Children* [1977] 1 All ER 589 at 607, [1978] AC 171 at 233 and in *Waugh v. British Railways Board* [1979] 2 All ER 1169 at 1175-1176, [1980] AC 521 at 535. But the drawback to that approach is that once any exception to the general rule is allowed, the client's confidence is necessarily lost. The solicitor, instead of being able to tell his client that anything which the client might say would never in any circumstances be revealed without his consent, would have to qualify his assurance. He would have to tell the client that his confidence might be broken if in some future case the court were to hold that he no longer had "any recognisable interest" in asserting his privilege. One can see at once that the purpose of the privilege would thereby be undermined.

As for the analogy with public interest immunity, I accept that the various classes of case in which relevant evidence is excluded may, as Lord Simon of Glaisdale suggested, be regarded as forming part of a continuous spectrum. But it by no means follows that because a balancing exercise is called for in one class of case, it may also be allowed in another. Legal professional privilege and public interest immunity are as different in their origin as they are in their scope. Putting it another way, if a balancing exercise was ever required in the case of legal professional privilege, it was performed once and for all in the sixteenth century, and since then has applied across the board in every case, irrespective of the client's individual merits.

In the course of his judgment in the Divisional Court, McCowan LJ indicated that he not only felt bound by *R v. Ataou*, but he also agreed with it. He continued:

> These further points were made by Mr Francis. He says that if a man charged with a criminal offence cannot go to a solicitor in the certainty that such matters as he places before him will be kept private for all time, he may be reluctant to be candid with his solicitors. Surely, however, it ought to be an incentive to him to tell the truth to his solicitors, which surely cannot be a bad thing. Mr Francis went on to suggest that his client's reputation would be damaged if the disclosures were to go to suggest that he was the murderer. For my part, I would be able to bear with equanimity that damage to his reputation. In the interests of justice and of the respondent, it would be a good thing that that reputation should be so damaged.

One can have much sympathy with McCowan LJ's approach, especially in relation to the unusual facts of this case. But it is not for the sake of the appellant alone that the privilege must be upheld. It is in the wider interests of all those hereafter who might otherwise be deterred from telling the whole truth to their solicitors. For this reason I am of the opinion that no exception should be allowed to the absolute nature of legal professional privilege, once established. It follows that *R v. Barton* [1972] 2 All ER 1192, [1973] 1 WLR 115 and *R v. Ataou* [1988] 2 All ER 321, [1988] QB 798 were wrongly decided, and ought to be overruled. I therefore consider these appeals should be allowed on both grounds and the case remitted to the High Court, with a direction that the decisions of the stipendiary magistrate dated 21 June and 8 August 1994 be quashed. ...

LORD LLOYD OF BERWICK: My Lords, I have had the advantage of reading in draft the speech which is to be delivered by my noble and learned friend Lord Taylor of Gosforth CJ. I agree with him on both issues, and wish only to add a few words on the second issue.

For the reasons which he gives, I regard *R v. Ataou* [1988] 2 All ER 321, [1988] QB 798 as having been wrongly decided. This is not, I think, because of any inherent difficulty in the balancing exercise proposed in that case. The task is no harder in the case of legal professional privilege than it is in other cases, for example, where there is a claim to withhold documents on the ground of public interest immunity: see *D. v. National Society for the Prevention of Cruelty to Children* [1977] 1 All ER 589 at 605-607, [1978] AC 171 at 231-233 per Lord Simon of Glaisdale. The reason is rather that the courts have for very many years regarded legal professional privilege as the predominant public interest. A balancing exercise is not required in individual cases, because the balance must always come down in favour of upholding the privilege, unless, of course, the privilege is waived.

What then about the cases where the client can be shown to have no "recognisable interest" in continuing to assert the privilege, to use the language first used by Cooke J in *R v. Craig* [1975] 1 NZLR 597, and subsequently adopted by the Court of Appeal in *R v. Ataou*? Historically, this has been treated as irrelevant. Thus in one case, *Bullivant v. A-G for Victoria* [1901] AC 196, [1901-3] All ER Rep 812, it was held that the privilege was not destroyed, even though the client himself was dead. It survived in favour of his executors (see [1901] AC 196 at 206, [1900-3] All ER Rep 812 at 816-817 per Lord Lindley). There must have been many other instances among the numerous cases decided in the 19th century and since, upholding legal professional privilege, in which the client no longer had any "recognisable interest" in asserting his claim. Yet it was never suggested that this might make a difference.

Mr Goldberg argued that times have changed, and that greater emphasis is now placed upon the court being put into possession of all relevant material, in order to arrive at the truth. But the principle remains the same; and that principle is that a client must be free to consult his legal advisers without fear of his communications being revealed. *R v. Cox and Railton* (1884) 14 QBD 153, [1881-5] All ER Rep 68 provides a well-recognised exception. Otherwise the rule is absolute. Once the privilege is established, the lawyer's mouth is "shut for ever": see *Wilson v. Rastall* (1792) 4 Term Rep 753 at 759, [1775-1802] All ER Rep 597 at 599 per Buller J. If the client had to be told that his communications were only confidential so long as he had "a recognisable interest" in preserving the confidentiality, and that some court on some future occasion might decide that he no longer had any such recognisable interest, the basis of the confidence would be destroyed or at least undermined. There may be cases where the principle will work hardship on a third party seeking to assert his innocence. But in the overall interests of the administration of justice it is better that the principle should be preserved intact.

For the above reasons, and the reasons given by Lord Taylor of Gosforth CJ, I would allow these appeals on both grounds. I would only add a reference to Bingham LJ's statement of the principle in *Ventouris v. Mountain, The Italia Express* [1991] 3 All ER 472 at 475, [1991] 1 WLR 607 at 611. The judgment of Schiemann LJ in *Barclays Bank plc v. Eustice* [1995] 4 All ER 511, [1995] 1 WLR 1238 came too late for our consideration. In any event, Mr Goldberg abandoned any argument based on *R v. Cox and Railton*. Finally, I would pay tribute to the careful analysis of Henry J in a ruling in *R v. Saunders* (10 January 1990, unreported). But he, unlike your Lordships, was bound by *R v. Ataou*. ...

LORD NICHOLLS OF BIRKENHEAD: My Lords, I have had the advantage of reading the speech of my noble and learned friend Lord Taylor of Gosforth CJ. I agree with the reasons he gives on the question concerning s 97 of the *Magistrates' Courts Act 1980*. I add some observations only on the legal professional privilege issue.

Legal professional privilege is concerned with the interaction between two aspects of the public interest in the administration of justice. The public interest in the efficient working of the legal system requires that people should be able to obtain professional legal advice on their rights and liabilities and obligations. This is desirable for the orderly conduct of everyday affairs. Similarly, people should be able to seek legal advice and assistance in connection with the proper conduct of court proceedings. To this end communications between clients and lawyers must be uninhibited. But, in practice, candour cannot be expected if disclosure of the contents of communications between client and lawyer may be compelled, to a client's prejudice and contrary to his wishes. That is one aspect of the public interest. It takes the form of according to the client a right, or privilege as it is unhelpfully called, to withhold disclosure of the contents of client–lawyer communications. In the ordinary course the client has an interest in asserting this right, in so far as disclosure would or might prejudice him.

The other aspect of the public interest is that all relevant material should be available to courts when deciding cases. Courts should not have to reach decisions in ignorance of the contents of documents or other material which, if disclosed, might well affect the outcome.

All this is familiar ground, well traversed in many authorities over several centuries. The law has been established for at least 150 years, since the time of Lord Brougham LC in *Greenough v. Gaskell* (1833) 1 My & K 98, [1824-34] All ER Rep 767: subject to recognised exceptions, communications seeking professional legal advice, whether or not in connection with pending court proceedings, are absolutely and permanently privileged from disclosure even though, in consequence, the communications will not be available in court proceedings in which they might be important evidence.

The principle has not lacked critics, from Jeremy Bentham onwards. Nevertheless in *Grant v. Downs* (1976) 135 CLR 674 at 685 Stephen, Mason and Murphy JJ accurately summarised the legal position thus:

> The rationale of this head of privilege, according to traditional doctrine, is that it promotes the public interest because it assists and enhances the administration of justice by facilitating the representation of clients by legal advisers, the law being a complex and complicated discipline. This it does by keeping secret their communications, thereby inducing the client to retain the solicitor and seek his advice, and encouraging the client to make a full and frank disclosure of the relevant circumstances to the solicitor. The existence of the privilege reflects, to the extent to which it is accorded, the paramountcy of this public interest over a more general public interest, that which requires that in the interests of a fair trial litigation should be conducted on the footing that all relevant documentary evidence is available. As a head of privilege legal professional privilege is so firmly entrenched in the law that it is not to be exorcised by judicial decision.

In *S v. Safatsa* 1988 (1) SA 868 at 886 Botha JA made the cautionary observation that any claim to relaxation of the privilege must be approached with the greatest circumspection.

Now, following the decisions of Caulfield J in *R v. Barton* [1972] 2 All ER 1192, [1973] 1 WLR 115, of Cooke J in *R v. Craig* [1975] 1 NZLR 597, of the Ontario Court of Appeal in *R v. Dunbar and Logan* (1982) 138 DLR (3d) 221 and of the English Court of Appeal in *R v. Ataou* [1988] 2 All ER 321, [1988] QB 798, your Lordships' House is being asked to re-examine the ambit of the privilege. The particular point raised was not expressly argued in the earlier authorities.

Encouraged by this and by comparatively recent developments in the related field of public interest immunity, Mr Goldberg QC and Mr Richards submitted that the balance between competing aspects of the public interest should not be struck once and for all on a generalised basis. The law should no longer adopt such a crude "all or nothing" approach. Instead, in each individual case the court should weigh the considerations for and against disclosure of the privileged material. The court should attach importance to any prejudice the client might suffer from disclosure. The court should also attach importance to the prejudice an accused person might suffer from non-disclosure. The court should then carry out a balancing exercise. The interest of the client in non-disclosure should be balanced against the public interest in seeing that justice is done. If disclosure were confined to truly exceptional cases, the public interest underlying legal professional privilege would not be at risk of serious damage.

This is a seductive submission, but in my view it should be resisted. The end result is not acceptable. Inherent in the suggested balancing exercise is the notion of weighing one interest against another. On this argument, a client may have a legitimate, continuing interest in non-disclosure but this is liable to be outweighed by another interest. In its discretion the court may override the privilege against non-disclosure. In *R v. Ataou* [1988] 2 All ER 321 at 326, [1988] QB 798 at 807 the Court of Appeal expressed the matter thus:

> The judge must … decide whether the legitimate interest of the defendant in seeking to breach the privilege outweighs that of the client in seeking to maintain it.

There are real difficulties here. In exercising this discretion the court would be faced with an essentially impossible task. One man's meat is another man's poison. How does one equate exposure to a comparatively minor civil claim or criminal charge against prejudicing a defence to a serious criminal charge? How does one balance a client's risk of loss of reputation, or exposure to public opprobrium, against prejudicing another person's possible defence to a murder charge? But the difficulties go much further. Could disclosure also be sought by the prosecution, on the ground that there is a public interest in the guilty being convicted? If not, why not? If so, what about disclosure in support of serious claims in civil proceedings, say, where a defendant is alleged to have defrauded hundreds of people of their pensions or life savings? Or in aid of family proceedings, where the shape of the whole of a child's future may be under consideration? There is no evident stopping place short of the balancing exercise being potentially available in support of all parties in all forms of court proceedings. This highlights the impossibility of the exercise. What is the measure by which judges are to ascribe an appropriate weight, on each side of the scale, to the diverse multitude of different claims, civil and criminal, and other interests of the client on the one hand and the person seeking disclosure on the other hand?

In the absence of principled answers to these and similar questions, and I can see none, there is no escaping the conclusion that the prospect of a judicial balancing exercise in this field is illusory, a veritable will-o'-the wisp. That in itself is a sufficient reason for not departing from the established law. Any development in the law needs a sounder base than this. This is of particular importance with legal professional privilege. Confidence in non-disclosure is essential if the privilege is to achieve its raison d'etre. If the boundary of the new incursion into the hitherto privileged area is not principled and clear, that confidence cannot exist.

Thus far I have been considering the case where the client retains some interest in insisting on non-disclosure and, in considering whether to direct disclosure, the court would have to carry out the so-called balancing exercise. There remains the case where the client no longer has any interest in maintaining his privilege. In many cases, once the transaction or proceedings have been concluded there is no conceivable reason why the lawyer–client communications should remain confidential. This is the type of situation Cooke J seems to have had in mind in *R v. Craig* [1975] 1 NZLR 597 at 599 when he referred to the possibility of proving that there was no ground on which the client could any longer be regarded as having a recognisable interest in asserting the privilege. Sir Rupert Cross adverted to this point in *Cross on Evidence* (5th edn, 1979) p 286:

> A time may come when the party denying the continued existence of the privilege can prove that the party relying on it no longer has any interest to protect, as where the solicitor for the unsuccessful plaintiff in a civil action takes a statement from a witness who is subsequently prosecuted for perjury, and the prosecution wish to ask the solicitor what the witness said to him.

In *R v. Dunbar and Logan* (1982) 138 DLR (3d) 221 at 252 Martin JA observed that no rule of policy requires the continued existence of the privilege when the person claiming the privilege no longer has any interest to protect. The court there drew a distinction between civil and criminal cases.

Non-availability of the privilege where the client no longer has an interest to protect would not depend upon carrying out any form of balancing exercise, weighing one interest against another. It would depend on proof that no rational person would regard himself as having any continuing interest in protecting the privilege of confidentiality in the originally privileged material. In other words, the privilege has become spent.

Mr Francis QC submitted that the client is the best judge of his own interests. He can waive the privilege if he sees fit. Confidence in the system would be eroded if the law were that someone else, namely a judge, may make this decision by holding that the privilege is spent. I see the force of the argument, but I have to say I am instinctively unattracted by an argument involving the proposition that a client can insist on non-disclosure, to the prejudice of a third party, when (*ex hypothesi*) disclosure would not prejudice the client. I would not expect a law, based explicitly on considerations of the public interest, to protect the right of a client when he has no interest in asserting the right and the enforcement of the right would be seriously prejudicial to another in defending a criminal charge or in some other way.

The point does not arise for determination in the present case. It cannot be said that no rational person would seek to maintain confidentiality in the circumstances confronting the appellant. In the pending criminal proceedings he is likely to be accused of having committed an horrific murder, a charge of which he has been publicly acquitted. He must have a legitimate interest in not disclosing material which would point in the opposite direction. Thus he is entitled to claim the privilege.

As to the "no interest" point, since this does not call for decision I prefer to reserve my final view on it.

Disposition

Appeal allowed.

NOTES AND QUESTIONS

1. Describe the cost–benefit analysis that is inherent in the decision in *Derby Magistrates' Court*. How does this analysis differ from that of the court in *Smith v. Jones* (reproduced in chapter 6)?

2. The House of Lords claims that "if a balancing exercise was ever required in the case of legal professional privilege, it was performed once and for all in the 16th century, and since then has applied across the board in every case, irrespective of the client's individual merits." How would you describe this "balancing of interests"? Is it sensible (or efficient) to refuse to allow those interests to be "rebalanced" in future cases? Why or why not?

3. At one point in its judgment, the House of Lords posed the following question: If an innocence-at-stake exception can be created—that is, if disclosure could be permitted based on the public interest in acquitting the innocent—"[c]ould disclosure also be sought by the prosecution, on the ground that there is a public interest in the guilty being convicted? If not, why not?" How would you answer this question? How might an economist answer this question?

4. Are the interests protected by the innocence-at-stake exception more or less "socially valuable" than the interests of a lawyer in collecting legal fees? Would it be surprising to learn that the English courts allow barristers to divulge confidential information in order to collect their fees? Can this be explained in terms of self-interest and utility maximization?

5. Can the House of Lords' decision in *Derby Magistrates' Court* be explained in terms of utility maximization? Can utility maximization explain the innocence-at-stake portion of the decision of the Supreme Court of Canada in *Smith v. Jones*? If the answer to both questions is "yes," why do the two decisions generate different outcomes? Does this undermine the usefulness of explaining legal rules by reference to economic notions?

6. Do you agree with the suggestion that the client at issue in *Derby Magistrates' Court* had no interest in maintaining confidentiality? If so, why did the client refuse to permit disclosure?

7. Which analysis do you prefer: that of the House of Lords in *Derby Magistrates' Court*, or that of the Supreme Court of Canada in *Smith v. Jones*? Why?

IV. Future Harm/Public Safety

If (as we observed in section II) Canadian courts and regulators allow the disclosure of confidential information in order to safeguard the ability of lawyers to collect outstanding legal fees, it is not surprising that courts also allow disclosure where a failure to disclose would likely lead to someone's death. If a lawyer's financial interest is sufficiently important to allow the disclosure of confidential information, surely an individual's interest in *survival* also outweighs whatever interest might be protected by non-disclosure. As we have seen, the Supreme Court of Canada reached this conclusion in *Smith v. Jones* (reproduced in chapter 6). As a result of that decision, Canadian courts recognize a general "future harm" or "public safety" exception to the lawyer's duty of confidentiality, pursuant to which disclosure is permitted (or even required) in cases in which the lawyer believes that disclosure will prevent serious, imminent harm to an identifiable class of individuals.

The nature and extent of the future-harm or public-safety exception have already been discussed in chapter 6, section III. Compare the policies furthered by that exception to the rationales of the other exceptions discussed in this chapter. Note that the future-harm exception has been included in Ontario's rules of professional conduct. According to Ontario's rule 2.03(3):

> Where a lawyer believes upon reasonable grounds that there is an imminent risk to an identifiable person or group of death or serious bodily harm, including serious psychological harm that substantially interferes with health or well-being, the lawyer may disclose, pursuant to judicial order where practicable, confidential information where it is necessary to do so in order to prevent the death or harm, but shall not disclose more information than is required.

Similar exceptions are found in other jurisdictions.

V. Disclosure Required by Law

Where disclosure of confidential information is required by legislation or court order, the rules of professional conduct permit (or require) the lawyer to disclose the confidential information. According to Ontario's rule 2.03(2), for example:

> When required by law or by order of a tribunal of competent jurisdiction, a lawyer shall disclose confidential information, but the lawyer shall not disclose more information than is required.

Similarly, commentary 13 to chapter IV of the CBA Code provides as follows:

> When disclosure is required by law or by order of a court of competent jurisdiction, the lawyer should always be careful not to divulge more information than is required.[1]

---

1   Note that commentary 13 is worded rather awkwardly. While it does not directly state that the lawyer is permitted (or required) to disclose the relevant information, it implies that such disclosure is authorized. Despite the ambiguity in this rule, Michel Proulx and David Layton, in *Ethics and Canadian Criminal Law* (Toronto: Irwin Law, 2001), 221, conclude that "[t]he better view, in light of a lawyer's duty to abide by the dictates of the law, is that counsel must disclose information where compelled by statute or court order."

Alberta's rules of professional conduct are more clear, providing (in chapter 7, rule 8(c)) that "a lawyer must disclose confidential information when required to do so by law." The effect of these rules is quite straightforward: where a lawyer is compelled (by legislation or court order) to disclose a client's otherwise confidential information, he or she must disclose that information. Disclosure of the information in such cases will not give rise to professional sanctions, unless the lawyer discloses more information than is required by the relevant statute or court order.

The rationale for this exception to the lawyer's duty of confidentiality is clear. It seems unfair to require lawyers to face the difficult choice of either (1) violating the rules of professional conduct by disclosing confidential information, or (2) violating a legislative provision or court order by refusing to disclose the information. In order to spare lawyers the burden of making such difficult choices, the rules of professional conduct instruct the lawyer to disclose client information wherever such disclosure is required by law.

The foregoing rules of professional conduct cannot, of course, guarantee that lawyers will comply with judicial or legislative directives to disclose a client's confidential information. As we observed throughout part I of this book, the lawyer's decision to embark on a particular course of action will inevitably be governed by the lawyer's own self-interest. Even when faced with legislative or judicial directives, lawyers (like all other individuals) will behave as though they are governed by the ethical equation developed in chapters 2 and 3. As a result, there may be cases in which the lawyer believes that *refusal* to comply with a legislative or judicial disclosure order promotes the lawyer's self-interest to a greater extent than disclosure of the client's information. In such cases (that is, where the lawyer prefers to face whatever penalties flow from refusal to disclose the information), the "efficient choice" (from the lawyer's perspective) will be to pay the requisite penalty and refuse to disclose the relevant information. A judicial or legislative directive cannot change the *nature* of the lawyer's decision. As we have seen throughout this book, the imposition of judicial or statutory penalties will simply change the math.

QUESTIONS

1. In what circumstances might a lawyer refuse to comply with a judicial order to disclose a client's confidential information? What if the lawyer believes that he or she can successfully appeal the relevant order? What if the lawyer believes that the relevant order is unjust?

2. Assume that a client offers a lawyer $100,000 to refuse to comply with a legislative directive to disclose the client's confidential information. Further assume that the only penalty for breach of the relevant legislative directive is $5,000. In what circumstances would such a legislative penalty be sufficient to ensure disclosure? Should the lawyer abide by the statute in such circumstances, or accept the client's payment and refuse to disclose the relevant information?

VI. Authorized Use or Disclosure

A. Rules of Professional Conduct

Perhaps the least controversial exception to the duty of confidentiality involves cases in which the client explicitly or impliedly authorizes the lawyer to divulge the client's private information. Where the client authorizes the lawyer to disclose information that would otherwise be considered confidential, rules of professional conduct uniformly (and rather sensibly) permit the lawyer to disclose the information. According to rule 1.6(a) of the ABA rules, for example, lawyers are entitled to divulge a client's information where "the client consents," or where the disclosure is "impliedly authorized in order to carry out the [lawyer's representation of the client]." Similarly, Ontario's rule 2.03(1) allows disclosure where such disclosure is "expressly or impliedly authorized by the client." Commentary 9 of chapter IV of the CBA Code is similar, providing that "[c]onfidential information may be divulged with the express authority of the client concerned and, in some situations, the authority of the client to divulge may be implied." As a result of these rules, disclosure that has been authorized (whether expressly or impliedly) by a client will not give rise to professional sanctions.

B. Rationale

The rationale for the authorized-disclosure exception to the lawyer's general duty of confidentiality is easy to articulate. As Proulx and Layton note:

> [T]he lawyer's duty of confidentiality is for the benefit of the client, and the rationale for maintaining confidentiality dissipates where the client can be said to permit disclosure. Authorized disclosure can be viewed either as an exception to the duty of confidentiality or instead as not coming within the scope of the duty to begin with.[2]

In other words, where the client wants (or allows) the lawyer to divulge the client's information, the original justification for keeping that information confidential disappears. As a result, where clients allow their lawyers to divulge or use the client's confidential information, the lawyer's use or disclosure of the relevant information is permitted.

VII. Public Knowledge

Some codes of professional conduct allow lawyers to divulge their client's information where the information in question is a matter of public knowledge. According to the CBA Code, chapter IV, commentary 8, for example, the rule of confidentiality "may not apply to facts that are public knowledge."[3] In jurisdictions that have exceptions of this nature,

---

2   Proulx and Layton, ibid., at 214.

3   Note, however, that the commentary goes on to state that "the lawyer should guard against participating in or commenting upon speculation concerning the client's affairs or business." The same language is found in the commentary to Ontario's rule 2.03(1).

the lawyer will not be sanctioned for divulging information that was already a matter of public knowledge.

Interestingly, the public-knowledge exception to the lawyer's duty of confidentiality is not accepted by all Canadian jurisdictions. In Alberta, for example, the rules of professional conduct provide that a lawyer must protect a client's confidential information "whether or not it is a matter of public record."[4] As a result, lawyers must be careful to consult their jurisdiction's specific rules of professional conduct before purporting to rely on a "public knowledge" exception to the duty of confidentiality.

In those jurisdictions where lawyers are permitted to disclose information that is a matter of public knowledge, an obvious question arises: How widely must information be known before it is considered to be within the public's knowledge? Is something public knowledge only when the information is *actually known* by a large segment of the community, or does it count as public knowledge when it is *accessible* by all members of the public, regardless of the number of people who actually have the information? Is my age public knowledge because I will happily reveal it to anyone who asks? Is my shoe size public knowledge because (1) I do not hide this information; (2) I volunteer it to selected individuals—namely, shoe salespersons, who have no duty of confidentiality; and (3) people could easily look at my feet and make a guess? Or does a matter only become public knowledge when it reaches a level of notoriety in the community such that most people might be *expected* to know the relevant information? A question of this nature was raised in *Ott v. Fleishman* (1983), below, in which the defendant lawyer disclosed the name of a man the lawyer's client was dating "openly but discreetly" while still married to someone else. Note that the court's decision is particularly useful in that it provides, at its outset, a clear summary of many of the principles governing the lawyer's duty of confidentiality.

Ott v. Fleishman
(1983) 46 BCLR 321

McEACHERN CJSC (orally): Apart from an indication of future unlawful conduct I regard it as settled law that any confidential information communicated to a lawyer and received by him in his professional capacity must not voluntarily be disclosed without either the consent of his client or a direction from the court. This is made apparent in the canons of the legal ethics which require a lawyer "scrupulously" to guard and not divulge his client's secrets or confidences (Canon 3[7]). But not all information received by a lawyer is privileged: *Zelinski v. Gordon*, (1983) 1 WWR 414 (BCSC).

Privilege in a practical sense arises in the course of legal or other proceedings, usually in the witness box, but also in discovery or in answering interrogatories, when a client or his solicitor is requested to disclose confidential information passing between them for the purpose of giving or receiving professional advice.

---

4   Alberta *Code of Professional Conduct*, chapter 7, rule 1 and commentary.

To put it bluntly, confidentiality prevents lawyers from talking about their clients' affairs out of court. Privilege prevents lawyers from disclosing certain types of confidential information during the course of proceedings.

Viewed this way it will be seen that confidentiality is a much broader concept than privilege, and it prohibits a solicitor as a professional matter, but at pain of liability for damages or injunction, from voluntarily disclosing confidential information. Such a breach may also give rise to disciplinary proceedings, and although these are matters for the Benchers, I have no doubt that such breaches are not just conduct unbecoming a member of the law society but rather professional misconduct.

In these matters a lawyer has very little discretion, if any, as it is not for him to decide whether he should tell the world, or anyone, what has been reported to him in his professional capacity.

The only other exception to this rule are those matters coming to the lawyer in his professional capacity which are obviously not confidential. This includes information which is already notorious, or the terms of settlement which a client will accept, or the basis upon which a client will contract, or other information which the lawyer must disclose generally or selectively in the management of his client's affairs, as in *Zelinski, supra.* In this connection, however, the lawyer, if challenged, carries the burden of establishing his right to disclose information and there may be an implied authority to disclose such information to some persons and not to others. While a test of reasonableness will usually be appropriate, careful and certain instructions are the lawyer's only real safeguard.

I pause to mention that it is not only information furnished to a lawyer by a client that is confidential. All information received on behalf of a client in a professional capacity, even if furnished anonymously, is also confidential. The real question is in what character the lawyer received the information: *In re Thomas Holloway: Young v. Holloway*, (1887) 12 P. 167 (CA). Further it must be remembered that the requirement of confidentiality continues indefinitely, even though the solicitor and client relationship may have terminated (3 Hals. 4th Edit., para. 1195).

The crucial question of course is to determine what is confidential information. I do not propose to attempt a comprehensive definition, but for practical purposes any information received by a lawyer in his professional capacity concerning his client's affairs is *prima facie* confidential unless it is already notorious or was received for the purpose of being used publicly or otherwise disclosed in the conduct of the client's affairs.

Lawyers also understand that it is their responsibility to train their staff and that they may well be liable for any breach of confidentiality committed by their agents or their staff.

The facts in this unusual case are not in dispute in any material particular. The defendant is a senior member of the Bar who has for many years confined his practice entirely to divorce and family law. The plaintiff was his client. The plaintiff retained the defendant to represent her with respect to unhappy differences which had arisen between her and her husband. She is a mature woman, now 47 years of age. The plaintiff had no evidence which entitled her to a divorce so that defendant introduced her to Mr. Britton, a private investigator to whom the defendant frequently referred such matters. Mr. Britton was engaged by the plaintiff or the defendant—it does not matter which—to obtain evidence of adultery but he was unable to succeed in such endeavour. As a consequence, or perhaps at the same time, the defendant commenced proceedings in this court under the *Family Relations Act* and a settlement was reached whereby the plaintiff received a substantial cash settlement.

In gratitude the plaintiff arranged a "thank you" dinner attended by the defendant's partner who had done some of the legal work in connection with the settlement, his wife, the defendant's secretary, her escort, Mr. Britton, and herself. For reasons which are not important, the defendant was not in attendance. The plaintiff commenced a romantic association with the investigator, Mr. Britton, at this time which is still continuing, and they have discreetly enjoyed each other's company and travelled together since that time.

Shortly after this the plaintiff requested Mr. Britton to resume his efforts to obtain evidence which would entitle her to a divorce. This evidence was obtained and the plaintiff was instructed to issue a Petition for divorce. The Answer filed by the plaintiff's husband did not dispute the adultery alleged against him. It was agreed before me that the evidence of the husband's adultery was genuine. Shortly after the Petition was served the plaintiff's husband's solicitor wrote the defendant's firm a letter in which he stated " ...my client has made no secret of his relationship [with the woman named] which has subsisted since May 1980." The defendant says he did not actually see that letter.

At about this time the plaintiff was casually discussing with the defendant's secretary the fact of the plaintiff's continuing relationship with Mr. Britton. The defendant's partner was also aware of this association but the defendant does not seem to have been aware of it for sometime.

Shortly before the hearing of the divorce petition the defendant's secretary informed the defendant that the plaintiff was having an affair with Mr. Britton. This greatly angered the defendant for two reasons and he called the plaintiff in, cross-examined her, and she readily admitted the association with Mr. Britton but she said she did not wish Mr. Britton to be hurt by her disclosure. The defendant gave her her file and sent her away.

The defendant was troubled for two main reasons: first, he was concerned this development might compromise the evidence in the pending divorce case. This was not a well-founded concern because, as already stated, the husband's adultery was not an issue (it was admitted again on discovery a few days later), and any professional concern the defendant had could easily have been managed by having the plaintiff in her role as Petitioner make a full disclosure to the court. The defendant, however, was entitled to be suspicious and to withdraw from the case in these circumstances, although I do not think most solicitors would likely have done so.

Secondly, the defendant was aware of two previous situations where he believed Mr. Britton had entered into romantic associations with parties who had retained him in his capacity as an investigator. Mr. Britton had in fact married one of those ladies and was still married to her at the time this association with the plaintiff commenced.

The defendant regarded this as outrageous conduct for a private investigator endangering the administration of justice, and he immediately sent a two and a half page letter to the RCMP which has supervisory jurisdiction or responsibility for private investigators. In this letter the defendant disclosed the details of the facts outlined above. The defendant sent a copy of this letter to the Deputy Attorney General, whom he regarded as the Queen's Proctor, and, for reasons which are not clear, he also sent a copy of this letter to the Law Society of British Columbia. He also called the plaintiff's husband's solicitor and informed him of the details of why he was withdrawing from the case.

As a consequence there was some kind of a hearing at which the plaintiff was a witness for Mr. Britton. The result of that hearing was that Mr. Britton's licence was suspended or cancelled. There was then an appeal at which the plaintiff was also a witness and Mr. Britton's licence was reinstated.

These hearings concerning Mr. Britton's licence were held in camera but they caused the plaintiff some concern because she did not wish her two grown up daughters to know the details of her relationship with Mr. Britton.

In these circumstances the plaintiff claims damages from the defendant.

The first question is to determine whether the plaintiff has a cause of action. I think she has although its precise ancestry is surprisingly vague and there are very few decided cases, although there is much writing on the subject. Counsel tell me the only cases they can uncover where damages were actually found to be payable for a breach of confidence are *Moore v. Terrell*, (1833) 110 ER 683, and *Taylor v. Blackwell*, (1836) 132 ER 401. Counsel also referred me to *Slavutych v. The Board of Governors of the University of Alberta*, (1975) 3 NR 587 at 595 where Spence J seems to confirm the validity of such a cause of action. I have no doubt that if there is a right to confidentiality there must be an appropriate sanction either by injunction to prevent a breach or damages where a breach has already occurred.

Applying the foregoing in this case it is my view that regardless of what went on before, the defendant received the plaintiff's admission and confirmation of the details of her relationship with Mr. Britton in the defendant's professional capacity, and there are no circumstances which permitted him to disclose such information as he did, particularly in view of the plaintiff's direct statement that she did not wish Mr. Britton to be harmed.

Counsel for the defendant sought to justify the disclosure of the information on a number of grounds. First, he said the information was not confidential because the plaintiff had openly but discreetly kept company with Mr. Britton. The defendant's communication to the RCMP and others went far beyond that. In any event, her admission of adultery to the defendant was expressly given in confidence and ought not to have been breached.

Secondly, Mr. Nuttall argued that the plaintiff disclosed this information to the defendant's partner and to his secretary. I regard those communications also to be confidential as they would not have been made if the recipients had not been engaged in the defendant's legal practice. But in any event, the information given to the defendant either by his partner or his secretary, as well as the information given to him by the plaintiff was received by him in his capacity as a solicitor and it was clearly confidential.

Thirdly, Mr. Nuttall argued that the defendant had a duty to disclose this information to prevent a possible fraud upon the court by the use of tainted evidence in the pending divorce trial and to prevent Mr. Britton from taking advantage of other women in the position of the plaintiff. These arguments cannot prevail in view of the fact that the defendant sent a copy of his letter to the Law Society, and because he furnished the same information to others.

Apart from that, I do not agree that the defendant, if he was under any such duty, was entitled to breach his primary duty of confidentiality to his former client. Many lawyers come into possession of information that could usefully be disclosed to police and other authorities and serious ethical questions sometimes arise in such cases. But the public interest has been declared to be that such information should be kept confidential, and the lawyer has no real discretion in these matters and his lips are sealed.

It was not necessary for the defendant to make this disclosure to prevent any fraud upon the court. If he was truly concerned, as I expect he was, about the validity of the evidence he could have examined the plaintiff's husband for discovery, and if he was still concerned that the evidence was fabricated he could, with his client's permission, make a full disclosure to the court and then call the plaintiff's husband as an adverse witness and possibly Mr. Britton. In these circumstances the court would either be satisfied with the evidence or would not be so satisfied but the defendant would have discharged his duty as an officer of the court without prejudicing any duty of confidentiality. Failing receipt of such instructions the defendant could have withdrawn from the case and no explanation would have been required or necessary.

While it is sometimes necessary, I think lawyers are sometimes too quick to withdraw from cases and they could better discharge their responsibility to the court and to their clients by staying in the case to ensure that it is properly presented. In any event, telling the RCMP about these matters would hardly protect the court. I reject the suggestion that the defendant had a duty to expose Mr. Britton by the use of information he received in confidence from his client.

Those of us who have practiced with the defendant are aware of his self-assumed responsibility for the protection of the courts. This is not the first case where he has conceived it to be his duty either to carry a case forward or to withdraw from it in defense of what he regards as the absolute necessity for the protection and preservation of the integrity of the court's processes.

If I may rely for a moment upon some personal observations made over many years of association with the defendant at the Bar I can say that I am satisfied that the defendant truly believes he has a continuing duty to expose any real or possible assault upon the purity of justice. This is commendable in one sense, but I regret to say in this case I believe the defendant overreacted under a misconception about the nature of his duty.

I find the defendant did breach his duty of confidentiality to the plaintiff.

The next question is whether this duty arises in contract or in tort because I am satisfied that, apart from some anxiety and embarrassment, the plaintiff suffered no actual damage. Damage is of course an essential ingredient to an action in tort, whereas any breach in contract gives rise to at least nominal damages. These historical distinctions sometimes do the law no credit and they are gradually disappearing. For there to be a consistent system of law, however, it is sometimes important that these distinctions be maintained. For the purpose of this case however I regard this

solicitor and client relationship to be contractual, with one of the implied terms necessarily being the assumption by the solicitor of the obligation of confidentiality. In
my view therefore the plaintiff is entitled to nominal damages which I assess in the
sum of $500.

The plaintiff asked that aggravated damages be allowed by reason of the
defendant's high-handed conduct. I do not think aggravated damages are properly
awarded in contract.

The plaintiff also asked for exemplary or punitive damages. They are similarly not
available in contract: *Cardinal Construction v. Queen*, (1981) 122 DLR (3rd) 703
(Ontario CA). In addition exemplary damages are only available in cases where the
conduct complained about is an act intentionally directed toward the injured person:
Kaytor v. Lions Driving Range Ltd., (1962) 40 WWR 173 at 180 (BCSC). The
defendant's conduct in this case was directly aimed not at the plaintiff but rather at
Mr. Britton.

I do not say that aggravated, exemplary or punitive damages may never be awarded
against a lawyer for a breach of confidence. If there were real damages so that a cause
of action could be founded in tort then in a proper case such additional damages
might also be assessed. Where there are only nominal damages, and the plaintiff must
rely on contract to sustain her cause of action then I think it proper not to award
damages that are only appropriate in cases where there is real serious injury. This of
course raises the further difficult question of whether it is possible, in a contractual
situation, to set aside the contract and rely upon a possible wider liability in tort.
Fortunately it is not necessary for me to decide that difficult question in this case.

NOTES AND QUESTIONS

1. According to the court in this case, the lawyer decided to disclose his client's
"private" information on the grounds that failure to do so would give rise to an "assault
upon the purity of justice." Assuming that this is true, how would you use the ethical
equation developed in chapters 2 and 3 to describe the lawyer's decision to disclose?

2. The court's decision makes it clear that the client in this case travelled openly with
Mr. Britton. Any member of the public who happened to see the client accompanying Mr.
Britton on a date could have become aware of the relevant relationship. Given that the
client dated Britton "openly but discreetly," and only hid this information from selected ·
individuals (such as her daughters and her husband), is it sensible to prevent the lawyer
from disclosing this relationship to the RCMP and the court? Why or why not? What
interest is protected by non-disclosure? What interests are protected by disclosure?

3. Note that the lawyer's decision to disclose was governed by a compensatory
framework: the client was able to sue the lawyer for breach of his ethical duties. In this
case, however, the court concluded that there were no damages suffered by the defendant
other than some anxiety or embarrassment. In other words, the pecuniary harm to the
plaintiff was valued (by the court) at $0. How, then, might an economist explain the court's
decision to award the plaintiff $500?

4. The possible public-knowledge exception to the lawyer's duty of confidentiality
was also discussed by the court in *Stewart v. Canadian Broadcasting Corp.* (1997), 150

DLR (4th) 24 (Ont. Ct. Gen. Div.), discussed in chapter 6, section IX. Proulx and Layton describe the effect of that decision as follows:

> In *Stewart*, defence counsel participated in a television broadcast that examined a former client's case. The information revealed by the broadcast was readily available in trial transcripts and had been the subject of widespread media coverage roughly twelve years previous. An important holding in *Stewart* is that defence counsel did not run afoul of Ontario's ethical rule of confidentiality by participating in the program. In the court's view, the only information disclosed by the broadcast was "public" within the meaning of Ontario's counterpart to the CBA Code commentary [regarding public information]: the information was therefore not confidential.[5]

5. Is the holding in *Ott* consistent with the holding in *Stewart* (question 4, above)? Why or why not? How would you compare the level of public knowledge in *Stewart* with the level of public knowledge in *Ott*? Does this justify any differences in the two courts' decisions?

VIII. A General Exception: Utility Maximization

Previous sections of this chapter have demonstrated several specific exceptions (or possible exceptions) to the lawyer's duty of confidentiality. Where such exceptions exist, the courts or regulators have decided that some important interest or policy (such as the public's right to be free from imminent danger or the lawyer's right to collect fees from a client) overcomes the interests protected by non-disclosure. In such cases, the courts or regulators permit the relevant lawyer to disclose or use the client's information, despite whatever harm may be caused to the relevant client (or despite whatever harm may be caused to the legal system).

Chapter 6, section VI, briefly raised the possibility of a broad, principled exception to confidentiality, involving "the pursuit of justice" or (more generally) the maximization of social utility. Given the various specific exceptions to confidentiality discussed in this chapter, would it make sense for courts and regulators to abandon their current "pigeon-hole" approach to such exceptions, and to simply accept a broader, general exception in cases where disclosure or use of a client's information would (on the balance) have the effect of maximizing social utility? Given the Supreme Court's decision in *Smith v. Jones* (chapter 6), does it appear that the Supreme Court of Canada is already moving in the direction of a general utility-maximization exception to confidentiality? What are the benefits of a more general exception? What are the costs? Before answering these questions, review the court's decision in *R v. Jack* (1992), 70 CCC (3d) 67 (Man. CA), discussed in chapter 6, section VI, together with the notes and questions following that decision.

In *Lawyers and Ethics*, Gavin MacKenzie expressly endorses a more general, principled method of considering lawyers' ability to disclose a client's private information. In MacKenzie's opinion, "an approach that weighs the competing interests in individual cases is preferable" to a rule-based or pigeonhole approach.[6] As MacKenzie astutely

---

5   Proulx and Layton, supra note 1, at 219.

6   Gavin MacKenzie, *Lawyers and Ethics: Professional Responsibility and Discipline*, 3d ed. (Toronto: Carswell, 2001), 3-18.

points out, such an approach would not only permit disclosure in cases that are not currently covered by the pigeonhole exceptions, but might also *prohibit* disclosure in cases where the pigeonholes would otherwise permit a lawyer to disclose the information. Where the policies advanced by an applicable pigeonhole appeared to be less important (or to generate less utility) than the interests that would be protected by non-disclosure, a principled approach to confidentiality would preclude disclosure, despite the fact that the relevant case would fit within the specific pigeonholes discussed above. In order to demonstrate this possibility, MacKenzie relies on the following hypothetical:

> The [lawyer's] client has AIDS. He has taken all reasonable precautions to prevent others from becoming infected. He is particularly vulnerable if the fact he has AIDS becomes known. His personal and business lives could be severely affected. In addition to the stigma of the disease, he may be the subject of false rumours of drug use or homosexuality, and may be fired from his job or lose clients or customers. Because of the significant potential for the infliction of severe damage to the reputation and livelihood of the client and his family, the principle of confidentiality should be strictly adhered to. Most if not all exceptions should be overridden. The fact that a dispute arises over the reasonableness of his lawyer's fees, for example, should not justify public disclosure of the client's condition, even if the work the lawyer did can be explained only by disclosing the client's condition.[7]

Do you agree with MacKenzie's conclusions? If so, should the courts (and regulators) abandon the specific pigeonhole exceptions to confidentiality in favour of a principled approach? Why or why not? Which approach has the greatest capacity to maximize social utility? Be sure to consider the judicial resources that would be expended in assessing claims of confidentiality on a case-by-case basis and the utility value of the predictability that is (or is not) generated by the existence of pigeonhole exceptions.

Finally, before accepting the value of a general utility-maximization exception to confidentiality, revisit the decision of the House of Lords in *Derby Magistrates' Court* (discussed above in section III). Based on that decision, what would the House of Lords say about the advisability of a general utility-maximization exception to the lawyer's duty of confidentiality? Do you agree with that analysis?

IX. Conclusion

Chapters 6 and 7 have demonstrated the general nature of (and exceptions to) the lawyer's duty of confidentiality, one of the core concepts of the lawyer's ethical universe. As we have seen throughout these chapters, the nature, content, and extent of the lawyer's duty of confidentiality (like all the lawyer's ethical obligations) can be explained through the use of economic tools. The next chapter applies these tools in the analysis of another core ethical duty of legal professionals: the duty to avoid conflicts of interest. The nature and extent of this duty, together with its implications for an economic theory of legal ethics, is the subject of chapter 8.

---

7   Ibid.

CHAPTER EIGHT

Conflicts of Interest

I. Introduction

A. Overview

Part I of this book demonstrated that rational people can be expected to act in pursuit of their own interests. One of the fundamental assumptions of economics is the assumption of self interest—in the process of utility maximization, individuals tend to ignore the preference sets of other people, choosing instead to give effect to their own preferences. Where a decision maker's interests come into conflict with the interests of another, the decision maker will tend to sacrifice the other person's interest in order to give effect to the decision maker's preferences.[1]

As we saw in chapter 3, section VII.B, lawyers are often said to act exclusively for the "best interests" of their clients. At first blush, this seems to conflict with the notion that lawyers (as rational actors) tend to maximize utility in pursuit of *their own interests*. As chapter 3, section VII.B explained, however, the notion of self-interest fits quite comfortably with the notion that lawyers must act in pursuit of their clients' interests. Even where the lawyer acts in a way that is beneficial to the client, the lawyer's behaviour is ultimately governed by the lawyer's perception of his or her own interests. Consider the following example.

Example 8.1

Anna Hamilton is a criminal defence lawyer in South Dakota. She is currently representing Patrick Huscroft, who has been charged with arson. Patrick is paying Anna $200 per hour for Anna's services.

Anna is aware that Patrick is factually guilty of the crime with which he is charged. He did, in fact, set fire to a flower shop in the middle of the night (happily, no one was injured). Anna does not approve of Patrick's actions. Nevertheless, Anna acts as a zealous advocate for her client, ably putting forth every argument that might secure his acquittal. Patrick is ultimately convicted.

---

1 As we have seen throughout this book, the notion of self-interest does not deny the possibility of altruistic behaviour. See chapter 1, section II.D for an explanation of the relationship between altruism and self-interest. This idea is further explored in chapter 2, section III.

A cursory review of the above example makes it appear that Anna is acting in pursuit of Patrick's interests rather than attempting to maximize her own utility. On a personal level, Anna disapproves of Patrick's actions, and probably thinks that arsonists should be punished (and securely locked away in non-flammable prison cells). Nevertheless, she attempts to secure Patrick's acquittal. One could argue that this is because Anna is putting Patrick's interests ahead of her own. While one *could* make this argument, one would be wrong to do so. Consider the example more carefully. On the facts of this example, Anna is being paid $200 per hour to further Patrick's legal objectives. Absent that financial incentive, Anna may not have taken Patrick's case. The legal fees that Patrick pays are designed to encourage Anna to act on Patrick's behalf. The effect of Anna's professional engagement (and the associated fees) is to ensure that the pursuit of Patrick's interest (that is, his interest in being acquitted) is now in Anna's interest as well—Anna is only entitled to payment if she does her job, and her job is to pursue her client's interests. As a result, the effect of a retainer is to make the lawyer's interests coincide with those of the client. Financial incentives (such as legal fees) provide lawyers with a direct interest in furthering their clients' legal objectives. If a lawyer will not pursue a client's goals without the financial incentive provided by the lawyer's fees, it can be seen that the lawyer's goal in pursuing the client's legal interests is, ultimately, the pursuit of the self-interest of the lawyer.

What if we change the facts of example 8.1 such that Anna will *not* be paid to represent Patrick? Assume, for example, that Anna has been appointed by the court to defend Patrick on a *pro bono* (or unpaid) basis. Further assume that, despite this lack of payment, Anna will do her best to secure her client's acquittal. Can Anna still be said to be acting in a self-interested manner?

Even if we modify the facts of example 8.1 to remove the financial incentive that is provided by legal fees, we can still explain Anna's behaviour by reference to self-interest. As a legal professional, one of Anna's most important assets is her professional reputation. In order to maximize her personal wealth, Anna must cultivate a reputation as a competent lawyer. Anna's performance on Patrick's behalf will be observed by many people, including Patrick, the prosecutor, the judge, and Anna's colleagues. If Anna does not do the job that she has agreed to do (that is, to undertake Patrick's defence to the best of her abilities), Anna's professional reputation may suffer. If her reputation suffers, she may find it more difficult to obtain clients in the future. Indeed, if her reputation suffers, Anna may have to lower her fees significantly if she is to have any clients at all. Once again, it is in Anna's interests to pursue her client's goals. Her decision to act as a zealous advocate for Patrick can accordingly be explained by reference to her personal interests. The suggestion that Anna is acting in pursuit of her client's interests is just another way of saying that, in these circumstances, Anna has a vested, personal interest in pursuing her client's goals. From this perspective, the interests of the client and the interests of the lawyer coincide.[2]

---

2   It is, perhaps, more accurate to say that actions taken in pursuit of the client's goals also further the lawyer's interests. The lawyer does not have precisely the same interests as the client—that is, the lawyer may not hope to see the client succeed—but the actions taken to ensure the client's success are also the actions that must be taken to further the lawyer's personal interests.

Even if we made the unlikely assumption that Anna was not concerned with her professional reputation, we may nonetheless explain her representation of Patrick by reference to the notion of self-interest. As we saw in chapter 3, section VI.B, many lawyers are motivated by the notion that they fill an important social role. When lawyers act on behalf of clients, they help to ensure that people (including those who hold unpopular ideas) have access to the rights and remedies offered by the law. Many lawyers gain utility by improving the public's access to the law. They *prefer* to have a legal system in which all people are entitled to competent representation. When assisting an individual whose goals the lawyer does not share, the lawyer is nevertheless pursuing his or her preference for an accessible legal system. In other words, the lawyer pursues his or her self-interest.

Whether the lawyer's preferences are grounded in the receipt of legal fees, in the improvement of the lawyer's reputation, or in a preference for an efficient and accessible legal system, lawyers typically have an interest in pursuing their clients' objectives to the best of their abilities. Thus, as self-interested economic actors, lawyers can generally be expected to promote their client's interests. Because or this, lawyers are said to be loyal (or to owe a "duty of loyalty") to their clients.

Despite the fact that lawyers typically have an interest in pursuing their client's interests, in many cases something happens that causes (or tempts) the lawyer to be disloyal toward a client. In such cases, the lawyer's personal interests appear to conflict with those of the client. Despite the incentives provided by legal fees or the lawyer's reputation, the lawyer may have an overriding interest in acting *against* the client's interests. Consider the following examples.

Example 8.2

Ramona Telfer is a lawyer representing two spouses (Fred and Ginger) jointly accused of robbing a bank. Since their first meeting with Ramona, both Fred and Ginger have steadfastly maintained their innocence. On the eve of trial, however, Ginger privately informs Ramona that she did, in fact, participate in the robbery, but did so only because Fred (an abusive spouse) threatened to kill her if she refused or if she divulged his threats to others. Fred intends to maintain his innocence at trial, but Ginger now wants Ramona to cast the blame for the crime on Fred. Ramona believes that, in the light of the Crown's evidence, the most likely way to secure Ginger's acquittal would be to cast the blame on Fred.

Both Fred and Ginger are Ramona's clients. Both are paying her fees. What should Ramona do? Do Ramona's personal interests continue to coincide with the interests of her clients? Is it possible for Ramona to be loyal to both of her clients?

Example 8.3

Linda Adams is in-house counsel for Widgetronics. Widgetronics is currently being sued in a class action for $30 million, stemming from damages caused by pollution emitted from Widgetronics' factory. Linda is representing Widgetronics in its defence against this claim. Widgetronics intends to deny liability.

Five of the plaintiffs named in this class action are Linda's parents and younger siblings. If their claim is successful, they each stand to gain several hundred thousand dollars from Widgetronics. Much of this money will be used to pay for health-care costs that have allegedly arisen as a result of Widgetronics' pollution-causing activities. If Widgetronics evades liability, the members of Linda's family will have to bear their own health-care expenses. Linda may have to use her own income to pay for her family's long-term care.

Do Linda's interests coincide with those of her client? Does this depend on the amount of money that Linda earns as Widgetronics' lawyer? Should Linda be permitted to represent Widgetronics in this case? What if, after learning of Linda's interest in the outcome of the proceedings, Widgetronics nonetheless *wants* Linda to be its lawyer?

Example 8.4

Jeff Hewitt is a lawyer representing Gerry Dingle, a 13-year-old boy who is charged with assault. All of the legal fees associated with Gerry's case are being paid by Gerry's parents, who retained Jeff to represent their son.

When interviewing Gerry in the absence of his parents, Jeff discovers that Gerry has been abused by his parents for several years. Jeff suspects that this abuse may lie at the heart of Gerry's anti-social behaviour, and that evidence of this abuse could play a role in securing Gerry's acquittal or minimizing his punishment if convicted. If this abuse is disclosed, however, Gerry's parents will likely be subjected to criminal sanctions.

Given that Jeff has been retained (and paid) by Gerry's parents, to whom does Jeff owe a "duty of loyalty"? Are Jeff's interests likely to coincide with Gerry's parents, or with Gerry himself? What should Jeff do in this situation?

In each of the foregoing examples, the lawyer's personal interests have (for one reason or another) come into conflict with the interests of one or more of the lawyer's clients. In example 8.2, Ramona has an interest in attempting to secure the acquittal of both of her clients. Unfortunately, the best route to securing the acquittal of one client is to cast the blame on another. If Ramona continues to act for both of these clients, she must either violate her duty to Ginger (by failing to raise the arguments that are most likely to lead to Ginger's acquittal), or violate her duty to Fred (by implicating him in the crime with which he is charged). Linda's personal interest in providing competent service (or zealous advocacy) for Ginger conflicts with Fred's personal interest in being acquitted. By the same token, Linda's personal interest in providing competent service to Fred conflicts with Ginger's interest in being acquitted. As a result, the lawyer's personal interests conflict with those of her clients.

In example 8.3, the lawyer's personal interests once again come into conflict with the interests of her client. The client, Widgetronics, has an interest in avoiding liability. The lawyer, by contrast, may be better off financially if the client is found liable. As a result, despite the payment of legal fees and the possible implications for the lawyer's reputation as a competent professional, the lawyer at issue in example 8.3 may be made better off by failing to vigorously pursue her client's interests. If we believe that lawyers are governed by self-interest, the lawyer is likely to act against her client if doing so would maximize her utility.

Finally, example 8.4 involves a case in which the lawyer appears to have conflicting loyalties. On the one hand, his personal interest may be served by pleasing the people who are responsible for paying his fees. If they are displeased with his professional services, they may end the retainer and stop providing a stream of income. The lawyer's client, however, has an interest in being acquitted, and this interest is best pursued by employing a strategy that could jeopardize the lawyer's stream of income. The lawyer's interest in preserving his stream of income is in conflict with the client's interest in (1) being acquitted, and (2) being removed from an abusive situation. In this instance, as in the other examples noted above, the lawyer's personal interests appear to conflict with those of his client, despite the general expectation that lawyers' interests will coincide with the interests of the clients they represent. In each of these situations, we have what is known (in legal parlance) as a "conflict of interest."

Why do we hope to avoid conflicts of interest? Consider what would happen if lawyers continued to act for clients where the lawyers had a personal interest in opposing the clients' objectives. If the lawyer continues to act for the client *without disclosing* the relevant conflict of interest, the likely result is market failure. Because the client is unaware of the lawyer's conflicting interests, the client will inadvertently trade resources that he or she values (namely, a sum of money) for resources that have little or no value to the client (namely, the services of a lawyer who will, in pursuit of his or her own self-interested objectives, ultimately act against the client). Had the client been made aware of the conflict of interest, the client would have deployed his or her resources in a more efficient manner, using his or her money to purchase the services of a lawyer who will promote (rather than undermine) the client's personal interests.[3] By squandering his or her resources on a lawyer who is likely to be disloyal, the client is using his or her resources in a less-than-optimal fashion, giving rise to the potential for overall losses in social utility. Since the conflict-of-interest problem can give rise to market failure, an efficient, market-correcting mechanism (such as rules designed to regulate conflicts of interest) may be needed.[4]

The situations in which a potential conflict of interest can give rise to market failure are not confined to the examples described above. Indeed, there are countless ways in which the lawyer's personal interests may conflict with those of the client, giving rise to the likelihood of market failure. Rather than exploring a large number of possible conflict-of-interest scenarios, this chapter (1) explores the general regulatory framework

---

[3] This is a variation on the "informational asymmetry" problem, explored in chapter 4, section I.C.

[4] For a more thorough discussion of the problem of market failure, and the role of regulation in addressing market failure, see chapter 4, section I.C.

governing lawyers' conflicts of interest (in the remainder of section I); (2) considers judicial responses to the conflict-of-interest problem (in section II), and (3) focuses on four of the most common and compelling situations in which the interests of the lawyer may conflict with those of the client (in sections III to VI). The goals of each section are to explore the economic basis of the rules regarding conflicts of interest and to assess the efficiency of the incentives that are provided by the conflict-of-interest rules.

B. Professional Regulations

The bodies charged with the task of regulating lawyers' professional conduct have promulgated rules designed to minimize the problems that may flow from conflicts of interest. Many of these rules are modelled on chapter VI(c) of the CBA's *Code of Professional Conduct*, which provides as follows:

> The lawyer shall not act for the client where the lawyer's duty to the client and the personal interests of the lawyer or an associate are in conflict.

The most thorough and recent treatment of this principle is found in rule 2.04 of Ontario's *Rules of Professional Conduct*, which provides (in part) as follows:

> 2.04(1) In this rule,
> a "*conflict of interest*" or a "*conflicting interest*" means an interest
>   (a) that would be likely to affect adversely a lawyer's judgment on behalf of, or loyalty to, a client or prospective client, or
>   (b) that a lawyer might be prompted to prefer to the interests of a client or prospective client. ...
>
>   . . .
>
> 2.04(3) A lawyer shall not act or continue to act in a matter when there is or is likely to be a conflicting interest unless, after disclosure adequate to make an informed decision, the client or prospective client consents.

The commentaries to Ontario's *Rules of Professional Conduct* explain the purpose of these rules in the following terms:

> Conflicting interests include, but are not limited to, the financial interest of a lawyer or an associate of a lawyer, including that which may exist where lawyers have a financial interest in a firm of non-lawyers in an affiliation, and the duties and loyalties of a lawyer to any other client, including the obligation to communicate information. For example, there would be a conflict of interest if a lawyer, or a family member, or a law partner had a personal financial interest in the client's affairs or in the matter in which the lawyer is requested to act for the client, such as a partnership interest in some joint business venture with the client. ...
>   A client or the client's affairs may be seriously prejudiced unless the lawyer's judgment and freedom of action on the client's behalf are as free as possible from conflict of interest.

In the United States, the model rules propounded by the American Bar Association contain similar rules regarding conflicts of interest. According to rule 1.7 of the ABA's model rules:

(a) A lawyer shall not represent a client if the representation of that client will be directly adverse to another client, unless:

(1) the lawyer reasonably believes the representation will not adversely affect the relationship with the other client; and

(2) each client consent[s] after consultation.

(b) A lawyer shall not represent a client if the representation of that client may be materially limited by the lawyer's responsibilities to another client or to a third person, or by the lawyer's own interests, unless:

(1) the lawyer reasonably believes the representation will not be adversely affected; and

(2) the client consents after consultation. When representation of multiple clients in a single matter is undertaken, the consultation shall include explanation of the implications of the common representation and the advantages and risks involved.

As a result of these provisions (and their counterparts in other jurisdictions), lawyers must take precautions before they agree to act in cases in which an impermissible conflict situation might arise.

American and Canadian rules of professional conduct make it clear that the rule requiring lawyers to avoid conflicts of interest is not absolute. This is sensible. Indeed, it would be impossible to prohibit lawyers from acting in any case in which a lawyer's interests conflicted with those of the client. Most lawyers have an interest in charging their clients as much as possible for legal services, and clients have a "conflicting" interest in paying as little as possible for the lawyer's professional service. Because some level of conflict between contracting parties (such as lawyers and their clients) is inevitable, the rules of professional conduct seek to minimize (rather than eliminate) conflicts of interest. As the commentary to Ontario's rule 2.04 explains, the goal of the rule is to ensure that "the lawyer's judgment and freedom of action on the client's behalf are *as free as possible* from conflict of interest" (emphasis added). As a result, some level of conflicting interest is inevitable and acceptable.

Even where a conflict of interest exceeds the "acceptable" level, the rules of professional conduct may allow the lawyer to act for the client despite the presence of conflicting interests. As noted above, Ontario's rule 2.04(3) explicitly grants the lawyer permission to act in cases involving conflicts of interest where "after disclosure adequate to make an informed decision, the client or prospective client consents" to having the lawyer act despite the conflict of interest. Similarly, rule 1.7 of the ABA's model code allows lawyers to act in the face of conflicting interests provided that "the client consents." This feature of the rules can be explained as follows:

As important as it is to the client that the lawyer's judgment and freedom of action on the client's behalf should not be subject to other interests, duties, or obligations, in practice this factor may not always be decisive. Instead, it may be only one of several factors that the client will weigh when deciding whether or not to give the consent referred to in the rule. Other factors might include, for example, the availability of another lawyer of comparable expertise and experience, the extra cost, delay and inconvenience involved in engaging another lawyer, and the latter's unfamiliarity with the client and the client's affairs. In some instances, each client's case may gather strength from joint representation. In the result, the client's interests may sometimes be better served by not engaging another lawyer, for example, when the client and another party to a commercial transaction are continuing clients of the same law firm but are regularly represented by different lawyers in that firm.[5]

This feature can also be explained by reference to economic principles. As we saw in section I.A, above, an *undisclosed* conflict of interest may give rise to market failure as a result of the unequal distribution of information—clients are likely to pay an inefficiently high price for legal services when they retain a lawyer who has an undisclosed conflict of interest. Where the client has *full information* regarding the lawyer's conflicting interests, he or she is able to make an informed decision. The client may choose to purchase the lawyer's legal services regardless of the conflict of interest, and may take the lawyer's conflict into account when setting the terms of the retainer. As a result, the rules recognize that there may be cases in which the client, even after becoming aware of the nature and extent of the lawyer's conflicting interests, may decide to avail himself or herself of the lawyer's professional services. In short, there may be cases in which the client prefers to retain a "conflicted" lawyer rather than (1) choosing another lawyer, or (2) going without legal representation.[6]

What is the general purpose of the rules regarding conflicts of interest? In section I.A, the need for such regulations was explained in terms of market failure. A failure to regulate conflicts of interest could give rise to inefficiency, causing clients to spend their money in ways that generate a less-than-optimal allocation of scarce resources. Not surprisingly, traditional ethical scholarship has not explained the conflict-of-interest rules in this manner. Instead, the rules have traditionally been explained by reference to the lawyer's duties of loyalty and confidentiality. The duty of confidentiality has already been addressed in chapters 6 and 7. The nature of the duty of loyalty, and its role in shaping the conflict-of-interest rules, is discussed in the following section of this chapter.

C. The Duty of Loyalty

The duty of loyalty is often said to lie at the heart of regulations precluding lawyers from acting in cases involving potential conflicts of interest. For example, Proulx and Layton state:

> The leitmotif of conflict of interest is the broader duty of loyalty. Where the lawyer's duty of loyalty is compromised by a competing interest, a conflict of interest will exist.[7]

According to Proulx and Layton:

> The client–lawyer relationship is based on the highest of trusts, where the lawyer's loyalty is unquestioned. The duty to be loyal, born of the fiduciary relationship between counsel and client, must guide and inform every aspect of the lawyer's dealing with a client, and it leads to important component duties such as the duty of confidentiality.[8]

---

5   Law Society of Upper Canada, *Rules of Professional Conduct*, rule 2.04, commentary.

6   At this point, it should be obvious that the decision whether to retain a conflicted lawyer is an economic decision and can be described through the $A-B=X$ equation developed in earlier chapters of this book.

7   Michel Proulx and David Layton, *Ethics and Canadian Criminal Law* (Toronto: Irwin Law, 2001), 287.

8   Ibid., at 286-87.

Similarly, Gavin MacKenzie explains the basis of the conflict-of-interest rules by reference to the combined effect of the lawyer's duties of loyalty and confidentiality:

> The most prominent of the immutable principles on the basis of which conflict of interest problems have traditionally been resolved are the two principles fundamental to the client–lawyer relationship: loyalty and confidentiality. The loyalty principle finds expression in Canadian rules of professional conduct that provide that "the reason" for the conflict of interest rule is that clients may suffer serious prejudice unless their lawyers' judgment and freedom of action on the clients' behalf are as free as possible from compromising influences. The principle of confidentiality is not expressed in the rules themselves to be a reason for the conflict of interest rule … . The importance of the confidentiality principle to the conflict of interest rule is nevertheless apparent. Clients whose options are either to conceal relevant information from their lawyer—thereby inhibiting the lawyer's ability to provide legal services effectively—or to divulge confidential information that will be disclosed to and perhaps used for the benefit of other parties, are placed in an intolerable position.[9]

In sum, the rules regarding conflicts of interest have typically been explained as follows: lawyers have an overriding duty to be loyal to their clients. This duty of loyalty is undermined where lawyers act in cases that involve undisclosed conflicts of interests. As a result, lawyers are generally prohibited from acting in cases involving undisclosed conflicts of interest. To allow lawyers to proceed in such cases would be to undermine the principle that lawyers must be loyal to their clients.

If the basis of the rules regarding conflicts of interest can truly be explained by reference to an overriding duty of loyalty, it should be noted that the word "loyalty," when used in the context of lawyer's conflicts of interest, bears an unusual meaning. As we saw in chapter 4, a lawyer need not agree with his or her client's position, nor even hope that the client succeeds in achieving his or her legal objectives. Indeed, a lawyer may desperately hope to see a particular client fail. The lawyer may represent a client whose position the lawyer abhors, or a client whose specific legal project the lawyer considers immoral. Consider, for example, a lawyer charged with the task of defending a factually guilty child molester. In cases of this nature, the lawyer may think that the world would be a better place if the client failed to achieve his or her goals. The lawyer in such cases does not share the client's objectives. As a result, the lawyer may be unlikely to characterize his or her feelings toward the client as feelings of loyalty.

How can a lawyer be expected to be loyal to a client whom he or she considers immoral? Such cases reveal that the lawyer's duty of loyalty does not truly imply loyalty to the client, or even loyalty to the client's legal objectives. Instead, the lawyer is loyal *to his or her position* as the client's legal advisor. If the lawyer fulfills the role of legal counsel, the lawyer will *act* as though he or she is loyal to the client. In reality, however, the lawyer's loyalty is to the job of lawyering. The lawyer's loyalty to his or her profession can be explained by reference to the lawyer's interests in (1) promoting access to justice by fulfilling a social role that the lawyer believes to be important; (2) promoting his or

---

9   Gavin MacKenzie, *Lawyers and Ethics: Professional Responsibility and Discipline*, 3d ed. (Toronto: Carswell, 2001), 22-2.

her own professional reputation as a skilled and zealous advocate; and (3) receiving legal fees for services rendered. As we can see, this explanation of the lawyer's duty of loyalty coincides with the economic underpinnings of the rules regarding conflicts of interest (explained above in section I.A). In sum, the duty of loyalty is nothing more than a useful shorthand for the economic analysis of conflict-of-interest rules that was put forward in the introductory portion of this chapter.

Now that we have considered the general nature of the professional regulations governing lawyers' conflicts of interest, it is useful to consider the manner in which these general principles have been applied and developed by Canadian courts. The seminal case concerning conflicts of interest is the decision of the Supreme Court of Canada in *MacDonald Estate v. Martin* (1990), reproduced below. That decision, and the insights that it offers into the regulation of conflicting interests, is the topic of the next section.

II. General Principles

The decision of the Supreme Court of Canada in *MacDonald Estate v. Martin*, below, explains the general nature of conflicts of interest, together with the judiciary's approach to conflict problems. On a more general level, the decision also demonstrates the role of the courts in regulating lawyers' ethical choices. As you will see from the court's decision, professional regulations are not the only factor precluding lawyers from acting in cases involving conflicts of interests. Lawyers must also contend with the courts' inherent jurisdiction to control the judicial process. One incident of this inherent jurisdiction is the courts' ability to disqualify a lawyer from acting in a particular matter where the matter may give rise to a conflict of interest. As a result, even where the lawyer is found to have complied with all of the relevant rules of professional conduct, the courts may nonetheless find that the lawyer is in a conflict position, and order that he or she be removed as counsel of record. The impact of this judicial power is discussed in the notes and question following the *MacDonald Estate* decision.

MacDonald Estate v. Martin
[1990] 3 SCR 1235

SOPINKA J (for the majority, with Dickson CJC and LaForest and Gonthier JJ concurring): This appeal is concerned with the standard to be applied in the legal profession in determining what constitutes a disqualifying conflict of interest. The issue arose in the context of a lawsuit in which a former junior solicitor for the appellant transferred her employment to the law firm acting for the respondent.

Facts

The respondent, Gray, is the plaintiff in an action for an accounting against the appellant and Rossmere Holdings. In 1983, the appellant retained the services of A. Kerr Twaddle, QC who served in the capacity of solicitor and counsel until his appointment to the bench in 1985. While acting for the appellant, Twaddle was assisted by

Kristin Dangerfield, a graduate articled student and later a junior member of his firm. She was actively engaged in the case and was privy to many confidences disclosed by the appellant to Twaddle. Dangerfield was in attendance at numerous meetings between Mr. Twaddle and the appellant Martin, assisted in the preparation of many documents, prepared and attended examinations for discovery, was present when a settlement was discussed by the parties and during discussions of a settlement with representatives of the law firm of Thompson, Dorfman, Sweatman, and participated in the taking of *de bene esse* evidence. Upon Twaddle's appointment to the bench in 1985, Dangerfield joined the firm of Scarth, Dooley. Eight out of eleven members of that firm, including Dangerfield, joined the Thompson firm in 1987. The Thompson firm represents the respondent in this action.

Both Dangerfield and senior members of Thompson, Dorfman, Sweatman have sworn affidavits that the case has not been discussed since Dangerfield joined the firm and will not be discussed.

The appellant brought an application in the Court of Queen's Bench in which he sought a declaration that the Thompson firm was ineligible to continue to act as solicitors of record for the respondent and an order removing that firm as solicitors of record. Hanssen J allowed the application.

The respondent's appeal from the decision of the motions judge was allowed by the Court of Appeal of Manitoba, Monnin CJM dissenting: (1989), 57 Man. R (2d) 161. ...

The Issue

The sole issue in this appeal is the appropriate standard to be applied in determining whether Thompson, Dorfman, Sweatman are disqualified from continuing to act in this litigation by reason of a conflict of interest.

Legal Ethics: Policy Considerations

In resolving this issue, the Court is concerned with at least three competing values. There is first of all the concern to maintain the high standards of the legal profession and the integrity of our system of justice. Furthermore, there is the countervailing value that a litigant should not be deprived of his or her choice of counsel without good cause. Finally, there is the desirability of permitting reasonable mobility in the legal profession. The review of the cases which follows will show that different standards have been adopted from time to time to resolve the issue. This reflects the different emphasis placed at different times and by different judges on the basic values outlined above. ...

Merger, partial merger and the movement of lawyers from one firm to another are familiar features of the modern practice of law. They bring with them the thorny problem of conflicts of interest. When one of these events is planned, consideration must be given to the consequences which will flow from loss of clients through conflicts of interest. To facilitate this process some would urge a slackening of the standard with respect to what constitutes a conflict of interest. In my view, to do so at the present time would serve the interest of neither the public nor the profession. The legal profession has historically struggled to maintain the respect of the public. This has been so notwithstanding the high standards that, generally, have been maintained. When the management, size of law firms and many of the practices of the legal profession are indistinguishable from those of business, it is important that the fundamental professional standards be maintained and indeed improved. This is essential if the confidence of the public that the law is a profession is to be preserved and hopefully strengthened. Nothing is more important to the preservation of this relationship than the confidentiality of information passing between a solicitor and his or her client. The legal profession has distinguished itself from other professions by the sanctity with which these communications are treated. The law, too, perhaps unduly, has protected solicitor and client exchanges while denying the same protection to others. This tradition assumes particular importance when a client bares his or her soul in civil or criminal litigation. Clients do this in the justifiable belief that nothing they say will be used against them and to the advantage of the adversary. Loss of this confidence would deliver a serious blow to the integrity of the profession and to the public's confidence in the administration of justice.

An important statement of public policy with respect to the conduct of barrister and solicitor is contained in the professional ethics codes of the governing bodies of the profession. The legal profession is self-governing. In each province there is a governing body usually elected by the lawyers practising in the province. The governing body enacts rules of professional conduct on behalf of those it represents. These rules must be taken as expressing the collective views of the profession as to the appropriate standards to which the profession should adhere.

While there exists no national law society, the Canadian Bar Association, a national society representing lawyers across the country, adopted a *Code of Professional Conduct* in 1974. The Code has been adopted by the Law Society of Manitoba and by the Law Societies of other provinces. Chapter V, entitled "Impartiality and Conflict of Interest," commences with the following rule:

> The lawyer must not advise or represent both sides of a dispute and, save after adequate disclosure to and with the consent of the client or prospective client concerned, he should not act or continue to act in a matter when there is or there is likely to be a conflicting interest. A conflicting interest is one which would be likely to affect adversely the judgment of the lawyer on behalf of or his loyalty to a client or prospective client or which the lawyer might be prompted to prefer to the interests of a client or prospective client.

The rule is followed by thirteen commentaries. The most relevant of these are Commentaries 11 and 12, which state:

> 11. A lawyer who has acted for a client in a matter should not thereafter act against him (or against persons who were involved in or associated with him in that matter) in the same or any related matter, or place himself in a position where he might be tempted or appear to be tempted to breach the Rule relating to Confidential Information. It is not, however, improper for the lawyer to act against a former client in a fresh and independent matter wholly unrelated to any work he has previously done for that person.

12. For the sake of clarity the foregoing paragraphs are expressed in terms of the individual lawyer and his client. However it will be appreciated that the term "client" includes a client of the law firm of which the lawyer is a partner or associate whether or not he handles the client's work.

A code of professional conduct is designed to serve as a guide to lawyers and typically it is enforced in disciplinary proceedings. See, for example, *Law Society of Manitoba v. Giesbrecht* (1983), 24 Man. R (2d) 228 (CA). The courts, which have inherent jurisdiction to remove from the record solicitors who have a conflict of interest, are not bound to apply a code of ethics. Their jurisdiction stems from the fact that lawyers are officers of the court and their conduct in legal proceedings which may affect the administration of justice is subject to this supervisory jurisdiction. Nonetheless, an expression of a professional standard in a code of ethics relating to a matter before the court should be considered an important statement of public policy. The statement in Chapter V should therefore be accepted as the expression by the profession in Canada that it wishes to impose a very high standard on a lawyer who finds himself or herself in a position where confidential information may be used against a former client. The statement reflects the principle that has been accepted by the profession that even an appearance of impropriety should be avoided.

The Law

The law in Canada and in other jurisdictions has adopted one of two basic approaches in determining whether a disqualifying conflict of interest exists: (1) the probability of real mischief, or (2) the possibility of real mischief. The term "mischief" refers to the misuse of confidential information by a lawyer against a former client. The first approach requires proof that the lawyer was actually possessed of confidential information and that there is a probability of its disclosure to the detriment of the client. The second is based on the precept that justice must not only be done but must manifestly be seen to be done. If, therefore, it reasonably appears that disclosure might occur, this test for determining the presence of a disqualifying conflict of interest is satisfied.

England

The "probability of real mischief" test is the traditional English approach based on *Rakusen v. Ellis, Munday & Clarke* [[1912] 1 Ch. 831]. Rakusen was terminated from his employment. He retained Mr. Munday to discuss his legal position. When several months later Rakusen instituted proceedings with the assistance of new solicitors, the defendant company retained Munday's associate, Clarke. The court accepted the evidence that Clarke knew nothing about what had transpired between Rakusen and Munday. The passages set out below are most often quoted in support of the "probability" test. Cozens-Hardy MR stated, at p. 835:

> I do not doubt for a moment that the circumstances may be such that a solicitor ought not to be allowed to put himself in such a position that, human nature being what it is, he cannot clear his mind from the information which he has confidentially obtained

from his former client; but in my view we must treat each of these cases, not as a matter of form, not as a matter to be decided on the mere proof of a former acting for a client, but as a matter of substance, before we allow the special jurisdiction over solicitors to be invoked, we must be satisfied that real mischief and real prejudice will in all human probability result if the solicitor is allowed to act.

Fletcher Moulton LJ expressed himself as follows, at p. 841:

As a general rule the Court will not interfere unless there be a case where mischief is rightly anticipated. I do not say that it is necessary to prove that there will be mischief, because that is a thing which you cannot prove, but where there is such a probability of mischief that the Court feels that, in its duty as holding the balance between the high standard of behaviour which it requires of its officers and the practical necessities of life, it ought to interfere and say that a solicitor shall not act.

There have been few cases in England since *Rakusen*, but the most recent case, *Re a Solicitor*, unreported, Chancery Division, March 31, 1987, summarized at 131 Sol. J 1063, reaffirmed "the probability of real mischief test." The court noted that it was not actually suggested that the solicitor had acquired "relevant knowledge concerning a former client" and the latter could not "think of any confidential information which he [had] communicated ... and which might be relevant in connection with" the case (p. 4).

United States

The courts in the United States have generally adopted the stricter "possibility of real mischief" test. According to this approach, once it is established that there is a "substantial relationship" between the matter out of which the confidential information is said to arise and the matter at hand, there is an irrebuttable presumption that the attorney received relevant information. If the attorney practises in a firm, there is a presumption that lawyers who work together share each other's confidences. Knowledge of confidential matters is therefore imputed to other members of the firm. This latter presumption can, however, in some circumstances, be rebutted. The usual methods used to rebut the presumption are the setting up of a "Chinese Wall" or a "cone of silence" at the time that the possibility of the unauthorized communication of confidential information arises. A "Chinese Wall" involves effective "screening" to prevent communication between the tainted lawyer and other members of the firm. A "cone of silence" is achieved by means of a solemn undertaking not to disclose by the tainted solicitor. Other means which would constitute clear and convincing evidence that no improper disclosure has or can take place are not ruled out. ...

In *Analytica, Inc. v. NPD Research, Inc.*, 708 F2d 1263 (7th Cir. 1983), Posner J set out the rationale for the "substantial relationship" test which gives rise to an irrebuttable presumption that confidences have been disclosed by the client. He states, at p. 1269:

The "substantial relationship" test has its problems, but conducting a factual inquiry in every case into whether confidences had actually been revealed would not be a satisfactory alternative, particularly in a case such as this where the issue is not just whether

they have been revealed but also whether they will be revealed during a pending litigation. Apart from the difficulty of taking evidence on the question without compromising the confidences themselves, the only witnesses would be the very lawyers whose
firm was sought to be disqualified (unlike a case where the issue is what confidences a
lawyer received while at a former law firm), and their interest not only in retaining a
client but in denying a serious breach of professional ethics might outweigh any felt
obligation to "come clean." While "appearance of impropriety" as a principle of professional ethics invites and maybe has undergone uncritical expansion because of its
vague and open-ended character, in this case it has meaning and weight. For a law firm
to represent one client today, and the client's adversary tomorrow in a closely related
matter, creates an unsavory appearance of conflict of interest that is difficult to dispel
in the eyes of the lay public—or for that matter the bench and bar—by the filing of
affidavits, difficult to verify objectively, denying that improper communication has
taken place or will take place between the lawyers in the firm handling the two sides.

The rigidity and overinclusiveness of the irrebuttable presumption have been criticized and some courts have departed from it in special circumstances. These criticisms are summarized in "Developments in the Law—Conflicts of Interest in the
Legal Profession" [(1981), 94 *Harvard Law Review* 1247], at pp. 1355-59:

> In situations involving large firms, the maintenance of an irrebuttable presumption of
> sharing among affiliates can become sorely strained. Suppose that a young litigator,
> now out on his own, was briefly associated with a big firm and that the firm included
> among its members a specialist in corporate law who once, perhaps many years before,
> represented a client in some affair. The young lawyer is now asked to represent a sec-
> ond client against the first in a suit involving a substantially related matter. If the firm is
> large enough, the corporate specialist may never have been more than a name on the
> letterhead to the young litigator, who was his nominal affiliate. In most instances, the
> affiliate will not have been familiar with the corporate lawyer's old client or with any
> of the details of that client's affairs during the affiliate's association with the firm. In
> this case, forbidding the young litigator's representation of a second client in a suit
> against the first client is an empty gesture.
>
> As the structure of legal practice changes and such cases become increasingly com-
> mon, one must ask whether the putative benefits of the strict rule justify its costs. Pro-
> scription of successive representation, including representation by a former affiliate,
> imposes significant losses on would-be clients, including effective deprivation of their
> first choice of counsel. A further objection to the categorical rule is its effect on the
> professional mobility of young attorneys, who frequently begin their careers with a
> stint at a large firm. A rule irrebuttably imputing to every former affiliate of such a firm
> synoptic knowledge of the matters it has handled is not merely unrealistic, but is poten-
> tially a serious impediment to an attorney (like the young litigator in the previous ex-
> ample) who seeks either to establish his own practice or to affiliate himself with a new
> firm. Especially when the former affiliate has specialized during his tenure with his old
> colleagues, an irrebuttable presumption may block his attempt to use his training to the
> advantage of new clients; indeed, it may transform his specialized skills from an asset
> into a serious liability. ...

The need for a more flexible approach to imputation of client confidences is widely acknowledged. The liberalized rule allows the traditional presumption to be rebutted in an enforcement proceeding by evidence suggesting a low probability that the lawyer who was materially involved in representing a client actually shared any relevant information with his affiliate. ...

Critics of a rebuttable imputation rule have generally relied on the need to prevent any representation that involves even an "appearance of impropriety." Operating on the view that appearances must be protected at nearly any price, some courts have rejected former affiliates' attempts to rebut the presumption of shared knowledge. Under the "appearance of impropriety" doctrine, the "non-existence of actual conflict is presumed," and the mere appearance of conflict is sufficient to taint the representation. Yet there seems to be a trend, even among those courts that accept the policy behind the doctrine, to allow "any initial inference of impropriety" to be "dispelled" by evidence rebutting the presumption that knowledge was shared among former affiliates. As the role of appearances in determining whether a given representation ought to be proscribed continues to decline, objections to a rebuttable presumption will presumably dissipate. This liberalized approach reduces unnecessary proscription and its associated costs while affording former clients a reasonable degree of security from the threat of fiduciary breach.

In support of this position, the author cites considerable authority. ...

Australia

In Australia as in Canada courts appear to vacillate as to the proper test. In *D & J Constructions Pty. Ltd. v. Head* (1987), 9 NSWLR 118, Bryson J approved of the *Rakusen* test. But in *National Mutual Holdings Pty. Ltd. v. Sentry Corp.* (1989), 87 ALR 539, Gummow J expressed the view that the Australian position was perhaps no less stringent than the American position. He also referred to a paper by Dr. Finn, "Conflicts of Interest and Professionals" (published by the New Zealand Legal Research Foundation in the volume *Professional Responsibility*) in which Dr. Finn refers to the *Rakusen* test as "untenable." Dr. Finn considers whether it is preferable to adopt the American concept of the irrebuttable presumption or the less rigid approach of a presumption rebuttable by the lawyer. The learned writer opts for the latter. ...

New Zealand

There are no reported cases on the point but, in "Conflicts of interest: When may a lawyer act against a former client?" Dean and Finlayson, [1990] NZLJ 43, the learned authors review several judicial statements and conclude, at p. 52:

It is the authors' submission that the appropriate test to be applied in this country in conflict of interest situations is the "possibility of real mischief or prejudice" test, developed by the American Courts and adopted and approved in at least the Canadian jurisdiction. Even if the American test is not followed to its fullest extent, it is at the very least essential that the Courts now place a greater onus on solicitors (and counsel) to avoid situations of conflict of interest including situations where there may be only the appearance of a conflict. Times have changed dramatically since *Rakusen*. As Bryson J observed in the *D & J Constructions* case "… each court must to some extent interpret its own times and manners and the conduct which it should expect or even fear from its practitioners" in deciding the degree of control to be exerted.

Canada

In Canada, some courts have applied *Rakusen* but the trend is to apply a stricter test which reflects the concern for the appearance of justice. P.W. Kryworuk ["Acting Against Former Clients—A Matter of Dollars and Common Sense" (1985), 45 CPC 1] points out that Canadian courts are largely applying the stricter American test or are applying a stricter version of *Rakusen* "in light of current attitude towards 'conflict of interest, justice and the appearance of justice and even the concept of "fairness." '"

A few statements from recent cases will serve to illustrate the judicial mood in Canada. In *Steed & Evans Ltd. v. MacTavish* (1976), 12 OR (2d) 236, Goodman J stated, at pp. 237-38:

> The applicant in proceedings of this kind must come to Court with clean hands and justice must not only be done but it must be seen to be done.
>
> … In my view it would be almost impossible for them to cleanse from their minds any information which they may have received while acting on behalf of any of the defendants in the past relating in any way to the subject-matter of these proceedings. It is true that there has been no allegation or submission made by counsel for the defendants herein indicating any specific use or misuse of information obtained confidentially by reason of a solicitor-and-client relationship, but the fact remains that the possibility of that occurring is very real.

In *Canada Southern Railway Co. v. Kingsmill, Jennings* (1978), 8 CPC 117, Southey J, after considering *Rakusen* and *Emle Industries v. Patentex* [478 F.2d 562 (1973)], concluded, at p. 122:

> It will be seen that the authorities emphasize the unfairness arising out of a solicitor acting against a former client where the solicitor might have received confidential information from that former client. That possibility, for all practical purposes, does not exist in the case at Bar, in my judgment.

In *Falls v. Falls* (1979), 12 CPC 270, Fanjoy Co. Ct. J applied *Rakusen* with the following caveat, at pp. 272-73:

> From this judgment [*Rakusen*] I come to the conclusion that the Court must be satisfied that real mischief and real prejudice will, in probability, result if the solicitor is allowed to act.
>
> I must apply this principle in light of present day practices and decisions with respect to conflict of interest, justice and the appearance of justice and even the concept of "fairness." My observation is that the Courts are requiring higher and stricter standards in all these areas.

In *Goldberg v. Goldberg* (1982), 141 DLR (3d) 133, Callaghan J (now CJHC), after reviewing the competing considerations with respect to the probability and possibility tests, stated, at pp. 135-36:

> Of more importance, however, is the fact that the principles involved herein are designed not only to protect the interests of the individual clients but they also protect the public confidence in the administration of justice. This is particularly so when the litigation involves a family dispute. Furthermore, when the public interest is involved, the appearance of impropriety overrides any private interest claimed by waiver.

In *Lukic v. Urquhart* (1984), 11 DLR (4th) 638 (Ont. HC), aff'd in part (1985), 15 DLR (4th) 639 (Ont. CA), a solicitor had been consulted by a party involved in a motor vehicle accident but swore that he had received no confidential information. O'Brien J, whose reasons were adopted by the Court of Appeal, stated, at p. 640:

> I am satisfied in this case there is a very real appearance of professional impropriety and this is clearly a situation where the solicitor might have received confidential information from the defendant, which could be used against the defendant in these proceedings.
>
> I think it would be difficult for the parties in this lawsuit to have confidence in a just result where the solicitor has been placed in that position and now intends to continue against one of his former clients. I am satisfied the solicitor should be removed from the record.

In *O'Dea v. O'Dea* (1987), 68 Nfld. & PEIR 67 (Nfld. Unif. Fam. Ct.), aff'd Nfld. CA June 6, 1988 (unreported), the solicitor, Mr. Day, was consulted by the defendant to obtain a second opinion with respect to the case. Subsequently, her husband retained another lawyer in the firm to act against his wife. Hickman CJ granted the wife's application. After referring to the relevant rule of professional conduct, he concluded as follows, at p. 75:

> In this case Mr. David C. Day, QC was given confidential information by the plaintiff [sic], based upon which he gave her professional advice on some, if not all the issues, which will be coming before this court during trial. He was paid a fee for such professional services. A solicitor–client relationship existed relating to the matters in dispute. While Mr. Day may never be in a position to pass on such confidential information to his partner, Ms. Dawe, yet, the perception is such that the defendant, as a reasonable person, could, in my view, conclude that her interests will be jeopardized should Ms. Dawe or any member of her firm continue to act for her husband in this case. That fact, coupled with the apprehension the defendant has toward the justice system, as a result of her husband's allegations of "connections within the legal profession" makes it all the more necessary that it be made clear that no possibility exists of a conflict of interest.
>
> I conclude, as well, that to permit the plaintiff's law firm to continue to act in this case would be perceived by the public as placing the defendant in an unfair position when this action goes to trial. The *sina qua non* of the justice system is that there be an unqualified perception of its fairness in the eyes of the general public. In order to sustain that salutary precept, it is essential that the integrity and absolute independence of the courts and its [sic] officers be maintained in such a way as to assure a discerning public that the principle of equality before the law is not in danger of being comprised

[sic]. The door must remain firmly shut against any possibility of comprising [sic] that principal [sic]. To allow the plaintiff's law firm to continue to act in this case would open that door, albeit ever so slightly, to the possibility of compromising the impartial administration of justice—something which a court is duty bound to prevent.

In *Fisher v. Fisher* (1986), 76 NSR (2d) 326, the Nova Scotia Court of Appeal disqualified a law firm which, while acting for a husband, was consulted by the wife. Different lawyers in the firm were involved. Although the court agreed that the conduct throughout was of the high standard expected in the legal profession, it refused to accept assurances that confidential information would not be shared.

In *Thomson v. Smith Mechanical Inc.*, [1985] CS 782, Gonthier J (now a member of this Court) found a conflict of interest where counsel for the plaintiff had previously advised both parties in respect of the transaction giving rise to the litigation. He stated, at p. 785:

> [TRANSLATION] This is the cost of ensuring that justice not only is done but is seen to be done, in accordance with the well-known maxim on which the integrity of the judicial system is based, and lawyers are an essential part of that system. Such a practice may also be contrary to the right of the parties to a full and equal hearing as required by s. 23 of the [Quebec] Charter.

In Canada v. Consortium Designers Inc. (1988), 72 Nfld. & PEIR 255 (PEISCTD), aff'd (1989), 80 Nfld. & PEIR 12, a lawyer who had been actively involved in the case for the plaintiff became a partner in the law firm representing the defendant. In acceding to the application to disqualify the defendant's law firm, McQuaid J propounded the following test, at pp. 257-62:

> ... [T]he court has a duty to balance the expected high standards of professional integrity against the realities of life. Where, in the opinion of the court, there exists, or may exist, or may be reasonably anticipated to exist a danger of a breach of confidentiality, then an injunction will issue. Strict proof of the likelihood of breach is not the standard; the standard is the perceived, or reasonably anticipated "danger" of such a breach.
>
> ... [I]f he [the transferred lawyer] has a duty to all parties to the litigation, as well as to the public, to avoid the very appearance of the possibility of any conflict of duty, which the law would appear to indicate that he has, then not only he, but his new colleagues as well, who are, may, or might be perceived to be, privy to the confidential information, then all would be tainted with the brush of conflict of interest.
>
> I consider the more appropriate approach to be, not the narrow and rigid approach of Cozens-Hardy MR "that real mischief and real prejudice will in all human probability result," but with the broader, and I think more relevant approach in today's society that "the court ought to be concerned not only with the actual possibility of a conflict of duty, but also with the appearance of such a possibility," as expressed by Saunders J, in *Brown*.
>
> The issue is: Can the court reasonably infer, given all of the facts, that it might reasonably be perceived primarily by the client, and secondarily, but possibly equally important, by the public, that such did, might, or could have taken place to the prejudice of the client, and to the prejudice of the public's perception and high expectations of the profession.

Finally, in *Morton v. Asper* [(1987), 49 Man. R (2d) 167], which was applied by Hanssen J in this case, Jewers J stated, at pp. 173-74:

> For myself, I prefer to follow those cases which have extended the principle in *Rakusen* to include considerations of public policy, the interest of the public in the proper administration of justice and the perception of fairness by the public and individual litigants. I see nothing in the appellate decisions which would prevent this approach and indeed, in my view, it is encouraged by *Re Speid* [(1984), 43 OR (2d) 596 (CA)] and *Fisher v. Fisher* (*supra*). I believe that these broad principles are reflected in the *Code of Professional Conduct*, in particular Clause 11 which speaks of a solicitor placing himself in a position where he might be tempted or appear to be tempted to breach the rule relating to confidential information.
>
> It reduces itself to a matter of appearance and perception: The plaintiffs' former solicitors have now joined the other side. They have a great deal of confidential information going to the very heart of the plaintiffs' case which would be of inestimable value to the opposition. I have already said that I am confident that they have not and will not divulge this information; however, the *Code of Ethics* says that they should not be in a position where they might be tempted or appear to be tempted to do so. I don't say they might be tempted to do so, but to the plaintiffs and to interested members of the public, they might very well appear to be tempted.

A number of courts, however, have continued to follow the *Rakusen* test. These decisions include: *Farmers Mutual Petroleums Ltd. v. United States Smelting, Refining & Mining Co.* (1961), 28 DLR (2d) 618 (Sask. CA); *R v. Burkinshaw* (1967), 60 DLR (2d) 748 (Alta. SC); *Devco Properties Ltd. v. Sunderland*, [1977] 2 WWR 664 (Alta. SC); *Mercator Enterprises Ltd. v. Mainland Investments Ltd.* (1978), 29 NSR (2d) 703 (SCTD); *Christo v. Bevan* (1982), 36 OR (2d) 797 (HC); *Schmeichel v. Saskatchewan Mining Development Corp.*, [1983] 5 WWR 151 (Sask. CA); and *International Electronics Corp. v. Woodside Developments Ltd.*, unreported, British Columbia Supreme Court, June 26, 1985.

Nevertheless it is evident from this review of authorities that the clear trend is in favour of a stricter test. This trend is the product of a strong policy in favour of ensuring not only that there be no actual conflict but that there be no appearance of conflict.

A number of cases have specifically addressed the question as to whether possession of confidential information on the part of one member of a firm should be imputed to the rest of the firm. The strict application of the appearance principle has led some courts to apply it so that the presumption that "the knowledge of one is the knowledge of all" is irrebuttable. In this category are *Davey v. Woolley, Hames, Dale & Dingwall* (1982), 35 OR (2d) 599 (CA); *Fisher v. Fisher, supra*; and *Morton v. Asper, supra*. Other courts have allowed the principle to be rebutted: see *United States Surgical Corp. v. Downs Surgical Canada Ltd.* (1982), 141 DLR (3d) 157 (FCTD), and *Law Society of Manitoba v. Giesbrecht, supra*. These cases are analyzed by Graham Steele in "Imputing Knowledge From One Member of a Firm to Another: 'Lead Us Not Into Temptation'" (1990), 12 *Adv. Q* 46. He concludes, at p. 58:

> Some judges (and lawyers) find the rigid application of test (2) to be too hard on lawyers and law firms, particularly in today's climate of mergers and megafirms. For the purpose

of determining whether there is a conflict of interest, they would advocate what might be called a "rebuttable imputation" of a lawyer's knowledge.

The Appropriate Test

What then should be the correct approach? Is the "probability of mischief" standard sufficiently high to satisfy the public requirement that there be an appearance of justice? In my opinion, it is not. This is borne out by the judicial statements to which I have referred and to the desire of the legal profession for strict rules of professional conduct as its adoption of the Canadian *Code of Professional Conduct* demonstrates. The probability of mischief test is very much the same as the standard of proof in a civil case. We act on probabilities. This is the basis of Rakusen. I am, however, driven to the conclusion that the public, and indeed lawyers and judges, have found that standard wanting. In dealing with the question of the use of confidential information we are dealing with a matter that is usually not susceptible of proof. As pointed out by Fletcher Moulton LJ in *Rakusen*, "that is a thing which you cannot prove" (p. 841). I would add "or disprove." If it were otherwise, then no doubt the public would be satisfied upon proof that no prejudice would be occasioned. Since, however, it is not susceptible of proof, the test must be such that the public represented by the reasonably informed person would be satisfied that no use of confidential information would occur. That, in my opinion, is the overriding policy that applies and must inform the court in answering the question: Is there a disqualifying conflict of interest? In this regard, it must be stressed that this conclusion is predicated on the fact that the client does not consent to but is objecting to the retainer which gives rise to the alleged conflict.

Typically, these cases require two questions to be answered: (1) Did the lawyer receive confidential information attributable to a solicitor and client relationship relevant to the matter at hand? (2) Is there a risk that it will be used to the prejudice of the client?

In answering the first question, the court is confronted with a dilemma. In order to explore the matter in depth may require the very confidential information for which protection is sought to be revealed. This would have the effect of defeating the whole purpose of the application. American courts have solved this dilemma by means of the "substantial relationship" test. Once a "substantial relationship" is shown, there is an irrebuttable presumption that confidential information was imparted to the lawyer. In my opinion, this test is too rigid. There may be cases in which it is established beyond any reasonable doubt that no confidential information relevant to the current matter was disclosed. One example is where the applicant client admits on cross-examination that this is the case. This would not avail in the face of an irrebuttable presumption. In my opinion, once it is shown by the client that there existed a previous relationship which is sufficiently related to the retainer from which it is sought to remove the solicitor, the court should infer that confidential information was imparted unless the solicitor satisfies the court that no information was imparted which could be relevant. This will be a difficult burden to discharge. Not only must the court's degree of satisfaction be such that it would withstand the scrutiny of the reasonably informed member of the public that no such information passed, but the burden must be discharged without revealing the specifics of the privileged communication.

Nonetheless, I am of the opinion that the door should not be shut completely on a solicitor who wishes to discharge this heavy burden.

The second question is whether the confidential information will be misused. A lawyer who has relevant confidential information cannot act against his client or former client. In such a case the disqualification is automatic. No assurances or undertakings not to use the information will avail. The lawyer cannot compartmentalize his or her mind so as to screen out what has been gleaned from the client and what was acquired elsewhere. Furthermore, there would be a danger that the lawyer would avoid use of information acquired legitimately because it might be perceived to have come from the client. This would prevent the lawyer from adequately representing the new client. Moreover, the former client would feel at a disadvantage. Questions put in cross-examination about personal matters, for example, would create the uneasy feeling that they had their genesis in the previous relationship.

The answer is less clear with respect to the partners or associates in the firm. Some courts have applied the concept of imputed knowledge. This assumes that the knowledge of one member of the firm is the knowledge of all. If one lawyer cannot act, no member of the firm can act. This is a rule that has been applied by some law firms as their particular brand of ethics. While this is commendable and is to be encouraged, it is, in my opinion, an assumption which is unrealistic in the era of the mega-firm. Furthermore, if the presumption that the knowledge of one is the knowledge of all is to be applied, it must be applied with respect to both the former firm and the firm which the moving lawyer joins. Thus there is a conflict with respect to every matter handled by the old firm that has a substantial relationship with any matter handled by the new firm irrespective of whether the moving lawyer had any involvement with it. This is the "overkill" which has drawn so much criticism in the United States to which I have referred above.

Moreover, I am not convinced that a reasonable member of the public would necessarily conclude that confidences are likely to be disclosed in every case despite institutional efforts to prevent it. There is, however, a strong inference that lawyers who work together share confidences. In answering this question, the court should therefore draw the inference, unless satisfied on the basis of clear and convincing evidence, that all reasonable measures have been taken to ensure that no disclosure will occur by the "tainted" lawyer to the member or members of the firm who are engaged against the former client. Such reasonable measures would include institutional mechanisms such as Chinese Walls and cones of silence. These concepts are not familiar to Canadian courts and indeed do not seem to have been adopted by the governing bodies of the legal profession. It can be expected that the Canadian Bar Association, which took the lead in adopting a *Code of Professional Conduct* in 1974, will again take the lead to determine whether institutional devices are effective and develop standards for the use of institutional devices which will be uniform throughout Canada. Although I am not prepared to say that a court should never accept these devices as sufficient evidence of effective screening until the governing bodies have approved of them and adopted rules with respect to their operation, I would not foresee a court doing so except in exceptional circumstances. Thus, in the vast majority of cases, the courts are unlikely to accept the effectiveness of these devices until the profession, through its governing body, has studied the matter and determined whether there are institutional guarantees that will satisfy the need to maintain confidence in the integrity of the profession. In this regard, it must be borne in mind that the legal profession is a self-governing profession. The Legislature has entrusted to it and not to the court the responsibility of developing standards. The court's role is merely supervisory, and its jurisdiction extends to this aspect of ethics only in connection with legal proceedings. The governing bodies, however, are concerned with the application of conflict of interest standards not only in respect of litigation but in other fields which constitute the greater part of the practice of law. It would be wrong, therefore, to shut out the governing body of a self-regulating profession from the whole of the practice by the imposition of an inflexible and immutable standard in the exercise of a supervisory jurisdiction over part of it.

A fortiori undertakings and conclusory statements in affidavits without more are not acceptable. These can be expected in every case of this kind that comes before the court. It is no more than the lawyer saying "trust me." This puts the court in the invidious position of deciding which lawyers are to be trusted and which are not. Furthermore, even if the courts found this acceptable, the public is not likely to be satisfied without some additional guarantees that confidential information will under no circumstances be used. In this regard I am in agreement with the statement of Posner J in *Analytica, supra,* to which I have referred above, that affidavits of lawyers difficult to verify objectively will fail to assure the public.

These standards will, in my opinion, strike the appropriate balance among the three interests to which I have referred. In giving precedence to the preservation of the confidentiality of information imparted to a solicitor, the confidence of the public in the integrity of the profession and in the administration of justice will be maintained and strengthened. On the other hand, reflecting the interest of a member of the public in retaining counsel of her choice and the interest of the profession in permitting lawyers to move from one firm to another, the standards are sufficiently flexible to permit a solicitor to act against a former client provided that a reasonable member of the public who is in possession of the facts would conclude that no unauthorized disclosure of confidential information had occurred or would occur.

Application to This Case

The answer to the first question in this case presents no problem. It is acknowledged that Kristin Dangerfield actively worked on the very case in respect of which her new firm is acting against her former client. She is therefore in possession of relevant confidential information.

With respect to the second question, there is nothing beyond the sworn statements of Sweatman and Dangerfield that no discussions of the case have occurred and undertaking that none will occur. In my opinion, while, as stated by the courts below, there is no reason not to accept the affidavits of apparently reputable counsel, this is not sufficient to demonstrate that all reasonable measures have been taken to rebut the strong inference of disclosure. Indeed, there is nothing in the affidavits to indicate that any independently verifiable steps were taken by the firm to implement any kind of screening. There is nothing to indicate that when Ms. Dangerfield joined the firm, instructions were issued that there were to be no communications directly or indirectly between Ms. Dangerfield and the four members of the firm working on the case. While these measures would not necessarily have been sufficient, I refer to them in order to illustrate the kinds of independently verifiable steps which, along with other measures, are indispensable if the firm intends to continue to act.

I would therefore allow the appeal with costs to the appellant both here and in the Court of Appeal, set aside the judgment of the Court of Appeal of Manitoba and restore the judgment of Hanssen J.

CORY J (for the minority, with Wilson and L'Heureux-Dube JJ concurring): I have read with interest the reasons of my colleague, Justice Sopinka. Although I agree with his disposition of the appeal, I would impose a stricter duty upon lawyers than that which he proposes. He puts his position in this way, at p. 1260:

> In my opinion, once it is shown by the client that there existed a previous relationship which is sufficiently related to the retainer from which it is sought to remove the solicitor, the court should infer that confidential information was imparted unless the solicitor satisfies the court that no information was imparted which could be relevant.

He observes that it will be difficult for a solicitor to meet that onus. He states that the position, taken by some courts, that if one lawyer in the firm cannot act, then no member of the law firm can act, is unreasonable in this era of mega-firms and mergers. Thus, he reasons that it should be open for a solicitor to show "that no information was imparted which could be relevant."

With respect, I disagree. Neither the merger of law firms nor the mobility of lawyers can be permitted to affect adversely the public's confidence in the judicial system. At this time, when the work of the courts is having a very significant impact upon the lives and affairs of all Canadians, it is fundamentally important that justice not only be done, but appear to be done in the eyes of the public.

My colleague stated that this appeal called for the balancing of three competing values, namely: the maintenance and integrity of our system of justice; the right of litigants not to be lightly deprived of their chosen counsel; and the desirability of permitting reasonable mobility in the legal profession.

Of these factors, the most important and compelling is the preservation of the integrity of our system of justice. The necessity of selecting new counsel will certainly be inconvenient, unsettling and worrisome to clients. Reasonable mobility may well be important to lawyers. However, the integrity of the judicial system is of such fundamental importance to our country and, indeed, to all free and democratic societies that it must be the predominant consideration in any balancing of these three factors.

Lawyers are an integral and vitally important part of our system of justice. It is they who prepare and put their clients' cases before courts and tribunals. In preparing for the hearing of a contentious matter, a client will often be required to reveal to the lawyer retained highly confidential information. The client's most secret devices and desires, the client's most frightening fears will often, of necessity, be revealed. The client must be secure in the knowledge that the lawyer will neither disclose nor take advantage of these revelations.

Our judicial system could not operate if this were not the case. It cannot function properly if doubt or suspicion exists in the mind of the public that the confidential information disclosed by a client to a lawyer might be revealed.

There can be no question that such a doubt would certainly be instilled if the public were to gather the perception that lawyers, by their actions, such as changing firms, create situations where the possibility of a conflict of interest exists.

Imagine a situation where a client involved in a contentious matter has divulged confidential information to a lawyer. If that lawyer practised with one partner, it would be perceived by the public as unfair and completely unacceptable if the partner were to act for the client's adversary. Similarly, if the lawyer moved to another firm which had been retained by those in opposition to the client, the most reasonable and fair-minded member of the public would find it intolerable for that firm to continue to act for those who opposed the client. In both situations the perception of unfairness would arise from the ease with which confidential information received from clients could be privately communicated between lawyers who are working together in the same firm.

Fortunately, partners rarely attempt to act for clients on both sides of a lawsuit. However, the problem more frequently arises when a lawyer, who has received confidential information, joins a firm that is acting for those opposing the interests of the former client. In such a situation there should be an irrebuttable presumption that lawyers who work together share each other's confidences with the result that a knowledge of confidential matters is imputed to other members of the firm. This presumption must apply to the members of the new firm the lawyer joins if public confidence in the administration of justice is to be maintained.

Indeed, this seems to be the purport of the Canadian Bar Association *Code of Professional Conduct* quoted by my colleague. ...

It is contended that it is too demanding to hold that the knowledge of one member of a law firm constitutes knowledge of all members of the firm in situations where there has been a merger of large firms or a lawyer has joined a "mega-firm." I cannot agree. It is the appearance of fairness in the eyes of the public that is fundamentally important. No matter how large the mega-firm, there will be innumerable occasions when a lawyer with a possible conflict of interest will be meeting with those lawyers in the firm who are in opposition to that lawyer's former client. Whether at partners' meetings or committee meetings, at lunches or the office golf tournament, in the boardroom or the washroom, the lawyer of the former client will be meeting with and talking to those who are on the other side of the client's case. To those who are not members of the legal profession, it must appear that the opportunities for private discussion are so numerous that the disclosure of confidential information, even if completely inadvertent, would be inevitable. Nor is it likely that disclosures of confidential information will ever be discovered. Further, if a lawyer even inadvertently discloses those weaknesses of the client that have been divulged to him or her, this may be sufficient to give the client's opponents an unfair advantage. This, I think, would be the inevitable conclusion of reasonable people.

That same conclusion would be drawn by the public no matter what form of restrictions were sought to be imposed on individual lawyers and law firms involved. No matter how carefully the Chinese Wall might be constructed, it could be breached without anyone but the lawyers involved knowing of that breach. Law has, after all, the historical precedent of Genghis Khan who, by subterfuge, breached the Great Wall of China, the greatest of Chinese walls. Nor would any system of cones of silence change the public's perception of unfairness. They do not change the reality that lawyers in the same firm meet frequently nor do they reduce the opportunities for the private exchange of confidential information. The public would, quite properly, remain skeptical of the efficacy of the most sophisticated protective scheme. ...

Let us consider again the two factors which are said to be the competing values to be weighed against the maintenance of the integrity of our system of justice. One of these was the desirability of permitting reasonable mobility in the legal profession. Yet, no matter how strong may be the current rage for mergers or how desirous the mega-firms may be to acquire additional lawyers, neither the large firms nor the lawyers who wish to join them or amalgamate with them should dictate the course of legal ethics. The latest available statistics (as of May 1990) from the Law Society of Upper Canada for the province of Ontario, where the greatest concentration of large law firms might be expected, demonstrate that lawyers in large firms do not comprise the majority of lawyers in that province. ...

This indicates that, although the large firms may be the movers and shakers on Bay Street, they do not represent the majority of lawyers soldiering on in the cause of justice.

The judicial system and the confidence of the public in its operation are too important to be put at risk by any appearance of unfairness. Unfortunately, no matter how scrupulously ethical an individual lawyer or firm may be, the appearance of unfairness will always be present when, as in this case, one or more lawyers who had a substantial relationship with a client become members of a firm acting for an opposing party. The opportunities for disclosure, even of an inadvertent nature, are too frequent and the possibility of discovering such disclosures too minimal to permit anything less than the irrebuttable presumption that the knowledge of one member of a law firm constitutes the knowledge of all of the lawyers in that firm. Only such a test will ensure the public's confidence in the administration of justice.

This conclusion should not be taken as an impediment to the mobility of lawyers, the merger of law firms or the growth of very large firms; rather, it is a recognition of a professional responsibility owed by lawyers to the litigation process so that the process may retain the respect of the public. It is a small price to pay for mobility of lawyers, mergers of law firms and the increasing size of law firms. It is no more than the fulfilment of a duty owed by members of the legal profession to the public to preserve the integrity of, and public confidence in, the judicial system.

The other factor to be weighed against maintaining the integrity of the justice system was that litigants ought not to be lightly deprived of their chosen counsel. It seems to me that to give undue weight to this factor would unduly benefit the large corporate clients who are said by my colleague to be the raison d'être of the larger firms. It is they who would retain counsel of their choice and primarily benefit from a change in the irrebuttable presumption of shared knowledge. I can see no reason for extending any special benefit or privilege to such clients of large firms. They, like any client who must seek new counsel, will suffer from inconvenience, loss of time and the inevitable worry and concern over such a change. However, the legal profession has many able counsel. The requirement of change imposed on a client is, on balance, a small price to pay for maintaining the integrity of our system of justice.

Conclusion

Where a lawyer who has had a substantial involvement with a client in an ongoing contentious matter joins another law firm which is acting for an opposing party, there is an irrebuttable presumption that the knowledge of such lawyer, including confidential information disclosed to him or her by the former client, has become the knowledge of the new firm. Such an irrebuttable presumption is essential to preserve public confidence in the administration of justice.

Potential conflict of interest is undoubtedly a factor which has to be taken into account when firms consider bringing in new lawyers or merging with other firms. However, the conflict of interest situations can be easily ascertained (a task readily accomplished with the use of computers) and a price fixed for the value of the files that will have to be turned over to other firms in order to avoid any appearance of conflict of interest. Such a procedure certainly does not impose an impossibly difficult burden on firms considering a merger; rather, it imposes a review that will lead to the cost assessment of the advantages and disadvantages of the merger.

It must be left for another occasion, when argument has been directed to the issue, to determine whether a lawyer, who has not personally been involved in any way with the client on the matter in issue and who moves to a firm acting for the opponent to the client, should also be irrebuttably presumed to have received and imparted confidential information to his new firm.

In the result, I reach the same conclusion as my colleague. I would allow the appeal with costs to the appellant here and in the Court of Appeal, set aside the judgment of the Court of Appeal of Manitoba and restore the judgment of Hanssen J.

NOTES AND QUESTIONS

1. Do you prefer the opinion of Sopinka J (for the majority) or the concurring opinion of Cory J (for the minority)? How would you characterize the fundamental difference(s) between these two opinions?

2. Note that the decision in *MacDonald Estates* makes it clear that the courts possess an "inherent jurisdiction" to disqualify lawyers who act in a conflict position. As a result, a party who feels that a lawyer is acting in a conflict position may bring a motion to have the lawyer disqualified from acting in the proceedings. Consider the effect of the courts' "inherent jurisdiction" to disqualify lawyers in cases of this nature. Should a court be quick to exercise this jurisdiction? Consider the possible motives that might govern motions for disqualification. Gavin MacKenzie offers the following insights:

Motions for disqualification orders may not always be sought for the purest of motives. Many such motions are undoubtedly brought by reason of genuine concerns about lawyers' loyalty or breaches of confidence. Others may be brought, however, to gain a tactical advantage by burdening a less well-financed adversary with additional costs, or by depriving the adversary of the services of a lawyer who is known to be effective in a particular type of case.[10]

In the light of MacKenzie's comments, what are the economic incentives provided by the courts' inherent jurisdiction to disqualify conflicted counsel? Are these efficient incentives? Is there a superior way of regulating conflict-of-interest situations?

  3. Justice Sopinka refers to the following quote from Justice Posner:

For a law firm to represent one client today, and the client's adversary tomorrow in a closely related matter, creates an unsavory appearance of conflict of interest that is difficult to dispel in the eyes of the lay public—or for that matter the bench and bar—by the filing of affidavits, difficult to verify objectively, denying that improper communication has taken place or will take place between the lawyers in the firm handling the two sides

Explain how the unsavory appearance referred to in this quote can (or cannot) be described as an economic cost that is borne by the general public. Can this economic cost be eliminated through a compensatory model of regulation, a punishment model of regulation, or some combination of the two?

  4. The appearance-of-impropriety test (referred to in *MacDonald Estate v. Martin*) has the effect of disqualifying lawyers (based on conflict-of-interest grounds) where it is *possible* (rather than certain or probable) that the relevant lawyers may breach the rule of confidentiality. What is the purpose of the appearance-of-impropriety test? If the public is satisfied that they will be compensated for any *actual* breach of the rules regarding confidentiality, is there any need for the test? If all direct victims of breaches of confidentiality will be fully compensated for any damage caused by the breach, is there any public utility lost through violations of the duty of confidentiality, or is the damage limited to the specific victim of the lawyer's violation? If the former, what is the point of the appearance-of-impropriety test? For a discussion of this issue, see chapter 4, section IV.B.

  5. Note that the court refers repeatedly to a screening mechanism known as the Chinese Wall. People often assume that this metaphor is a reference to the Great Wall of China. (Cory J.'s minority opinion reinforces this suggestion by referring to the breach of the Great Wall by Genghis Khan.) In fact, the phrase "Chinese Wall" refers to a wall of paper. In the context of lawyer screening, this refers to a series of documents (or a paper trail), such as sworn affidavits, that are designed to prevent the flow of confidential information from a conflicted lawyer and to prove that no such confidential information flowed throughout a firm to which the conflicted lawyer has transferred.

  6. The court refers repeatedly to the "irrebuttable presumption" approach to conflicts of interest (that is, the presumption that a lawyer in possession of confidential information will inevitably share that information with other lawyers at his or her firm). Under

---

10   Ibid., at 5-3.

this presumption, a lawyer who transfers from one firm to another would automatically be held to "infect" the new firm's lawyers with confidential information, effectively disqualifying the firm from participating in certain transactions or acting against particular clients. What are the economic costs and benefits of the irrebuttable-presumption approach? Is this the optimal approach for regulating conflicts of interest? When answering this question, consider the following observation:

> To deprive clients, who may have invested a great deal of time, energy and money in litigation, of counsel of their choice is a necessary—though often disruptive and expensive—consequence of a process that must ensure that other parties are protected against such improprieties as disloyalty and breaches of confidentiality. To deprive clients of the right to be represented by counsel of their choice—and in some cases to inflict on them the burdens of disruption, duplication of effort, and added expense—based on a mere appearance of impropriety that does not in fact exist, may be intolerable.[11]

7. Can the conflict-of-interest rule be explained (in economic terms) as a mechanism for overcoming the fact that, in cases involving potential conflicts of interest, actual violations of the confidentiality rule will be extremely difficult to detect? In other words, does the conflict-of-interest rule overcome the low probability of detecting and punishing breaches of confidentiality? How so?

8. Justice Cory notes that "[n]either the merger of law firms nor the mobility of lawyers can be permitted to affect adversely the public's confidence in the judicial system." Presumably, law firms merge and become megafirms because it is profitable for them to do so. This, of course, implies that clients are availing themselves of megafirms' services. If the public wants megafirms (and demonstrates this desire by purchasing their services), and a necessary incident of the growth of megafirms is the transfer of lawyers from one firm to another, should we take this as an indication that the public is willing to accept the greater likelihood that possible conflicts of interest will arise? If this is the case, should we accept Cory J.'s suggestion that the transfer of a lawyer from one firm to another gives rise to a perception of impropriety, or a lessening of the public's confidence in the legal system?

9. When considering the problems that flow from the transfer of a lawyer between two firms, Cory J makes the following observation:

> Whether at partners' meetings or committee meetings, at lunches or the office golf tournament, in the boardroom or the washroom, the lawyer of the former client will be meeting with and talking to those who are on the other side of the client's case. To those who are not members of the legal profession, it must appear that the opportunities for private discussion are so numerous that the disclosure of confidential information, even if completely inadvertent, would be inevitable.

If this truly lessens the esteem in which the public holds the legal profession, would the public's confidence in the legal system also be eroded by (1) the marriage of two lawyers at different firms, where those firms often find themselves on opposite sides of transactions

---

11   Ibid.

or court proceedings; or (2) close friendships between lawyers of two competing firms? Would the public be surprised to learn that a lawyer at one megafirm had a close (or even familial) relationship with a lawyer at another (competing) firm? If not, is Cory J wrong to believe that the public's confidence in the legal system would dissipate where lawyers change firms while bearing confidential information? Why or why not? Do differing policy concerns arise in the different cases described above?

10. Assume that a prosecutor has married a defence lawyer. Would Sopinka J.'s formulation of the conflict-of-interest rule ever allow these spouses to appear on opposite sides of the same case? Would Cory J.'s decision allow this? Should this be allowed?

11. The Law Society of Upper Canada has promulgated specific rules regarding the situation described in *MacDonald Estate v. Martin* (the transfer of lawyers from one firm to another). These are found in rule 2.05 of the Law Society's *Rules of Professional Conduct*. Review the rules (available online at http://www.lsuc.on.ca/) and consider the following questions:

a. Do this rules successfully address the problems inherent in conflict cases?

b. Would compliance with these rules allow lawyers to avoid a motion for disqualification?

c. Do these rules provide lawyers with efficient economic incentives?

III. Joint Retainer

One of the most common sources of conflicting interests is the "joint retainer"—that is, the lawyer's agreement to act on behalf of multiple parties to a transaction or dispute. The most obvious conflict that could arise in cases of joint retainer, also called "multiple representation," involves the case in which a lawyer represents *opposing* parties. It seems unlikely that a lawyer's interests could coincide with the interests of two or more people who are on opposite sides of a transaction or legal proceeding. As a result, lawyers are generally prohibited from acting for parties on opposite sides of any transaction or claim.[12]

Even where two or more parties appear to share a common interest, a lawyer should be wary of representing multiple parties. Consider, for example, the lawyer who represents two people who are jointly accused of criminal conduct. While both parties share an interest in opposing the Crown's case and being acquitted, the best strategy for each client could well conflict with the interests of the other. Perhaps each client could hope to gain an advantage by offering the authorities information concerning the other client's activities. Perhaps each client could generate reasonable doubt by claiming that the other client was responsible for the crime. Thus, even though both clients appear to be on the same side of the dispute (opposing the Crown in this example), the interests of the parties may diverge. Where jointly represented clients' interests do diverge, the lawyer will find himself or herself in a position involving a conflict of interest.

According to many commentators, it is rare to find two parties whose interests truly coincide. As a result, a decision to accept a joint retainer is fraught with ethical conun-

---

12   See, for example, chapter V of the CBA's *Code of Professional Conduct*, which provides that "[t]he lawyer shall not advise or represent both sides of a dispute." Similarly, rule 2.04(2) of Ontario's *Rules of Professional Conduct* provides that "[a] lawyer shall not advise or represent more than one side of a dispute."

drums. As Proulx and Layton note (in the context of criminal representation), joint retainer "presents one of the most common and dangerous conflict-of-interest dilemmas" for the lawyer.[13] Where a lawyer agrees to accept a joint retainer, the lawyer enters a minefield of potential conflicts of interest, where he or she is likely to face perplexing ethical choices.

As a result of the frequency with which joint retainers give rise to conflicting interests, regulatory bodies have put forth specific rules designed to regulate cases of multiple representation. The Law Society of Upper Canada, for example, has promulgated the following rules:

2.04(6) Before a lawyer accepts employment from more than one client in a matter or transaction, the lawyer shall advise the clients that:

(a) the lawyer has been asked to act for both or all of them,

(b) no information received in connection with the matter from one can be treated as confidential so far as any of the others are concerned, and

(c) if a conflict develops that cannot be resolved, the lawyer cannot continue to act for both or all of them and may have to withdraw completely.

2.04(9) Save as provided by subrule (10), where clients have consented to a joint retainer and an issue contentious between them or some of them arises, their lawyer shall:

(a) not advise them on the contentious issue, and

(b) refer the clients to other lawyers, unless

(i) no legal advice is required, and

(ii) the clients are sophisticated,

in which case, the clients may settle the contentious issue by direct negotiation in which the lawyer does not participate.

2.04(10) Where clients consent to a joint retainer and also agree that if a contentious issue arises their lawyer may continue to advise one of them and a contentious issue does arise, the lawyer may advise the one client about the contentious matter and shall refer the other or others to another lawyer.[14]

The policies underlying these rules are obvious: where a lawyer acts for two or more parties to a transaction or dispute, the lawyer may find himself or herself unable to act in the best interests of both clients. Proulx and Layton explain this problem as follows:

The danger arising from multiple representation is simply a function of the increased likelihood of conflicting demands on counsel's loyalty where he or she represents two clients in the same matter. It follows that the right to effective counsel is especially susceptible to harm in cases of multiple representation.[15]

---

13   Proulx and Layton, supra note 7, at 297.

14   The American Bar Association addresses this problem in rule 1.7(b)(2), which states:

When representation of multiple clients in a single matter is undertaken, the consultation shall include explanation of the implications of the common representation and the advantages and risks involved.

15   Proulx and Layton, supra note 7, at, 297.

The economic account of the problems inherent in joint retainers is similarly intuitive. If two clients' interests diverge, it will be impossible for the lawyer's interests to coincide with the interests of both clients. As we noted in section I, a conflict between the lawyer's interests and those of one or more of the lawyer's clients may give rise to market failure. As a result, some market correcting mechanism (such as subrules 2.04(6), (9), and (10)) may be effective in promoting a more near-optimal allocation of scarce resources. The foregoing rules pursue this purpose by requiring disclosure of potential conflicts of interest and withdrawal in cases where an unacceptable level of conflict is inevitable.

The decision of the Ontario Court of Appeal in *R v. Widdifield* (1995), below, provides a useful example of the conflicts that may arise in cases involving joint retainer. The case also deals with the standard of review that courts apply in determining whether a conflict of interest exists. Notes and questions concerning both aspects of the court's decision are found after the case.

R v. Widdifield
(1995), 25 OR (3d) 161

DOHERTY JA:

I. The Issues

The appellants, who are husband and wife, were represented by the same counsel at trial. They were convicted. They now contend that their joint representation at trial placed trial counsel in a position of having to choose between conflicting interests and that, as a consequence, their convictions constitute a miscarriage of justice and must be quashed. The appellants also appeal their sentences.

II. Overview

There were five counts in the indictment. L.W., Mr. Widdifield's niece, was the complainant in all five charges. Mr. Widdifield was charged in all counts and Mrs. Widdifield was charged in counts 1 and 2. Counts 4 and 5 alleged that Mr. Widdifield indecently and sexually assaulted L.W. between June 1981 and June 1987. Mr. Widdifield was also charged with sexual assault, sexual intercourse with a female under 14 years of age, and threatening (counts 1, 2, and 3). These three charges arose out of incidents which allegedly occurred over a three-day period at the appellants' cottage in the summer of 1987. Mrs. Widdifield was jointly charged with Mr. Widdifield in respect of the charges of sexual assault and sexual intercourse with a female under 14 years of age arising out of the events at the cottage in the summer of 1987 (counts 1 and 2). The Crown alleged that Mrs. Widdifield assisted Mr. Widdifield in the commission of these offences.

Mr. Widdifield was convicted of all counts and received a total sentence of three years, Mrs. Widdifield was convicted of both charges brought against her and received a total sentence of one year.

. . .

V. The Right to the Effective Assistance of Counsel

An accused who is represented by counsel at trial is entitled to receive the effective assistance of counsel. That entitlement has common law, statutory, and constitutional roots: *R v. Silvini* [(1991), 5 OR (3d) 545 (CA)], at p. 549 OR, p. 257 CCC; *R v. Garofoli* [[1990] 2 SCR 1421; 43 OAC 1], at p. 152; *Criminal Code*, s. 650(3). If an accused does not receive the effective assistance of counsel at trial, the adversary system cannot function properly, the appearance of fairness suffers, and the reliability of the verdict is called into question. Ineffective legal assistance at trial may result in a miscarriage of justice necessitating the quashing of the conviction.

Counsel must be competent in order to render effective assistance. No one suggests that the appellants' counsel was incompetent. The accused is, however, entitled to more than competence. A lawyer can render effective assistance only when that lawyer gives the accused's cause the undivided loyalty which is a prerequisite to proper legal representation. Within the limits imposed by legal and ethical constraints, the lawyer must champion the accused's cause without regard to counsel's personal interests or the interests of anyone else: G.A. Martin, "The Role and Responsibility of the Defence Advocate" (1970), 12 *Crim. LQ* 376 at pp. 383-86; W.F. Schroeder, "Some Ethical Problems in the Criminal Laws," Special Lectures of the Law Society of Upper Canada 1963, Part IV: *Representing an Arrested Client and Police Interrogation* (Toronto: de Boo, 1963), at pp. 100-04. This duty of undivided loyalty not only serves and protects the client, but is essential to the maintenance of the overall integrity of the justice system: *MacDonald Estate v. Martin*, [1990] 3 SCR 1235, 77 DLR (4th) 249 per Sopinka J at p. 1243 SCR, p. 254 DLR, per Cory J (in dissent) at pp. 1264-65 SCR, pp. 271-72 DLR.

While there can be no absolute bar against the joint representation of co-accused, joint representation puts counsel's obligation of undivided loyalty to each client at risk: *R v. Silvini, supra*, at p. 549 OR, p. 257 CCC. In attempting to serve two masters, counsel may do a disservice to the interests of one or both. Counsel who undertake the joint representation of co-accused assume the heavy burden of ensuring that they are not placed in a position of representing interests which are or may be in conflict: Rules of Professional Conduct of the Law Society of Upper Canada (1992), Rule 5. Where counsel fails to perform that duty and undertakes the representation of interests which do or may conflict, the court will order counsel removed from the record: *R v. Speid* (1983), 43 OR (2d) 596, 8 CCC (3d) 18 (CA); *R v. Robillard* (1986), 28 CCC (3d) 22, 23 CRR 364 (Ont. CA).

In this case, the issue of joint representation was not raised at trial. Trial counsel apprehended no conflict of interests until well after the appellants were convicted. The trial judge was not called upon to consider whether counsel could properly represent both accused. Thus, the issue on appeal is not whether counsel should have been allowed to continue to act for both appellants. Rather, the issue is whether, on a review of the trial record supplemented by the fresh evidence, the appellants have demonstrated that their joint representation resulted in a miscarriage of justice.

The judgment of this court in *R v. Silvini, supra*, is directly on point. There, the appellant and his co-accused were jointly represented at trial. The appellant was convicted. On appeal, he contended that his interests and those of his co-accused were opposed at trial. In trying to represent both interests, trial counsel had failed to render effective legal assistance to the appellant. This court accepted that submission and quashed the conviction. Lacourcière JA, for the court, held that the interests of the appellant and the co-accused were in conflict and set out four specific instances where, as a result of that conflict counsel's effectiveness on behalf of the appellant had been compromised (pp. 551-52 OR, pp. 259-60 CCC). Lacourcière JA summarized his conclusion (pp. 556-57 OR, p. 264 CCC):

> ... I am satisfied that trial counsel failed to provide reasonably effective legal assistance to the appellant, by reason only of the conflict of interest. The performance of trial counsel was adversely affected, impairing the appellant's right to present full answer and defence. Thus, the proper functioning of the adversarial process was undermined and the verdict resulting from a trial lacking in fairness cannot be relied upon.

The approach formulated in *Silvini* requires that the appellant demonstrate:

— an actual conflict of interest between the respective interests represented by counsel

   AND

— as a result of that conflict, some impairment of counsel's ability to represent effectively the interests of the appellant.

If both criteria are established, then the appellant has been denied the right to make full answer and defence and a miscarriage of justice has occurred. The appellant need not demonstrate that, but for the ineffective representation of counsel, the verdict could have been different. The absence of any need to show prejudice in terms of an adverse impact on the verdict flows from characterizing the product of ineffective representation flowing from a conflict of interests as a miscarriage of justice. By its own terms, the curative proviso in s. 683(1)(b)(iii) can have no application.

The approach taken in *Silvini* is borrowed from a formidable line of American authority, and has also been followed in this country: *Cuyler v. Sullivan*, 446 US 335 (1980); *Strickland v. Washington*, 466 US 668 (1986); *Burger v. Kemp*, 483 US 776 (1987); *R v. Graff* (1993), 80 CCC (3d) 84 at p. 90 (Alta. CA), leave to appeal to SCC. refused (1993), 83 CCC (3d) vi.

Counsel for the appellants cited and relied on *Silvini*. They also submitted that if they could demonstrate a potential or apparent conflict of interests, as opposed to an actual conflict of interests, the appellants were entitled to have their convictions quashed. This contention is contrary to *Silvini* and was expressly rejected in *Cuyler v. Sullivan, supra*, at p. 348, one of the American authorities relied on in *Silvini*.

In support of this submission, counsel relied on *R v. Bullis* (1990), 57 CCC (3d) 438 (BCCA), a case decided before *Silvini*, but not referred to in *Silvini*. Parts of the judgment in *Bullis* suggest that an appellant need only demonstrate "an appearance of a conflict of interest" or "an apparent conflict of interest" (pp. 441-42). Before considering the effects of those passages, however, I observe that in the end result Gibbs JA, for the court, found an actual conflict of interests as between the three accused who were represented by the same counsel at trial. He further held at p. 443 that:

> ... I am forced to the conclusion that the one counsel for all three collectively must necessarily have been inhibited in the performance of his duty towards each separately.

The result in *Bullis* is consistent, therefore, with the approach taken in *Silvini*. However, if *Bullis* does hold that an appearance of a conflict of interest is enough to warrant reversal on appeal, then I must disagree with that conclusion. The two authorities from this province relied on in *Bullis* do not support that conclusion. In both cases, this court found an actual conflict of interests which inhibited counsel's performance on behalf of the appellant. With respect, it seems to me that the judgment in *Bullis* wrongly equates an "apparent conflict of interests" with "a conflict of interests that is apparent." An apparent conflict refers to a conflict which seems to exist, but which in fact may not; a conflict that is apparent (the phrase used by McKay JA in *R v. DePatie* [[1971] OR 698 (CA)], at p. 699 OR, p. 340 CCC) refers to a conflict which does exist and is plainly observable: *New Shorter Oxford English Dictionary*, vol. 1 (Oxford: Clarendon Press, 1993) at p. 97.

It is important to distinguish between the respective functions of a trial judge and an appellate court when faced with a conflict of interests claim. Where the issue is raised at trial, the court must be concerned with actual conflicts of interests and potential conflicts that may develop as the trial unfolds. In deciding whether counsel should be permitted to act for co-accused, trial judges must, to some degree, speculate as to the issues which may arise and the course the trial will take. The trial judges' task is particularly difficult since they cannot be privy to the confidential discussions which may have passed between the clients and counsel and which may reveal the source of potential conflicts. Given those circumstances, trial judges must proceed with caution and when there is any realistic risk of a conflict of interests they must direct that counsel not act for one or perhaps either accused.

Where the allegation of a conflict of interests is raised for the first time on appeal, the perspective is very different. The appellate court looks backward at the completed trial. The court has the full trial record and may have further material detailing the circumstances surrounding the joint representation and the effects of that representation on counsel's ability to defend the appellant. Unlike the trial court, the appellate court is not concerned with prophylactic measures intended to avoid the potential injustice which may flow from compromised representation. Instead, the appellate court must determine whether counsel's representation was in fact compromised in such a way as to result in a miscarriage of justice. The concern on appeal must be with what happened and not with what might have happened. It makes no more sense to find ineffective representation based on the possibility of a conflict of interest, than it does to find ineffective representation based on the mere possibility of incompetent representation.

I am satisfied that a standard which would require appellate reversal of a conviction whenever it could be said that there was an appearance of a conflict of interests, could do significant harm to the criminal justice system. If that standard were adopted, it would either virtually eliminate the joint representation of co-accused, or it would permit accused to avail themselves of the advantages of joint representation at trial, secure in the knowledge that if the verdict went against them, reversal on appeal was a virtual certainty.

The approach developed in *Silvini*, requiring that an appellant demonstrate an actual conflict of interests which produced some adverse effect on counsel's representation of that appellant, offers full protection against ineffective representation flowing from counsel's divided loyalties. In my view, *Silvini* is a correct statement of the applicable law.

In the context of joint representation of co-accused, an actual conflict of interests exists where a course of conduct dictated by the best interests of one accused would, if followed, be inconsistent with the best interests of the co-accused: *Cuyler v. Sullivan, supra*, per Marshall J (dissenting in part) at p. 355, fn 3; *Baty v. Balkcom*, 661 F2d 391 at p. 395 (5th Cir., 1981), cert. denied 405 US 1011 (1982); *Tate v. State*, 515 NE 2d 1145 at pp. 1147-48 (Ind. App. 2 Dist., 1987); *United States v. Boling*, 869 F2d 965 at pp. 971-72 (6th Cir., 1989). Obviously, if the interests of both clients dictate that the same course of conduct should be followed, albeit for different reasons, there is a coincidence rather than a conflict of interests: *United States v. Gambolino*, 864 F2d 1064 at pp. 1070-71 (3rd Cir., 1988).

It is incumbent on an appellant to point to a specific instance or instances where the appellant's interests and those of the co-accused diverged, requiring counsel to choose between them: *Thomas v. Foltz*, 818 F2d 476 at p. 481 (6th Cir., 1987). That is not to say that an appellant must demonstrate that counsel consistently favoured the co-accused's interests. If, at any point in the course of the joint retainer, counsel, when faced with conflicting interests, took a course of action which adversely impacted on the effectiveness of counsel's representation of the appellant, then the appellant has established the necessary adverse effect.

Much time was spent during the appellants' submissions suggesting different trial tactics which might have been employed, and the various benefits which may have accrued to either or both of the appellants, had they been separately represented at trial. Counsel for Mrs. Widdifield suggested, for example, that had Mrs. Widdifield been separately represented, she would have enjoyed the benefit of a "friendly" cross-examination of Mr. Widdifield by her own counsel.

This submission misses the point. Assuming that Mrs. Widdifield would have benefited from such a cross-examination, the loss of that benefit neither demonstrates nor creates the necessary conflict of interests between Mrs. Widdifield and her husband. Counsel's representation is not rendered ineffective because counsel, if acting for only one of the appellants, may have rendered more effective assistance. The question is not whether the appellants could have been more effectively represented by separate counsel, but whether their joint representation placed counsel in a conflict of interests such that the assistance provided to either or both clients was adversely affected.

The appellants' submission that they need only show that trial counsel gave less consideration to possible defence strategies available to each accused than counsel acting for only one of the accused might have given also misses the mark. A failure to give adequate consideration to possible defence strategies can lead to a finding that counsel provided ineffective assistance if that failure can properly be characterized as incompetence within the meaning of the prevailing case-law: see, e.g., *R v. Collier* (1992), 77 CCC (3d) 570 (Ont. CA), leave to appeal to SCC. refused (1994), 91 CCC (3d) vi. That contention is not made here. Absent incompetence, the appellants can succeed only if they can link the alleged failure to give adequate individual consideration to each appellant's defence to an existing conflict between the interests of the appellants.

I have stressed the need to demonstrate both an actual conflict of interests and an adverse effect on counsel's performance flowing from that conflict. The two requirements are distinct and together produce a miscarriage of justice. Where, however, a conflict of interests exists between jointly tried co-accused, an action by counsel which gives preference to the interests of one accused will almost inevitably produce the required adverse effect on counsel's representation of the other accused: *Tate v. State*, *supra*, at p. 1148; *Sullivan v. Cuyler*, 553 F. Supp. 1236 at p. 1242 (ED Pa., 1982), affirmed 723 F2d 1077 at pp. 1085-86 (3rd Cir., 1983); W. LaFave and J. Israel, *Criminal Procedure*, vol. 2 (St. Paul: West Publishing, 1984) at pp. 92-93. Consequently, in most cases involving allegations of conflicts of interests arising out of the joint defence of co-accused who are jointly tried, the real issue on appeal will be whether there was an actual conflict of interests. If that conflict is demonstrated, the conclusion that at least one of the co-accused did not receive effective representation will follow in most cases.

VI. Was There a Conflict of Interests in This Case?

Trial counsel had been a lawyer for some 18 years at the time of trial. He is a general practitioner and regularly appears on behalf of persons charged with criminal offences. Trial counsel was familiar with and understood the prohibition against representing clients with conflicting interests. He perceived no potential conflict of interests when first retained by the appellants or at any point throughout his joint representation of them. In trial counsel's initial conversations with appellate counsel, he did not suggest any potential conflict. After appellate counsel raised the possibility of a conflict of interests and referred to *Silvini*, trial counsel wrote to appellate counsel indicating that he "may well have placed [himself] in a conflict of interests." In his affidavit executed on August 25, 1994, counsel stated that the conclusion set out in his earlier correspondence had been "reinforced" by further consideration of his position. In cross-examination, trial counsel testified that he had come to the view that he was in a conflict of interests from the outset of his representation of the two appellants.

Trial counsel candidly acknowledged that his retrospective determination that he had operated under a conflict of interests was significantly affected by what he regarded as the injustice of the verdicts returned by the jury. The following passage from his cross-examination is pertinent:

> A. Let me put it to you this way, just so you understand my feelings. I am troubled with the verdict. I have to think back about what went wrong as far as the trial is concerned. I honestly believe in the innocence of these individuals. I know these individuals as a result of spending a lot of time with them in terms of preparing for this particular case, and I thought that the verdict was wrong. I just honestly believe that.

Q. Is there a natural tendency for trial counsel to look back on a trial that had a surprising outcome and second guess some of the tactical decisions that were made?

A. Certainly.

Q. And is it fair that a large part of your concern over what you didn't do or might have done really reflects the fact that you were very surprised by this verdict and feel that it's an unjust verdict?

A. That's a fair statement.

Q. And that leads you to assume that there must have been something you could have done differently?

A. Well, certainly it causes me to pause and give a lot of thought to that, yes.

Trial counsel indicated that he was retained by both appellants shortly after they were charged in April 1991. Both appellants were at the initial meeting. Counsel recalled that he advised the appellants of their right to separate representation. He stated that it was his practice, when approached by co-accused, to explain the possible benefits of joint representation and to advise both accused that if any conflict developed he could not continue to act for both of them. Trial counsel did not urge the appellants to obtain separate representation as he did not perceive any potential conflict of interests.

The appellants made it clear that both wished to be represented by trial counsel. There were several reasons for their decision. Trial counsel had previously represented Mr. Widdifield in a civil matter and had developed a good rapport with him. Trial counsel had also successfully defended L.W.'s stepfather on a charge of sexual assault made by her, and had represented the stepfather and his wife in family court proceedings arising out of L.W.'s allegations. As a result of this prior involvement, trial counsel was familiar with much of the background to these charges and had previously (apparently successfully) cross-examined the complainant. The appellants also had a financial reason for seeking joint representation. Their defence was funded by the Legal Aid Plan and they were required to place a lien in favour of the Plan on their jointly owned property. They were anxious, therefore, to minimize the costs associated with their defence.

From the first meeting with trial counsel, both appellants denied that the acts complained of ever took place. Their position did not change throughout the almost two years they were represented by counsel. While Mr. Widdifield dominated the meetings involving both clients, Mrs. Widdifield never took exception to anything said by her husband. Trial counsel explained his relationship with his clients in these terms:

Q. When you made the decision throughout the course of the trial that I referred to, at that time, what was in your mind?

A. Well, in my mind was the instructions of my client and there was sort of a strategy that was agreed upon before trial. As I said previously, that strategy came essentially from William Widdifield in the presence of Ivana [Mrs. Widdifield].

Q. And when you made those decisions, were you taking into account the fact that you were representing two clients?

A. Well, one thing you have to understand. I wasn't making decisions, I was giving advice and taking instructions. I gave advice based on my instructions.

Q. From both—

A. And my advice was in a large part based on what was being told to me about the ability of Ivana to give evidence and also with respect to what transpired.

Q. And was that information that you received from both Widdifields?

A. Yes.

Significantly, the position of the appellants has not changed in the two years that they have been separately represented. Neither appellant filed any material on this appeal purporting to alter, even by one iota, the positions both had taken with trial counsel throughout his retainer. Nor have the appellants filed any material suggesting that their ability to communicate with and instruct trial counsel was in any way fettered by their joint representation. Having had the benefit of separate representation for some two years, neither appellant has suggested that had they been separately represented prior to or at trial, they would have provided their trial counsel with further or different information or instructions.

Based on the appellants' instructions, the disclosure provided by the Crown and the evidence adduced at the preliminary inquiry, trial counsel advanced the same defence on behalf of both appellants. Through cross-examination, defence evidence, and closing argument, he contended that the alleged assaults had not occurred and that the complainant could not be believed for a variety of reasons. The defence submissions were consistent with the position taken by the appellants throughout their relationship with trial counsel and applied with equal force to both. This was clearly not a situation in which there could be any conflict with respect to the fundamental positions advanced by the appellants. Their cause was a common cause.

The interests of co-accused who advance the same defence and share the same factual position may still come into conflict in the course of the criminal process. The appellants contend that despite their common position their interests did come into conflict at several specific points. They further contend that at those points counsel did not render effective assistance to either or both of them.

Counsel for Mrs. Widdifield submits that the facts presented in this case suggest that Mrs. Widdifield, who was obviously less culpable than her husband, may have been able to negotiate a favourable settlement of her case with the Crown. It is argued that trial counsel's representation of Mr. Widdifield prevented him from pursuing this course on her behalf.

Plea negotiations on behalf of Mrs. Widdifield was not an available option. Mrs. Widdifield had denied (and apparently continues to deny) any involvement in or knowledge of the alleged assaults. Any attempt to negotiate a plea in view of her instructions may well have been contrary to the prevailing rules of professional conduct. More importantly, any such attempt was doomed to failure. The absence of any effort to undertake plea negotiations on behalf of Mrs. Widdifield was not a decision tainted by a conflict of interests. It was instead a decision dictated by, and wholly consistent with, Mrs. Widdifield's instructions to counsel.

Counsel next submit that trial counsel should have moved for severance and that he failed to do so because of the conflicting interests he was trying to serve at trial. Both appellants contend that they were adversely affected by the failure to apply for severance.

In his cross-examination, trial counsel acknowledged that he gave some, but not much, consideration to a severance application. He went on to say that in looking back on the matter he would have considered more seriously the possibility of bringing a motion for severance had he acted for only one of the appellants. Trial counsel referred to the severance of counts 1, 2 and 3 from counts 4 and 5, and the severance of the accused.

In my view, a severance of counts was not a realistic option. I do not think that Mr. Widdifield could have avoided a single trial on all counts. The allegations arose out of an ongoing course of conduct between him and the complainant. The evidence concerning the earlier allegations of sexual misconduct would have been admissible on the counts relating to the events at the cottage in 1987. I will, therefore, address this argument only in the context of a potential application for severance of the accused on counts 1 and 2.

Were the interests of the appellants in conflict in so far as the advisability of a motion for severance was concerned? I think not. There were advantages and disadvantages to both appellants associated with either a joint or a separate trial. At a joint trial, for example, Mr. Widdifield would suffer the potential prejudice associated with the risk that the jury would, contrary to the trial judge's instructions, use Mrs. Widdifield's statement against him. On the other hand, Mr. Widdifield stood to gain by standing shoulder to shoulder with his wife in joint denial of the allegations. Their solidarity may have been particularly beneficial given the nature of the charges and the familial connection with the complainant. With respect to Mrs. Widdifield, a joint trial meant that she had to suffer the potential prejudice of the admission of the evidence of the earlier assaults which had nothing to do with her. That potential prejudice could be minimized but not necessarily erased by the appropriate instructions from the trial judge. There were, however, benefits accruing to Mrs. Widdifield by virtue of a joint trial. She apparently would not have made a very good witness. At a joint trial, she could let her husband, the more intelligent and verbally skilled of the two, take the witness stand and put forward the defence on behalf of both. This advantage was particularly significant in relation to Mrs. Widdifield's statement. Mr. Widdifield, in his evidence, advanced a plausible exculpatory explanation for the statement made by his wife to the police. In a joint trial, Mrs. Widdifield could have that explanation put before the jury without undergoing the risks associated with testifying.

I cannot say that either separate trials or a joint trial was in the best interests of one appellant, but not the other. Severance had its pros and cons from the perspective of both appellants. When the potential benefit and harm to each appellant associated with severance or a joint trial is assessed, I do not see any significant difference in the net position of either appellant. Whatever may be said of the wisdom of counsel's decision to proceed with a joint trial, I am satisfied that counsel did not labour under a conflict of interests when making that decision.

Counsel for Mr. Widdifield next submitted that Mr. Widdifield's best interests conflicted with his wife's best interests in so far as the approach to be taken to her statement to police was concerned. Counsel submits that it would have been in Mr. Widdifield's best interests to argue that the evidence of the police officers should not be believed and that the jury should conclude that Mrs. Widdifield did not make the statement. Counsel contends that trial counsel could not make that argument on behalf of Mr. Widdifield because, as regards Mrs. Widdifield, the statement was exculpatory. It was in her best interests, therefore, to accept the evidence that she had made the statement.

Trial counsel tried unsuccessfully to have the statement excluded. After the statement was admitted he advanced three arguments in an effort to neutralize its effect. Counsel pointed out that the statement was, on its face, a denial and not an admission. He further argued that Mrs. Widdifield was under a severe strain when she made the statement and could not be expected to provide a comprehensive and articulate outline of her position. Trial counsel observed that the police officers, who were under no such stress, did not request any clarification or elaboration from Mrs. Widdifield. Finally, counsel relied on Mr. Widdifield's evidence that he had previously told his wife about the nature of the complainant's allegation as providing an innocuous explanation for her statement.

Counsel's attempt to exclude the statement and the positions advanced once the statement was admitted were all in the best interests of Mrs. Widdifield. She would have been better off had the jury never heard the statement. Once the statement was adduced in evidence it was clearly in her best interests that the jury view it as exculpatory or, at worst, neutral. Although Mrs. Widdifield's statement was not admissible against Mr. Widdifield, he no doubt would have preferred that the jury not hear the statement. It was in his best interests also that counsel move to exclude it. Once the statement was admitted it was in Mr. Widdifield's best interests that the jury view the statement as a denial of culpability or, at worst, an innocuous statement.

I cannot agree that counsel did not advance the further argument that the statement was not made because he regarded it as in Mrs. Widdifield's best interests to accept the evidence that it was made. Counsel's efforts to exclude the statement indicate that he did not regard it as exculpatory in so far as Mrs. Widdifield was concerned. I think that his assessment was an accurate one. Had it been viable to argue that the statement was not made, that argument would also have served the best interests of both appellants. In my view, without any evidence to contradict the evidence of the officer, an argument that the statement was not made was at best a very weak one. To raise it could only have detracted from the stronger arguments advanced on behalf of both appellants by trial counsel. I see no conflict of interests as between the appellants with respect to the approach to be taken to Mrs. Widdifield's statement. The approach taken by trial counsel served the best interests of both clients.

I turn next to the contention made on behalf of Mrs. Widdifield that counsel's advice to her that she should not testify was motivated by a desire to protect Mr. Widdifield from any adverse consequences of her testimony. Counsel submits that trial counsel sacrificed Mrs. Widdifield's opportunity to tell her version of events to the jury in the service of Mr. Widdifield's defence.

In his initial correspondence with appellate counsel a few days after the verdict, trial counsel wrote:

> Michael [William] Widdifield gave evidence at trial on behalf of the defence. Ivana Widdifield did not take the stand due to the fact that it was felt that she would have considerable difficulty with cross-examination in light of her background/ antecedents.

In a subsequent letter sent to appellate counsel in January 1993, trial counsel wrote:

Mike [William] was called as a witness at the jury trial. Ivana was not called as a witness due to the fact that it was believed she would not leave a favourable impression on the jury.

In his affidavit sworn in August 1994, trial counsel said:

William Widdifield testified at the trial, Ivana Widdifield did not. I considered her to be of weaker character, a person who could easily be confused and became flustered under cross-examination. It was both my opinion, and that of her husband, that she should not testify, and she went along with this decision. It is impossible, in hindsight, to say that I would have advised her to testify if I had been representing only her. Given my assessment of Ivana Widdifield, I believe that she would have relied upon me to make the decision for her had she been my sole client. It is very possible that I would have counselled her to testify had I not also represented her husband as my attention would have been focussed only on her and her best interests. It was my opinion at trial that she may have harmed the cause of her husband if she testified.

In trial counsel's cross-examination on his affidavit, he was asked why he was of the opinion that Mrs. Widdifield would not make a good witness. He responded:

The problem for Ivana is she had, in my view, relatively low intelligence. She was not particularly articulate. She had difficulty in being particularly responsive to questions, and she was extremely nervous about taking the stand as well. She didn't want to take the stand. It would have been very difficult for her emotionally, in my opinion, for her to take the stand.

The cross-examination of counsel on this point culminated with this exchange:

Q. Well, the factors which you state led you to conclude that she should not take the stand were all factors that were personal to Ivana Widdifield; they related to how she would fare in the witness box, her ability to answer questions. Would you agree that none of those factors would have been any different if she had been your sole client?
A. Well, that is accurate, yes.
Q. So, given that the factors in the equation would have been identical, is it fair to assume that the outcome of the equation would likely have been the same?
A. I don't know. That's where I run into a problem. I really don't know. If I was representing Ivana by herself, I would have been seeing her by myself. I don't know if the instructions would have been different. I don't know if there would have been a different coloration to the version that I in fact received from the Widdifields. I just honestly don't know the answer to that question.

The suggestion in trial counsel's final answer, that Mrs. Widdifield's instructions or version of events may have been different had she been separately represented, can be safely discounted. She has been separately represented for over two years and there is no indication that her position has changed. I am left, therefore, to consider a decision to advise Mrs. Widdifield not to testify based on factors which would have applied with equal force had Mrs. Widdifield been separately represented. Trial counsel made a considered decision that Mrs. Widdifield would have made a poor witness and would have hurt her own cause had she testified. Based on that assessment, it was clearly in her best interests not to testify. The fact that she may also have done harm to Mr. Widdifield's defence had she done so does not detract from the conclusion that it was not in her best interests to testify. Nor does it create a conflict of interests. To the contrary, the concerns about the impact on Mr. Widdifield's defence, should Mrs. Widdifield testify, led to the same conclusion as that reached when the question was considered from the vantage point of Mrs. Widdifield's best interests. From both perspectives, it was unwise for Mrs. Widdifield to testify. Counsel's advice to Mrs. Widdifield that she should not testify served the best interests of both appellants.

Counsel for Mrs. Widdifield also submits that had she been separately represented, her counsel could have submitted that, while Mr. Widdifield may have committed the assaults, Mrs. Widdifield was not a party to them. Clearly, if this argument could have been made at trial, the interests of the appellants were in conflict. I do not, however, regard this position as one which was realistically available to Mrs. Widdifield in the circumstances of this case.

In order to advance the argument now put forward on appeal, counsel for Mrs. Widdifield would have had to invite the jury to accept the complainant's evidence when she testified that she was assaulted by Mr. Widdifield, but to reject her evidence when she testified that Mrs. Widdifield assisted in that assault. While a jury is always at liberty to accept only part of a witness's testimony, I can see no rational basis in the context of this complainant's evidence for a jury making the distinction that this argument would have entailed. How, I wonder, could counsel suggest, with one breath, that the complainant told the truth about Mr. Widdifield's assaults on her, and with the next breath contend that she totally fabricated her allegation that Mrs. Widdifield assisted in those same assaults? Had counsel made this argument, counsel's credibility before the jury would have been destroyed and with it any hope that Mrs. Widdifield may have been acquitted. The suggestion that it may have been to Mrs. Widdifield's benefit to contend that her husband had committed the assaults, but that she had not assisted him in doing so is untenable on the evidence adduced before this jury. This argument seems to me designed more to create the appearance of conflict on appeal than to suggest a course of conduct that may have been in Mrs. Widdifield's best interests at trial.

Lastly, counsel advanced an omnibus argument predicated on the contention that the joint representation of the appellants at trial "linked" the appellants in the eyes of the jury. Trial counsel put it this way in his affidavit:

> I am concerned that the jury may have linked both appellants in rendering their verdicts because of my joint representation of them. This linkage, in particular, could have harmed the appellant Ivana Widdifield given that the allegations against her suggested that she acted as a party to her husband's crimes.

Where two persons who are alleged to have jointly committed a crime are tried together there is always a danger that the case against one accused will infect the jury's assessment of the case against the other. The danger necessitates an appropriate limiting instruction from the trial judge. That instruction was given in this case. The danger of improper "linkage" may increase where the co-accused are represented by the same counsel, but it exists regardless of whether the co-accused are in a position of conflict of interests. Indeed, it is arguable that the danger is greatest when the co-accused share the same position. Absent a showing of an actual conflict of interests, the suggestion that the jury may have improperly "linked" the appellants on account of their joint representation does not advance the claim that the appellants received ineffective legal representation as a result of joint representation. In any event, there is no basis in this record, apart from trial counsel's speculation, that the jury did improperly "link" the two appellants in striving at its verdicts. I see no reason to think that the jury did not follow the instructions of the trial judge and consider the case against each appellant separately.

VII. Conclusion

I would dismiss the appeals from conviction.

VIII. The Sentence Appeals

Mr. Widdifield was sentenced to three years in the penitentiary. He has no criminal record, has always been steadily employed and has worked hard to raise his own family since his marriage in 1987. The family's lot has not been an easy one. The Widdifields have a son and a daughter. Their son, Alex, has significant behavioural problems which require constant attention. Alex has also had difficulty learning to speak. We were provided with fresh evidence updating the family's progress since conviction. That material indicates that Mr. Widdifield and Mrs. Widdifield continue to try their best to keep the family together and to provide whatever help they can in attending to the special needs of Alex. It is said that both Mr. and Mrs. Widdifield are very involved parents who display a real commitment to their children and family life.

Despite these mitigating factors and Alex's special needs, denunciation and general deterrence must be given predominate consideration in determining the appropriate sentence. I am satisfied that the sentence imposed was a fit one. The sexual abuse perpetrated by Mr. Widdifield occurred over a very long period of time, beginning with inappropriate touching and escalating to actual sexual intercourse. The complainant was very young when the assaults began. She was entitled to look to Mr. Widdifield for protection and support, but instead suffered continuous abuse at his hands.

Mrs. Widdifield received a sentence of one year. She has no criminal record. She is also working very hard to be a good mother to her children and to help Alex with his special problems. Mrs. Widdifield was physically abused as a child by her own father and has only recently come to terms with the ongoing effect of that abuse on her. The impact of the charges and prosecution on Mrs. Widdifield has been very severe. Apparently, she lost some 100 pounds in the course of the proceedings.

Mrs. Widdifield assisted in the most severe assault perpetrated by Mr. Widdifield on the complainant. It must, however, be acknowledged that Mrs. Widdifield came into an ongoing abusive relationship. She is apparently more passive and less intelligent than her husband. It is a fair inference that Mr. Widdifield initiated the assaults to which Mrs. Widdifield was a party.

Mrs. Widdifield's case presents a very difficult sentencing problem. It is important to try to preserve the Widdifield family unit. The longer the sentence imposed on Mrs. Widdifield the greater the risk to the ongoing viability of that family unit. As in the case of Mr. Widdifield, however, denunciation and deterrence must be given primary consideration. I cannot say that the sentence imposed on Mrs. Widdifield was outside of the appropriate range. Concerns with respect to the adverse impact of Mrs. Widdifield's incarceration on her family must be addressed to the appropriate correctional and parole authorities.

I would grant leave to appeal against sentence to both appellants, but would dismiss both appeals.

Appeal dismissed.

NOTES AND QUESTIONS

1. According to the court in *Widdifield*, a breach of the lawyer's duty of loyalty (at least in the criminal context) may lead to a finding of "ineffective counsel." The court went on to describe the costs associated with ineffective counsel as follows:

> If an accused does not receive the effective assistance of counsel at trial, the adversary system cannot function properly, the appearance of fairness suffers, and the reliability of the verdict is called into question.

How would you describe these costs in economic terms? What is the best method of combating these costs: a compensatory model of regulation, a punishment model of regulation, or some combination of the two? How would the appropriate model function in this context?

2. According to the court in *Widdifield*:

> A lawyer can render effective assistance only when that lawyer gives the accused's cause the undivided loyalty which is a prerequisite to proper legal representation. Within the limits imposed by legal and ethical constraints, the lawyer must champion the accused's cause without regard to counsel's personal interests or the interests of anyone else.

Is this an accurate statement? Does the lawyer truly abandon his or her own personal interests in pursuit of a client's goals? When answering this question, consider whether *free* legal advice would advance the client's goals more than legal advice in exchange for fees. Is the lawyer undermining the client's interests (in favour of the lawyer's personal interests) by charging the client for advice? Even aside from the question of fees, is it ever sensible to expect a person to set aside his or her self-interest in favour of the interests of another? In the context of the lawyer–client relationship, is it not more accurate to suggest that, to the greatest extent possible, the lawyer should ensure that his or her interests coincide with those of the client? For a discussion of this issue, see section I.

3. Based on the court's decision in *Widdifield*, construct an economic account of the decision to accept or reject a joint retainer. Describe this decision from the lawyer's perspective as well as from the perspective of the client.

4. When considering whether to interfere with the trial court's decision, the court in *Widdifield* held that "[t]he question is not whether the appellants could have been more effectively represented by separate counsel, but whether their joint representation placed counsel in a conflict of interests such that the assistance provided to either or both clients was adversely affected." What does this passage mean?

5. In this case, Mr. and Mrs. Widdifield were supported by their former lawyer's affidavit, in which the lawyer asserted that he had, in fact, acted in a situation involving a conflict of interest. Assuming that this admission could expose the Widdifields' former lawyer to professional sanctions or disciplinary proceedings, why would he make this admission? Is he truly sacrificing his best interests in favour of those of his clients?

6. If the original lawyer in *Widdifield* had not supported the Widdifields' claim that the joint retainer had given rise to a conflict of interest, would it be proper for him to give evidence *opposing* the Widdifields' claim? For example, could the lawyer submit an affidavit (for the Crown) in which he claimed that no conflict of interest had arisen? Would this be an instance of the lawyer preferring his own interests (for example, his interest in avoiding professional sanctions) over those of the clients (who hope to be acquitted)? If so, should we nonetheless allow lawyers to oppose their former clients in such situations? Consider the impact of the codes of professional conduct on this decision. Also revisit chapter 7, section II, "Lawyer Self-Interest."

IV. Acting Against Former Clients

A. Introduction

Where a lawyer has acted for a particular client, should that lawyer be permitted to act *against* the same client in subsequent matters? In other words, does the so-called duty of loyalty, like the lawyer's duty of confidentiality, continue beyond the conclusion of a retainer? This question is addressed by the rules of professional conduct of several jurisdictions. Ontario's *Rules of Professional Conduct*, for example, provide as follows:

> 2.04(4) A lawyer who has acted for a client in a matter shall not thereafter act against the client or against persons who were involved in or associated with the client in that matter:
>
>> (a) in the same matter,
>>
>> (b) in any related matter, or
>>
>> (c) save as provided by subrule (5), in any new matter,
>
> if the lawyer has obtained from the other retainer relevant confidential information unless the client and those involved in or associated with the client consent.[16]
>
> 2.04(5) Where a lawyer has acted for a former client and obtained confidential information relevant to a new matter, the lawyer's partner or associate may act in the new matter against the former client if:

---

16   The commentary to this rule provides that "[i]t is not improper for the lawyer to act against a client in a fresh and independent matter wholly unrelated to any work the lawyer has previously done for that person and where previously obtained confidential information is irrelevant to that matter."

(a) the former client consents to the lawyer's partner or associate acting, or

(b) the law firm establishes that it is in the interests of justice that it act in the new matter, having regard to all relevant circumstances, including

(i) the adequacy and timing of the measures taken to ensure that no disclosure of the former client's confidential information to the partner or associate having carriage of the new matter will occur,

(ii) the extent of prejudice to any party,

(iii) the good faith of the parties,

(iv) the availability of suitable alternative counsel, and

(v) issues affecting the public interest.

The text of these rules reveals their purpose. Rule 2.04(4) makes it clear that the rules relate to the lawyer's possession of confidential information. Having represented the former client in an earlier transaction or proceeding, the lawyer will have collected confidential information concerning that client. If allowed to act against the former client in later proceedings, the lawyer may be tempted to use this confidential information (to the extent that it is relevant) *against* the former client. The source of this temptation should be obvious. The use or disclosure of the former client's information may enable the lawyer to better pursue the interests of the lawyer's current client. Since, as we have seen in section I, lawyers have a vested interest in pursuing the interests of their current clients, the lawyer may have a personal interest in divulging a former client's confidential information. Indeed, divulging the former client's information may be the fastest way of achieving the legal objectives of the current client. To the extent that the lawyer is thought to remain loyal to former clients, he or she is tempted to violate this duty of loyalty. As a result, a conflict of interest is said to exist. Since this conflict of interest relates to the lawyer's possession of confidential information, exceptions to the rule against opposing former clients relate to cases in which the lawyer is *not* in possession of relevant confidential information.

In chapters 6 and 7 we saw that lawyers owe their clients a continuing duty of confidentiality. Generally speaking, lawyers are prohibited from divulging or using their clients' (or former clients') confidential information. Since the use or disclosure of former clients' confidential information is already prohibited by the rules of professional conduct, it may seem unnecessary to further prevent the use of confidential information by preventing lawyers from acting against former clients in subsequent matters. As we saw in chapter 6, if the lawyer *does* divulge or use the former client's private information (whether in subsequent proceedings or any other context), the lawyer will be subjected to tort liability and disciplinary measures. Why, then, do we need the added protection provided by the rule against opposing former clients? Is this rule redundant, given the fact that confidentiality is already protected by other rules of professional conduct? Consider the answer to these questions when reviewing the cases that follow.[17]

---

17   Some possible answers to this question are presented in the notes and questions following the account of *MacDonald Estate v. Martin*, above, section II.

R v. Zwicker
(1995), NBJ no. 502

THE COURT: Bucky Dean Zwicker pleaded guilty to the theft of a fishing vessel, an offence under s. 334(a) of the *Criminal Code* of Canada. The vessel was damaged to the extent of $22,000.00 as a result of the theft. On April 5, 1995, Mr. Zwicker was sentenced to 12 months imprisonment to be followed by two years of probation. In addition, pursuant to s. 725 of the *Criminal Code*, the sentencing Judge ordered Mr. Zwicker to pay $22,000.00 to the owner of the vessel as compensation for the damage caused to the vessel resulting from the theft. He now seeks leave to appeal his sentence. We grant leave.

Although this is a sentence appeal, Mr. Zwicker submits that the conviction should be quashed because counsel for the Crown at the sentencing hearing, Randall Wilson, had represented Mr. Zwicker when he entered a plea of guilty to the charge. While counsel should never place himself or herself in a position of conflict, the situation here is exacerbated by the forceful representations made by Mr. Wilson both when he was representing Mr. Zwicker and when he was representing the Crown.

Following Mr. Zwicker's plea of guilty on March 15, 1995, Mr. Wilson made a strong plea for a non-custodial sentence. After outlining the events that led to the theft and damage of the boat, he pointed out that Mr. Zwicker made a statement implicating himself without which the charge could not have been laid. He concluded his remarks by saying:

> ... [Mr. Zwicker] realizes that the owner has had substantial losses; had substantial down time. He knows that the people on Grand Manan are outraged at his behaviour and he thinks this is a—an opportunity for himself to go back to Grand Manan and to get work and to pay this individual back which he fully intends to do. And he wishes that in lieu of incarceration.

The sentencing Judge requested a pre-sentence report and adjourned the sentencing hearing to April 5, at which time Mr. Wilson appeared for the Crown. He opened his remarks on sentencing as follows:

> It is the crown's position that, ah, Mr. Zwicker should go to jail, and should go to jail for a significant period of time. We base this on the magnitude of the crime that was committed and also upon the impact that it had on the victim. ...

Mr. Wilson then cited two decisions in which imprisonment for one year was imposed for theft of an automobile. He went on to describe Mr. Zwicker as having "a very poor work record" and a "very poor reputation." He pointed out that Mr. Zwicker was then imprisoned for other offences. He concluded his remarks as follows:

> ... This man should go to jail, Your Honour. He should go to jail for a long time. ...

An example of an inadvertent conflict that might not attract sanction is found in *R v. Dobrotic* (1995), NBR (2d) Advance Sheets, No. 62, August 6, 1995, p. 63 at p. 68. The conflict here, as illustrated by the above passages, is much more serious. Mr. Wilson made strong representations for a non-custodial sentence on behalf of Mr.

Zwicker on March 15 and on April 5, on behalf of the Crown, was strongly urging a "significant" jail sentence.

The Crown concedes that Mr. Wilson's dual representation violated Mr. Zwicker's s. 7 Charter right not to be deprived of his liberty except in accordance with the principles of fundamental justice. Mr. Wilson's actions, in our view, amount to a breach of the solicitor–client relationship formed by virtue of Mr. Wilson's March 15 representation of Mr. Zwicker as well as prosecutorial misbehaviour. A lawyer acquires confidential information, which becomes privileged, when engaged by a client. A lawyer should not advise or represent different parties to a dispute. As a result of Mr. Wilson's actions in representing both Mr. Zwicker and the Crown, Mr. Zwicker is entitled to a remedy under s. 24(1) of the Charter.

Before considering the remedy, we would note that Mr. Zwicker was 21 years old when the offence occurred, that he has a criminal record both as a young offender and as an adult and that his Pre-Sentence Report was not favourable. Mr. Zwicker pleaded guilty and acknowledged damaging the vessel to the extent of at least $22,000.00. In our view, the appropriate s. 24(1) remedy is to reduce the sentence imposed on Mr. Zwicker to the time that he has now served and set aside the Probation Order. We would, however, maintain the conviction and Compensation Order.

For the above reasons, we allow the appeal and reduce the sentence of imprisonment of one year imposed on Mr. Zwicker to time now served and set aside the Probation Order.

NOTES AND QUESTIONS

1. Assume, for the moment, that someone other than Zwicker's former lawyer had made submissions (for the Crown) regarding the appropriate sentence. Would this have had a material impact on the outcome of the proceedings? In other words, did the identity of the lawyer for the Crown make a difference in this case? If not, was it appropriate to grant Zwicker a remedy under the Charter?

2. Was the accuracy, persuasiveness, or content of the submissions made by Zwicker's former lawyer affected in any way by the conflict of interest that was identified in this case? Does this matter?

3. At one point in the *Zwicker* case, the Crown conceded: "Mr. Wilson's dual representation violated Mr. Zwicker's s. 7 Charter right not to be deprived of his liberty except in accordance with the principles of fundamental justice." Do you agree? Specifically, do you agree that (1) access to a non-conflicted counsel is a principle of fundamental justice; and (2) that principle was violated (in a material way) in the *Zwicker* case?

4. If we believe in lawyers' integrity and accept that lawyers can act as zealous advocates for causes with which they do not agree, why are we bothered when an advocate switches sides? If we assume that Zwicker's former lawyer refrained from abusing his prior position as Zwicker's former lawyer, and made the same submissions that any competent Crown attorney would have made, should we be bothered by his decision to switch sides?

5. If the advocate is merely the mouthpiece of the client, does the identity of the mouthpiece *really* matter? Is an advocate really nothing more than a mouthpiece for the

client? For a review of the principles governing the lawyer's "zealous representation" of clients and the role the lawyer's personal ethical choices may play when the lawyer functions as a client's advocate, see chapter 3. A more general discussion of duties that arise when a lawyer functions as an advocate is presented in chapter 9.

6. Did the problem in *Zwicker* relate to the lawyer's possession of confidential information? Did the lawyer appear to use confidential information against Zwicker? If not, what is the purpose of preventing the lawyer from acting against Zwicker? Do the rules against opposing former clients pursue some policy other than the protection of confidential information? Do the rules simply relate to the appearance of impropriety? Is this adequate justification for granting a remedy under the Charter?

B. Lateral Moves

In *R v. Zwicker*, above, the question before the court involved a criminal-defence lawyer who performed an "about face," abandoning his client's defence and choosing instead to prosecute his former client. In other words, at various stages of the proceedings, the lawyer in *Zwicker* acted for parties with opposing interests. The ethical issues arising from such a maneuver should be obvious. A more difficult issue arises when the lawyer performs a "lateral move"—that is, when the lawyer withdraws from the representation of one client in a particular transaction or dispute, only to start representing a *different client on the same side* of that transaction or dispute. Should the lateral move be prohibited? Perhaps not. After all, a lateral move does not appear to require the lawyer to act *against* a former client. On the contrary, the lawyer's current and former clients are on the same side of the transaction or dispute. As a result, it is tempting to conclude that lateral moves do not entail conflicts of interest.

The case of *R v. J. (G.P.)* (2001), below, raises the issue of lateral moves. In that case, a lawyer who had represented a criminal complainant (that is, the alleged victim of the relevant crime) at the trial of the accused subsequently appeared as the lawyer for the Crown when the case was appealed. The court's decision in *R v. J. (G.P.)* reveals the conflicts of interest that may arise in such situations, showing how an apparent lateral move may ultimately lead a lawyer to act against his or her former client.

R v. J. (G.P.)
(2001), 151 CCC (3d) 382

PHILP JA:

Introduction

The accused was acquitted at trial before Oliphant ACJQB, sitting without a jury, of five counts of decades-old sexual offences (rape, sexual intercourse with a person under 14 years of age, indecent assault, buggery, and gross indecency) against the complainant, the youngest sister of his wife. The Crown has appealed, raising as questions of law orders made by the trial judge pursuant to ss. 278.1 to 278.91 of the *Criminal Code* with respect to the production of the complainant's counselling records.

At his trial, the accused was convicted of a sixth count in the indictment charging him with the offence of indecent assault of his niece, the daughter of another of his wife's sisters, and he was sentenced to a term of imprisonment of six months, to be served conditionally. That conviction was not appealed and is not before the Court.

The Issues

The principal issues before the Court on the appeal are the orders of the trial judge ordering production of counselling records for his review (s. 278.5) and production of a part of them to the accused (s. 278.7). These issues raise questions of law because Parliament has said so (s. 278.91). A final ground of appeal—the manner in which the trial judge used the counselling records that had been produced in assessing the complainant's credibility—sounds at best as one of mixed law and fact. ...

The Role of Counsel

The participation of the complainant's counsel at trial and her later appearance as counsel for the Crown on the appeal are matters that were not raised or argued at the appeal hearing and they play no part in the Court's disposition of the appeal. Nevertheless, they are matters on which I wish to make a few comments.

At common law, a witness who was not a party to the proceedings was not entitled to have his or her own counsel. See *Halsbury's Laws of England*, vol. 3, 3rd ed. (London: Butterworth & Co. (Publishers) Ltd., 1953) at 70, para. 104. In Canada, the *Canadian Bill of Rights* recognized an exception to that principle. Section 2(d) provides, in part:

> 2. ... [N]o law of Canada shall be construed or applied so as to. ...
> (d) authorize a court ... to compel a person to give evidence if he is denied counsel, protection against self crimination or other constitutional safeguards.

Judicial consideration of that provision is sparse. What comment there has been, however, suggests that the role of a witness's counsel is a limited one. See, for example, *R v. Hawke* (1975), 7 OR (2d) 145, 22 CCC (2d) 19 (CA), in which Dubin JA (as he then was), writing for the court, observed (at p. 183):

> ... [A] witness is not a party to the proceedings and does not become a party by the appointment of counsel on his or her behalf. The issue as to the relevancy and admissibility of evidence in a criminal case is one solely to be considered on the basis of the submissions of Crown counsel and defence counsel. It has been the traditional role of the judiciary to see that every witness is treated courteously and fairly. A witness does not need counsel to see that that right is preserved.

See also *Vapor Canada Ltd. v. MacDonald (No. 2)*, [1971] FC 465 (TD), in which Noël ACJ commented (at p. 467) that the intervention of counsel for a witness "should occur in exceptional cases only and only when [the fundamental rights of a witness] are infringed."

The role of counsel for a complainant or witness in a sexual assault case where production of his or her therapeutic records is sought was not discussed in *R v.*

O'Connor or in *R v. Mills*. (It is noted that in *R v. Mills*, the complainant, L.C., was the appellant to whom leave to appeal had been granted by the Supreme Court. However, she had been granted intervener status at trial for the purpose of the accused's challenge to the constitutionality of *Bill C-46*. It was her status *qua* intervener, not *qua* complainant or witness, that was recognized by the Supreme Court and which entitled her counsel to participate.)

However, in A. (L.L.) v. B. (A.), [1995] 4 SCR 536, 103 CCC (3d) 92, a decision released at the same time as *R v. O'Connor*, the Court considered its jurisdiction to entertain a third party's appeal from a trial judge's interlocutory ruling in a sexual assault case. L'Heureux-Dubé J, for a unanimous Court on this issue, wrote (at paras. 27 and 28):

> The one question that remains is whether both a complainant, a third party to the proceedings (whether or not an appellant, but here one of the appellants), and the Crown, a party to the proceedings, have standing in third party appeals. There is no doubt in my mind that they do. The *audi alteram partem* principle, which is a rule of natural justice and one of the tenets of our legal system, requires that courts provide an opportunity to be heard to those who will be affected by the decisions. ...
>
> Here, both the complainant and the Crown possess a direct and necessary interest in making representations. Both would be directly affected by a decision regarding the production of the complainant's private records. The decision is susceptible of affecting the course of the criminal trial. Both, therefore, must be afforded an opportunity to be heard.

That decision has been drawn upon to support the right of a complainant's counsel to participate at the hearing of an accused's application for production of third-party records. See *R v. Lee*, [1997] OJ No. 5574 (QL) (Gen. Div.) [summarized 36 WCB (2d) 257]. But in *R v. A.M.*, [1998] BCJ No. 1910 (QL) (SC) [summarized 39 WCB (2d) 291], Bennett J cautioned (at para. 13):

> This legislation gives complainants more rights in criminal cases than they have previously held. However, they have not been elevated to the position of a party in the litigation.

Under s. 278.3(5), the persons upon whom the accused must serve his application include the complainant or witness to whom the record relates. Section 278.4(2) provides that the person to whom the record relates "may appear and make submissions at the hearing." In Manitoba, those rights, in the case of a "victim," are supplemented by s. 4(2) of the *Victims' Rights Act*, SM 1998, c 44—Cap. V55, which provides:

> **Right to free independent counsel**
>
> 4(2) Victims are entitled to be given access to free, independent counsel when access to personal information about them is sought under section 278.3 of the *Criminal Code* (Canada).

It flows naturally from those rights that a complainant is entitled to the assistance of counsel when her constitutional rights are in the balance during the in camera hearing that must be held under s. 278.4(1). In my view, the participation of a complainant's counsel during her cross-examination at trial, limited, of course, to matters touching on the admissibility of the record, is also appropriate where an application under s. 278.3 is pending before the court. The complainant's testimony in those circumstances may well be part of the evidentiary foundation for the accused's application.

That is what happened in this case. The accused's second application seeking production of the complainant's counselling records had been filed before the commencement of the trial and was scheduled to be heard at the close of the Crown's case. The complainant's counsel was present and participated in the trial proceedings during the cross-examination of the complainant, at the in camera hearing, and during the subsequent proceedings leading up to the trial judge's order that part of the records be produced to the accused. She then withdrew. Her participation was limited to matters affecting the production of her client's counselling records. Her participation was, in my view, proper and appropriate.

It is counsel's appearance as counsel for the Crown on the appeal that is troubling to me. In my view, her appearance ignores the unique role of counsel for the Crown in the criminal justice system and raises serious conflict of interest concerns.

In *Boucher v. The Queen*, [1955] SCR 16, 110 CCC 263, Taschereau J had this to say of the position and duty of counsel for the Crown (at p. 21):

> [TRANSLATION] The position held by counsel for the Crown is not that of a lawyer in civil litigation. His functions are quasi-judicial. His duty is not so much to obtain a conviction as to assist the judge and jury in ensuring that the fullest possible justice is done. His conduct before the Court must always be characterized by moderation and impartiality. He will have properly performed his duty and will be beyond all reproach if, eschewing any appeal to passion, and employing a dignified manner suited to his function, he presents the evidence to the jury without going beyond what it discloses.

That comment was quoted in *R v. S. (F.)* (2000), 144 CCC (3d) 466 (Ont. CA), in which the unique role of Crown counsel was reviewed again. Labrosse JA, writing for the court, concluded that Crown counsel at trial had breached his duty, *inter alia*, by stating that it was his role to obtain a conviction, and by referring "to the complainant as 'notre victime', as if she were his client and inferring there was some bond between the jury and himself against the accused" (at para. 14).

It goes without saying that Crown counsel at trial could not accept a retainer from a complainant or a witness in the proceedings. Conflicts would abound! It is enough to mention the discretion Crown counsel enjoys in relation to the prosecution of a criminal offence. That responsibility is incompatible with the interests of a witness, particularly a complainant, when production of his or her record is sought by the accused in a s. 278.3 application. The duty of a prosecutor to produce to the accused all relevant information, both favourable and unfavourable, collides with the retainer of counsel representing a witness or a complainant in a s. 278.3 application—to oppose the production of his or her client's record.

It is not an answer to say that in this case counsel's retainer by the complainant ended when the trial judge ordered the production of her counselling records. A lawyer's absolute duty of confidentiality survives the termination of his or her retainer. More specific to the circumstances in this case, however, is the confidence of the public in the integrity of the profession and in the administration of the criminal justice system. There is, in my view, an appearance of impropriety in counsel's role as Crown counsel on the appeal.

The complainant alleged that the accused had committed serious sexual offences against her. Counsel represented the complainant during her cross-examination at trial, and in the subsequent proceedings on the accused's s. 278.3 application. The accused sought production of the complainant's counselling records in furtherance of his right to make full answer and defence. Counsel opposed the production of her client's records. Then she appeared as counsel on the Crown's appeal against the accused's acquittal.

There is, in my view, flowing from counsel's latter role the likely perception both in the eyes of the accused and in those of the informed and reasonable person, that the Crown and the complainant share a common purpose in seeking the conviction of the accused. That may well be the purpose of the complainant, but it is no part of the public duty of a prosecutor exercising his quasi-judicial functions.

· · ·

Disposition

The appeal should be dismissed.

NOTES AND QUESTIONS

1. Did the changing role of counsel in *R v. J. (G.P.)* constitute a lateral move? Why or why not?

2. In what sense could it be argued that the lawyer in this case was acting *against* the interests of her former client?

3. The court noted that counsel's changing role could give rise to "the likely perception both in the eyes of the accused and in those of the informed and reasonable person, that the Crown and the complainant share a common purpose in seeking the conviction of the accused." The court felt that this perception was wrong: the complainant had the purpose of seeking conviction, while the prosecutor had the "quasi-judicial" purpose of seeking the truth. Is there really a divergence between the interests of the complainant and the Crown? Does the complainant have an interest in convicting the accused *regardless of the accused's guilt*? If not, do the complainant and the Crown share a common purpose—that is, the conviction of the guilty? When answering this question, consider whether the Crown has an interest in convicting guilty persons based on improperly gathered evidence.

4. A central feature of the court's discussion of conflict of interest involved the court's perception of the lawyer's duty of confidentiality. At one point, the court stated that "[a] lawyer's absolute duty of confidentiality survives the termination of his or her retainer." Given the many exceptions to confidentiality noted in chapters 6 and 7, what might the judge have meant when referring to the "absolute duty of confidentiality"?

5. Is there such a thing as an "innocuous" lateral move, in which the interests of the lawyer's current and former clients could not come into conflict? If so, should such moves be permitted? If not, how should we regulate lateral moves?

C. MacDonald Estate revisited

In both *Zwicker* and *J. (G.P.)*, above, lawyers acted against their former clients in connection with the very matter in which they had appeared for the former clients: the lawyer who had defended Zwicker at trial acted on behalf of the Crown in the sentencing portion of Zwicker's trial, and the lawyer who had acted for the complainant in *J. (G.P.)* acted for the Crown on appeal. These cases are highly unusual. Lawyers rarely "switch clients" in the context of a single set of ongoing judicial proceedings. Most conflicts involving former clients arise when lawyers act against their former clients in *new proceedings* that bear little or no relationship to the proceedings in which the lawyer initially represented the former client. The most thorough recent analysis of the conflicts that arise in such cases is provided by the decision of the Supreme Court of Canada in *MacDonald Estate v. Martin* (1990), above, section II. Review that case and compare the court's decision to the rules of professional conduct set out in section IV.A, above.

V. Payment of Fees

A. Introduction

Section I demonstrated that one of the major reasons for a lawyer's loyalty to a client involves the receipt of legal fees. The lawyer appears to act in his or her client's best interests (rather than in pursuit of the lawyer's personal interests) because the lawyer is paid to do so: the payment of legal fees ensures that the lawyer's interest in monetary gain leads the lawyer to act for the benefit of the client. In other words, legal fees ensure that actions advancing a client's personal interests will also be in the interests of the lawyer. Legal fees accordingly cause the interests of lawyers and their clients to coincide.

In some cases, legal fees have the effect of causing the interests of the lawyer and the client to diverge. Consider the case in which someone *other* than the client pays the lawyer's fee. Here, the lawyer might feel obliged to please the party paying the fee rather than acting exclusively for the benefit of the client. According to Gavin Mackenzie:

> Lawyers must be vigilant in such cases to ensure that their loyalty to their clients is not compromised by loyalty to the interests of the persons who are paying their fees. The lawyer's duty in such [a] case is to pursue the client's interests singlemindedly. To pursue the interests of the party who is paying the lawyer's fee to the detriment of the client would be improper.[18]

As a result, cases in which the lawyer's fee is paid by someone other than the client may give rise to conflicting interests.

The decision of the BC Court of Appeal in *R v. Stork and Toews* (1975), discussed below, involves a case of third-party payments.[19]

---

18   MacKenzie, *supra* note 9, at 5-37.

19   Initially, *Stork and Toews* does not appear to involve a true third-party payment. The lawyer in the case acted for several accused persons whose legal bills were paid by one of the accused. Because of this, those payments count as third-party payments as far as the non-paying accused are concerned. The problem in

R v. Stork and Toews
(1975), 24 CCC (2d) 210 (BCCA)

FARRIS CJBC: This is an application by the two appellants to withdraw their pleas of guilty to a charge of conspiracy to traffic in cannabis resin. Both accused were represented at the trial (but not on this appeal) by Mr. N. N also represented the third accused by the name of Stenson. Stenson paid N fees which totalled $10,000 to defend him and also to defend Stork and Toews. A fourth accused, Bruce, was separately represented. Miss Norma Christie appeared for the Crown. In para. 17 of Mr. N's affidavit filed on this appeal he states:

> 17. THAT prior to the preliminary and during the preliminary, I had pressed MISS NORMA CHRISTIE and CORPORAL BEITEL and other senior members of the RCMP to accept the proposition that I was offering; the Crown should stay against BRUCE and STENSON and allow guilty pleas to be entered by STORK and TOEWS at the Provincial Court level,

This course was followed. In para. 27, Mr. N states:

> 27. THAT in fairness to the accused, STORK and TOEWS, I believe that they accepted my estimation of the case and accepted my advice that they should plead guilty. I believe that I influenced them in this regard and that they relied upon my judgment and upon my advice in deciding to plead guilty.

In my opinion, Mr. N was in a position of hopeless conflict of interest. Here, the man who was paying him goes free while the other two accused go to jail for five or eight years. While there is no attack on Mr. N's good faith, or indeed, upon the soundness of his advice, it does not seem to me that the plea of guilty obtained under such circumstances can stand when the accused ask to withdraw it. See *Adgey v. The Queen* (1973), 13 CCC (2d) 177 at pp. 189-90, 39 DLR (3d) 553, [1975] 2 SCR 426, where Mr. Justice Dickson in the Supreme Court of Canada said:

> This Court in *R v. Bamsey* (1960), 125 CCC 329 at p. 333, [1960] SCR 294, 32 CR 218, held that an accused may change his plea if he can satisfy the appeal Court "that there are valid grounds for his being permitted to do so." It would be unwise to attempt to define all that which might be embraced within the phrase "valid grounds." I have indicated above some of the circumstances which might justify the Court in permitting a change of plea. The examples given are not intended to be exhaustive.

There are valid grounds where the plea of guilty is obtained under circumstances that have such an appearance of unfairness as there is here. For these reasons I would allow the appeal and give permission for the withdrawal of the plea of guilty and direct a new trial be held.

Appeal allowed.

---

this case accordingly parallels the classic third-party payment problem. Rather than observing the duties owed to each of the lawyer's other clients, he or she is tempted to show allegiance only to the payor of the fees.

NOTES AND QUESTIONS

1. Do you agree with the court's finding that there was a "hopeless" conflict of interest in this case? Why or why not? What was the source of this apparent conflict?

2. If you believe that the lawyer in this case breached his duty of loyalty, what caused him to do so? If there was a breach of the duty of loyalty in this case (and a violation of the rules regarding conflict of interest), should this lawyer be subjected to professional sanctions? Why or why not?

3. Does the court's decision imply that lawyers' loyalty is for sale? If so, should that be troubling or surprising? Why or why not?

4. Is there any sense in which it could be argued that Mr. N's interests coincided with those of Stork and Toews at any point in the proceedings? If not, should the rules of professional conduct preclude lawyers from acting in situations of this nature? Do they?

B. Contingency Fees

Cases involving third-party payments are not the only ones in which the lawyer's fees can lead to conflicts of interest. In some cases, the lawyer may be paid a fee (often referred to as a contingency fee) only if he or she achieves a specified result for the client. For example, a litigator's retainer may provide that the litigator becomes entitled to payment only if he or she succeeds in obtaining a judgment for the client. If the litigator is successful, he or she will be paid a fee (perhaps based on a percentage of the value of the judgment). If the litigator is unsuccessful in obtaining a judgment for the client, he or she will not be paid at all. In this sense, the lawyer's payment is "contingent" on the results of the client's case.

Like third-party payments, contingency fees may result in conflicting interests. If the lawyer is in immediate need of cash, for example, a litigator working for contingency fees may have an interest in securing an early (and perhaps inadequate) settlement for the client, rather than fighting for a higher amount through long-term litigation. Where the client's interest would best be served by taking the matter to trial, and the lawyer's interest would best be served by accepting an immediate offer to settle, the interests of the client and the lawyer come into conflict. As a result, rules regulating contingency fee arrangements (and the conflicts of interests that such arrangements may cause) may be necessary.

Despite the ethical problems they may cause, contingency fee arrangements may be rather beneficial. As Gavin MacKenzie notes, "the main justification for allowing contingency fees is that they enable persons who might otherwise be unable to obtain redress for legal wrongs to finance litigation."[20] Stated simply, a client may be unable to afford to pay a lawyer unless the client's claim succeeds. If the client's claim is successful, the client can pay the lawyer out of the proceeds of the relevant settlement or judgment. If the client's claim is defeated, the client cannot afford to pay. If the client's case is likely to succeed (because the client is legally entitled to a payment, for example), it seems unfair to preclude the client from asserting his or her rights due to the fact that the client

---

20   MacKenzie, supra note 9, at 12-10.

cannot afford a lawyer. Contingency fees can help avoid this problem. Where a client has a meritorious claim but lacks the funds to hire a lawyer, the lawyer can help to vindicate the impoverished client's rights by agreeing to receive payment only if the client succeeds. Because contingency fee arrangements may increase access to justice, it may be advisable to permit contingency fees despite the ethical problems that such fees may cause.

While contingency fee arrangements have been permitted throughout most of North America for many years, the Law Society of Upper Canada has only recently allowed Ontario lawyers to enter into contingency fee arrangements. Ontario's new rules of professional conduct allow contingency fee arrangements under rule 2.08,[21] which provides (in part) as follows:

> 2.08(3) Subject to subrules (1), (4) and (5), except in family law or criminal or quasi-criminal matters, a lawyer may enter into a written agreement signed by the lawyer and his or her client, or where the client is under a disability, by the client's litigation guardian or other duly appointed representative, that provides that the lawyer's fee is contingent, in whole or in part, on a specified disposition of the matter for which the lawyer's services are to be provided.

> 2.08(4) An agreement under subrule (3) shall contain:

> (a) a statement of the method by which the fee is to be determined, including the percentage that may accrue to the lawyer in the event of settlement, trial or appeal, and

> (b) a statement that the client may apply to the Superior Court of Justice for a determination of whether the contingent fee is fair and reasonable.

> 2.08(5) Except as permitted by the *Class Proceedings Act*, 1992, or any order made under it, an agreement under subrule (3) shall not:

> (a) require the lawyer's consent if the client decides to discontinue or settle his or her claims, or

> (b) include a term that prevents the client from changing lawyers or ending the lawyer and client relationship at any time.

Having reviewed Ontario's rules regarding contingency fee arrangements, consider the following questions:

1. Should contingency fee arrangements be allowed? Does the policy of increasing access to justice outweigh the ethical problems that contingency fees may cause? If not, should contingency fees be banned altogether, or (as they are in Ontario) be subjected to judicial review on a case-by-case basis?

2. Rule 2.08 prohibits contingency arrangements in cases involving family law. Why? When answering this question, consider divorce proceedings. Specifically, consider (a) the lawyer's interest in being paid upon the successful completion of divorce proceedings, and (b) the parties' interests in reconciling. Should a lawyer have an interest in encouraging his or her client to go through with a divorce?

---

21   This rule was promulgated in October 2002.

3. Rule 2.08 precludes contingency fee arrangements in criminal cases. Why? What economic incentives does a rule against contingency fees provide?

4. Should contingency fees be made available only to clients who could not otherwise afford to pay for a lawyer's services? In other words, should wealthy clients pay their lawyers on an hourly basis, while impoverished parties pay contingency fees? What are the policy implications of this choice? Note that New Brunswick's *Judicature Act*, SNB 1978, c. J-2, s. 72.1 takes this approach, making contingency fee arrangements available only to clients who cannot otherwise afford to pay a lawyer.

5. Do contingency fees increase a lawyer's interest in "winning" the client's case? Do lawyers who are paid on an hourly basis (regardless of the outcome) have an interest in winning the client's case, or are they perfectly happy to lose?

6. Do hourly rates (as opposed to contingency fees) encourage lawyers to be inefficient (that is, to spend unwarranted time on a client's file in order to render a larger bill)? Do contingency fees provide more efficient incentives?

VI. The Lawyer's Personal Interest

Most of the conflicts of interest discussed in earlier portions of this chapter have arisen as a result of competing duties owed by lawyers. Where lawyers represent multiple clients, for example, the duties owed to the various clients may conflict with one another, generating an unacceptable conflict of interest. Similarly, where a lawyer acts against a former client, the duties owed to the former client may come into conflict with the duties owed to the lawyer's current clients. Finally, where lawyers' fees are paid by someone other than the lawyers' current clients, lawyers may owe competing allegiances to their clients and to the party who pays the fees. In each of these conflicting-duty cases, the lawyer's allegiance to the client comes into conflict with the lawyer's allegiance to another individual. In other words, the conflict-of-interests arise because of duties owed to competing individuals.

In many cases, a conflict of interest arises in the absence of conflicting obligations owed to clients or third parties. Consider the following example.

Example 8.6

Claudia Doyle is launching a bid to acquire 100 percent of the issued and outstanding shares of HugeCo, a company listed on the New York stock exchange. Her lawyer, Jack Davis (a takeover-bid specialist) is helping her by drafting the relevant legal documentation. In reliance on Jack's advice, Claudia offers to purchase the shares at a price of $90 per share (the current market price is $75 per share).

Unbeknownst to Claudia, Jack owns a large number of HugeCo's shares through an offshore holding company. Through clever legal means, Jack has ensured that his interest in HugeCo's shares is undetectable.

In the above example, Jack's interests conflict with the interests of his client. Jack has an interest in obtaining the highest possible price for his HugeCo shares, and Claudia has an interest in acquiring the shares for the lowest possible price. When advising Claudia as to the appropriate price to offer for HugeCo shares, Jack's advice is likely to be coloured by his own financial interests. Because Jack's interests are opposed to those of his client, this gives rise to a conflict-of-interest.

Example 8.6 differs from the conflicting-duty examples discussed above. In those examples, the conflict of interest arose because of duties owed to competing individuals. In example 8.6, by contrast, the conflict arises because the lawyer has a *direct, personal interest* in the affairs of the lawyer's client.[22] Despite this apparent difference, example 8.6 raises many of the same policy issues that are raised in the conflicting-duty cases. The lawyer in example 8.6, like the lawyers discussed throughout the earlier portions of this chapter, is tempted to harm the client in order to advance competing goals. As a result, he is tempted to be disloyal toward his client, just as the lawyers discussed throughout this chapter have been tempted to undermine their clients' interests. As we saw in section I, this temptation to undermine the client's interests can give rise to market failure. As a result, the problems that arise in cases implicating the lawyer's personal interests seem to parallel the problems that arise in cases involving conflicting duties.

There is another sense in which a personal-interest problem is no different than a competing-duty problem. As we saw in section I.A above, all conflict-of-interest problems ultimately implicate the lawyer's personal interests. Even where the lawyer is tempted to prefer the interests of a third party to the interests of a client, the lawyer is doing so in order to advance his or her personal interests. In the case of third-party payments, for example, the lawyer may sacrifice the interests of a client in favour of those of the party paying the lawyer's fees in order to give effect to the lawyer's preference for a steady stream of income. Similarly, where the lawyer acts against a former client, the lawyer does so because the lawyer has an interest in pursuing the legal objectives of the lawyer's current client. As a result, where the lawyer appears to be faced with a choice between competing duties, the lawyer is ultimately making a choice concerning the best way to pursue the lawyer's interests. As a result, one could argue that cases involving conflicting duties owed to clients and third parties are no different than cases in which the lawyer's direct personal interests come into conflict with the interests of a client.

There is one viable distinction between competing-duty cases and cases implicating the lawyer's self-interest. Where the conflict of interest arises because of a lawyer's competing duties, we may be more inclined to sympathize with the lawyer. In competing-duty cases, the lawyer has to choose between the interests of two persons to whom he or she owes a professional duty of loyalty. In cases of this nature, the lawyer often appears to be in an involuntary bind. The nature of the lawyer's employment requires him or her to choose between competing individuals. The lawyer did not ask to be burdened with this difficult choice. In self-interest cases, by contrast, the lawyer merely chooses be-

---

22   The problems relating to contingency fees, discussed in section V.D, also relate to the lawyer's personal interests.

tween his or her personal interests and the interests of a client whom the lawyer agreed to serve. To many people, the "moral choice" in cases involving the lawyer's personal interest seems quite obvious. The lawyer should sacrifice his or her personal interests in favour of the interests of the client. When reviewing the cases that follow, consider whether the choice between the interests of the client and the interests of the lawyer is as easy as it appears. More importantly, consider whether competing-duty cases ought to be treated any differently than the cases in which the lawyer's personal interests are directly opposed to the interests of a client.

The decision of the court in *Regina v. Laperrière* (1995), below, provides a useful example of a conflict rooted in a lawyer's personal interests. Unfortunately, the facts of the case are presented in an unduly complex fashion. Broadly speaking, *Laperrière* concerns a criminal trial involving various charges including trafficking in narcotics and assault. During the course of the trial, defence counsel (Mr. Petit) allegedly bribed two of the prosecution's witnesses, paying the witnesses to refuse to offer evidence.[23] When the lawyer for the Crown discovered the bribery in question, the Crown threatened to launch an investigation into Mr. Petit's behaviour. In order to avoid this investigation, Mr. Petit pressured his client to plead guilty. In short, Mr. Petit had a direct, personal interest in convincing his client to plead guilty to the offences with which the client had been charged. Does this give rise to an impermissible conflict of interest?

Regina v. Laperrière
(1995), 101 CCC (3d) 462 (Que. CA)

BISSON JA (dissenting) [TRANSLATION]: On December 8, 1994, a bench of our court was seized with the appellant's two motions:

1. A motion for leave to appeal mixed questions of fact and law;

2. A motion to introduce fresh evidence on appeal, as provided for by s. 683(1)(b) of the *Criminal Code*.

On the first motion, leave was granted to the appellant to appeal all the guilty pleas that he had entered on October 19, 1994, before a judge of the Court of Quebec, Criminal and Penal Division, for the District of Quebec. ...

The Procedural Context

At the hearing, counsel for the appellant informed us that he was seeking to have the guilty pleas in all the cases quashed and that if the court, for one reason or another, was rather inclined to only permit the withdrawal of certain pleas, the appeal should be dismissed.

---

23   The decision to bribe a witness, of course, raises its own ethical issues.

This statement by counsel for the appellant was part of a certain logic which one will better understand after referring to what will be done in the circumstances of the present case.

The cases in which the appellant pleaded guilty can be grouped into three categories.

First Category

They are the following cases for offences committed in November and December, 1992, and for which the appellant was charged in 1992 and at the beginning of 1993 ... . In all these cases, the proceedings were all at the trial stage by June, 1994.

Second Category

... The incidents took place on December 3, 1993, the charges were laid shortly thereafter, but it was only in June, 1994, that the appellant was arrested in respect of these two cases.

After his arrest in June, 1994, the appellant was jailed for several days but then he decided to plead guilty in all the cases.

However, the appellant preferred to spend the summer outside and he obtained from the prosecution permission to only enter his guilty pleas on September 23, 1994.

As the agreement reached satisfied the prosecution, it no longer objected to bail for the appellant, and on June 23, 1994, he was granted interim release up until September 23, 1994.

The appellant expressed himself as follows in this regard in a solemn declaration given on November 13, 1994, ex. A-1, which was provided in support of the motions which our court ruled on December 8, 1994:

> On June 23, 1994, all my cases were called by the court to enter a plea of guilty. At my request, both counsel agreed to adjourn everything over to September 23, 1994. This date allowed me to be at large until after my birthday on September 20. In return, I had to plead guilty to all the counts.

Third Category

... On September 20, 1994, the appellant was arrested for a bar room brawl and charged in two cases, one containing three counts of violation of a condition on release and the other, one count of aggravated assault contrary to s. 268 of the *Criminal Code*.

In light of these repeat offences—two of the three 1993 cases were also for assault—the Crown was no longer inclined to agree to a global sentence of less than two years.

It insisted then that the sentence for the charge of trafficking in narcotics in November, 1992, be 45 months, although it agreed that all the other sentences, although less lengthy, be concurrent with the trafficking sentence.

Counsel for the appellant, Jean Petit, found this proposition acceptable and agreed to submit it to the appellant, but the latter refused and, on September 27th or 28th, the Crown was informed of this decision.

It was then agreed to proceed in October with the preliminary inquiry in the case of the September 20, 1994 aggravated assault, and that trial dates would be set for all the other cases.

On September 29th, the parties appeared before a judge where counsel Petit had his client testify that he no longer agreed to plead guilty: "… I cannot accept the deal being offered to me."

October 19th was then set for the preliminary inquiry in case 200-01-008954-947, with an agreement to proceed to trial in the other cases later.

The events which gave rise to the present appeal took place on the morning of October 19th.

Counsel who then acted for the Crown, Georges Letendre, learned that the prosecution witnesses on the September 20th brawl were not present and that they had been bribed.

Furious, counsel Letendre informed counsel Petit that he would have both Petit and the appellant investigated.

Counsel Petit, who had previously been charged with, but acquitted of, obstructing justice, panicked, in his words, met his client—then detained since September 20th—who in turn panicked and the two agreed that the appellant would immediately plead guilty and accept the sentence of 45 months offered by the Crown in September.

It was at that point that counsel Petit returned to see counsel Letendre who suggested to him that they wait until the next day for the pleas in order to allow the appellant time to reflect, which was not agreed to by counsel Petit, who wanted the matter done with.

Finally, on October 19th, towards the end of the morning, the parties attended before Andre Plante J and guilty pleas were entered in all of the cases except for the September 20th assault cases where the charge was reduced to assault causing bodily harm (Code, s. 267(1)(b)).

Counsel Letendre then informed Plante J of his recommendation and the judge, at the end, turned to counsel Petit who simply answered: "Nothing to say, Your Honour." After sentence was pronounced, the last words were spoken by counsel Petit: "Thank you, Your Honour, Counsel Letendre."

In all the cases and for all the charges, except the case of trafficking in narcotics on November 10, 1992, the sentences varied from six months to two years. …

Shortly after the October 19, 1994 hearing, it seems the very same day, counsel Petit questioned himself as to the appropriateness of his actions that morning, and began to put in place, with the appellant, the proceedings which we now have before us, the motions being drafted in the second half of November, 1994.

The Fresh Evidence

… At the hearing before this court, counsel for the appellant fairly admitted that a certain number of the November, 1994 declarations were no longer reliable and as a result that his application to quash the guilty pleas was only based on the following allegations in the motion:

(J) Your APPELLANT was immediately met by his attorney, who, completely rattled by the situation, and quite understandably upset by the prospect of being the subject of a criminal investigation, pressured his client to plead guilty and accept the 45 month sentence;

(K) The attorney for the APPELLANT also advanced the argument that one of the persons suspected of having conspired to obstruct justice was the brother of your APPELLANT, Mr. LABRECQUE, and that your APPELLANT owed it to his brother to plead guilty in order to avoid having his brother, a man with a family to care for, experience any problems; ...

(R) It therefore results from the foregoing that the guilty pleas entered by your APPELLANT in the above cases should be quashed for the following reasons:

· · ·

(b) They were entered as a result of extreme pressure put on him by the attorney for your APPELLANT when this attorney (1) had an interest in the your APPELLANT pleading guilty in order to avoid being investigated himself, and (2) argued that your APPELLANT should plead guilty in order to avoid having his brother, who had a family to care for, upset;

In short, what the appellant no longer bases his appeal on are all the circumstances in which the September 20, 1994 brawl took place and the steps taken in the days which followed, at the instigation of the appellant's half-brother, Alain Labrecque.

As counsel for the appellant summarized in his submissions, regardless of the appellant's guilt or innocence on any of the charges in the eight cases, it only remains a question of determining whether, on October 19, 1994, the appellant pleaded guilty, in an informed manner, or rather, to use the words of counsel for the appellant, whether the appellant was pushed to the wall by his then counsel who would have, so to speak, forced him to plead guilty.

In short, counsel for the appellant says that on October 14, 1994, guilty pleas were extorted from his client and, that the appeal should be granted so that the appellant can be released from his guilty pleas.

Viewed from this new perspective suggested by counsel for the appellant, the issue of the admissibility of the fresh evidence becomes less complex.

This new evidence is admissible in so far as it meets the following well-known tests:

— it was not available at the trial;

— it is relevant;

— it is credible; and

— it may affect the decision taken at first instance.

The decision at first instance is the acceptance by the trial judge of the guilty pleas, but includes the decision taken on the morning of October 19th by the appellant and his counsel to offer to plead guilty.

I will come back to the fourth test.

With respect to the other three tests, they present little difficulty because, obviously, the evidence was not available for the judge on the morning of October 19, 1994, and it appears to me relevant to the appellant's change of heart with respect to the fate of the charges against him; in addition, the narrative of what took place on the morning of October 19th appears to me to be credible.

From this perspective, I will only accept, however, the November, 1994, declarations and the testimony of the appellant and of counsel Petit, and therefore I refuse the remainder of the fresh evidence.

I now return to the fourth test and I am ready to accept that, if the exchanges between counsel Letendre and counsel Petit, and between the latter and the appellant on October 19th had not taken place, Yves Laperriere would not have gone back on his decision which he communicated to the court on September 29th, to not plead guilty.

I am therefore of the view that, within these limits, the fresh evidence should be admitted and form part of the appeal record and, as a result, I would grant the appellant's motion in so far as it concerns the appellant and counsel Petit.

The Appeal

Should the appeal be granted and should the appellant be authorized to withdraw his guilty pleas—in short, to quash the pleas—and the cases be returned to the Court of Quebec in the same state as they were before the morning of October 19, 1994?

I note in passing that all the six-month sentences have been served because the appellant has been incarcerated since October 19, 1994.

With respect to the others except for the 45-month sentence, they are either 12-month sentences or two-year sentences.

With respect to the others, contrary to other cases which we have been referred to by the appellant (*R v. Toussaint* (1984), 16 CCC (3d) 544, 40 CR (3d) 230 (Que. CA), and *R v. Lamoureux* (1984), 13 CCC (3d) 101, 40 CR (3d) 370 (Que. CA)), the present case does not put the integrity of the criminal justice system in issue.

The appellant does not argue that he is not guilty of the offences for which he is charged except the one for the possession of narcotics for the purpose of trafficking on November 10, 1992 (case No. 200-01-013884-923). It was on this charge that the appellant was sentenced to 45 months' imprisonment on October 19, 1994.

In his solemn declaration of November 13, 1994, he said that he drove the vehicle in which the narcotics were found, with the mandate to see that the car was repaired.

After he was stopped, the car was searched and the police found in it the narcotics that the appellant says he did not know were there.

With reason, counsel for the appellant asks the court to beware of the temptation to ask ourselves whether or not the 45-month sentence, imposed on October 19, 1994, was a good deal for the appellant.

I would note that the record shows that prior to October 19, 1994, the appellant never had thought of pleading guilty in return for a 45-month sentence.

It is true that up until September 20, 1994, the appellant agreed to plead guilty and to be sentenced to less than two years, but this did not necessarily involve an admission of the appellant's guilt.

Experience shows that faced with several charges—which was the appellant's situation between June and September, 1994—a person may decide to plead guilty in return for a negotiated sentence which will be suggested to the judge.

This is what happened in the present case.

What is more, as soon as the new charges were brought following the September 20, 1994 events, the appellant refused straight away to plead guilty and to be sentenced to 45 months. He told this himself to the judge at the hearing on September 29, 1994.

One must necessarily conclude that the appellant's October 19, 1994 decision was not taken in an enlightened manner and that the appellant pleaded guilty only under pressure from his then counsel.

I will summarize then what happened:

1. More than three weeks before the October 19, 1994 court date, the appellant, faced with a new situation, had decided to no longer plead guilty and, on September 29th, he so informed the judge.

2. While the appellant pleaded guilty on October 19th, it was under the pressure, which was almost unavoidable, put on him that same day by his then counsel: this is a new element which should cause us to be very wary of the new pleas of guilty.

3. The situation is exacerbated when one notes that the reason why the attorney acted as he did is in large part personal to him: he had just learned that as a result of certain acts which the Crown alleged that he had posed, he was under investigation for his presumed participation in manoeuvres designed to obstruct justice in relation to the crimes for which his client was charged following the events of September 20, 1994.

4. Therefore, not only the attorney put pressure which caused the appellant to suddenly change the decision which he had taken three weeks earlier, but this pressure was dictated in large part by the personal interests of the attorney, who previously had to go through with criminal charges—which he was however acquitted of—for obstruction of justice.

5. In my view, this situation leads to the conclusion that the guilty pleas entered by the appellant were not really his own.

In passing, the appellant does not ask for the withdrawal of the pleas because he is not satisfied with the sentence that he received: it was exactly what he was told; he asks to have the pleas withdrawn because the act of October 19th was not his own.

I would grant the motion to produce fresh evidence to the extent previously mentioned; I would grant the appeal, quash all the guilty pleas entered on October 19, 1994, except in case No. 200-01-013886-928 where this court does not have jurisdiction.

I would quash the sentences imposed on October 19, 1994, and return the cases to the Court of Quebec, Criminal and Penal Division, District of Quebec, so that they can be continued from where they left off before the hearing of October 19, 1994.

NOTES AND QUESTIONS

1. Note that the judgment set out above was a dissenting opinion (written by Bisson JA of the Quebec Court of Appeal). On appeal to the Supreme Court of Canada (in *Laperrière v. The Queen* (1996), 109 CCC (3d) 347, (SCC)), the court overturned the majority's

decision and (without providing further reasons) simply adopted the reasons of Bisson JA, set out above.

2. How would you describe the nature of the conflict of interest at issue in *Laperrière*? Does it differ (in any material respect) from the conflicts identified in the other cases discussed throughout this chapter? If so, how?

3. Ignoring, for the moment, the suggestion that Laperrière's lawyer may have bribed potential witnesses, should that lawyer be prosecuted for violating his professional obligations and acting in a case that involved a conflict of interest?

4. What was the nature of the harm caused by the conflict of interest that was described by the court in *Laperrière*? What regulatory model provides the most effective method for eliminating (or preventing) this harm?

5. Assuming that Petit did, in fact, bribe the prosecution's witnesses, can his decision to do so be described in economic terms? Can Petit's decision to continue acting for Laperrière (despite the conflict of interest) be described in economic terms? What costs and benefits were weighed in these decisions? Is it unreasonable to assume that Petit was governed by rational self-interest in the circumstances of this case?

6. When a conflict of interest relates directly to the lawyer's personal interests, rather than to the interests of another client, should the penalty for failing to avoid that conflict of interest be more serious? Why or why not? Are there economic reasons to support your decision?

Regina v. Henry
(1990), 61 CCC (3d) (Que. CA)

GENDREAU JA [TRANSLATION]: At the end of a trial before a judge and jury, Louis Henry, along with three accomplices, was found guilty of two counts of importing cocaine into Canada and one count of conspiracy for the purposes of importing this narcotic.

Henry appealed this verdict. Although his notice of appeal and his application for leave to appeal on questions of mixed law and fact and of fact alone contain several grounds of appeal, the appellant now only argues a single ground: his trial was unfair "because of his counsel's lack of independence and the conflict of interest between the appellant and his counsel."

In order to succeed, the appellant asks this court to receive in evidence the testimony of counsel Rock which we have already permitted be taken. He thereby intends to demonstrate that the attitude and conduct of his counsel at trial were dictated by his desire to protect his own reputation and this to the detriment of his client's defence.

The Admissibility of the Fresh Evidence

In order to understand this application, it is necessary to know that the Crown's evidence is principally found in the testimony of an informer and in the transcription of a recording of telephone conversations intercepted on the basis of a judicial authorization. This authorization covers calls received by, or originating from, telephones located in the residences of the four co-accused and several other persons including

Daniel Rock, counsel for the appellant. The affidavit filed in support of the application for authorization to intercept, which was only disclosed at trial, mentions counsel Rock in terms which would lead one to believe that he was an active participant in the plan to import cocaine. Police officer Gervais, the affiant, affirmed therein that he had received his information from his colleague Arcand to whom one Beauchamp had revealed the cocaine import plan that the appellant and his companions had developed and for which they are today before the courts.

This affidavit, part of the sealed packet, was disclosed at trial following an order of the judge and the appellant submits in his application not to have been aware of its contents until after his conviction. He also reproaches his counsel for being in a conflict of interest and he finds evidence of this in the failure of counsel Rock and his colleagues to cross-examine the witness Beauchamp and the affiant Gervais on the voir dire and at the trial in order to protect his own reputation. It is on this basis that he makes his application to have counsel Rock and the lawyers for the other accused testify before this court, which was done, and their testimony was filed in the record. Also before the court is the transcript of the testimony of the appellant who was examined by the Crown on his affidavit filed in support of his application.

We are now at this stage in the application.

This case is distinguishable from many others where fresh evidence was submitted. Even if the appellant had relied on s. 610(1) of the *Criminal Code* (now s. 683(1)), the evidence which he intended to call was not in itself directly related to his defence as in *Palmer v. The Queen* (1979), 50 CCC (2d) 193, 106 DLR (3d) 212, [1980] 1 SCR 759, and *R v. Stolar* (1988), 40 CCC (3d) 1, [1988] 1 SCR 480, 62 CR (3d) 313. He does not seek to establish that this fresh evidence, even if it had been called at trial and believed, would have influenced the result in this case. Here, the appellant wants to demonstrate to this court that exceptional circumstances that he was unaware of, placed his counsel in a position that he could not ensure his full answer and defence.

The reproach made by the appellant to his counsel is so serious and its consequences so grave that it is necessary that this evidence be received, which we permitted to be gathered in order to verify whether there was a conflict of interests, whether it had been disclosed and in the affirmative, whether the appellant had waived his right to invoke it.

The Conflict of Interests

… From this lengthy but necessary review of the facts, I would note the following:

— that the accused and in particular, Mr. Henry, knew that the residence and office of counsel Rock were being wiretapped and that this covert interception required the authorization of a judge, which could only be granted in so far as criminal activity was in issue: here, conspiracy to import a narcotic;

— that the affidavit in support of the application for authorization to intercept telephone conversations at the residence and office of counsel, which was disclosed and filed at trial at the request of counsel for the accused, was never shown to Mr. Henry nor to anyone else until after they had been convicted;

— that the allegations of the participation of counsel Rock in the conspiracy were specific and serious;

— that while the defence attempted unsuccessfully to have the informer Beauchamp testify at the voir dire to show that the allegations in the affidavit were false, he was never cross-examined at trial in this regard nor, moreover, were Police Officers Gervais and Arcand;

— that well before the start of the trial, counsel Rock had offered to his client to withdraw from the case, which Mr. Henry refused;

— that the judge, as soon as he knew the contents of the affidavit, informed the accused that the document revealed facts which placed counsel Rock "in a situation quite close or near or proximate to the events which are the subject of the present case"; there is no indication whether these observations were discussed by counsel and the accused.

Was counsel Rock in a situation where his interests, here his reputation, could influence the conduct of his client's trial? The appellant affirms this and finds evidence of this in the absence of cross-examination of the informer Beauchamp on his statements made to the police officers which were reported in the affidavit.

The independence of counsel has on numerous occasions been affirmed by the courts and is found in every code of ethics: see s. 3.05 of the Quebec Bar Association *Code of Ethics*; see also the Canadian Bar Association *Code of Ethics*. It is a principle at the very heart of our adversarial legal system without which the guarantees of independence and justice could not be offered and could not thereby fulfil its irreplaceable role in the maintenance of individual and democratic freedoms. The rule of law and of equality before the law could no longer be ensured if counsel could not advance the interests of his client and combat the opposing theory without, at the same time, taking into consideration his own interests or those of a third party. Professor David Luban admirably expressed these principles in *Lawyers and Justice, an Ethical Study* (1988), Princeton University Press, Princeton, New Jersey. I would note that the author's use of the feminine is intentional; see the introduction, p. XXVI, where he wrote at pp. 56-7:

> What, then, is the adversary system? We may distinguish narrow and wide senses of the term. In the narrow sense, it is a method of adjudication characterized by three things: an impartial tribunal of defined jurisdication, formal procedural rules and, most importantly for the present discussion, assignment to the parties of the responsibility to present their own cases and challenge their opponents' (see Murray L. Schwartz (1), p. 672; Fuller(1), pp. 30-32; Golding, p. 105). The attorneys are their clients' agents in this task. The duty of a lawyer in an adversary proceeding is therefore one-sided partisan zeal in advocating her client's position. This in turn carries with it familiar collateral duties, the most important of which are disinterestedness and confidentiality (On disinterestedness, see ABA Code, Canon 5, and Model Rules 1.7-1.11; on confidentiality, see ABA Code, Canon 4, and Model Rule 1.6). Each of these duties is best viewed as a prophylactic designed to enhance the quality of partisan advocacy. Forbidding lawyers

who have conflicts of interest from advocating a client's cause is meant to forestall the possibility of diluted zeal, and forbidding lawyers from divulging clients' confidences and secrets is meant to encourage clients to give their lawyers information necessary for effective advocacy. These duties of zeal, disinterestedness, and confidentiality form the core of an attorney's professional obligations.

In common law jurisdictions, the solicitor–client relationship has been generally characterized as "a fiduciary relationship." Stephen M. Grant and Linda R. Rothstein, in *Lawyers' Professional Liability*, propose a definition of this concept which is taken from the case of *Hospital Products Ltd. v. United States Surgical Corp.*, [1984] 58 ALJR. 587. They also wrote at p. 32:

> [A] fiduciary relationship is established "when a person is entrusted with powers for another's benefit ... (and) in the exercise of those powers (is) not subject to the direct and immediate control of (the) other."

Even if this notion is absent in the civil law, where the mandate or agency approach is preferred, it none the less remains that the obligations that the courts have imposed on counsel in applying this principle in their relationship with their clients are universal. Grant and Rothstein note these in the following terms (at p. 32):

> As previously noted, in many of the decisions involving lawyers, the courts impose fiduciary obligations without discussion of the underlying rationale. Accordingly, it is important to recall that the numerous obligations that are characterized as "fiduciary" can be seen as flowing from essentially three principles:
>
> (i) a lawyer must represent his or her client with undivided loyalty:
>
> (ii) a lawyer must preserve his or her client's confidences; and
>
> (iii) a lawyer must make full disclosure of all relevant and material information relating to his or her client's interests.

In addition, while counsel is bound by a duty of undivided loyalty and of complete confidentiality, he also has a duty to make full disclosure to his client of all relevant and material information. This is why, because of the importance of the interests and principles in issue, that the courts, in my view, must verify the scrupulous application of this duty to disclose the facts which give rise to a conflict of interests. There is not, in my view, any reason to infringe this principle.

This is what I find from reading *R v. Robillard* (1986), 28 CCC (3d) 22, 23 CRR 364, 14 OAC 314. In that case, a lawyer, one Ms. Roy, had represented another accused in a matter related to that of her client Robillard. She had obtained from her former client a document in which the client declared knowing the rules of the Law Society of Upper Canada and releasing her counsel from all obligation towards her. She even added: "I further recognize that counsel Daniele Roy will be in adversarial position against me with respect to a matter allegedly related to the matter I was charged when I consulted her." The judge presiding over the preliminary inquiry had ordered the removal of counsel from the record even though the former client acknowledged that the rules permitted her to submit her waiver for review by independent counsel, but she expressly waived that right. The High Court and the Court of Appeal upheld this decision. Lacourciere JA, on behalf of the Court of Appeal, wrote (at p. 26):

His submission was to the effect that the waiver of Doris Goudreault was irrevocable and had the effect of terminating any duty of confidentiality arising from the solicitor-and-client relationship. Accordingly, the solicitor would not be in a conflict of interest position in cross-examining her former client. There was no probability of real mischief within the meaning of the conflict of interest principle in civil cases.

We cannot agree. As stated by Dublin JA speaking for this Court in *Re Regina and Speid* (1983), 8 CCC (3d) 18 at p. 21, 3 DLR (4th) 246, 43 OR (2d) 596, it is:

> … axiomatic that no client has a right to retain a counsel if that counsel, by accepting the brief, puts himself in a position of having a conflict of interest between his new client and a former one.

This flows from the accused's right to professional advice and services by one who has not placed himself or herself in a position where he or she cannot act professionaly and ethically. The public respect for, and the societal interest in, the administration of justice would be reduced if it were otherwise. The right of an accused to retain and instruct counsel of his choice has long been recognized as a fundamental right at common law and is now inferentially entrenched in the *Canadian Charter of Rights and Freedoms* by ss. 7, 10(b) and 11(d). It is, however, not an absolute right and is subject to reasonable limitations.

The Quebec Bar Association *Code of Ethics* deals with conflicts of interests in the following terms:

> 3.05.04 The advocate may not represent conflicting interests. He must at all times safeguard his professional independence and avoid any situation in which he would be in conflict of interest. Without restricting the generality of the foregoing, an advocate:
>
> (a) is not an objective advisor if he derives a direct or indirect, real or possible, personal benefit from a given act;
>
> (b) is in conflict of interest:
>
> (i) when the interests in question are such that he might tend to favour certain of them over those of his client or where his judgment and his loyalty towards the latter may be unfavourably affected;
>
> (ii) if he acts as the advocate of a syndic or a liquidator, except as an advocate or liquidator, appointed under the *Winding-up Act* (RSQ, c. L-4), and represents the debtor, company or partnership that is winding-up, a secured creditor or a creditor whose claim is contested or has represented one of these persons in the 2 preceding years, unless he gives written notice to the creditors or inspectors of any previous mandate received from the debtor, company or partnership or from their creditors during that period.

In *Thomson v. Smith Mechanical Inc.*, [1985] CS 782, Gonthier J (as he then was) wrote [at p. 784] that the prohibition was absolute:

> This provision contains an absolute prohibition against representing conflicting interests. It adds thereto a duty to safeguard at all times professional independence and avoid any situation in which he would be in a conflict of interest. No exception is provided to this rule. In particular, no exception is even provided in the case where the fact of not acting would cause serious and irreparable prejudice to the client, an exception

which is provided for in respect of the prohibition against accepting a mandate where counsel will be called upon to testify.

However, examining the scope of art. 3.05.06 of the *Code of Ethics*, Gonthier J distinguished the situation of a true conflict of interests from that where there is "an overlapping of the roles of attorney and witness." He wrote [at 784-85]:

> [3.05.06] The advocate must not, personally, accept a mandate or continue the execution thereof in a dispute if he knows or if it is evident that he shall be called upon as witness. However, he may accept or continue such mandate if the fact of not filing (acting) it is of a nature to cause serious and irrevocable (irreparable) prejudice to the client, or if his testimony only refers to:
>
> (a) an uncontested matter;
>
> (b) a question of form and where there is no reason to believe that serious proof shall be offered to contradict such testimony;
>
> (c) the nature of the legal services he or his law firm have rendered the client.
>
> This provision seeks to avoid an overlapping of the roles of attorney and witness and the personal involvement of counsel in the dispute and not a conflict of interests as such, although, as in the circumstances of the present case, the testimony of counsel for the plaintiffs could highlight the existence of a conflict of interests, notably where professional secret is involved.
>
> In addition, the exception in article 3.05.06 can not apply where there is a conflict of interests no more so than in matters of professional secret which only the client can waive.

In our case, it would therefore be appropriate to attempt to characterize the situation of counsel Rock. Counsel's interest here was to protect his reputation and the question that must be answered is the following: Was counsel Rock in a conflict of interest because the preservation of his honour and his respectability could unfavourably affect his judgment and his loyalty towards his client, Henry, to paraphrase art. 3.05.04(b)(i) of the *Code of Ethics*?

In my view, the situation of counsel Rock, vis-a-vis his client, was considerably modified as soon as the latter was informed that a judicial authorization had allowed the wiretapping on the basis of reasonable grounds to believe in the participation of his counsel and himself, in a conspiracy to import a narcotic. He then found himself in a position which negatively affected his role as counsel—independent, impartial and free from all interest. This was, moreover, implicitly acknowledged when he offered to Mr. Henry to withdraw from the case.

The statement by Crown counsel that there was no evidence which allowed him to charge him, although important, does not completely rectify his situation. The authorization to wiretap necessitated the submission by the applicant to a judge of information which demonstrated reasonable grounds to believe that the interception sought would be useful in the investigation of the commission of a crime. That counsel Rock knew, as he moreover testified. Therefore, even if this information was false, it risked having the name of counsel mentioned throughout the trial, thereby mixing him up with his client's matter. In addition, his conduct and the decisions that he would have to make during the course of the trial, could be perceived as seeking to remove the taint from his reputation while forgetting or neglecting the interests of his client.

Such very understandable attitude could manifest itself in efforts to sweep all reference to himself under the carpet or on the contrary, by directing his efforts towards adducing evidence which would exculpate himself entirely.

This is even more important in the present case in that a large part of the evidence against the accused is found in the testimony of the informer Beauchamp, the author of the allegations which provided the grounds for the authorization to wiretap counsel Rock. The credibility of this witness was, therefore, of capital importance and one of the means of testing it remained cross-examination. Cross-examination, if it needs to be repeated, is a formidable tool in the hands of counsel. Its effective use, however, necessitates perfect knowledge of the case and the complete freedom of the person conducting it to ask all admissible questions. This is why he must not be hampered, and even less so, by some psychological restriction. McWilliams in *Canadian Criminal Evidence*, 2nd ed. (1984), Canada Law Book, p. 771, wrote:

> Cross-examination is the most powerful weapon of the defence, often its sole weapon. In *R v. Anderson* (1938), 70 CCC 275 (Man. CA), at p. 279, Dennistoun JA quoted from the headnote in *R v. Simmons and Greenwood*, [1923] 3 WWR 749 (BCCA), as follows:
>
> > It is the right of the prisoner, at a criminal trial, that his counsel should have the right of cross-examination in the fullest and widest sense of the word so long as he does not abuse the right. ...

And the author added, relying for that proposition on an important line of jurisprudence: "Any improper interference with the right (to cross-examine) is an error which will result in a conviction being quashed": see also, *Preuve penale*, Jacques Fortin, Editions Themis, pp. 195ff.

This is why Lacourciere JA in *R v. Robillard* wrote at pp. 27-8:

> Public confidence in the criminal justice process would surely be undermined by any appearance of impropriety in the conduct of the trial or any lack of fairness in the cross-examination of a witness.

Our case, I admit, differs substantially from that described in *Robillard*. None the less, can one not think that in the present case, counsel conducted his cross-examination affected by "diluted zeal," to use the expression of Luban, knowing that the questions would be related back to his own conduct?

Counsel Rock answers this question as follows:

> At trial, because the affidavit had been shown to us at trial ... I did not take the document and turn around and show it to clients; I think that I would not have had the time to do it. However, the thing I said, I said quite clearly to the four accused in the box that it was a question of me and that the affirmations were lies. I was perhaps not explicit as to the details of what were those affirmations; I did not see the use. What we had done up to that point, which had been planned, I asked three things of Mr. Justice Boilard. I asked first to be able to testify which was something which would have helped the others because I calculated that it had been illegally obtained and I saw the possibility that by testifying, it would support that position. Secondly, I asked to examine the Mr. Beauchamp in question in order to show that the statements contained in the affidavit

were false, but this was refused. I then offered to the Court to file the testimony of Beauchamp at the preliminary inquiry in order to demonstrate that the judge who had given the authorization had not been informed of the witness's wrong doings, which did not meet the test in Sing in the Supreme Court of Canada.

Q. And was that also refused?

A. All three were refused.

Contrary to his affirmation, the record does not reveal that counsel offered to testify but he none the less informed us that he wanted to call Beauchamp and to offer affidavits, without however indicating who would sign them. The judge refused to admit this evidence, as he was of the view that at that stage, only the admissibility of the wiretap evidence had to be decided. This decision obviously did not close the door to examination at trial in order to attack Beauchamp's credibility, which could have found support in the revelations made to Police Officer Arcand, whose affidavit made mention of them. The judge moreover expressly recognized this.

In other words, the affirmations of counsel Rock, who is at the same time counsel and the sole subject of the conflict of interest, are insufficient in order to decide whether he acted with complete independence and freedom. In fact, the test must be objective and not subjective. It is less important to know that counsel was convinced that he could conduct the trial adequately and properly to ensure his client's defence than to define the situation of counsel on the basis of the perception of an informed objective observer. Lacourciere JA repeated that confidence in the criminal justice process must not be undermined by any appearance of impropriety. In short, the credibility of the judicial system must not suffer from the slightest doubt as to the quality of its operations. As I mentioned earlier, one of these fundamental aspects is the adversarial system which necessarily is given effect to by the freedom and the appearance of that most complete freedom that counsel has in presenting his case and in meeting that of his adversary.

The respondent submits that counsel only chose to offer evidence that the allegations in the affidavit were false at the voir dire and that he decided not to attack the credibility of the witnesses by referring to its contents. It even seems that counsel Rock was of the view that this evidence was not possible on the *voir dire*. The first ground of appeal in his notice of appeal—he was still on the record at that point—would lead one to believe so:

> The trial judge, he wrote, should have permitted the applicant to submit evidence to contradict the affidavit filed as exhibit R-7, and which was sworn by officer Jean-Pierre Gervais. The applicant wanted at that point either to call a witness and/or to file extracts from the transcript of the preliminary inquiry in order to demonstrate that the allegations contained in the affidavit were false and to point out the omissions which had influenced His Honour Judge Jean-Pierre Bonin.

Whether it was a well-thought-out decision, an omission, or even an error, it does not eliminate the appearance of conflict of interest, if one exists. While the quality of professional services may be affected by counsel's conflict of interest, this is not necessarily so.

From this review, I conclude that it is not doubtful that counsel was personally implicated in the trial of Mr. Henry. But I cannot convince myself that this is a case of a conflict of interest which his client is not entitled to waive. It is what I would term a relative conflict of interests, that is a situation where it may seem or appear that the accused, because he is uninformed, would not have been appropriately and correctly defended and may have had a trial which did not offer all the guarantees of fairness and justice. The reproach that one could make to counsel Rock flows from appearances and not from a situation where he would be called upon to choose between his own interests or those of a third party and those of his own client Henry. It is, moreover, from this perspective that the appellant presented his case to us. His grievance lies not in the fact that the telephone conversations of counsel Rock were wiretapped, nor even that suspicions were entertained with regard to his conduct, but rather from his ignorance of the precise allegations of participation in the conspiracy with which he was charged. In summary, his grievance stems from the failure to have been informed and thereby to have been unable to evaluate his counsel's situation.

I do not doubt that counsel, in the circumstances of our case, had a duty to fully inform his client of all the facts as they came to his knowledge.

In the present case, these facts became manifest on two occasions: first, when it became known that the telephones at counsel Rock's residence and office were being wiretapped, which signified the existence of allegations of illegal acts and, secondly at the time that the affidavit was disclosed.

Up until the filing of the affidavit, counsel Rock could only warn his client about the existence of a delicate situation where necessarily serious suspicions were entertained about him. But for the rest, he could only speculate, which he moreover did: "I informed my clients that it was certain that in this affidavit they would say things, I told them immediately that I believed that they were lies, but that's what happened."

I believe that counsel Rock fulfilled his duty to inform his client and that he cannot properly be reproached at this first stage. His testimony is telling and uncontradicted. He wanted to withdraw from the case; the appellant objected. In addition, Mr. Henry attached no importance to the incident. Again today, he does not really complain because his counsel was being wiretapped.

However, did he have a duty after the affidavit was filed to inform his client of its contents? The appellant submits that he did on the ground that counsel Rock then found himself in a new conflict of interests.

Whether counsel Rock then found himself at the centre of a new conflict of interests or whether the same one was continuing, his duty to inform his client of all the relevant facts was not thereby reduced and it required that he immediately communicate these allegations, especially here because of their importance and their specificity. A brief review of the document convinces us of that. One learns, *inter alia*, that on October 17, 1986, at 6062 Sherbrooke, premises occupied by Planigest Durock Inc., Conrad Bouchard and counsel Rock discussed over the telephone, in the presence of several persons including the appellant and the other accused, the "*modus operandi*" of the import project, departure and arrival dates, contacts established in Peru, in Jamaica, and at the customs office at the Toronto Airport and the risks of moving too quickly. It is not here a question of the confirmation of a few minor details but rather the recital of serious and specific facts which place counsel Rock at the centre of the project which would result in the arrest and trial of the accused. In addition, in these circumstances, I cannot convince myself that counsel Rock could remain silent and not inform his client of these facts and I believe that he failed to fulfil his duty to inform him.

There now remain the comments of the judge who presided over the trial. It should be remembered that the court addressed every-one, counsel and accused, *proprio motu*, and informed them that the affidavit that he had just read revealed facts which placed "counsel Rock in a situation quite close to, or near, or proximate to the events which are the subject of the present case." He gave them the stern warning that he would not permit separate trials or an adjournment because a lawyer would have to testify "or find himself in an analogous situation to having to give exculpatory testimony." Unaware of, and with reason, the relationship between solicitor and client, and the defence that was proposed to be advanced, he could hardly go further except to offer the appellant a copy of the affidavit or to inform him of its contents. Although he may have thought of doing so, he did not in fact do so. In a supplementary report addressed to the Chief Justice pursuant to s. 682 of the *Criminal Code*, the trial judge wrote:

> I also remember raising the issue, in the presence of the other counsel and the accused, and asking him whether he did not feel that he was in a conflict of interest in light of the allegations in the affidavit. To the best of my memory, it seems to me that I also asked that the accused be informed of these allegations.

However, it remains that the warning given by the presiding judge was serious. The place and the time at which he gave it, and the words that he used, confer on it force and an obvious importance. The judge manifestly wanted the accused to know that counsel Rock had been named in the affidavit and especially that certain facts were alleged against him which linked him to the facts which gave rise to their trial.

Mr. Henry heard these comments. He surely understood them as he had known for seven or eight months that the telephone conversations of his counsel had been wire-tapped. This is why he was not really "surprised" by the remarks of the judge and he added (Book 1, p. 32):

> Q. Did you actually know, like ... that he was being wiretapped?
> A. Yes, I was aware of that.
> Q. In respect obviously, of the same transactions which brought you before the Court?
> A. In respect of a police investigation, yes.

What he was unaware of, he stated: "It was that they spoke of Mr. Rock as one of the organizers of a conspiracy to import heroin into Canada. I was totally unaware of these facts during the trial."

If the remarks of the judge, whatever their value and effect, did not in themselves have the effect of ending the conflict in which counsel had placed himself, they created a new situation for the appellant. They were obviously made in order to alert the accused and more particularly, the appellant Henry. A failure to react does not mean that they were insufficient.

The serious, direct, and inhabitual comments of the judge must be examined in the context of the case. The accused is a few steps from his counsel and they conferred amongst themselves several times during the hearing. They met in private daily. Mr. Henry had known for several months that his counsel was the subject of a wiretap authorized by a judge to whom the facts of a police investigation into a conspiracy to import narcotics were revealed and for which he is today charged.

Mr. Henry is therefore not totally ignorant, but rather just the contrary. Moreover, he does not argue that he misunderstood the allegations of illegal acts made against counsel Rock revealed by the witness Beauchamp, but only that the details that the witness provided had not been disclosed to him. The appellant knew that while these revelations had resulted in him being charged, they had, on the other hand, not led to any charges being laid against counsel Rock. He also knew that the Crown's proof was based on telephone conversations which were intercepted starting on October 23, 1986, in respect of a conspiracy to import 13 kilos of cocaine over a period extending from October 15th until November 6th; 7 kilos were brought into the country between November 1st and 4th, and the other six, on November 6th. Finally, he knew, as I already pointed out, that counsel Rock had offered to withdraw from the case.

It is in this context that the accused received the comments addressed to him by the judge. He was in my view able to evaluate them and to react. He had every opportunity to discuss them with his counsel, even then and there since the judge adjourned the sitting as soon as his comments were made. He chose not to do so, if only summarily or even superficially.

While the accused was entitled to know all the facts which go to establish that his counsel could have had a conflict of interests, he also had an obligation to inform himself as soon as the judge formally and publicly drew his attention to the contents of this statement, which was the subject of argument over a two-day period. The judge manifestly believed that the absence of reaction from the accused to what was a clear warning, constituted the manifestation of their consent to the continuation of the trial as it was. And in my view, he was correct.

In summary, I believe that the judge correctly took the necessary precautions to ensure that the accused had a fair trial. That was his role. The appellant, for some unexplained reason, did not seize this opportunity. On the contrary, he acted as if he was fully satisfied with his counsel in respect of this incident. In the circumstances, I do not believe that we should intervene because the appellant was fully capable of instructing himself either through his counsel, or even by addressing the judge. He freely and voluntarily refused to do so, for no apparent or stated reason. In addition, I am of the view that if a conflict of interests did exist, the remarks of the judge, when examined in the context prevailing at that moment permitted the appellant to better understand the conflict because he was already aware of it, and to take steps to change lawyers, which he refused to do.

I would conclude by quoting Tjoflat J of the United States Court of Appeal, Fifth circuit, in *USA v. Villarreal*, 554 F2d 235 (1977):

> Moreover, a defendant may choose to be represented by counsel with possible or real conflicts. *United States v. Garcia*, 517 F2d (5th Cir, 1975). The fact that Villarreal

continued to employ the firm after judge Garza had explicitly noted the conflict conclusively demonstrates a knowing, intelligent waiver of conflict-free representation.

(See, to the same effect, *USA v. Partin*, 601 F2d 1000 (1979) (9th Cir.).

I would therefore find that the only ground of appeal has no merit and would therefore propose that the appeal be dismissed.

Proulx JA concurs with Gendreau JA.

Appeal dismissed.

NOTES AND QUESTIONS

1. Do you agree or disagree with the court's decision? Do you believe that the accused was denied the opportunity to make "full answer and defence" as a result of his lawyer's conflict of interest? In what circumstances might a conflict of interest undermine the accused's ability to make full answer and defence?

2. According to the court in *Henry*, the independence of counsel "is a principle at the very heart of our adversarial legal system without which the guarantees of independence and justice could not be offered and could not thereby fulfil its irreplaceable role in the maintenance of individual and democratic freedoms. The rule of law and of equality before the law could no longer be ensured if counsel could not advance the interests of his client and combat the opposing theory without, at the same time, taking into consideration his own interests or those of a third party." Is this an accurate statement or an overstatement? Given the economic assumption of self-interest, is it sensible to assume that counsel proceed without regard for their own interests?

3. According to the court in *Henry*, "[c]ross-examination, if it needs to be repeated, is a formidable tool in the hands of counsel. Its effective use, however, necessitates perfect knowledge of the case and the complete freedom of the person conducting it to ask all admissible questions. This is why he must not be hampered, and even less so, by some psychological restriction." Does this mean that it is improper for counsel to refuse to ask certain questions on *moral* grounds? For example, is a lawyer committing professional misconduct if he or she refuses to vigorously cross-examine a nervous, truthful witness for the purpose of undermining the truthful witness' credibility? What if the lawyer believes that it is *immoral* to publicly undermine the credibility of a person who the lawyer knows to be telling the truth? Does this amount, in the words of the court in *Henry*, to an impermissible "psychological restriction" on cross-examination?

4. The court in *Henry* claimed that "the credibility of the judicial system must not suffer from the slightest doubt as to the quality of its operations." In the real world, does the public have doubts about the quality of the judicial system's operations? Can concerns about judicial credibility be expressed in terms of economic costs? How? Refer to chapter 4 for an answer to this question.

5. The court in *Henry* held that Rock had failed "to fulfil his duty to inform" his client of his personal interest in the case. What level of disclosure would be sufficient to fulfil this duty? In other words, what information would Rock have to provide to Henry in order to avoid a charge of professional misconduct?

VII. Conclusion

Chapter 8 has demonstrated a variety of cases in which the interests of a lawyer may conflict with those of a client. As we have seen throughout the chapter, the tension between the lawyer's interests and those of a client are nowhere more evident than in those cases in which the lawyer is called upon to serve as an advocate for the client. While solicitors certainly find themselves burdened by difficult ethical choices flowing from conflict situations and related questions of confidentiality, many of the most difficult ethical burdens are most evident when the lawyer represents (or prepares to represent) a client in court. Indeed, lawyers who play the role of "advocate" find themselves subjected to a host of peculiar ethical conundrums that are not experienced by lawyers who do not take on this role. Ethical problems that are unique to the advocacy context are the topic of chapter 9.

CHAPTER NINE

The Ethics of Advocacy

I. Introduction

The ethical codes of most jurisdictions impose distinctive ethical duties on lawyers who act as advocates for their clients. Chapter IX of the CBA *Code of Professional Conduct*, for example, sets out the following rule:

> When acting as an advocate, the lawyer must treat the tribunal with courtesy and respect and must represent the client resolutely, honourably and within the limits of the law.

The provincial bodies responsible for regulating lawyers' professional conduct have adopted this rule with minor modifications. In Ontario, for example, rule 4.01(1) of the Law Society's *Rules of Professional Conduct* provides as follows:

> When acting as an advocate, a lawyer shall represent the client resolutely and honourably within the limits of the law while treating the tribunal with candour, fairness, courtesy, and respect.

While the text of these rules does not explain what it means for a lawyer to act "as an advocate," the meaning of this phrase can be gleaned from context. Because the rule imposes ethical duties relating to the treatment of tribunals, we can safely conclude that a lawyer is said to act as an advocate where he or she appears before a tribunal. As a result, the special ethical duties imposed by chapter IX of the CBA Code (and the parallel rules in provincial codes of conduct) arise when lawyers represent clients in proceedings before courts or other adjudicative tribunals.

The language of chapter IX of the CBA Code draws attention to the balancing act lawyers must engage in when they appear before tribunals. Lawyers must be resolute in representing the interests of their clients, but must temper their resolve by reference to (1) the limits of the law; (2) the limits of "honour"; and (3) the limits imposed by "fairness," "courtesy," and "respect" for the tribunal. Some of the elements of this balancing act are clarified by commentary 1 to chapter IX, which provides (in part) as follows:

> The advocate's duty to the client "fearlessly to raise every issue, advance every argument and ask every question, however distasteful, which he thinks will help his client's case" and to endeavour "to obtain for his client the benefit of any and every remedy and defence which is authorized by law" must always be discharged by fair and honourable means, without illegality and in a manner consistent with the lawyer's duty to treat the court with candour, fairness, courtesy and respect.

In other words, while lawyers must act in furtherance of their client's legal objectives, the lawyer's ability to pursue these objectives has limitations. While the lawyer must (generally speaking) do all that he or she can in pursuit of the client's interests, some actions that *might* advance the client's interests are prohibited. Even where the optimal way to advance the client's objectives is to engage in an unfair practice or a dishonourable activity, the lawyer is prohibited from adopting this course of action.

Consider a lawyer who bribes a judge. Assuming that the judge is willing to accept the lawyer's bribe, the bribe may ensure that the judge decides a case in favour of the lawyer's client. By ensuring that the judge decides a case in the client's favour, the lawyer could be said to be advancing the client's interests (indeed, the cost of the bribe may be much lower than the cost of protracted litigation, making bribery the financially optimal way of helping the client.) Bribery, however, is illegal; it is also inconsistent with the notions of honour and fairness.[1] As a result, even though a particular course of action (such as bribery) might advance the client's interests, the lawyer is prohibited from engaging in that action where the action is inconsistent with honour and fairness (or the other virtues mentioned in chapter IX of the CBA Code). The lawyer must find some other (permissible) way to advance the client's aims, a way that conforms to the limits of the law as well as to the undefined dictates of fairness, honour, candour, courtesy, and respect for the tribunal.

The ethical limits created by chapter IX of the CBA Code are largely undefined. Some of the limits are intuitive. The reference to the "limits of the law," for example, simply suggests that lawyers may not undertake illegal actions in pursuit of their client's objectives. At the very least, the client's objectives (and the lawyer's methods of achieving them) must be arguably legal in order to be permitted by the rules of professional conduct. The other limits imposed by chapter IX and its commentaries are less clear. What precise limitations are imposed by the requirement to act fairly and honourably, or the requirement that the lawyer treat the tribunal with respect? Commentary 2 to chapter IX provides some guidance. According to commentary 2, the lawyer must not

(b) knowingly assist or permit the client to do anything that *the lawyer considers* to be dishonest or dishonourable; [emphasis added][2] ...

(d) attempt or allow anyone else to attempt, directly or indirectly, to influence the decision or actions of a tribunal or any of its officials by any means except open persuasion as an advocate;

(e) knowingly attempt to deceive or participate in the deception of a tribunal or influence the course of justice by offering false evidence, misstating facts or law, presenting or relying upon a false or deceptive affidavit, suppressing what ought to be disclosed or otherwise assisting in any fraud, crime or illegal conduct;

(f) knowingly misstate the contents of a document, the testimony of a witness, the substance of an argument or the provisions of a statute or like authority; ...

1   Commentary 2(d) to chapter IX of the Code makes this clear.

2   This rule is interesting in that it appears to allow the lawyer to establish his or her own definition of honourable and honest. This section prohibits only those activities that *the lawyer* considers dishonourable or dishonest.

(j) knowingly permit a witness to be presented in a false or misleading way or to impersonate another;

(k) needlessly abuse, hector or harass a witness;[3]

(l) needlessly inconvenience a witness.

As a result of this list (which is largely replicated in provincial codes of professional conduct),[4] commentary 2 prohibits lawyers from engaging in the listed activities when acting as an advocate, whether or not the act in question would promote the client's objectives.

When introducing the foregoing list of prohibited actions, commentary 2 makes it clear that the relevant actions are simply examples[5] of activities that are prohibited by the general rule created by chapter IX. In other words, the listed activities are examples of conduct that is considered "unfair," "dishonourable," "discourteous," or "disrespectful." The list is not exhaustive. No doubt, there are other activities that qualify as dishonourable, unfair, discourteous, and disrespectful in the context of chapter IX. Although these unlisted activities are not specifically noted in the commentaries to chapter IX of the CBA Code, they are nonetheless prohibited by the general language of the relevant rule of professional conduct.

The ethical rules established by chapter IX of the CBA Code (and its provincial counterparts) apply to all cases in which lawyers appear as advocates for their clients. Whether the lawyer is involved in criminal trials, civil actions, or administrative proceedings, the rules regarding the ethics of advocacy apply. Whether the lawyer cross-examines a witness, makes submissions before a jury, or argues a point of law before a court of appeal, he or she must comply with the rules regarding the ethics of advocacy. Indeed, whenever a lawyer commits an act of advocacy, the rules regarding the ethics of advocacy are engaged. While these rules apply to a wide array of situations, there are two particular situations in which they become especially relevant, seriously curtailing the behaviour of legal professionals. These situations are cases in which (1) a criminal lawyer defends a guilty client, and (2) the lawyer's client offers (or plans to offer) perjured testimony. These two difficult situations, which are dealt with by specific rules of professional conduct, are discussed in the following sections of this chapter.

II. Defending the Guilty

A. Introduction

How can criminal defence lawyers justify the defence of guilty clients? Does a truly guilty person deserve a lawyer's professional services? Should a lawyer feel *good* about helping a dangerous child molester avoid going to prison? Should (or can) a lawyer *refuse* to act

---

3   The presence of the word "needlessly" in this commentary suggests that, from time to time, it may be necessary to abuse, hector, or harass witnesses.

4   See, for example, the Law Society of Upper Canada's *Rules of Professional Conduct*, rule 4.01(2).

5   See the opening words of commentary 2, chapter IX.

for a client who has committed a crime the lawyer considers particularly distasteful? From a layperson's perspective (and from the perspective of at least half the students enrolled in a typical legal ethics course), these questions strike at the heart of the legal system. From the perspective of most lawyers, however, these questions are simply "boring and irrelevant."[6] Indeed, the "fundamental mindset of most criminal defence lawyers toward defending the guilty is one of staggering indifference to the question."[7] Rather than grappling with the ethical issues inherent in the defence of guilty clients, many criminal defence lawyers avoid the question of whether the defence of guilty clients carries ethical implications.

How can a criminal defence lawyer avoid the question of whether or not it is moral to help a guilty person escape punishment? Some lawyers change the focus of the question by resorting to glib pronouncements concerning the legal nature of guilt. "My client is not *guilty*," one might argue, "until her guilt has been declared by a court of competent jurisdiction." This type of response is disingenuous and unhelpful, simply avoiding a problematic moral issue. What the lay public wants to know is this: if you know that your client has committed a prohibited act, and that your client is *morally culpable* for that act and deserving of punishment, how can you morally justify the decision to help that client avoid the relevant penal sanction? Happily, many defence lawyers and ethicists willingly grapple with this question, and a rich body of literature has developed on the issue.[8] Generally speaking, most of that literature attempts to justify the defence of guilty clients by reference to the lawyer's institutional role as an element of the criminal justice system. The following section discusses these "systemic justifications" for the defence of guilty clients.

B. Justifications for Defending the Guilty

Many lawyers and ethicists contend that those who question the propriety of defending guilty clients simply fail to understand the nature of the legal system. According to Beverley Smith, for example:

> [W]hat of the situation where a lawyer retained by a person accused of a crime is fixed with information given in the confidence of the lawyer-client relationship which points to the client's guilt? This is the point at which the public so often parts company with the legal profession, believing it to be a moral impossibility to defend someone apparently guilty of a

---

6   Gavin MacKenzie, *Lawyers and Ethics: Professional Responsibility and Discipline*, 3d ed. (Toronto: Carswell, 2001), 7-2.

7   Barbara Babcock, "Defending the Guilty" (1985), vol. 33, no. 2 *Cleveland State Law Review*, quoted in Mackenzie, supra note 6.

8   See, for example, B. Babcock, "Commentary: Defending the Guilty" (1983-1984), 32 *Cleveland State Law Review* 175; J. Mitchell, "The Ethics of the Criminal Defense Attorney—New Answers to Old Questions" (1980), 32 *Stanford Law Review* 293; M. Freedman, "Professional Responsibility of the Criminal Defense Lawyer: The Three Hardest Questions" (1966), 64 *Michigan Law Review* 1469; A. Hutchinson, *Legal Ethics and Professional Responsibility* (Toronto: Irwin Law, 1999); and Michel Proulx and David Layton, *Ethics and Canadian Criminal Law* (Toronto: Irwin Law, 2001).

crime. The public, along with Jeremy Bentham it seems, in taking that position does not. understand the nature of the criminal law system under which it lives.[9]

What the public and Jeremy Bentham fail to understand, Smith argues, is that the lawyer who defends a guilty client is not simply attempting to help a villain avoid a just penalty. On the contrary, the defence lawyer's objective is much grander—the fair and efficient functioning of the criminal justice system. The lawyer pursues this goal by helping the client take advantage of rights that are guaranteed by law but obscured by the law's complexity. According to Smith:

> [I[t may not be inappropriate to describe generally the role of the defence lawyer as being that of a protector to the accused. The protection envisaged is from possible hurt to an accused arising out of a justice system, with the operations of which the accused is unfamiliar. Such person may accordingly be unable by her/himself to adequately see to their own legitimate interests, interests which the system itself acknowledges. The defence lawyer is trained to meet that situation.[10]

These arguments are familiar. As we saw in chapter 3, many of the decisions lawyers make are justified by reference to the lawyer's institutional role. The role of counsel is to eradicate the unintentional barriers that are created by the complexity of the law. The legal system is unduly complicated. The lawyer (whether drafting a simple agreement or defending a serial killer) simply allows the client to access rights and remedies that are available to all people but obscured by the legal system's inherent complexity. The lawyer provides a morally neutral conduit through the complexity of the system, allowing clients to gain access to whatever benefits the law provides. Because the lawyer's *raison d'etre* is to *enhance* the public's access to the benefits of the law, the lawyer has no business refusing to act for a client whom the lawyer has judged to be guilty. The lawyer's role is to *remove* barriers that impede a client's access to the law, not to impose a barrier based on the lawyer's personal views regarding who deserves to receive the benefits of the law.

In the context of criminal defence, the neutral conduit argument seems especially appealing. In pursuing their neutral-conduit function, defence lawyers not only help their clients, but also help protect the rights of all individuals. As Proulx and Layton note:

> The lawyer who vigorously defends the accused who is known to be guilty sends a message to police and prosecution alike that fair and complete evidence will be needed if they hope to secure a conviction, with an attendant benefit for all accused. Such a defence also recognizes an inherent dignity and autonomy in even the culpable accused, who is deserving of fair procedures as he or she goes through the criminal justice process. The result may

---

9   Beverley Smith, *Professional Conduct for Lawyers and Judges*, 2d ed. (Fredericton, NB: Maritime Law Book, 2002), 8:23. The reference to Bentham relates to Bentham's famous suggestion that lawyers who decide to defend the guilty should be considered "accessories after the fact" (or accomplices) and are as morally guilty as the guilty clients they represent.

10   Smith, ibid., at 8:25.

be the acquittal of persons who have committed criminal offences—in a sense, the over-protection of the guilty—but society has deemed this to be an acceptable price to pay in exchange for the adequate protection of individual rights.[11]

Gavin MacKenzie carries this sentiment even further. In his opinion:

> Resolute partisan advocacy on behalf of those accused of crimes is the *greatest safeguard against encroachment by the state*. The right to counsel is essential whether or not the accused person is guilty. To suggest that defence counsel represent only people who are innocent (or any other category of people) is to open the door to a system in which the government decides who is, and who is not, entitled to a defence.[12] [Emphasis added.]

As a result of arguments of this nature, many ethicists conclude that the defence of guilty clients promotes the fundamental rights of all individuals. By defending guilty clients, we protect the rights of the innocent as well.

Not surprisingly, the Bar's commitment to the defence of guilty clients can be evaluated through the application of economic tools. Consider the values that are at stake when lawyers defend guilty clients. The following is a partial list (based, in part, on the justifications identified above).

Benefits of Defending Guilty Clients

1. Protection of the innocent.[13] If lawyers are not permitted to defend guilty clients, clients who *wrongly* believe that they are guilty may refrain from giving their lawyers full accounts of the facts relating to the crimes with which they are charged. Such clients may have a valid defence (duress and self-defence are typical examples). By giving their lawyers incomplete information, such clients (who are *innocent*) may be convicted of the crimes with which they are charged. This would undermine the reliability of judicial decisions, imposing a wide array of economic costs.[14]

2. Enhanced dignity and autonomy for participants in the criminal justice system.[15]

3. Enhanced wealth for criminal defence lawyers (whose client-base increases if we allow or require the defence of guilty clients).[16]

---

11   Proulx and Layton, supra note 8, at 35. Proulx and Layton go on to contend that lawyers who do their best to defend the guilty help to ensure the reliability of the verdicts that are rendered by the courts, thereby promoting "public confidence in the administration of justice."

12   MacKenzie, supra note 6, at 7-3.

13   For a more thorough account of the impact of full information on the outcome of judicial decisions, see chapter 6.

14   For example, the cost of imprisoning an innocent person is a massive waste of resources.

15   This particular benefit is difficult to quantify (or, in many cases, to understand). However, out of deference to those who consider it one of the fundamental values generated through the defence of guilty clients, it is included in this list.

16   This "benefit" enures only to criminal defence lawyers—wealth is simply transferred from clients to their lawyers. It does, however, help to explain why many defence lawyers are in favour of the guilty client's right to representation.

4. Fewer tax dollars spent on imprisonment. If we assume that the defence of guilty clients lowers the number of convictions, fewer people will be imprisoned. Imprisonment is expensive. By allowing guilty people to go free (as a result of the intervention of a lawyer), we save the money we would have spent imprisoning inmates.

Costs of Defending Guilty Clients

1. Increased danger. If we assume that the defence of guilty clients enhances the likelihood that they will avoid punishment, there is an increased likelihood that dangerous offenders will go free. These offenders (through additional offences) may impose a wide array of economic costs, such as losses of life and property.

2 Lost fines. The defence of guilty clients should (in theory) lower the likelihood that the guilty will be convicted. To the extent that guilty parties would have been punished by fines, the state loses the income of these fines when the guilty escape punishment.

3. Diminished deterrence. To the extent that legal representation lowers the likelihood that criminals will be convicted, the defence of guilty clients diminishes deterrence. As we saw in chapter 4, deterrence is measured (in part) by multiplying the cost of a punishment by the likelihood that the punishment will be imposed. Where the likelihood of punishment drops, deterrence drops as well.

The foregoing list is far from exhaustive. It does, however, provide a general sense of the costs and benefits flowing from the decision to allow (or require) the defence of guilty clients. To the extent that Canadian courts and regulatory bodies *do* allow (or require) the defence of guilty clients, it appears that they have decided that, from their perspective, the benefits of defending guilty clients outweigh the costs.

As noted above, some ethicists[17] conclude that those who do not support the defence of morally guilty clients fail to understand the criminal justice system. This argument is presumptuous. It assumes that all people who understand the workings of the criminal justice system place the same value on each of the costs and benefits flowing from the defence of guilty clients. This seems unlikely. Some people who *do* understand the justice system believe that the benefits that arise through the defence of guilty clients fail to justify (for example) the possibility that a murderer will go free. The decision of whether the guilty should be defended is a difficult moral (and economic) choice—a choice that, like other moral choices, is grounded in the decision maker's subjective assessment of relevant costs and benefits.

Before moving on to consider judicial decisions that demonstrate the ethical issues arising from the defence of guilty clients, it is important to review the specific rules of professional conduct that apply when a lawyer defends a guilty client. The relevant rules of professional conduct are discussed in the following section of this chapter.

---

17   Supra note 9.

C. Relevant Rules of Professional Conduct

The commitment of the criminal defence Bar to the defence of accused persons (regardless of the accused's guilt or innocence) is reflected in the rules of professional conduct. According to the CBA Code, chapter IX, commentary 10, for example:

> When defending an accused person, the lawyer's duty is to protect the client as far as possible from being convicted except by a court of competent jurisdiction and upon legal evidence sufficient to support a conviction for the offence charged. Accordingly, and notwithstanding the lawyer's private opinion as to credibility or merits, the lawyer may properly rely upon all available evidence or defences including so-called technicalities not known to be false or fraudulent.[18]

While this reflects a strong commitment to the defence of accused persons, the commentaries to chapter IX go on to impose important limits on the defence of any client whom the lawyer knows to be guilty. According to commentary 11:

> Admissions made by the accused to the lawyer may impose strict limitations on the conduct of the defence and the accused should be made aware of this. For example, if the accused clearly admits to the lawyer the factual and mental elements necessary to constitute the offence, the lawyer, if convinced that the admissions are true and voluntary, may properly take objection to the jurisdiction of the court, or to the form of the indictment, or to the admissibility or sufficiency of the evidence, but must not suggest that some other person committed the offence, or call any evidence that, by reason of the admissions, the lawyer believes to be false. Nor may the lawyer set up an affirmative case inconsistent with such admissions, for example, by calling evidence in support of an alibi intended to show that the accused could not have done, or in fact had not done, the act. Such admissions will also impose a strict limit upon the extent to which the lawyer may attack the evidence for the prosecution. The lawyer is entitled to test the evidence given by each individual witness for the prosecution and argue that the evidence taken as a whole is insufficient to amount to proof that the accused is guilty of the offence charged, but the lawyer should go no further than that.

As a result, the rules of professional conduct make it clear that, while defence lawyers are permitted (and expected) to defend guilty clients, they must do so in a way that conforms with honour, fairness, candour, and respect for the tribunal. Specifically, the lawyer must not set up an affirmative defence for guilty clients, leading the tribunal to accept or rely on facts that the lawyer knows to be false.

The limits that are imposed where lawyers defend guilty clients are explored in the cases set out in the following sections of this chapter. When reviewing those decisions, consider the economic nature of the legal profession's commitment to the defence of guilty clients. In each case, consider the nature of the values that are promoted through the lawyer's decision to defend (or abandon) a guilty client. What values are eroded? Can these values be expressed using the tools of economics? If so, does the benefit of

---

18   A similar statement is found in the commentaries to rule 4.01(1) of the *Rules of Professional Conduct* of the Law Society of Upper Canada.

defending a guilty client outweigh the costs? These issues will be explored in greater detail in the notes and questions following each of the cases below.

Tuckiar v. The King
(1934), 52 CLR 335

[The decision of the High Court of Australia in *Tuckiar v. The King* (1934) is set out in chapter 3. Review that decision now, keeping in mind the CBA Code's rules regarding the defence of guilty clients.][19]

NOTES AND QUESTIONS

1. Assume that the CBA's *Code of Professional Conduct* applied to Tuckiar's counsel. Did the actions of Tuckiar's counsel comply with the rule set out in chapter IX? Were the actions of Tuckiar's counsel ethical? Can the actions of Tuckiar's counsel by explained by reference to economic reasoning?

2. How *should* Tuckiar's lawyer have proceeded?

3. Assuming that Tuckiar knew, in advance, that a confession to his lawyer would be made public, would Tuckiar have confessed to his lawyer? How might the trial have gone differently in the absence of this confession?

4. Why might a lawyer decide to violate the ethical rule found in chapter IX of the CBA Code? In what circumstances might such a violation be justified? What benefits might a lawyer gain by violating the rule of chapter IX?

5. Chapter IX of the CBA Code allows lawyers to defend guilty clients. Does it also *require* lawyers to defend guilty clients? In other words, can a lawyer, upon learning that his or her client is guilty of the crime with which the client has been charged, withdraw from the case on the ground that he or she refuses to represent guilty clients? Why or why not? Should lawyers be allowed to refuse to act for guilty clients?[20] Might your answer depend on the nature of the crime and the identity of the lawyer? For example, should a Jewish lawyer be required to defend a client who is factually guilty of spreading anti-Semitic hate literature?

6. Review commentary 11 to chapter IX of the CBA Code (set out above, as well as in appendix A). That commentary places severe restrictions on the manner in which a lawyer may defend a guilty client. The lawyer who knows that his or her client is guilty may challenge the sufficiency of the prosecution's case, test the admissibility of evidence, or rely on technicalities, but the lawyer may not present an affirmative defence. What would happen if these restrictions were known by members of the public? Assume, for example, that you are a juror in a murder trial. The prosecutor presents a thorough case including DNA evidence, eye witness testimony, and other compelling evidence pointing toward the accused's guilt. The accused's lawyer raises no affirmative defence.

---

19   Obviously, the CBA Code did not apply to Australian lawyers in 1934.

20   See chapter 3, sections II to III for a thorough analysis of this issue.

Instead, the defence simply argues that (1) the prosecutor has not discharged the burden of proof, and (2) the evidence against the accused was gathered improperly, undermining its reliability. Assuming that you know the restrictions imposed by chapter IX of the CBA Code, are you (as the juror) likely to conclude that the defence lawyer's strategy flows from the fact that the accused made an admission of guilt to his or her lawyer? If jurors are likely to make this mental leap, should we repeal the restrictions on the behaviour of defence counsel? What are the costs and benefits associated with this decision?

7. The restrictions imposed by commentary 11 to chapter IX arise where the lawyer's knowledge of the accused's guilt is based on "[a]dmissions made by the accused to the lawyer." What if the accused makes no admissions to the lawyer, but the lawyer knows that the accused is guilty based on other evidence (such as incontrovertible, yet inadmissible, videotape evidence that was discovered by the prosecution and disclosed to the defence)? Should the restrictions imposed by commentary 11 apply in cases of this nature? Why or why not?

R v. Li
[1993] BCJ 2312 (CA)

[Mr. Li was convicted of two counts of robbery. On appeal, Li argued that his trial lawyer (Mr. Brooks) had been unable to provide him with a competent defence because Brooks had been laboring under a conflict of interest. In dismissing the appeal, the Court of Appeal considered the constraints imposed on Brooks's behaviour as a result of the fact that Li had privately admitted his guilt to Brooks before the trial.]

McEACHERN CJBC: ... [I]t is not necessary to pronounce on the fascinating question of whether Mr. Brooks should have called the accused to give evidence. While no binding or other authorities were cited, the common understanding of most legal writers, lawyers and judges is that counsel who is told by his client that he "did it" cannot call the accused or any witness to say otherwise. This view is an ancient one. I shall mention only a few authorities.

In *Legal Ethics* by Mark M. Orkin (Toronto: Cartwright & Sons Ltd., 1957), the author at p. 112 refers to the well-known case of *R v. Courvoisier*. Mr. Courvoisier was a Swiss valet who was convicted of murder. He was tried by Tindal CJ with Baron Parke sitting with him. In the course of the trial, the accused admitted to his counsel that he had committed the murder but nevertheless required his counsel to defend him "to the utmost."

Being unsure of his duty, counsel consulted Baron Parke who, upon being informed that the accused wished his counsel to continue, advised counsel that he was "bound to do so, and to use all fair arguments arising on the evidence."

In "Counsel's Duties to the Court and to the Client—Is There a Conflict" by J. Mathew, QC, published in *The Advocates' Society Journal* for August, 1984, p. 3, it is stated at p. 4:

> The rule that his belief, however strong, is immaterial is not an example of the lawyer's
> ability to perform mental gymnastics, for the decision is reversed if the advocate knows

the defendant is guilty of the offence with which he is charged, because his client has told him so. This is no longer a matter of belief or opinion, but a matter of instruction from the client. Here there is a direct conflict with his duty to the court and he must decline to put forward a case that he knows to be false, for that would make him a party to deceiving the court.

All he is permitted to do is to allow his client to enter a plea of not guilty and challenge the prosecution to prove its case. He has full rein to test the case against his client, but he must be careful in cross-examination and in his speech not to suggest anything he knows to be untrue. It follows from this that he must not call his client or any other witness into the witness box to swear to what is false, for that would make him a party to perjury.

In a text, *Professional Conduct for Canadian Lawyers* by B.G. Smith (Toronto: Butterworths, 1989), the author states that Commentary 11 to the Rule in Chap. IX of the Canadian Bar Association Code was largely influenced by an essay, *The Ethics of Advocacy*, by Lord MacMillan, which is repeated in part in an article by the same name in the 1981 Pitblado Lectures, p. 30. The Commentary states:

> 11. Admissions made by the accused to the lawyer may impose strict limitations on the conduct of the defence and the accused should be made aware of this. For example, if the accused clearly admits to the lawyer the factual and mental elements necessary to constitute the offence, the lawyer, if convinced that the admissions are true and voluntary, may properly take objection to the jurisdiction of the court, or to the form of the indictment, or to the admissibility or sufficiency of the evidence, but must not suggest that some other person committed the offence, or call any evidence that, by reason of the admissions, the lawyer believes to be false. Nor may the lawyer set up an affirmative case inconsistent with such admissions, for example, by calling evidence in support of an alibi intended to show that the accused could not have done, or in fact had not done, the act. Such admissions will also impose a limit upon the extent to which the lawyer may attack the evidence for the prosecution. The lawyer is entitled to test the evidence given by each individual witness for the prosecution and argue that the evidence taken as a whole is insufficient to amount to proof that the accused is guilty of the offence charged, but the lawyer should go no further than that.

From the above, I would conclude, if it were necessary to do so, that Mr. Brooks was not required to withdraw from the defence if the accused wished him to continue. When there is time, as in this case, counsel in such circumstances must instruct the client that such admission may compromise the defence and seek instructions whether the client wishes him or her to continue with the defence.

As there is no evidence on whether the accused wished Mr. Brooks to continue to act for him, I must assume that Mr. Brooks had proper instructions to continue with the defence.

Having received an admission from the accused that he robbed the store, Mr. Brooks was required to refrain from setting up any inconsistent defence. He was entitled, however, indeed under a duty, to test the proof of the case in every proper way. Thus, in my view, it was not improper for Mr. Brooks to call two independent witnesses who gave uncontroversial evidence about the hairstyle of the accused, and about his fluency in English. Those matters might have raised a doubt about the reliability of the identification evidence given by the jewellery store clerks.

On this point, I agree with Mr. Crossin's argument that if the evidence of the Crown was that an assailant was about 6 feet in height, a counsel defending an accused who has privately admitted guilt, could properly call evidence to prove the real height of the accused was less or more than that.

Thus, it does not appear that Mr. Brooks breached any ethical rule by continuing to act after the accused admitted he participated in the Burnaby robbery. He cross-examined the witnesses and sought to raise a doubt about identification (which was the only hope the accused had). He did not call the accused or put up any defence inconsistent with the facts believed by him to be true. ...

I would accordingly dismiss this appeal.

NOTES AND QUESTIONS

1. The court in *Li* made it clear that it was permissible (and perhaps necessary) for Brooks to challenge identification evidence that was offered by Li's victims. Obviously, the identification evidence that was offered by Li's victims was truthful and accurate: the victims identified Li as the culprit, and Li admitted (to Brooks) that he had committed the crime in question. Given that Li's victims were offering accurate, truthful evidence, should Li's lawyer be permitted to try to convince the court that the evidence in question is *inaccurate*? Should this count as participating "in the deception of a tribunal" (see CBA Code, chapter IX, commentary 2)? If a lawyer is not permitted to make untruthful submissions, should the lawyer be permitted to make another person's truthful submissions appear to be false?

2. How far should counsel in Brooks' position go in undermining the credibility of a nervous, truthful witness who offers accurate identification evidence? Can counsel suggest that the witness is lying? Can counsel suggest that the witness is insufficiently intelligent to offer reliable evidence? If the witness is nervous or vulnerable, can the lawyer attempt to "trick" the witness into making inconsistent statements on the stand? When answering these questions, consider the following statement by the US Supreme Court:

> If [the lawyer] can confuse a witness, even a truthful one, or make him appear at a disadvantage, unsure or indecisive, that will be his normal course. Our interest in not convicting the innocent permits counsel to put the State to its proof, to put the State's case in the worst possible light, regardless of what he thinks or knows to be the truth. Undoubtedly, there are some limits which defence counsel must observe but more often than not, defence counsel will cross-examine a prosecution witness, and impeach him if he can, even if he thinks the witness is telling the truth, just as he will attempt to destroy a witness whom he thinks is lying. In this respect, as part of our modified adversary system and as part of the duty imposed on the most honourable defence counsel, we countenance or require conduct which in many instances has little, if any, relation to the search for truth.[21]

Is this a sensible approach? What are the economic costs and benefits of this approach?

---

21   *United States v. Wade*, 388 US 218, at 257-58 (1967).

3. If defence lawyers do not wish to be encumbered by the limitations imposed by the CBA Code, chapter IX, commentary 11 (or the related provincial rule of professional conduct), should they inform their clients, in advance, that any confession the client makes to a lawyer could limit the lawyer's ability to put forward affirmative defences? Could counsel say, for example, "If you tell me that you committed the crime, I will not be able to argue that you have an alibi, and an alibi is a very effective way of avoiding conviction"? Can counsel refrain from discussing the facts of the case with the client, but suggest an exculpatory story (without worrying about the truth or falsity of the story in question)? This practice, known as "woodshedding" or "the lesson," is considered by most ethicists to violate the spirit (if not the letter) of the rules of professional conduct.[22] Should woodshedding be considered dishonest, dishonourable, or unfair? Is wood-shedding ethical? What might a lawyer gain by woodshedding his or her client (assuming that the lawyer is paid the same amount regardless of the outcome of trial)?

4. Note that the restrictions imposed on the conduct of the defence arise only when the lawyer is certain that the client is guilty.[23] The decision of the court in *R v. Delisle* (1999), 133 CCC (3d) 541 (Que. CA) reveals the problems that arise when counsel leaps to the conclusion that his or her client is guilty. That decision is set out in chapter 3.

5. The court in *Li* cited an article that stated that lawyers are permitted to plead "not guilty" on behalf of clients whom the lawyers know to be guilty. Is this a dishonest plea? Does this involve deceiving the tribunal? Why or why not? This issue is explored in greater detail in the following section.

III. Client Perjury

Section 131 of the *Criminal Code* describes the crime of perjury as follows:

> [E]very one commits perjury who, with intent to mislead, makes ... a false statement under oath or solemn affirmation, by affidavit, solemn declaration or deposition or orally, knowing that the statement is false.

At the time of writing, the punishment for perjury (set out in s. 132 of the *Criminal Code*) includes up to 14 years imprisonment. The heavy penalty reflects the fact that perjury is considered a serious crime—an attack on the administration of justice, undermining the reliability of judicial decisions.

What should a lawyer do when his or her client expresses an intention to give false evidence? There are several possibilities (some of which are violations of the rules of professional conduct):

1. *Proceed as usual.* The lawyer could simply allow the client to offer perjured testimony. The lawyer could elicit the client's testimony through normal questioning, and even rely on the perjured testimony when summing up the case in closing arguments. This would constitute participation by the lawyer in a deception of the tribunal—this

---

22   See, for example, Proulx and Layton, supra note 8, at 49.

23   Based on the words of commentary 11, the restrictions arise only where the accused has made admissions to the lawyer.

action is accordingly forbidden by Chapter IX of the CBA code (and related provincial rules of professional conduct).

2. *Free-and-open narrative.* The lawyer could conduct the examination-in-chief in the usual manner with respect to issues concerning which the client has not expressed an intention to lie. However, when the lawyer comes to the issues concerning which the client intends to commit perjury, the lawyer ends the examination-in-chief. At this stage, the lawyer simply asks the client if he or she has anything else to add. The client then introduces the perjured evidence without any help (in the form of supplementary questions) from the lawyer. Counsel may then refrain from relying on the perjured testimony when summing up the case for the trier of fact.

3. *Refuse to call the client.* The lawyer could refuse to call the client to the stand. This prevents the client from offering perjured evidence, but may unduly interfere with the client's right to testify. It should be noted, however, that clients have a right to testify, not a right to testify *falsely*.

4. *Steer the client away from the relevant issues.* If the client intends to lie about a particular issue, the lawyer may steer the client away from that issue and ask no questions concerning that issue while the client is on the stand. This approach has several problems. It may result in unexplained (and rather suspicious) "gaps" in the client's case, and it denies the client the chance to have a last minute "change of heart" while on the stand.

5. *Dissuade or withdraw.* The lawyer could (privately) attempt to dissuade the client from committing perjury, and threaten to withdraw if the client persists with the intention to lie on the stand. Note that withdrawal may, in certain circumstances, be prevented by the court or by the ethical rules regarding withdrawal (see chapter XII, CBA *Code of Professional Conduct*, found in appendix A of this book). If the lawyer is precluded from withdrawing from the case, he or she will have to select one of the other options described in this list.

6. *Expose the client's intentions.* The lawyer might inform the court that the client intends to commit perjury. This choice is problematic. The client migiht have had a last minute change of heart had the lawyer refrained from exposing the client's plan. More importantly, exposure may constitute a serious violation of the rules regarding confidentiality.[24]

Each of the foregoing options raises its own ethical issues and carries its own costs and benefits. When deciding among these options, the lawyer must balance several important considerations, including (1) loyalty to the client, (2) the duty of confidentiality, (3) the duty to render competent service,[25] (4) the client's constitutional right to

---

24   According to Proulx and Layton, supra note 8, at 390, "disclosure represents a huge incursion against the duty of confidentiality normally owed to the client. Disclosing the intended perjury may require the revelation of a whole raft of confidential information, especially if the client disputes counsel's allegations and an evidentiary hearing is held. Clients may therefore react by refusing to be candid in their dealings with lawyers, with the result that the overall quality of representation suffers."

25   The lawyer has a duty to render competent service to the client (see chapter II of the CBA *Code of Professional Conduct*). This may include the duty to proceed with full information concerning the client's case. If the client believes that the lawyer will not be loyal, he or she may be unwilling to provide the lawyer with full information.

testify on his or her own behalf, (5) the lawyer's role as an officer of the court, and (6) the lawyer's potential liability for assisting in the commission of an offence (namely, perjury).

Academic opinion is somewhat divided as to which of the foregoing options a lawyer should choose when his or her client expresses an intention to commit perjury. Most scholars agree that the "dissuade-and-withdraw" option is a logical first step. This option is endorsed by the CBA's *Code of Professional Conduct*. According to commentary 4, chapter IX:

> If the client wishes to adopt a course that would involve a breach of this Rule, the lawyer must refuse and do everything reasonably possible to prevent it. If the client persists in such a course the lawyer should, subject to the Rule relating to withdrawal, withdraw or seek leave of the court to do so.

Unfortunately, there are many cases in which the court will not allow the lawyer to withdraw: only where the client will not be unduly prejudiced will the court allow the lawyer to withdraw from the client's case. What should the lawyer do if he or she is prevented from withdrawing and fails to convince the client to be truthful on the stand? This is where scholars disagree. According to Monroe Freedman,[26] for example, a lawyer who can neither withdraw from the case nor dissuade a client from committing perjury is required to proceed as if the client's testimony is true, eliciting the testimony in the normal manner and relying on that evidence when summing up the case for the trier of fact. In Freedman's view, a failure to follow this course of action constitutes a violation of the lawyer's duty of loyalty to the client and unduly prejudices the client's interests. Other commentators disagree. According to Gavin MacKenzie, for example:

> The duty of confidentiality, like the client-lawyer privilege, does not extend to clients' intentions to commit crimes [including the crime of perjury]. For policy reasons, moreover, lawyers should not have any duty to assist clients to carry out their expressed intentions to commit crimes. To require lawyers to do so is to corrupt the appropriate role of criminal defence lawyers in the administration of criminal justice.[27]

MacKenzie's view is correct. Lawyers are retained to fulfill the role of counsel by pursuing the client's interests within the limits of the law. It is never the role of counsel to help clients carry out plans to *break* the law.[28] A lawyer whose client states an intention to commit perjury should inform the client that all lawyers are prohibited (by virtue of the

---

26 See "Professional Responsibility of the Criminal Defence Lawyer: The Three Hardest Questions" (1966), 64 *Michigan Law Review* 1469 and *Understanding Lawyers' Ethics* (New York: Matthew Bender, 1990).

27 MacKenzie, supra note 6, at 7-13–7-14.

28 Some of the most shocking ethical problems arise when lawyers step outside the role of counsel. Consider, for example, the case of *R v. Murray* (2000), 48 OR (3d) 544 (Sup. Ct. J). In that case, Ken Murray actively searched for physical evidence of his client's involvement in a violent crime, and then kept the relevant evidence from the police. Murray stepped outside the role of counsel and became a private investigator. The ensuing ethical problems are discussed in chapter 3. Of course, the question of whether a lawyer will step outside the role of counsel, lead perjurious evidence, or otherwise run afoul of the rules regarding the ethics of advocacy, will depend upon the lawyer's subjective assessment of the optimal route to utility maximization.

rules of professional conduct and the *Criminal Code*) from participating in the commission of perjury.[29] If the client continues to express an intention to commit perjury, the lawyer can threaten to expose any false evidence that the client ultimately leads. This threat can be persuasive, as the lawyer's exposure of perjury will (1) undermine the client's credibility; and (2) expose the client to prosecution for perjury, leading to a possible prison sentence of 14 years. Once counsel has made this threat, the client is free to (1) adopt another (permissible) strategy, or (2) fire the lawyer who refuses to lead false evidence.

The options discussed in the preceding paragraphs are available only where the client informs the lawyer (in advance) of an intention to lie in court. In many instances, of course, clients commit perjury without giving advance notice. What should a lawyer do in this situation? How should the lawyer deal with the client who unexpectedly lies when testifying? What should the lawyer do if he or she learns, after the client has finished giving evidence, that the testimony the client gave was false? These situations are addressed (somewhat clumsily) by the CBA Code, chapter IX, commentary 3:

> The lawyer who has unknowingly done or failed to do something that, if done or omitted knowingly, would have been in breach of this Rule and discovers it, has a duty to the court, subject to the Rule relating to confidential information, to disclose the error or omission and do all that can reasonably be done in the circumstances to rectify it.[30]

A lawyer who has unknowingly helped a client lead false evidence has "unknowingly done ... something that, if done ... knowingly, would have been a breach" of chapter IX. As a result, commentary 3 applies. Unfortunately, this commentary is clumsy in its application because of the phrase "subject to the Rule relating to confidential information." If a client commits perjury, the lawyer recognizes the false evidence as perjury only because he or she has access to confidential information that contradicts the client's evidence. One could accordingly argue that any disclosure of client perjury constitutes a prohibited use of confidential information and violates the rules regarding confidentiality. Because the rule requiring disclosure is "subject to" the rule of confidentiality, disclosure of client perjury would be prohibited. Despite this problem, most commentators agree that lawyers must not allow the court to rely on a client's perjured evidence. Instead, the lawyer must first attempt to convince the client to correct the false evidence; if the client refuses to do so, the lawyer must disclose the client's perjury.[31] To do otherwise would result in the deception of the tribunal.

The decision of the House of Lords in *Meek v. Flemming* (1961) (reproduced below) provides an interesting analysis of the nature of deception and counsel's role in ensuring that a tribunal is not deceived. In *Meek*, counsel for the defendant allowed the court to proceed on the assumption that the defendant was a chief inspector (a high-ranking

---

29   As we have seen, this prohibition is found in the CBA Code, chapter IX, commentary 2(3), reproduced above (as well as in appendix A).

30   This rule is largely replicated by rule 4.01(5) of the Law Society of Upper Canada's *Rules of Professional Conduct*.

31   Proulx and Layton, supra note 8, at 401. See also MacKenzie, supra note 6, at 7-14 ("a lawyer who has innocently introduced false evidence has a duty to correct the false evidence as soon as possible even if the lawyer knows of the falsity of the evidence as a result of a confidential communication with the client").

police officer), when in fact the defendant had been demoted to the rank of sergeant shortly before the commencement of the hearing.[32] The defendant's counsel did not specifically mention their client's rank, nor did they directly rely on his rank or status in their submissions. Nevertheless, by concealing the defendant's change of status, the lawyers were found to have participated in the deception of the court. When reading the Law Lords' decisions, consider whether the lawyers' conduct is an ethical breach or simply resolute representation of the client.

Meek v. Flemming
[1961] 2 QB 366 (HL)

At the trial with a jury, in October, 1960, of an action brought in November, 1958, by a press photographer against "Chief Inspector "F." of the Metropolitan Police, claiming damages for alleged assault and wrongful imprisonment, the plaintiff's virtually unsupported evidence on the incident alleged to constitute the assault and on the other matters complained of was in direct conflict with that of the defendant, whose evidence as to the events before and after the alleged assault were supported by other police officers in uniform.

Between November, 1958, when the plaintiff issued his writ, and October, 1960, when the trial took place, the defendant had been reduced in rank by a disciplinary board to station sergeant for being party to an arrangement to practise a deception on a court of law in the course of his duty as a senior police officer. That was known to the defendant's legal advisers, but a decision, for which leading counsel for the defence assumed full responsibility, was taken not to make it known to the court, and deliberate steps to that end were taken in the conduct of the defence.

HOLROYD PEARCE LJ: The plaintiff appeals from the judgment of Streatfeild J sitting with a jury given on October 21, 1960, after a trial lasting five days. The jury, after an absence of four hours, gave answers to certain questions on which the judge dismissed the action and entered judgment for the defendant. The plaintiff by his notice of appeal complains that the verdict was against the weight of evidence, and makes certain unsubstantial criticisms of the summing-up. These have not been stressed, and in my judgment no criticism can be made of the conduct of the judge or the verdict of the jury on the evidence before them. The real ground of this appeal is stated in the notice of appeal as follows: "(6) That at the trial the rank and status of the defendant was by implication represented to be that of a chief inspector when in fact between the date of the matters complained of in the action and the date of the trial he had been reduced to the rank of a station sergeant by reason of misconduct and that the credit of the parties was a crucial issue at the trial." A further notice of motion for leave to give fresh evidence alleges that on the question of credit the defendant deceived or misled the court, and thereby occasioned a miscarriage of justice.

---

32   Interestingly, the defendant was demoted because of a previous case in which he had misled a tribunal.

The plaintiff was claiming damages for assault and wrongful imprisonment in respect of an incident that happened on Guy Fawkes night, November 5, 1958. There was a disorderly crowd in Trafalgar Square, and many police officers had been detailed to deal with it. They made a number of arrests that night, and removed the arrested persons in a police tender to Cannon Row police station where they charged them and then, as a rule, released them. The defendant was the chief inspector at Cannon Row police station, and was actively engaged in helping to control the disorder in Trafalgar Square. The plaintiff, a press photographer with a good record, was there with his camera for the purpose of taking photographs. At about 9.40 p.m. the defendant arrested him on a charge of obstructing the police, and took him in a tender to Cannon Row police station where he was kept in a cell until 1.30 a.m.

If the plaintiff's story was correct, the defendant arrested him without proper cause, used considerable violence to him which caused physical injury, and without justification locked him up for some hours instead of charging him straight away and releasing him. If the defendant's story was correct, he acted with propriety; he was justified in arresting the plaintiff, and the subsequent violence (which was far less than the plaintiff alleged) was wholly occasioned by the plaintiff's own violence and resistance.

On November 17, 1958, the plaintiff issued the writ in this action. On December 17 he appeared at the magistrates' court and was convicted of obstructing the police and fined £5. Another charge was dismissed.

On December 16, 1959, while this action was pending, certain events occurred which at the trial were unknown to the plaintiff's advisers, and which they had no reason to know or to suspect. These events were deliberately concealed at the trial by the defendant and his legal advisers. It is on this concealment that the plaintiff relies in this appeal. He asks for a new trial in order that these facts may be proved by fresh evidence. The facts have been agreed between the parties for the purpose of this appeal in the following terms: "(1) At the date when the defendant gave evidence at the trial of the action, his true rank in the Metropolitan Police Force was station sergeant. (2) The defendant was reduced from the rank of chief inspector to station sergeant on December 16, 1959. (3) On December 16, 1959, the defendant appeared before a disciplinary board on the following charges: (i) Acting in a manner prejudicial to discipline by being a party to an arrangement with a police constable whereby that officer purported to have arrested a street bookmaker on October 26, 1959, when in fact you were the officer who made the arrest. (ii) Without good and sufficient cause did omit promptly and diligently to attend to a matter which was your duty as a constable, that is to say having arrested … for street betting on October 26, 1959, you did not attend the hearing of the case against him at Thames Metropolitan Magistrates' Court on October 27, 1959.

The defendant was reduced in rank to station sergeant on each charge, but on appeal to the commissioner on December 30, the punishment on the second charge was reduced to a reprimand, but there was no variation in the first punishment."

It is conceded that those facts were known to the defendant's legal advisers and his counsel, and that as a matter of deliberate policy they were not put before the court. A letter written by the defendant's solicitor on November 21, 1960, pending the appeal, says: "The learned Queen's Counsel instructed by me was throughout, as

I believe you are aware, in full possession of all the facts relating to my client's past and present status and the reasons for his reduction in rank, and conducted the case in full knowledge of these facts in the manner he felt was consistent with his duty to his client and the court, and he is fully prepared to defend and justify his handling of the case at the proper time if called upon to do so."

It having been decided not to reveal these facts, the following things occurred at the trial. The defendant attended the trial not in uniform, but in plain clothes, whereas all the other police witnesses were in uniform. Thus there was no visible sign of the defendant's altered status. He was constantly addressed by his counsel as "Mr." and not by his rank of sergeant. Counsel tells us that he would so address a sergeant in the normal case. When the defendant entered the witness-box, he was not asked his name and rank in the usual manner. No suspicions were aroused since no one had any reason to suspect. The plaintiff's counsel, however, and the judge frequently addressed the defendant, or referred to him, as "inspector" or "chief inspector," and nothing was done to disabuse them.

The defendant started his evidence with a brief summary of his career up to the time when he was chief inspector at Cannon Row police station, but no reference was made to his reduction in rank. In cross-examination he was asked: "You are a chief inspector, and you have been in the force, you told us, since 1938? (A) Yes, that is true." That answer was a lie. Later: "(Q) You realise, as chief inspector, the importance of the note being accurate? (A) The importance of it conveying to me what I want to give in evidence." He was asked further: "Let us understand this. You are a chief inspector. How old are you? (A) I am forty-six years of age." and again: "(Q) I am not asking you whether you took part in the inquiries, but whether you as a responsible and senior adult man—never mind about your being a chief inspector—had no anxiety about this case, no concern or interest? (A) No. I can only repeat I have nothing to fear."

The judge referred to the defendant as "inspector" or "chief inspector Fleming" many times in his summing-up to the jury. It is clear that he reasonably considered that the defendant's rank and status were relevant on credibility in a case where there was oath against oath, and where there was a question of the defendant's conduct in the course of his duty. No doubt he felt what Singleton LJ expressed in *Mohahir Ali v. Ellmore* when, in dealing with a matter concerning evidence, he said: "It appears to me that that evidence was irrelevant and unnecessary. The fact that a witness who is also a defendant is a superintendent of Leeds City Police shows that he is of good standing, and that he has the confidence of his superior officers."

Nor was the defendant's counsel prepared to forgo the advantage to be derived from the status in the police force of his witnesses in general. The parties have, fortunately, in the interests of economy been able to use the reports of the case in "The Times" newspaper. These show that in his opening speech for the defence, counsel stated that the jury had not yet had an opportunity of listening to persons against whom it was at times fashionable to make wild hysterical allegations, but who could not have reached their positions unless they had shown to those who controlled the Metropolitan Police a substantial degree of responsibility. They were not concerned here with some newcomer to the force who had only just finished his course, and was out on the street full of enthusiasm to arrest the first person he could.

"The Times" report of the final speech of defendant's counsel shows that he said in reference to the allegations of the plaintiff: "That was un-English, and not what the jury would expect of any police officer who had passed through the sieve, been trained and risen to any rank in the Metropolitan Police." He then went on to contrast unfavourably the plaintiff's background in Fleet Street where "words come out in very large letters, and the range of adjectives and description is so wide as to make us callous." I accept from counsel that he was intending to refer to the generality of his seven or eight witnesses, all of whom had attained some rank above that of constable. Nevertheless, such references must inevitably have connoted in the minds of judge and jury a reference to the status of the defendant, who was the leading person in the case, and held (in their erroneous belief) the highest rank of all the witnesses.

The fact that the defendant's advisers were prepared to act as they did showed the great importance which they attached to the facts concealed. If one leaves aside for the moment any question of ethics, the hazards of such a course were extremely great. With so many police witnesses who might well know the truth (since the defendant's demotion was circulated in police orders) the chance of somebody in cross-examination referring to the defendant by his present rank of sergeant, or letting the truth out in some other way, was not negligible. Had that occurred, or had the plaintiff's counsel known the facts, and elicited them in cross-examination, it seems very unlikely that the jury would accept the defendant's case when they found how they had been deceived. Even without knowing the facts, the jury took four hours for their deliberations; and since the plaintiff's evidence was, broadly speaking, that of one against so many, one must, I think, conclude that he did well in the witness-box.

How then does the matter stand now that the truth has come out? This court is rightly loth to order a new trial on the ground of fresh evidence. *Interest reipublicae ut sit finis litium.* The cases show that this court has given great weight to that maxim. There would be a constant succession of retrials if judgments were to be set aside merely because something fresh that might have been material has come to light. In the case of fresh evidence relating to an issue in the case, the court will not order a new trial unless such evidence would probably have an important influence on the result of the case, though such evidence need not be decisive … . Such evidence must also, of course, be apparently credible and such that it could not have been obtained with due diligence. But in the present case the fresh evidence is agreed, and it could not have been found out with due diligence since there was no reason to suspect it. In the present case, therefore, these two latter considerations are not in issue.

Where, however, the fresh evidence does not relate directly to an issue, but is merely evidence as to the credibility of an important witness, this court applies a stricter test. It will only allow its admission (if ever) where "the evidence is of such a nature and the circumstances of the case are such that no reasonable jury could be expected to act upon the evidence of the witness whose character had been called in question" … or where the court is satisfied that the additional evidence *must* have led a reasonable jury to a different conclusion from that actually arrived at in the case": *per* Cohen LJ Mr. Neville Faulks claims that the fresh evidence in the present case satisfies even that strict test. But whether that be so, it is not necessary for us to decide.

Where the judge and jury have been misled, another principle makes itself felt. Lord Esher MR in *Praed v. Graham* said: "If the court can see that the jury in assessing damages have been guilty of misconduct, or made some gross blunder, or have been misled by the speeches of the counsel, those are undoubtedly sufficient grounds for interfering with the verdict."

In *Tombling v. Universal Bulb Co. Ltd.* it was sought to adduce fresh evidence on the ground that there had not been revealed to the judge the fact that a highly material witness was at the time of the trial serving a prison sentence for a motoring offence. Counsel had allowed him to give in evidence a residential address which was his normal home, and asked him questions which indicated that he had in the past held a responsible position. The appeal was dismissed; but Singleton LJ described the case as "near the line." Denning LJ there said: "This raises an important question of professional duty. I do not doubt that, if a favourable decision has been obtained by any improper conduct of the successful party, this court will always be ready to grant a new trial. The duty of counsel to his client in a civil case—or in defending an accused person—is to make every honest endeavour to succeed. He must not, of course, knowingly mislead the court, either on the facts or on the law, but, short of that, he may put such matters … as in his discretion he thinks will be most to the advantage of his client." I respectfully agree with those words. He then discussed the facts of that case, and came to the conclusion that there had been nothing improper in the conduct of the case for the plaintiffs. In that case the failure to reveal was not a premeditated line of conduct. Nor was conviction for a motoring offence so relevant on credibility as the demotion of a chief inspector (who is a party to the case) for an offence which consisted in deceiving a court of law as to the accurate facts relating to an arrest. There is no authority where the facts have been at all similar to those of the present case, but in my judgment the principles on which we should act are clear.

Where a party deliberately misleads the court in a material matter, and that deception has probably tipped the scale in his favour (or even, as I think, where it may reasonably have done so), it would be wrong to allow him to retain the judgment thus unfairly procured. *Finis litium* is a desirable object, but it must not be sought by so great a sacrifice of justice which is and must remain the supreme object. Moreover, to allow the victor to keep the spoils so unworthily obtained would be an encouragement to such behaviour, and do even greater harm than the multiplication of trials.

In every case it must be a question of degree, weighing one principle against the other. In this case it is clear that the judge and jury were misled on an important matter. I appreciate that it is very hard at times for the advocate to see his path clearly between failure in his duty to the court, and failure in his duty to his client. I accept that in the present case the decision to conceal the facts was not made lightly, but after anxious consideration. But in my judgment the duty to the court was here unwarrantably subordinated to the duty to the client. It is no less surprising that this should be done when the defendant is a member of the Metropolitan Police Force on whose integrity the public are accustomed to rely.

It was argued that there were several other police witnesses against the plaintiff's story; that although part of the issue depended on the evidence of the parties alone,

the greater part of the defence depended on other witnesses than the defendant, and
that therefore the concealment did not have any substantial result. But since the defendant and his advisers thought fit to take so serious a step, they must, in the light of
their own intimate knowledge of their case, have regarded the concealment as being
of overwhelming importance to their success. Therefore I am not prepared to counte-
nance their present argument that it may have made no difference to the result.

It was argued that the defendant was justified in that a party need not reveal something to his discredit; but that does not mean that he can by implication falsely pretend
(where it is a material matter) to a rank and status that are not his, and, when he
knows that the court is so deluded, foster and confirm that delusion by answers such
as the defendant gave. *Suggestio falsi* went hand in hand with *suppressio veri*. It may
well be that it was not so clear in prospect as it is in retrospect how wide the web of
deceit would be woven before the verdict came to be given. But in the event it spread
over all the evidence of the defendant. It affected the summing-up of the judge, and it
must have affected the deliberations of the jury. The defendant and his legal advisers,
and probably some at least of his witnesses, on the one hand, were aware of the facts,
and intent not to reveal them, in order that on the other hand the plaintiff and his
counsel and the jury and the judge might remain in ignorance, and that the defendant
might be thereby enabled to masquerade as a chief inspector of unblemished reputation enjoying such advantage as that status and character would give him at the trial.
It would be an intolerable infraction of the principles of justice to allow the defendant
to retain a verdict thus obtained. I would, accordingly, allow the appeal with costs,
and order a new trial.

WILLMER LJ: I agree. In saying that, I wish to make it clear that not only do I concur
in the result, but that I agree with and subscribe to the reasons which my Lord has so
clearly stated.

The course which the defendant took resulted in the judge and the jury, as well as
the plaintiff and his advisers, being deceived into thinking that the defendant was,
and remained, a highranking officer of unblemished reputation. In view of the nature
of the charges brought against him the character of the defendant was, in my judgment,
a matter of vital importance for the proper determination of the case. We now know
not only that the defendant has been reduced in rank to station sergeant, but that this
was done in consequence of a disciplinary offence which involved the deception of a
court of law. This is, therefore, the second occasion on which the defendant's conduct
has had the result of deceiving the court. It is in these circumstances that the plaintiff
now asks for an order for a new trial, basing himself on the submission that there has
been a miscarriage of justice.

We are not dealing here with an ordinary case of an application to adduce fresh
evidence. The plaintiff's contention involves something much more fundamental, and
I regard this case as a wholly exceptional one, as was, I think, conceded in argument
by Mr. Durand, counsel for the defendant. ... [H]ere we are concerned with evidence
relating to the character of one of the parties to the suit, and it is a case in which the
character of the parties was of peculiarly vital significance, so that failure to disclose

the defendant's record amounted in effect to presenting the whole case on a false basis. ... Here the matter sought to be proved against the defendant was an offence involving not only the deception of a court of law, but also a question of police discipline, a matter which, I should have thought, was of crucial importance having regard to the issues to be determined.

Lastly, in Tombling's case what was done was not done knowingly to deceive the court; see *per* Denning LJ. Had it been done knowingly, Denning LJ would have regarded it as improper; and it is to be inferred that he would have concurred in the view of Singleton LJ that a new trial should have been directed.

In the present case there is no doubt that the course taken, which had the effect of deceiving the court, was taken deliberately. Counsel for the defendant has so informed us with complete candour. I accept his assurance that the decision was not taken lightly, but after careful consideration, and in the belief that the course taken was proper in all the circumstances. But for my part I am in no doubt that it was a wrong decision. I would venture to follow the example of Singleton LJ in *Tombling's* case in quoting from Lord Macmillan on "The Ethics of Advocacy." This is what Lord Macmillan said: "In the discharge of his office the advocate has a duty to his client, a duty to his opponent, a duty to the court, a duty to the State and a duty to himself." It seems to me that the decision which was taken involved insufficient regard being paid to the duty owed to the court and to the plaintiff and his advisers.

The result of the decision that was taken was that the trial proceeded in a way that it should not have done. Where the court has been thus deceived in relation to what I conceive to be a matter of vital significance, I think it would be a miscarriage of justice to allow a verdict obtained in this way to stand. For these additional reasons, as well as for the reasons already stated by my Lord, I agree that this appeal must be allowed.

DURAND QC: I indicated last week in the course of my argument before your Lordships that I took responsibility for the decision; I hope that the words I used then left the court under no misunderstanding as to my personal responsibility. It is right that I should say as emphatically and clearly as I can that the decision not to make disclosure of the defendant's change of status was mine, and mine alone. Having come to the conclusion that this course was justifiable, I determined and dictated the policy which was thereafter followed during the course of the trial. Neither my learned junior counsel, Mr. Stabb, nor my instructing solicitor was responsible for initiating or pursuing that policy, and indeed they expressed their disapproval of it. I thought it right, having regard to the observations made last week, to make that statement before your Lordships in open court, and I am very grateful to your Lordships for allowing me to make it.

NOTES AND QUESTIONS

1. If the lawyers for the defendant in *Meek v. Flemming* had been bound by the language of chapter IX of the CBA Code, would they have been found to have violated the Code? Why or why not?

2. According to the court in *Meek v. Flemming*:

> [I]t is very hard at times for the advocate to see his path clearly between failure in his duty to the court, and failure in his duty to his client. I accept that in the present case the decision to conceal the facts was not made lightly, but after anxious consideration. But in my judgment the duty to the court was here unwarrantably subordinated to the duty to the client.

Do you agree? Should counsel's duty to the court have overridden their duty to the client in this case, or was the minor deception of the court justified in order to bolster the defendant's credibility? Note that Flemming's counsel, Durand QC, explicitly stated that he believed his conduct to be justifiable.

3. Assume that Flemming's lawyers knew, in advance, that their conduct would be found to violate rules of professional conduct. Might they nonetheless have decided to proceed with the strategy they adopted? What did they hope to gain (for themselves) by concealing Flemming's rank? Can the decision of Flemming's counsel be explained in terms of rational self-interest?

4. According to Flemming's lead counsel, Durand QC, the other lawyers involved with Mr. Flemming's defence did not approve of Durand's "deceptive" strategy. Given that these lawyers were aware of the deception, did they have a duty to report Durand's conduct to the court or to the Bar? Consider the language of commentary 1 to rule XV of the CBA Code of professional conduct, which provides (in part) as follows:

> [I]t is ... proper ... for a lawyer to report to a governing body any occurrences involving a breach of this Code. Where, however, there is a reasonable likelihood that someone will suffer serious damage as a consequence of an apparent breach ... the lawyer has an obligation to the profession to report the matter unless it is privileged or otherwise unlawful to do so.

5. What kinds of actions should qualify as a deception of a tribunal? Should a lawyer helping a factually guilty client plead "not guilty" count as an act of deception? Beverley Smith provides the following answer:

> An apparent potential for perjury arises very early in the courtroom setting of a criminal trial. Is a plea of "not guilty" a perjury on behalf of an accused in a case where the defence lawyer is reasonably certain that, to use the words of the CBA Code, "the necessary factual and mental elements" required to constitute the offence charged are present? The answer appears to be no. There are at least two reasons for this. The first is that an accused person is presumed to be innocent until proven guilty. The second, an extension of the first, is the recognition that conviction may only take place under "a court of competent jurisdiction and upon legal evidence sufficient to support a conviction for the offence charged." Until these elements are in place the accused is in law not guilty, and may justifiably plead so.[33]

6. Throughout this chapter we have seen that one way of dealing with client perjury is for counsel to withdraw. The decision of the Ontario Superior Court of Justice in *Re Jenkins and the Queen* (2001) (reproduced below) deals with the nature of the lawyer's right to withdraw in cases involving client perjury.

---

33   Smith, supra note 9, at 8:48.

Re Jenkins and The Queen
(2001), 152 CCC (3d) 426 (Ont. Sup. Ct. J)

ABBEY J: These reasons are given following my decision, upon an application made during trial, to permit counsel for the accused to withdraw.

The accused is charged with first degree murder.

This trial began, following jury selection, on October 4. The Crown completed its case on November 16. The defence began with the testimony of the accused on November 21. Cross-examination of the accused began November 23 and was adjourned that day for continuation the following day. Defence counsel had provided an estimate of no more than one week for defence evidence and it was therefore anticipated that the evidentiary portion of the trial would be completed by November 28.

On the morning of November 24 Mr. Powell, counsel for the accused, informed the court that a matter had arisen following the cross-examination the previous day which necessitated a request for adjournment until Monday, November 27.

On November 27, Mr. Peel appeared as counsel for Mr. Powell requesting that Mr. Powell be permitted to withdraw as counsel for the accused. The application, therefore, was made after approximately eight weeks of trial and, based upon the estimates of counsel, one or two weeks before its anticipated conclusion.

There had been two previous attempts to conduct a trial of this charge. The first ended in September 1999, days before jury selection when then counsel for the accused was removed, upon application by the crown, as a result of a conflict of interest. The accused retained new counsel. The second attempt was in the spring of this year. After a number of weeks of *voir dire* proceedings and on the eve of commencement of the trial with a jury previously selected the accused discharged his counsel, necessitating a further postponement to September of this year.

Mr. Peel, in addressing the application on Mr. Powell's behalf, advised the court that information had been provided by the accused to Mr. Powell following the cross-examination of November 23, the nature and particulars of which could not be disclosed without breaching solicitor–client confidentiality. He took the position that any continued participation by Mr. Powell as counsel for the accused while maintaining the confidentiality of the information would result in a deception of the court.

Counsel for the Crown, while acknowledging the obligation of solicitor–client confidentiality attaching to the communication, took the position that Mr. Powell ought not to be permitted to withdraw.

When I became aware of the application on November 27, I requested the attendance of duty counsel to assist the accused in having independent counsel for the purpose of the application. On November 28 Miss Strain appeared prepared to address the court on behalf of the accused.

All counsel, including Miss Strain were advised of the possibility that, should Mr. Powell be permitted to withdraw, consideration would then be given to a continuation of the trial with other counsel on behalf of the accused or without counsel for the accused. Miss Strain, with that information and after speaking with the accused and obtaining his instructions, advised that no position would be taken by the accused in respect to the application on behalf of Mr. Powell to withdraw.

It appeared to me that time was of the essence in the determination of the application. The jury had last heard evidence November 23. The cross-examination of the accused was yet to be completed. There existed a rather narrow window of opportunity in which to complete the trial either with or without Mr. Powell. In those circumstances I considered it prudent to put in place some advance planning. The local director of legal aid was requested to attend the court. I outlined to him the circumstances and requested whatever assistance he might provide in investigating the availability of counsel to complete the trial should the application prove successful and should the accused make a request to Legal Aid to have another counsel continue in the place of Mr. Powell. I also advised the accused, as well as Miss Strain, that he might consider it prudent to himself make inquiries in regard to other counsel. I took those precautionary steps in order to minimize any further delay after determination of the application in the event that the outcome of the application might result in the withdrawal of Mr. Powell.

On November 29, I was informed by Mr. Peel that Mr. Michael McArthur, an experienced and certified specialist in criminal law was agreeable, if requested by the accused, to complete the trial and to begin the following week. I again provided to all counsel, including Miss Strain, the opportunity of further submissions. Mr. Peel, on behalf of Mr. Powell and Mr. Bailey for the Crown did so, each maintaining the positions originally taken. Miss Strain, speaking for the accused, again said that the accused took no position.

With that as background, I come to the determination of the application.

Certainly there is no absolute right to withdraw. Rule 25 of the Criminal Proceedings Rules, SI/92-99, requires an application to the court to be removed and which, in the case of the matter arising at trial, is to the trial judge. The *Rules of Professional Conduct*, adopted by convocation of the Law Society of Upper Canada (LSUC), June 22, 2000, recognize, as well, the discretionary role of the court. Rule 2.09(7) of the rules although under the heading "mandatory withdrawal" reads, in part, as follows:

> 2.09(7) Subject to the rules about criminal proceedings and the direction of the tribunal, a lawyer shall withdraw ...
>
>> (d) if it becomes clear that the lawyer's continued employment will lead to a breach of these rules.

I pause to note, on the subject of the role of the court in the event of counsel seeking to withdraw the decision of the Alberta Court of Appeal in *R v. C. (D.D.)* (1996), 110 CCC (3d) 323, which, commenting upon on a contrary view expressed by McKay J in *Leask v. Cronin* (1985), 18 CCC (3d) 315 (BCSC), put the obligation to seek leave in plain language, at pp. 327-8 saying:

> We do not agree with McKay J in *Leask v. Cronin Prov. J*, [1985] 3 WWR 152, 18 CCC (3d) 315 (BCSC) when he categorized the traditional request for leave to withdraw as merely a matter of "politeness and courtesy" elevated by repetition "... into a discretionary power in the judge to grant or refuse leave to withdraw." If he is right, it would not be contempt for a lawyer simply to walk out of Court in the middle of a hearing, provided he utters a polite goodbye. We think not. It certainly can be contempt to fail,

barring good reason, to come when bid by the Court to come. See *R v. Aster (No. 1)* (1980), 57 CCC (2d) 450 (Que. SC) at 451 (not cited by counsel); *R v. Fox* (1976) 70 DLR (3d) 577, 30 CCC (2d) 330 (Ont. CA) (not cited by counsel); *Re Andreachuk* (1984), 120 AR 156 (Alta. CA) (not cited by counsel). And it follows that it can be contempt to fail, barring good reason, to remain when bid to stay.

The sole authority relied upon by McKay J was the decision of the BC Court of Appeal in a civil case where Taggart JA said that, in his Court, "… there is no obligation on counsel who finds himself in the position of being unable to continue with an appeal to seek leave of the court to withdraw": *Boult Enterprises Ltd. v. Bisset*, [1985] 3 WWR 669 (BCCA) at 671. That was a case where unhappy differences arose between client and counsel. So far as we can determine from the brief report, the point made was that, in such a circumstance, it was sufficient for counsel to appear to say he must withdraw, and he needed the permission of nobody. With respect, we are of a contrary view, although in such a circumstance we are bound to add that a Court is under a duty to grant the request. In the result, the difference between us and Taggart JA is minuscule. But this nicety was the tiny acorn with which McKay J built his tree.

The position taken by McKay J is against the weight of authority. See for example, this recent comment by our brother Côté J in *R v. Le (V.)* (1994), 162 AR 4 (Alta. CA) at 5 (not cited by counsel):

> I must point out that when counsel goes on the record for the appellant on a criminal appeal and gets bail for his client, he thereby incurs some very serious obligations to keep the matter moving. Those obligations cannot be delegated, and if he wants to get out of them, he should apply to be relieved of them … or to have himself taken off the record as counsel.

Nor is this position in any way novel. It was also taken in two earlier reported Alberta cases, not cited. *R v. ATC Consulting Ltd.* (1982), 48 AR 238 (Alta. QB) (not cited by counsel) and *R v. Mosychuk* (1978), 21 AR 339 (Alta. Dist. Ct.) (not cited by counsel). It has been taken by the Saskatchewan Court of Appeal: *Mireau v. Saskatchewan (Minister of Justice)*, [1995] 4 WWR 389 (Sask. CA) (not cited by counsel). See also *Dooling v. Banfield* (1978), 22 Nfld. & PEIR 413 (Nfld. Dist. Ct.) (not cited by counsel), *R v. Bunbury*, [1995] YJ No. 103 (QFL) (YTSC) (not cited by counsel), *Weldo Plastics Ltd. v. Communication Press Ltd.* (1987), 19 CPC (2d) 36 (Ont. Dist. Ct.) (not cited by counsel), *Duca Community Credit Union v. Tay* (1995), 26 OR (3d) 172 (Ont. Ct. (Gen. Div.)) (not cited by counsel). Unlike Alberta, Ontario now has *Criminal Proceedings Rules*, SI/92-99, and Rule 25 requires leave to withdraw. And, finally, it is the rule in the United States; *Corpus Juris Secandum*, vol. 7A (Brooklyn: American Law Book, 1957) at 393 and 400.

Nothing need be said here in justification of the duty owed by an advocate to a client but, of course, that duty does not exist in isolation. Rule 4 of the LSUC *Rules of Professional Conduct* and in particular Rule 4.01(1) deals with the relationship of counsel to the administration of justice and recognizes both the duty of a lawyer to provide effective representation and the significant duty owed to the court.

Rule 4.01(1) provides:

4.01(1) When acting as an advocate, a lawyer shall represent the client resolutely and honourably within the limits of the law while treating the tribunal with candor, fairness, courtesy and respect.

Rule 4.01(2), focusing upon the duty to the court, reads, in part, as follows:

When acting as an advocate, a lawyer shall not: ...

(e) knowingly attempt to deceive a tribunal or influence the course of justice by offering false evidence, misstating facts or law, presenting or relying upon a false or deceptive affidavit, suppressing what ought to be disclosed, or otherwise assisting in any fraud, crime, or illegal conduct;

(f) knowingly misstate the contents of a document, the testimony of a witness, the substance of an argument, or the provisions of a statute or like authority;

(g) knowingly assert as true a fact when its truth cannot reasonably be supported by the evidence or as a matter of which notice may be taken by the tribunal. ...

In some circumstances, of course, the duty of counsel owed to the client and the duty owed to the court may conflict. In this regard, I was referred to a panel discussion entitled "Problems in Ethics and Advocacy" (1969), *Spec. Lect. LSUC* 279 (hereinafter *Lecture*). The lecture title is "Defending a Criminal Case." Those participating in the panel discussion included Chief Justice, at the time, George A. Gale, and the then-noted practitioner G. Arthur Martin, QC, later, of course, Justice Martin of the Ontario Court of Appeal. Recognizing that the various duties of counsel may, at times, conflict, in his introductory remarks to the panel discussion S.L. Robbins, QC said:

The preamble to the *Canon of Ethics* states that "the lawyer is more than a mere citizen. He is a minister of justice, an officer of the Courts, his client's advocate, and a member of an ancient, honourable and learned profession. In these several capacities it is his duty to promote the interest of the State, serve the cause of justice, maintain the authority and dignity of the courts, be faithful to his clients, candid and courteous in his intercourse with his fellows and true to himself." These various duties owed by us as lawyers inevitably and frequently are in apparent conflict and sometimes in very real conflict. As Chief Justice Cartwright once pointed out, "to find and maintain the right balance between these opposing claims is apt to prove a task of difficulty and delicacy."

Indeed, Rule 4.01(1) of the LSUC *Rules of Professional Conduct, supra*, also recognizes that, at times, there are limits that must be imposed upon a lawyer's duty to provide effective advocacy in order to recognize and comply with the duty owed to the court.

In the *Lecture, supra*, at 297-298, Mr. Martin (as he then was) discussed specifically whether a counsel might withdraw if something came to his or her attention that prevented being able to continue to act in good faith or in good conscience. In the course of answering the question, particularly in reference to the withdrawal of counsel near the date for commencement of trial, he said:

... [I]f it comes close to the trial then counsel should continue to represent the accused to the extent of asking for an adjournment for him so that he can get other counsel, and to get the court's permission to withdraw. If the court considers that the interests of justice require the case to go on and refuses to permit him to withdraw then, he must go on and do the best he can within the limitations imposed by this information that has come to him. I think a court should not lightly refuse an application by counsel to withdraw if the court is satisfied that the application is made in good faith, that there is a serious problem, and counsel has acted promptly.

Although this passage addresses withdrawal prior to commencement of the trial, there is no doubt that even when the situation arises during the trial, in the interests of justice, counsel may, in some circumstances, be required to continue "to do the best he can within the limitations imposed by the information that has come to him." Dictated by the circumstances and consistent with the duty of candor owed by counsel to the court, limited representation is in many cases an acceptable alternative to withdrawal.

Mr. Powell and Mr. Peel are both very experienced trial counsel. In his submissions, Mr. Peel recalled that in neither of their long careers had a situation such as this presented itself. Indeed, neither counsel were able to present to me any authority directly addressing the circumstances of this case.

The jury in this trial, to the point that the application was made, had heard, as I said, approximately eight weeks of testimony. Mr. Powell, as counsel for the accused, had conducted the trial on behalf of the accused with a particular plan consistent with his being able to advance, at the end of the trial, that the Crown had failed to prove, beyond reasonable doubt, the guilt of the accused.

Mr. Peel, in his submissions to me, emphasized that the information which the accused had conveyed to Mr. Powell was such that it was fundamentally inconsistent with the very essence of the case which had been advanced to the jury on behalf of the accused. It was his view that, should Mr. Powell be required to continue his representation of the accused, any active participation whatsoever would raise the potential of Mr. Powell misleading the court. In fact, Mr. Peel submitted that, as counsel to Mr. Powell, should Mr. Powell be required to continue, he would advise, in order to comply with his duty to the court, that he not actively participate:

- in the presentation of further evidence for the defence,
- in the cross-examination of any reply witness called by the Crown, or
- in the presentation of a closing address except to advance the most basic of principles.

Further than that, the position advanced by Mr. Peel was that even without active participation in the continuation of the trial there would be a serious risk of Mr. Powell being seen to deceive the court.

Mr. Peel was in the awkward position of being unable to set forward the precise factual underpinning for the application. He could go no further than to say to me that the information communicated by the accused was such that any involvement by Mr. Powell in the continuation of this trial would raise the hazard of a deception of the court.

Whatever, therefore, may have been the information conveyed by the accused to his counsel, I am convinced that it was contrary to the very core of the case which had been presented on behalf of the accused through the cross-examinations of Crown witnesses and the testimony of the accused himself.

There are, as far as I have been made aware, few authorities that have addressed the subject of silence, in relation to deception, although I note that rule 4.01(2) of the LSUC *Rules of Professional Conduct*, in particular paragraph (e), prohibits a counsel from knowingly attempting to deceive a tribunal by suppressing what ought to be disclosed.

McLennan JA for the Ontario Court of Appeal in *Re The Ontario Crime Commission*, [1963] 1 OR 391, 37 DLR (2d) 382, [1963] 1 CCC 117 (cited to DLR), in commenting upon the responsibility of counsel appearing before the commission, at 391 stated that:

> If he knows that his client is making false statements under oath and does nothing to correct it his silence indicates, at the very least, a gross neglect of duty.

In making the statement, McLennan JA noted the House of Lords decision of *Myers v. Elman*, [1939] 4 All ER 484. In that case, a solicitor was found guilty of professional misconduct in not insisting on clients disclosing relevant documents as soon as they were in their possession and further, in filing affidavits of documents he knew were inadequate. The original action in which that solicitor was acting alleged fraud. Although not specifically quoted by the Ontario Court of Appeal, in affirming the finding of misconduct, Viscount Maugham in his opinion at 491 wrote:

> If the defendants are guilty of the alleged frauds, it is hardly to be expected that they will make adequate affidavits without considerable pressure. However guilty they may be, an honourable solicitor is perfectly justified in acting for them and doing his very best in their interests, with, however, the important qualification that he is not entitled to assist them in any way in dishonorable conduct in the course of the proceedings. The swearing of an untrue affidavit of documents is perhaps the most obvious example of conduct which his solicitor cannot knowingly permit. He must assist and advise his client as to the latter's bounden duty in that matter, and, if the client should persist in omitting relevant documents from his affidavit, it seems to me plain that the solicitor should decline to act for him any further. He cannot properly, still less can he consistently with duty to the court, prepare and place upon the file a perjured affidavit.
>
> A further observation should be made here. Suppose that, in such a case, the client swears an affidavit of documents which discloses nothing relating to the frauds alleged in the statement of claim, and suppose that the solicitor has previously given his client full and proper advice in the matter, but has no good reason to suppose that the affidavit is untrue. It may be asked, what else ought the most punctilious solicitor to do? My answer is: Nothing, at that time. However, suppose that, before the action comes on for trial, facts come to the knowledge of the solicitor which show clearly that the original affidavit by his client as defendant was untrue, and that important documents were omitted from it. What then is the duty of the solicitor? I cannot doubt that his duty to the plaintiff, and to the court, is to inform his client that he, the solicitor, must inform the plaintiff's solicitor of the omitted documents, and, if this course is not assented to, he must cease to act for the client. He cannot honestly contemplate the plaintiff failing in the action owing to his client's false affidavit. That would, in effect, be to connive at a fraud, and to defeat the ends of justice. A solicitor who has innocently put on the file an affidavit by his client which he has subsequently discovered to be certainly false

owes it to the court to put the matter right at the earliest date, if he continues to act as solicitor upon the record. The duty of the client is equally plain. I wish to say with emphasis that I reject the notion that it is justifiable in such a case to keep silence, and to wait and wait till the plaintiff succeeds, if he can, in obtaining an order for a further and better affidavit. To do so is, in the language of SINGLETON J, to obstruct the interest of justice, to occasion unnecessary costs, and, even if disclosure is ultimately obtained, to delay the hearing of the action in a case where an early hearing may be of great importance.

As well, the Divisional Court of the Ontario Court of Justice (General Division) in *Supreme Signs Ltd. v. Chartex Construction Ltd.* (1992), 2 CLR (2d) 305, in dealing with the responsibility of counsel to make known to the court a fact which other counsel, at trial, had forgotten, said this [at 306]:

> Counsel for [the defendants] was under no obligation to Supreme or to the court to remind counsel for Supreme about the fact that he had forgotten. He was, however, under an obligation to not mislead in any way (including by silence) either the court or counsel for Supreme about that fact.

I have before me no guidance as to the interpretation which the Law Society of Upper Canada may place upon its *Rules of Professional Conduct* in relation to the obligation of counsel in continuing to represent the accused in the circumstances presented in this case. Of course, the *Rules of Professional Conduct* are not, in any event, the sole basis by which to determine the duty owed by counsel to the court.

It was the position of the Crown that, even should the accused, in the continuation of this trial, testify contrary to the disclosure made to Mr. Powell, the duty which Mr. Powell owes to the court would be fulfilled provided he did not, to use the Crown's words, advance the lie. As I understood his position, it was that as long as Mr. Powell remained silent it would not matter that silence in the face of what had gone before would have the effect of deceiving the court nor would it matter that even further testimony would have that effect, so long as Mr. Powell did not actively do anything to advance the deception.

Respectfully, I disagree. It is important to note that this was not a case where the application was made before trial so that deception might be avoided by counsel, to borrow the Crown's words, not advancing the lie in the way in which the case was then presented. Rather, the deception in this case would arise from silence alone on the part of counsel in the face of what had already been presented to the court.

My view is that, quite apart from the obvious prejudicial inferences that might be taken by the jury as a result of Mr. Powell continuing as counsel while virtually tied to his chair, even silence on the part of Mr. Powell would have the potential of placing him in jeopardy in respect to his duty to the court, remembering that the communication made to Mr. Powell cuts to the very core and essence of the defence that had been presented in the trial. Silence on the part of counsel may not in all circumstances be deception, but in these circumstances, I believe that it would be. Limited representation on the part of Mr. Powell would not be an acceptable alternative. To borrow the words of Mr. Martin (as he then was) from 1969, the application has been made in good faith, there is a serious problem and counsel has acted promptly. I am, therefore, reluctantly compelled to the conclusion that the application must be granted.

I might add that Mr. Peel on behalf of Mr. Powell, at my request assured the court that all necessary arrangements would be made to comply with the provisions of rule 2.09(8) and (9) pertaining to the obligations of counsel to facilitate the orderly transfer of the case to a successor lawyer should it become necessary that other counsel be instructed to complete the trial.

NOTES AND QUESTIONS

1. Chapter XII of the CBA *Code of Professional Conduct* (reproduced in appendix A) provides the following rule in respect of the lawyer's ability to withdraw from a client's case:

> The lawyer owes a duty to the client not to withdraw services except for good cause and upon notice appropriate in the circumstances.

The commentaries to this rule go on to provide as follows:

> 1. Although the client has a right to terminate the lawyer–client relationship at will the lawyer does not enjoy the same freedom of action. Having once accepted professional employment the lawyer should complete the task as ably as possible unless there is justifiable cause for terminating the relationship. …
>
> 4. In some circumstances the lawyer will be under a duty to withdraw. The obvious example is following discharge by the client. Other examples are (a) if the lawyer is instructed by the client to do something inconsistent with the lawyer's duty to the court and, following explanation, the client persists in such instructions; (b) if the client is guilty of dishonourable conduct in the proceedings or is taking a position solely to harass or maliciously injure another; (c) if it becomes clear that the lawyer's continued employment will lead to a breach of these Rules such as for example a breach of the Rules relating to conflict of interest; or (d) if it develops that the lawyer is not competent to handle the matter. In all these situations there is a duty to inform the client that the lawyer must withdraw.

As we saw in the *Jenkins* case, the lawyer's ability to withdraw is also subject to the discretion of the court.

2. In asserting his right to withdraw, Jenkins' lawyer (through his own counsel) "advised the court that information had been provided by the accused to Mr. Powell following the cross-examination of November 23, the nature and particulars of which could not be disclosed without breaching solicitor–client confidentiality. He took the position that any continued participation by Mr. Powell as counsel for the accused while maintaining the confidentiality of the information would result in a deception of the court." Did this submission provide the court with too much information? Did this submission undermine Jenkins's interests, or run the risk of leading the judge to prejudge Jenkins's guilt or innocence? Could Jenkins's lawyer have phrased his submission in such a way as to avoid leaving the court with the impression that Jenkins planned to commit perjury?

3. The court in *Jenkins* made it clear that counsel is not permitted to mislead the court "by silence." If counsel cannot mislead the court by silence, why can counsel mislead the

court by convincing the court that the accurate evidence of a reliable, truthful witness is unreliable? Should counsel be permitted to undermine the credibility of a reliable, truthful witness who offers evidence that the lawyer knows to be true? Is this ethical? Are there economic justifications for permitting the lawyer to undermine the credibility of a reliable, truthful witness?

IV. Conclusion

The purpose of this chapter has been to consider the ethical issues that arise when lawyers act as advocates for their clients. As we have seen, these ethical issues can be explained by reference to economic principles. This should come as no surprise: throughout this book we have found that all ethical choices, regardless of the context in which they arise, can be described and evaluated using the tools of economics. Indeed, *all* rational choices, whether or not we choose to portray them as involving "ethical" issues, are made through the use of cost–benefit analysis. This form of analysis is best described and evaluated through the use of economic tools. As a result, all rational choices—even those relating to ethics, morals, or other so-called metaphysical concepts—are best analyzed through the application of economic principles. Economics allows us to engage in a rigorous assessment of decisions made by rational individuals. By deploying economics in the realm of lawyers' *ethical* decisions, we augment our ability to assess the motivations underlying ethical choices, and situate the lawyer's ethical choices within a comprehensive model of human behaviour. As we continue to collect empirical data concerning the costs and benefits that flow from lawyers' ethical choices, the economic account of legal ethics will continue to grow in importance.

APPENDIX A

The Canadian Bar Association, Code of Professional Conduct

Adopted by Council, August 1987*

CONTENTS

---

* Published with the Permission of the Canadian Bar Association. The Canadian Bar Association's Code of Professional Conduct is undergoing extensive revisions and additions as this book goes to press. It is expected that a substantially revised code will be adopted in future editions of this publication.

INTERPRETATION

In this Code the field of professional conduct and ethics is divided into twenty chapters, each of which contains a short statement of a rule or principle followed by commentary and notes. Although this division gives rise to some overlapping of subjects, the principle of integrity enunciated in Chapter I underlies the entire Code, so that some of the rules in subsequent chapters represent particular applications of the basic rule set out in Chapter I. Again there are instances where substantially the same comment appears more than once. Such duplication is considered desirable in order to provide clarity and emphasis and to reduce cross-references.

The commentary and notes to each rule contain a discussion of the ethical considerations involved, explanations, examples and other material designed to assist in the interpretation and understanding of the rule itself. Each rule should therefore be read with and interpreted in the light of the related commentary and notes.

Certain terms used in the Code require definition as follows:

"client"   means a person on whose behalf a lawyer renders or undertakes to render professional services;

"court"   includes conventional law courts and generally all judicial and quasi-judicial tribunals;

"Governing Body"   means the body charged under the laws of a particular jurisdiction with the duty of governing the legal profession (e.g., the Benchers, General Council, Convocation or Council);

"lawyer"   means an individual who is duly authorized to practise law;

"legal profession" refers to lawyers collectively;

"person"   includes a corporation or other legal entity, an association, partnership or other organization, the Crown in right of Canada or a province and the government of a state or any political subdivision thereof.

It will be noted that the term "lawyer" as defined above extends not only to those engaged in private practice but also to those who are employed on a full-time basis by governments, agencies, corporations and other organizations. An employer–employee relationship of this kind may give rise to special problems in the area of conflict of interest, but in all matters involving integrity and generally in all professional matters, if the requirements or demands of the employer conflict with the standards declared by the Code, the latter must govern.

CHAPTER I
INTEGRITY

RULE

The lawyer must discharge with integrity all duties owed to clients, the court, other members of the profession and the public.

Commentary

Guiding Principles

1. Integrity is the fundamental quality of any person who seeks to practise as a member of the legal profession. If the client is in any doubt about the lawyer's trustworthiness, the essential element in the lawyer-client relationship will be missing. If personal integrity is lacking the lawyer's usefulness to the client and reputation within the profession will be destroyed regardless of how competent the lawyer may be.

2. The principle of integrity is a key element of each rule of the Code.

Disciplinary Action

3. Dishonourable or questionable conduct on the part of the lawyer in either private life or professional practice will reflect adversely upon the lawyer, the integrity of the legal profession and the administration of justice as a whole. If the conduct, whether within or outside the professional sphere, is such that knowledge of it would be likely to impair the client's trust in the lawyer as a professional consultant, a governing body may be justified in taking disciplinary action.

Non-Professional Activities

4. Generally speaking, however, a governing body will not be concerned with the purely private or extra professional activities of a lawyer that do not bring into question the integrity of the legal profession or the lawyer's professional integrity or competence.

CHAPTER II
COMPETENCE AND QUALITY OF SERVICE

RULE

(a) The lawyer owes the client a duty to be competent to perform any legal services undertaken on the client's behalf.

(b) The lawyer should serve the client in a conscientious, diligent and efficient manner so as to provide a quality of service at least equal to that which lawyers generally would expect of a competent lawyer in a like situation.

Commentary

Knowledge and Skill

1. Competence in the context of the first branch of this Rule goes beyond formal qualification to practise law. It has to do with the sufficiency of the lawyer's qualifications to deal with the matter in question. It includes knowledge, skill, and the ability to use them effectively in the interests of the client.

2. As members of the legal profession, lawyers hold themselves out as being knowledgeable, skilled and capable in the practice of law. The client is entitled to assume that the lawyer has the ability and capacity to deal adequately with any legal matters undertaken on the client's behalf.

3. The lawyer should not undertake a matter without honestly feeling either competent to handle it, or able to become competent without undue delay, risk or expense to the client. The lawyer who proceeds on any other basis is not being honest with the client. This is an ethical consideration and is to be distinguished from the standard of care that a court would apply for purposes of determining negligence.

4. Competence involves more than an understanding of legal principles: it involves an adequate knowledge of the practice and procedures by which such principles can be effectively applied. To accomplish this the lawyer should keep abreast of developments in all branches of law wherein the lawyer's practice lies.

5. In deciding whether the lawyer has employed the requisite degree of knowledge and skill in a particular matter, relevant factors will include the complexity and specialized nature of the matter, the lawyer's general experience, the lawyer's training and experience in the field in question, the preparation and study the lawyer is able to give the matter and whether it is appropriate or feasible to refer the matter to, or associate or consult with, a lawyer of established competence in the field in question. In some circumstances expertise in a particular field of law may be required; often the necessary degree of proficiency will be that of the general practitioner.

Seeking Assistance

6. The lawyer must be alert to recognize any lack of competence for a particular task and the disservice that would be done the client by undertaking that task. If consulted in such circumstances, the lawyer should either decline to act or obtain the client's instructions to retain, consult or collaborate with a lawyer who is competent in that field. The lawyer should also recognize that competence for a particular task may sometimes require seeking advice from or collaborating with experts in scientific, accounting or other non-legal fields. In such a situation the lawyer should not hesitate to seek the client's instructions to consult experts.

Quality of Service

7. Numerous examples could be given of conduct that does not meet the quality of service required by the second branch of the Rule. The list that follows is illustrative, but not by any means exhaustive:

    (a) failure to keep the client reasonably informed;

    (b) failure to answer reasonable requests from the client for information;

(c) unexplained failure to respond to the client's telephone calls;

(d) failure to keep appointments with clients without explanation or apology;

(e) informing the client that something will happen or that some step will be taken by a certain date, then letting the date pass without follow-up information or explanation;

(f) failure to answer within a reasonable time a communication that requires a reply;

(g) doing the work in hand but doing it so belatedly that its value to the client is diminished or lost;

(h) slipshod work, such as mistakes or omissions in statements or documents prepared on behalf of the client;

(i) failure to maintain office staff and facilities adequate to the lawyer's practice;

(j) failure to inform the client of proposals of settlement, or to explain them properly;

(k) withholding information from the client or misleading the client about the position of a matter in order to cover up the fact of neglect or mistakes;

(l) failure to make a prompt and complete report when the work is finished or, if a final report cannot be made, failure to make an interim report where one might reasonably be expected;

(m) self-induced disability, for example from the use of intoxicants or drugs, which interferes with or prejudices the lawyer's services to the client.

Promptness

8. The requirement of conscientious, diligent and efficient service means that the lawyer must make every effort to provide prompt service to the client. If the lawyer can reasonably foresee undue delay in providing advice or services, the client should be so informed.

Consequences of Incompetence

9. It will be observed that the Rule does not prescribe a standard of perfection. A mistake, even though it might be actionable for damages in negligence, would not necessarily constitute a failure to maintain the standard set by the Rule, but evidence of gross neglect in a particular matter or a pattern of neglect or mistakes in different matters may be evidence of such a failure regardless of tort liability. Where both negligence and incompetence are established, while damages may be awarded for the former, the latter can give rise to the additional sanction of disciplinary action.

10. The lawyer who is incompetent does the client a disservice, brings discredit to the profession, and may bring the administration of justice into disrepute. As well as damaging the lawyer's own reputation and practice, incompetence may also injure the lawyer's associates or dependants.

CHAPTER III
ADVISING CLIENTS

RULE

The lawyer must be both honest and candid when advising clients.

Commentary

Scope of Advice

1. The lawyer's duty to the client who seeks legal advice is to give the client a competent opinion based on sufficient knowledge of the relevant facts, an adequate consideration of the applicable law and the lawyer's own experience and expertise. The advice must be open and undisguised, clearly disclosing what the lawyer honestly thinks about the merits and probable results.

2. Whenever it becomes apparent that the client has misunderstood or misconceived what is really involved, the lawyer should explain as well as advise, so that the client is informed of the true position and fairly advised about the real issues or questions involved.

3. The lawyer should clearly indicate the facts, circumstances and assumptions upon which the lawyer's opinion is based, particularly where the circumstances do not justify an exhaustive investigation with resultant expense to the client. However, unless the client instructs otherwise, the lawyer should investigate the matter in sufficient detail to be able to express an opinion rather than merely make comments with many qualifications.

4. The lawyer should be wary of bold and confident assurances to the client, especially when the lawyer's employment may depend upon advising in a particular way.

Second Opinion

5. If the client so desires, the lawyer should assist in obtaining a second opinion. Compromise or Settlement

6. The lawyer should advise and encourage the client to compromise or settle a dispute whenever possible on a reasonable basis and should discourage the client from commencing or continuing useless legal proceedings.

Dishonesty or Fraud by Client

7. When advising the client the lawyer must never knowingly assist in or encourage any dishonesty, fraud, crime or illegal conduct, or instruct the client on how to violate the law and avoid punishment. The lawyer should be on guard against becoming the tool or dupe of an unscrupulous client or of persons associated with such a client.

Test Cases

8. A *bona fide* test case is not necessarily precluded by the preceding paragraph and, so long as no injury to the person or violence is involved, the lawyer may properly advise and represent a client who, in good faith and on reasonable grounds, desires to challenge or test a law and this can most effectively be done by means of a technical breach giving rise to a test case. In all such situations the lawyer should ensure that the client appreciates the consequences of bringing a test case.

Threatening Criminal Proceedings

9. Apart altogether from the substantive law on the subject, it is improper for the lawyer to advise, threaten or bring a criminal or quasi-criminal prosecution in order to secure some civil advantage for the client, or to advise, seek or procure the withdrawal of a prosecution in consideration of the payment of money, or transfer of property to, or for the benefit of the client.

Advice on Non-Legal Matters

10. In addition to opinions on legal questions, the lawyer may be asked for or expected to give advice on non-legal matters such as the business, policy or social implications involved in a question, or the course the client should choose. In many instances the lawyer's experience will be such that the lawyer's views on non-legal matters will be of real benefit to the client. The lawyer who advises on such matters should, where and to the extent necessary, point out the lawyer's lack of experience or other qualification in the particular field and should clearly distinguish legal advice from such other advice.

Errors and Omissions

11. The duty to give honest and candid advice requires the lawyer to inform the client promptly of the facts, but without admitting liability, upon discovering that an error or omission has occurred in a matter for which the lawyer was engaged and that is or may be damaging to the client and cannot readily be rectified. When so informing the client the lawyer should be careful not to prejudice any rights of indemnity that either of them may have under any insurance, client's protection or indemnity plan, or otherwise. At the same time the lawyer should recommend that the client obtain legal advice elsewhere about any rights the client may have arising from such error or omission and whether it is appropriate for the lawyer to continue to act in the matter. The lawyer should also give prompt notice of any potential claim to the lawyer's insurer and any other indemnitor so that any protection from that source will not be prejudiced and, unless the client objects, should assist and co-operate with the insurer or other indemnitor to the extent necessary to enable any claim that is made to be dealt with promptly. If the lawyer is not so indemnified, or to the extent that the indemnity may not fully cover the claim, the lawyer should expeditiously deal with any claim that may be made and must not, under any circumstances, take unfair advantage that might defeat or impair the client's claim. In cases where liability is clear and the insurer or other indemnitor is prepared to pay its portion of the claim, the lawyer is under a duty to arrange for payment of the balance.

Giving Independent Advice

12. Where the lawyer is asked to provide independent advice or independent represen-tation to another lawyer's client in a situation where a conflict exists, the provision of such advice or representation is an under- taking to be taken seriously and not lightly assumed or perfunctorily discharged. It involves a duty to the client for whom the independent advice or representation is provided that is the same as in any other lawyer and client relationship and ordinarily extends to the nature and result of the transaction.

CHAPTER IV
CONFIDENTIAL INFORMATION

RULE

The lawyer has a duty to hold in strict confidence all information concerning the business and affairs of the client acquired in the course of the professional relationship, and should not divulge such information unless disclosure is expressly or impliedly authorized by the client, required by law or otherwise permitted or required by this Code.

Commentary

Guiding Principles

1. The lawyer cannot render effective professional service to the client unless there is full and unreserved communication between them. At the same time the client must feel completely secure and entitled to proceed on the basis that without any express request or stipulation on the client's part, matters disclosed to or discussed with the lawyer will be held secret and confidential.

2. This ethical rule must be distinguished from the evidentiary rule of lawyer and client privilege with respect to oral or written communications passing between the client and the lawyer. The ethical rule is wider and applies without regard to the nature or source of the information or to the fact that others may share the knowledge.

3. As a general rule, the lawyer should not disclose having been consulted or retained by a person unless the nature of the matter requires such disclosure.

4. The lawyer owes a duty of secrecy to every client without exception, regardless of whether it be a continuing or casual client. The duty survives the professional relationship and continues indefinitely after the lawyer has ceased to act for the client, whether or not differences have arisen between them.

Confidential Information Not To Be Used

5. The fiduciary relationship between lawyer and client forbids the lawyer to use any confidential information covered by the ethical rule for the benefit of the lawyer or a third person, or to the disadvantage of the client. The lawyer who engages in literary works, such as an autobiography, memoirs and the like, should avoid disclosure of confidential information.

6. The lawyer should take care to avoid disclosure to one client of confidential information concerning or received from another client and should decline employment that might require such disclosures.

7. The lawyer should avoid indiscreet conversations, even with the lawyer's spouse or family, about a client's affairs and should shun any gossip about such things even though the client is not named or otherwise identified. Likewise the lawyer should not repeat any gossip or information about the client's business or affairs that may be overheard by or recounted to the lawyer. Apart altogether from ethical considerations or questions of good taste, indiscreet shop-talk between lawyers, if overheard by third parties able to identify the matter being discussed, could result in prejudice to the client. Moreover, the respect of the listener for the lawyers concerned and the legal profession generally will probably be lessened.

8. Although the Rule may not apply to facts that are public knowledge, the lawyer should guard against participating in or commenting upon speculation concerning the client's affairs or business.

Disclosure Authorized by Client

9. Confidential information may be divulged with the express authority of the client concerned and, in some situations, the authority of the client to divulge may be implied. For example, some disclosure may be necessary in a pleading or other document delivered in litigation being conducted for the client. Again, the lawyer may (unless the client directs otherwise) disclose the client's affairs to partners and associates in the firm and, to the extent necessary, to non-legal staff such as secretaries and filing clerks. This implied authority to disclose places the lawyer under a duty to impress upon associates, students and employees the importance of non-disclosure (both during their employment and afterwards) and requires the lawyer to take reasonable care to prevent their disclosing or using any information that the lawyer is bound to keep in confidence.

Disclosure Where Lawyer's Conduct in Issue

10. Disclosure may also be justified in order to establish or collect a fee, or to defend the lawyer or the lawyer's associates or employees against any allegation of malpractice or misconduct, but only to the extent necessary for such purposes. (As to potential claims for negligence, see commentary 10 of the Rule relating to Advising Clients.)

Disclosure To Prevent a Crime

11. Disclosure of information necessary to prevent a crime will be justified if the lawyer has reasonable grounds for believing that a crime is likely to be committed and will be mandatory when the anticipated crime is one involving violence.

12. The lawyer who has reasonable grounds for believing that a dangerous situation is likely to develop at a court facility shall inform the person having responsibility for security at the facility and give particulars. Where possible the lawyer should suggest solutions to the anticipated problem such as:

    (a) the need for further security;

    (b) that judgement be reserved;

    (c) such other measures as may seem advisable.

Disclosure Required by Law

13. When disclosure is required by law or by order of a court of competent jurisdiction, the lawyer should always be careful not to divulge more information than is required.

14. The lawyer who has information known to be confidential government information about a person, acquired when the lawyer was a public officer or employee, shall not represent a client (other than the agency of which the lawyer was a public officer or employee) whose interests are adverse to that person in a matter in which the information could be used to the material disadvantage of that person.

CHAPTER V
IMPARTIALITY AND CONFLICT OF INTEREST BETWEEN CLIENTS

RULE

The lawyer shall not advise or represent both sides of a dispute and, save after adequate disclosure to and with the consent of the clients or prospective clients concerned, shall not act or continue to act in a matter when there is or is likely to be a conflicting interest.

Commentary

Guiding Principles

1. A conflicting interest is one that would be likely to affect adversely the lawyer's judgement or advice on behalf of, or loyalty to a client or prospective client.

2. The reason for the Rule is self-evident. The client or the client's affairs may be seriously prejudiced unless the lawyer's judgement and freedom of action on the client's behalf are as free as possible from compromising influences.

3. Conflicting interests include, but are not limited to the duties and loyalties of the lawyer or a partner or professional associate of the lawyer to any other client, whether involved in the particular transaction or not, including the obligation to communicate information.

Disclosure of Conflicting Interest

4. The Rule requires adequate disclosure to enable the client to make an informed decision about whether to have the lawyer act despite the existence or possibility of a conflicting interest. As important as it is to the client that the lawyer's judgement and freedom of action on the client's behalf should not be subject to other interests, duties or obligations, in practice this factor may not always be decisive. Instead it may be only one of several factors that the client will weigh when deciding whether to give the consent referred to in the Rule. Other factors might include, for example, the availability of another lawyer of comparable expertise and experience, the extra cost, delay and inconvenience involved in engaging another lawyer and the latter's unfamiliarity with the client and the client's affairs. In the result, the client's interests may sometimes be better served by not engaging another lawyer. An example of this sort of situation is when the client and another party to a commercial transaction are continuing clients of the same law firm but are regularly represented by different lawyers in that firm.

5. Before the lawyer accepts employment from more than one client in the same matter, the lawyer must advise the clients that the lawyer has been asked to act for both or all of them, that no information received in connection with the matter from one can be treated as confidential so far as any of the others is concerned and that, if a dispute develops that cannot be resolved, the lawyer cannot continue to act for both or all of them and may have to withdraw completely. If one of the clients is a person with whom the lawyer has a continuing relationship and for whom the lawyer acts regularly, this fact should be revealed to the other or others at the outset with a recommendation that they obtain independent representation. If, following such disclosure, all parties are content that the lawyer act for them, the lawyer should obtain their consent, preferably in writing, or record their consent in a separate letter to each. The lawyer should, however, guard against acting for more than one

client where, despite the fact that all parties concerned consent, it is reasonably obvious that an issue contentious between them may arise or their interests, rights or obligations will diverge as the matter progresses.

6. If, after the clients involved have consented, an issue contentious between them or some of them arises, the lawyer, although not necessarily precluded from advising them on other non-contentious matters, would be in breach of the Rule if the lawyer attempted to advise them on the contentious issue. In such circumstances the lawyer should ordinarily refer the clients to other lawyers. However, if the issue is one that involves little or no legal advice, for example a business rather than a legal question in a proposed business transaction, and the clients are sophisticated, they may be permitted to settle the issue by direct negotiation in which the lawyer does not participate. Alternatively, the lawyer may refer one client to another lawyer and continue to advise the other if it was agreed at the outset that this course would be followed in the event of a conflict arising.

Lawyer as Arbitrator

7. The Rule will not prevent a lawyer from arbitrating or settling, or attempting to arbitrate or settle, a dispute between two or more clients or former clients who are *sui juris* and who wish to submit the dispute to the lawyer.

Acting Against Former Client

8. A lawyer who has acted for a client in a matter should not thereafter act against the client (or against persons who were involved in or associated with the client in that matter) in the same or any related matter, or take a position where the lawyer might be tempted or appear to be tempted to breach the Rule relating to confidential information. It is not, however, improper for the lawyer to act against a former client in a fresh and independent matter wholly unrelated to any work the lawyer has previously done for that person.

9. For the sake of clarity the foregoing paragraphs are expressed in terms of the individual lawyer and client. However, the term "client" includes a client of the law firm of which the lawyer is a partner or associate, whether or not the lawyer handles the client's work. It also includes the client of a lawyer who is associated with the lawyer in such a manner as to be perceived as practising in partnership or association with the first lawyer, even though in fact no such partnership or association exists.

Acting for More Than One Client

10. In practice, there are many situations where even though no actual dispute exists between the parties their interests are in conflict. Common examples in a conveyancing practice are vendor and purchaser, or mortgagor and mortgagee. In cases where the lawyer is asked to act for more than one client in such a transaction, the lawyer should recommend that each party be separately represented. In all such transactions the lawyer must observe the rules prescribed by the governing body.

11. There are also many situations where more than one person may wish to retain the lawyer to handle a transaction and, although their interests appear to coincide, in fact a potential conflict of interest exists. Examples are co-purchasers of real property and persons forming a partnership or corporation. Such cases will be governed by commentaries 4 and 5 of this Rule.

12. A lawyer who is employed or retained by an organization represents that organization acting through its duly authorized constituents. In dealing with the organization's directors, officers, employees, members, shareholders or other constituents, the lawyer shall make clear that it is the organization that is the client when it becomes apparent that the organization's interests are adverse to those of the constituents with whom the lawyer is dealing. The lawyer representing an organization may also represent any of the directors, officers, employees, members, shareholders or other constituents, subject to the provisions of this Rule dealing with conflicts of interest.

Burden of Proof

13. Generally speaking, in disciplinary proceedings arising from a breach of this Rule the lawyer has the burden of showing good faith and that adequate disclosure was made in the matter and the client's consent was obtained.

CHAPTER VI
CONFLICT OF INTEREST BETWEEN LAWYER AND CLIENT

RULE

(a) The lawyer should not enter into a business transaction with the client or knowingly give to or acquire from the client an ownership, security or other pecuniary interest unless:

(i) the transaction is a fair and reasonable one and its terms are fully disclosed to the client in writing in a manner that is reasonably understood by the client;

(ii) the client is given a reasonable opportunity to seek independent legal advice about the transaction, the onus being on the lawyer to prove that the client's interests were protected by such independent advice; and

(iii) the client consents in writing to the transaction.

(b) The lawyer shall not enter into or continue a business transaction with the client if:

(i) the client expects or might reasonably be assumed to expect that the lawyer is protecting the client's interests;

(ii) there is a significant risk that the interests of the lawyer and the client may differ.

(c) The lawyer shall not act for the client where the lawyer's duty to the client and the personal interests of the lawyer or an associate are in conflict.

(d) The lawyer shall not prepare an instrument giving the lawyer or an associate a substantial gift from the client, including a testamentary gift.

Commentary

Guiding Principles

1. The principles enunciated in the Rule relating to impartiality and conflict of interest between clients apply *mutatis mutandis* to this Rule.

2. A conflict of interest between lawyer and client exists in all cases where the lawyer gives property to or acquires it from the client by way of purchase, gift, testamentary disposition or otherwise. Such transactions are to be avoided. When they are contemplated, the

prudent course is to insist that the client either be independently represented or have independent legal advice.

3. This Rule applies also to situations involving associates of the lawyer. Associates of the lawyer within the meaning of the Rule include the lawyer's spouse, children, any relative of the lawyer (or of the lawyer's spouse) living under the same roof, any partner or associate of the lawyer in the practice of law, a trust or estate in which the lawyer has a substantial beneficial interest or for which the lawyer acts as a trustee or in a similar capacity, and a corporation of which the lawyer is a director or in which the lawyer or an associate owns or controls, directly or indirectly, a significant number of shares.

Debtor–Creditor Relationship To Be Avoided

4. The lawyer should avoid entering into a debtor-creditor relationship with the client. The lawyer should not borrow money from a client who is not in the business of lending money. It is undesirable that the lawyer lend money to the client except by way of advancing necessary expenses in a legal matter that the lawyer is handling for the client.

Joint Ventures

5. The lawyer who has a personal interest in a joint business venture with others may represent or advise the business venture in legal matters between it and third parties, but should not represent or advise either the joint business venture or the joint venturers in respect of legal matters as between them. When Person to be Considered a Client

6. The question of whether a person is to be considered a client of the lawyer when such person is lending money to the lawyer, or buying, selling, making a loan to or investment in, or assuming an obligation in respect of a business, security or property in which the lawyer or an associate of the lawyer has an interest, or in respect of any other transaction, is to be determined having regard to all the circumstances. A person who is not otherwise a client may be deemed to be a client for purposes of this Rule if such person might reasonably feel entitled to look to the lawyer for guidance and advice in respect of the transaction. In those circumstances the lawyer must consider such person to be a client and will be bound by the same fiduciary obligations that attach to a lawyer in dealings with a client. The onus shall be on the lawyer to establish that such a person was not in fact looking to the lawyer for guidance and advice.

CHAPTER VII

OUTSIDE INTERESTS AND THE PRACTICE OF LAW

RULE

The lawyer who engages in another profession, business or occupation concurrently with the practice of law must not allow such outside interest to jeopardize the lawyer's professional integrity, independence or competence.

Commentary

Guiding Principles

1. The term "outside interest" covers the widest possible range and includes activities that may overlap or be connected with the practice of law, such as engaging in the mortgage business, acting as a director of a client corporation, or writing on legal subjects, as well as activities not so connected such as a career in business, politics, broadcasting or the performing arts. In each case the question of whether the lawyer may properly engage in the outside interest and to what extent the lawyer will be subject to any applicable law or rule of the governing body.

2. Whenever an overriding social, political, economic or other consideration arising from the outside interest might influence the lawyer's judgement, the lawyer should be governed by the considerations declared in the Rule relating to conflict of interest between lawyer and client.

3. Where the outside interest is in no way related to the legal services being performed for clients, ethical considerations will usually not arise unless the lawyer's conduct brings either the lawyer or the profession into disrepute or impairs the lawyer's competence as, for example, where the outside interest occupies so much time that clients suffer because of the lawyer's lack of attention or preparation.

4. The lawyer must not carry on, manage or be involved in any outside business, investment, property or occupation in such a way that makes it difficult to distinguish in which capacity the lawyer is acting in a particular transaction, or that would give rise to a conflict of interest or duty to a client. When acting or dealing in respect of a transaction involving an outside interest in a business, investment, property or occupation, the lawyer must disclose any personal interest, must declare to all parties in the transaction or to their solicitors whether the lawyer is acting on the lawyer's own behalf or in a professional capacity or otherwise, and must adhere throughout the transaction to standards of conduct as high as those that this Code requires of a lawyer engaged in the practice of law.

5. The lawyer who has an outside interest in a business, investment, property or occupation:

(a) must not be identified as a lawyer when carrying on, managing or being involved in such outside interest; and

(b) must ensure that monies received in respect of the day-to-day carrying on, operation and management of such outside interest are deposited in an account other than the lawyer's trust account, unless such monies are received by the lawyer when acting in a professional capacity as a lawyer on behalf of the outside interest.

6. In order to be compatible with the practice of law the other profession, business or occupation:

(a) must be an honourable one that does not detract from the status of the lawyer or the legal profession generally; and

(b) must not be such as would likely result in a conflict of interest between the lawyer and a client.

CHAPTER VIII
PRESERVATION OF CLIENTS' PROPERTY

RULE

The lawyer owes a duty to the client to observe all relevant laws and rules respecting the preservation and safekeeping of the client's property entrusted to the lawyer. Where there are no such laws or rules, or the lawyer is in any doubt, the lawyer should take the same care of such property as a careful and prudent owner would when dealing with property of like description.

Commentary

Guiding Principles

1. The lawyer's duties with respect to safekeeping, preserving and accounting for the clients' monies and other property are generally the subject of special rules. In the absence of such rules the lawyer should adhere to the minimum standards set out in the note. "Property", apart from clients' monies, includes securities such as mortgages, negotiable instruments, stocks, bonds, etc., original documents such as wills, title deeds, minute books, licences, certificates, etc., other papers such as clients' correspondence files, reports, invoices, etc., as well as chattels such as jewellery, silver, etc.

2. The lawyer should promptly notify the client upon receiving any property of or relating to the client unless satisfied that the client knows that it has come into the lawyer's custody.

3. The lawyer should clearly label and identify the client's property and place it in safekeeping separate and apart from the lawyer's own property.

4. The lawyer should maintain adequate records of clients' property in the lawyer's custody so that it may be promptly accounted for, or delivered to, or to the order of, the client upon request. The lawyer should ensure that such property is delivered to the right person and, in case of dispute as to the person entitled, may have recourse to the courts.

5. The duties here expressed are closely related to those concerning confidential information. The lawyer should keep clients' papers and other property out of sight as well as out of reach of those not entitled to see them and should, subject to any right of lien, return them promptly to the clients upon request or at the conclusion of the lawyer's retainer.

Privilege

6. The lawyer should be alert to claim on behalf of clients any lawful privilege respecting information about their affairs, including their files and property if seized or attempted to be seized by a third party. In this regard the lawyer should be familiar with the nature of clients' privilege, and with relevant statutory provisions such as those in the *Income Tax Act*, the *Criminal Code*, the *Canadian Charter of Rights and Freedoms* and other statutes.

CHAPTER IX
THE LAWYER AS ADVOCATE

RULE

When acting as an advocate, the lawyer must treat the tribunal with courtesy and respect and must represent the client resolutely, honourably and within the limits of the law.

Commentary

Guiding Principles

1. The advocate's duty to the client "fearlessly to raise every issue, advance every argument, and ask every question, however distasteful, which he thinks will help his client's case" and to endeavour "to obtain for his client the benefit of any and every remedy and defence which is authorized by law" must always be discharged by fair and honourable means, without illegality and in a manner consistent with the lawyer's duty to treat the court with candour, fairness, courtesy and respect.

Prohibited Conduct

2. The lawyer must not, for example:

(a) abuse the process of the tribunal by instituting or prosecuting proceedings that, although legal in themselves, are clearly motivated by malice on the part of the client and are brought solely for the purpose of injuring another party;

(b) knowingly assist or permit the client to do anything that the lawyer considers to be dishonest or dishonourable;

(c) appear before a judicial officer when the lawyer, the lawyer's associates or the client have business or personal relationships with such officer that give rise to real or apparent pressure, influence or inducement affecting the impartiality of such officer;

(d) attempt or allow anyone else to attempt, directly or indirectly, to influence the decision or actions of a tribunal or any of its officials by any means except open persuasion as an advocate;

(e) knowingly attempt to deceive or participate in the deception of a tribunal or influence the course of justice by offering false evidence, misstating facts or law, presenting or relying upon a false or deceptive affidavit, suppressing what ought to be disclosed or otherwise assisting in any fraud, crime or illegal conduct;

(f) knowingly misstate the contents of a document, the testimony of a witness, the substance of an argument or the provisions of a statute or like authority;

(g) knowingly assert something for which there is no reasonable basis in evidence, or the admissibility of which must first be established;

(h) deliberately refrain from informing the tribunal of any pertinent adverse authority that the lawyer considers to be directly in point and that has not been mentioned by an opponent;

(i) dissuade a material witness from giving evidence, or advise such a witness to be absent;

(j) knowingly permit a witness to be presented in a false or misleading way or to impersonate another;

(k) needlessly abuse, hector or harass a witness;

(l) needlessly inconvenience a witness.

Errors and Omissions

3. The lawyer who has unknowingly done or failed to do something that, if done or omitted knowingly, would have been in breach of this Rule and discovers it, has a duty to the court, subject to the Rule relating to confidential information, to disclose the error or omission and do all that can reasonably be done in the circumstances to rectify it.

Duty To Withdraw

4. If the client wishes to adopt a course that would involve a breach of this Rule, the lawyer must refuse and do everything reasonably possible to prevent it. If the client persists in such a course the lawyer should, subject to the Rule relating to withdrawal, withdraw or seek leave of the court to do so.

The Lawyer as Witness

5. The lawyer who appears as an advocate should not submit the lawyer's own affidavit to or testify before a tribunal save as permitted by local rule or practice, or as to purely formal or uncontroverted matters. This also applies to the lawyer's partners and associates; generally speaking, they should not testify in such proceedings except as to merely formal matters. The lawyer should not express personal opinions or beliefs, or assert as fact anything that is properly subject to legal proof, cross-examination or challenge. The lawyer must not in effect become an unsworn witness or put the lawyer's own credibility in issue. The lawyer who is a necessary witness should testify and entrust the conduct of the case to someone else. Similarly, the lawyer who was a witness in the proceedings should not appear as advocate in any appeal from the decision in those proceedings. There are no restrictions upon the advocate's right to cross-examine another lawyer, and the lawyer who does appear as a witness should not expect to receive special treatment by reason of professional status.

Interviewing Witnesses

6. The lawyer may properly seek information from any potential witness (whether under subpoena or not) but should disclose the lawyer's interest and take care not to subvert or suppress any evidence or procure the witness to stay out of the way. The lawyer shall not approach or deal with an opposite party who is professionally represented save through or with the consent of that party's lawyer.

Unmeritorious Proceedings

7. The lawyer should never waive or abandon the client's legal rights (for example an available defence under a statute of limitations) without the client's informed consent. In civil matters it is desirable that the lawyer should avoid and discourage the client from resorting to frivolous or vexatious objections or attempts to gain advantage from slips or oversights not going to the real merits, or tactics that will merely delay or harass the other side. Such practices can readily bring the administration of justice and the legal profession into disrepute.

Encouraging Settlements

8. Whenever the case can be settled fairly, the lawyer should advise and encourage the client to do so rather than commence or continue legal proceedings.

Duties of Prosecutor

9. When engaged as a prosecutor, the lawyer's prime duty is not to seek a conviction, but to present before the trial court all available credible evidence relevant to the alleged crime in order that justice may be done through a fair trial upon the merits. The prosecutor exercises a public function involving much discretion and power and must act fairly and dispassionately. The prosecutor should not do anything that might prevent the accused from being represented by counsel or communicating with counsel and, to the extent required by law and accepted practice, should make timely disclosure to the accused or defence counsel (or to the court if the accused is not represented) of all relevant facts and known witnesses, whether tending to show guilt or innocence, or that would affect the punishment of the accused.

Duties of Defence Counsel

10. When defending an accused person, the lawyer's duty is to protect the client as far as possible from being convicted except by a court of competent jurisdiction and upon legal evidence sufficient to support a conviction for the offence charged. Accordingly, and notwithstanding the lawyer's private opinion as to credibility or merits, the lawyer may properly rely upon all available evidence or defences including so-called technicalities not known to be false or fraudulent.

11. Admissions made by the accused to the lawyer may impose strict limitations on the conduct of the defence and the accused should be made aware of this. For example, if the accused clearly admits to the lawyer the factual and mental elements necessary to constitute the offence, the lawyer, if convinced that the admissions are true and voluntary, may properly take objection to the jurisdiction of the court, or to the form of the indictment, or to the admissibility or sufficiency of the evidence, but must not suggest that some other person committed the offence, or call any evidence that, by reason of the admissions, the lawyer believes to be false. Nor may the lawyer set up an affirmative case inconsistent with such admissions, for example, by calling evidence in support of an alibi intended to show that the accused could not have done, or in fact had not done, the act. Such admissions will also impose a limit upon the extent to which the lawyer may attack the evidence for the prosecution. The lawyer is entitled to test the evidence given by each individual witness for the prosecution and argue that the evidence taken as a whole is insufficient to amount to proof that the accused is guilty of the offence charged, but the lawyer should go no further than that.

Agreement on Guilty Plea

12. Where, following investigation,

(a) the defence lawyer bona fide concludes and advises the accused client that an acquittal of the offence charged is uncertain or unlikely,

(b) the client is prepared to admit the necessary factual and mental elements,

(c) the lawyer fully advises the client of the implications and possible consequences of a guilty plea and that the matter of sentence is solely in the discretion of the trial judge, and

(d) the client so instructs the lawyer, preferably in writing, it is proper for the lawyer to discuss and agree tentatively with the prosecutor to enter a plea of guilty on behalf of the client to the offence charged or to a lesser or included offence or to another offence appropriate to the admissions, and also on a disposition or sentence to be proposed to the court. The public interest and the client's interests must not, however, be compromised by agreeing to a guilty plea.

Undertakings

13. An undertaking given by the lawyer to the court or to another lawyer in the course of litigation or other adversary proceedings must be strictly and scrupulously carried out. Unless clearly qualified in writing, the lawyer's undertaking is a personal promise and responsibility.

Courtesy

14. The lawyer should at all times be courteous and civil to the court and to those engaged on the other side. Legal contempt of court and the professional obligation outlined here are not identical, and a consistent pattern of rude, provocative or disruptive conduct by the lawyer, even though unpunished as contempt, might well merit disciplinary action.

Role in Adversary Proceedings

15. In adversary proceedings, the lawyer's function as advocate is openly and necessarily partisan. Accordingly, the lawyer is not obliged (save as required by law or under paragraphs 2(h) or 7 above) to assist an adversary or advance matters derogatory to the client's case. When opposing interests are not represented, for example in *ex parte* or uncontested matters, or in other situations where the full proof and argument inherent in the adversary system cannot be obtained, the lawyer must take particular care to be accurate, candid and comprehensive in presenting the client's case so as to ensure that the court is not misled.

Communicating with Witnesses

16. When in court the lawyer should observe local rules and practices concerning communication with a witness about the witness's evidence or any issue in the proceeding. Generally, it is considered improper for counsel who called a witness to communicate with that witness without leave of the court while such witness is under cross-examination.

Agreements Guaranteeing Recovery

17. In civil proceedings the lawyer has a duty not to mislead the court about the position of the client in the adversary process. Thus, where a lawyer representing a client in litigation has made or is party to an agreement made before or during the trial whereby a plaintiff is guaranteed recovery by one or more parties notwithstanding the judgement of the court, the lawyer shall disclose full particulars of the agreement to the court and all other parties.

Scope of the Rule

18. The principles of this Rule apply generally to the lawyer as advocate and therefore extend not only to court proceedings but also to appearances and proceedings before boards, administrative tribunals and other bodies, regardless of their function or the informality of their procedures.

CHAPTER X
THE LAWYER IN PUBLIC OFFICE

RULE

The lawyer who holds public office should, in the discharge of official duties, adhere to standards of conduct as high as those that these rules require of a lawyer engaged in the practice of law.

Commentary

Guiding Principles

1. The Rule applies to the lawyer who is elected or appointed to legislative or administrative office at any level of government, regardless of whether the lawyer attained such office because of professional qualifications. Because such a lawyer is in the public eye, the legal profession can more readily be brought into disrepute by failure on the lawyer's part to observe its professional standards of conduct.

Conflicts of Interest

2. The lawyer who holds public office must not allow personal or other interests to conflict with the proper discharge of official duties. The lawyer holding part-time public office must not accept any private legal business where duty to the client will or may conflict with official duties. If some unforeseen conflict arises, the lawyer should terminate the professional relationship, explaining to the client that official duties must prevail. The lawyer who holds a full-time public office will not be faced with this sort of conflict, but must nevertheless guard against allowing the lawyer's independent judgement in the discharge of official duties to be influenced by the lawyer's own interest, or by the interests of persons closely related to or associated with the lawyer, or of former or prospective clients, or of former or prospective partners or associates.

3. In the context of the preceding paragraph, persons closely related to or associated with the lawyer include a spouse, child, or any relative of the lawyer (or of the lawyer's spouse) living under the same roof, a trust or estate in which the lawyer has a substantial beneficial interest or for which the lawyer acts as a trustee or in a similar capacity, and a corporation of which the lawyer is a director or in which the lawyer or some closely related or associated person holds or controls, directly or indirectly, a significant number of shares.

4. Subject to any special rules applicable to a particular public office, the lawyer holding such office who sees the possibility of a conflict of interest should declare such interest at the earliest opportunity and take no part in any consideration, discussion or vote with respect to the matter in question.

Appearances Before Official Bodies

5. When the lawyer or any of the lawyer's partners or associates is a member of an official body such as, for example, a school board, municipal council or governing body, the lawyer should not appear professionally before that body. However, subject to the rules of the official body it would not be improper for the lawyer to appear professionally before a committee of such body if such partner or associate is not a member of that committee.

6. The lawyer should not represent in the same or any related matter any persons or interests that the lawyer has been concerned with in an official capacity. Similarly, the lawyer should avoid advising upon a ruling of an official body of which the lawyer either is a member or was a member at the time the ruling was made.

Disclosure of Confidential Information

7. By way of corollary to the Rule relating to confidential information, the lawyer who has acquired confidential information by virtue of holding public office should keep such information confidential and not divulge or use it even though the lawyer has ceased to hold such office. (As to the taking of employment in connection with any matter in respect of which the lawyer had substantial responsibility or confidential information, see commentary 3 of the Rule relating to avoiding questionable conduct.)

Disciplinary Action

8. Generally speaking, a governing body will not be concerned with the way in which a lawyer holding public office carries out official responsibilities, but conduct in office that reflects adversely upon the lawyer's integrity or professional competence may subject the lawyer to disciplinary action.

CHAPTER XI
FEES

RULE

The lawyer shall not
   (a) stipulate for, charge or accept any fee that is not fully disclosed, fair and reasonable;
   (b) appropriate any funds of the client held in trust or otherwise under the lawyer's control for or on account of fees without the express authority of the client, save as permitted by the rules of the governing body.

Commentary

Factors To Be Considered

1. A fair and reasonable fee will depend on and reflect such factors as:
   (a) the time and effort required and spent;
   (b) the difficulty and importance of the matter;
   (c) whether special skill or service has been required and provided;
   (d) the customary charges of other lawyers of equal standing in the locality in like matters and circumstances;
   (e) in civil cases the amount involved, or the value of the subject matter;
   (f) in criminal cases the exposure and risk to the client;
   (g) the results obtained;
   (h) tariffs or scales authorized by local law;
   (i) such special circumstances as loss of other employment, urgency and uncertainty of reward;
   (j) any relevant agreement between the lawyer and the client.

A fee will not be fair and reasonable and may subject the lawyer to disciplinary proceedings if it is one that cannot be justified in the light of all pertinent circumstances, including the factors mentioned, or is so disproportionate to the services rendered as to introduce the element of fraud or dishonesty, or undue profit.

2. It is in keeping with the best traditions of the legal profession to reduce or waive a fee in cases of hardship or poverty, or where the client or prospective client would otherwise effectively be deprived of legal advice or representation.

Avoidance of Controversy

3. Breaches of this Rule and misunderstandings about fees and financial matters bring the legal profession into disrepute and reflect adversely upon the administration of justice. The lawyer should try to avoid controversy with the client over fees and should be ready to explain the basis for charges, especially if the client is unsophisticated or uninformed about the proper basis and measurements for fees. The lawyer should give the client an early and fair estimate of fees and disbursements, pointing out any uncertainties involved, so that the client may be able to make an informed decision. When something unusual or unforeseen occurs that may substantially affect the amount of the fee, the lawyer should forestall misunderstandings or disputes by explaining this to the client.

Interest on Overdue Accounts

4. Save where permitted by law or local practice, the lawyer should not charge interest on an overdue account except by prior agreement with the client and then only at a reasonable rate.

Apportionment and Division of Fees

5. The lawyer who acts for two or more clients in the same matter is under a duty to apportion the fees and disbursements equitably among them in the absence of agreement otherwise.

6. A fee will not be a fair one within the meaning of the Rule if it is divided with another lawyer who is not a partner or associate unless (a) the client consents, either expressly or impliedly, to the employment of the other lawyer and (b) the fee is divided in proportion to the work done and responsibility assumed.

Hidden Fees

7. The fiduciary relationship that exists between lawyer and client requires full disclosure in all financial matters between them and prohibits the lawyer from accepting any hidden fees. No fee, reward, costs, commission, interest, rebate, agency or forwarding allowance or other compensation whatsoever related to the professional employment may be taken by the lawyer from anyone other than the client without full disclosure to and consent of the client. Where the lawyer's fees are being paid by someone other than the client, such as a legal aid agency, a borrower, or a personal representative, the consent of such other person will be required. So far as disbursements are concerned, only bona fide and specified payments to others may be included. If the lawyer is financially interested in the person to whom the disbursements are made, such as an investigating, brokerage or copying agency, the lawyer shall expressly disclose this fact to the client.

Sharing Fees with Non-Lawyers

8. Any arrangement whereby the lawyer directly or indirectly shares, splits or divides fees with notaries public, law students, clerks or other non-lawyers who bring or refer business to the lawyer's office is improper and constitutes professional misconduct. It is also improper for the lawyer to give any financial or other reward to such persons for referring business.

9. The lawyer shall not enter into a lease or other arrangement whereby a landlord or other person directly or indirectly shares in the fees or revenues generated by the law practice.

Contingent Fees

10. Except where prohibited by the laws of the jurisdiction in which the lawyer practises, it is not improper for the lawyer to enter into an arrangement with the client for a contingent fee, provided such fee is fair and reasonable and the lawyer adheres to any rules of court or local practice relating to such an arrangement.

CHAPTER XII
WITHDRAWAL

RULE

The lawyer owes a duty to the client not to withdraw services except for good cause and upon notice appropriate in the circumstances.

Commentary

Guiding Principles

1. Although the client has a right to terminate the lawyer-client relationship at will the lawyer does not enjoy the same freedom of action. Having once accepted professional employment the lawyer should complete the task as ably as possible unless there is justifiable cause for terminating the relationship.

2. The lawyer who withdraws from employment should act so as to minimize expense and avoid prejudice to the client, doing everything reasonably possible to facilitate the expeditious and orderly transfer of the matter to the successor lawyer.

3. Where withdrawal is required or permitted by this Rule the lawyer must comply with all applicable rules of court as well as local rules and practice.

Obligatory Withdrawal

4. In some circumstances the lawyer will be under a duty to withdraw. The obvious example is following discharge by the client. Other examples are (a) if the lawyer is instructed by the client to do something inconsistent with the lawyer's duty to the court and, following explanation, the client persists in such instructions; (b) if the client is guilty of dishonourable conduct in the proceedings or is taking a position solely to harass or maliciously injure another; (c) if it becomes clear that the lawyer's continued employment will lead to a breach of these Rules such as for example a breach of the Rules relating to conflict of interest; or (d) if it develops that the lawyer is not competent to handle the matter. In all these situations there is a duty to inform the client that the lawyer must withdraw.

Optional Withdrawal

5. Situations where a lawyer would be entitled to withdraw, although not under a positive duty to do so, will as a rule arise only where there has been a serious loss of confidence between lawyer and client. Such a loss of confidence goes to the very basis of the relationship. Thus, the lawyer who is deceived by the client will have justifiable cause for withdrawal. Again, the refusal of the client to accept and act upon the lawyer's advice on a significant point might indicate such a loss of confidence. At the same time, the lawyer should not use the threat of withdrawal as a device to force the client into making a hasty decision on a difficult question. The lawyer may withdraw if unable to obtain instructions from the client.

Non-Payment of Fees

6. Failure on the part of the client after reasonable notice to provide funds on account of disbursements or fees will justify withdrawal by the lawyer unless serious prejudice to the client would result.

Notice to Client

7. No hard and fast rules can be laid down as to what will constitute reasonable notice prior to withdrawal. Where the matter is covered by statutory provisions or rules of court, these will govern. In other situations the governing principle is that the lawyer should protect the client's interests so far as possible and should not desert the client at a critical stage of a matter or at a time when withdrawal would put the client in a position of disadvantage or peril.

Duty Following Withdrawal

8. Upon discharge or withdrawal the lawyer should:

(a) deliver in an orderly and expeditious manner to or to the order of the client all papers and property to which the client is entitled;

(b) give the client all information that may be required about the case or matter;

(c) account for all funds of the client on hand or previously dealt with and refund any remuneration not earned during the employment;

(d) promptly render an account for outstanding fees and disbursements;

(e) co-operate with the successor lawyer for the purposes outlined in paragraph 2. The obligation in clause (a) to deliver papers and property is subject to the lawyer's right of lien referred to in paragraph 11. In the event of conflicting claims to such papers and property, the lawyer should make every effort to have the claimants settle the dispute.

9. Co-operation with the successor lawyer will normally include providing any memoranda of fact and law that have been prepared by the lawyer in connection with the matter, but confidential information not clearly related to the matter should not be divulged without the express consent of the client.

10. The lawyer acting for several clients in a case or matter who ceases to act for one or more of them should co-operate with the successor lawyer or lawyers to the extent permitted by this Code, and should seek to avoid any unseemly rivalry, whether real or apparent.

Lien for Unpaid Fees

11. Where upon the discharge or withdrawal of the lawyer the question of a right of lien for unpaid fees and disbursements arises, the lawyer should have due regard to the effect of its enforcement upon the client's position. Generally speaking, the lawyer should not enforce such a lien if the result would be to prejudice materially the client's position in any uncompleted matter.

Duty of Successor Lawyer

12. Before accepting employment, the successor lawyer should be satisfied that the former lawyer approves, or has withdrawn or been discharged by the client. It is quite proper for the successor lawyer to urge the client to settle or take reasonable steps toward settling or securing any account owed to the former lawyer, especially if the latter withdrew for good cause or was capriciously discharged. But if a trial or hearing is in progress or imminent, or if the client would otherwise be prejudiced, the existence of an outstanding account should not be allowed to interfere with the successor lawyer acting for the client.

Dissolution of Law Firm

13. When a law firm is dissolved, this will usually result in the termination of the lawyer- client relationship as between a particular client and one or more of the lawyers involved. In such cases, most clients will prefer to retain the services of the lawyer whom they regarded as being in charge of their business prior to the dissolution. However, the final decision rests in each case with the client, and the lawyers who are no longer retained by the client should act in accordance with the principles here set out, and in particular commentary.

CHAPTER XIII
THE LAWYER AND THE ADMINISTRATION OF JUSTICE

RULE

The lawyer should encourage public respect for and try to improve the administration of justice.

Commentary

Guiding Principles

1. The admission to and continuance in the practice of law imply a basic commitment by the lawyer to the concept of equal justice for all within an open, ordered and impartial system. However, judicial institutions will not function effectively unless they command the respect of the public. Because of changes in human affairs and the imperfection of human institutions, constant efforts must be made to improve the administration of justice and thereby maintain public respect for it.

2. The lawyer, by training, opportunity and experience, is in a position to observe the workings and discover the strengths and weaknesses of laws, legal institutions and public authorities. The lawyer should, therefore, lead in seeking improvements in the legal system, but any criticisms and proposals should be bona fide and reasoned.

Scope of the Rule

3. The obligation outlined in the Rule is not restricted to the lawyer's professional activities but is a general responsibility resulting from the lawyer's position in the community. The lawyer's responsibilities are greater than those of a private citizen. The lawyer must not subvert the law by counselling or assisting in activities that are in defiance of it and must do nothing to lessen the respect and confidence of the public in the legal system of which the lawyer is a part. The lawyer should take care not to weaken or destroy public confidence in legal institutions or authorities by broad irresponsible allegations of corruption or partiality. The lawyer in public life must be particularly careful in this regard because the mere fact of being a lawyer will lend weight and credibility to any public statements.

For the same reason, the lawyer should not hesitate to speak out against an injustice. (As to test cases, see commentary 8 of the Rule relating to advising clients.)

Criticism of the Tribunal

4. Although proceedings and decisions of tribunals are properly subject to scrutiny and criticism by all members of the public, including lawyers, members of tribunals are often prohibited by law or custom from defending themselves. Their inability to do so imposes special responsibilities upon lawyers. Firstly, the lawyer should avoid criticism that is petty, intemperate or unsupported by a *bona fide* belief in its real merit, bearing in mind that in the eyes of the public, professional knowledge lends weight to the lawyer's judgements or criticism. Secondly, if the lawyer has been involved in the proceedings, there is the risk that any criticism may be, or may appear to be, partisan rather than objective. Thirdly, where a tribunal is the object of unjust criticism, the lawyer, as a participant in the administration of justice, is uniquely able to and should support the tribunal, both because its members cannot defend themselves and because the lawyer is thereby contributing to greater public understanding of and therefore respect for the legal system.

Improving the Administration of Justice

5. The lawyer who seeks legislative or administrative changes should disclose whose interest is being advanced, whether it be the lawyer's interest, that of a client, or the public interest. The lawyer may advocate such changes on behalf of a client without personally agreeing with them, but the lawyer who purports to act in the public interest should espouse only those changes that the lawyer conscientiously believes to be in the public interest.

CHAPTER XIV
ADVERTISING, SOLICITATION AND MAKING LEGAL
SERVICES AVAILABLE

RULE

Lawyers should make legal services available to the public in an efficient and convenient manner that will command respect and confidence, and by means that are compatible with the integrity, independence and effectiveness of the profession.

Commentary

Guiding Principles

1. It is essential that a person requiring legal services be able to find a qualified lawyer with a minimum of difficulty or delay. In a relatively small community where lawyers are well known, the person will usually be able to make an informed choice and select a qualified lawyer in whom to have confidence. However, in larger centres these conditions will often not obtain. As the practice of law becomes increasingly complex and many individual lawyers restrict their activities to particular fields of law, the reputations of lawyers and their competence or qualification in particular fields may not be sufficiently well known to enable a person to make an informed choice. Thus one who has had little or no contact with lawyers or who is a stranger in the community may have difficulty finding a lawyer with the special skill required for a particular task. Telephone directories, legal directories and referral services may help find a lawyer, but not necessarily the right one for the work involved. Advertising of legal services by the lawyer may assist members of the public and thereby result in increased access to the legal system. Where local rules permit, the lawyer may, therefore, advertise legal services to the general public.

2. When considering whether advertising in a particular area meets the public need, consideration must be given to the clientele to be served. For example, in a small community with a stable population a person requiring a lawyer for a particular purpose will not have the same difficulty in selecting one as someone in a newly established community or a large city. Thus the governing body must have freedom of action in determining the nature and content of advertising that will best meet the community need.

3. Despite the lawyer's economic interest in earning a living, advertising, direct solicitation or any other means by which the lawyer seeks to make legal services more readily available to the public must comply with any rules prescribed by the governing body, must be consistent with the public interest and must not detract from the integrity, independence or effectiveness of the legal profession. They must not mislead the uninformed or arouse unattainable hopes and expectations, because this could result in distrust of legal institutions and lawyers. They must not adversely affect the quality of legal services, nor must they be so undignified, in bad taste or otherwise offensive as to be prejudicial to the interests of the public or the legal profession.

Finding a Lawyer

4. The lawyer who is consulted by a prospective client should be ready to assist in finding the right lawyer to deal with the problem. If unable to act, for example because of lack of qualification in the particular field, the lawyer should assist in finding a practitioner who is qualified and able to act. Such assistance should be given willingly and, except in very special circumstances, without charge.

5. The lawyer may also assist in making legal services available by participating in legal aid plans and referral services, by engaging in programs of public information, education or advice concerning legal matters, and by being considerate of those who seek advice but are inexperienced in legal matters or cannot readily explain their problems.

6. The lawyer has a general right to decline particular employment (except when assigned as counsel by a court) but it is a right the lawyer should be slow to exercise if the

probable result would be to make it very difficult for a person to obtain legal advice or representation. Generally speaking, the lawyer should not exercise the right merely because the person seeking legal services or that person's cause is unpopular or notorious, or because powerful interests or allegations of misconduct or malfeasance are involved, or because of the lawyer's private opinion about the guilt of the accused. As stated in commentary 4, the lawyer who declines employment should assist the person to obtain the services of another lawyer competent in the particular field and able to act.

Enforcement of Restrictive Rules

7. The lawyer should adhere to rules made by the governing body with respect to making legal services available and respecting advertising, but rigid adherence to restrictive rules should be enforced with discretion where the lawyer who may have infringed such rules acted in good faith in trying to make legal services available more efficiently, economically and conveniently than they would otherwise have been.

CHAPTER XV
RESPONSIBILITY TO THE PROFESSION GENERALLY

RULE

The lawyer should assist in maintaining the integrity of the profession and should participate in its activities.

Commentary

Guiding Principles

1. Unless the lawyer who tends to depart from proper professional conduct is checked at an early stage, loss or damage to clients or others may ensue. Evidence of minor breaches may, on investigation, disclose a more serious situation or may indicate the beginning of a course of conduct that would lead to serious breaches in the future. It is, therefore, proper (unless it be privileged or otherwise unlawful) for a lawyer to report to a governing body any occurrences involving a breach of this Code. Where, however, there is a reasonable likelihood that someone will suffer serious damage as a consequence of an apparent breach, for example where a shortage of trust funds is involved, the lawyer has an obligation to the profession to report the matter unless it is privileged or otherwise unlawful to do so. In all cases, the report must be made *bona fide* without malice or ulterior motive. Further, subject to local rules, the lawyer must not act on a client's instructions to recover from another lawyer funds allegedly misappropriated by that other lawyer unless the client authorizes disclosure to the governing body and the lawyer makes such disclosure.

2. The lawyer has a duty to reply promptly to any communication from the governing body.

3. The lawyer should not in the course of a professional practice write letters, whether to a client, another lawyer or any other person, that are abusive, offensive or otherwise totally inconsistent with the proper tone of a professional communication from a lawyer.

Participation in Professional Activities

4. In order that the profession may discharge its public responsibility of providing independent and competent legal services, the individual lawyer should do everything possible to assist the profession to function properly and effectively. In this regard, participation in such activities as law reform, continuing legal education, tutorials, legal aid programs, community legal services, professional conduct and discipline, liaison with other professions and other activities of the governing body or local, provincial or national associations, although often time-consuming and without tangible reward, is essential to the maintenance of a strong, independent and useful profession.

CHAPTER XVI
RESPONSIBILITY TO LAWYERS INDIVIDUALLY

RULE

The lawyer's conduct toward other lawyers should be characterized by courtesy and good faith.

Commentary

Guiding Principles

1. Public interest demands that matters entrusted to the lawyer be dealt with effectively and expeditiously. Fair and courteous dealing on the part of each lawyer engaged in a matter will contribute materially to this end. The lawyer who behaves otherwise does a disservice to the client, and neglect of the Rule will impair the ability of lawyers to perform their function properly.

2. Any ill feeling that may exist or be engendered between clients, particularly during litigation, should never be allowed to influence lawyers in their conduct and demeanour toward each other or the parties. The presence of personal animosity between lawyers involved in a matter may cause their judgement to be clouded by emotional factors and hinder the proper resolution of the matter. Personal remarks or references between them should be avoided. Haranguing or offensive tactics interfere with the orderly administration of justice and have no place in our legal system.

3. The lawyer should accede to reasonable requests for trial dates, adjournments, waivers of procedural formalities and similar matters that do not prejudice the rights of the client. The lawyer who knows that another lawyer has been consulted in a matter should not proceed by default in the matter without enquiry and warning.

Avoidance of Sharp Practices

4. The lawyer should avoid sharp practice and not take advantage of or act without fair warning upon slips, irregularities or mistakes on the part of other lawyers not going to the merits or involving any sacrifice of the client's rights. The lawyer should not, unless required by the transaction, impose on other lawyers impossible, impractical or manifestly unfair conditions of trust, including those with respect to time restraints and the payment of penalty interest.

5. The lawyer should not use a tape-recorder or other device to record a conversation, whether with a client, another lawyer or anyone else, even if lawful, without first informing the other person of the intention to do so.

6. The lawyer should answer with reasonable promptness all professional letters and communications from other lawyers that require an answer and should be punctual in fulfilling all commitments.

Undertakings

7. The lawyer should give no undertaking that cannot be fulfilled, should fulfill every undertaking given, and should scrupulously honour any trust condition once accepted. Undertakings and trust conditions should be written or confirmed in writing and should be absolutely unambiguous in their terms. If the lawyer giving an undertaking does not intend to accept personal responsibility, this should be stated clearly in the undertaking itself. In the absence of such a statement, the person to whom the undertaking is given is entitled to expect that the lawyer giving it will honour it personally. If the lawyer is unable or unwilling to honour a trust condition imposed by someone else, the subject of the trust condition should be immediately returned to the person imposing the trust condition unless its terms can be forthwith amended in writing on a mutually agreeable basis.

8. The lawyer should not communicate upon or attempt to negotiate or compromise a matter directly with any party who is represented by a lawyer except through or with the consent of that lawyer.

Acting Against Another Lawyer

9. The lawyer should avoid ill-considered or uninformed criticism of the competence, conduct, advice or charges of other lawyers, but should be prepared, when requested, to advise and represent a client in a complaint involving another lawyer.

10. The same courtesy and good faith should characterize the lawyer's conduct toward lay persons lawfully representing others or themselves.

11. The lawyer who is retained by another lawyer as counsel or adviser in a particular matter should act only as counsel or adviser and respect the relationship between the other lawyer and the client.

CHAPTER XVII
PRACTICE BY UNAUTHORIZED PERSONS

RULE

The lawyer should assist in preventing the unauthorized practice of law.

Commentary

Guiding Principles

1. Statutory provisions against the practice of law by unauthorized persons are for the protection of the public. Unauthorized persons may have technical or personal ability, but they are immune from control, regulation and, in the case of misconduct, from discipline

by any governing body. Their competence and integrity have not been vouched for by an independent body representative of the legal profession. Moreover, the client of a lawyer who is authorized to practise has the protection and benefit of the lawyer-client privilege, the lawyer's duty of secrecy, the professional standards of care that the law requires of lawyers, as well as the authority that the courts exercise over them. Other safeguards include group professional liability insurance, rights with respect to the taxation of bills, rules respecting trust monies, and requirements for the maintenance of compensation funds.

Suspended or Disbarred Persons

2. The lawyer should not, without the approval of the governing body, employ in any capacity having to do with the practice of law (a) a lawyer who is under suspension as a result of disciplinary proceedings, or (b) a person who has been disbarred as a lawyer or has been permitted to resign while facing disciplinary proceedings and has not been reinstated.

Supervision of Employees

3. The lawyer must assume complete professional responsibility for all business entrusted to the lawyer, maintaining direct supervision over staff and assistants such as students, clerks and legal assistants to whom particular tasks and functions may be delegated. The lawyer who practises alone or operates a branch or part-time office should ensure that all matters requiring a lawyer's professional skill and judgement are dealt with by a lawyer qualified to do the work and that legal advice is not given by unauthorized persons, whether in the lawyer's name or otherwise. Furthermore, the lawyer should approve the amount of any fee to be charged to a client.

Legal Assistants

4. There are many tasks that can be performed by a legal assistant working under the supervision of a lawyer. It is in the interests of the profession and the public for the delivery of more efficient, comprehensive and better quality legal services that the training and employment of legal assistants be encouraged.

5. Subject to general and specific restrictions that may be established by local rules and practice, a legal assistant may perform any task delegated and supervised by a lawyer so long as the lawyer maintains a direct relationship with the client and assumes full professional responsibility for the work. Legal assistants shall not perform any of the duties that lawyers only may perform or do things that lawyers themselves may not do Generally speaking, the question of what the lawyer may delegate to a legal assistant turns on the distinction between the special knowledge of the legal assistant and the professional legal judgement of the lawyer, which must be exercised whenever it is required.

6. A legal assistant should be permitted to act only under the supervision of a lawyer. Adequacy of supervision will depend on the type of legal matter, including the degree of standardization and repetitiveness of the matter as well as the experience of the legal assistant, both generally and with regard to the particular matter. The burden rests on the lawyer who employs a legal assistant to educate the latter about the duties to which the legal assistant may be assigned and also to supervise on a continuing basis the way in which the legal assistant carries them out so that the work of the legal assistant will be shaped by the lawyer's judgement.

CHAPTER XVIII
PUBLIC APPEARANCES AND PUBLIC STATEMENTS BY LAWYERS

RULE

The lawyer who engages in public appearances and public statements should do so in conformity with the principles of the Code.

Commentary

Guiding Principles

1. The lawyer who makes public appearances and public statements should behave in the same way as when dealing with clients, fellow practitioners and the courts. Dealings with the media are simply an extension of the lawyer's conduct in a professional capacity. The fact that an appearance is outside a courtroom or law office does not excuse conduct that would be considered improper in those contexts.

Public Statements Concerning Clients

2. The lawyer's duty to the client demands that before making a public statement concerning the client's affairs, the lawyer must first be satisfied that any communication is in the best interests of the client and within the scope of the retainer. The lawyer owes a duty to the client to be qualified to represent the client effectively before the public and not to permit any personal interest or other cause to conflict with the client's interests.

3. When acting as an advocate, the lawyer should refrain from expressing personal opinions about the merits of the client's case.

Standard of Conduct

4. The lawyer should, where possible, encourage public respect for and try to improve the administration of justice. In particular, the lawyer should treat fellow practitioners, the courts and tribunals with respect, integrity and courtesy. Lawyers are subject to a separate and higher standard of conduct than that which might incur the sanction of the court.

5. The lawyer who makes public appearances and public statements must comply with the requirements of commentary 3 of the Rule relating to advertising, solicitation and making legal services available.

Contacts with the Media

6. The media have recently shown greater interest in legal matters than they did formerly. This is reflected in more coverage of the passage of legislation at national and provincial levels, as well as of cases before the courts that may have social, economic or political significance. This interest has been heightened by the enactment of the *Canadian Charter of Rights and Freedoms*. As a result, media reporters regularly seek out the views not only of lawyers directly involved in particular court proceedings but also of lawyers who represent special interest groups or have recognized expertise in a given field in order to obtain information or provide commentary.

7. Where the lawyer, by reason of professional involvement or otherwise, is able to assist the media in conveying accurate information to the public, it is proper for the lawyer

to do so, provided that there is no infringement of the lawyer's obligations to the client, the profession, the courts or the administration of justice, and provided also that the lawyer's comments are made bona fide and without malice or ulterior motive.

8. The lawyer may make contact with the media in a non-legal setting to publicize such things as fund-raising, expansion of hospitals or universities, promoting public institutions or political organizations, or speaking on behalf of organizations that represent various racial, religious or other special interest groups. This is a well established and completely proper role for the lawyer to play in view of the obvious contribution it makes to the community.

9. The lawyer is often called upon to comment publicly on the effectiveness of existing statutory or legal remedies, on the effect of particular legislation or decided cases, or to offer an opinion on causes that have been or are about to be instituted. It is permissible to do this in order to assist the public to understand the legal issues involved.

10. The lawyer may also be involved as an advocate for special interest groups whose objective is to bring about changes in legislation, government policy or even a heightened public awareness about certain issues, and the lawyer may properly comment publicly about such changes.

11. Given the variety of cases that can arise in the legal system, whether in civil, criminal or administrative matters, it is not feasible to set down guidelines that would anticipate every possible situation. In some circumstances, the lawyer should have no contact at all with the media; in others, there may be a positive duty to contact the media in order to serve the client properly. The latter situation will arise more often when dealing with administrative boards and tribunals that are instruments of government policy and hence susceptible to public opinion.

12. The lawyer should bear in mind when making a public appearance or giving a statement that ordinarily the lawyer will have no control over any editing that may follow, or the context in which the appearance or statement may be used.

13. This Rule should not be construed in such a way as to discourage constructive comment or criticism.

CHAPTER XIX
AVOIDING QUESTIONABLE CONDUCT

RULE

The lawyer should observe the rules of professional conduct set out in the Code in the spirit as well as in the letter.

Commentary

Guiding Principles

1. Public confidence in the administration of justice and the legal profession may be eroded by irresponsible conduct on the part of the individual lawyer. For that reason, even the appearance of impropriety should be avoided.

2. Our justice system is designed to try issues in an impartial manner and decide them upon the merits. Statements or suggestions that the lawyer could or would try to circumvent

the system should be avoided because they might bring the lawyer, the legal profession and the administration of justice into disrepute.

Duty After Leaving Public Employment

3. After leaving public employment, the lawyer should not accept employment in connection with any matter in which the lawyer had substantial responsibility or confidential information prior to leaving, because to do so would give the appearance of impropriety even if none existed. However, it would not be improper for the lawyer to act professionally in such a matter on behalf of the particular public body or authority by which the lawyer had formerly been employed. As to confidential government information acquired when the lawyer was a public officer or employee, see commentary 14 of the Rule relating to confidential information.

Retired Judges

4. A judge who returns to practice after retiring or resigning from the bench should not (without the approval of the governing body) appear as a lawyer before the court of which the former judge was a member or before courts of inferior jurisdiction thereto in the province where the judge exercised judicial functions. If in a given case the former judge should be in a preferred position by reason of having held judicial office, the administration of justice would suffer; if the reverse were true, the client might suffer. There may, however, be cases where a governing body would consider that no preference or appearance of preference would result, for example, where the judge resigned for good reason after only a very short time on the bench. In this paragraph "judge" refers to one who was appointed as such under provincial legislation or section 96 of the Constitution Act, 1982 and "courts" include chambers and administrative boards and tribunals.

5. Conversely, although it may be unavoidable in some circumstances or areas, generally speaking the lawyer should not appear before a judge if by reason of relationship or past association, the lawyer would appear to be in a preferred position.

Inserting Retainer in Client's Will

6. Without express instructions from the client, it is improper for the lawyer to insert in the client's will a clause directing the executor to retain the lawyer's services in the administration of the estate.

Duty To Meet Financial Obligations

7. The lawyer has a professional duty, quite apart from any legal liability, to meet financial obligations incurred or assumed in the course of practice when called upon to do so. Examples are agency accounts, obligations to members of the profession, fees or charges of witnesses, sheriffs, special examiners, registrars, reporters and public officials as well as the deductible under a governing body's errors and omissions insurance policy.

Dealings with Unrepresented Persons

8. The lawyer should not undertake to advise an unrepresented person but should urge such a person to obtain independent legal advice and, if the unrepresented person does not do so, the lawyer must take care to see that such person is not proceeding under the impres-

sion that the lawyer is protecting such person's interests. If the unrepresented person requests the lawyer to advise or act in the matter, the lawyer should be governed by the considerations outlined in the Rule relating to impartiality and conflict of interest between clients. The lawyer may have an obligation to a person whom the lawyer does not represent, whether or not such person is represented by a lawyer.

Bail

9. The lawyer shall not stand bail for an accused person for whom the lawyer or a partner or associate is acting, except where there is a family relationship with the accused in which case the person should not be represented by the lawyer but may be represented by a partner or associate.

Standard of Conduct

10. The lawyer should try at all times to observe a standard of conduct that reflects credit on the legal profession and the administration of justice generally and inspires the confidence, respect and trust of both clients and the community.

CHAPTER XX
NON-DISCRIMINATION

RULE

The lawyer shall respect the requirements of human rights and constitutional laws in force in Canada, and in the respective provinces and territories thereof, and shall not discriminate on grounds, including, but not limited to, of race, language, national or ethnic origin, colour, religion, age, sex, sexual orientation, marital status, family status, or disability.

Commentary

Duty of Non-Discrimination

1. The lawyer has a duty to respect the dignity and worth of all persons and to treat persons equally, without discrimination. Discrimination is defined as any distinction that disproportionately and negatively impacts on an individual or group identifiable by the grounds listed in the Rule, in a way that it does not impact on others. This duty includes, but is not limited to:

(a) the requirement that the lawyer does not deny services or provide inferior services on the basis of the grounds noted in the Rule;

(b) the requirement that the lawyer not discriminate against another lawyer in any professional dealings;

(c) the requirement that the lawyer act in accordance with the legal duty to accommodate and not engage in discriminatory employment practices; and

(d) the requirement that the lawyer prohibit partners, co-workers and employees and agents subject to the lawyer's direction and control from engaging in discriminatory practices.

Extent of Duty of Non-Discrimination

2. As a member of the legal profession, the lawyer must ensure that he or she is at all times acting in compliance with the law. The law applicable in this context is human rights legislation. According to the law, discrimination can be constituted by the effect of action or omission.

Intent to discriminate is not a prerequisite to a finding of discrimination. Discrimination can also arise though the adverse impact of neutral practices on the basis of the grounds noted in the Rule. Failure by the lawyer to take reasonable steps to prevent or stop discrimination by the lawyer's partner, co-worker or by any employee or agent also violates the duty of non-discrimination.

Special Programs

3. Discrimination does not include special programs designed to relieve disadvantage for individuals or groups on the grounds noted in the Rule.

Responsibility

4. Discriminatory attitudes on the part of partners, employees, agents or clients do not diminish the responsibility of the lawyer to refrain from discrimination in the provision of service or employment.

Discrimination in Employment

5. The Rule applies to discrimination by the lawyer in any aspect of employment and working conditions, including recruitment, promotion, training, allocation of work, compensation, receipt of benefits, dismissal, lay-offs, discipline, performance appraisal and hours of work.

It applies to all discrimination with repercussions for employment and workplace conditions including physical work sites, washrooms, conferences, business travel and social events. Examples of discrimination in employment include:

(a) setting unnecessary or unfair hiring criteria that tend to exclude applicants on prohibited grounds;

(b) asking questions during an employment or promotion interview that are not logically related to the essential requirements of the job;

(c) assigning work on the basis of factors or assumptions other than individual ability or denying work to lawyers on the basis of prohibited grounds;

(d) failing to provide appropriate maternity and parental leave thereby discriminating on the basis of sex or family status;

(e) failing to accommodate religious holidays or religious practices thereby discriminating on the basis of religion;

(f) requiring billable hour targets or workload expectations which effectively exclude those who have child care responsibilities and adversely affect such persons on the basis of family status or sex.

It is not considered discrimination when distinctions are made as a result of a reasonable and bona fide occupational qualification or requirement. For example, if an applicant for a position is not sufficiently proficient in the language(s) required for the competent performance of the essential duties and responsibilities required in that position, it would not constitute discrimination to deny the applicant employment solely on the ground of language. Where facility in a particular language is clearly an essential requirement for the position, the employer is not prevented from demanding the necessary proficiency.

Duty of Accommodation

6. One aspect of the duty of non-discrimination is the duty to accommodate the diverse needs of lawyers on the basis of grounds noted in the Rule.

Such accommodation is required unless it would cause undue hardship to the lawyer. Examples of this type of accommodation include:

(a) the provision of flexible hours to accommodate family responsibilities or to accommodate transportation difficulties for persons with disabilities;

(b) the modification of the physical workplace to include wheelchair access, modified furniture and assistive devices;

(c) a benefits policy that includes same sex couples;

(d) adjusting the billable hour or workload expectations to accommodate family responsibilities;

(e) accommodation of religious holidays or religious practices.

Sexual Harassment and Harassment

7. Sexual harassment and harassment are forms of discrimination. The lawyer should refrain from engaging in vexatious comment or conduct that is known or reasonably ought to be known to constitute sexual harassment or harassment in all areas of professional conduct.

(a) Sexual harassment includes the use of a position of power to import sexual requirements into the workplace thereby negatively altering the working conditions of employees;

(b) Harassment includes all conduct which has the effect of eroding the dignity and equality of opportunity of the victim, particularly based on the grounds noted in the Rule.

Discriminatory Activities

8. The lawyer must refrain from participating in discriminatory activities in his or her professional life.

Law Society Act

RSO 1990, c. L.8

Amended by: 1991, c. 41; 1992, c. 7; 1993, c. 27, s. 5; 1993, c. 27, Sched.; 1994, c. 11, s. 389; 1994, c. 27, s. 49; 1996, c. 25, s. 7; 1997, c. 26, Sched.; 1998, c. 18, Sched. B, s. 8; 1998, c. 21; 1998, c. 26, s. 106; 2000, c. 42, Sched., ss. 20-23; 2001, c. 8, ss. 46-50; 2002, c. 18, Sched. A, s. 12.

PART I

Interpretation

1(1) In this Act,

"Appeal Panel" means the Law Society Appeal Panel established under Part II;

"bencher" means a bencher of the Society, other than an honorary bencher;

"by-laws" means the by-laws made under this Act;

"certificate of authorization" means a certificate of authorization issued under this Act authorizing the professional corporation named in it to practise law;

"Chief Executive Officer" means the Chief Executive Officer of the Society;

"Convocation" means a regular or special meeting of the benchers convened for the purpose of transacting business of the Society;

"document" includes a paper, book, record, account, sound recording, videotape, film, photograph, chart, graph, map, plan, survey and information recorded or stored by computer or by means of any other device;

"elected bencher" means a person who is elected as a bencher under subsection 15(1) or holds the office of elected bencher under subsection 15(3);

"Hearing Panel" means the Law Society Hearing Panel established under Part II;

"lay bencher" means a person appointed as a bencher by the Lieutenant Governor in Council under section 23;

"life bencher" means a person who is a bencher under paragraph 3 of subsection 12(1);

"member" means a member of the Society and includes a life member and a temporary member but does not include an honorary member or a student member;

"physician" means a member of the College of Physicians and Surgeons of Ontario or a person who is authorized to practise medicine in another province or territory of Canada;

"professional corporation" means a corporation incorporated under the *Business Corporations Act* that holds a valid certificate of authorization under this Act;

"psychologist" means a member of the College of Psychologists of Ontario or a person who is authorized to practise psychology in another province or territory of Canada;

"regulations" means the regulations made under this Act;

"rules of practice and procedure" means the rules of practice and procedure made under this Act;

"Secretary" means the Secretary of the Society;

"Society" means The Law Society of Upper Canada;

"Treasurer" means the Treasurer of the Society.

Documents in possession or control

(2) For the purposes of this Act, a document is in the possession or control of a person if the person is entitled to obtain the original document or a copy of it.

Hearings

(3) A hearing is not required before making any decision under this Act, the regulations, the by-laws or the rules of practice and procedure unless the Act, regulations, by-laws or rules of practice and procedure specifically require a hearing.

The Society

Law Society continued

2(1) The Law Society of Upper Canada (previously referred to in French as Société du barreau du Haut-Canada) is continued under the name of The Law Society of Upper Canada in English and Barreau du Haut-Canada in French.

Status

(2) The Society is a corporation without share capital composed of the Treasurer, the benchers and the other members from time to time.

Annual meeting

3. A meeting of the members shall be held annually at such place and at such time as is determined from time to time in Convocation, notice of which shall be given by publication as provided by the by-laws.

Seat

4. The permanent seat of the Society shall continue to be at Osgoode Hall in the City of Toronto.

Powers of society

Acquisition and disposition of property

5(1) The Society may purchase, acquire, take by gift, bequest, devise, donation or otherwise any real or personal property for its purposes, and it may hold, sell, mortgage, lease or dispose of any of its real or personal property.

Trustee powers

(2) The Society has and may exercise all powers of trustees under the laws of Ontario.

Borrowing power

(3) The Society may borrow money for its purposes.

Capacity to hold an interest in an insurance corporation

(4) The Society may own shares of or hold a membership interest in an insurance corporation incorporated for the purpose of providing professional liability insurance to members and to persons qualified to practise law outside Ontario in Canada.

Application of Corporations Act

No proxies on dissolution

6(1) Sections 84 and 317 of the *Corporations Act* do not apply to the Society.

Conflict

(2) In the event of conflict between any provision of this Act and any provision of the *Corporations Act*, the provision of this Act prevails.

Treasurer

7. The Treasurer is the president and head of the Society.

Chief Executive Officer

8(1) The Chief Executive Officer shall, under the direction of Convocation, manage the affairs and functions of the Society.

Secretary

(2) The Secretary shall carry out his or her duties under this Act, the regulations, by-laws and rules of practice and procedure, and such other duties as the Secretary may be instructed to undertake by the Chief Executive Officer.

Liability of benchers, officers and employees

9. No action or other proceedings for damages shall be instituted against the Treasurer or any bencher, official of the Society or person appointed in Convocation for any act done in good faith in the performance or intended performance of any duty or in the exercise or in the intended exercise of any power under this Act, a regulation, a by-law or a rule of practice and procedure, or for any neglect or default in the performance or exercise in good faith of any such duty or power.

Benchers

Government of the Society

10. The benchers shall govern the affairs of the Society, including the call of persons to practise at the bar of the courts of Ontario and their admission and enrolment to practise as solicitors in Ontario.

Honorary benchers

11. Every person,
(a) who is an honorary bencher on the 1st day of October, 1970; or
(b) who after that day is made an honorary bencher,
is an honorary bencher but as such has only the rights and privileges prescribed by the by-laws.

Benchers by virtue of their office

12(1) The following, if and while they are members, are benchers by virtue of their office:

1. The Minister of Justice and Attorney General for Canada.
2. The Solicitor General for Canada.
3. Every person who has held the office of elected bencher for at least 16 years.

Same: attorneys general

(2) The following, whether or not they are members, are benchers by virtue of their office:

1. The Attorney General for Ontario.
2. Every person who has held the office of Attorney General for Ontario.

Same

(3) Subsection (2) does not apply to a person whose membership is in abeyance under section 31.

Rights and privileges

(4) Benchers by virtue of their office under subsection (1) or (2) have the rights and privileges prescribed by the by-laws but, except as provided in subsection (5), may not vote in Convocation or in committees.

Voting

(5) The following voting rights apply:

1. The Attorney General for Ontario may vote in Convocation and in committees.
2. Benchers by virtue of their office under paragraph 3 of subsection (1) or paragraph 2 of subsection (2) may vote in committees.

Elected bencher's choice

(6) An elected bencher who becomes qualified as a bencher under subsection (1) or (2) shall choose whether to continue in office as an elected bencher or to cease to hold office as an elected bencher and serve as a bencher under subsection (1) or (2).

Same

(7) If a bencher chooses under subsection (6) to continue in office as an elected bencher, he or she is eligible to be re-elected in any subsequent election of benchers without prejudice to his or her right to become a bencher under subsection (1) or (2) at any time so long as he or she is still an elected bencher.

Attorney General, guardian of the public interest

13(1) The Attorney General for Ontario shall serve as the guardian of the public interest in all matters within the scope of this Act or having to do with the legal profession in any way, and for this purpose he or she may at any time require the production of any document or thing pertaining to the affairs of the Society.

Admissions

(2) No admission of any person in any document or thing produced under subsection (1) is admissible in evidence against that person in any proceedings other than proceedings under this Act.

Protection of Minister

(3) No person who is or has been the Attorney General for Ontario is subject to any proceedings of the Society or to any penalty imposed under this Act for anything done by him or her while exercising the functions of such office.

Former Treasurers

14. Every member who previously held the office of Treasurer is a bencher by virtue of his or her office.

Election of benchers

15(1) Forty benchers shall be elected in accordance with the by-laws.

Regions

(2) The benchers elected under subsection (1) shall be elected for regions prescribed by the by-laws.

Vacancies

(3) Any vacancies in the offices of elected benchers may be filled in accordance with the by-laws.

Removal for non-attendance

22. The benchers may remove from office any elected bencher who fails to attend six consecutive regular Convocations.

Lay benchers

23(1) The Lieutenant Governor in Council may appoint eight persons who are not members as benchers.

Term of office

(2) Every appointment under subsection (1) expires immediately before the first regular Convocation following the first election of benchers that takes place after the effective date of the appointment.

Reappointment

(3) A person appointed under this section is eligible for reappointment.

Deemed reappointment

(4) A person whose appointment expires under subsection (2) shall be deemed to have been reappointed until his or her successor takes office.

Quorum

24. Ten benchers present and entitled to vote in Convocation constitute a quorum for the transaction of business.

Election of Treasurer

25(1) The benchers shall annually, at such time as the benchers may fix, elect an elected bencher as Treasurer.

Bencher by virtue of office

(2) The Treasurer is a bencher by virtue of that office and ceases to hold office as an elected bencher.

Re-election

(3) The Treasurer is eligible for re-election as Treasurer, despite having ceased to hold office as an elected bencher, but, after a new election of benchers takes place under subsection 15 (1), the Treasurer may be re-elected only if he or she is an elected bencher.

Advisory Council

Meeting

26. The Treasurer shall convene a meeting in each year consisting of,
    (a) the chair and the vice-chair of each standing committee;
    (b) the president of each county or district law association, or his or her nominee, being a member of his or her association; and
    (c) one member who is a full-time teacher at each law school in Ontario approved by the Society, to be appointed annually by the faculty of the law school,
to consider the manner in which the members of the Society are discharging their obligations to the public and generally matters affecting the legal profession as a whole.

Admission of Members

Admission to the Society

Form of applications

27(1) Every application for admission to the Society shall be on the prescribed form and be accompanied by the prescribed fees.

Good character

(2) An applicant for admission to the Society shall be of good character.

Where no refusal

(3) No applicant for admission to the Society who has met all admission requirements shall be refused admission.

Hearing

(4) An application for admission to the Society may be refused only by the Hearing Panel after holding a hearing.

Parties

(5) The parties to a hearing under subsection (4) are the applicant, the Society and any other person added as a party by the Hearing Panel.

Subsequent applications

(6) If an application for admission to the Society is refused, another application may be made at any time based on fresh evidence or a material change in circumstances.

Definition

(7) In this section,

"admission to the Society" means,
    (a) admission as a student member, or
    (b) admission as a member other than as a temporary member.

Notice of admission, etc.

27.1 The Secretary shall give the local registrar of the Superior Court of Justice at Toronto notice of every admission to membership and of every revocation, suspension, resignation, readmission or other change in the status of a member or student member and of every name of a professional corporation that holds a valid certificate of authorization under this Act and of every suspension or revocation of the corporation's certificate of authorization.

Classes of Members

Classes of members

28. Subject to sections 30, 31 and 32 and to any order made under Part II,

honorary members
    (a) the persons,
        (i) who are honorary members of the Society on the 31st day of December, 1990, or
        (ii) who after that day are made honorary members of the Society,
are honorary members with only the rights and privileges prescribed by the by-laws;

life members
    (b) the persons, being Canadian citizens or permanent residents of Canada,
        (i) who are honorary life members on the 31st day of December, 1990, or
        (ii) who after that day become life members,
are life members with the rights and privileges of members, and such additional rights and privileges as are prescribed by the by-laws;

members
    (c) the persons, being Canadian citizens or permanent residents of Canada,
        (i) who are members on the 31st day of December, 1990,
        (ii) who after that day successfully complete the Bar Admission Course and are called to the bar and admitted and enrolled as solicitors,
        (iii) who after that day transfer from a jurisdiction outside Ontario and are called to the bar and admitted and enrolled as solicitors, or
        (iv) who, as deans or members of the faculty of a law school in Ontario, are called to the bar and admitted and enrolled as solicitors without examination in accordance with the by-laws,
are members and entitled to practise law in Ontario as barristers and solicitors;

student members

(d) the persons,

(i) who are students-at-law in the Bar Admission Course on the 31st day of December, 1990, or

(ii) who after that day become students-at-law in the Bar Admission Course,

are student members, with the rights and privileges prescribed by the by-laws, until they cease to be students-at-law in the Bar Admission Course.

Admission of temporary members

28.1(1) On the request of the Attorney General, a person who is of good character and who is qualified to practise law outside Ontario may be admitted as a temporary member of the Society for a specified period.

Canadian citizenship or residency not required

(2) A person need not be a Canadian citizen or a permanent resident of Canada to be admitted as a temporary member of the Society.

Hearing

(2.1) A request for admission of a temporary member of the Society may be refused only by the Hearing Panel after holding a hearing.

Parties

(2.2) The parties to a hearing under subsection (2.1) are the Attorney General, the person for whom temporary membership is requested, the Society and any other person added as a party by the Hearing Panel.

Limited right to practise

(3) For the period specified under subsection (1), a temporary member of the Society who has taken the oaths or given the affirmations prescribed for temporary members by the by-laws shall be deemed to be called to the bar and admitted and enrolled as a solicitor and is entitled to act and practise as a barrister and solicitor in the employ of the Attorney General for Ontario or, if appointed under the *Crown Attorneys Act*, as a Crown Attorney or as an assistant Crown Attorney.

Termination of temporary membership

(4) A person admitted as a temporary member of the Society for a specified period ceases to be a member at the end of the period.

Members are officers of the courts

29. Every member is an officer of every court of record in Ontario.

Resignation

30(1) A member or student member may apply in writing to resign his or her membership in the Society.

Acceptance of resignation

(2) A resignation is effective when the application to resign is accepted in accordance with the by-laws.

Application for readmission following resignation

(3) If a person resigned his or her membership in the Society as a member or student member, the Hearing Panel may, on the application of the person, make an order readmitting the person as a member or student member.

Appointment to judicial office

31(1) The membership of a person is in abeyance while the person holds office,
    (a) as a full-time judge of any federal, provincial or territorial court, as a full-time master of the Superior Court of Justice, as a full-time case management master, or as a full-time prothonotary of the Federal Court of Canada; or
    (b) as a full-time member of the Ontario Municipal Board or as a full-time member of a tribunal that has a judicial or quasi-judicial function and that is named in the regulations for the purposes of this section.

Restoration

(2) Upon ceasing to hold an office described in subsection (1), a person whose membership is in abeyance may apply to the Secretary to have the membership restored and, subject to subsection (3), the Secretary shall restore it.

Exception

(3) The Hearing Panel may refuse to restore the membership of a person whose membership is in abeyance if, after holding a hearing, the Panel finds that the person was removed or resigned from an office described in subsection (1) because of,
    (a) conduct that was incompatible with the due execution of the office;
    (b) failure to perform the duties of the office; or
    (c) conduct that, if done by a member, would be professional misconduct or conduct unbecoming a barrister and solicitor.

Parties

(4) The parties to a hearing under subsection (3) are the person whose membership is in abeyance, the Society and any other person added as a party by the Hearing Panel. ...

Effect of losing Canadian citizenship

32(1) When a member ceases to be a Canadian citizen or a permanent resident of Canada, he or she ceases to be a member.

Transition re British subjects

(2) Any member who is not a Canadian citizen or a permanent resident of Canada on the 1st day of July, 1989 ceases to be a member on that day.

Readmission

(3) Any person who ceases to be a member under subsection (1) or (2) may, on becoming a Canadian citizen or a permanent resident of Canada, make application for readmission as a member.

Hearing

(4) An application for readmission may be refused only by the Hearing Panel after holding a hearing.

Parties

(5) The parties to a hearing under subsection (4) are the applicant, the Society and any other person added as a party by the Hearing Panel.

PART II
CONDUCT

Prohibited conduct

Prohibited conduct: members

33(1) A member shall not engage in professional misconduct or conduct unbecoming a barrister or solicitor.

Prohibited conduct: student members

(2) A student member shall not engage in conduct unbecoming a student member.

Conduct application

34(1) With the authorization of the Proceedings Authorization Committee, the Society may apply to the Hearing Panel for a determination of whether a member or student member has contravened section 33.

Parties

(2) The parties to the application are the Society, the member or student member who is the subject of the application, and any other person added as a party by the Hearing Panel.

Restriction

(3) If a complaint is referred to the Complaints Resolution Commissioner in accordance with the by-laws, no application relating to the subject matter of the complaint may be made under this section while the Commissioner is dealing with the complaint.

Conduct orders

35(1) Subject to the rules of practice and procedure, if an application is made under section 34 and the Hearing Panel determines that the member or student member has contravened section 33, the Panel shall make one or more of the following orders:

1. An order revoking the member's or student member's membership in the Society and, in the case of a member, disbarring the member as a barrister and striking his or her name off the roll of solicitors.
2. An order permitting the member or student member to resign his or her membership in the Society.
3. An order suspending the rights and privileges of the member or student member,
    i. for a definite period,
    ii. until terms and conditions specified by the Hearing Panel are met to the satisfaction of the Secretary, or
    iii. for a definite period and thereafter until terms and conditions specified by the Hearing Panel are met to the satisfaction of the Secretary.
4. An order imposing a fine on the member or student member of not more than $10,000, payable to the Society.
5. An order that the member or student member obtain or continue treatment or counselling, including testing and treatment for addiction to or excessive use of alcohol or drugs, or participate in other programs to improve his or her health.
6. An order that the member or student member participate in specified programs of legal education or professional training or other programs to improve his or her professional competence.
7. In the case of a member, an order that the member restrict his or her practice to specified areas of law.
8. In the case of a member, an order that the member practise only,
    i. as an employee of a member or other person approved by the Secretary,
    ii. in partnership with and under the supervision of a member approved by the Secretary, or
    iii. under the supervision of a member approved by the Secretary.
9. In the case of a member, an order that the member co-operate in a review of the member's practice under section 42 and implement the recommendations made by the Secretary.
10. In the case of a member, an order that the member maintain a specified type of trust account.
11. In the case of a member, an order that the member accept specified co-signing controls on the operation of his or her trust accounts.
12. In the case of a member, an order that the member not maintain any trust account in connection with his or her practice without leave of the chair or a vice-chair of the standing committee of Convocation responsible for discipline matters.

13. In the case of a member, an order requiring the member to refund to a client all or a portion of the fees and disbursements paid to the member by the client or, in the case of a student member, an order requiring the student member to pay to a person an amount equal to all or a portion of the fees and disbursements paid by the person in respect of work done by the student member.

14. In the case of a member, an order requiring the member to pay to the Society, for the Lawyers Fund for Client Compensation, such amount as the Hearing Panel may fix that does not exceed the total amount of grants made from the Fund as a result of dishonesty on the part of the member.

15. In the case of a member, an order that the member give notice of any order made under this section to such of the following persons as the order may specify:
    i. The member's partners or employers.
    ii. Other members working for the same firm or employer as the member.
    iii. Clients affected by the conduct giving rise to the order.

16. In the case of a student member, an order that the student member give notice of any order made under this section to his or her articling principal.

17. In the case of a student member, an order revoking any credit in the Bar Admission Course to which the student member would otherwise be entitled.

18. An order that the member or student member report on his or her compliance with any order made under this section and authorize others involved with his or her treatment or supervision to report thereon.

19. An order that the member or student member be reprimanded.

20. An order that the member or student member be admonished.

21. Any other order that the Hearing Panel considers appropriate.

Same

(2) The failure of subsection (1) to specifically mention an order that is provided for elsewhere in this Act does not prevent an order of that kind from being made under paragraph 21 of subsection (1).

Test results

(3) If the Hearing Panel makes an order under paragraph 18 of subsection (1), specific results of tests performed in the course of treatment or counselling of the member or student member shall be reported pursuant to the order only to a physician or psychologist selected by the Secretary.

Report to Secretary

(4) If test results reported to a physician or psychologist under subsection (3) relate to an order made under paragraph 5 of subsection (1), the Secretary may require the physician or psychologist to promptly report to the Secretary his or her opinion on the member's or student member's compliance with the order, but the report shall not disclose the specific test results.

Invitation to attend

36(1) If an application has been made under section 34, the Hearing Panel may invite the member or student member in respect of whom the application was made to attend before the Panel for the purpose of receiving advice from the Panel concerning his or her conduct.

Dismissal of application

(2) The Hearing Panel shall dismiss the application if the member or student member attends before the Panel in accordance with the invitation.

Capacity

Incapacity

Interpretation—"incapacitated": members

37(1) A member is incapacitated for the purposes of this Act if, by reason of physical or mental illness, other infirmity or addiction to or excessive use of alcohol or drugs, he or she is incapable of meeting obligations as a member.

Interpretation—"incapacitated": student members

(2) A student member is incapacitated for the purposes of this Act if, by reason of physical or mental illness, other infirmity or addiction to or excessive use of alcohol or drugs, he or she is incapable of serving under articles or of participating in the Bar Admission Course.

Determinations under other Acts

(3) Subject to subsections (4) and (5), the Hearing Panel may determine that a person is incapacitated for the purposes of this Act if the person has been found under any other Act to be incapacitated within the meaning of that Act.

Conditions controlled by treatment or device: members

(4) The Hearing Panel shall not determine that a member is incapacitated for the purposes of this Act if, through compliance with a continuing course of treatment or the continuing use of an assistive device, the member is capable of meeting his or her obligations as a member.

Same: student members

(5) The Hearing Panel shall not determine that a student member is incapacitated for the purposes of this Act if, through compliance with a continuing course of treatment or the continuing use of an assistive device, the student member is capable of serving under articles and of participating in the Bar Admission Course.

Same

(6) Despite subsections (4) and (5), the Hearing Panel may determine that a person who is the subject of an application under section 38 is incapacitated for the purposes of this Act if,

(a) the person suffers from a condition that would render the person incapacitated were it not for compliance with a continuing course of treatment or the continuing use of an assistive device; and

(b) the person has not complied with the continuing course of treatment or used the assistive device on one or more occasions in the year preceding the commencement of the application.

Capacity application

38(1) With the authorization of the Proceedings Authorization Committee, the Society may apply to the Hearing Panel for a determination of whether a member or student member is or has been incapacitated.

Parties

(2) The parties to the application are the Society, the member or student member who is the subject of the application, and any other person added as a party by the Hearing Panel.

Medical or psychological examinations

39(1) If an application is made under section 38, the Hearing Panel may, on motion by a party to the application or on its own motion, make an order requiring the member or student member who is the subject of the application to be examined by one or more physicians or psychologists.

Panel to specify examiners

(2) The examining physicians or psychologists shall be specified by the Hearing Panel after giving the parties to the proceeding an opportunity to make recommendations.

Purpose of examination

(3) The purpose of the examination is,

(a) to assess whether the member or student member is or has been incapacitated;

(b) to assess the extent of any incapacity and the prognosis for recovery; and

(c) to assist in the determination of any other medical or psychological issue in the application.

Questions and answers

(4) The member or student member shall answer the questions of the examining physicians or psychologists that are relevant to the examination.

Same

(5) The answers given under subsection (4) are admissible in evidence in the application, including any appeal, and in any proceeding in court arising from the application, but are not admissible in any other proceeding.

Failure to comply

(6) If the member or student member fails to comply with an order under this section, the Hearing Panel may make an order suspending his or her rights and privileges until he or she complies.

Appeal

(7) A party to the proceeding may appeal an order under this section or a refusal to make an order under this section to the Appeal Panel.

Grounds: parties other than Society

(8) A party other than the Society may appeal under subsection (7) on any grounds.

Grounds: Society

(9) The Society may appeal under subsection (7) only on a question that is not a question of fact alone.

Time for appeal

(10) An appeal under subsection (7) shall be commenced within the time prescribed by the rules of practice and procedure.

Capacity orders

40(1) Subject to the rules of practice and procedure, if an application is made under section 38 and the Hearing Panel determines that the member or student member is or has been incapacitated, the Panel may make one or more of the following orders:

1. An order suspending the rights and privileges of the member or student member,
    i. for a definite period,
    ii. until terms and conditions specified by the Hearing Panel are met to the satisfaction of the Secretary, or
    iii. for a definite period and thereafter until terms and conditions specified by the Hearing Panel are met to the satisfaction of the Secretary.
2. An order that the member or student member obtain or continue treatment or counselling, including testing and treatment for addiction to or excessive use of alcohol or drugs, or participate in other programs to improve his or her health.
3. In the case of a member, an order that the member restrict his or her practice to specified areas of law.
4. In the case of a member, an order that the member practise only,
    i. as an employee of a member or other person approved by the Secretary,
    ii. in partnership with and under the supervision of a member approved by the Secretary, or
    iii. under the supervision of a member approved by the Secretary.

5. An order that the member or student member report on his or her compliance with any order made under this section and authorize others involved with his or her treatment or supervision to report thereon.

6. Any other order that the Hearing Panel considers appropriate.

Same

(2) The failure of subsection (1) to specifically mention an order that is provided for elsewhere in this Act does not prevent an order of that kind from being made under paragraph 6 of subsection (1).

Test results

(3) If the Hearing Panel makes an order under paragraph 5 of subsection (1), specific results of tests performed in the course of treatment or counselling of the member or student member shall be reported pursuant to the order only to a physician or psychologist selected by the Secretary.

Report to Secretary

(4) If test results reported to a physician or psychologist under subsection (3) relate to an order made under paragraph 2 of subsection (1), the Secretary may require the physician or psychologist to promptly report to the Secretary his or her opinion on the member's or student member's compliance with the order, but the report shall not disclose the specific test results.

Professional Competence

Interpretation—standards of professional competence

41 A member fails to meet standards of professional competence for the purposes of this Act if,

(a) there are deficiencies in,
  (i) the member's knowledge, skill or judgment,
  (ii) the member's attention to the interests of clients,
  (iii) the records, systems or procedures of the member's practice, or
  (iv) other aspects of the member's practice; and
(b) the deficiencies give rise to a reasonable apprehension that the quality of service to clients may be adversely affected.

Practice reviews

42(1) The Society may conduct a review of a member's practice in accordance with the by-laws for the purpose of determining if the member is meeting standards of professional competence.

Restriction

(2) A review may be conducted under this section only if,

(a) the review is required under section 49.4;

(b) the member is required by an order under section 35 to co-operate in a review under this section; or

(c) the member consents.

Recommendations

(3) On completion of the review, the Secretary may make recommendations to the member.

Proposal for order

(4) The Secretary may include the recommendations in a proposal for an order.

Contents of proposal

(5) A proposal for an order may include orders like those mentioned in section 44 and any other order that the Secretary considers appropriate.

Acceptance by member

(6) If the Secretary makes a proposal for an order to the member and the member accepts the proposal within the time prescribed by the by-laws, the Secretary shall notify the chair or a vice-chair of the standing committee of Convocation responsible for professional competence and the chair or vice-chair shall appoint an elected bencher to review the proposal.

Approval by bencher

(7) The bencher who reviews the proposal may make an order giving effect to the proposal if he or she is of the opinion that it is appropriate to do so.

Modifications to proposal

(8) The bencher may include modifications to the proposal in an order under subsection (7) if the member and the Secretary consent in writing to the modifications.

Application of subss. (4)-(8)

(9) Subsections (4) to (8) do not apply if the member is required by an order under section 35 to co-operate in a review of the member's practice under this section and implement the recommendations made by the Secretary.

Professional competence application

43(1) With the authorization of the Proceedings Authorization Committee, the Society may apply to the Hearing Panel for a determination of whether a member is failing or has failed to meet standards of professional competence.

Parties

(2) The parties to the application are the Society, the member who is the subject of the application and any other person added as a party by the Hearing Panel.

Professional competence orders

44(1) Subject to the rules of practice and procedure, if an application is made under section 43 and the Hearing Panel determines that the member is failing or has failed to meet standards of professional competence, the Panel shall make one or more of the following orders:

1. An order suspending the rights and privileges of the member,
    i. for a definite period,
    ii. until terms and conditions specified by the Hearing Panel are met to the satisfaction of the Secretary, or
    iii. for a definite period and thereafter until terms and conditions specified by the Hearing Panel are met to the satisfaction of the Secretary.
2. An order that the member institute new records, systems or procedures in his or her practice.
3. An order that the member obtain professional advice with respect to the management of his or her practice.
4. An order that the member retain the services of a person qualified to assist in the administration of his or her practice.
5. An order that the member obtain or continue treatment or counselling, including testing and treatment for addiction to or excessive use of alcohol or drugs, or participate in other programs to improve his or her health.
6. An order that the member participate in specified programs of legal education or professional training or other programs to improve his or her professional competence.
7. An order that the member restrict his or her practice to specified areas of law.
8. An order that the member practise only,
    i. as an employee of a member or other person approved by the Secretary,
    ii. in partnership with and under the supervision of a member approved by the Secretary, or
    iii. under the supervision of a member approved by the Secretary.
9. An order that the member report on his or her compliance with any order made under this section and authorize others involved with his or her treatment or supervision to report thereon.
10. Any other order that the Hearing Panel considers appropriate.

Same

(2) The failure of subsection (1) to specifically mention an order that is provided for elsewhere in this Act does not prevent an order of that kind from being made under paragraph 10 of subsection (1).

Test results

(3) If the Hearing Panel makes an order under paragraph 9 of subsection (1), specific results of tests performed in the course of treatment or counselling of the member shall be reported pursuant to the order only to a physician or psychologist selected by the Secretary.

Report to Secretary

(4) If test results reported to a physician or psychologist under subsection (3) relate to an order made under paragraph 5 of subsection (1), the Secretary may require the physician or psychologist to promptly report to the Secretary his or her opinion on the member's compliance with the order, but the report shall not disclose the specific test results.

Failure to Comply with Order

Suspension for failure to comply with order

45(1) On application by the Society, the Hearing Panel may make an order suspending the rights and privileges of a member or student member if the Panel determines that the member or student member has failed to comply with an order under this Part.

Parties

(2) The parties to the application are the Society, the member or student member who is the subject of the application, and any other person added as a party by the Hearing Panel.

Nature of suspension

(3) An order under this section may suspend the rights and privileges of the member or student member,

   (a) for a definite period;

   (b) until terms and conditions specified by the Hearing Panel are met to the satisfaction of the Secretary; or

   (c) for a definite period and thereafter until terms and conditions specified by the Hearing Panel are met to the satisfaction of the Secretary.

Summary Orders

Summary suspension for non-payment

46(1) An elected bencher appointed for the purpose by Convocation may make an order suspending a member's rights and privileges if, for the period prescribed by the by-laws, the member has been in default for failure to pay a fee or levy payable to the Society.

Length of suspension

(2) A suspension under this section remains in effect until the member pays the amount owing in accordance with the by-laws to the satisfaction of the Secretary.

Discharge from bankruptcy

(3) A suspension under this section is not terminated by the member's discharge from bankruptcy, but the member may apply to the Hearing Panel under subsection 49.42 (3).

Summary suspension for failure to complete or file

47(1) An elected bencher appointed for the purpose by Convocation may make an order suspending a member's rights and privileges if, for the period prescribed by the by-laws,

(a) the member has been in default for failure to complete or file with the Society any certificate, report or other document that the member is required to file under the by-laws; or

(b) the member has been in default for failure to complete or file with the Society, or with an insurer through which indemnity for professional liability is provided under section 61, any certificate, report or other document that the member is required to file under a policy for indemnity for professional liability.

Length of suspension

(2) A suspension under this section remains in effect until the member completes and files the required document in accordance with the by-laws to the satisfaction of the Secretary.

Summary revocation

48. An elected bencher appointed for the purpose by Convocation may make an order revoking a member's membership in the Society, disbarring the member as a barrister and striking his or her name off the roll of solicitors if an order under section 46 or clause 47(1)(a) is still in effect more than 12 months after it was made.

Summary suspension relating to continuing legal education

49(1) An elected bencher appointed for the purpose by Convocation may make an order suspending a member's rights and privileges if the member has failed to comply with the requirements of the by-laws with respect to continuing legal education.

Length of suspension

(2) A suspension under this section remains in effect until the member complies with the requirements of the by-laws with respect to continuing legal education to the satisfaction of the Secretary.

Failure to make use of legal skills

49.1(1) An elected bencher appointed for the purpose by Convocation may make an order prohibiting a member from engaging in the private practice of law if it has been determined in accordance with the by-laws that the member has not made substantial use of legal skills on a regular basis for such continuous period of time as is specified by the by-laws.

Restriction

(2) An order shall not be made under subsection (1) more than 12 months after the end of the continuous period of time during which the member did not make substantial use of legal skills on a regular basis.

Termination of order

(3) The Secretary may certify that a member who is the subject of an order under subsection (1) has met the requalification requirements specified by the by-laws, and the order thereupon ceases to have effect, subject to such terms and conditions authorized by the by-laws as may be imposed by the Secretary.

Application to Hearing Panel

(4) If the Secretary refuses to certify that a member has met the requalification requirements or imposes terms and conditions under subsection (3), the member may apply to the Hearing Panel for a determination of whether the requalification requirements have been met or of whether the terms and conditions are appropriate.

Parties

(5) The parties to an application under subsection (4) are the applicant, the Society and any other person added as a party by the Hearing Panel.

Powers

(6) The Hearing Panel shall,

(a) if it determines that the requalification requirements have been met, order that the order made under subsection (1) cease to have effect, subject to such terms and conditions authorized by the by-laws as may be imposed by the Panel; or

(b) if it determines that the requalification requirements have not been met, order that the order made under subsection (1) continue in effect.

Audits, Investigations, etc.

Audit of financial records

49.2(1) The Secretary may require an audit to be conducted of the financial records of a member or group of members for the purpose of determining whether they comply with the requirements of the by-laws.

Powers

(2) A person conducting an audit under this section may,

(a) enter the business premises of the member or group of members between the hours of 9 a.m. and 5 p.m. from Monday to Friday or at such other time as may be agreed to by the member or by any member in the group of members;

(b) require the production of and examine the financial records maintained in connection with the practice of the member or group of members and, for the purpose of understanding or substantiating those records, require the production of and examine any other documents in the possession or control of the member or group of members, including client files; and

(c) require the member or members, and people who work with the member or members, to provide information to explain the financial records and other documents examined under clause (b) and the transactions recorded in those financial records and other documents.

Investigations

Investigations: members' conduct

49.3(1) Subject to section 49.5, the Secretary may require an investigation to be conducted into a member's conduct if the Secretary receives information suggesting that the member may have engaged in professional misconduct or conduct unbecoming a barrister or solicitor.

Powers

(2) A person conducting an investigation under subsection (1) may require the person under investigation and people who work with the person to provide information that relates to the matters under investigation and, if the Secretary is satisfied that there is a reasonable suspicion that the person under investigation may have engaged in professional misconduct or conduct unbecoming a barrister or solicitor, the person conducting the investigation may,

(a) enter the business premises of the person under investigation between the hours of 9 a.m. and 5 p.m. from Monday to Friday or at such other time as may be agreed to by the person under investigation; and

(b) require the production of and examine any documents that relate to the matters under investigation, including client files.

Investigations: student members' conduct

(3) Subject to section 49.5, the Secretary may require an investigation to be conducted into a student member's conduct if the Secretary receives information suggesting that the student member may have engaged in conduct unbecoming a student member.

Powers

(4) A person conducting an investigation under subsection (3) may require the person under investigation and people who work with the person to provide information that relates to the matters under investigation and, if the Secretary is satisfied that there is a reasonable suspicion that the person under investigation may have engaged in conduct unbecoming a student member, the person conducting the investigation may,

(a) enter the business premises of the person under investigation between the hours of 9 a.m. and 5 p.m. from Monday to Friday or at such other time as may be agreed to by the person under investigation; and

(b) require the production of and examine any documents that relate to the matters under investigation, including client files.

Investigations: capacity

(5) Subject to section 49.5, the Secretary shall require an investigation to be conducted into a member's or student member's capacity if the Secretary is satisfied that there are reasonable grounds for believing that the member or student member may be or may have been incapacitated.

Powers

(6) A person conducting an investigation under subsection (5) may,

(a) enter the business premises of the person under investigation between the hours of 9 a.m. and 5 p.m. from Monday to Friday or at such other time as may be agreed to by the person under investigation;

(b) require the production of and examine any documents that relate to the matters under investigation, including client files; and

(c) require the person under investigation and people who work with the person to provide information that relates to the matters under investigation.

Mandatory reviews of professional competence

49.4(1) Subject to section 49.6, the chair or a vice-chair of the standing committee of Convocation responsible for professional competence shall direct that a review of a member's practice be conducted under section 42 if the circumstances prescribed by the by-laws exist.

Powers

(2) A person conducting a review under this section may,

(a) enter the business premises of the member between the hours of 9 a.m. and 5 p.m. from Monday to Friday or at such other time as may be agreed to by the member;

(b) require the production of and examine documents that relate to the matters under review, including client files, and examine systems and procedures of the member's practice; and

(c) require the member and people who work with the member to provide information that relates to the matters under review.

Investigations of benchers and Society employees

49.5(1) A reference in section 49.3 to the Secretary shall be deemed, with respect to any matter that concerns the conduct or capacity of a bencher or employee of the Society, to be a reference to the Treasurer.

Outside investigator

(2) The Treasurer shall appoint a person who is not a bencher or employee of the Society to conduct any investigation under section 49.3 that concerns the conduct or capacity of a bencher or employee of the Society.

Reviews of professional competence of benchers

49.6(1) The Treasurer shall exercise the authority of the chair or a vice-chair of the standing committee of Convocation responsible for professional competence under section 49.4 in respect of any matter that concerns the professional competence of a bencher.

Outside review

(2) The Treasurer shall appoint a person who is not a bencher or employee of the Society to conduct any review under section 49.4 that concerns the professional competence of a bencher.

Access to information

49.7 A person appointed under section 49.5 or 49.6 to conduct an investigation or review that concerns a bencher or employee of the Society is entitled to have access to,

(a) all information in the records of the Society respecting the bencher or employee of the Society; and

(b) all other information within the knowledge of the Society with respect to the matter under investigation or review.

Privilege

Disclosure despite privilege

49.8(1) A person who is required under section 49.2, 49.3, 49.4 or 49.15 to provide information or to produce documents shall comply with the requirement even if the information or documents are privileged or confidential.

Admissibility despite privilege

(2) Despite clause 15(2)(a) and section 32 of the *Statutory Powers Procedure Act*, information provided and documents produced under section 49.2, 49.3, 49.4 or 49.15 are admissible in a proceeding under this Act even if the information or documents are privileged or confidential.

Privilege preserved for other purposes

(3) Subsections (1) and (2) do not negate or constitute a waiver of any privilege and, even though information or documents that are privileged must be disclosed under subsection (1) and are admissible in a proceeding under subsection (2), the privilege continues for all other purposes.

Removal for copying

49.9(1) A person entitled to examine documents under section 49.2, 49.3, 49.4 or 49.15 may, on giving a receipt,

(a) remove the documents for the purpose of copying them; and

(b) in the case of information recorded or stored by computer or by means of any other device, remove the computer or other device for the purpose of copying the information.

Return

(2) The person shall copy the documents or information with reasonable dispatch and shall return the documents, computer or other device promptly to the person from whom they were removed.

Order for search and seizure

49.10(1) On application by the Society, the Superior Court of Justice may make an order under subsection (2) if the court is satisfied that there are reasonable grounds for believing,

(a) that circumstances exist that authorize or require an investigation to be conducted under section 49.3 or that require a review to be conducted under section 49.4;

(b) that there are documents or other things that relate to the matters under investigation or review in a building, dwelling or other premises specified in the application or in a vehicle or other place specified in the application; and

(c) that an order under subsection (2) is necessary because of urgency or because use of the authority in subsection 49.3 (2), (4) or (6) or 49.4 (2) is not possible, is not likely to be effective or has been ineffective.

Contents of order

(2) The order referred to in subsection (1) may authorize the person conducting the investigation or review, or any police officer or other person acting on the direction of the person conducting the investigation or review,

(a) to enter, by force if necessary, any building, dwelling or other premises specified in the order, or any vehicle or other place specified in the order;

(b) to search the building, dwelling, premises, vehicle or place;

(c) to open, by force if necessary, any safety deposit box or other receptacle; and

(d) to seize and remove any documents or other things that relate to the matters under investigation or review.

Terms and conditions

(3) An order under subsection (2) may include such terms and conditions as the court considers appropriate.

Assistance of police

(4) An order under subsection (2) may require a police officer to accompany the person conducting the investigation or review in the execution of the order.

Application without notice

(5) An application for an order under subsection (2) may be made without notice.

Removal of seized things

(6) A person who removes any thing pursuant to an order under this section shall,

(a) at the time of removal, give a receipt to the person from whom the thing is seized; and

(b) as soon as practicable, bring the thing before or report the removal to a judge of the Superior Court of Justice.

Order for retention

(7) If the judge referred to in clause (6)(b) is satisfied that retention of the thing is necessary for the purpose of the investigation or review or for the purpose of a proceeding under this Part, he or she may order that the thing be retained until,

(a) such date as he or she may specify; or

(b) if a proceeding under this Part has been commenced, until the proceeding, including any appeals, has been completed.

Extension of time

(8) A judge of the Superior Court of Justice may, before the time for retaining a thing expires, extend the time until,

(a) such later date as he or she may specify; or

(b) if a proceeding under this Part has been commenced, until the proceeding, including any appeals, has been completed.

Return

(9) If retention of a thing is not authorized under subsection (7) or the time for retaining the thing expires, it shall be returned to the person from whom it was seized.

Seizure despite privilege

(10) An order under this section may authorize the seizure of a thing even if the thing is privileged or confidential.

Admissibility despite privilege

(11) Despite clause 15(2)(a) and section 32 of the *Statutory Powers Procedure Act*, a thing seized under this section is admissible in a proceeding under this Act even if the thing is privileged or confidential.

Privilege preserved for other purposes

(12) Subsections (10) and (11) do not negate or constitute a waiver of any privilege and, even though a thing that is privileged may be seized under subsection (10) and is admissible in a proceeding under subsection (11), the privilege continues for all other purposes.

Identification

49.11 On request, a person conducting an audit, investigation, review, search or seizure under this Part shall produce identification and proof of his or her authority.

Confidentiality

49.12(1) A bencher, officer, employee, agent or representative of the Society shall not disclose any information that comes to his or her knowledge as a result of an audit, investigation, review, search, seizure or proceeding under this Part.

Exceptions

(2) Subsection (1) does not prohibit,

(a) disclosure required in connection with the administration of this Act, the regulations, the by-laws or the rules of practice and procedure;

(b) disclosure required in connection with a proceeding under this Act;

(c) disclosure of information that is a matter of public record;

(d) disclosure by a person to his or her counsel; or

(e) disclosure with the written consent of all persons whose interests might reasonably be affected by the disclosure.

Testimony

(3) A person to whom subsection (1) applies shall not be required in any proceeding, except a proceeding under this Act, to give testimony or produce any document with respect to information that the person is prohibited from disclosing under subsection (1).

Disclosure to public authorities

49.13(1) The Society may apply to the Superior Court of Justice for an order authorizing the disclosure to a public authority of any information that a bencher, officer, employee, agent or representative of the Society would otherwise be prohibited from disclosing under section 49.12.

Restrictions

(2) The court shall not make an order under this section if the information sought to be disclosed came to the knowledge of the Society as a result of,

(a) the making of an oral or written statement by a person in the course of the audit, investigation, review, search, seizure or proceeding that may tend to criminate the person or establish the person's liability to civil proceedings;

(b) the making of an oral or written statement disclosing matters that the court determines to be subject to solicitor-client privilege; or

(c) the examination of a document that the court determines to be subject to solicitor-client privilege.

Documents and other things

(3) An order under this section that authorizes the disclosure of information may also authorize the delivery of documents or other things that are in the Society's possession and that relate to the information.

No appeal

(4) An order of the court on an application under this section is not subject to appeal.

Complaints Resolution Commissioner

Appointment

49.14(1) Convocation shall appoint a person as Complaints Resolution Commissioner in accordance with the regulations.

Restriction

(2) A bencher or a person who was a bencher at any time during the two years preceding the appointment shall not be appointed as Commissioner.

Term of office

(3) The Commissioner shall be appointed for a term not exceeding three years and is eligible for reappointment.

Removal from office

(4) The Commissioner may be removed from office during his or her term of office only by a resolution approved by at least two thirds of the benchers entitled to vote in Convocation.

Restriction on practice of law

(5) The Commissioner shall not engage in the practice of law during his or her term of office.

Functions of Commissioner

49.15(1) The Commissioner shall,

(a) attempt to resolve complaints referred to the Commissioner for resolution under the by-laws; and

(b) review and, if the Commissioner considers appropriate, attempt to resolve complaints referred to the Commissioner for review under the by-laws.

Investigation by Commissioner

(2) If a complaint is referred to the Commissioner under the by-laws, the Commissioner has the same powers to investigate the complaint as a person conducting an investigation under section 49.3 would have with respect to the subject matter of the complaint, and, for that purpose, a reference in section 49.3 to the Secretary shall be deemed to be a reference to the Commissioner.

Access to information

(3) If a complaint is referred to the Commissioner under the by-laws, the Commissioner is entitled to have access to,

(a) all information in the records of the Society respecting a member or student member who is the subject of the complaint; and

(b) all other information within the knowledge of the Society with respect to the subject matter of the complaint.

Delegation

49.16(1) The Commissioner may in writing delegate any of his or her powers or duties to members of his or her staff or to employees of the Society holding offices designated by the by-laws.

Terms and conditions

(2) A delegation under subsection (1) may contain such terms and conditions as the Commissioner considers appropriate.

Identification

49.17 On request, the Commissioner or any other person conducting an investigation under subsection 49.15 (2) shall produce identification and, in the case of a person to whom powers or duties have been delegated under section 49.16, proof of the delegation.

Confidentiality

49.18(1) The Commissioner and each member of his or her staff shall not disclose,

(a) any information that comes to his or her knowledge as a result of an investigation under subsection 49.15 (2); or

(b) any information that comes to his or her knowledge under subsection 49.15 (3) that a bencher, officer, employee, agent or representative of the Society is prohibited from disclosing under section 49.12.

Exceptions

(2) Subsection (1) does not prohibit,

(a) disclosure required in connection with the administration of this Act, the regulations, the by-laws or the rules of practice and procedure;

(b) disclosure required in connection with a proceeding under this Act;

(c) disclosure of information that is a matter of public record;

(d) disclosure by a person to his or her counsel; or

(e) disclosure with the written consent of all persons whose interests might reasonably be affected by the disclosure.

Testimony

(3) A person to whom subsection (1) applies shall not be required in any proceeding, except a proceeding under this Act, to give testimony or produce any document with respect to information that the person is prohibited from disclosing under subsection (1).

Decisions final

49.19 A decision of the Commissioner is final and is not subject to appeal.

Proceedings Authorization Committee

Proceedings Authorization Committee

Establishment

49.20(1) Convocation shall establish a Proceedings Authorization Committee in accordance with the by-laws.

Functions

(2) The Committee shall review matters referred to it in accordance with the by-laws and shall take such action as it considers appropriate in accordance with the by-laws.

Decisions final

(3) A decision of the Committee is final and is not subject to appeal or review.

Hearing Panel

Establishment of Hearing Panel

49.21(1) There is hereby established a panel of benchers to be known in English as the Law Society Hearing Panel and in French as Comité d'audition du Barreau.

Members of Panel

(2) Every bencher is a member of the Hearing Panel, except the following benchers:

1. Benchers who are members of the Proceedings Authorization Committee.
2. Benchers who hold office under paragraph 1 or 2 of subsection 12 (1) or under subsection 12 (2).

Chair

49.22(1) Convocation shall appoint one of the members of the Hearing Panel who is an elected bencher as chair of the Hearing Panel.

Term of office

(2) Subject to subsection (3), the chair holds office for a term of one year and is eligible for reappointment.

Appointment at pleasure

(3) The chair holds office at the pleasure of Convocation.

Hearings

49.23(1) An application to the Hearing Panel under this Part shall be determined after a hearing by the Panel.

Assignment of members

(2) The chair shall assign members of the Hearing Panel to hearings.

Composition at hearings

(3) A hearing before the Hearing Panel shall be heard and determined by such number of members of the Panel as is prescribed by the regulations.

French-speaking panelists

49.24(1) A person who speaks French who is a party to a proceeding before the Hearing Panel may require that any hearing in the proceeding be heard by panelists who speak French.

Assignment of members as panelists

(2) If a hearing before the Hearing Panel is required to be heard by panelists who speak French and, in the opinion of the chair of the Panel, it is not practical to assign the required number of French-speaking benchers to the hearing, he or she may appoint one or more French-speaking members as temporary panelists for the purposes of that hearing, and the temporary panelists shall be deemed, for the purposes of subsection 49.23 (3), to be members of the Hearing Panel.

Powers

49.25 The Hearing Panel may determine any question of fact or law that arises in a proceeding before it.

Terms and conditions

49.26 An order of the Hearing Panel may include such terms and conditions as the Panel considers appropriate.

Interlocutory orders

49.27 The Hearing Panel may make an interlocutory order authorized by the rules of practice and procedure, but no interlocutory order may be made suspending the rights and privileges of a member or student member or restricting the manner in which a member may practise law unless the Panel is satisfied that the order is necessary for the protection of the public.

Costs

49.28(1) Subject to the rules of practice and procedure, the costs of and incidental to a proceeding or a step in a proceeding before the Hearing Panel are in the discretion of the Panel, and the Panel may determine by whom and to what extent the costs shall be paid.

Society expenses

(2) Costs awarded to the Society under subsection (1) may include,

(a) expenses incurred by the Society in providing facilities or services for the purposes of the proceeding; and

(b) expenses incurred by the Society in any audit, investigation, review, search or seizure that is related to the proceeding.

Appeal Panel

Establishment of Appeal Panel

49.29(1) There is hereby established a panel of benchers to be known in English as the Law Society Appeal Panel and in French as Comité d'appel du Barreau.

Composition

(2) The Appeal Panel shall consist of at least seven benchers appointed by Convocation.

Elected and lay benchers

(3) The Appeal Panel must include at least three elected benchers and at least one lay bencher.

Benchers by virtue of their office

(4) A bencher who holds office under paragraph 1 or 2 of subsection 12 (1) or under subsection 12 (2) may not be appointed to the Appeal Panel.

Life benchers

(5) The number of life benchers who are members of the Appeal Panel shall not exceed one-third of the total number of members of the Appeal Panel.

Former Treasurers

(6) Not more than one bencher who holds office under section 14 may be a member of the Appeal Panel.

Term of office

(7) Subject to subsection (8), an appointment to the Appeal Panel shall be for such term, not exceeding two years, as Convocation may fix.

Appointment at pleasure

(8) A bencher appointed to the Appeal Panel holds office as a member of the Appeal Panel at the pleasure of Convocation.

Reappointment

(9) A bencher may not be reappointed to the Appeal Panel until after the next regular election of benchers.

Chair

49.30(1) Convocation shall appoint one of the members of the Appeal Panel as chair of the Appeal Panel.

Term of office

(2) Subject to subsection (3), the chair holds office for a term of one year.

Appointment at pleasure

(3) The chair holds office at the pleasure of Convocation.

Reappointment

(4) A member of the Appeal Panel may not be reappointed as chair until after the next regular election of benchers.

Hearing of appeals

49.31(1) An appeal to the Appeal Panel shall be determined after a hearing by the Appeal Panel.

Assignment of members

(2) The chair shall assign members of the Appeal Panel to hearings.

Composition at hearings

(3) An appeal to the Appeal Panel shall be heard and determined by at least five members of the Appeal Panel, of whom at least three must be elected benchers and at least one must be a lay bencher.

Temporary members

(4) If, in the opinion of the chair, it is not practical for five members of the Appeal Panel to be assigned to a hearing, he or she may appoint one or more benchers as temporary members of the Appeal Panel for the purposes of that hearing, and the temporary members shall be deemed, for the purposes of subsection (3), to be members of the Appeal Panel.

Restriction

(5) The chair may not appoint a bencher who holds office under paragraph 1 or 2 of subsection 12 (1) or under subsection 12 (2) as a temporary member of the Appeal Panel.

Appeals to Appeal Panel

49.32(1) A party to a proceeding before the Hearing Panel may appeal a final decision or order of the Hearing Panel to the Appeal Panel.

Appeal from costs order

(2) A party to a proceeding before the Hearing Panel may appeal any order of the Hearing Panel under section 49.28 to the Appeal Panel, but the appeal may not be commenced until the Hearing Panel has given a final decision or order in the proceeding.

Appeal from summary orders of elected bencher

(3) A person who is subject to an order under section 46, 47, 48, 49 or 49.1 may appeal the order to the Appeal Panel.

Grounds

Grounds: parties other than Society

49.33(1) A party other than the Society may appeal under section 49.32 on any grounds.

Grounds: Society

(2) The Society may appeal under section 49.32 only on a question that is not a question of fact alone, unless the appeal is from an order under section 49.28, in which case the Society may appeal on any grounds.

Time for appeal

49.34 An appeal under section 49.32 shall be commenced within the time prescribed by the rules of practice and procedure.

Jurisdiction of Appeal Panel

49.35(1) The Appeal Panel may determine any question of fact or law that arises in a proceeding before it.

Powers on appeal

(2) After holding a hearing on an appeal, the Appeal Panel may,
  (a) make any order or decision that ought to or could have been made by the Hearing Panel or person appealed from;
  (b) order a new hearing before the Hearing Panel, in the case of an appeal from a decision or order of the Hearing Panel; or
  (c) dismiss the appeal.

Stay

49.36(1) An appeal to the Appeal Panel does not stay the decision or order appealed from, unless, on motion, the Appeal Panel orders otherwise.

Terms and conditions

(2) In making an order staying a decision or order, the Appeal Panel may impose such terms and conditions as it considers appropriate on the rights and privileges of a person who is subject to the decision or order.

Application of other provisions

49.37(1) Sections 49.24, 49.26, 49.27 and 49.28 apply, with necessary modifications, to the Appeal Panel.

French-speaking panelists

(2) In exercising authority under subsection 49.24 (2), the chair of the Appeal Panel may appoint one or more French-speaking benchers as temporary panelists or, if the chair is of the opinion that it is not practical to appoint benchers as temporary panelists, he or she may appoint one or more French-speaking members as temporary panelists.

Costs

(3) The authority of the Appeal Panel under section 49.28 includes authority to make orders with respect to steps in the proceeding that took place before the Hearing Panel.

Appeals to the Divisional Court

Appeals to Divisional Court

49.38 A party to a proceeding before the Appeal Panel may appeal to the Divisional Court from a final decision or order of the Appeal Panel if,
   (a) the Appeal Panel's final decision or order was made on an appeal from a decision or order of the Hearing Panel under subsection 31 (3); or
   (b) the proceeding was commenced under subsection 30 (3), section 34, section 38 or subsection 49.42 (4).

Grounds for appeal to court

Grounds: parties other than Society

49.39(1) A party other than the Society may appeal under section 49.38 on any grounds.

Grounds: Society

(2) The Society may appeal under section 49.38 only on a question that is not a question of fact alone, unless the appeal is from an order under section 49.28, in which case the Society may appeal on any grounds.

Payment for documents

49.40 The Society may require a party to an appeal under section 49.38 to pay the Society for providing the party with copies of the record or other documents for the purpose of the appeal.

Stay

49.41(1) An appeal under section 49.38 does not stay the decision or order appealed from, unless, on motion, the Divisional Court orders otherwise.

Terms and conditions

(2) In making an order staying a decision or order, the court may impose such terms and conditions as it considers appropriate on the rights and privileges of a person who is subject to the decision or order.

Reinstatement and Readmission

Application for reinstatement and readmission

Application for reinstatement

49.42(1) If an order made under this Act suspended the rights and privileges of a member or student member or restricted the manner in which a member may practise law, the Hearing Panel may, on application by the member or student member, make an order discharging or varying the order on the basis of fresh evidence or a material change in circumstances.

Exceptions

(2) Subsection (1) does not apply to an interlocutory order or an order made under section 46, 47, 49 or 49.1.

Discharge from bankruptcy

(3) If an order made under section 46 suspended the rights and privileges of a member, the Hearing Panel may, on application by the member, make an order discharging or varying the order on the basis that the member has been discharged from bankruptcy.

Application for readmission

(4) If an order made under this Act revoked a person's membership in the Society as a member or student member, the Hearing Panel may, on the application of the person, make an order readmitting the person as a member or student member.

Parties

(5) The parties to an application under this section are the applicant, the Society and any other person added as a party by the Hearing Panel.

Terms and conditions

(6) Without limiting the generality of section 49.26, the terms and conditions that may be included in an order under this section include the following:

1. That a member or student member successfully pass examinations in specified subjects.
2. That a member not practise law in Ontario as a barrister or solicitor.
3. That the manner in which a member may practise law be restricted as specified by the Hearing Panel.

Dispute over satisfaction of terms and conditions

49.43(1) A member or student member may apply to the Hearing Panel for a determination of whether terms and conditions specified in an order under this Part have been met if,

(a) the order suspended the rights and privileges of the member or student member until the terms and conditions were met to the satisfaction of the Secretary; and

(b) the Secretary is not satisfied that the terms and conditions have been met.

Powers

(2) The Hearing Panel shall,

(a) if it determines that the terms and conditions have been met, order that the order suspending the rights and privileges of the member or student member cease to have effect; or

(b) if it determines that the terms and conditions have not been met, order that the order suspending the rights and privileges of the member or student member continue in effect.

Parties

(3) The parties to an application under this section are the applicant, the Society and any other person added as a party by the Hearing Panel.

Freezing Orders and Trusteeship Orders

Application

49.44(1) Sections 49.45 to 49.52 apply to property that is or should be in the possession or control of a member in connection with,

(a) the practice of the member;

(b) the business or affairs of a client or former client of the member;

(c) an estate for which the member is or was executor, administrator or administrator with the will annexed;

(d) a trust of which the member is or was a trustee;

(e) a power of attorney under which the member is or was the attorney; or

(f) a guardianship under which the member is or was the guardian.

Same

(2) Sections 49.45 to 49.52 apply to property wherever it may be located.

Same

(3) An order under section 49.46 or 49.47 applies to property that is or should be in the possession or control of the member before or after the order is made.

Grounds for order

49.45 An order may be made under section 49.46 or 49.47 with respect to property that is or should be in the possession or control of a member only if,

(a) the member's membership in the Society has been revoked;

(b) the member's rights and privileges are under suspension or the manner in which the member may practise law has been restricted;

(c) the member has died or has disappeared;

(d) the member has neglected or abandoned his or her practice without making adequate provision for the protection of clients' interests;

(e) there are reasonable grounds for believing that the member has or may have dealt improperly with property that may be subject to an order under section 49.46 or 49.47 or with any other property; or

(f) there are reasonable grounds for believing that other circumstances exist in respect of the member or the member's practice that make an order under section 49.46 or 49.47 necessary for the protection of the public.

Freezing order

49.46 On the application of the Society, the Superior Court of Justice may order that all or part of the property that is or should be in the possession or control of a member shall not be paid out or dealt with by any person without leave of the court.

Trusteeship order

49.47(1) On the application of the Society, the Superior Court of Justice may order that all or part of the property that is or should be in the possession or control of a member be held in trust by the Society or another person appointed by the court.

Purpose of order

(2) An order may be made under subsection (1) only for one or more of the following purposes, as specified in the order:

1. Preserving the property.
2. Distributing the property.
3. Preserving or carrying on the member's practice.
4. Winding up the member's practice.

Property subject to freezing order

(3) An order under subsection (1) may supersede an order under section 49.46.

Use of agent

(4) If the Society is appointed as trustee, it may appoint an agent to assist it or act on its behalf.

Search and seizure

(5) An order under subsection (1) may authorize the trustee or the sheriff, or any police officer or other person acting on the direction of the trustee or sheriff,

(a) to enter, by force if necessary, any building, dwelling or other premises, or any vehicle or other place, where there are reasonable grounds for believing that property that is or should be in the possession or control of the member may be found;

(b) to search the building, dwelling, premises, vehicle or place;

(c) to open, by force if necessary, any safety deposit box or other receptacle; and

(d) to seize, remove and deliver to the trustee any property that is or should be in the possession or control of the member.

Assistance of police

(6) An order under this section may require a police officer to accompany the trustee or sheriff in the execution of the order.

Compensation

(7) In an order under subsection (1) or on a subsequent application, the court may make such order as it considers appropriate for the compensation of the trustee and the reimbursement of the trustee's expenses out of the trust property, by the member, or otherwise as the court may specify.

Application for directions

49.48 The Society, at the time of making an application for an order under section 49.46 or 49.47, or the trustee appointed under subsection 49.47 (1), may apply to the Superior Court of Justice for the opinion, advice or direction of the court on any question affecting the property.

Application without notice

49.49 An application for an order under section 49.46 or 49.47 may be made without notice.

Requirement to account

49.50 An order under section 49.46 or 49.47 may require the member to account to the Society and to any other person named in the order for such property as the court may specify.

Variation or discharge

49.51(1) The Society, the member or any person affected by an order under section 49.46 or 49.47 may apply to the Superior Court of Justice to vary or discharge the order.

Notice

(2) In addition to any person specified by the rules of court, notice of an application under this section shall be given to,

(a) the Society, if the Society is not the applicant; and

(b) the trustee, if an order has been made under section 49.47 and the applicant is not the trustee.

Former members

49.52(1) Sections 49.44 to 49.51 also apply, with necessary modifications, in respect of former members.

Same

(2) Sections 49.44 to 49.51 apply to property that is or should be in the possession or control of a former member before or after the former member ceases to practise law.

Outside Counsel

Outside counsel

49.53 The Society shall be represented by a person who is not a bencher or employee of the Society in any proceeding under this Part before the Hearing Panel, the Appeal Panel or a court that concerns a bencher or employee of the Society.

PART III

PROHIBITIONS AND OFFENCES

Prohibition as to practice, etc.

50(1) Except where otherwise provided by law,

(a) no person, other than a member whose rights and privileges are not suspended, shall act as a barrister or solicitor or hold themself out as or represent themself to be a barrister or solicitor or practise as a barrister or solicitor; and

(b) no temporary member shall act as a barrister or solicitor or practise as a barrister or solicitor except to the extent permitted by subsection 28.1 (3).

Offence: unauthorized practice

50.1(1) Every person who contravenes section 50 is guilty of an offence and on conviction is liable to a fine of not more than $10,000.

Offence: foreign legal advice

(2) Every person who gives legal advice respecting the law of a jurisdiction outside Canada in contravention of the by-laws is guilty of an offence and on conviction is liable to a fine of not more than $10,000.

Compensation or restitution

(3) The court that convicts a person of an offence under this section may prescribe as a condition of a probation order that the person pay compensation or make restitution to any person who suffered a loss as a result of the offence.

Limitation

(4) A proceeding shall not be commenced in respect of an offence under this section after two years after the date on which the offence was, or is alleged to have been, committed.

Application to prohibit contravention

50.2(1) The Society may apply to the Superior Court of Justice for an order prohibiting a person from contravening section 50 or from giving legal advice respecting the law of a jurisdiction outside Canada in contravention of the by-laws, if,
    (a) the person has been convicted of an offence under section 50.1; or
    (b) the person was a member of the Society and,
        (i) the person's membership in the Society has been revoked, or
        (ii) the person has been permitted to resign his or her membership in the Society.

Same

(2) An order may be made under clause (1)(b) if the court is satisfied that the person is contravening or has contravened section 50 or is giving or has given legal advice respecting the law of a jurisdiction outside Canada in contravention of the by-laws, whether or not the person has been prosecuted for or convicted of an offence under section 50.1.

Variation or discharge

(3) Any person may apply to the Superior Court of Justice for an order varying or discharging an order made under subsection (1).

Lawyers Fund for Client Compensation

Lawyers Fund for Client Compensation

51(1) The Compensation Fund is continued as the Lawyers Fund for Client Compensation.

Same

(1.1) The Society shall maintain the Fund and shall hold it in trust for the purposes of this section.

Composition of Fund

(2) The Fund shall be made up of,
    (a) all money paid by members of the Society under subsection (3);
    (b) all money earned from the investment of money in the Fund;
    (c) all money recovered under subsection (7); and
    (d) all money contributed by any person.

Fund levy

(3) Every member, other than those of a class exempted by the by-laws, shall pay to the Society, for the Fund, such sum as is prescribed from time to time by the by-laws.

Insurance

(4) The Society may insure with any insurer licensed to carry on business in Ontario for such purposes and on such terms as Convocation considers expedient in relation to the Fund, and, in such event, the money in the Fund may be used for the payment of premiums.

Grants

(5) Convocation in its absolute discretion may make grants from the Fund in order to relieve or mitigate loss sustained by any person in consequence of dishonesty on the part of any member in connection with such member's law practice or in connection with any trust of which the member was or is a trustee, although after the commission of the act of dishonesty the member may have died or ceased to administer the member's affairs or to be a member.

Conditions of grants

(6) No grant shall be made out of the Fund unless notice in writing of the loss is received by the Secretary within six months after the loss came to the knowledge of the person suffering the loss or within such further time, not exceeding eighteen months, as in any case may be allowed by Convocation.

Subrogation

(7) If a grant is made under this section, the Society is subrogated to the amount of the grant to any rights or remedies to which the person receiving the grant was entitled on account of the loss in respect of which the grant was made against the dishonest member or any other person, or, in the event of the death or insolvency or other disability of the member or other person, against the personal representative or other person administering the estate.

Grantees' rights conditionally limited

(8) A person to whom a grant is made under this section, or, in the event of death or insolvency or other disability, the personal representative or other person administering the estate, has no right to receive anything from the dishonest member or the member's estate in respect of the loss in respect of which the grant was made until the Society has been reimbursed the full amount of the grant.

Reimbursement from bankrupt's estate

(9) Where a grant has been made under this section and the dishonest member has been declared a bankrupt, the Society is entitled to prove against the bankrupt's estate for the full amount of the claim of the person to whom the grant was made and to receive all dividends on such amount until the Society has been reimbursed the full amount of the grant.

Delegation of powers to committee or referee or both

(10) Convocation may delegate any of the powers conferred upon it by this section to a committee of Convocation and, whether or not Convocation has made any such delegation, it may appoint any member as a referee and delegate to the member any of the powers conferred upon it by this section that are not delegated to a committee.

Reports

(11) Where Convocation has delegated any of its powers under this section to a committee or to a referee, the committee or referee, as the case may be, shall report as required to Convocation but, where there is a delegation to both a committee and a referee, the referee shall report as required to the committee.

Summons

(11.1) For the purposes of this section, the Secretary may require any person, by summons,

(a) to give evidence on oath or affirmation at a hearing before Convocation, a committee or a referee; and

(b) to produce in evidence at a hearing before Convocation, a committee or a referee documents and things specified by the Secretary.

Application of Public Inquiries Act

(11.2) Section 4, subsection 7 (2) and sections 8 and 13 of the *Public Inquiries Act* apply, with necessary modifications, if a summons is issued under subsection (11.1).

Costs of administration

(12) There may be paid out of the Fund the costs of its administration, including the costs of investigations and hearings and all other costs, salaries and expenses necessarily incidental to the administration of the Fund.

The Law Foundation of Ontario

Definitions

52. In this section and in sections 53 to 59.5,

"board" means the board of trustees of the Foundation;

"class proceeding" means a proceeding certified as a class proceeding on a motion made under section 2 or 3 of the *Class Proceedings Act, 1992*;

"Committee" means the Class Proceedings Committee referred to in section 59.2;

"defendant" includes a respondent;

"Foundation" means The Law Foundation of Ontario referred to in section 53;

"plaintiff" includes an applicant;

"trustee" means a trustee of the board.

Foundation continued

53(1) The corporation known as The Law Foundation of Ontario is continued as a corporation without share capital under the name The Law Foundation of Ontario in English and Fondation du droit de l'Ontario in French and shall consist of the trustees for the time being of the board.

Corporations Act inapplicable

(2) The *Corporations Act* does not apply to the Foundation.

Board of trustees

54(1) The affairs of the Foundation shall be managed and controlled by a board of trustees consisting of five trustees of whom two shall be appointed by the Attorney General and three shall be appointed by the Society.

Quorum

(2) Three trustees constitute a quorum.

Vacancies

(3) Where there are not more than two vacancies in the membership of the board, the remaining trustees constitute the board for all purposes.

Remuneration

(4) The trustees shall serve without remuneration, but each trustee is entitled to receive his or her actual disbursements for expenses incurred for any services rendered by him or her at the direction of the board.

Audit

(5) The accounts and financial transactions of the Foundation shall be audited annually by an auditor or auditors appointed by the board.

Annual report

(6) The board shall make a report annually to the Attorney General on the activities of the Foundation, including the report of the auditor under subsection (5), and the Attorney General shall lay the report before the Assembly if it is in session or, if not, at the next session.

Objects and funds

Objects

55(1) The objects of the Foundation are to establish and maintain a fund to be used for any or all of the following purposes:

1. Legal education and legal research.
2. Legal aid.

3. The establishment, maintenance and operation of law libraries.

4. The provision of costs assistance to parties to class proceedings and to proceedings commenced under the *Class Proceedings Act, 1992.*

Derivation of funds

(2) The funds of the Foundation shall be derived from,

    (a) money received from members under section 57;

    (b) gifts, bequests and devises referred to in section 56;

    (b.1) money received as interest or other gain on joint accounts held under section 57.1;

    (b.2) money paid to the Foundation under subsection 59.7 (3); and

    (c) money resulting from the use, disposal or investment of property received under clauses (a), (b), (b.1) and (b.2).

Application of funds

(3) The board shall apply the funds of the Foundation for such of its purposes as the board considers appropriate, but at least 75 per cent of the net revenue received in each year under clauses (2)(a), (b.1) and (b.2) shall be paid to Legal Aid Ontario established under the *Legal Aid Services Act, 1998.*

Investment strategy

(4) In making investments and entering agreements under clauses 56(1)(a), (d) and (e), the board shall use its best efforts to maximize the return to the Foundation within the bounds of prudent financial management.

Powers of Foundation

56(1) In addition to the powers and privileges mentioned in section 27 of the *Interpretation Act*, the Foundation has power,

    (a) to invest the funds of the Foundation;

    (b) to pay out of the funds of the Foundation the costs, charges and expenses necessarily incurred in the administration of the Foundation and in carrying out its objects;

    (c) to enter into agreements with any person and pay and apply any of its funds for the implementation of its objects;

    (d) to invest the funds that it holds on joint account under section 57.1;

    (e) to enter into agreements with financial institutions related to the consolidation for investment purposes of funds held on joint accounts under section 57.1 and related to the use of those funds;

    (f) to borrow such funds as it considers appropriate for the purpose of making investments and entering into agreements under clauses (a), (d) and (e).

Investment

(1.1) Sections 27 to 31 of the *Trustee Act* apply, with necessary modifications, to the investment of funds under clauses (1)(a) and (d).

Gifts, devises, etc.

(2) The Foundation has power to receive gifts, bequests and devises of property, real or personal, and to hold, use or dispose of such property in furtherance of the objects of the Foundation, subject to the terms of any trust affecting the same.

Idem

(3) Any form of words is sufficient to constitute a gift, bequest or devise to the Foundation so long as the person making the gift, bequest or devise indicates an intention to contribute presently or prospectively to the Foundation.

Service charges

(3.1) The following rules apply to service charges and other fees charged in relation to a joint account held under section 57.1:

1. Service charges and other fees that are prescribed by the regulations shall be paid out of the funds of the Foundation.
2. Amounts charged for issuing certified cheques against the joint account shall be paid by the member.
3. All other service charges and fees shall be paid by the member.

Accounting

(3.2) All interest and other profits under the investments and agreements authorized under clauses (1)(d) and (e) accrue to and become funds of the Foundation and not to any member or any client of any member or to any person claiming through any member or client of a member.

Protection of joint accounts

(3.3) Despite subsection (3.2), the Foundation is responsible for all losses resulting from investments and agreements under clauses (1)(d) and (e) and shall ensure that losses in respect of particular investments are paid out of the funds of the Foundation and not out of funds held for the benefit of any client of a member.

Member's responsibility

(3.4) A member is responsible to his or her clients for the operation of a joint account established by the member under section 57.1 as if it were a trust account held solely by the member and the Foundation is not responsible to any person in respect of the joint account except to the extent that its exercise of its powers under clause (1)(d) or (e) has caused a loss to the person.

Powers of the board

(4) The board may pass by-laws not contrary to this Act to achieve the objects of the Foundation and to regulate and govern its procedure and the conduct and administration of the affairs of the Foundation.

Interest on trust funds

Trust funds to bear interest

57(1) Every member who holds money in trust for or on account of more than one client in one fund shall hold the money in an account at a bank listed in Schedule I or II to the *Bank Act* (Canada), provincial savings office, credit union or a league to which the *Credit Unions and Caisses Populaires Act, 1994* applies or registered trust corporation, bearing interest at a rate approved by the trustees.

Interest in trust

(2) The interest accruing on money held in an account referred to in subsection (1) shall be deemed to be held in trust for the Foundation.

Payment to Foundation

(3) Every member to whom subsection (1) applies shall,

(a) file reports with the Foundation as to the interest referred to in subsection (2); and

(b) remit or cause to be remitted to the Foundation all interest money referred to in subsection (2),

in the manner and at the times prescribed by the regulations.

Immunity

(4) Subject to subsection (5), a member is not liable, whether as solicitor or as trustee, to account to any person as client or as settlor or beneficiary of the trust other than the Foundation, for interest on money held under subsection (1).

Exceptions

(5) Nothing in this section shall be deemed to affect,

(a) any arrangement in writing between a member and the person for whom the member holds money in trust as to the disposition of the interest accruing thereon; or

(b) any entitlement by a client to the interest accruing on money held in trust in an account separate from any other money.

Joint trust accounts

57.1(1) A member who maintains an account to which subsection 57(1) applies at a financial institution designated by the regulations shall establish it as a joint account in the name of the member and the Foundation, and shall immediately notify the Foundation that the account has been established and provide such details as may be required by the regulations and by the Foundation.

Same

(2) The member shall execute such documents as the Foundation considers necessary,

(a) to permit the financial institution to pay interest accruing on money held in the joint account directly to the Foundation;

(b) to permit the Foundation to consolidate the funds in the joint account with other funds in which the Foundation has an interest.

Same

(3) The Foundation shall ensure that the member retains the power in his or her relationship with the financial institution in which a joint account is established to deposit funds to and make payments out of the joint account in the same manner as if it were a trust account solely in the name of the member.

Same

(4) Subsections 57(4) and (5) apply to the joint accounts but subsections 57(2) and (3) do not.

Immunity

57.2(1) The Foundation is not liable to any person for any failure of any member to fulfil his or her obligations under section 57 or 57.1 or in respect of any dealing by a member with trust funds and no proceeding shall be commenced against the Foundation in respect thereof.

Same

(2) No action or other proceeding for damages shall be commenced against a member of the board for an act done in good faith in the performance or intended performance of a duty or in the exercise or intended exercise of a power under this Act or a regulation, or for any neglect or default in the performance or exercise in good faith of such a duty or power.

Reports

Report by Society

58(1) The Society shall in each year report to the Foundation the name and office or residence address shown by the records of the Society of every member who files a report with the Society that shows the member holds money on deposit in a trust account for or on account of clients.

Report by member

(2) The Foundation may require a member whose name is contained in a report by the Society under subsection (1) to file a report with the Foundation stating whether or not the member has received or been credited with interest on money held in a trust account for or on account of clients.

Regulations

59. Subject to the approval of the Lieutenant Governor in Council, the board may make regulations,

(a) governing the form, content and filing of the reports required under section 57;

(b) governing the time and manner of remitting the interest money referred to in section 57 to the Foundation;

(b.1) prescribing the information that must be provided to the Foundation when a joint account is established under section 57.1 and prescribing and governing information that must be provided by a member from time to time in respect of the joint account after it is established;

(c) prescribing the form and the time of filing of reports required under section 58.

Class Proceedings Fund

59.1(1) The board shall,

(a) establish an account of the Foundation to be known as the Class Proceedings Fund;

(b) within sixty days after this Act comes into force, endow the Class Proceedings Fund with $300,000 from the funds of the Foundation;

(c) within one year after the day on which the endowment referred to in clause (b) is made, endow the Class Proceedings Fund with a further $200,000 from the funds of the Foundation; and

(d) administer the Class Proceedings Fund in accordance with this Act and the regulations.

Purposes of the Class Proceedings Fund

(2) The Class Proceedings Fund shall be used for the following purposes:

1. Financial support for plaintiffs to class proceedings and to proceedings commenced under the *Class Proceedings Act, 1992*, in respect of disbursements related to the proceeding.
2. Payments to defendants in respect of costs awards made in their favour against plaintiffs who have received financial support from the Fund.

Application of s. 56

(3) Funds in the Class Proceedings Fund are funds of the Foundation within the meaning of section 56, but payments out of the Class Proceedings Fund shall relate to the administration or purposes of the Fund.

Class Proceedings Committee

59.2(1) The Class Proceedings Committee is established and shall be composed of,

(a) one member appointed by the Foundation;

(b) one member appointed by the Attorney General; and

(c) three members appointed jointly by the Foundation and the Attorney General.

Term of office

(2) Each member of the Class Proceedings Committee shall hold office for a period of three years and is eligible for re-appointment.

Quorum

(3) Three members of the Committee constitute a quorum.

Vacancies

(4) Where there are not more than two vacancies in the membership of the Committee, the remaining members constitute the Committee for all purposes.

Remuneration

(5) The members of the Committee shall serve without remuneration, but each member is entitled to compensation for expenses incurred in carrying out the functions of the Committee.

Applications by plaintiffs

59.3(1) A plaintiff to a class proceeding or to a proceeding commenced under section 2 of the *Class Proceedings Act, 1992* may apply to the Committee for financial support from the Class Proceedings Fund in respect of disbursements related to the proceeding.

Idem

(2) An application under subsection (1) shall not include a claim in respect of solicitor's fees.

Committee may authorize payment

(3) The Committee may direct the board to make payments from the Class Proceedings Fund to a plaintiff who makes an application under subsection (1), in the amount that the Committee considers appropriate.

Idem

(4) In making a decision under subsection (3), the Committee may have regard to,
    (a) the merits of the plaintiff's case;
    (b) whether the plaintiff has made reasonable efforts to raise funds from other sources;
    (c) whether the plaintiff has a clear and reasonable proposal for the use of any funds awarded;
    (d) whether the plaintiff has appropriate financial controls to ensure that any funds awarded are spent for the purposes of the award; and
    (e) any other matter that the Committee considers relevant.

Supplementary funding

(5) A plaintiff who has received funding under subsection (3) may apply to the Committee at any time up to the end of the class proceeding for supplementary funding and the Committee may direct the board to make further payments from the Class Proceedings Fund to the plaintiff if the Committee is of the opinion, having regard to all the circumstances, that it is appropriate to do so.

Board shall make payments

(6) The board shall make payments in accordance with any directions given by the Committee under this section.

Applications by defendants

59.4(1) A defendant to a proceeding may apply to the board for payment from the Class Proceedings Fund in respect of a costs award made in the proceeding in the defendant's favour against a plaintiff who has received financial support from the Class Proceedings Fund in respect of the proceeding.

Board shall make payments

(2) The board shall make payments applied for in accordance with subsection (1) from the Class Proceedings Fund, subject to any limits or tariffs applicable to such payments prescribed by the regulations.

Plaintiff not liable

(3) A defendant who has the right to apply for payment from the Class Proceedings Fund in respect of a costs award against a plaintiff may not recover any part of the award from the plaintiff.

Regulations

59.5(1) The Lieutenant Governor in Council may make regulations,

(a) respecting the administration of the Class Proceedings Fund;

(b) establishing procedures for making applications under sections 59.3 and 59.4;

(c) establishing criteria in addition to those set out in section 59.3 for decisions of the Committee under section 59.3;

(d) establishing limits and tariffs for payments under sections 59.3 and 59.4;

(e) prescribing conditions of awards under section 59.3;

(f) providing for the assessment of costs in respect of which a claim is made under section 59.4;

(g) providing for levies in favour of the Class Proceedings Fund against awards and settlement funds in proceedings in respect of which a party receives financial support from the Class Proceedings Fund.

Idem

(2) A regulation made under clause (1)(d) may provide for different limits and tariffs for different stages and types of proceedings.

Idem

(3) A regulation made under clause (1)(g) may provide for levies that exceed the amount of financial support received by the parties to a proceeding.

Idem

(4) A regulation made under clause (1)(g) may provide for levies based on a formula that takes the amount of an award or settlement fund into account.

Idem

(5) A levy under clause (1)(g) against a settlement fund or monetary award is a charge on the fund or award.

Unclaimed Trust Funds

Unclaimed trust funds

59.6(1) A member who has held money in trust for or on account of a person for a period of at least two years may apply in accordance with the by-laws for permission to pay the money to the Society, if,

(a) the member has been unable to locate the person entitled to the money despite having made reasonable efforts throughout a period of at least two years; or

(b) the member is unable to determine who is entitled to the money.

Approval of application

(2) If the Secretary approves an application under subsection (1), the member may pay the money to the Society, subject to such terms and conditions as the Secretary may impose.

Financial records

(3) A member who pays money to the Society under subsection (2) shall provide the Society with copies of financial records relating to the money that are in the member's possession or control.

Member's liability

(4) Payment of money to the Society under subsection (2) extinguishes the member's liability as trustee or fiduciary with respect to the amount paid to the Society.

Society becomes trustee

59.7(1) Money paid to the Society under section 59.6 shall be held in trust by the Society in perpetuity for the purpose of satisfying the claims of the persons who are entitled to the money.

One or more accounts

(2) Money held in trust under this section may be held in one or more accounts.

Trust income

(3) Subject to subsections (5) and (6), all income from the money held in trust under this section shall be paid to the Law Foundation.

Passing accounts

(4) The Society shall from time to time apply to the Superior Court of Justice under section 23 of the *Trustee Act* to pass the accounts of the trust established by this section and the court's order on each application shall specify a date before which the Society must make its next application to pass the accounts.

Trustee compensation

(5) Subject to subsection (6), the Society may take compensation from the trust property in accordance with orders made under subsection 23(2) of the *Trustee Act*.

Same

(6) Compensation may be taken under subsection (5) only from the income of the trust.

First application

(7) The Society shall make its first application under subsection (4) not later than two years after this section comes into force.

Transfer to trust fund

59.8(1) Despite section 59.6, the Society may transfer to the trust established by section 59.7 any money received in trust by the Society from a member after the day the *Law Society Amendment Act, 1998* came into force, if,

(a) immediately before the money was received by the Society, the member was holding the money in trust for or on account of a person; and

(b) the Secretary is satisfied that the Society is unable to locate the person entitled to the money or to determine who is entitled to the money.

Exception

(2) Money held in trust by the Society pursuant to an order made under section 49.47 shall not be transferred under subsection (1) without the approval of the Superior Court of Justice provided for in the order made under section 49.47 or obtained on an application under section 49.48 or 49.51.

Money held before *Law Society Amendment Act, 1998*

(3) The Society may transfer to the trust established by section 59.7 any money held in trust by the Society immediately before the *Law Society Amendment Act, 1998* came into force, if,

(a) the money was received by the Society from a member who held the money in trust for or on account of a person; and

(b) the Secretary is satisfied that the Society is unable to locate the person entitled to the money or to determine who is entitled to the money.

Transferred money to be held in trust

(4) Money transferred under this section to the trust established by section 59.7 shall be held in trust by the Society under section 59.7.

Member's liability

(5) The transfer of money under this section extinguishes the member's liability as trustee or fiduciary with respect to the amount transferred.

Notice

59.9(1) The Secretary shall publish a notice annually in *The Ontario Gazette* listing the name and last known address of every person entitled to money that, during the previous year, was paid to the Society under section 59.6 or transferred under section 59.8 to the trust established by section 59.7.

Exception

(2) Subsection (1) does not require publication of any name or address of which the Society is not aware.

Other steps

(3) The Society shall take such other steps as it considers appropriate to locate the persons entitled to money held in trust by the Society under section 59.7.

Claims

59.10(1) A person may make a claim in accordance with the by-laws for payment of money held in trust by the Society under section 59.7.

Payment of claims

(2) Subject to sections 59.12 and 59.13, the Society shall pay claims in accordance with the by-laws.

Application to court

59.11 Subject to sections 59.12 and 59.13, if a claim under section 59.10 is denied by the Society in whole or in part, the claimant may apply to the Superior Court of Justice for an order directing the Society to pay the claimant any money to which the claimant is entitled.

No entitlement to interest

59.12 A claimant to whom money is paid under section 59.10 or 59.11 is not entitled to any interest on the money that was held in trust by the Society.

Limit on payments

59.13 (1) The total of all payments made to claimants under sections 59.10 and 59.11 in respect of money paid to the Society by a particular member under section 59.6 shall not exceed the amount paid to the Society under section 59.6 by that member.

Money transferred to trust fund

(2) Subsection (1) also applies, with necessary modifications, in respect of money transferred under section 59.8 to the trust established by section 59.7.

Former members

59.14 Sections 59.6 to 59.13 also apply, with necessary modifications, in respect of money held in trust by former members.

Legal Education, Degrees

Bar Admission Course and law degrees

Bar Admission Course

60(1) The Society may maintain the Bar Admission Course and programs of continuing legal education.

Law degrees

(2) The Society may grant degrees in law.

Indemnity for Professional Liability

Indemnity for professional liability

61. The Society may make arrangements for its members respecting indemnity for professional liability and respecting the payment and remission of premiums in connection therewith and prescribing levies to be paid by members or any class thereof and exempting members or any class thereof from all or any part of any such levy.

Professional corporations

61.0.1 Subject to the by-laws, a member or two or more members practising law as individuals or as a partnership may establish a professional corporation for the purpose of practising law, and the provisions of the *Business Corporations Act* that apply to professional corporations within the meaning of that Act apply to such a corporation.

Register

61.0.2(1) The Secretary shall establish and maintain a register of professional corporations that have been issued certificates of authorization.

Contents of registry

(2) The register shall contain the information set out in the by-laws.

Notice of change of shareholder

61.0.3 A professional corporation shall notify the Secretary within the time and in the form and manner determined under the by-laws of a change in the shareholders of the corporation.

Application of Act, etc.

61.0.4 (1) This Act, the regulations, the by-laws and the rules of practice and procedure apply to a member, student member and all other persons authorized to practise law despite the fact that the practice of the member, student member or other person is carried on through a professional corporation.

Exercise of powers of Society against corporation

(2) Sections 35, 36, 45 to 48 and 49.2, subsections 49.3(1) and (2) and sections 49.7 to 49.10, 49.44 to 49.52, 57 to 59, 61 and 61.0.7 apply with necessary modifications to professional corporations as if a reference to a member in those provisions were a reference to a professional corporation, a reference to membership were a reference to a certificate of authorization, a reference to a revocation of membership were a reference to the revocation of a certificate of authorization and a reference to a restriction of manner of practice were a reference to the attachment of conditions to a certificate of authorization.

Professional, fiduciary and ethical obligations to clients

61.0.5(1) The professional, fiduciary and ethical obligations of a member, student member and all other persons practising law to a person on whose behalf they are practising law,
    (a) are not diminished by the fact that they are practising law through a professional corporation; and
    (b) apply equally to the corporation and to its directors, officers, shareholders, agents and employees.

Audit, etc.

(2) If an action or the conduct of a member, student member or another person practising law on behalf of a professional corporation is the subject of an audit, investigation or review,
    (a) any power that may be exercised under this Act in respect of the member, student member or other person may be exercised in respect of the corporation; and
    (b) the corporation is jointly and severally liable with the member, student member or other person for all fines and costs that he or she is ordered to pay.

Restrictions on certificate of authorization

61.0.6 A term, condition or limitation imposed on a person practising law through a professional corporation applies to the certificate of authorization of the corporation in relation to the practice of law through the person.

Prohibitions, professional corporations

61.0.7(1) A corporation shall not act as a barrister or practise as a solicitor unless it is a professional corporation that holds a valid certificate of authorization under this Act.

Same, representations

(2) A corporation shall not represent or hold out expressly or by implication that is a professional corporation under this Act unless the corporation holds a valid certificate of authorization under this Act.

Prohibition, professional misconduct

(3) In the course of practising law, a professional corporation shall not engage in professional misconduct or conduct unbecoming a barrister or solicitor.

Prohibition, contraventions

(4) A professional corporation shall not contravene any provision of this Act.

Same

(5) A professional corporation shall not contravene a term, condition or limitation imposed on its certificate of authorization.

Prohibition, corporate matters

(6) A professional corporation shall not practise law when it does not satisfy the requirements for a professional corporation under subsection 3.2(2) of the *Business Corporations Act* or under this Act.

Trusteeships permitted

61.0.8 Clause 213(2)(b) of the *Loan and Trust Corporations Act* does not prevent a professional corporation from acting as a trustee in respect of services normally provided by members.

References to barrister, etc.

61.0.9 A reference in any other Act or any regulation, rule or order made under any other Act to a barrister, solicitor or member shall be deemed to include a reference to a professional corporation.

Limited Liability Partnerships

Limited liability partnerships

61.1 Subject to the by-laws, two or more members may form a limited liability partnership or continue a partnership as a limited liability partnership within the meaning of the *Partnerships Act* for the purpose of practising law.

Rules of Practice and Procedure

Rules

61.2(1) Convocation may make rules of practice and procedure applicable to proceedings before the Hearing Panel and the Appeal Panel and to the making of orders under sections 46, 47, 48, 49 and 49.1.

Examples

(2) Without limiting the generality of subsection (1), Convocation may make rules of practice and procedure,

(a) governing the circumstances in which orders may be made under this Act;

(b) authorizing and governing interlocutory orders in a proceeding or intended proceeding, including interlocutory orders suspending the rights and privileges of a member or student member or restricting the manner in which a member may practise law;

(c) authorizing appeals from interlocutory orders;

(d) prescribing circumstances in which an interlocutory order suspending the rights and privileges of a member or student member may be deemed to be a final order if the member or student member does not appear at the hearing of an application;

(e) governing the admissibility of evidence in proceedings, including the admissibility in evidence of documents and other information disclosed under this Act or under the regulations, by-laws or rules;

(f) authorizing orders that a hearing or part of a hearing be held in the absence of the public and authorizing orders that specified information relating to a proceeding not be disclosed;

(g) authorizing the Hearing Panel, in applications under section 34, to deal, with the consent of the parties, with matters that would otherwise have to be the subject of an application under section 38, and to make any order referred to in section 40;

(h) governing the administration of reprimands and admonitions;

(i) governing the awarding of costs under section 49.28.

Rules under SPPA

(3) Rules made under this section shall be deemed, for the purposes of the *Statutory Powers Procedure Act*, to have been made under section 25.1 of that Act.

Conflict with SPPA

(4) In the event of a conflict between the rules made under this section and the *Statutory Powers Procedure Act*, the rules made under this section prevail, despite section 32 of that Act.

By-laws

By-laws

62(0.1) Convocation may make by-laws,

1. relating to the affairs of the Society;
2. providing procedures for the making, amendment and revocation of the by-laws;

3. governing honorary benchers, persons who are benchers by virtue of their office and honorary members, and prescribing their rights and privileges;

4. governing members and student members or any class of either of them, and prescribing their rights and privileges;

5. governing the handling of money and other property by members and student members;

6. requiring and prescribing the financial records to be kept by members and providing for the exemption from such requirements of any class of members;

7. requiring and providing for the examination or audit of members' financial records and transactions and for the filing with the Society of reports with respect thereto;

8. requiring members and student members to register an address with the Society and to notify the Society of any changes in the address;

9. requiring members and student members, or any class of either of them specified in the by-laws or specified by the Secretary, to provide the Society with information relating to the Society's functions under this Act;

10. authorizing and providing for the preparation, publication and distribution of a code of professional conduct and ethics;

11. authorizing and providing for the preparation, publication and distribution of guidelines for professional competence;

12. respecting the reporting and publication of the decisions of the courts;

13. authorizing officers or employees of the Society holding offices specified by the by-laws to exercise powers or perform duties of the Secretary under this Act, the regulations, the by-laws or the rules of practice and procedure, subject to such terms and conditions as may be specified by the by-laws or imposed by the Secretary;

14. prescribing fees and levies relating to the functions of the Society, including fees for late compliance with any obligation, that must be paid to the Society by,

    i.   members and student members or any class of either of them,

    ii. applicants for membership in the Society or any class of them,

    iii. limited liability partnerships that practise law and applicants for licences for limited liability partnerships to practise law,

    iii.1 professional corporations and applicants for certificates of authorization for professional corporations,

    iv. persons who give legal advice respecting the law of a jurisdiction outside Canada, and applicants for licences to give such advice,

    v.   persons authorized to practise law outside Ontario who are permitted to appear as counsel in a specific proceeding in an Ontario court, and applicants for such permission,

    vi. persons authorized to practise law in other provinces and territories of Canada who are permitted to engage in the occasional practice of law in Ontario, and applicants for such permission,

    vii. partnerships, corporations and other organizations that provide legal services and that maintain one or more offices outside Ontario and one or more offices in Ontario, and applicants for licences to provide such services, and

    viii. persons, partnerships, corporations and other organizations that practise law and also practise another profession, and applicants for licences relating to such practices;

15. governing the payment and remission of fees and levies prescribed under paragraph 14 and exempting any class of persons from all or any part of any fee or levy;

16. providing for the payment to the Society by a member or student member of the cost of an audit, investigation, review, search or seizure under Part II;

17. requiring the payment of interest on any amount owed to the Society by any person and prescribing the interest rate;

18. providing for and governing meetings of members or representatives of members;

19. defining and governing the employment of student members while under articles and the employment of other law students;

20. defining and governing the employment of barristers and solicitors clerks;

21. governing degrees in law;

22. providing and governing bursaries, scholarships, medals and prizes;

23. respecting legal education, including the Bar Admission Course;

24. providing for and governing extension courses, continuing legal education and legal research, and prescribing continuing legal education requirements that must be met by members, subject to such exemptions as may be provided for by the by-laws;

25. governing the call to the bar of barristers and the admission and enrolment of solicitors, including prescribing the qualifications required;

26. prescribing oaths and affirmations for members and student members or any class of either of them;

27. providing for and governing libraries;

28. governing the practice of law by limited liability partnerships, including requiring those partnerships to maintain a minimum amount of liability insurance for the purposes of clause 44.2(b) of the *Partnerships Act*, requiring the licensing of those partnerships, governing the issuance, renewal, suspension and revocation of licences and governing the terms and conditions that may be imposed on licences;

28.1 governing the practice of law through professional corporations, including, without limiting the generality of the foregoing, requiring the certification of those corporations, governing the issuance, renewal, surrender, suspension and revocation of certificates of authorization, governing the terms, conditions, limitations and restrictions that may be imposed on certificates and governing the names of those corporations and the notification of a change in the shareholders of those corporations;

29. providing for persons authorized to practise law outside Ontario to be permitted to appear as counsel in a specific proceeding in an Ontario court, subject to the approval of the court, governing the granting of permission and the terms

and conditions to which the permission may be subject, and making any provision of this Act applicable, with necessary modifications, to those persons;

30. providing for persons authorized to practise law in other provinces and territories of Canada to be permitted to engage in the occasional practice of law in Ontario, governing the granting of permission and the terms and conditions to which the permission may be subject, and making any provision of this Act applicable, with necessary modifications, to those persons;

31. governing the provision of legal services by any partnership, corporation or other organization that maintains one or more offices outside Ontario and one or more offices in Ontario, including requiring the licensing of those partnerships, corporations and other organizations, governing the issuance, renewal, suspension and revocation of licences and governing the terms and conditions that may be imposed on licences;

32. governing the practice of law by any person, partnership, corporation or other organization that also practises another profession, including requiring the licensing of those persons partnerships, corporations and other organizations, governing the issuance, renewal, suspension and revocation of licences and governing the terms and conditions that may be imposed on licences;

33. regulating the giving of legal advice respecting the law of a jurisdiction outside Canada, including requiring a licence issued by the Society, governing the issuance, renewal, suspension and revocation of licences and governing the terms and conditions that may be imposed on licences;

34. providing for the establishment, maintenance and administration of a benevolent fund for members and the dependants of deceased members;

35. governing the acceptance of resignations under section 30;

36. respecting the Lawyers Fund for Client Compensation;

37. governing applications to pay trust money to the Society under section 59.6 and governing the making of and determination of claims under section 59.10;

38. governing the referral of complaints to the Complaints Resolution Commissioner and governing the performance of duties and the exercise of powers by the Commissioner;

39. designating offices held by employees of the Society to which the Complaints Resolution Commissioner may delegate powers or duties;

40. prescribing circumstances in which a direction must be made under section 49.4 requiring that a review of a member's practice be conducted under section 42;

41. governing reviews under section 42;

42. governing the appointment of persons to conduct audits, investigations and reviews under Part II;

43. prescribing a period for the purposes of subsection 46(1) and governing the payment of amounts owing for the purposes of subsection 46(2);

44. prescribing a period for the purposes of subsection 47(1) and governing the completion and filing of documents for the purposes of subsection 47(2);

45. governing the criteria to be applied and the method to be used under subsection 49.1(1) in determining whether members have made substantial use of

legal skills on a regular basis and prescribing the length of the continuous period of time referred to in that subsection;

46. prescribing the requalification requirements that must be met for the purpose of section 49.1, governing the determination of whether those requirements have been met and prescribing terms and conditions that may be imposed under section 49.1;

47. governing the implementation of agreements with the responsible authorities in other jurisdictions relating to the practice of law;

48. prescribing forms and providing for their use.

Same

(1) Without limiting the generality of paragraph 1 of subsection (0.1), by-laws may be made under that paragraph, ...

2. prescribing the seal and the coat of arms of the Society;

3. providing for the execution of documents by the Society;

4. respecting the borrowing of money and the giving of security therefor;

5. fixing the financial year of the Society and providing for the audit of the accounts and transactions of the Society;

6. governing the election of benchers under section 15, including prescribing regions for the purpose of subsection 15(2), prescribing the terms of office of elected benchers, prescribing the number of benchers to be elected for each region, governing the qualifications required to be a candidate or vote in elections and providing for challenges of election results;

6.1 governing the filling of vacancies in the offices of elected benchers;

7. governing the election of and removal from office of the Treasurer, the filling of a vacancy in the office of Treasurer, the appointment of an acting Treasurer to act in the Treasurer's absence or inability to act, and prescribing the Treasurer's duties;

8. providing for the appointment of and prescribing the duties of the Chief Executive Officer and of the Secretary, one or more deputy secretaries and assistant secretaries and such other officers as are considered appropriate;

9. respecting Convocation;

10. providing for the establishment, composition, jurisdiction and operation of the Proceedings Authorization Committee;

11. providing for the establishment, composition, jurisdiction and operation of standing and other committees, including standing committees responsible for discipline matters and for professional competence, and delegating to any committee such of the powers and duties of Convocation as may be considered expedient.

General or particular

(1.1) A by-law made under this section may be general or particular in its application.

Interpretation of by-laws

(2) The by-laws made under this section shall be interpreted as if they formed part of this Act.

Availability of copies of by-laws

(3) A copy of the by-laws made under this section, as amended from time to time,
    (a) shall be filed in the office of the Attorney General; and
    (b) shall be available for public inspection in the office of the Secretary.

Regulations

Regulations

63(1) Convocation, with the approval of the Lieutenant Governor in Council, may make regulations, ...

  8. providing for the establishment, operation and dissolution of county and district law associations and respecting grants and loans to such associations; ...
11. prescribing service charges and other fees, other than amounts charged for issuing certified cheques against the joint account, for the purpose of paragraph 1 of subsection 56(3.1);
12. designating any or all of the following, or any class or classes thereof, as financial institutions in which joint accounts must be established for the purposes of section 57.1,
    i. banks listed in Schedule I or II to the *Bank Act* (Canada),
    ii. registered trust corporations,
    iii. provincial savings offices,
    iv. credit unions and leagues to which the *Credit Unions and Caisses Populaires Act, 1994* applies;
13. governing the appointment of the Complaints Resolution Commissioner;
14. governing the assignment of members of the Hearing Panel to hearings, including the number of persons required to hear and determine different matters;
15. naming, for the purpose of section 31, tribunals that have a judicial or quasi-judicial function.

General or particular

(2) A regulation made under this section may be general or particular in its application.

French Name, Transitional

Reference to name

64. A reference in any Act, regulation, contract or other document to Société du barreau du Haut-Canada shall be deemed to be a reference to Barreau du Haut-Canada.

Citation of Act

65. This Act may be cited in French as *Loi sur le Barreau*.

Index

617